JUDGING

by

Robert E. Keeton
Langdell Professor Emeritus
Harvard Law School

WEST PUBLISHING CO.
ST. PAUL, MINN., 1990

COPYRIGHT 1990 by WEST PUBLISHING CO.

All rights reserved.
Printed in the United States of America

ISBN 0-314-76285-X

Acknowledgements

I gratefully acknowledge the benefit of constructive criticisms offered by my most faithful and benign reader, Betty, whom you may hold accountable if you find less legal jargon in these pages than suits your taste.

I gratefully acknowledge also the generous and patient persistence of my secretary, Lillian Di Blasi, as well as her incomparable proficiency, at deciphering even vaguely manifested intentions and translating them into copy.

Finally, I acknowledge my debt to my court staff during the years I have been judging; to counsel who have appeared with, against, or before me in court; to colleagues in judging and law teaching; and to the judges and scholars whose opinions, lectures, and articles have taught us about the work of professionals in trial courts. Together, they have inspired my interest, and I hope yours as well, in what we have yet to understand about judging.

February, 1990   Robert E. Keeton

TABLE OF CONTENTS

Acknowledgements..iii

Part One
An Introduction to Judicial Decisionmaking

Chapter 1. Commitments and Perspectives.....................1
   A. The Obligation of Reasoned Decision.....................1
   B. Perspectives for Understanding Law and Judging........3
      1. The Perspective of a Trial Judge....................3
      2. Law in Action..4
         Case 1.1 The Injured Inmate.....................5
         Case 1.2 The Battered Child.....................8
      3. Law in Development..................................9
   C. Professional Commitment..............................10
      1. Judging as Professional Conduct....................10
      2. Representation of Interests
         Other Than One's Own..............................15
   D. The Method of Reasoned Choice........................17
      1. Legal and Factual Premises........................17
      2. Reason, Choice, Policy and Rationality............20
         Case 1.3 The Favored Older Resident............24

Chapter 2. Law and Facts in the Administration
         of Justice..28
   A. Introduction...28
   B. Who Decides Disputes of Law?.........................28
      1. Identification of Lawmakers.......................28
         Case 2.1 An Infant Vaccine Victim..............31
      2. Changing Roles of Different Types of
        Lawmakers...35
   C. Who Decides Disputes of Fact?........................38
         Case 2.2 Knowledge of Asbestos Hazards.........40
   D. Truth, Fact, and Justice.............................43
      1. Truth in Being.....................................43
      2. Truth Becoming....................................43
      3. Truth Unknown.....................................46
      4. Truth and Proclamation............................48

E. Law and Justice...50
　　　　1. Law in Being..50
　　　　2. Law Becoming..50
　　　　3. Law Unknown...54
　　　　4. Law and Proclamation................................55
　　F. Ways of Classifying Facts and Disputes of Fact.........56
　　G. Mixed Questions of Law and Fact........................60
　　H. Borderland Between Law and Fact........................61

　　　　　　　　　　　Part Two
　　　　　Making and Explaining Lawmaking Choices

Chapter 3. Tailoring Tests for Deciding Cases...............66
　　A. Words and Meanings.....................................66
　　　　1. Introduction..66
　　　　2. Different Kinds of Legal Tests
　　　　　 and How We Describe Them............................67
　　　　3. Subjective and Objective Tests.....................74
　　B. State-of-Mind Elements in Tests
　　　 for Legal Accountability...............................79
　　　　1. In General..79
　　　　2. The Changing Significance of
　　　　　 State-of-Mind Tests.................................83
　　　　3. Tailoring State-of-Mind Tests
　　　　　 to Individual Cases.................................85
　　　　4. Entity State-of-Mind Tests.........................87
　　C. Objective Tests for Accountability....................90
　　　　1. The Meaning of "Objective".........................90
　　　　2. Tailoring the Multitude of
　　　　　 Objective Tests.....................................91
　　　　3. Factors, "Totality of the
　　　　　 Circumstances," and Related Tests..................93
　　D. Immunities and Privileges.............................95
　　　　1. Introduction..95
　　　　　 Case 3.1 A Cost Containment
　　　　　 Controversy...95
　　　　2. Terminology...96
　　　　3. The Scope of Protection
　　　　　 and Ways of Defining It............................97
　　E. Burdens as Techniques for Decisionmaking..............99

F. Duty, Cause, and Scope of Accountability............102
    1. Duty and Cause as Conclusions....................102
    2. Uncertain Meaning of Tests on Scope
       of Accountability..............................103
    3. Tailoring to Cases the Tests on
       Scope of Accountability........................106
          Case 3.2 The Ruptured Spleen..................106

Chapter 4. Values in Reasoned Decisionmaking.............112
    A. Introduction....................................112
          Case 4.1 The Adult Vaccine Victim............114
          Case 4.2 Gypsy Moths and Honeybees...........115
    B. Probing Premises for Value Implications..........118
    C. Deductive and Informative Reasoning..............122
    D. Individual Entitlement and Social Calculus.......124
    E. Lawmaking Choices Affecting Who Pays.............128
       1. Introduction.................................128
       2. Burdens, Costs, and Incomplete
          Decisionmaking..............................131

Chapter 5. A Judge's Writing and Speaking................137
    A. Introduction....................................137
    B. When and How Much to Write......................139
    C. How the Decision is Reasoned....................139
    D. Interpreting Communications: Problems
       of Manifested Meaning and Intent................142
    E. Combining Substance With Style..................143
    F. The Jury Charge.................................144
    G. Conclusion......................................145

Chapter 6. Judging Statutes..............................146
    A. Introduction....................................146
          Case 6.1 Rich, Cabbie, and Luce..............146
          Case 6.2 After Luce's Settlement.............148
          Case 6.3 Wrongful Death and
          Punitive Damages.............................149
          Case 6.4 Electronic Eavesdropping............149
    B. Determining Manifested Meaning..................149
    C. Guidelines for Deciding Issues Regarding
       Statutory Meaning...............................151
    D. The Contrast Between Intent and
       Objectively Manifested Meaning..................152
    E. A Proposed Analysis of Cases 6.1 and 6.5........154
          Case 6.5 Toxic Waste Disposal................165
    F. A Proposed Analysis of Case 6.2.................169
    G. Suggestions About How to Search
       for Manifested Meaning..........................170
    H. Transitory Premises and Outmoded Statutes.......171

Part Three
Case Development and Disposition

Chapter 7. Judging in Pretrial Proceedings.............177
  A. Judging Under Rules of Procedure...................177
    1. Objectives of Rules of Procedure................177
    2. Questions Not Answered by Rules.................178
  B. Rule and Discretion in Trial Procedure.............180
  C. Incentive Structures and Professional Conduct......182
  D. Discretionary Judicial Management
     of Pretrial Proceedings...........................184
  E. Judicial Intervention to Promote
     Disposition Without Trial.........................188
  F. Choices Committing Judicial and Party
     Resources to a Particular Case....................198
    1. A Problem of Limited Public
       and Private Resources..........................198
    2. A Sequence of Choices...........................200
    3. Decisions Based on Incomplete
       Information....................................202
    4. A Qualitative Perspective.......................207

Chapter 8. Conducting Jury and Nonjury Trials...........209
  A. Incentive Structures and
     Judicial Management Revisited.....................209
  B. Tailored Trials....................................216
  C. Judging Proof.....................................240
  D. Charges and Verdict Forms.........................244
  E. Post-Trial Proceedings............................252

Table of Cases

The principal cases are in bold. Cases cited or discussed in the text are not underlined. References are to pages. Cases cited in principal cases and within other quoted materials are not included.

Amalgamated Ass'n of Street, Electric Ry. & Motors Coach Employees v. Lockridge, 67
American Broadcasting-Paramount Theatres, Inc. v. Simpson, 46
Asbestos Litigation, In re, 41, 55, 58, **395** mc

Bank of New England, N.A., United States v., 538 mc
Bazley v. Tortorich, 155
Bishop v. E.A. Strout Realty Agency, Inc., 92, **574** mc
Breland v. Schilling, 159
Brown v. Board of Education, 39
Browning-Ferris Industries of Vermont v. Kelco Disposal, Inc., 84, 87
Bull v. McCuskey, 750 mc

C & J Fertilizer, Inc. v. Allied Mut. Ins. Co., 133
Cabell v. Markham, 141
Carapellucci v. Town of Winchester, 62
Carolene Products Co., United States v., 176
Chamberlain v. Mathis, 95, 98, **580** mc
Chastleton Corp. v. Sinclair, 175
Citizen v. Daigle, 155, 156
Cody v. Connecticut General Life Ins. Co., 134

Dance v. Ripley, 101
Daniels v. Williams, 5, 6, **265** mc
Dartmouth College v. Woodward, 87
Davis v. Wyeth Laboratories, Inc., 114, **662** mc

DeShaney v. Winnebago County Department of Social Services, 8, **279** mc
Diggs v. Hood, 169

EEOC v. Trabucco, 59
Elliott, United States v., 173

Faithful Liability Insurance Company v. Edward Edwards and the Pub, Inc., 686
First National Bank of Boston v. Bellotti, 87
Frigaliment Importing Co. Ltd. v. B.N.S. International Sales Corp., 142

Gulden v. Crown Zellerbach Corporation, 702 mc

Hardy v. United States, 82
Harlow v. Fitzgerald, 99
Heileman Brewing Co., Inc. v. Joseph Oat Corporation, 709 mc
Hooker Chemicals & Plastics Corp., United States v., 72

Hustler Magazine v. Falwell, 37, 76, 83, **458** mc, 681
Hybritech, Inc. v. Abbott Laboratories, 73

Insurance Co. of North America v. Pasakarnis, 162
International Paper Co. v. Inhabitants of the Town of Jay, Maine, 12

TABLE OF CASES

Janklow v. Newsweek, Inc., 74
Jones v. Davis, 511, 513, 520

Kassel v. Consolidated Freightways Corp., 176
Kavadas v. Lorenzen, 693 mc
Koos v. Roth, 76

Langan v. Valicopters, Inc., 446 mc
Lowe v. Estate Motors Ltd., 162

Mattyasovsky v. West Towns Bus Co., 149
McDonnell Douglas Corp. v. Green, 101
McKee v. American Home Products Corporation, 594 mc
Montplaisir v. Leighton, 67

NAACP v. Claiborne Hardware Co., 37
New England Tractor-Trailer Training of Connecticut, Inc. v. Globe Newspaper Company, 77, 93, 562 mc
New York Times Company v. Sullivan, 37, 83, 93

Olmstead v. United States, 50
Oxford Shipping Co., Ltd. v. New Hampshire Trading Corp., 16, 88, 527 mc
O'Neill v. Dell Publishing Co., 58, 60

Philadelphia Newspapers, Inc. v. Hepps, 46, 100
Pique v. Saia, 158
Planned Parenthood League of Massachusetts v. Bellotti, 73

Reyes v. Wyeth Laboratories, Inc., 114
Rochin v. California, 14
Rossell v. Volkswagen of America, 757 mc

Salinas v. Roadway Express, Inc., 19, 302 mc
San Juan Dupont Plaza Hotel Fire Litigation, In re, 215
Sandstrom v. Montana, 57, 80, 81, 82, 470 mc
Shackil v. Lederle Laboratories, 31, 342 mc, **681**
Siegler v. Kuhlman, 58
Sinram v. Pennsylvania Railroad, 103, 128
Six Carpenters' Case, 125
Smith v. Westland Life Ins. Co., 133
Sonesta International Hotels Corp. v. Wellington Associates, 73
Southern Pacific Co. v. Jensen, 52
Spier v. Barker, 162

Texas Department of Community Affairs v. Burdine, 101
Time, Inc. v. Hill, 83

Vest, United States v., 149
Vlandis v. Kline, 26

Wallace v. United States, 17
Wards Cove Packing Company, Inc. v. Atonio, 77, 102, 626 mc
Warren's Community Health Center, Inc. v. Cohen, 73

Zobel v. Williams, 24, 26, 312 mc

PART ONE

AN INTRODUCTION TO JUDICIAL DECISIONMAKING

CHAPTER 1

COMMITMENTS AND PERSPECTIVES

A. The Obligation of Reasoned Decision

Judging is choice. Choice is power. Power is neither good nor evil, except as it is allocated and used.

Judging in a legal system is professional. Professionals, including judges, represent interests other than their own. One who accepts a professional role in a legal system accepts an obligation to confine the exercise of power within the limits of authority. For each professional role, the limits of authority are defined by law. One cannot fully understand the conduct of a professional without fully understanding the defined professional role.

The quality of judging in a legal system depends on commitment. It depends, first, on commitment to the aim of justice. Second, it depends on commitment to professionalism. The declared beliefs of all professionals in the system -- including advocates, counsellors, and academic critics as well as judges -- affect the quality of judging in the system. Third, the quality of judging depends on commitment to method. Judicial choice, at its best, is reasoned choice, candidly explained.

Ch. 1 COMMITMENTS AND PERSPECTIVES

The most common method of reasoning to a choice depends less on deductive reasoning than on informative reasoning. An example of deductive reasoning is a judge's use of reason to work out what an authoritative statement of law means for the case before the court. The truth is, however, that when the meaning of the authoritative statement is not clear, deductive reasoning alone cannot tell the judge which of two or more suggested interpretations to choose. In this circumstance, the judge may turn to informative reasoning -- that is, to the use of reason to explore the practical consequences of each of the two or more different interpretations suggested. When choosing one interpretation over others after this kind of reasoning, the judge makes a better informed choice -- a choice illumined by informative reasoning.

Also, a judge may use informative reasoning when two or more different and clashing statements of law are cited, and the judge must choose which one to apply to the case at hand.

Another method of reasoned choice is what we call analogy. Logic draws sharp, bright lines. In contrast, analogy deals with ranges and shadings. If life -- or what we call experience -- has seams, or bright lines of separation between one kind of experience and another, the seams are few and far between. What we perceive or report as a seam -- a bright line between contrasts -- is more often the gloss of our interpretation of life experiences than an inherent contrast in their nature. Two life experiences seldom, if ever, are either exactly alike or totally different. They tend to be more or less alike, and more or less different. Analogy, more often than logic, is the principal method by which we compare and contrast different experiences, and assimilate and differentiate them.

Folk wisdom supports these observations about judging. People call judges good not because they are good at logic but because they are good at making hard choices.

The community holds judges accountable for their choices. Community critics attack a judge's decision when they notice a choice perceived to be bad. Often they do so because they also believe, or assume, that it was within the judge's authority to make a better choice. If community critics are less sensitive than they should be to the distinction between power (what a judge can do and get away with it) and authority (what the judge can legitimately do), perhaps legal professionals -- all of us and not just the judges among us -- have been less candid and resourceful than we should be in explaining judging both among ourselves and to others.

Judging tends to be burdensome. If choices are too easy, making them becomes repetitive and boring. In current circumstances, however, judging is more likely to be burdensome in another way. The load of cases is heavy. Delays produced by excessive caseloads encourage more settlements. The small percentage of cases left for decision, after settlements have disposed of the great majority, are selectively the more difficult. The judge's choices are often hard and must be made under time pressures. Judging in these circumstances is both difficult and challenging, but less fulfilling than it might have been if each judge were free to take more time for reflection about each issue that must be decided.

These, I believe, are fundamental truths about judging. If you agree, I hope not to dissuade you. But even at that risk and regardless of your agreement or disagreement with these assertions, I ask you to reexamine what you believe about judging.

Whether or not you are a judge or ever expect to be one, it makes a difference how well you understand judging in our legal system and what you believe about commitment to the aim of justice, to professionalism, and to method in judging.

B. Perspectives for Understanding Law and Judging

1. The Perspective of a Trial Judge

This book concerns decisionmaking in both trial and appellate courts. I speak primarily, however, from the perspective of a trial judge, even when speaking of appellate decisionmaking. In part I do so because of the nature of my personal experience. I do so as well because of my central purpose in preparing this book. That purpose is to encourage you to examine law in action. Viewing law from the perspective of the lawyers and the judge participating in a trial helps us think about how well a rule of law works when human actors try to apply it, and whether a somewhat different rule might work better.

There is, of course, great risk that a trial judge's reflections on appellate decisionmaking will be understood -- and in this specific instance I will assert misunderstood -- as petulant criticism of higher authority. I would not deny having felt impulses of that kind, but I intend and believe that the ideas I wish to express in this book are free of that taint. They are meant to be reflections on the inherent nature of judicial decisionmaking rather than criticisms of the performance of particular judges -- either appellate or trial judges.

Published materials on the nature of judging are voluminous. This book does not purport to present all the conflicting views worthy of study, or even to cite to sources that do so. Rather, it is aimed, first, at identifying fundamental issues a judge in the American legal system encounters. Second, it presents some reflections on how judges may resolve those issues consistently with their professional commitments. Third, it presents some problem cases, judicial opinions, and other materials that illustrate the issues and serve as a basis for your own personal reflection. Though my purpose is to encourage you to develop your own considered views, I have not hesitated to state my own views, including views developed earlier but reinforced by the experience of serving as a trial judge.

2. Law in Action

Trying to understand law without ever thinking about its application to particular transactions and relationships is an undertaking with inherent limitations. We cannot fully understand law, or any aspect of it, until we know how it works. Theories, principles, doctrines, rules of law, standards of conduct, and legal tests for determining accountability mean, in the real world, what they come to mean when human actors, with all their strengths and failings, bring them to bear in shaping transactions and relationships and resolving controversies. For this reason, in order to sharpen particular issues for examination I will also make generous use of real cases, decided by real people, first at trial and later on appeal. In addition, I will use hypothetical cases before hypothetical judges. My purpose in using real cases as part of the subject matter is not to evaluate or rate individual judges. Instead, the purpose is to examine law in action -- to test abstract ideas, including theories and principles of judicial decisionmaking, by evaluating attempts to apply them to real as well as hypothetical cases.

For the purpose of testing principles against practice and practice against principles, I will often interrupt a train of thought about principles with comments about cases -- some of them real cases and some of them hypothetical. The time has come for the first of such interruptions.

Case 1.1
The Injured Inmate

In a case that came before the Supreme Court in 1986,[1] Daniels claimed that, while an inmate at a city jail, he slipped on a pillow negligently left on the stairs by a correctional deputy stationed at the jail. Claiming under 42 U.S.C. §1983, Daniels argued that this negligence deprived him of his liberty interest in freedom from bodily injury. Because the defendant asserted a defense of sovereign immunity against tort liability under state law, Daniels argued that he was without an adequate state remedy and that the deprivation of his liberty was without "due process of law." Affirming the Court of Appeals' affirmance of a summary judgment against Daniels, the Supreme Court concluded "that the Due Process Clause is simply not implicated by a <u>negligent</u> act of an official causing unintended loss of or injury to life, liberty or property."[2]

The Court added:

> Despite his claim about what he might have pleaded, petitioner concedes that respondent was at most negligent. Accordingly, this case affords us no occasion to consider whether something less than intentional conduct, such as

---

[1] <u>Daniels</u> v. <u>Williams</u>, 474 U.S. 327 (1986).

[2] 474 U.S. at 328 (emphasis in Court opinion).

recklessness or "gross negligence," is enough to trigger the protections of the Due Process Clause.[3]

Assume that, in a §1983 action based on an incident occurring after the Court's decision in Daniels, an injured inmate proffers evidence on which reasonable jurors could find either way on issues of intent, recklessness, or gross negligence. What question or questions about intent, recklessness, or gross negligence of the state officer should the trial court submit to the jury?

The Court's decision in Daniels v. Williams removed any doubt about whether a trial court need submit a negligence question in relation to this kind of §1983 claim; it need not.

You will observe, however, that the question presented in the hypothetical Case 1.1 is an issue not decided by the Supreme Court. Thus, to understand the law as applied to the issue presented in Case 1.1, a federal trial judge must look first to any relevant decisions of the court of appeals for the circuit in which the trial court is located and, if finding no clear answer there, to other court decisions that might provide guidance.

In the period immediately after Daniels v. Williams was decided, the precedents to be found left unanswered many questions about potentially applicable standards of conduct that might be used as tests for determining legal responsibility -- gross negligence, recklessness, or intent, and if intent, then intent in what sense and in relation to what consequence or consequences.

Moreover, quite apart from issues regarding the standard of conduct -- that is, about intent, recklessness, and gross negligence -- one may read the opinion in Daniels as suggesting that, on an appropriate occasion, the Supreme Court may fashion a test for determining the scope of liability for violation of whatever standard of conduct is used as a test for determining liability. Tests for determining the scope of liability are sometimes fashioned

---

[3]Id. at 334, n.3.

under the rubric of "legal cause." The Court stated:

> The only tie between the facts of this case and anything governmental in nature is the fact that respondent was a sheriff's deputy at the Richmond city jail and petitioner was an inmate confined in that jail.[4]

Might the Court fashion a test for determining "legal cause" that is different from the tests stated or implicitly suggested in other precedents?

The conclusion stated by the Court immediately following the quoted passage was only that the Due Process Clause of the Fourteenth Amendment does not require any procedure for awarding compensation for harm caused by a state officer's lack of due care. But if the absence of some "tie" other than inmate status in a city jail is fatal to a negligence claim, may it likewise be fatal to a claim based on violation of some standard of conduct other than negligence -- for example, recklessness or intent? And what other kind of "tie," or test for determining "legal cause," might be relevant to a claim under any of the possible standards of conduct that might be invoked? Will it make a difference whether some more substantial or different kind of "tie" is shown? For example, suppose the claimant in custody was disabled by intoxication, or by a diabetic condition that was mistaken for intoxication? In these circumstances, does the Due Process Clause of the Fourteenth Amendment require any procedure for compensating harm caused by recklessness, or by deliberate indifference to the claimant's need for medical attention, or by recklessness or deliberate indifference about his safety when using a stairway in the jail? These are questions that advocates may present, and that trial judges must resolve when they are presented, either with guidance in circuit and district court precedents or as issues of first impression.

One reason for calling attention to these unresolved issues is to underscore the point that we begin to understand much more about the meaning of law laid down in an authoritative source, and about the scope and nature of questions left unresolved, as we consider how that authoritative declaration will be brought to bear in a trial

---

[4] Id. at 332.

court to help resolve a pending case. Nuances of the authoritative declaration will be exploited in advocacy when the circumstances of a pending case present the opportunity. One of the contexts of law in action that is most likely to illumine the meaning of authoritative declarations is that in which the trial judge and the advocates in a pending case consider how statutes and precedents are to be invoked and interpreted in tailoring interrogatories or instructions to the jury at trial. This book will return to that context often.

Consider, briefly, a second illustration.

Case 1.2
The Battered Child[5]

The mother of Joshua brought this action, pursuant to 42 U.S.C. §1983, against social workers and other local officials. She alleged that the defendants had received complaints that Joshua's father had beaten Joshua repeatedly and that they failed to remove Joshua from the father's custody, causing him, at age four, to be exposed to a beating that left him brain-damaged and profoundly disabled for the rest of his life. The legal theory of the claim is that defendants deprived Joshua of his liberty interest without due process of law in violation of his rights under the Fourteenth Amendment.

Is a §1983 claim stated?

When thinking about Case 1.2, every former first-year law student will recall an early exposure to tort cases concerning when, if at all, one has a duty to act to aid another in peril. The student is aware of centuries of evolving legal precedents on this subject in what, only as recently as about a century ago, we came to refer to as the law of torts. The former student who recalls some of this legal history will naturally be curious about how the claim that Joshua has been deprived of a constitutionally protected interest relates to that large body of tort law. One

---

[5]Based on DeShaney v. Winnebago County Department of Social Services, ___ U.S. ___, 109 S. Ct. 998 (1989).

question that comes to mind is this: Out in the real world, what practical difference will it make whether the claim, if supportable on any ground, is recognized as just a "tort," or instead as a "constitutional tort," or as both? Is this a question that is, or ought to be, explicitly and candidly considered by judicial decisionmakers in trial and appellate courts as Joshua's case is decided? My answer is yes.

My reasons are so intimately associated with all I wish to present for your consideration that for the moment I postpone any explanation beyond what I have stated above.[6]

Having stated two cases and a few questions about them in order to give some context for introducing ideas about judicial decisionmaking generally, I proceed to some additional comments on perspective and then some tentative generalizations about judicial decisionmaking in all cases, these included.

3. Law in Development

To understand judging, one must first understand that law is always developing.

Trial lawyers and trial judges have less to do with the immediate shaping of transactions and ongoing relationships than do other members of the legal profession, whose clients seek advice and representation long before litigation has developed. Good advice may enable the client to shape transactions to serve the client's purposes while also avoiding risks of dispute that may lead to litigation. Nevertheless, because of daily involvement in resolving controversies, trial judges and trial lawyers are acutely aware of a characteristic of law and the legal system that is critical to fully understanding judicial decisionmaking at all levels. Law is developing. It is not a complete and closed system. Implications of this point will appear again and again in this book.[7]

---

[6] Section A, this Chapter, supra.

[7] See, e.g., Chapter 2, Section 2, infra.

Ch. 1 COMMITMENTS AND PERSPECTIVES

C. Professional Commitment

1. Judging as Professional Conduct

One who is cynical about the legal system may tell you that cases are decided for reasons different from those disclosed by judges -- even for reasons that judges do not appreciate cognitively, such as the state of their digestion.

Both as a trial judge and as an observer of trial and appellate judging generally, I assert with conviction that although some cases may be decided in one or the other of those two ways -- unknowingly by the state of the judge's digestion, or knowingly for reasons deliberately concealed -- most are not. Of course, even though judging ranks quite favorably in public perception as to integrity, no human institution is entirely free of corruption. It seems beyond reasonable challenge, however, that in the American legal system the percentage of cases corruptly decided for reasons other than those disclosed is quite small. In a greater number of cases, no doubt, though still a low percentage, judges deliberately stop short of candidly explaining all the reasons for decision because they think fully candid explanation is inappropriate. Also, probably a still more substantial number of cases are decided for reasons not adequately explained, either simply because judges, too, are human or because when a case is decided by a panel of two or more members of a court it may be difficult to determine precisely what are the reasons that persuade at least a majority of the court. Despite all these reasons for less than full and candid explanation, most cases are decided for the very reasons the court states. The fact that no court's statement of reasons ever answers all the questions that occur to the minds of thoughtful readers does not disprove this point. Instead, that fact is one more confirmation of the developing quality of law.

I am acutely aware of many expressions of cynicism about the stated reasons for judicial decisions. Those who express cynicism on this subject include lawyers and law teachers, and even some judges -- especially trial judges. Of course, judge-bashing (even one judge's bashing another judge, at least if it is discreet and professional) has always received protection and for very good reasons, not only under the First Amendment but more broadly as well, under other legal authority. I would not have it otherwise. I emphasize, however, a different point. It is that professionals of the legal system have it in their power to use their freedom of comment to affect the quality of judging. What lawyers, law teachers, and judges say to each other and to students about the quality of judging may tend to be self-fulfilling prophecy. It will have an influence on the quality of judging in the future.

An illustration reinforces the point. A curious thing happened in the law of torts, commencing in the late 1950s. Noticeably, the number of decisions of state courts of last resort that candidly overruled precedents increased. Within a ten-year span commencing in 1958, the count of such decisions in American state courts of last resort rose to a hundred.[1] The count for any preceding ten-year period in Anglo-American legal history was no more than a small fraction of this number. How and why did this happen?

No doubt there were many influences. An important one, I believe, was that many of the judges of the 1960s had in the 1930s sat in the classes of Realists. Realists were stridently critical of decisions they perceived to be grounded on reasons other than those stated in judicial opinions. Realists -- at least most of them -- were also reformers. The message they conveyed to their students was that judging could be and should be improved -- by candid, policy-based reasoning, both in deciding cases and in drafting the courts' opinions explaining the decisions.

More than criticism of individual judges, the Realists' position was criticism of the way the legal system defined the professional role of judging -- placing constraints, as they correctly perceived it did, upon a judge's freedom to recognize the developing nature of law. The professional tradition preceding the Realist critique did not openly recognize a reality -- the fact that, by necessity, in order to decide cases before them, judges had to make choices and sometimes had to make lawmaking choices. Under the pre-Realist tradition, judges were not free to be candidly explicit in their opinions about what they were doing and why. Thus, that tradition grossly understated the lawmaking role of judges. It tended to foster a myth that even when deciding cases of first impression judges were just finding the law -- deriving it from authoritative sources by logical deduction -- rather than making law by informed choice.

---

[1] The cases are collected in R. Keeton, <u>Venturing to Do Justice</u> 169-79 (1969).

Ch. 1   COMMITMENTS AND PERSPECTIVES

By the 1960s, the Realists' preference for candor about judicial lawmaking (though certainly not all their criticisms of the legal system) had taken hold. A perceptive trial judge, writing about judging, would draw little criticism for observing not only that judges make law but as well that they do so on value-based reasoning.[2] More and more judges acknowledged, even in writing their judicial opinions, that judges often make law in deciding cases. By the 1980s, the inevitability of lawmaking by judges -- including trial judges[3] -- was quite generally accepted even if sometimes acknowledged uneasily because of concern that public awareness might undermine public confidence in law and courts.

---

[2] See C. Wyzanski, Whereas -- A Judge's Premises xiii (1965) ("Value is not merely, as it always has been, inherent in the process. It is at the forefront of explicit considerations."). The role of value-based reasoning is a recurring theme in this book and is the principle theme of Chapter 4, infra.

[3] E.g., International Paper Co. v. Inhabitants of the Town of Jay, Maine, 887 F.2d 338, 344-45 (1st Cir. 1989); Nuesse v. Camp, 385 F.2d 694, 702 (D.C. Cir. 1967). In International Paper, an issue before the court was whether the adverse impact of stare decisis may alone be sufficient to satisfy the practical impairment requirement for intervention as of right under Fed. R. Civ. P. 24(a)(2), and thus warrant reversal of the trial court's denial of the State of Maine's petition for intervention. The First Circuit held that the trial court did not abuse discretion in denying intervention, noting that the stare decisis effect is greatly lessened where there are parties already in the suit whose position on the issues is the same as the absent party's. The First Circuit, 887 F.2d at 345, also quoted with approval the following passage from Nuesse regarding a trial court's decision of an issue of first impression.

> [W]e may expect that a decision by the [Federal] District Court here, the first judicial treatment of this question, would receive great weight, whether the question arose again in this jurisdiction or in the federal court in Wisconsin. Should this court on appeal render a decision in the Commissioner's [proposed intervenor's] absence, and contrary to his view, he would presumably be hampered in seeking to vindicate his approach in another court.

385 F.2d at 702.

Nor is it just law professors and judges who recognize this point. Even before judges became more candid in judicial opinions about the inevitability of lawmaking in deciding cases, lawyers were heard, and still today may be heard, to say of a kind of case they most enjoy talking about, "We made some law in that case!" Typically the emphasis is on "made some law." No need to emphasize "we," because it is self-evident that at least the winning advocate, and sometimes the loser as well, has a hand in the making.

If we accept that point of view, as I do, then legal professionals are lawmakers all, and accountable to the community for the lawmaking we do in professional roles.

The professional commitment of the judge -- what the judge believes about what he or she is doing -- makes a difference. If any judge believes with the cynics that reasons for decisions are different from those publicly stated -- as some judges have occasionally proclaimed -- the potential contributions of that judge to justice are in some degree limited by the lack of commitment to the principle of reasoned decisionmaking, candidly explained. One of the limitations concerns the way advocates are likely to respond to a perception of lack of commitment by a judge. Stated more generally, the point is that the advocates' perception of the judge's commitment makes a difference also.

If, as an advocate, you believe that the judge whom you are trying to persuade is firmly committed to reasoned decisionmaking, you tailor your advocacy to appeal to that point of view. You show the judge, in your briefs and arguments, a reasoned way the judge can responsibly decide for your client. Because it would be at least unfruitful and perhaps even counterproductive to seem to be appealing to the judge to violate professional obligations, including an oath of office to do justice according to law and fact, you never submit a brief or argument that simply appeals to prejudice or advances only strident arguments no responsible judge could use in explaining a decision your way. Briefs and arguments of that kind make it harder for the judge to decide your way, because the judge is left with no help (except that of good law clerks) in preparing the reasoned explanation of a decision your way. It is not only cynical but, I believe, ill-advised advocacy to hope that the judge will decide in ignorance of relevant authority, or will ignore relevant authority in delivering an oral opinion or drafting a written opinion for the content of which neither advocate has made any suggestion -- both advocates making instead only more strident arguments that a responsible judge could not comfortably adopt.

To underscore this point, I call attention to some wise but often misinterpreted advice about emphasizing the facts in briefs and oral arguments. The eloquent advice of distinguished advocates about incorporating in your brief a good statement of facts is advice in which I join without hesitation. I emphasize another point as well, however, lest good advice be misunderstood and misapplied.

Compare two kinds of statements of facts.

First, imagine a full paragraph of colorful prose that makes only two factual points -- that the plaintiff is in desperate financial straits and that the defendant is a large corporation. If you write that kind of statement of facts, you tell the court that you are appealing for sympathy and not for reasoned decisionmaking. By writing such a statement, you weaken your appeal to a judge who is committed to reasoned decisionmaking, candidly explained.

Second, imagine a statement of facts that eloquently marshals the factual premises of your legal position and exposes implications of your opponent's legal position that are likely to "shock the conscience."[4] That is one of the most telling legal arguments an advocate can make.

Note, then, that when wisely practiced, the advice to include an eloquent statement of facts in a brief or oral argument -- either to an appellate court or to a trial court -- is not cynical advice to try to persuade the decisionmaker to disregard sworn obligations. It is instead advice to use facts to expose premises for evaluation -- to expose any harsh unstated implications of an opponent's legal argument. It is advice to use advocacy to help the court make a wiser, better informed choice that is also consistent with the court's obligation of reasoned decisionmaking.

---

[4] Of course, authoritative sources of law include references to things perceived as shocking, either to the "conscience of the court" or to the "conscience of the community" that it is the court's obligation to respect. See, e.g., Rochin v. California, 342 U.S. 165 (1952) (stomach pumping). See also the next subsection, infra.

2. Representation of Interests Other Than One's Own

All of the professionals of the legal system are actors in lawmaking. I use the term "actors" descriptively, not pejoratively. Professionals are representatives of interests other than their own. They have professional responsibilities. They occupy defined roles.

Acting in an assigned role, a professional often must place the interests of others ahead of the professional's own personal interests. Occasionally a defined role may demand of a professional -- a lawyer or a judge, among others -- actions that are compatible with moral premises held by the person or persons whose interests the professional is charged to represent, despite incompatibility with moral premises the professional would apply in purely personal decisions. If the incompatibility is so severe that the lawyer or the judge cannot perform in the defined role, the required response may be withdrawal from the role rather than action contrary to the demands of the role. And, of course, even withdrawal is not a choice free of constraints, given the potential harm that withdrawal may cause to interests that the lawyer or the judge was charged to serve while acting in the defined professional role.

No doubt the hard choice of withdrawing from the role of judging or else reaching a decision contrary to the judge's sense of justice does sometimes confront a judge. No doubt, also, when confronting such a dilemma, the judge usually concludes that the contribution one may make as a judge, committed to professionalism in judging, outweighs personal discomfort and leads to the choice to reach a result offensive to the judge's personal sense of justice. Far more often, however, judging presents no such dilemma. One reason is that closer scrutiny of the legal arguments for an outcome that the judge initially perceives to be contrary to the judge's sense of justice discloses fallacies in the legal arguments.[5] In such circumstances, even though resourceful advocacy has presented the appearance of a genuine dilemma for the judge, deeper probing convinces the judge that the law applicable to the case at hand supports an outcome

---

[5] For additional comment on this subject, see Chapter 2, Section E2, infra.

Ch. 1 COMMITMENTS AND PERSPECTIVES

entirely compatible with the judge's sense of justice.[6]

Each of the many roles of actors in the legal system is defined by law. That legal definition of role often leaves great range for the exercise of discretion by the actor, and an individual actor's performance may enhance or reduce the significance of the role. But it is law that defines both the role and the scope and limits of the

---

[6]See, e.g., Oxford Shipping Co. v. New Hampshire Trading Corp., 697 F.2d 1 (1st Cir. 1983) (Breyer, J.). The court observed:

> Oxford Shipping Co., Ltd. ("Oxford"), is a subsidiary of a large Hong Kong commercial firm. Oxford's assets consist principally of one cargo ship, the "Eastern Saga." Oxford claims that it was hurt when its ship was seized by South Korean authorities as a result of a scheme to cheat a Korean firm, Yulsan. Yulsan had bought about 20,000 tons of scrap metal, which applicable bills of lading represented to be aboard the "Eastern Saga," but the ship actually contained only about 17,000 tons of metal.
>
> . . .
>
> Since Oxford itself seems to have been innocent of wrongdoing (although the captain and crew of its ship may have known of the plot), while several of the defendants seem to have been guilty of conduct ranging from simple breach of fiduciary duty to what approaches criminal behavior, one might believe at first glance that it would be fairly easy for Oxford (the company and its shareholders) to recover for the harms suffered. The record reveals, however, a highly complicated set of legalistic arguments, made by the defendants' lawyers and by Oxford's lawyers in response, that led the district court to conclude that the defendants were entitled to judgment on all counts. Oxford appeals. <u>Our review of the case convinces us that the law should, and does, correspond with one's elementary sense of justice</u>: namely, as between Oxford and most of these defendants, the defendants rather than Oxford and its shareholders should pay for the damage caused.

<u>Id.</u> at 2 (emphasis added). The legal issue involved is one of many problems that have arisen with respect to "entity state-of-mind" standards. <u>See generally</u> Chapter 3, Section B4, <u>infra</u>.

discretion of the actor in that role.

To perform in the most effective way, any actor in the legal system -- including a lawyer or a judge -- must understand the different demands, constraints, and potentialities of each of the different roles he or she is called upon to occupy, either in sequence[7] or, sometimes, simultaneously.[8]

Professional commitment to the judicial role is essential, but, of course, it does not guarantee good judging. The professional commitment is both to the objective of doing justice and to the method of law -- that is, the method of using law to achieve justice, and doing so in an evenhanded way that treats like cases alike, regardless of who the litigants are. Thus, to understand the role of judge fully, one must understand the judge's use of law. Exploration of the method -- or methods if you prefer -- of judging lawfully is the principal subject matter of this book.

D. The Method of Reasoned Choice

1. Legal and Factual Premises

Judges must make choices in deciding cases.

To reach a reasoned choice about the final judgment in a case a judge must use both legal and factual grounds --

---

[7]An illustration of occupying different roles in sequence is the trial lawyer who must at different times in the same case occupy the roles of zealous advocate, skilled negotiator, and wise counselor to the client about settlement.

[8]The necessity of occupying two roles simultaneously is illustrated in a decisionmaker's application of the test commonly used in deciding value when no market exists -- the price upon which a willing buyer and willing seller would agree. The decisionmaker must envision a bargaining session between these two hypothetical creatures who, unlike real-life negotiators, always reach agreement. It is as if the decisionmaker were taking both roles simultaneously, and bargaining until agreement. See Wallace v. United States, 566 F. Supp. 904, 910-12, 917-21 (D. Mass. 1981).

or, as we commonly say, "premises." Either acting alone, or as part of a decisionmaking panel, the judge considers competing contentions and chooses among conflicting potentially applicable legal premises. As to factual premises, the judge either chooses which among the disputed assertions of fact is correct -- and thus decides the facts -- or chooses among methods of regulating and reviewing fact decisions made by others.

Assume these circumstances: first, the case is one in which finding the distinctive facts of the case on trial is the judge's responsibility; second, alleged fact "x" is material to the outcome of the case; and, third, the evidence is such that reasonable persons may draw either the inference that "x" is true or the inference that it is not true. In these circumstances, the judge must choose which of these two inferences to draw. For example, if Case 1.1 is tried before a judge without a jury, the judge is supposed to make this choice with respect to the alleged fact that the defendant was grossly negligent in leaving the pillow on the jail stairway. A contrast between the judge's role as factfinder and a jury's role as factfinder is that the judge must disclose a reasoned explanation for the choice made.

A jury is directed to make a reasoned choice, based on evidence and in conformity with instructions on the applicable law, but the jury need not explain its choice, may even be forbidden to explain in any proceeding before a court, and, if jurors try to explain, what they say may be legally irrelevant. Thus, if Case 1.1 is tried before a jury, the jury decides whether or not to draw from the conflicting evidence the inference that the defendant was grossly negligent. The jury need not disclose its reasons.

In a nonjury trial of Case 1.1, this factfinding choice of the judge is subject to review not simply by a test concerned with whether a reasonable person could reach the choice the judge made, but by a more demanding test concerned with whether a reasonable person could reach the choice in the way the judge reached it. Thus, if the trial judge has failed to offer a reasoned explanation that passes muster, a higher court may remand with directions that the trial judge reconsider and either make the same ultimate finding on reasoning that does pass muster (perhaps including additional, subsidiary findings) or else make a different finding on reasoning that is acceptable.[1]

When an issue of law material to disposition of a case is in dispute, the judge must choose among the possible ways of resolving that issue. The range of choice is not unfettered, however. Judges are not free to make choices expressing their own personal values. Their professional obligation is one of reasoned choice -- or as it is often described -- principled adjudication.[2]

The obligation of principled adjudication refers to principles that are consistent with a community standard. It is not enough that the principles on which a decision is based are acceptable to some individuals, or even to the entire group serving as judges at the time and place of decision. The judge's obligation is to apply rules of law that are expressed in the community's authoritative sources of law -- chiefly constitutions, statutes, and precedents. Also, the judge's obligation is to respect not only the explicit mandates but as well the manifestations of principle and policy found in the authoritative sources. Even when these manifestations are incomplete and imperfect -- that is, when they do not answer one or more of the questions that must be answered to decide the case at hand -- they nevertheless offer substantial guidance. The judge must make a choice among different suggested answers to any previously unanswered question that must be answered to decide the case, but both the framing of the question and the range of possible answers are constrained by the guidance that is either explicit or implicit in the authoritative sources. When the guidance is thus incomplete or ambiguous and the judge must make a choice, candid disclosure of the reasons for choice contributes to clarity of law and promotes understanding.

---

[1] E.g., Salinas v. Roadway Express, Inc., 735 F.2d 1574 (5th Cir. 1984).

[2] See H. Hart & A. Sacks, The Legal Process: Basic Problems in the Making and Application of Law 588-89 (tent. ed. 1958). This traditional obligation is reinforced in some specific contexts by formal rules, such as Fed. R. Civ. P. 52(a) (trial court's obligation to express findings and conclusions in nonjury trials) and federal sentencing guidelines.

2. Reason, Choice, Policy and Rationality

The requirement that the judge's choice in resolving a dispute over an issue of law be reasoned and impartial is not a requirement that it be value-free. No ruling on an issue of law is value-free.[3] Invariably, if we press the analysis deeply enough, we find that any ruling of law (even, for example, one on a narrow issue regarding a burden of production of evidence) has a set of consequences not only for the case at hand but also, under the doctrine of precedent, for other cases as well. That set of consequences is different from the set that would be produced by a different ruling. Examined from the perspective of the extent to which those different sets of consequences serve or disserve various interests that different people value in different ways, the ruling is value-laden. This is so whether or not the judge's reasoning explicitly takes the value implications of the decision into account.

Essentially the same point is expressed in the statement that legal decisionmaking inevitably involves moral choice. Thus, the point made above -- that judges are not free to make choices expressing their own personal values -- may also be expressed another way: judges are not free to make choices on the basis of personal moral views that they perceive to be in conflict with the moral views expressed or implied in the authoritative declarations they are professionally obligated to apply.

I do not suggest that this position is universally accepted. Indeed, debates about it are ongoing. I believe, however, that much of the apparent conflict becomes less difficult to understand and resolve when the issue is framed as I have stated it -- in terms of the inevitability that rulings are value-laden rather than in terms of differences over moral principles. In any event, references to the issue in this book are usually framed in terms of the value implications of decisions.

The form of judicial reasoning that explores considerations of principle and policy underlying constitutional, statutory and decisional declarations of law results in a choice that is neither more nor less value-laden than reasoning that contains no reference to principle or policy. Being more explicit about value implications of a

---

[3] *See* Chapter 4, *infra*.

choice does make an important difference, however. It more clearly exposes for criticism both the choice and the reasons for the choice. Openly acknowledging that courts make value-laden choices will, in the long run, contribute to a sharper focus on issues of principle and policy, and to wiser choices.[4]

When policy choices and their value-laden implications are openly debated, the reasoning in which the decisionmaker engages is not primarily deductive reasoning from pre-selected declarations of law found in authoritative sources. That is, rather than choosing authoritative declarations first, to serve as what we commonly call "premises" for legal reasoning, and then using reason to derive the outcomes that are implicit in the chosen premises, the decisionmaker is bringing reason to bear upon the choice of premises. This kind of reasoning serves an informative function. It develops the implications of alternative sets of premises and their consequences.[5]

Informative reasoning makes use of logic as it explores the necessary implications of each of the potential rules or rulings among which a choice is to be made. Logic by itself can never produce decision, however, because logic requires premises and logic alone cannot determine all of the premises to be used.

It is true that a premise used in one step of reasoning may have been derived from a previous step of reasoning, in which some form of logic was used. That is, reasoned decisionmaking is seldom a one-step process, and logic is used in some way in each step. Thus, when a second step of reasoning takes as one of its premises a proposition derived from the first step, that premise of the second step was derived by the use of logic in the first step. It may be possible, then, in making a reasoned decision, to move through several steps of reasoning for which a legal premise has been supplied by logical deduction in a preceding step of reasoning. In every instance, however, in which the decision of an issue of law is subject to reasonable dispute,

---

[4] More detailed development of the basic theme of this paragraph and the two preceding paragraphs appears in Chapter 4, infra.

[5] This point was introduced in Section A, this Chapter, supra, and it appears again later in this section and in later Chapters of this book.

if we probe deeply enough we find at some step of the reasoning some legal premise that the judge has chosen rather than deriving it from the outcome of a preceding logical deduction. For premises that must be chosen, logic alone does not supply the answer and cannot explain the choice.

When choice is inevitable, it is prudent to turn to analogy as a method of reasoning aimed at keeping as closely as possible in touch with sources of authority. When those sources do not supply the answer, they nevertheless supply guidance that we perceive by examining the aptness of the most illuminating analogies we may imagine. The most difficult choices judges must make are illumined more by analogy than by logic.

"Rational" and related terms, such as "rationally" and "rationality," are used to express ideas about whether a judge's methods of reasoning to a choice measure up to the judge's obligations.

Consider what "rational" means. At the least it means "reasoned." If a decision is reasoned, rather than being made in some other way (the flip of a coin, for example), it is "rational" in this limited sense. One who says a decision is not "rational," however, may not be using "rational" in this limited sense. As already noted,[6] one cannot reason without using premises, and the essence of wise "judgment" is in the choice of premises, not in the deductive reasoning from them. One who says a decision is "irrational" may be criticizing the premises rather than the logic. Indeed, we more often differ with another person's decision because we reject the premises that the decisionmaker chose as authoritative, or because we reject the analogies invoked by the decisionmaker. Far less often do we differ because we believe the decisionmaker made an error of logical deduction.

This is not to say that logic is unimportant. Logic is, indeed, a powerful instrument for exposing what has been unstated but is implicit. Examples will appear in the discussion of Case 1.3, below. An unstated but implicit proposition that reason helps to expose may be either an unstated premise or an unstated set of consequences of accepting that premise. Curiously, the jargon we use to describe decisions with which we disagree only occasionally refers to "false" or "incorrect" or "indefensible" premises;

---

[6]Section A, this Chapter, *supra*, and this Section, *supra*.

more often a decision is characterized as "illogical" (that is, not reached by a correct use of logic) or "irrational" (that is, not reasoned, or not reasoned correctly).

An argument cast in the unexplained jargon -- "it's illogical," or "it's irrational" -- probably occurs more frequently in trial courts than in appellate courts. By the time a case reaches the appellate level an opposing advocate or a judge has challenged the assertion of irrationality and thus has encouraged a focus on premises and their implications.

In any event, whatever the reasons for the phenomenon may be, a point about good advocacy remains valid -- in trial courts as well as on appeal. An advocate needs to think through premises and implications and, even if electing not to state them fully in the initial argument, written or oral, needs at least to be prepared to do so when challenged. A judge who takes seriously the obligation of reasoned decisionmaking will recognize a meritorious argument more quickly when premises are disclosed. And if reasoned exploration of previously unstated premises and their implications exposes lack of merit, the advocate should recognize that circumstance in advance -- as a result of evaluating the argument before making it -- and look for a better argument, or if there is none, for a settlement.

To illustrate these observations about reason and choice, and about unstated premises and implications, as they come to bear upon both good judging and good advocacy, I turn to an "Equal Protection" case that worked its way through the courts to a final resolution before the Supreme Court in 1982. Bear in mind two points as you consider this illustration. First, premises and implications have become clearer and more explicit by the time the case reaches the highest level of appellate argument. Second, even though Supreme Court opinions tend to be clearer and more explicit on these matters than opinions of lower courts and arguments of advocates in lower courts -- nevertheless, public criticisms of Supreme Court opinions (and references to them in later arguments of advocates in lower courts) tend to fall back often to the form of statement that appears to speak of the logic of the decision rather than the legitimacy of premises.

Ch. 1   COMMITMENTS AND PERSPECTIVES

Case 1.3
The Favored Older Resident[7]

A state statute makes a distinction between old residents of the state and new residents of the state, and prescribes different burdens or benefits for the old and the new.

The case arises from the 1967 discovery of large oil reserves on state-owned land in Alaska, with resulting oil revenues to the state in 1981 of $3.7 billion. The total budget of the state in 1969 had been $124 million. The state established a Permanent Fund into which the state must deposit at least 25% of mineral income each year. In 1980, the legislature enacted, in addition to a tax credit, a dividend program to distribute annually to adult residents a portion of the Fund's earnings on investment of the Fund's principal. Each adult received one dividend unit for each year of residency in Alaska subsequent to 1959, the first year of statehood.

Does the Act violate constitutional rights of the newer residents of the state?

The Supreme Court held that the Act violated the guarantees of the Equal Protection Clause of the Fourteenth Amendment.

My immediate purpose in using this example focuses less upon the substantive issue of Equal Protection than upon how we communicate our views about this and other substantive issues -- upon the professional jargon commonly used in criticizing sources of authority such as statutes and judicial opinions.

Compare the following criticisms of the challenged statutory provision distinguishing between old and new residents, and consider their explicit or implicit meanings: (1) The distinction between old and new residents is irrational; (2) the distinction is illogical; (3) the

---

[7]This case is based on <u>Zobel</u> v. <u>Williams</u>, 457 U.S. 55 (1982).

distinction does not meet the minimum rationality test imposed by decisions of the Supreme Court applying the Equal Protection Clause in cases not involving suspect classifications; (4) the distinction does not rationally further a legitimate state purpose; (5) the distinction is not rationally related to the statutorily declared purpose of rewarding citizen contributions, tangible and intangible, to the public good; and (6) the distinction is in violation of the Constitution because the objective to which it is alleged to be rationally related -- to reward citizens for past contributions to the public good -- is not a legitimate state purpose.

In each of these six instances, what is the target of criticism -- logic, choice of premises, or both?

As you may have observed, the first two of these criticisms, on the surface at least, appear to be criticisms of logic, not choice of premises. The third and fourth are quite ambiguous as to whether they are critical of logic, of choice of premises, or both. The fifth is an unambiguous criticism of logic. The sixth is an unambiguous criticism of the premise.

I refer to this case, and to critics' descriptions of its holding, to illustrate points I try to make in this book about (1) clarity, (2) speaking English at least in addition to, if not in substitution for, jargon, (3) the roles of reason and choice in decisionmaking, and (4) the sensitivity of good advocates to the judge's obligation of reasoned decisionmaking.

None of the four opinions handed down by Justices of the Supreme Court in this case left us to wonder, as the first and second of these six criticisms do, what were the premises of the critic's reasoning. Each of the third through the sixth of the formulations is adapted from a passage or passages in one or more of the opinions. For example, consider this statement of the criterion for scrutiny under the Equal Protection Clause:

Apart from "particularly invidious distinctions [that] are subject to more rigorous scrutiny," when a state law distributes benefits or imposes burdens unequally, generally that law will survive scrutiny under the Equal Protection Clause of the Fourteenth Amendment "if the distinction it makes <u>rationally furthers a legitimate state purpose</u>."[8]

The Alaska statute contained a statement of the purposes of the Act, to which the Court looked rather than speculating about other possible state purposes claimed to be legitimate. Note that the allegedly legitimate state purposes are the premises the Court is examining. The Court's decision is that none of these premises is legitimate. Consistently with the customary way of speaking -- that is, our professional jargon -- the Court states the decisive issue to be whether the state law can "pass even the minimum rationality test proposed by the State."[9] This is an instance, however, in which the Court also explained in English that they were rejecting the state's premises rather than holding that the state's logic was flawed. For example, the Court said, "The only apparent justification for the retrospective aspect of the program, 'favoring established residents over new residents,' is constitutionally unacceptable."[10]

The Court is quite explicit also in its rejection of premises in relation to another of the state's arguments:

> The last of the State's objectives -- to reward citizens for past contributions -- alone was relied upon by the Alaska Supreme Court to support the retrospective application of the law to 1959. However, that objective is not a legitimate state purpose.[11]

Also, near the end of his separate concurring opinion, Justice Brennan is quite explicit in the rejection of a premise:

---

[8] <u>Zobel</u> v. <u>Williams</u>, 457 U.S. 55, 60 (1982) (opinion of the Court, delivered by Burger, C.J., in which Brennan, White, Marshall, Blackmun, Powell and Stevens joined) (emphasis added). Justices Brennan and O'Connor wrote concurring opinions, and Justice (later Chief Justice) Rehnquist dissented on grounds consistent with the formulation of the Equal Protection criterion quoted here.

[9] <u>Id.</u> at 60-61. The State's contentions are recited <u>id.</u> at 61-64.

[10] <u>Id.</u> at 65, <u>citing</u> <u>Vlandis</u> v. <u>Kline</u>, 412 U.S. 441, 450 (1973).

[11] <u>Id.</u> at 63.

> In my view, it is difficult to escape from the recognition that underlying any scheme of classification on the basis of duration of residence, we shall almost invariably find the unstated premise that "some citizens are more equal than others." We rejected that premise and, I believe, implicitly rejected most forms of discrimination based upon length of residence, when we adopted the Equal Protection Clause.[12]

I have used an Equal Protection case for illustration. In Equal Protection cases, the nature of an argument or statement of grounds of decision tends to be starkly evident. That is, it is usually quite clear to one who looks closely that the argument or statement of grounds of decision does or does not disclose underlying premises and examine their implications. But I emphasize that the point I am making about the usefulness and the persuasiveness of the opinion or the brief that is explicit about premises and their implications applies generally and not just to Equal Protection cases. Examples appear elsewhere in this book.[13]

The more fully advocates and judges expose and examine the factual and legal premises of decision -- the more fully they become explicit rather than proceeding on unarticulated implicit premises -- the more likely it is that the inescapable element of judicial choice in decisionmaking is both evenhanded and wise. It is, of course, a fundamental premise of an adversary system that good advocacy will contribute significantly to evenhanded and wise decisionmaking because it will cause the choices made by judges to be better illumined, wiser, and fairer.

---

[12] Id. at 71.

[13] See, e.g., Case 2.1, Chapter 2, Section B, infra.

CHAPTER 2

LAW AND FACTS IN THE ADMINISTRATION OF JUSTICE

A. Introduction

We commonly assert that the aim of our legal system is to do justice according to the law and the facts. By "the law" we mean, more precisely, the law as determined by whatever actor the legal system charges with responsibility for determining the applicable law. By "the facts" we mean, more precisely, the facts as determined by whatever actor the legal system charges with responsibility for determining the facts. Before knowing whether we succeed in doing justice, we must take account of some fundamental characteristics of both law and facts, and of our ways of determining them.

In sketching relationships among law, facts, and justice, this chapter starts with some basic ideas about who decides law and who decides facts. Then it identifies three truths about facts, identifies and develops briefly a fourth truth, and only then identifies parallel or nonparallel truths about law in the same four respects.

B. Who Decides Disputes of Law?

   1. Identification of Lawmakers

At the beginning of the 20th century the body of law commonly called "private law" was overwhelmingly common law. Claims in contract and tort were together the greater part of this body of law. Disputes over the law governing these claims were decided by judges through the common law process of case-by-case decisional development.

It is true that statutes had intervened to govern some

particular issues. For example, statutes of frauds made some oral promises unenforceable; statutes on insurable interest enabled insurers to renounce some contracts -- even written contracts -- because they were in violation of legislatively declared public policies against wagering; survival and wrongful death acts abrogated the common law rules under which death of an injured person terminated all rights of recovery for tortious bodily injuries; and statutes proscribing conduct and fixing criminal penalties occasionally had an impact on tort claims, through the doctrine of negligence per se or in some other way. Nevertheless, all the exceptional instances together added up to a small percentage of contract and tort litigation, which was the greater part of the caseload in the principal trial and appellate courts of the states. The caseload in federal trial and appellate courts included many of the same kinds of cases as those that made up the greater part of state caseloads. These kinds of cases came into the federal courts by reason of diversity jurisdiction. The remainder of the caseload in federal courts -- though the greater percentage of _federal_ cases -- was nevertheless a very small part of the _total_ caseload in all the courts of the nation.

The predominance of common-law claims in the caseload of the courts continued into mid-century, though the picture had begun to change with disproportionate increases in criminal cases, public law cases, and cases in courts of specialized jurisdiction, all of which tended to depend more on statutes than did contract and tort cases.

By the 1990s, the picture regarding the mix of issues of common law and statutory law bearing upon cases in the principal trial courts, state and federal, had changed in several ways.

The most apparent and pervasive change was a marked increase in legislation and in the percentage of court cases affected by legislation. A fundamental characteristic of judging in American courts of the late 20th century is that very few cases depend solely on common law grounds. Legislatures have enacted so many statutes on so many subjects that in most cases before the courts at least one party invokes at least one statute. This change has increased the significance of problems of judging statutes, which are discussed in Chapter 6.

It nevertheless remains true that the judge (or panel of judges) deciding each particular case makes the final reasoned choice that decides any dispute of law in that case. Even when there is no issue of "first impression," the judge makes a choice that decides what rule or rules within the established body of law will be invoked to resolve each dispute of law in the particular case at hand. In this sense of making the final choice, a judge (or a court consisting of a panel of judges) decides every dispute of law.

In a deeper sense, however, other lawmakers have participated in the decision. By adopting constitutions, enacting statutes, and deciding cases within a legal system that treats decisions as precedents, they have created the body of law to which the decisionmaker in the particular case turns for guidance.

An increase in the percentage of issues to which some statute is relevant does not change the necessity of reasoned choice by the judge or court deciding the particular case. It does, however, affect the answer to questions about who created the body of law to which that decisionmaker turns for guidance. The answer to this latter set of questions has been changed not only by the increase in legislation but also by other developments.

In the earlier period of American legal history, judges of state courts of last resort were the principal lawmakers, making state law through the common-law process of case-by-case decisional development. It always has been an inherent characteristic of our federal legal system, however, that others would participate in the process. Thus, the change is not in identity of other lawmakers but in the scope and influence of their work. To understand current and future lawmaking, we need to understand both the identity of the participants and the circumstances that bear upon what the scope of their participation in lawmaking has been and will be.

Presented below in summary form is a suggested structure for thinking about who makes law that becomes a part of the sources of authority that judges are professionally committed to using for guidance in deciding disputes of law in particular cases. Before presenting that summary, however, I state another case that poses some concrete issues addressed in the summary.

WHO DECIDES DISPUTES OF LAW? Sec. B

Case 2.1
An Infant Vaccine Victim[1]

Plaintiffs are a thirteen-year-old child and her parents. They assert medical malpractice and products liability claims for injuries arising out of the inoculation of the child, before her second birthday, with a combined diphtheria-pertussis- tetanus vaccine (DPT). They are unable to identify the manufacturer of the vaccine. It is undisputed that at and before the time of the inoculation five manufacturers were manufacturing DPT, and at the time of trial only two were doing so. Plaintiffs assert that there was a common design defect in the product of all manufacturers. Plaintiffs ask the court to disregard traditional cause-in-fact requirements and apply a rule of "alternative liability" or "market share liability" to hold all manufacturers liable.

State products liability legislation has been enacted, and a dispute exists as to whether any provision of that legislation applies to any issue in this case. Also, Congress enacted the 1986 National Childhood Vaccine Injury Act. That Act, as amended, provides that a person who has suffered illness, injury, or death may submit a petition to the United States Claims Court for compensation by the United States to the extent specified in the Act. Under the Act, a presumption of vaccine-relatedness arises if the injury suffered is listed in the Vaccine Injury Table and the first symptoms occur within a specified time period.

Who has made or will make the law that determines whether the manufacturers' motion for summary judgment should be allowed? Will the answer depend on whether the case is pending in a state court or instead is filed or removed to a United States district court

---

[1]Adapted from <u>Shackil</u> v. <u>Lederle Laboratories</u>, 561 A.2d 511 (N.J. 1989).

on the basis of diversity-of-citizenship jurisdiction?

Here is a structure for thinking about who makes law, both as that question may arise in Case 2.1 and also more generally.

(1) <u>Judges of state courts</u>. Most lawmaking by judges of state courts is done by those serving on a state court of last resort. Of course, in cases involving legal issues of first impression, trial judges must face these issues first. Even the trial judge who declares firmly that he or she will leave all lawmaking to the court of last resort is nevertheless deciding an issue of first impression. The trial judge may act on an implicit premise that in the absence of controlling precedent favoring a claim (or defense) the law precludes that claim (or defense). Or the trial judge may act on an implicit premise that absence of precedent precluding the claim (or defense) means the claim (or defense) is not precluded. In short, when in its nature the case presents an issue that has not previously been decided, refusing to recognize the issue is deciding it, one way or the other. For example, even when the court says it will leave choice to the legislature, it has decided the case before the court on an unstated implicit premise that determines who wins cases like this one until the legislature acts. Thus, issues of first impression that bear upon the outcome of the case are decided not by choice but by inherent necessity. Moreover, what the trial judge does in response to such an issue is a precedent, though of a sort having far less force than a decision by a court of last resort.[2]

In a state with a caseload so modest that no system of intermediate appeal is needed, the only judges making law are trial judges and judges of the court of last resort. In state after state, however, as caseloads have grown, one or more intermediate appellate courts have been created. Their lawmaking role is more substantial than that of a trial judge, because typically it is an understood part of the system that at least all trial judges whose judgments may be appealed to an intermediate appellate court are bound by that court's previous decisions.

(2) <u>Entities with power to adopt and amend state constitutions</u>. In many instances, the conventions, the

---

[2] <u>See</u> Chapter 1, Section C1, <u>supra</u>.

representative bodies, the electorate or other entities empowered to participate in enacting or amending state constitutions have adopted constitutional provisions that (among other things) modify ordinary contract and tort law. They have done so to far greater extent than one might have expected before examining their product.[3] Such state constitutional provisions not only make a new body of legal rules but also cast them into a form more difficult to change than are statutes and judicial precedents.

(3) <u>State legislatures</u>. Because of gaps or unanswered questions characteristic of legislation as well as other writings (including contracts and judicial opinions),[4] the intrusion of legislation is more likely merely to change than to reduce the lawmaking role of judges.

(4) <u>Judges of federal courts</u>. The most visible and significant lawmaking by federal courts is, of course, that done by the Justices of the Supreme Court of the United States. Well into the 20th century, it was still possible for the Court to function with jurisdiction that included appeals of right from inferior federal courts and from state courts of last resort (even if, under the state system, that might be a justice of the peace). In later years, however, the caseload has risen so dramatically that some restrictions on litigants' rights of access have become essential. Long ago, United States courts of appeals became an intermediate appellate system that in practical effect is the last resort for most cases in the federal courts.

Because many influences toward higher caseloads tend to reinforce each other, the rate of increase tends to rise, absent some dramatic intervention. One foreseeable consequence is that the percentage of all federal lawmaking that is done by the Supreme Court will tend to be lower, and the percentage done by lower federal courts, and by state courts, will rise. A state court necessarily is a participant in this process of federal law development when, for example, a state court decides a federal issue of first

---

[3] For some examples, see R. Keeton, <u>Statutes, Gaps, and Values in Tort Law</u>, 44 J. Air L. & Com. 1, 16-19 (1978) (Texas constitutional provisions bearing upon wrongful death actions, and having gaps characteristic of statutory and constitutional mandates, even though with distinctive Texas qualities).

[4] <u>See</u> Chapters 5 and 6, <u>infra</u>.

impression. Indeed, in some circumstances, even though a federal substantive right is involved, Congress has provided for enforcement in state courts, and the losing party in the highest state court with jurisdiction over the case may not have an appeal of right; if the Supreme Court of the United States declines to take the case, on petition for certiorari, the state court decision on the federal law issue is the final decision in that case.

Just as state judges sometimes participate in federal lawmaking, so too federal judges -- both those on courts of appeals and those in district courts -- sometimes participate in state lawmaking, and especially so in cases within the diversity jurisdiction of the federal courts.

(5) <u>Entities with power to adopt and amend the Constitution of the United States</u>. The percentage of the caseloads of all courts in which at least one party invokes some federal constitutional claim or defense had plainly become greater by the 1990s than it was at the beginning of the 20th century. It is interesting to speculate about the reasons, and about whether this increase will become an ongoing trend. More about that appears later.[5]

(6) <u>Congress</u>. More federal statutes are enacted in each session of Congress. As with state legislation, so too federal legislation has not reduced the lawmaking work of federal and state courts. Of course, legislation places new constraints on courts because the courts must respect its mandates. The point that I emphasize here, however, is that legislation usually does not effect a net reduction in the workload of the courts -- not even in that part of the courts' workload that is lawmaking. Rather, the addition to the workload because judges must construe legislation and fill gaps is greater than the reduction incident to having statutory mandates that answer previously disputable questions of law. Moreover, influences toward preemptive legislation have produced other changes in lawmaking roles, to which we will return later.[6]

This six-part summary identifying lawmakers in the American legal system, though including those who account for the most lawmaking, is not exhaustive. It has not included,

---

[5] <u>See, e.g.</u>, Section B2(4), this Chapter, <u>infra</u>.

[6] <u>See</u> Section B2(5), this Chapter, <u>infra</u>.

for example, the chief executive officers, federal and state, who have a veto power over legislation as well as an even more pervasive influence throughout the development of proposed legislation. Also, it has not included municipal authorities, or administrative officials, state and federal. Nor has it included the advocates before all these tribunals and legislative entities who, as noted before, participate in lawmaking by influencing lawmaking decisions.[7]

2. Changing Roles of Different Types of Lawmakers

Bearing in mind the large number of participants in lawmaking, consider briefly how the roles and influence of different groups of participants have changed and may be expected to change in the future. Allusions to some changes and trends have appeared in the foregoing discussion. The following summary of developments and trends that have substantial effect on the lawmaking work of judges includes others, too, that have become increasingly apparent in the latter part of the 20th century.

(1) <u>An increase in legislation</u>. As already noted, this development has sharply affected the agenda of the courts in lawmaking, but it has not reduced the lawmaking work of judges. As will be more fully developed in Chapter 6, it has instead increased the lawmaking work of judges because statutes have the fundamental characteristic that they have gaps -- unanswered questions -- that must be answered by courts before particular cases governed by the new legislation can be decided.

(2) <u>An increase in caseloads per state</u>. This phenomenon of the ever-increasing caseload leads to the creation of an intermediate level or levels of appellate decisionmaking. That development, in turn, tends to more decentralization of judicial lawmaking as more and more cases are finally decided short of the state court of last resort. Of course, there are many other consequences as well -- including needs for more judicial resources that, if not met, have significant impacts on the work of judges with increasing individual caseload responsibilities. Efforts to address these problems by developing and encouraging the use of methods of alternative dispute resolution have helped, but only a little.

---

[7] <u>See</u> Chapter 1, Section C2, <u>supra</u>.

(3) <u>An increase in the total federal caseload</u>. This phenomenon has many consequences for federal judges like those of increased state caseloads for state judges. One significant difference, however, is that Congress may respond by transferring part of the caseload to state courts, as it has done by reducing to some extent the scope of federal jurisdiction in diversity cases.

(4) <u>An increase in the complexity of legal and factual disputes</u>. This increase is partly the product of lawmaking. One influence on lawmakers is toward rules and standards that provide for finer tuning of the decision in the particular case to the distinctive characteristics of that case. One way this may be done is by creating more numerous and more complex rules that take account of more and more characteristics of cases, and in the process inherently create more and more decision points. A second way fine tuning may occur is by the use of tests for legal accountability that leave discretion to a decisionmaker, on the premise that a system of wisely exercised discretion works better than a system of intricately detailed rules. Either of these methods of aiming for more refined justice tends to increase the transaction costs of decisionmaking. Thus, viewed from another perspective, these are influences toward greater complexity in the administration of justice -- toward the adoption of tests of legal accountability that require more judicial and party resources for the resolution of each controversy. A system of fewer and more objective rules has the disadvantage of cutting corners, and the advantage of reducing the cost of administering justice. It is often difficult for a lawmaker to decide how far to press the effort at finer tuning of decisionmaking (either by refining rules or by allowing discretion). When should that effort yield to the interest in reducing -- or at least not increasing -- complexity and expense of adjudication?

If the lawmaker chooses a more complex set of <u>legal</u> rules, or a set of rules more expensive to administer because of the scope of discretion they allow, almost certainly this choice leads to greater complexity of the <u>fact</u> disputes that are material to the outcome.

For example, Case 2.1 is easily and quickly decided for the defendant manufacturers if the court applies the traditional cause-in-fact rules. In contrast, several additional issues of fact and law, some of which may turn out to be quite complex, must be decided if the court concludes that some version of alternative liability or market share liability is to be applied.

Beyond these tendencies of increasing complexity of law, and increasing complexity of fact disputes incident to lawmaking trends, is another influence toward complexity with its source outside the legal system. Human relations and transactions become more complex as the population increases and greater density of population in metropolitan centers produces more and different interactions. Also, scientific and economic changes tend to produce more complex human interactions that in turn tend to present more complex disputes for resolution. The legal system did not need to have a rule for DPT cases (such as Case 2.1) until DPT vaccine was developed. More cases arise, and more complex cases per unit of population arise, with scientific and economic changes.

(5) *Change occurs in the balance of influences toward local autonomy, on the one hand, and national uniformity, on the other*. At least for a substantial period of time, we have experienced a trend toward federal preemption. Developments in labor law have long illustrated this point, and recent developments regarding the law of pensions have underscored it. Similar developments have occurred, and more may be expected, in environmental law. Debates over proposals for more preemptive federal legislation regarding products liability have been proceeding, year by year. Defamation was generally regarded as exclusively a state-law field before New York Times v. Sullivan.[8] Now federal preemption is sometimes avoided only by the creation of a new body of state law (including state constitutional law) in which state-law privileges afford more protection against liability than would the First Amendment. Moreover, the scope of this development is yet to be determined, as reasons for extending First Amendment protection beyond defamation are explored.[9]

The potential consequences of growing federal preemption upon the work of judges, state and federal, are clearly enormous, even though they are unpredictable in

---

[8] 376 U.S. 254 (1964).

[9] See, e.g., Hustler Magazine v. Falwell, 485 U.S. 46 (1988); NAACP v. Claiborne Hardware Co., 458 U.S. 886 (1982).

detail.

Is the 1986 National Childhood Vaccine Injury Act preemptive? If so, in what sense and to what extent? If it is not preemptive, is it nevertheless a fact -- a "premise fact"[10] -- that a state court would take into account in its state lawmaking? To answer this last question, we will need to consider some ideas about who decides disputes of fact.

C. Who Decides Disputes of Fact?

We are accustomed to thinking that in jury trials in state and federal courts, if judge and jury perform their respective functions well, the jury ordinarily decides all genuine disputes of fact that are material to disposition of the case. Expressed another way, our common belief is that any party to a dispute over a material fact ordinarily is entitled to have a jury decide that issue unless, on the evidence received in the trial court, jurors could not reasonably differ about the answer.[1]

This way of thinking is appropriate for disputes about facts that are simply the facts of a particular case -- disputes, for example, about whether the light facing the defendant driver was red or green as the defendant's car entered the intersection, or whether the driver was negligent in driving too fast, even though within the posted speed limit, because the roadway was slippery. Facts that are used in this way in deciding a case -- that is, facts used just to decide the particular case on trial and not for a more general purpose -- are commonly called "adjudicative facts."[2]

---

[10]With respect to the meaning of "premise fact" as used here, see Section C, this Chapter, infra.

[1]For a report of an audience's response to a lecturer's questions, confirming these views, see R. Keeton, Legislative Facts and Similar Things: Deciding Disputed Premise Facts, 73 Minn. L. Rev. 1, 4 (1988) (hereinafter cited as "Premise Facts").

[2]The term "adjudicative facts" appears, for example, in Fed. R. Evid. 201. Roughly defined, "adjudicative facts" are facts distinctive to a particular case as distinguished from those common to all cases of a class or type. In the use of this rough definition, however, it is important to bear in mind the reason why the fact dispute needs to be

WHO DECIDES DISPUTES OF FACT? Sec. C

The idea that any party to a dispute over a material fact ordinarily is entitled to have that dispute decided by a jury turns out to be incorrect for disputes of fact that a court concludes it needs to resolve in order to arrive at a <u>lawmaking</u> choice. Thus, for example, as a basis for deciding controlling issues of constitutional law in <u>Brown v. Board of Education</u>,[3] the Supreme Court made its own fact determinations about effects of segregation on education. Facts that are used in this more general way -- in order to decide a rule of law that will govern many cases and not just the case before the court -- are commonly called "legislative facts."[4] This book often refers to them as "premise facts."[5]

The distinction between "adjudicative facts" and "premise facts" is very important because legal precedents have authorized methods for deciding "premise facts" that are very different from the methods authorized for deciding "adjudicative facts." Stated another way, the point is that far more constraints on method apply to deciding "adjudicative facts." For example, all the constraints on method that are incident to constitutional rights to trial by jury apply only to "adjudicative facts." Some constraints on method apply to deciding "premise facts," but courts have much more freedom, for example, to consider matters outside the formal "record" of evidence offered at trial when they are deciding "premise facts."

Because of this contrast between authorized methods for deciding "adjudicative facts" and authorized methods for deciding "premise facts," the choice among methods by which facts are decided in each instance of a material dispute of fact depends on the anticipated use of the facts -- whether as premises for adopting a legal rule that affects the outcome of many cases or instead as facts that affect outcome only in the case at hand (and perhaps in closely related

---

decided. This is explained further in the text that follows.

[3] 347 U.S. 483 (1954).

[4] The phrase was first suggested by Professor Kenneth Davis, in <u>An Approach to Problems of Evidence in the Administrative Process</u>, 55 Harv. L. Rev. 364, 402-10 (1942).

[5] I gratefully acknowledge my indebtedness to Judge Frank Coffin for suggesting the phrase "premise facts." <u>See</u> <u>Premise Facts</u>, 73 Minn. L. Rev. at 8, n.2.

cases within the scope of claim preclusion and issue preclusion).

Having different methods for deciding disputes of fact may also mean having different decisionmakers. Thus, to determine who will decide a particular dispute of fact in the course of reaching a final judgment in a case, we need to know the purpose for which the fact determination is being made -- whether or not the fact determination is part of the court's reasoning in arriving at a lawmaking choice.

Another case will serve to illustrate the problem and some of its difficulties.

Case 2.2
Knowledge of Asbestos Hazards

Numerous plaintiffs filed claims in the United States District Court for the District of New Jersey for personal injury caused by exposure to asbestos products. In many of these cases defendants asserted a "state-of-the-art" defense against strict products liability. If a court recognizes the defense, a defendant may escape liability for an injury caused by the defendant's product. The defendant, however, must prove that, although defective by present-day standards of knowledge and understanding, the product measured up to the state of the art at the time it was manufactured.

The New Jersey Supreme Court had rejected the defense shortly before the present cases were filed in federal court. The defendants, however, challenged on a federal constitutional ground the New Jersey judge-made law precluding use of the defense. Plaintiffs argued that because the New Jersey Supreme Court had not created a special rule precluding the use of the state-of-the-art defense for asbestosis cases, the defendants had based their constitutional claims on an erroneous premise. Rather, plaintiffs argued, the Supreme Court had merely determined <u>as a fact</u> that the hazards of asbestos exposure were <u>knowable</u> to the industry at all relevant times. Therefore, plaintiffs alleged, it was this factual determination (and not a special legal rule, for asbestos cases only) that precluded application of the state-of-the-art defense in asbestos cases.

If plaintiffs' argument is correct, then in New Jersey the answer to the question "who decides" whether asbestos hazards were knowable in the 1930s is the Supreme Court of New Jersey. Should the federal courts accept that answer?[6]

In the Third Circuit case on which Case 2.2 is based, the majority of a divided panel concluded that the New Jersey court-made rules allowing a state-of-the-art defense in products liability cases generally but not in asbestos cases was not in violation of the Equal Protection Clause of the Fourteenth Amendment. The opinion of the court, delivered by Judge Weis, applies the rational-basis standard of scrutiny.[7] The opinion concludes that the asbestos manufacturers failed to meet their burden of convincing the federal court that the factual assumptions on which the state-law classification "is apparently based could not reasonably be conceived as true by the governmental decision maker."[8] Only one of the three Third Circuit panel opinions, Judge Becker's concurrence, explicitly addresses the question stated in Case 2.2 regarding who decides the dispute of fact as to whether asbestos hazards were knowable in the 1930s. His answer is that the New Jersey Supreme Court decided that question, and by a method permissible for what I have

---

[6] Premise Facts, 73 Minn. L. Rev. at 4-5 (footnote omitted). This case is based on In re Asbestos Litigation, 829 F.2d 1233 (3d Cir. 1987), cert. denied, 108 S. Ct. 1586 (1988). In that litigation, the district court consolidated the pending asbestos cases for argument and disposition of the federal constitutional issue. Because the district court, sitting en banc, was closely divided, it certified the following question to the Court of Appeals for the Third Circuit pursuant to 28 U.S.C. 1292(b): do "decisions of the New Jersey Supreme Court violate the Equal Protection Clause in abolishing the state-of-the-art defense in asbestos personal injury cases" while still allowing that defense in other product liability cases, including drug cases? 829 F.2d at 1235.

[7] 829 F.2d at 1235-40.

[8] Id. at 1243.

referred to as "premise facts,"[9] even though a different answer would have been appropriate for "adjudicative facts."[10]

"Premise facts," or "legislative facts" as Professor Kenneth Davis[11] and many others have chosen to call them, are used as premises for lawmaking decisions by legislatures when they enact statutes, by courts when they render opinions that establish precedents, by administrative agencies when they make decisions that are to be used as guides for later decisions, and by any other entities that adopt official rules for practice, procedure, or decisionmaking. When fact determinations are made to serve as part of the foundation for the reasoned choice to adopt a particular rule of law, they are fundamental facts relevant to a rule that governs many cases, not just the case before the court. Fact determinations that serve this purpose are premises for the reasoned explanation of the decision of a legal issue. These fact determinations are made by the lawmaker who is deciding that legal issue. Thus, neither the choice of decisionmaker nor the methods of decisionmaking that govern adjudicative-fact disputes apply to premise-fact disputes. Some constraints regarding method are appropriate. Some form of notice to parties and opportunity for response is appropriate when the court is considering matters outside the "record" of evidence at trial in resolving a dispute about a fact that bears upon the adoption of a legal rule (for example, a dispute about the scope and extent of the risks to persons and property on adjacent farms, which bears on whether the court should adopt a legal rule of strict liability for crop dusting by aircraft on one farm, resulting in harm to person or property on an adjacent farm). But the nature and degree of the constraints differ markedly from those applicable to adjudicative facts.[12]

---

[9] More commonly referred to as "legislative facts." See this Section, note 4, supra.

[10] 829 F.2d at 1249, n.6. See also id. at 1245.

[11] See this Section, note 4, supra.

[12] See Premise Facts, 73 Minn. L. Rev. at 13-44.

D. Truth, Fact, and Justice

1. Truth in Being

Truth is. Assertions about some fact -- allegations "of fact" -- on the other hand, may be true or false. These observations are part of the truth but not the whole truth. In order to understand the central role of seeking truth, through law in action, as a means of doing justice, we need to understand additional truths about truth itself.

2. Truth Becoming

I believe, and I suppose you believe, that at least most, if not all, of the physical laws of the universe are immutable.

Apart from immutable laws of nature, and perhaps of human nature, however, it is also true that in the physical universe around us, and even more so in human relations, nothing is constant but change. Thus, the truth is always becoming. The whole truth includes the fact that when we look at what is, we do not fully understand it unless we perceive motion. The astute observer of a still photograph perceives evidence of motion from which inferences may be drawn about what changes are likely to be seen in another still photograph taken sometime later. Inferences are, of course, just interpretations of truth and not truth itself. They may or may not be correct or accurate -- the "facts" inferred may or may not be true.

As a very practical matter, then, a search for the whole truth must be very sensitive to time and motion -- to change.

This point applies with special force to determining the truth or falsity of that kind of allegation that concerns not a single historical fact -- such as whether a light was red or green -- but instead some alleged characteristic or consequence of a whole set of facts. An example is an allegation of crisis as to cost and availability of malpractice liability insurance -- such as may be advanced as a legislative fact, as a reason for enacting legislation. A crisis is by its very nature likely to produce change -- not only in other respects but also in the crisis itself. It is likely to deepen, or to abate, with or without the intervention of legal processes.

A perceived crisis, even if correctly perceived to exist at one time, may no longer exist at another time, whether or not a legal remedy designed to meet the crisis has been effective. Also, if someone prematurely thought that a crisis existed before it actually did, it may happen that a decisionmaker may appropriately determine that, as of a particular time later, a crisis has come into existence. Should a statute be invalidated because a legislature acted too soon -- because no crisis existed when the legislature acted, even if a crisis has developed before the mills of justice have finally ground to a decision?

How, if at all, does the truth about change bear upon adjudication of claims of unconstitutionality of statutes, of administrative regulations, or of judicially adopted rules of law such as that in Case 2.2 regarding a state-of-the-art defense in asbestosis cases?

One important factor to be considered as we think about these questions is the transitory nature of factual premises of lawmaking.

When a dispute of fact is being decided to serve as an adjudicative fact, ordinarily there is little reason to be concerned about the likelihood that the truth about the fact is changing. An exception is the "factfinding" of future loss -- for example, loss of earning capacity in the future. It is both a potential embarrassment to the legal system and an apparent failure to do justice in a precise and refined way if a factfinding of future loss turns out to be grossly excessive or grossly inadequate, when better evidence of the truth becomes available. But it is only in exceptional circumstances (such as findings of future loss to support a present judgment binding for all time) that the transitory nature of _adjudicative_-fact premises poses a serious problem of method of doing justice through law.

Far more often, the transitory nature of a _premise_ fact presents a serious problem of method. The legal rule that is based upon a premise-fact determination is expected to be binding in many cases -- ordinarily in all cases to which the rule will be applied until it is abrogated by statute or by an overruling judicial opinion. If that "fact" is changing, how does the change affect the legal rule?

An illustration of this problem of transitory premises of lawmaking occurs when a statute, once determined to be valid, is challenged again, decades later, on the ground that circumstances have changed so materially that the court should no longer enforce the statute. That issue will be discussed in Chapter 6.[13]

The problem of transitory premises is even more pervasive, however, than just the issue presented by a second, later challenge to constitutionality of a statute. The problem sometimes arises even in the first challenge to constitutionality of a statute in court. Stated another way, an example of the problem is this: In applying a "rational basis" test, is a court limited to considering information ("evidence"?) about "legislative facts" that were in existence (and known to the legislature?) at the time the legislature acted? Or may the court also consider information ("evidence"?) about those "legislative facts" that are in existence and known to the court at the time of the challenge? The latter facts may either tend to support assumptions about "legislative facts" for which there may have been no "rational basis" at the time the legislation was enacted, or tend so strongly to rebut the claimed "legislative facts" that no longer can a litigant show an existing "rational basis" for the statute even if able to show that a rational basis appeared to exist at the time the legislation was enacted. Questions about transitory premises are rarely addressed directly. They are important issues that deserve further exploration.[14]

In relation to judge-made law, it has long been part of the common law tradition that a court may overrule or candidly disregard a precedent that it holds to have been founded on outmoded premises. The reason supporting a rule of law having disappeared, the rule itself no longer applies. Thus, for example, development of the printing press, radio, and television, each in its own time, changed some of the questions that had to be answered in the law of defamation. The latter two developments led one court to invent the term "defamacast" as a new category rather than to attempt to fit new forms of publication into one or the other of the two categories of libel and slander previously established in

---

[13] Chapter 6, Section H, <u>infra</u>.

[14] For additional comments in relation to statutes based on transitory premises, <u>see</u> Chapter 6, Section H, <u>infra</u>.

Ch. 2   **LAW AND FACTS**

precedents.[15] Within two more decades after defamacasts presented new issues for the courts, developments in computer science presented new issues in the context of computerized bulletin boards that will enable hundreds, thousands, and in time millions of participants to spread scurrilous imputations against their favorite targets.

It is symptomatic of the pace of change affecting transitory premises of lawmaking that three of these four developments (from printing press to radio to television to computerized bulletin boards) occurred within the 20th century.

3. Truth Unknown

One of the realities -- the truths -- that our legal system must confront if we are to succeed in doing justice is that we shall never know the whole truth about any dispute that one of the parties brings into the legal system for resolution.[16]

---

[15] See, e.g., American Broadcasting-Paramount Theatres, Inc. v. Simpson, 106 Ga. App. 230, 126 S.E.2d 873 (1962):

> As Holmes said, "[The law] is forever adopting new principles from life at one end, and it always retains old ones from history at the other, which have not yet been absorbed or sloughed off. It will become entirely consistent only when it ceases to grow." The Common Law, 36 (1881). And Cardozo: "Unique situations can never have their answers ready made as in the complete letter-writing guides or the manuals of the art of conversation." The Growth of the Law, 133 (1924). "Modification implies growth," said Brandeis, "It is the life of the law." State of Washington v. Dawson & Co., 264 U.S. 219, 236, 44 S. Ct. 302, 308, 68 L.Ed. 646 (dissenting opinion). And see the excellent collection of authorities in Shor v. Billingsley, 4 Misc.2d 857, 158 N.Y.S.2d 476, supra.

Id. at 878-79.

[16] Cf. Philadelphia Newspapers, Inc. v. Hepps, 475 U.S. 767 (1986), and especially the folllowing passage from the opinion of the Court, delivered by Justice O'Connor:

The long-range effectiveness of any human institution requires some form of planning for future uncertainties. Wise managers develop ways of managing ignorance. The current terminology, "risk management," is an attractive and potentially deceptive name, if not a euphemism, for this process. In the risk management context, the problem is ignorance about future events -- about whether in fact harmful events will or will not occur. Our society has devised many means of dealing with lack of knowledge about events of the future. Among them is our whole system of insurance.

In striving to do justice, as in other human affairs, we seek to develop sensible ways of managing our ignorance. In this context the problem is not only our inability to know what events will occur in the future but also our inability to know the whole truth about what has occurred in the past. The administration of justice depends not only on fair and accurate fact determinations but also on developing ways of allocating fairly the risks incident to our inability to know the whole truth about either the past or the future. Among the methods we have developed for this purpose are presumptions, burdens of persuasion and production,[17] and various standards of proof (for example, proof by a preponderance of the evidence, proof by clear and convincing evidence, and proof beyond reasonable doubt). They are accommodations that law in action makes with the reality that our ability to determine the truth or falsity of assertions of fact is limited.

One of the participants in a dispute alleges a crisis of some kind as a factual premise for a reasoned decision

---

> There will always be instances when the factfinding process will be unable to resolve conclusively [in a defamation case] whether [the defamatory innuendo of] the speech is true or false; it is in those cases that the burden of proof is dispositive.... Under either rule [as to the burden], then, the outcome of the suit will sometimes be at variance with the outcome that we would desire if all speech were either demonstrably true or demonstrably false.

Id. at 776.

[17] Examples are discussed in Chapter 3, Section F, infra.

that the rights alleged are legally protected rights. Someone must determine whether it is true that such a crisis exists, or else must determine that the law makes that fact question irrelevant -- perhaps even that the law does so for the very reason that it is too hard to determine the truth or falsity of the allegation of crisis.

Of course, the things we have done to, for, or without consideration for, each other may help to create a context -- whether a crisis or not -- within which the realities of the physical universe and the realities of human relations operate in a particular instance. It is true, also, that to understand the full truth about the circumstances of a particular dispute, we would need to understand all the truth about context -- not just some of the facts but the whole truth. But we never do know that much. In striving to do justice we do as much as we sensibly can in the conviction that we come closer to our aim as we come closer to full understanding of the context of the particular dispute as well as full understanding of fundamental truths of a more general nature. In some instances, however, we decide, as a matter of law, to adopt a legal rule managing ignorance rather than purporting to determine truth or falsity of factual allegations that we cannot reliably determine to be true or false. One may view an argument for either "alternative liability" or "market share liability" in Case 2.1 (An Infant Vaccine Victim) as urging precisely this kind of legal rule -- one aimed at managing the economic and social problems arising from ignorance about which manufacturer supplied the DPT used to inoculate the child rather than either purporting to determine the truth or denying relief to the child and the parents because of the impossibility of determining the truth.

4. Truth and Proclamation

When the governor of a state issues a proclamation that the gopher is the state animal, or the lady slipper is the state flower, or a particular day is the State Widget Recognition Day, so it is -- unless the governor lacked authority to issue the proclamation.

In resolving disputes in court, occasions arise, of course, when the authority of an executive official, or a legislature, or an administrative agency, is challenged. To determine the truth about whether the lady slipper is the state flower we must determine an issue of authority to make the proclamation. Once that issue is itself authoritatively determined in favor of the proclaimer's authority, we know the truth. The truth is, by proclamation.

More often than not, however, truth exists independently of proclamation. The laws of the physical universe exist independently of what we proclaim them to be. No matter whether we understand and state them correctly, or misunderstand or misrepresent them, they continue to function. They are. We do not make them less so or more so by perceiving and describing them either correctly or incorrectly.

I believe also, and (whether you join me in so believing or not) I invite you to consider some of the practical implications of believing, that some realities of human relations exist independently of what we perceive and proclaim about them, correctly or incorrectly. For example, I believe human behavior is influenced by incentives. An incentive structure may be established by the laws of the physical universe. You do not ordinarily jump out of a third floor window once you understand the law of gravity. But you might jump, of course, if because of some other law of the physical universe, combined with other facts you perceive, such as a raging fire around you, you have an incentive to take the risks of jumping in preference to the alternatives.

Another kind of truth that *is* because it *is*, and not because somebody proclaimed it to be so, is the truth about what may be called historical facts. The light was red or the light was green, it was on or it was off, and whichever it was, so it was, regardless of who proclaims what.

Likewise, the state of mind some actor had, when acting, was what it was, regardless of what either that actor, or somebody else, later proclaims about that state of mind.

What I have just been saying may seem a bit abstract. Before we return to problem cases to test the validity of these generalizations about facts as aids to deciding particular disputes, however, consider briefly some parallel and nonparallel observations about law.

Ch. 2   LAW AND FACTS

E. Law and Justice

   1.   Law in Being

   Whatever may have been the reality for our most primitive predecessors, for us the reality is that we have law. Regardless of the differing conceptions of law we may hold, ranging from the most natural of natural law theories to the most positivist of positivist theories, in common we believe law exists in some form. Law is. For the moment, that's all I ask you to accept about law in being. Just as truth is, regardless of how we may perceive or misperceive it, law is, regardless of how much we may agree or disagree in our efforts to understand and explain it.

   2.   Law Becoming

   Law is becoming. It is developing.

   It does not yet, and never will, provide answers to all the questions that will arise as it is applied to the transactions, relationships, and disputes that will occur in the future. Both the power and the authority to choose when judging in relation to such unanswered questions are profound. This point is less often declared in judicial opinions than in commentary, but judicial opinions in which it is expressed include some written by very distinguished judges.[1]

---

   [1]See the dissenting opinions of Justices Holmes and Brandeis in Olmstead v. United States, 277 U.S. 438, 469-85 (1928), and in particular the following passages in Justice Holmes' opinion:

   My brother BRANDEIS has given this case so exhaustive an examination that I desire to add but a few words. While I do not deny it, I am not prepared to say that the penumbra of the Fourth and Fifth Amendments covers the defendant, although I fully agree that Courts are apt to err by sticking too closely to the words of a law where those words import a policy that goes beyond them. Gooch v. Oregon Short Line R. R. Co., 258 U.S. 22, 24. But I think, as Mr. Justice Brandeis says, that apart from the Constitution the Government ought not to use evidence obtained and only obtainable by a criminal act. There is no body of precedents by which we are bound, and which confines us to logical deduction from

Trial lawyers are constantly reminded of the incompleteness of law as they read sources of authority in search of support for the arguments they advance on behalf of their clients. Trial judges are reminded, too, as they search for guidance in deciding disputed issues. Cases 1.1 (The Injured Inmate) and 1.2 (The Battered Child) illustrate the point. They present questions that the Supreme Court did not answer in the decisions on which they are based -- questions that remain to be answered, first by trial judges, in cases arising after these authoritative but incomplete declarations of the law applicable to two kinds of §1983 cases.

Most disputes, of course, are resolved by settlement. The ones most likely to be resolved by settlement are those that opposing counsel evaluate in much the same way. Those are the cases that judges and juries would find the easiest to decide.

The disputes that settlement negotiations leave for juries to decide are commonly those as to which the facts are most disputed and debatable. The disputes left for judges to decide (in addition to nonjury cases of disputed facts) are commonly those involving the most debatable issues of law -- those as to which, even if each advocate argues "precedents go my way," the trial judge may conclude that in truth precedents go neither way. Instead they leave unanswered some question courts must answer to decide the case -- a trial court in the first instance, and an appellate court if the losing party appeals.

I do not wish the allusions to unanswered questions to be misunderstood as a suggestion that individual lawmakers, either in legislatures or on appellate courts,

---

established rules. Therefore we must consider the two objects of desire, both of which we cannot have, and make up our minds which to choose....

... I have said that we are free to choose between two principles of policy. But if we are to confine ourselves to precedent and logic the reason for excluding evidence obtained by violating the Constitution seems to me logically to lead to excluding evidence obtained by a crime of the officers of the law.

Id. at 469-71.

deserve criticism whenever they fail to provide answers to all the questions of law that trial judges must answer in deciding cases before them.

A lawmaking body -- either a legislative body or a court -- may for good reason leave unanswered some of the questions its members foresee. For example, the lawmakers may believe it better to have the answers worked out over time, through case-by-case development. Also, any lawmaking body will leave other questions unanswered simply because human foresight cannot anticipate all the problems that will arise as a statutory or decisional rule of law is applied to human affairs. Thus, the phenomenon of unanswered questions of law is a fundamental characteristic of any legal system. It is so not alone by choice but as well by necessity. Viewing law as if it does, or is meant to, provide ready answers for all conflicting claims is to misunderstand law fundamentally.

Emphasizing the perspectives of law in action and law in development will not eliminate the phenomenon of unanswered questions of law. It may, however, reduce their number. More to the point, it may help us improve the quality of judicial decisionmaking, at all levels, when previously unanswered questions are critical to the outcome.

There was a time when the two phrases "law is" and "law is becoming" might have been taken as fighting slogans -- rallying cries for two opposing schools of thought about the legal system and the nature of law. That was the time when one of the raging debates of legal theorists was between those who believed in natural law and those who were positivists. Many of the believers in natural law have included within their legal philosophy the belief that law has foundations of divine creation. On the other hand, positivists hold that law consists exclusively of commands of human sovereigns. In the words of a positivist-leaning Justice, Oliver Wendell Holmes, Jr., "The common law is not a brooding omnipresence in the sky but the articulate voice of some sovereign or quasi-sovereign that can be identified ...."[2]

---

[2]<u>Southern Pacific Co.</u> v. <u>Jensen</u>, 244 U.S. 205, 222 (1917) (Holmes, J., dissenting). The Court held that application of New York's workers' compensation law to a Southern Pacific Co. employee, injured while operating an electric freight truck in unloading cargo from a vessel (owned by Southern Pacific) to a dock, was preempted as inconsistent with

Even when ringing debates between natural-law adherents and positivists were in vogue in the academic community, however, protagonists of the view that "law is" could be found among both camps of academics. A natural-law sympathizer might have said that law _is_ what it _is_ by nature or by divine creation. A positivist might have insisted that law is what the authorized lawmaker has declared its positive mandates to be.

Protaganists of both those contrasting views could, and often did, argue alike that law is existing, that the judge should find it, not make it, and that having found it the judge should apply it faithfully.

But law as existing positivist mandates and law as existing mandates of divine or natural origin are not the only alternatives, and certainly not the whole truth.

Professor Lon Fuller, among others, taught us that both these points of view leave unstated at least, if not implicitly rejected, another part of the whole truth about law. "Law is," of course, but also "law is becoming." Inherent in the nature of law[3] itself is its capacity for growth. The point is not merely that law can be changed by whoever has the authority to make law or change it but rather that the seeds of adaptability to new times and circumstances already exist in the law that is. I do not dwell more on the point here; I pause only to note that it has a bearing on how a judge perceives his or her responsibility for reaching decisions while striving to do justice lawfully.

Because law reflects the community's standards of decisiomaking about debatable issues, including disputes over conflicting values and moral issues, any one person in the community may hold a view, on moral or other grounds, that the community's standards are not what they should be and that the law ought to be different in some respect from what it is. For this reason, a judge, acting in the judicial role as a representative of the community interest in having the

---

the Constitution and laws of the United States and the "policy of Congress to encourage investments in ships manifested in [enacted statutes] which declare a limitation upon the liability of their owners." 244 U.S. at 218.

[3]_E.g._, L. Fuller, The Law in Quest of Itself, 4-10, 132-40 (1940).

community's law faithfully administered, may sometimes conclude that law compels a result different from the result the judge would prefer. Putting the point most strongly, we may say that the judge sometimes determines that the law compels what the judge sees as an unjust result. But it is the community's standards of justice -- the community's law -- that the judge is sworn to administer, not the judge's own.

The obligation sometimes to reach a result one considers unjust, by one's own standards of right and wrong, is inherent in the role of judging lawfully. It is a constraint that is part of the definition of the judicial role. One who is unwilling to accept that constraint cannot fully accept the responsibility of being the community's representative as judge. To be a representative of any interest, one must be willing to disregard conflicting personal interest. In this respect, even if differing in degree, judging is similar in principle to occupying some other representative role in society -- a role as an advocate, counselor, trustee of a private trust, an officer of a private entity, or a governmental official, executive, legislative, or administrative.

The point I emphasize, however, is that the occasions when a judge is presented with this agonizing circumstance are far fewer than they would be if we rejected the idea that law is becoming.[4] If judges were taught to look only to the mandates of declared law without taking account of the objectively manifested purposes[5] that give law its living quality -- its capacity for new growth -- they would more often reach decisions they thought unjust. This living quality of law is the characteristic that is suggested, even if inadequately described, in the phrase, "law is becoming."

3. Law Unknown

Like existing facts, existing law may sometimes be hard to discover and determine. If you doubt, ask a law student, or even a professor. You would, however, be less

---

[4] See Chapter 1, Section C2, supra.

[5] For an explanation of what I mean by "objectively manifested," see Chapter 5, Section D2, and Chapter 6, Sections D and G, infra.

likely to receive the same answer from a lawyer, at least if you asked it about any issue affecting a client's interests. An advocate is very leery of telling a judge that the claim or defense the advocate asserts on behalf of a client is not supported in precedent and is advanced merely in good faith argument for an extension or modification of precedent. The point remains that law is sometimes hard to determine, and what is law existing, but inherently becoming something more, may be even harder to determine or predict.

In another respect, however, there is a contrast rather than a parallel between unknown law and unknown facts. Legislatures or judges may adopt rules on burden of persuasion or burden of production to aid in doing justice in the circumstance of unknown or even unknowable facts. In contrast, the legal system does not permit judges this luxury in relation to unknown law. If the unknown law is essential to disposition of a dispute within the jurisdiction of the court, the judge of the trial court or judges of the appellate court must search to discover the needed law, and, if discovering none that decides the issue, must create it. The dispute must be decided, and it must be decided lawfully. When the reasoned explanation for that decision is stated, it is precedent. It is law.[6]

4. Law and Proclamation

The point just stated calls attention also to a contrast between facts and law in relation to proclamation. Some facts exist independently of and regardless of proclamation; others exist by reason of authorized proclamation. In contrast, unless you believe in some version of natural law, you are likely to agree that all law exists not independently of proclamation but by reason of proclamation by an authorized lawmaking entity -- constitutional convention, electorate, legislature, administrative agency, court, or other authorized institution or official. In deciding a particular dispute, a court is guided by discerning the mandates of those authorized proclamations. Taking account as well of the objectively manifested purposes of existing law, the court must make law

---

[6]Cf. In Re Asbestos Litigation, 829 F.2d at 1238 ("the Supreme Court has continued to use the word 'laws' in its broader sense, reflecting to a degree the influence of Legal Realism and its conclusion that courts do, in fact, 'make' law").

Ch. 2   LAW AND FACTS

to fill in the gaps -- the interstices that cause us to say some cases are cases of first impression.

F. Ways of Classifying Facts and Disputes of Fact

An assertion of fact is an assertion that, in common usage, can be said to be true or false.

The introduction to an earlier section of this book[1] calls attention to one way of classifying facts, distinguishing between "legislative" or "premise" facts on the one hand and "adjudicative" facts on the other hand. As explained there, this classification draws attention to the way a fact is to be used, once the fact dispute has been decided. If the fact is to be used just to decide the case at hand, it is an "adjudicative fact." If instead the fact is to be used as a reason for deciding what rule of law shall be adopted to decide many cases, it is a "premise fact."

Another way of classifying facts concerns the nature of the issue that must be decided in order to determine the outcome of a dispute of fact. Bearing in mind that in ordinary usage an assertion of fact can be said to be true or false, we may observe that such assertions are commonly made not only about acts and events of the past and present but also about interpretations and evaluations of those acts and events. From the perspective of the nature of the assertion that is to be determined to be true or false, it will be useful to recognize two different kinds of assertions about present or past "facts," as to which different methods of fact-determination may sometimes be justified. They are:

    (1) assertions about events, commonly called historical facts; and

    (2) evaluative (interpretive) assertions about the past or the present (sometimes called "evaluative facts").

Assertions about the future are also sometimes referred to as assertions of "fact." These third and fourth types differ both from each other and from the first two categories just listed. They are:

---

[1]Section C, this Chapter, <u>supra</u>.

(3) predictions of future events; and

(4) evaluative predictions -- that is, assertions about the future that are evaluative rather than simply predicting future events.

It is possible to have a dispute about an event (historical fact) that, when decided, serves as a premise for a court's adoption of a rule of law. For example, in Case 2.2, to determine whether asbestos hazards were knowable to the industry in the 1930s, or at some other particular time, a court must decide some historical facts about the state of scientific knowledge in the 1930s, even though the court must also decide some evaluative facts. That is, in addition to deciding disuptes over historical facts as to how much was known about the properties of asbestos, the court must apply an evaluative test to determine the degree of inquiry required of manufacturers and the degree of understanding of "hazards" required to support a determination that asbestos hazards were "knowable."

It is possible, also, to have a dispute about an event or historical fact that, when decided, serves as a premise for a legislature's enactment of a statute. Indeed, legislative bodies sometimes state historical factual premises in the text of an introductory section of a statute -- for example, the nation is at war, or unemployment has been 6% or higher each of the last twelve months. Even more often the legislative history recites historical factual premises, such as the examples just given. Many historical-fact disputes, however, are those the determination of which serves to decide only one particular case. These historical-fact determinations serve the function of adjudicative facts rather than premise facts. Typical of such disputes concerning historical facts that serve the function of adjudicative facts are disputes about who did what, when, and where, and about whether a person acted with a defined state of mind. For example, a rule of law may require a factfinding as to the state of mind of a defendant in a criminal case, rather than allowing the imposition of criminal liability for presumed intent.[2]

A typical dispute of interpretive or evaluative

---

[2]Sandstrom v. Montana, 442 U.S. 510, 521-23 (1979); see also Fed. R. Evid. 201, advisory committee's note, subdivision (a), for other examples and additional explanation.

adjudicative fact deals with whether a person's act violated a legal test for evaluating conduct. For example, a finding that conduct satisfied a prerequisite of liability, such as the negligence standard or the proximate cause standard, is a finding of adjudicative fact.[3] So, too, is a finding of substantial similarity in a copyright case.[4]

The treatment of evaluative-fact issues in tort law illustrates that courts determine the purpose for which an evaluative determination is made and that this purpose is decisive as to whether the evaluative determination is a finding of an adjudicative fact or instead is a premise-fact decision.[5] For example, courts treat as a premise-fact issue the evaluative issue concerning whether the transportation of explosives on the highways is abnormally dangerous in the sense that supports strict liability.[6] In contrast, courts treat as an adjudicative-fact question the evaluation of a driver's allegedly negligent conduct in driving a truck loaded with explosives at a speed barely within posted limits.[7] Another type of evaluative determination in tort law occurs in the large body of precedents bearing on whether juries or courts determine disputes over proximate cause. The legal decisionmaking includes not only laying down rules

---

[3] See Restatement (Second) of Torts §§291, 431 (1965).

[4] See O'Neill v. Dell Publishing Co., 630 F.2d 685, 687 (1st Cir. 1980) (concluding that ultimate finding of substantial similarity in copyright case is mixed question of fact and law, not to be decided on summary judgment if evidence must be weighed).

[5] See Premise Facts, 73 Minn. L. Rev. 1, 19 (1988). Judge Becker commented in Asbestos Litigation: "The state-of-the-art defense decides not what the defendant or another party knew -- a fact relating to a particular party -- but what was knowable -- a fact about the state of the world." In re Asbestos Litigation, 829 F.2d 1233, 1246 (3d Cir. 1987) (Becker, J., concurring), cert. denied, 108 S. Ct. 1586 (1988).

[6] See, e.g., Siegler v. Kuhlman, 81 Wn.2d 448, 502 P.2d 1181 (1972); Restatement (Second) of Torts, §484 (1965). The term ultrahazardous served the same function in the first Restatement.

[7] For discussion of these and other illustrations of evaluative determinations in tort law, see R. Keeton, Venturing to Do Justice 64-77 (1969); R. Keeton Legal Cause in the Law of Torts 49-60, 88-90, 105-17 (1963); Keeton, Creative Continuity in the Law of Torts, 75 Harv. L. Rev. 463, 498-506 (1962).

and standards that are precedents but also establishing patterns of decisionmaking in the evaluative determinations as to whether the issue goes to the jury. These patterns serve as precedents that enable lawyers and lower courts to understand how a higher court will address the issue in a particular case.[8] Thus, the evaluative determinations that establish these patterns, if regarded as fact determinations rather than rulings "as a matter of law," serve the function of premise-fact determinations.

In contrast with adjudicative-fact disputes, which usually involve historical facts and often involve evaluative facts as well, premise-fact disputes less often concern historical facts. That is, disputes of premise fact do not usually focus on happenings, such as who did what, when, or where. Even when data are introduced, the emphasis of the dispute is not on the uninterpreted multitude of historical facts that constitute the data but on disputed assertions about whether the data are complete and what interpretive inferences or evaluative determinations courts properly may derive from them.[9]

Courts and legislatures also often use data as a basis for predicting the future. For example, a legislature may say, "On the basis of data relating to the last three years, it appears that malpractice insurance rates have been rising at an averge annual rate of 17%, and we predict they will rise at the same rate for the next three years unless we enact a 'cap' on noneconomic damages." Such use demonstrates that a dispute over a prediction about the future that may serve as a factual premise for the decision of an issue of law (deciding whether to enact a "cap" on damages) may involve both predicted events (predictions about data) and evaluative predictions (including inferences drawn from the data by extrapolation or otherwise). Thus, a court may base a legal decision in part on the decision of a dispute about evaluative inferences but also in part on the decision of a dispute about predicted future events (malpractice claims payments), which, after they occur, may be organized and counted as data. In part, then, the decision of an issue of

---

[8] See R. Keeton, Legal Cause in the Law of Torts 49-60, 88-90, 105-17 (1963).

[9] Cf. EEOC v. Trabucco, 791 F.2d 1, 2 (1st Cir. 1986) (describing starting point of stare decisis analysis as determination of "database" available to court).

law may depend on predictions about the future -- what will become, from a perspective even farther into the future, historical facts.

It bears emphasis that the essence of the distinction between premise facts and adjudicative facts is the purpose for which they are used in deciding a case. The illustrations considered above demonstrate that to determine whether a fact is an adjudicative fact or a premise fact we must probe more deeply than simply determining which among the four types of facts is involved in a dispute. We must answer the questions: "Why, under the reasoning of the court, is the disputed fact material to disposition of the case before the court? Is it, or was it, material to decision of an issue of law?"

G. Mixed Questions of Law and Fact

The phrase "mixed question of law and fact" is commonly used to describe an issue involving the application of an evaluative test for deciding cases.[1] This phrase most often appears in relation to an issue framed in a way that makes it difficult, if not impossible, to disentangle the factual element from the legal element. If disentanglement is impossible or very difficult, then it is likewise impossible or very difficult to decide separately the legal and factual issues, using the different methods ordinarily applicable to legal and factual disputes.

---

[1]Concerning evaluative tests generally, see Chapter 3, Section A, infra. The opinion in O'Neill v. Dell Publishing Co., 630 F.2d 685 (1st Cir. 1980), illustrates the application of an evalutive test. To determine who decides a dispute over an evaluative determination, and how, one must distinguish between the mixed question of law and fact in which all factual elements concern adjudicative facts and the mixed question of law and fact in which one or more of the factual elements concern premise facts. The factual element in applying the "substantial similarity" test to a copyright case, if reasonably disputed, is adjudicative. O'Neill, 630 F.2d at 687. In contrast, the factual element in deciding the dispute about the knowability of asbestos hazards in Case 2.2 is a premise fact. The distinction lies not in the nature of the disputed facts, but in the purpose for which the disputed fact is material under the precedents the court invokes in reaching its decision. See Section C, this Chapter, supra.

If a mixed question of law and fact is submitted to a jury in a way that does not explicitly and clearly explain the law to be applied by the jury in deciding the issue, then there is risk that, in effect, the court is surrendering effective control over whether the jury's verdict is reached by a route of reasoning involving no error of law.

If a mixed question of law and fact is decided by a trial judge, distinctive problems are presented to the appellate court with respect to its standard of review. Unless the appellate court requires of the trial judge a set of findings and conclusions sufficiently detailed and explicit to make clear that no errors of law were involved in the reasoned basis for the decision, there is, again, a risk of surrendering effective control over whether the outcome involves no error of law.

These risks may be to some extent reduced by closer judicial scrutiny of jury verdicts and closer appellate scrutiny of trial court findings and conclusions resolving "mixed questions of law and fact." The risks are not eliminated, however, if the form of scrutiny never succeeds in separating the legal issues from the factual. Separation is essential if a higher court is to review legal determinations by a no-deference standard and, in contrast, is to review fact determinations only to determine that they are not "clearly erroneous" or not supported by the evidence.

H. Borderland Between Law and Fact

The contrast between law and fact, like most other contrasts of legal discourse, is easy to recognize at the extremes but difficult at the borderline.

One reason for the difficulty is that a dispute may center on what is commonly called a mixed question of law and fact. That difficulty is discussed in the next preceding section.

A second reason for the difficulty is that courts, commentators, and advocates often refer to disputes over "legislative" or "premise" facts as issues of law, because they are usually decided by courts rather than by juries and in ways resembling, if not identical with, the ways issues of law are decided. One must be careful, then, to observe which of the ways of using the fact decision is involved (whether as a "premise" fact or instead as an "adjudicative" fact), when considering whether the decision is precedent that controls either a fact dispute in another case or the method of resolving a fact dispute in another case.

A third reason for difficulty in deciding whether an issue in the borderland area is one of law or one of fact concerns the nature of the issue itself and how it is appropriately defined under applicable law (either as established in authoritative sources or as decided in the case at hand as an issue of first impression). If the dispute is over historical facts only, the nature of the issue is plainly factual, even when confusion or difficulty may arise because of lack of clarity as to whether it is being resolved for use as a "premise" fact or as an "adjudicative" fact. If, on the other hand, the dispute is over whether proof of historical facts satisfies a legal test, more risk of confusion arises. For example, if the dispute is over whether proof of a custodian's knowledge of historical facts about bizarre behavior of a detainee supports a finding of "deliberate indifference" of the custodian to a "known, serious need of the detainee for medical attention," the nature of the issue itself presents difficulties of classification for the purpose of determining who decides the issue and how.[1] By its nature, the issue is not exclusively one of historical fact. It is, instead, at least in part one of evaluation. Similarly, the issue of "knowability" of asbestos hazards in Case 2.2 involves both historical facts about what had been published at the relevant time and the application of an evaluative test of "knowability."[2]

Any dispute over definition of the test to be applied in making the evaluation is plainly a dispute of law, not fact. For example, it is a question of law whether the test of "knowability" is defined in a way that makes historical facts known only to a certain kind of experts in the field "knowable" to manufacturers, or instead makes historical facts "knowable" only if ordinarily prudent manufacturers would have consulted experts of that kind.

---

[1] See, e.g., Carapellucci v. Town of Winchester, 707 F. Supp. 611 (D. Mass. 1989) (appeal pending).

[2] A more detailed discussion of this set of questions appears in Premise Facts, 73 U. Minn. L. Rev. 1, 63-65 (1988).

On the other hand, any dispute over the historical facts is a dispute of fact (regardless of whether the answer will be used in decisionmaking as a premise fact or instead as an adjudicative fact). For example, the dispute over how widely articles about asbestos hazards were circulated in the 1930s is a dispute of historical fact, even though it is never submitted to a jury if the lawmaking court decides to adopt a rule of law that invokes strict liability against a manufacturer without regard to whether evidence is offered to prove that the manufacturer knew of asbestos hazards.

If the case presents disputes both over the definition of the evaluative test and over determination of the historical facts (as, for example, a dispute over "knowability" in Case 2.2 does), it presents a mixed question of law and fact.

If there is no dispute over the definition of the test to be applied, but there is dispute both over the historical facts and the evaluation, the mixture is not necessarily one of law and fact. It is a dispute of historical fact and evaluation. A tort case arising from a motoring accident typically involves this kind of dispute over negligence (for example, what was the speed, and was proceeding at that speed negligent). There remains a possibility, however, that an evaluation will be treated not as a fact determination (as in most negligence cases) but as a legal ruling or as a premise for a legal ruling (as in the decision that crop dusting by airplane is an abnormally dangerous activity).

That part of a dispute over an evaluative question that concerns whether reasonable persons, correctly applying the test to the undisputed historical facts, could differ in answering the evaluative question is always treated as one of law. Thus, when a court decides that reasonable persons could reach only one answer, that decision is commonly called a "ruling" of law, not fact. It is precedent, though one of less general force than, for example, the "rule"[3] of strict liability for abnormally dangerous activities.

If the court decides that reasonable persons might differ in their answers to the evaluative question, usually the evaluative question is treated as one of fact to be

---

[3] See Chapter 3, Section A2, infra, regarding the distinction sometimes made between a "ruling" and a "rule."

resolved by adjudicative-fact procedures. That is the way, as just noted, that a determination of negligence is usually treated. In some contexts, however, courts have treated evaluative questions as questions for the court to decide. Two examples, noted just above as well as previously, are the evaluative questions as to whether the transportation of explosives on the highways is abnormally dangerous, and whether the use of an airplane in crop dusting is abnormally dangerous.[4]

One reason for doubt as to the meaning of some decisions is lack of clarity in the definition of an evaluative test. Lack of clarity is especially likely to result when a court fails to be explicit about whether all relevant historical facts are undisputed and, if not, precisely what bearing resolution of the historical fact disputes has upon decision of the evaluative question.

Allowing this kind of ambiguity to remain in a court's opinion tends to support an interpretation of the legal test as one under which the jury (or the trial judge as factfinder) is allowed very broad discretion. Relatively few cases applying the test can be decided "as a matter of law," and outcomes in particular cases are quite difficult to predict. Tests of "legal cause" commonly have this characteristic.[5]

The decision of a court as to whether to adopt a loosely defined evaluative test of uncertain meaning is, of course, an important decision of law. Allowing such broad discretion in the application of the test, case by case, allows the decisionmaker in the individual case to take account of all the distinctive characteristics of the particular case -- to fine tune the administration of justice to the distinctive characteristics of that particular case. It works strongly, however, against the public interest in assuring like outcomes in like cases, and the public interest in clarity of law and predictability of outcomes, because the discretionary decisions are largely unpoliced and may reflect differences among decisionmakers (whether juries or judges) more than they reflect differences among the cases themselves. This concern will again be considered in

---

[4] See Section F, this Chapter, supra.

[5] See Chapter 3, Section F, infra.

relation to those kinds of lawmaking decisions that involve choice of an "evaluative" test over a "bright-line" test.[6]

---

[6]See Chapter 3, Section A, infra.

PART TWO

MAKING AND EXPLAINING LAWMAKING CHOICES

CHAPTER 3

TAILORING TESTS FOR DECIDING CASES

A. Words and Meanings

    1. Introduction

    Stone walls do not a prison make,
    Nor iron bars a cage;
    ....[1]

Poetic expression has much in common with creative labeling. Just as one may, with the romantic poet Lovelace (writing while committed to the Gatehouse at Westminster in 1642), believe that the human spirit can transcend any physical barrier, so one may hope (as advocate writing a brief, or judge writing an opinion) through labeling to transcend any substantive barrier to persuading others to accept a proposed outcome. It happens, however, that before a perceptive audience

    creative   labeling   cannot   carry   the   day.

---

[1] Richard Lovelace (under the pen name "Lucasta"), To Althea: From Prison, st. 4, republished in Bartlett, <u>Familiar Quotations</u> (15th ed. Little, Brown & Co. 1980).

> Rather, the needed ... [focus is upon] "the conduct being regulated, not the formal description of governing legal standards ...."[2]

Nevertheless, the words used to state and explain a thought are important, because they have a significant bearing on whether the intended meaning is communicated.

Differences over terminology sometimes interfere with communication. The risk of misunderstanding is especially high if writer and reader, or speaker and listener, are not alert to each other's usages. You can use a word or phrase with any meaning you choose to give it, but you cannot force others to understand it that way. Moreover, if you propose a meaning different from ordinary usage, the risk that others will misunderstand what you mean rises dramatically.

In the hope of reducing the risks of misunderstanding of this discussion of tests for deciding cases, I begin with some explanation of meanings I wish to convey.

2. Different Kinds of Legal Tests and How We Describe Them

I use the word "test" to include all kinds of legal criteria for deciding any of the many issues in any case. Some legal tests define requirements a plaintiff must satisfy to establish a claim, or eligibility for a benefit. Others concern the elements of a defense, or privilege, or immunity from suit, or immunity from liability, or of a limit upon the scope of liability under rubrics such as "legal" or "proximate" cause, or "duty."

A distinction is sometimes made between rules and rulings. Whether or not a formal distinction is explicitly declared, in common usage "legal ruling" (or simply "ruling") is a term ordinarily used to signify the outcome of applying a legal test when that outcome is one of relatively narrow impact. The immediate effect is to decide an issue in a

---

[2]<u>Montplaisir</u> v. <u>Leighton</u>, 875 F.2d 1, 4 (1st Cir. 1989), <u>quoting</u> <u>Amalgamated Ass'n of Street, Electric Ry. & Motors Coach Employees</u> v. <u>Lockridge</u>, 403 U.S. 274, 292 (1971) (labor-law pre-emption issue). Applying the principle to the case at hand, the opinion for the First Circuit, Selya, J., explains: "That appellants chose not to couch their complaint as an unfair labor practice cuts no mustard." 87 F.2d at 4.

single case. This meaning contrasts, for example, with the usual meaning of "legal rule" (or simply "rule"). The term "rule" ordinarily refers to a legal proposition of general application.[3] A "ruling" may have force as precedent, but ordinarily it has that force because the conclusion it expresses (for example, "objection sustained") explicitly depends upon and implicitly reiterates a "rule" -- a legal proposition of more general application (for example, that a question seeking to elicit hearsay testimony is objectionable unless some exception to the hearsay rule applies). Ordinarily, I use "ruling" in the relatively narrow sense stated in this paragraph. The meaning of "rule" requires more explanation.

"Rule" is sometimes used in a sense as broad as that of legal "test," as I am using the latter term. At other times it is used with somewhat less breadth of meaning, to refer to every kind of legal "test" that is expressed in a formal body of "Rules" such as the Federal Rules of Evidence or the Federal Rules of Civil Procedure. At still other times "rule" has been used in a distinctively narrower sense as a contrast with "standard." A "rule" in this sense is a "bright-line" test; in contrast, a "standard" is an "evaluative" (or "on-balance") test requiring consideration of two or more factors or elements. For example, the legal criterion for determining the age of competency to contract is ordinarily a "rule" specifying a chronological age (usually 21 or 18), but the criterion for determining

---

[3]<u>Cf.</u> Fed. R. Evid. 201, Judicial Notice of Adjudicative Facts, Notes of Advisory Committee. Observe the context and apparent meanings of "rules" and "ruling" in the following explanation of the kinds of facts that are judicially noticed:

> The phrase "propositions of generalized knowledge," found in Uniform Rule 9(1) and (2) is not included in the present rule.... While judges use judicial notice of "propositions of generalized knowledge" in a variety of situations: determining the validity and meaning of statutes, formulating common law <u>rules</u>, ... all are essentially nonadjudicative in nature.... There is a vast difference between <u>ruling</u> on the basis of judicial notice that radar evidence of speed is admissible and explaining to the jury its principles and degree of accuracy....

<u>Id.</u>, Subdiv. (b) (emphasis added).

capacity to consent to a potentially harmful or offensive touching is ordinarily a "standard" making effectiveness of the consent depend on whether the person was mature enough to understand the nature and quality of the touching to which consent was purportedly given.[4]

An "evaluative" (or "on-balance") test never makes a single finding of historical fact decisive. In contrast, a "bright-line" test may direct the decisionmaker who applies it in a particular case to make a finding of truth or falsity with respect to a single alleged historical fact. An example is a test making the legal effect of consent depend on whether the person allegedly consenting was (or was not) at that time at least 21 years of age.

A "bright-line" test may, however, direct the decisionmaker who applies it in a particular case to make findings of truth or falsity with respect to two or more alleged historical facts. An example is a test, used in a criminal case, in which the jury, in order to convict, must find beyond reasonable doubt both that the defendant did an act alleged and that when doing that act the defendant had the alleged intent (a defined state of mind). In the context of a criminal trial, the different parts of such a bright-line test are commonly called "elements" of the offense charged. One may also describe the different parts of such a test in other ways, in both civil and criminal contexts -- as "components" or "prongs" of the legal test, or in some other expression of similar connotation, as I have just done in the first phrase of this sentence, referring to them as "parts."

An "evaluative" test always involves at least two, and usually more numerous, elements or components, or, in another expression quite commonly used, "factors." The most significant contrast between "bright-line" tests and "evaluative" tests, however, concerns not the number of components or factors involved but the way in which they are considered and used by the decisionmaker.

A "bright-line" test involving two or more elements requires the person applying it to a particular case to consider each element separately and make a true-false

---

[4] Cf. 2 R. Pound, _Jurisprudence_ 124-28 (1959). See also Keeton, _Creative Continuity in the Law of Torts_, 75 Harv. L. Rev. 463, 493-506 (1962).

finding as to each, or at least as to enough of the different elements (whether one or more) to decide the outcome. Thus, for example, if the test requires the plaintiff to prove the truth of three separate allegations of historical facts, a finding that the plaintiff has failed as to any one will be decisive and may lead the decisionmaker to conclude it is unnecessary to consider closely debatable issues regarding the other two.

In contrast, an "evaluative" test requires the person applying it to consider two or more elements together and arrive at an answer, "on balance," to a single question defined in the test -- a question to be answered only after considering and weighing all the elements identified as things to be weighed. Thus, for example, a trial judge applying the law of a state that adheres to the test for "scope of employment" expressed in the Restatement (Second) of Agency tells the jury to consider all of the listed factors as to which evidence has been presented and then decide whether the plaintiff has proved by a preponderance of the evidence whatever the court declares to be necessary to show that the employee of the defendant was acting within the scope of employment at the relevant time.[5]

As already noted, the term "factors" is commonly used to describe the different components of an evaluative test. This usage is quite common, for example, in relation to the "scope of employment" test. The "factors" to be weighed may include one or more historical facts, along with other "factors" each of which is itself evaluative rather than merely a determination of historical fact.[6] Thus, the decisionmaker who is applying the test to a case must engage in a rather complex process of making an evaluative weighing to assess one or more separate factors and then proceed to make another more comprehensive weighing that sweeps those factors into the decision.

In thinking about this more complex kind of evaluative test, it may be useful to observe another contrast -- that

---

[5] Restatement (Second) of Agency, §§219, 229, 235 (1965). For further discussion of this illustration, see Section C3 of this Chapter, infra.

[6] Regarding historical facts and evaluative determinations, see generally Chapter 2, Section F, supra.

is, a contrast between "one-choice" tests and "multi-choice" tests. A legal test specifying chronological age of 21 as decisive of competency to consent is a "one-choice, bright-line" test. Another "one-choice" test is a legal test specifying that the decisive matter is capacity to understand the nature and quality of the touching to which consent was purportedly given. This test is, however, a "one-choice, evaluative" test. Consider, in contrast with both of these types of "one-choice" tests, a test that makes criminal liability depend on the government's proving beyond reasonable doubt both that the defendant committed an act alleged and that he did so willfully. This is a "multi-choice" test. Whether it is simply a "two-choice" test, each part of which is "bright-line" historical fact, or instead is more complex, depends on how the lawmaker establishing the test defines each of the two choices. For example, if "willfully" is defined as requiring both "intent" to cause a defined consequence such as deception of a person to whom a false statement was made and "knowledge" that the act of making such a statement is unlawful, then the test involves at least three choices. This is so regardless of whether we view it as a two-choice test, the second part of which ("willfully"), in turn, has two sub-choices, or instead we view the test as having three choices, the second and third of which are sometimes collapsed into one ("willfully") for convenience of communication or analysis.

"Multi-choice" tests may also be more complex in another way. The different choices may be a mixture of "bright-line" and "evaluative" choices. For example, in motoring accident cases, state law applicable to a case may have adopted a multi-choice legal test for accountability for speed under which: (1) choice one is made under a bright-line rule directing that a factfinder decide whether speed was in excess of 55 miles per hour; (2) if yes, a second choice is an "evaluative" or "on-balance" standard directing the factfinder to determine whether emergency circumstances were so compelling that they satisfied the legal definition of an "excuse" or "justification," with the legal consequence that the doctrine of "negligence per se" does not apply to this case; and (3) a third choice is an "evaluative" determination as to whether driving at the speed used in the emergency circumstances was "unreasonably risky" and thus in violation of the negligence standard.

Another illustration of a complex multi-choice test came before the Second Circuit in the form of a challenge to the interpretation and application of Rule 24(a)(2) of the

Federal Rules of Civil Procedure, regarding intervention as of right. In an opinion by Judge Friendly, the court declared:

> The various components of the Rule are not bright lines, but ranges -- not all 'interests' are of equal rank, not all impairments are of the same degree, representation by existing parties may be more or less adequate.... Application of the Rule requires that its components be read not discretely, but together.... Finally, although the Rule does not say so in terms, common sense demands that consideration also be given to matters that shape a particular action or particular type of action.[7]

In this passage Judge Friendly was using "Rule" to mean one of the Federal Rules of Civil Procedure -- a quite different meaning from "rule" as used in the distinction between "rule" and "standard." In the latter usage, Fed. R. Civ. P.24(a)(2) established a "standard." Thus a "rule" commonly makes one or more separately determined historical facts decisive. In contrast, a "standard" commonly requires an evaluative weighing of two or more facts, often along with other factors that are not themselves merely historical facts, in order to answer a single question identified in the legal test as decisive.

Discussion of additional implications of the use of "evaluative" tests, especially when they require consideration of the "totality of the circumstances," appears in a later section.[8]

Of course, a "multi-choice" legal test with some choices "bright-line" in nature and other choices "evaluative" in nature tends to be more difficult than a one-choice test to describe, to understand, and to apply without error. The risks of misunderstanding and misapplication rise, and sometimes quite dramatically, as a legal test is fashioned to involve more choices and more variance in the nature of the different choices. Concern about the

---

[7]United States v. Hooker Chemicals & Plastics Corp., 749 F.2d 968, 983 (2d Cir. 1984).

[8]Section C3, this Chapter, infra.

likelihood of incorrect application of more complex tests is one of the policy considerations lawmakers do and should take into account when deciding what kind of legal test to fashion in order to achieve the substantive objectives of the lawmaking decision.

The potential significance of the distinction between a one-choice test and a multi-choice test is illustrated by apparently conflicting precedents regarding the test for determining whether a preliminary injunction should be issued. Many precedents generated in many different contexts identify four elements as relevant. They are commonly described as a plaintiff's showing four things: (1) a likelihood of success on the merits at trial, (2) irreparable harm to the plaintiff absent injunction, (3) a balance of hardships in which plaintiff's hardship is greater, and (4) consistency of the proposed injunction with public interest. Some precedents may be interpreted as establishing such a four-part test under which there are four discrete requirements, as to each of which a plaintiff has the burden of proof; failure to satisfy any one of them is fatal to the claim for preliminary injunction.[9] Other precedents may be interpreted as establishing a one-choice, evaluative test under which these four elements are "factors"; no single factor, taken individually, is dispositive.[10] That is, the court is to consider these factors together in a single "evaluative" or "on-balance" determination rather than

---

[9] See, e.g., Planned Parenthood League of Massachusetts v. Bellotti, 641 F.2d 1006, 1009 (1st Cir. 1981), quoting with approval the statement in Warren's Commmunity Health Center, Inc. v. Cohen, 477 F. Supp. 542, 544 (D. Me. 1979), that the plaintiff "must satisfy [these] four criteria." In Cohen, the court added: "In order to prevail, plaintiff must satisfy each of the four criteria." 477 F. Supp. at 544. A "more flexible" standard has been adopted in other circuits, however. Id. at n.1, citing Sonesta International Hotels Corp. v. Wellington Associates, 483 F.2d 247 (2d Cir. 1973).

[10] See, e.g., Hybritech, Inc. v. Abbott Laboratories, 849 F.2d 1446 (Fed. Cir. 1988) (patent case).

> These factors, taken individually, are not dispositive; rather, the district court must weigh and measure each factor against the other factors and against the form and magnitude of the relief requested.

Id. at 1451.

considering each separately as one of four distinct elements, each of which must be established independently of the others in order for the plaintiff to succeed in the claim for preliminary injunction.

Precedents treating the four elements as separate requirements, all of which must be met, tend to produce more structured and more rigorous appellate review of a trial court's determination to grant or deny a preliminary injunction. Precedents treating the four elements as factors to be weighed in a one-choice determination tend to produce more deferential appellate review, with the consequence that the trial court has more discretionary authority and is less likely to be reversed.

3. Subjective and Objective Tests

The adjectives "subjective" and "objective" are often used in describing tests for deciding cases. These adjectives may be used to identify opposites in two quite different senses, however, and it is sometimes necessary to examine the context closely to determine which contrast is meant. The first contrast focuses on who is judging; the second, on whose conduct is being judged.

In the first contrast, a test is "subjective" if it provides so little constraint upon the decisionmaker who is applying it to a particular case that the decisionmaker is free to make virtually any decision he or she wishes. For example, the dissenting judges in a First Amendment case were criticizing as too "subjective" in this sense the court's test for distinguishing between "fact" and "opinion" when they said: "[b]eauty is in the eye of the beholder, and it would appear that the result to be obtained through the application [of the test elaborated in the opinion of Arnold, J.] is in the eye of the judge."[11] In this usage, the less a test leaves to the discretion (or choice) of the judge or jury -- the less it leaves to the eye of the beholder -- the more "objective" it is. Another example of a test that is objective in this sense is the legal proposition, used in statutory rape cases, that makes the legal effect of a person's manifestation of consent to a physical contact depend on chronological age of that person. Under this

---

[11] Janklow v. Newsweek, Inc., 788 F.2d 1300, 1307 (8th Cir. 1986) (en banc) (Bowman, Ross, and Fagg, Circuit Judges, dissenting).

"objective" test the decisionmakers have strong guidance and little discretion (merely that implicit in resolving any dispute about chronological age). Described in the form of another distinction noted above, this legal proposition making effectiveness of consent depend on age is a "bright-line" test (a "rule") in contrast with an "evaluative" test (a "standard"). Bright-line tests tend more than evaluative tests to produce decisionmaking that is "objective" in the sense described in this paragraph.

A legal proposition that makes the legal effect of a person's manifestation of consent depend instead on the capacity of that person to understand the nature and quality of the proposed physical contact is more "subjective" because it leaves much discretion to the decisionmakers. They have discretion both in evaluating evidence, whether disputed or not, and in determining whether that evidence, together with any set of historical facts it tends to prove, does or does not show capacity to understand the nature and quality of the proposed physical contact. In the rule-standard distinction noted above, the contrast between the more "objective" criterion of chronological age and the more "subjective" criterion of capacity to understand is described as a contrast between a rule (age) and a standard (capacity).

Sometimes a court deliberately rejects a standard and adopts a rule because of concern about leaving too much discretion to decisionmakers case by case. Thus, for example, the Supreme Court declined to allow a cause of action for malicious parody where the jury found no false statement of fact about the public-figure plaintiff, even though the jury found that the publishers intended to cause severe emotional distress and that the standard of "outrageousness" was satisfied.

> "Outrageousness" in the area of political and social discourse has an inherent <u>subjectiveness</u> about it which would allow a jury to impose liability on a basis of the jurors' tastes or views, or perhaps on the basis of their dislike of a particular expression. An "outrageousness" standard thus runs afoul of our longstanding refusal to allow damages to be awarded because the speech in question may have an adverse emotional

impact on the audience.[12]

To describe a test as "subjective" in this sense is to say that it allows the decisionmakers who apply it to make a decision based on the decisionmakers' own tastes and values, rather than rigorously requiring that the decisionmakers adhere to the community values that the legal formulation they are applying is designed to serve. The distinction is focused on whether the test being applied allows decisions "subjectively" related to the characteristics and views of <u>the decisionmaker</u>, or instead constrains each decisionmaker to be more "objective."[13]

Of course, standards for decisionmaking are neither entirely "subjective" nor entirely "objective" in the sense of this contrast. They range across the spectrum from tending strongly toward being "objective" to tending strongly toward being "subjective."

In a very different usage, the distinction between "subjective" and "objective" is related to whether the standard is "subjectively" related to the characteristics <u>of the person whose conduct is being judged</u>. In this second

---

[12] <u>Hustler Magazine</u> v. <u>Falwell</u>, 485 U.S. 46, 55 (1988) (emphasis added).

[13] <u>Cf.</u> <u>Koos</u> v. <u>Roth</u>, 293 Or. 670, 652 P.2d 1255 (1982) (holding a farmer who employed "field burning" strictly liable to pay damages when the fire entered upon and destroyed a neighbor's property). Justice Linde, writing for the court, was critical of a shift of emphasis that occurred when the <u>Restatement (Second) of Torts</u> moved from using the phrase "extrahazardous" or "ultrahazardous" to using the phrase "abnormally dangerous" in §§519, 520. "The older phrases kept the focus on the hazardous character of the activity, on its essentially irreducible potential for causing substantial harm." 652 P.2d at 1260. "But the newer phrase lends itself to invoking social as well as physical norms, as if it read 'abnormal and dangerous activities,' thereby mixing questions of cause and effect, or probabilities and magnitudes of harm in the natural world, with what may be called societal considerations" such as value of the dangerous activity to the community. <u>Id.</u> One reason "not to judge civil liability for unintended harm by a court's views of the utility or value of the harmful activity" is that "[u]tility and value often are <u>subjective</u> and controversial." 652 P.2d at 1261 (emphasis added). "Our cases have not required courts and counsel to enter upon such philosophical issues in deciding whether a defendant is strictly liable for harm from a hazardous activity." 652 P.2d at 1262.

usage, a test is "objective" to the extent that it uses criteria that are independent of the characteristics (including state of mind) of the person whose conduct is being judged and subjective to the extent that it uses that person's own characteristics.[14] "Standards" tend more than "rules" to produce decisionmaking that is "objective" in this sense.

In this sense, too, tests used in law need not necessarily be totally "subjective" or totally "objective." Thus, for example, even though the negligence test does not depend on the intent of the actor (which is "subjective") in relation to the consequences for which claim is made, the negligence test has a "subjective" element when it is fashioned to take account of age, or a physical characteristic such as blindness, or a state-of-mind element such as specialized knowledge. The negligence test (commonly referred to as a "standard") is invariably to some extent objective, however, because "ordinary" care is the measure of the conduct.[15] Of course, not only the negligence test (or "standard") but many others as well are partly subjective and partly objective in this sense.

The precise sense in which the subjective-objective contrast is used becomes a bit more difficult to disentangle and explain when a court is considering, first, the nature of private decisionmaking and, second, the nature of decisionmaking in court (by jurors and judges) about the private decisionmaking. A case based on a claim of employment discrimination illustrates the point. In Wards Cove Packing Co. v. Atonio,[16] nonwhite employees challenged both the employer's use of "objective" criteria of hiring (nepotism, separate hiring channels, and rehire preferences) and "subjective decisionmaking" by the employer in the selection of persons for positions in one part of the

---

[14] E.g., New England Tractor-Trailer Training of Connecticut, Inc. v. Globe Newspaper Co., 395 Mass. 471, 480 N.E.2d 1005, 1007-12 (1985) (adopting "objective" negligence standard for the "of and concerning plaintiff" issue in a defamation case rather than "subjective" standard concerned with publisher's "intent").

[15] See generally Seavey, Negligence -- Subjective or Objective, 41 Harv. L. Rev. 1 (1927). See also Section C1, this Chapter, infra.

[16] ___ U.S. ___, 109 S. Ct. 2115 (1989).

workforce.[17] Thus, the subjective-objective contrast was focused on the extent to which the employer decisionmaking was "subjective" in relation to characteristics of the persons acting for the employer in the decisionmaking (rather than being more constrained by "objective" criteria those decisionmakers were expected to apply). Described in another way, in the sense of a who-is-deciding (or who-is-judging) contrast, the employer's decisionmaking for one segment of its work force was "subjective" and for another segment of its work force was "objective." It does not follow, of course, that the decisionmaking in court would likewise be "subjective" or "objective" in the sense of the who-is-judging contrast. Indeed, in reviewing the decisions of the District Court and the Court of Appeals as it did, and in fashioning instructions as to how they should proceed on remand, the Supreme Court was making lawmaking choices that allowed some leeway for "subjective decisionmaking" by the employer in the sense of the who-is-deciding contrast (that is, the contrast focusing on the employer as decisionmaker), but much less leeway for "subjective decisionmaking" by the courts in that sense (that is, the contrast focusing on the court as decisionmaker rather than the whose-conduct-is-judged contrast).

In the materials that follow, unless otherwise stated, I will be using the contrast between the more "subjective" and the more "objective" tests in the second sense -- that is, in the sense concerned with the extent to which the test depends on characteristics of the person whose conduct is being judged ("subjective") and the extent to which it is independent of that person's characteristics ("objective").

In this usage a state-of-mind element of any test is "subjective." Thus, a test that declares a person accountable for consequences that person "intended" when acting is "subjective." In contrast, a test that declares a person accountable for consequences that were foreseeable to a hypothetical ordinarily prudent person, regardless of what the actor's state of mind with respect to those consequences may have been, is primarily "objective," even if, as noted above, it may have some "subjective" element in it, such as age of the actor whose conduct is being judged.

The tests in common use in the legal system that are most "subjective" in this sense are those that depend most

---

[17]Id. at ___, 109 S. Ct. at 2125.

heavily upon a factfinding as to some specified state of mind of the person whose conduct is being judged.

Of course, a lawmaking choice, in any given context, to use a state-of mind test rather than a more objective test, or vice versa, is likely to be heavily value-laden.[18] As a general proposition, we are most likely to be comfortable with the use of a state-of-mind test, and uncomfortable without it, in criminal law. Even so, pragmatic interests in effective deterrence and enforcement lead to lawmaking choices to establish some "crimes without intent." In other legal contexts, objective tests of accountability are more prominent. The tests for negligence and legal cause in tort actions are illustrations. A court may make the lawmaking choice to adopt such a test, or may explicitly acknowledge in applying such a test in a particular case that "fiat" or partly unexplained "choice" is involved, and yet conclude that this more "objective" test better serves the interests of justice than would a state-of-mind test.[19] Also, variations in the relative prominence of subjective and objective tests occur over time and in changing social and economic conditions.

Examining in more detail legal tests for determining accountability, we turn first to those that have significant state-of-mind elements.

B. State-of-Mind Elements in Tests for Legal Accountability

1. In General

Probably the single greatest source of confusion about tests for legal accountability is lack of clarity about whether a test is exclusively objective or instead has one or more state-of-mind elements. To be precise and clear, the definition of a test that does include a state-of-mind element must also indicate exactly how that state-of-mind

---

[18] Regarding value implications of lawmaking choices, more generally, see Chapter 4, infra.

[19] With respect to the element of "fiat," see, e.g., Judge Learned Hand's opinion in Sinram, discussed in Chapter 4, Section D, n.5, infra. Regarding choice more generally, see Chapter 1, Sections A and D, supra.

element is to be framed for the judge or jury applying it. Any confusion about these matters in the authoritative statement of a test substantially affects the work of advocates, trial judges, and juries.

If the advocates of conflicting positions in a case press the interests of their respective clients as zealously as they are legally entitled to do, at least one of the advocates may force the trial judge to take a position on any material question left unanswered by statutes or precedents that are inexplicit as to whether some state-of-mind element is included in the applicable test for accountability. In a jury trial, the advocate may do so by appropriate requests for instruction (or for interrogatories to the jury) or by objections to the court's charge (or to interrogatories). In a nonjury trial, the advocate may do so by proposed findings and conclusions, or by objections to findings and conclusions. Moreover, the advocate may similarly press the trial judge to define the state-of-mind element precisely where lack of precision adversely affects the client's interests. At the least, the advocate will have preserved an argument for appeal that the lack of precision both in precedents and in the trial court's charge (or in findings and conclusions in a nonjury trial) is a failure to provide clarification, to which the client is entitled.

An illustration in point is <u>Sandstrom</u> v. <u>Montana</u>.[1] The trial court's charge to the jury in a prosecution for murder included the hoary fallacy that "a man is presumed to intend the natural and probable consequences of his act." A moment's reflection will tell you that literal application of this proposition converts what sounds like a state-of-mind test (because it includes the word "intend") into an objective test with no state-of-mind element. The test becomes simply an objective one, application of which requires no finding about the defendant's state of mind but only a finding that a relevant consequence of the defendant's conduct (death of the decedent) was "a natural and probable consequence" of the defendant's conduct. That is, the instruction tells the jury that if they find (beyond reasonable doubt, of course, under other instructions in the charge) that death of the decedent was a natural and probable consequence, then they need not consider the state of mind of the defendant -- whether he intended that his act cause the death -- because he is presumed to have intended it

---

[1] 442 U.S. 510 (1979).

regardless of whether or not he did so in fact.

Countless convictions in cases in which the trial judge gave such a presumed-intent charge survived appellate review before the Supreme Court of the United States, in Sandstrom, held that the Due Process Clause of the Fourteenth Amendment forbids a state's elimination, in this way, of the state-of-mind element from the charge to the jury in a murder trial.

Sequels to Sandstrom illustrate another source of confusion about applying tests for accountability that include a state-of-mind element. This source of confusion is failure to distinguish between "irrebuttable presumptions" and "permissive inferences." The trial court charge in Sandstrom applied what was in effect an "irrebuttable presumption" that if death was "a natural and probable consequence" of the defendant's conduct, then defendant intended the death. If the court had, instead, merely told the jury they were permitted (but not required) to draw this inference, the Due Process challenge would have failed. Even when a test for accountability plainly does have a state-of-mind element, the factfinder (jury or judge) may make the essential factfinding without direct evidence to support it and in the face of the actor's sworn testimony to the contrary.

> The factfinder need not credit the actor's assertion that the actor did not intend the result in question. One of the common lines of argument against crediting the actor's assertion is (1) that, given the circumstances disclosed in the evidence, a reasonable person in the actor's position would have known that the consequence in question was substantially certain to follow the act, (2) that the evidence shows that the actor was even brighter and shrewder than most others, and (3) that the inference is therefore compelling that the actor knew even though testifying otherwise. If the factfinder credits inference (1) but not inferences (2) and (3), the finding is negligence. But if the factfinder credits all three inferences, the finding is intent to produce the consequence in question. Expressed another way the point is this: Since intent is a state of mind, it is plainly incorrect for a court to instruct

> a jury that an actor is presumed to intend the natural and probable consequences of the actor's conduct; but it is correct to tell the jury that, relying on circumstantial evidence, they may infer that the actor's state of mind was the same as a reasonable person's state of mind would have been.[2]

Thus, even though a presumed-intent charge like that given by the trial court in Sandstrom violates the Due Process Clause, the trial court may instruct the jury that they are permitted, though not required, to draw the inference from the evidence before them that death of the decedent was a natural and probable consequence of defendant's conduct, that defendant so realized, and that defendant intended the death.[3]

Another source of confusion and lack of clarity is that many words and phrases are sometimes used to refer to a state of mind and at other times are used to refer to a state of fact involving no state-of-mind element. Among such words and phrases are "wanton" and "reckless." Of course, if a court uses a word such as "intentionally" or "willfully," or a phrase such as "reckless disregard," or "deliberate indifference" -- each of which sounds like a state-of-mind test -- but applies a presumption like that repudiated by the Supreme Court in Sandstrom, then even words and phrases that seem unambiguously to refer to a state of mind must be included, along with "wanton" and "reckless," in the list of the ambiguous.

The problems such ambiguities create in the application of tests to particular cases are illustrated in the discussion elsewhere of questions as to whether one or more of the concepts of intent, deliberate indifference, recklessness, and gross negligence should be included in the test for determining whether a state official's conduct toward a person in the official's custody deprived that person of liberty or property without due process of law.[4]

---

[2] W. Prosser & W. Keeton, Torts 36, §8 (5th ed. 1984) (footnote omitted).

[3] E.g., Hardy v. United States, 691 F.2d 39 (1st Cir. 1982).

[4] See discussion of Case 1.1, Chapter 1, Sections B2 and D1, supra.

2. The Changing Significance of State-of-Mind Tests

If the principles and policies a lawmaker wishes to serve in fashioning a test for accountability are best served by strict liability or negligence, ordinarily there is no need for invoking any state-of-mind test. The critical line between liability and nonliability is drawn on an objective basis. Unless some additional legal consequence is at stake, beyond liability for harm caused, no state-of-mind finding of fact need be made.

As tort litigation in the courts developed in the early part of the 20th century, most cases involved negligence claims. Interest in state-of-mind tests waned, both in law schools and in courts. Moreover, as the incidence of strict liability increased, the center of interest in accident compensation cases shifted even farther away from state-of-mind tests.

Developments of the 1960s and later years, however, have made state-of-mind tests more significant than before.

First, the Supreme Court's decision in New York Times Company v. Sullivan[5] introduced into defamation cases a First Amendment protection against tort liability that depends upon a state-of-mind test commonly called "reckless disregard." Many reported trial and appellate decisions in defamation cases since 1964 have concerned problems encountered in applying the "reckless disregard" test to individual cases. Also, later developments have extended this state-of-mind test beyond defamation into other areas of litigation, thus increasing the practical significance of state-of-mind tests in the administration of justice.[6]

Second, in the 1960s and 1970s a set of problems always inherent in liability insurance and occasionally litigated earlier came to be increasingly significant. When first appearing late in the 19th century, liability insurance itself was thought to be problematic because it had the appearance of relieving "wrongdoers" -- as tort defendants

---

[5] 376 U.S. 254 (1964).

[6] See, e.g., Time, Inc. v. Hill, 385 U.S. 374 (1967). As to another extension of First Amendment protection, involving other issues rather than application of the "reckless disregard" standard, see Hustler Magazine v. Falwell, 485 U.S. 46 (1988).

were then generally perceived to be -- of responsibility for their wrongs. The legal system soon rejected that challenge to the legitimacy of liability insurance. A challenge of greater significance emerged, however, when tort defendants sought to use liability insurance coverage as protection against liability for intended consequences of their conduct. Currently, decisions by courts on claims of liability insurance coverage often depend on state-of-mind tests concerned with whether consequences for which the tort defendant is sued were intended by the tort defendant -- or, in the language of many insurance policies, were "expected or intended from the standpoint of the insured."[7] Also, courts commonly invoke state-of-mind tests in deciding disputes over coverage for punitive damages.

Third, in the 1970s and 1980s occasional awards of punitive damages high enough to place a defendant in bankruptcy and the spectre of a crippling succession of awards in mass tort cases have brought to the surface and exposed for public debate lawmaking issues regarding fairness of process as well as result. Some of these issues reach federal constitutional dimensions.[8] Because state-of-mind tests are commonly applied to claims for punitive damages, the increased interest in these developments relating to punitive damages results also in more concern with the application of state-of-mind tests generally. In addition, claims for punitive damages raise new concerns -- or at least concerns new in dimension -- about application of state-of-mind tests to legal entities that, in a strictly factual sense, can never have a state of mind.[9]

Fourth, although from earliest times claims of fraud have often depended on state-of-mind tests, the incidence of fraud claims as a percentage of litigation in the court system has increased significantly in the 1960s and later decades. Securities fraud litigation has increased substantially, and claims under state and federal consumer fraud statutes are now common. Although many statutes include remedies for violation of objective tests (negligent

---

[7] R. Keeton and A. Widiss, Insurance Law §5.4(d) (1988).

[8] See, e.g., Browning-Ferris Ind. v. Kelco Disposal, ___ U.S. ___, 109 S. Ct. 2909 (1989).

[9] See Section D4, this Chapter, infra, regarding entity state-of-mind standards.

or reckless misrepresentation, defined objectively) most statutes also allow added relief based on violation of a state-of-mind test (intent to deceive).

Fifth, federal courts, led of course by the Supreme Court, have fashioned a substantial body of law commonly referred to as the law of "constitutional torts." Many of the tests of accountability developed in this context are state-of-mind tests. "Deliberate indifference" is an example.

The combined impact of all these developments has dramatically increased the importance of state-of-mind tests in current litigation. A general understanding of state-of-mind tests is therefore now a more significant part of a full understanding of judging than it was in time past.

3. Tailoring State-of-Mind Tests to Individual Cases

A general understanding of state-of-mind tests is only a first step to understanding their use in judging. Because state-of-mind tests typically focus on the state-of-mind of some particular person, existing at the time of some particular conduct of that person, a full statement of the state-of-mind test used in resolving a dispute tends to be tailored to the particular issue in the particular case.

Did the defendant reporter, at the time of writing for publication the article stating that plaintiff teacher "used a ruler to whack the knuckles of any student who crossed her," act with reckless disregard for whether the statement the reporter made about the teacher was true or false? Did the driver, when swerving his car as it struck the bicycle plaintiff was riding, do so with the purpose of causing bodily injury to the plaintiff, or with knowledge that bodily injury to the plaintiff was substantially certain to result? Did the defendant, when negotiating for sale of a used car to the plaintiff, say to the plaintiff, "Our service department checked the brakes, and they are A-OK," and, if so, did the defendant when making that statement know that it was false and that the brakes pulled the car to the left when applied hard? Did the town police officer place the decedent in a cell, unattended, while the decedent was behaving strangely even for a person under the influence of alcohol, and, if so, did the officer act with deliberate indifference to a known serious need for immediate medical attention?

Each of the formulations of a state-of-mind test in the illustrations stated immediately above might be appropriate for a particular case, but quite inappropriate for another case invoking the same body of substantive law in a setting quite different in detail. The formulation of the test used in a particular case need not include every qualification or exception that might be needed for use in some other case. Especially if the formulation is used as an interrogatory to a jury or as part of the court's instructions to the jury, it is ordinarily better that it not tell the jury about inapplicable exceptions, qualifications, or any other kind of modifications that might be appropriate if the formulation were being stated in a statute or a judicial opinion as a proposition applicable generally. Telling the jury things about the law that they do not need to know in order to decide the material disputes of fact in the case before them is ordinarily more likely to impede than to aid them in their task.[10]

Because of the need to tailor a state-of-mind test to the particulars of the case and of the issue within that case that is to be resolved by its use, the number of state-of-mind formulations used in judging is countless. Also, because of this need for tailoring, general formulations advanced in treatments of the substantive law, both in authoritative sources (such as statutes and precedents) and in commentaries on the meaning of the sources, are likely to be framed at a level of generality or abstraction that leaves room for debate or disagreement about how they should be adapted to the factfinder's need for guidance in applying the test to a particular issue in a particular case.

If the factfinder is a jury, it is the responsibility of the trial judge to provide this added guidance by giving instructions that appropriately tailor the test to each material state-of-mind dispute in the case. If the trial judge fails to provide the added guidance, and instead merely repeats a general formulation of the state-of-mind test, the jury is left to do the tailoring themselves. Of course, they are less likely than the trial judge to succeed in doing it consistently with the underlying premises of the lawmaker who created the test. Jurors lack the access that the trial judge has to the whole body of legal materials that may help

---

[10] For additional discussion of this point about jury instructions, see Chapter 8, Section D, infra.

one understand those premises.

One or another of the parties to any case is likely to be disadvantaged by a trial judge's failure to formulate interrogatories or instructions that provide needed additional guidance -- that is, failure to tailor a state-of-mind test for use in the particular case. The fuller explanation, by giving more explicit directions, tends to reduce risks of misunderstanding and misapplication of the more general statement of the test. In most cases these risks of misunderstanding tend to favor one party or the other rather than having neutral impact. This circumstance creates a need for the attorney for each party to submit requests for instruction that will serve the client's interests consistently with precedent, and perhaps to object to any instruction that is framed in such general terms that it leaves ambiguities that might be resolved by the jury in a way adverse to the client. In every case clearly involving application of a state-of-mind test, a critical part of the advocate's effective representation of the client is giving careful attention to how any state-of-mind interrogatories or instructions will be framed for the jury. And, of course, the judge's charge is likely to be better when the advocates have performed their functions well.

4. Entity State-of-Mind Tests

A "legal entity" other than a natural person is a creature of the law. It does not exist outside the legal system.[11]

Being this kind of creature, a "legal entity" has no "mind" in the usual sense of that word and cannot have a

---

[11] Cf. Dartmouth College v. Woodward, 4 Wheat. 518, 636 (1819) (opinion of the Court, delivered by Marshall, C.J., observing, "A corporation is an artificial being, invisible, intangible, and existing only in contemplation of law."). See also Browning-Ferris Industries of Vermont v. Kelco Disposal, Inc., ___ U.S. ___, ___, 109 S. Ct. 2909, 2925 (1989) (opinion of O'Connor, J., concurring in part and dissenting in part, observing that a corporation "is not entitled to '"purely personal" guarantees' whose '"historic function" ... "has been limited to the protection of individuals,"'" citing First National Bank of Boston v. Bellotti, 435 U.S. 765, 779, n.14 (1978), and, for example, has no Fifth Amendment privilege against self-incrimination or right to privacy, but it does have many other legally enforceable rights).

"state of mind" in the usual sense of that phrase. For these reasons, a corporation, a municipality, an organized club, or any other form of organization or association of natural persons has legal rights and obligations (as distinct from the legal rights and obligations of the individuals in the organization or association) only to the extent that the law recognizes the organization or association as an entity -- thus conferring on it the status of a "legal entity."

When a state-of-mind test is invoked against a legal entity, the court applying the test must at some point determine whether to hold the entity accountable for the state of mind of one or more natural persons. This can be a troubling issue.[12]

---

[12]See, e.g., Oxford Shipping Co. v. New Hampshire Trading Corp., 697 F.2d 1 (1st Cir. 1983), which is discussed also in Chapter 1, Section C2, note 6, supra, where the basic facts are stated. As noted there, bills of lading represented that 20,000 tons of scrap metal were aboard a vessel that in fact had aboard only about 17,000 tons. Was the vessel owner legally accountable if one of its agents knew, or should have known, of the short tonnage? In a passage that focuses upon negligence ("should have known"), but may be applicable as well to the state-of-mind issue ("knew"), the court concluded:

> The legal question presented is simply whether an innocent principal (Oxford) is barred from collecting for damages caused by one set of negligent agents (Tager) because another set of agents has also been negligent (the captain and first officer) -- in other words, whether one agent's contributory negligence is to be imputed to his principal to bar the principal from recovering from another negligent agent. The courts that have faced this question have divided in their responses....
>
> Our conclusion rests on our view that in the cases in which the contributory negligence of one agent has been held to bar an innocent principal from recovering against another, the courts have simply reasoned by analogy from a different situation without recognizing the difference. The different situation is that in which the principal seeks to recover from a third party, such as when Firm A seeks to recover from a driver of a car who negligently collides with Firm A's truck. In such circumstances, courts often have held that the

A "legal entity" in the sense defined above is to be distinguished from a "conspiracy." The purpose for which courts determine whether a conspiracy existed is to determine criminal or civil responsibility of the conspirators (either natural persons or other "legal entities" in the sense stated above). The "conspiracy," even when proved to be in existence up to and at the time of judgment, ordinarily has no assets to be reached for enforcement of a judgment and no status as a legally accountable "entity." Instead, the existence of the conspiracy during a relevant period of time is part of the legal basis for holding members of the conspiracy accountable to criminal and civil sanctions. It may also be a basis for forfeiture of assets (of members) that were used in furtherance of the conspiracy.

>contributory negligence of Firm A's driver, if sufficient to bar the driver's own recovery, is sufficient to bar recovery by Firm A as well. The servant's or agent's contributory negligence is "imputed" to the master or principal. See Restatement (Second) of Agency § 317 (principal-agent); Restatement (Second) of Torts § 486 (master-servant).
>
>This general rule of imputation presumably is grounded in the desire to require the principal to recover from his agent, rather than allowing him to pursue the third party as well. If so, that rationale is defeated rather than furthered if two negligent agents are allowed to impute each other's negligence and bar recovery against either: instead of being remitted to his agents for relief, the principal is barred from recovering against them altogether. We have not found any other plausible rationale underlying the imputing of contributory negligence that would require imputation in this case. Given the basic legal rule that a principal can recover for damages caused by an agent's breach of his duties of trust and care, we see no reason why the principal should be barred by the fact that injuries were caused by two agents or two sets of agents. To allow each to set up that breach of duty of the other as a defense to the principal's claim is, in effect, to disallow the principal's recovery where more than one agent defaults in his duty. We see no rational basis for such a distinction.

Id. at 6-7.

Speaking of an entity state of mind in the sense referred to above is quite distinct from another usage, which may be introduced by the following questions. What does a court, or brief-writer or commentator mean, when saying (a) that a proposed interpretation of a statute is consistent with (or contrary to) "Congressional intent," or (b) that a proposed interpretation of a contract is consistent with (or contrary to) the "intent of the contracting parties"? These are matters discussed in later chapters of this book.[13]

C. Objective Tests for Accountability

1. The Meaning of "Objective"

As explained in an earlier section,[1] the distinction between "objective" and "subjective" as those terms are used here refers not to who is judging but instead to who is being judged. A test is "objective" to the extent that it requires that the decisionmaker applying it measure conduct of the actor who is being judged by a test external to that actor -- a test that disregards, in material respects, the particular characteristics of the "subject" who is being judged.

A classic illustration of an "objective" test is that applied by judge and jury in determining whether a person (either plaintiff or defendant) was negligent. The law regarding negligence also illustrates two more points: (1) in some respects the law creates a separate negligence test for each person whose conduct is being judged, and (2) the test created is neither totally "objective" nor totally "subjective." We call negligence tests "objective" because they so strongly emphasize factors external to the particular person ("subject") to whom the test is being applied. They emphasize the characteristics of "an ordinarily prudent person." It is nevertheless true that if the person (the "subject") being judged has distinctly abnormal physical characteristics (for example, blindness) or mental capacity (not just a little below normal but severely below, to the point of "incompetence"), the test used takes this factor

---

[13] See Chapters 5 and 6, infra.

[1] Section A3, this Chapter, supra.

2. Tailoring the Multitude of Objective Tests

The law has developed a multitude of objective tests for legal accountability. It is not my purpose here to examine the substantive content of various objective tests in detail. A judge must do that, of course, in deciding cases. The purpose here, however, is to invite reflection on some of the problems a judge (and the advocates) encounter as they undertake to determine what test or tests to apply in a particular case, and how to make the application.

One set of problems arises from the necessity of tailoring the test to be applied to each actor whose conduct is being judged, and in relation to the conduct at issue. The necessity of tailoring a case-specific and conduct-specific test is inherent in the point, already noted, that the test is seldom if ever totally objective. To the extent, for example, that a negligence test takes account of characteristics of the "subject" being judged, it must be tailored to those characteristics even though it is expressed as measuring that person's conduct by the standard of "ordinary care" or the care of "an ordinarily prudent person" having certain characteristics in common with the subject.

A second set of problems arises from the fact that the law has developed many tests that are different, one from another, with respect to the degree of deviation from the "ordinary." Sometimes that deviation is expressed as a level of care different from "ordinary care." At other times, the terminology of "ordinary care" is retained but the definition of what must be done to measure up to "ordinary care" deviates from the usual definition. An example of a deviation expressed as a different level of care occurs when a common carrier is said to be liable for "slight negligence" (or failure to exercise that "high degree of care that an ordinarily prudent carrier" exercises to protect the safety of passengers). Another example is that a host driver is said to be liable only for "gross negligence" (or deviation from that less demanding test that some jurisdictions apply to guest-host claims). "Recklessness" is deviation from an even less demanding standard, but one that is nevertheless

---

[2] See Section A3, this Chapter, supra.

"objective." It differs from "reckless disregard," which is a state-of-mind test. A test imposing legal accountability only for failure to heed the "obvious" is still less demanding; it deviates farther from a test requiring ordinary care.

Confusion is likely when a court or advocate refers to one of the less demanding tests as "objective" and fails to observe that it is not a test of "ordinary care" in the usual sense. Because "ordinary care" is the most commonly used objective test, there is risk that the meaning "ordinary care" is conveyed whenever the phrase "objective test" is used without an explanation that it refers to a test that deviates from the ordinary and is therefore either more or less demanding than an "ordinary care" test in what it requires.

The test of "obviousness" probably is the most difficult to state clearly and apply correctly. It is used most often in relation to circumstances in which falsity of a statement of fact or danger of physical harm would be recognized by all but the most careless or foolish. Thus, in an action for damages for misrepresentation, a plaintiff may be barred from recovering for harm suffered in reliance upon a "representation _obviously_ false," even though the effect is that a knave has wronged a fool, and the latter has no legal remedy.[3] Also, in that kind of action for defamation in which a state is free to apply a test for fault short of the state of mind of "reckless disregard," state law may hold a defendant liable for making a statement that was "obviously false" -- that is, a statement that all but the most careless or foolish of persons in the position of the defendant would have realized was false. Thus, the defendant would be subject to liability, even though he or she did not have either the state of mind of knowing the statement was false or the state of mind of "reckless disregard" for its truth or falsity.

Another kind of problem arises in the application of an objective test when the court or jury applying it does not focus adequately on the element of the case to which the test applies. The point is illustrated by a problem that arises in applying the requirement of the law of defamation that the plaintiff prove that the defendant published a defamatory

---

[3] _See generally_ Bishop v. E.A. Strout Realty Agency, 182 F.2d 503 (4th Cir. 1950).

statement "of and concerning" the plaintiff. At least when the plaintiff and defendant are private persons (as distinguished from "public officials," "public figures," and publishing media) and the statement does not relate to an issue of public concern, states are free to fashion a test (or various tests) for fault less demanding than those that New York Times Company v. Sullivan and its progeny prescribe for claims by public officials and public figures in actions against media. A test used in the law of some states is sometimes described as imposing liability for negligently publishing defamatory words that reasonably could be interpreted to refer to the plaintiff. This description is ambiguous, however, because it merges two issues -- one focusing on the publisher's conduct and the other on the reader's interpretation. A sensible and helpful clarification is that, first, the trial judge must decide whether readers or listeners could reasonably interpret the statement as referring to the plaintiff and whether the evidence is sufficient to support a finding that some did, second, the jury must decide whether in fact some did so interpret it, and, if so, third, the jury must decide whether the publisher, in publishing, was negligent in the sense that the publisher unreasonably failed to anticipate that one or more persons would reasonably understand that the statement referred to the plaintiff.[4]

3. Factors, "Totality of the Circumstances," and Related Tests

A previous section calls attention to the distinction between "bright-line" and "evaluative" legal tests.[5] Every evaluative test requires that the decisionmaker (a) take note of at least two and usually more factors (or "elements" or "components"), (b) consider them together rather than discretely, and (c) then answer a single question. The evaluative tests that go to the extreme in this respect require that the decisionmaker consider the "totality of the circumstances." Of course, there is no magic in the phrase "totality of the circumstances." Essentially the same meaning may be expressed in other phrases -- for example, "the congeries of facts," or "all matters that bear upon the

---

[4]See, e.g., New England Tractor-Trailer Training of Connecticut, Inc. v. Globe Newspaper Co., 395 Mass. 471, 480 N.E.2d 1005 (1985).

[5]Section A2, this Chapter, supra.

decision."

When a test for legal accountability is expressed or explained as one involving either specified "factors" or the "totality of the circumstances," there is a high risk of ambiguity and a special need for clarity in distinguishing between identifying the factors or circumstances the decisionmaker may (or must) consider and what precisely is the question the decisionmaker must answer after considering all the identified factors or the "totality of the circumstances." A familiar example from the common law of agency illustrates the point. The test for determining whether an employee was acting within the scope of employment for the employer, with the legal consequence that the employer is liable in tort for harm the employee negligently caused, as this test developed in the common law, required the decisionmaker to consider evidence with respect to many factors. The Restatement (Second) of Agency lists ten.[6] The Restatement also specifies that the question the jury is to answer after considering all the evidence before them with respect to these factors is whether the conduct was "of the same general nature as that authorized, or [was] incidental to the conduct authorized."[7]

A jury is left with a little less guidance if they are told only to consider all of a set of listed factors (or at least all as to which there is any evidence before them in the case on trial), and then decide whether the employee was in the scope of employment.

---

[6] Restatement (Second) of Agency §229(2) (1958). The introductory phrase of §229(2) directs that "the following matters of fact are to be considered." It does not say either that these _are_ the only "matters of fact" to be considered, or that these _are not_ the only "matters of fact" to be considered. Curiously, §220(2), listing ten "matters of fact" bearing on whether "one acting for another is a servant or [instead] an independent contractor," directs that "the following matters of fact, among others, are to be considered." (Emphasis added.) Was the omission of the phrase "among others" from §229(2) meant to carry significance?

[7] Id., §229(1). Compare §220(1), specifying that the question the jury is to answer in determining whether one acting for another is a "servant" is whether he or she was "employed to perform services in the affairs of [the other and] and with respect to the physical conduct in the performance of the services is subject to the other's control or right to control."

Even when an added definition of "scope of employment" is supplied, and it is framed consistently with the Restatement, one may be very uneasy about whether this added definition of the test for determining whether an employee was in the "scope of employment" provides enough guidance to juries to cause like cases to be decided alike, rather than according to the views and tendencies of different juries. Nevertheless, the Restatement does address explicitly the need to define a test for "scope of employment" as well as telling the decisionmaker the factors to be considered. If the authoritative statement of a test for "scope of employment" fails to provide any definition other than the phrase "scope of employment" itself, the guiding quality of the authoritative statement is limited indeed, and the risk is greater that different decisionmakers will reach decisions that fail to fit a pattern of like treatment of like cases.

D. Immunities and Privileges

1. Introduction

The focus of this section is not upon issues of substantive law that controversies regarding immunity and privilege raise in the many varied contexts in which they have arisen but upon the nature of lawmaking choices expressed in fashioning legal tests for use in deciding claims of immunity or privilege. A hypothetical case will set a context for introducing some central and recurring issues of lawmaking method.

Case 3.1
A Cost Containment Controversy[1]

Plaintiff is an accountant employed by the State Department of Health. Defendant is the Director of the Department. Plaintiff participated with others in performing an audit of health care costs and filing with the defendant a draft report and recommendations. Reporters demanded access to the draft report. Defendant refused to release the draft report, commenting in the presence of reporters:

---

[1]This hypothetical case is adapted from Chamberlain v. Mathis, 151 Ariz. 551, 729 P.2d 905 (1986).

> The draft report was prepared by Department of Health employees who are incompetent and unqualified as auditors. I think these employees have a rich fantasy life. Charges of a cover-up have been made by uninformed dissidents in my own department. I would be sued by our independent contractors if I released this audit before the Attorney General has reviewed it.

These comments were published in the State Gazette. Plaintiff filed a civil action for defamation, alleging that defendant made the statements maliciously, knowing they were false.

Defendant, a gubernatorial appointee, serving at the governor's pleasure, moved to dismiss on grounds of immunity and privilege. The trial court dismissed and the matter is on appeal.

Should the dismissal be affirmed? Why?

2. Terminology

A distinction is sometimes made between the terms "immunity" and "privilege" and among variants such as "immunity from suit," "immunity from liability for damages," "absolute immunity," "qualified immunity," "absolute privilege," "complete privilege," "unconditional privilege," "qualified privilege," "incomplete privilege," and "conditional privilege." As noted in another section of this book,[2] you can use a word or phrase with any meaning you choose to give it, but you cannot force others to understand it the way you mean it. Unfortunately the words "immunity" and "privilege" and phrases including them have been used with such varied meanings that a reader needs always to examine context closely to avoid misunderstanding.

In earlier writings (at least through the middle of

---

[2] Section A, this Chapter, <u>supra</u>.

the 20th century), "immunity" was commonly used to designate the kind of protection against legal accountability available to the sovereign (or the government as an entity), to judges, to legislators, high level executives, and to charities and other eleemosynary entities. "Privilege" was commonly used to designate the somewhat less sweeping protection against legal accountability available to individuals acting in self-defense, in defense of property, in defense of the person or property of others, in the exercise of legally protected interests in freedom of expression and freedom of action not threatening harm to person or tangible property of others, and even in acting for the public interest in cases of "public necessity" or for private interests in cases of "private necessity." This distinction has not been well maintained, however, and in some instances substantive distinctions previously expressed as contrasts between "immunity" and "privilege" are expressed as contrasts between "absolute" (or "complete" or "unconditional") immunity or privilege, on the one hand, and on the other hand "qualified" (or "incomplete" or "conditional") immunity or privilege.

3. The Scope of Protection and Ways of Defining It

The most sweeping form of protection against legal accountability is usually called an immunity. "Sovereign" or "governmental" immunity is the classic example. At least in modern times, however, if not earlier as well, even this form of protection against legal accountability has limits. No immunity is truly unlimited in scope. The United States and all states have enacted formal "waivers" of immunity of defined scope. Tort Claims Acts are examples.

The immunities or privileges of individuals, even when designated as "absolute," "complete," or "unqualified," nevertheless have their bounds. A judge's immunity applies only to "judicial" conduct; a legislator's, only to "legislative" conduct. Debatable issues are presented by a judge's conduct that allegedly is clearly beyond jurisdiction, or by a legislator's conduct that allegedly is clearly not within the scope of legislative concerns.

Also, some immunities and privileges are, by the law that creates them, defined in a way that makes the claim of immunity or privilege subject to being defeated by proof of abuse or by proof that the person asserting the immunity or privilege acted solely (or primarily, or in part) for a purpose other than the purpose authorized by law. Sometimes this idea is expressed in the form of a statement that the person asserting the immunity or privilege may do so by showing that the "occasion" of the challenged act or speech was a "privileged occasion." The opponent may then show that the immunity or privilege, unless absolute, was lost by abuse, or by the person's acting for a purpose other than an authorized purpose.

To understand a body of law with respect to an asserted immunity or privilege, we must first understand the legal test that determines who may invoke it and in what circumstances -- the legal definition of the immunity or privilege. Next, we must understand whether the legal test allows for an opponent's response. That is, does it allow the opponent to defeat the immunity or privilege on the ground that the person asserting it acted for an improper purpose or in an improper manner. Finally, we must understand the precise terms of both the test for invoking the immunity or privilege and the test for asserting abuse. Like all other tests of accountability, these tests may range widely from those primarily subjective to those primarily objective, and with many different combinations in between the polar extremes. Case 3.1 illustrates these points.

A threshold issue in Case 3.1 is whether the state law definition of the immunity or privilege of a cabinet-level officer of state government is such that its protection can be invoked by a motion to dismiss. An important lawmaking choice for a legislature enacting a statutory cabinet-level immunity or a court adopting a cabinet-level immunity is whether the cabinet-level officer should be protected not only against having to pay damages for defamation in circumstances like those of Case 3.1 but also against having to bear the cost and burden of pretrial and trial proceedings. "If executive officials are denied immunity, they may elevate personal interest above official duty.... Ultimately, government, including good government, may be hampered and qualified individuals may be hesitant to serve...."[3] On the other hand, "arguments favoring official immunity are countered by the legitimate complaints of those injured by government officials."[4] In a carefully reasoned opinion, the Supreme Court of Arizona concluded that although "absolute immunity" may be appropriate for some very high

---

[3] Chamberlain v. Mathis, 729 P.2d at 908-09.

[4] 729 P.2d at 909.

level officers, "qualified immunity" is appropriate for a state cabinet officer such as the Director of the Arizona Department of Health Services.[5]

Addressing the question as to what a plaintiff must show to establish that the official invoking the qualified immunity acted for an improper purpose or in an improper manner, the Arizona Court declared that the official invoking the qualified immunity is protected "unless the official knew or should have known" that he or she "was acting in violation of established law or acted in reckless disregard" of another person's rights.[6] This formulation of the test for deciding claims of abuse of the qualified immunity was further refined, however, at least for defamation actions, by a requirement that the claimant show "objective malice" of the official,[7] in a sense consistent with the court's interpretation of that phrase as used by the Supreme Court of the United States in <u>Harlow</u> v. <u>Fitzgerald</u>[8] and its progeny. The determination of the full meaning of "objective malice" and its impact on potential disposition of cases by motions to dismiss and motions for summary judgment are matters that have occupied and will in the future continue to occupy very substantial lawmaking energies of state courts and federal circuit and district courts as well as the Supreme Court.

E. Burdens as Techniques for Decisionmaking

Ordinarily a decisionmaker, judge or jury, feels better about a decision made squarely on substantive merits, according to facts proved to the decisionmaker's satisfaction, than about a decision made on the ground that the facts are unknown and the law says the party with the burden of proof loses. I cannot cite authority for this proposition. I state it as my own observation, and I ask you to consider whether it squares with your observations about human nature.

---

[5] 729 P.2 at 912-14.

[6] 729 P.2d at 912.

[7] 729 P.2d at 913.

[8] 457 U.S. 800, 816-17 (1982).

If I am correct in this observation, it follows that most decisionmakers will be trying hard to decide factual disputes on the merits, as shown by the evidence, and not on the basis that one party or the other failed to meet a burden of proof.

Of course, a decisionmaker who prefers to decide on the merits may sometimes be tempted to be less candid in explaining the decision because candor may require a blunt statement of a finding that the loser lied on the witness stand. Even so, the point remains that the decisionmaker will have made the decision, if possible, on the merits and not on the burden.

Nevertheless, there will be occasions when the facts are unknown not only to the decisionmaker but even to the parties, whose inducements to disclose whatever they know will have been affected by the rules of law about burdens of proof and production. The law must provide for deciding all cases. Insofar as possible, lawmakers aim to fashion the rules of law so as little injustice as possible results from inability to discover all the material facts.

The problem of fashioning appropriate rules regarding burdens is complicated when a lawmaker senses that the interests at stake are high value interests on both sides. First Amendment cases illustrate the point.

One element of a First Amendment problem is like that of any other problem regarding a burden. Under either rule as to which party has the burden, the outcome of particular cases will sometimes differ from the outcome we would desire if we knew the facts.[9]

The problem is at least different in degree if not in kind, however, whenever (as in typical First Amendment cases) interests of extraordinarily high value, by community standards, are at stake on both sides. Interests of high value will be sacrificed, whichever way the burden is placed. In a defamation case, for example, the burden of proof as to truth or falsity of a defamatory statement will determine liability for speech that is unknowably true or false, and "we cannot know how much of the speech affected by the allocation of the burden of proof is true and how much is

---

[9]Cf. Philadelphia Newspapers, Inc. v. Hepps, 475 U.S. 767, 776 (1986).

false."[10] In some, at least, of the configurations of type of plaintiff (public or private), type of defendant (publishing medium or nonmedium), and type of statement (concerning matters of public concern or instead only private concern), the Supreme Court has placed the burden on the plaintiff, explicitly fashioning this legal rule on the burden of proof "[t]o ensure that true speech on matters of public concern is not deterred, ..."[11]

Commencing with McDonnell Douglas,[12] Supreme Court decisions, together with a host of lower court decisions interpreting and applying them, have developed a special set of rules on burdens of production and persuasion for application in litigation over claims of various forms of discrimination in violation of constitutional and statutory standards. From these decisions have emerged a number of significant issues about lawmaking choices.

A problem that emerged quite early is whether the seminal lawmaking decisions of this sequence created firm mandates that must be followed or instead only guidelines that are to be followed absent some articulable ground for discretionary departure. Probably the answer implicit, if not explicit, in the current state of the relevant precedents is that some discretion for departure is allowed. This conclusion is supported both in judicial opinions[13] and in principle. The structure of analysis directed by McDonnell Douglas, as refined in Burdine,[14] is less adaptable to jury than to nonjury trials, and poses serious issues regarding whether a trial judge should even tell a jury about the plaintiff's initial burden of showing a "prima facie case" in order to trigger a defendant's burden of producing an articulable nondiscriminatory reason for its challenged

---

[10] Id.

[11] Id.

[12] McDonnell Douglas Corp. v. Green, 411 U.S. 792 (1973).

[13] See, e.g., Dance v. Ripley, 776 F.2d 370, 373 (1st Cir. 1985) ("This circuit, along with other circuits, has rejected the argument that McDonnell Douglas and Burdine set forth a 'rigid, three-step proof process in Title VII cases.'").

[14] Texas Department of Community Affairs v. Burdine, 450 U.S. 248 (1980).

decision, when the trial court concludes that both these procedural burdens have been met. For example, is such an explanation, even if fashioned to perfection, more likely to confuse than to help a jury to understand the burden of proof it must apply in its factfinding?

Another problem of growing dimension is the increased complexity of this body of law as more and more precedents fashion a new structure (or new interpretations of an established structure) of burdens of various kinds (including, for example, burdens of showing a "prima facie" case, however that concept may be defined, burdens of production, burdens of articulation of reasons for decision, burdens defining how a decisionmaker is to resolve "mixed motive" cases, and burdens regarding "but-for" or other definitions of causal links between motive and "bottom line" decision). New dimensions of complexity, and of the likelihood of conflict among lower federal courts as they attempt to understand and apply mandates of the Supreme Court, were added by the opinions of the closely-divided Court in Ward's Cove Packing Co., Inc. v. Atonio.[15]

From the perspective of trial judges and trial lawyers who must fashion answers to the unanswered questions about the meaning of precedents for cases on trial, issues regarding burdens in litigation of claims of discrimination are increasing in number and complexity to an extent that seriously impairs the likelihood that cases will ordinarily be tried without reversible error.

F. Duty, Cause, and Scope of Accountability

1. Duty and Cause as Conclusions

Every decision of duty (or no duty) and every decision of cause (or no cause) is at least in part a conclusion of law. Occasionally decisions of duty (or no duty) and usually decisions of cause (or no cause) are also in part findings of fact. Thus, a minority of the decisions on duty and most decisions on cause are mixed law and fact decisions. As noted elsewhere,[1] making a decision on a mixed question of

---

[15] ___ U.S. ___, 109 S. Ct. 2115 (1989).

[1] Chapter 2, Section G, supra.

law and fact is difficult. At least as difficult, and perhaps more so, is explaining such a decision unambiguously.

Some problems associated with this difficulty are discussed immediately below.

2. Uncertain Meaning of Tests on Scope of Accountability

Causation tests of the legal system have tended to lack both precision and clarity. One reason for lack of clarity is that, although causation tests are always at least in part legal conclusions, they are typically phrased in language that connotes historical fact. Moreover, the likelihood of confusion is often enhanced by the use of "the" before "cause." Nothing in human experience is ever, in fact, "the" cause of anything that follows. Yet a practice persists, though to less extent currently than in previous generations, of using phrases such as "the proximate cause." The first constructive step toward making your communications about "cause" less ambiguous is to be wary of using phrases such as "the cause," "the proximate cause," and "the legal cause." I propose that you be wary, rather than proposing that you banish these phrases from the vocabulary you use in writing, because there will be times when the precedents you are interpreting and applying use them. In those circumstances, use them respectfully, but also consider doing your best to explain, in a less misleading way, the meaning you infer the precedents have.

In many contexts in which the language of causation is used, human experience and common perceptions support to a significant extent the connotation of historical connection that the language of causation carries. Stated another way, the point is that legal decisions regarding scope of accountability are influenced by our perceptions regarding the degree to which the conduct being judged was in some significant way "connected with" the events or harms for which a legal remedy is being sought. Considerations of principle and policy support the legal conclusion that such a factual connection is relevant to a legal decision about the scope of accountability.[2]

---

[2] For extended development of this point, see R. Keeton, Legal Cause in the Law of Torts 20-24 (1963) (hereinafter cited as Legal Cause). Cf. Sinram v. Pennsylvania R. R., 61 F.2d 767, 770 (2d Cir. 1932) (opinion

Legal concepts of causation tend nevertheless to be quite misleading because, in addition to being influenced by common sense notions of connection between conduct and harms for which claims are brought, legal concepts of causation are also heavily influenced by other public policy considerations of very different and varied kinds.[3]

Together, all of the varied influences on notions of causation in law that can be identified in precedents support the view that unlimited liability (or liability the scope of which is quite fortuitous) is offensive to community values. In the precedents, considered together, is strong support for a principle of tailoring the scope of legal responsibility to make it compatible with the reasons for imposing that responsibility.

Duty concepts, like causation concepts, lack precision and clarity. Partly this is so for a reason quite similar to one of those noted about causation. That is, duty concepts, like causation concepts, conceal a varied array of public policy reasons for reaching a legal conclusion. Those public policy reasons could be more candidly and clearly expressed in other ways, but a long and respected legal tradition supports expression in terms of "duty" and "cause" when liability is allowed, and lack of duty or lack of causal connection when liability is denied.

The similarity between "duty" and "cause" in the way just noted becomes even more striking in contexts in which legal theorists battle as if to the death over whether "duty," or instead "cause," is the only legally correct usage.[4]

Another set of reasons for lack of clarity of concepts of duty is more distinctive to the idiom of duty. This set of reasons derives from the fact that a legal duty may range all the way from one demanding very little of the actor to one that results in some version of strict liability. Yet a determination of applicability of any one of these different versions, of quite different practical consequence,

---

of Learned Hand, J.).

[3] See, e.g., Legal Cause at 47-78.

[4] See, e.g., Legal Cause at 79-86 (discussing debates in the American Law Institute and in scholarly articles).

is commonly called simply an instance of duty, rather than, for example, an instance of a "duty of ordinary care," or an instance of a "duty of slight care" or an instance of a "duty of extreme care." In the same way, the rejection of an argument for one or another kind of duty is often described simply as a determination of "no duty," rather than, more precisely, a determination of "no duty of ordinary care," which may leave open an issue as to whether a duty of at least "slight care" might be recognized, thus imposing liability for "gross negligence," or for "recklessness," or for "intended harm."[5]

When one seeks to clarify and reduce the imprecision and ambiguity of the common language of duty, the problem may be attacked in several ways.

First, it is helpful to distinguish among different versions of duty, such as those illustrated in the discussion immediately above.

Second, it is helpful to distinguish between "duty when acting" and "duty to act." Usually one is subject to liability for acting carelessly. Another way of stating this point is to say one has a "duty of ordinary care when acting" (or a duty of ordinary care with respect to what one does). In contrast, the scope of liability for carelessly failing to act is more limited. At common law the general rule was that a person has no duty to exercise ordinary care in deciding whether to take affirmative action. A duty to act to aid another in peril whenever an ordinarily prudent person would have done so was exceptional. Stated in still another way, liability for negligently failing to act was the exception. Over time, however, the exceptions have grown in number and scope, and it may reasonably be argued that today exceptions apply to more of human experience than does the rule of "no duty" of ordinary care to act in aid of others in peril.

Third, it is helpful to take note of interests, principles, and policies at stake in a lawmaking choice about "duty," as is also true of a lawmaking choice about "cause." Every lawmaking decision explained either as part of the law of "duty" or as part of the law of "cause" inevitably involves some value-laden lawmaking choice. Wiser choices

---

[5] See this Chapter, section D, above, for additional comments on the meaning of these different tests.

Ch. 3   TAILORING TESTS

will be made if this reality is openly recognized.[6]

3. Tailoring to Cases the Tests on Scope of Accountability

The need for tailoring legal tests to particular issues in particular cases has been stated previously.[7] Also, the usefulness of probing premises and their implications has been stated previously.[8] Both these points apply when it becomes necessary for a trial judge to instruct a jury regarding a test on the scope of accountability. An illustration may be useful.

Case 3.2
The Ruptured Spleen

    The plaintiff sues under 42 U.S.C. §1983 and state tort law, claiming that police officers used excessive force while arresting him, and specifically that one of the officers kicked him, causing a ruptured spleen. It is undisputed that, immediately after the incident, the plaintiff had a ruptured spleen that led to an operation and extended hospitalization and disability. There is sharp dispute as to how he got it -- whether in boisterous activity, including assaults on others, by reason of which the police were called to the scene, or instead as plaintiff alleges.

    How should the trial judge instruct the jury with respect to the dispute in the evidence about how the plaintiff sustained the ruptured spleen?

In Case 3.2, it is easy indeed for the trial judge to conclude that the jury should be told that if plaintiff sustained the ruptured spleen before the police arrived and they did nothing to aggravate it, defendants are not liable

---

[6] See Chapter 4, infra.

[7] See Sections B3, C2, this Chapter, supra.

[8] See Chapter 1, Section D, supra.

for the ruptured spleen even if they did use excessive force. Stated in plain English rather than in the traditional but-for formulation, the point is that plaintiff would have suffered the hospitalization and disability anyway.

If the trial judge and trial lawyers share an inclination toward plain English instructions and a leaning toward doing no more special tailoring for circumstances like those of Case 3.2, the "proximate cause" instructions to the jury might be something like this illustration:

> Just a moment ago I used the phrase "proximate cause."
>
> Now I will explain "proximate cause." If you will look at the verdict form, you will see a slight variation of this phrase "proximate cause" used in the introductory paragraph, which applies to all of the separate questions. Also, in these instructions I may sometimes use some similar phrase such as "proximately resulting from." The explanation I am now giving to you applies wherever the phrase "proximate cause" or some similar phrase is used.
>
> Proximate cause is a technical legal term, the meaning of which I will now explain. You cannot extract that meaning from the phrase "proximate cause" itself. So you will need to pay close attention to my explanation.
>
> Keep these ideas in mind. First, if an element of loss would have happened anyway for other reasons regardless of defendants' negligent act or omission then that act or omission is not a proximate cause of that element of loss. This idea is more often expressed as a "but-for" rule rather than a "would-have-happened-anyway" rule. These are two different ways of expressing the same idea. Lawyers and judges seem to prefer the double negative form -- that is, the way of speaking that says: to find proximate cause you must find that the element of loss would not have occurred but for the defendants' negligence. Another way of expressing the point is to say, if this element of loss would

have happened anyway -- regardless of defendants' negligence -- then defendants' negligence was not a proximate cause.

Second, loss of this type must have been reasonably foreseeable in a general sense -- not precisely the way it happened, but a loss of this general type or kind must be reasonably foreseeable to an actor in defendants' position at the time of defendants' negligence. This idea is also expressed by the phrase "natural and probable consequence."

Third, in order to find that a defendants' negligence proximately caused an element of loss, you must find that the negligence was a substantial factor in bringing about that element of loss. "Substantial" is used here in its ordinary sense, which requires no further explanation.

Now, putting these three ideas together in one definition of proximate cause, I instruct you as follows:

You will find that an element of loss was proximately caused by defendants' negligence if you find, from a preponderance of the evidence in the case, first, that the element of loss would not have occurred but for the defendants' negligence, second, that the element of loss was a natural and probable consequence of the defendants' negligence, and third, that the defendants' negligence was a substantial factor in bringing about that element of loss.

As this definition implies, an element of loss may have more than one proximate cause.

It is the obligation of the plaintiff to prove by a preponderance of the evidence the causal relationship between defendants' negligence and each element of loss of which the plaintiff complains. You are not allowed to speculate on the question of causal relationship.

The mere occurrence of an element of loss is not sufficient to establish that the defendants' negligence was in any way a proximate cause of that element of loss.

As I stated earlier, an element of loss may have more than one proximate cause. A proximate cause of injury or loss is one that causes or contributes to cause loss of the type claimed by a plaintiff. However, some events, circumstances and conduct of others that contribute in some way to bringing about an element of loss may be found by a jury to be what in law we call independent intervening causes of some part or all of an element of loss, and not merely causes that, along with others, are proximate causes.

An independent intervening cause is one that (a) occurs independently of the defendants' negligence, and (b) was not "reasonably foreseeable." By "reasonably foreseeable" we mean something that an ordinarily prudent person in the position of the defendant would foresee and take into account in weighing the utility and the risks of conduct, at or before the time of the conduct.

In Case 3.2, it is easy to see, also, that if requested to do so the trial judge should instruct the jury that if they find that one of the defendants kicked plaintiff deliberately in anger, after the arrest had been effected, and that's when the spleen was ruptured, then the kicking defendant (at least) is liable for the ruptured spleen.

If the advocates address only these extreme positions, the court has quite a large middle ground to explore alone when preparing the charge to the jury. Suppose one of the advocates (for the plaintiff) goes one step farther and asks the court to charge:

Even if plaintiff had sustained a damaging blow or blows to the spleen before the police arrived, you will award damages for the disability and for the hospitalization for treatment of the ruptured spleen if you find that the defendants used more force than they reasonably believed necessary to arrest and detain plaintiff and thereby aggravated a previous injury to the spleen.

That proposed instruction covers a multitude of different factual premises, as to which the legal rules -- some settled and some unsettled -- might be different. Among the possible rules of law that might be invoked would be some supporting full liability, some supporting partial liability, and some making the extent of liability depend on which of the factual premises may be selected by the jury as consistent with a preponderance of the evidence. Consider just two of the possibilities.

First. The spleen had been bruised but not ruptured before a policeman's kick. The kick caused a rupture. Most courts would be likely to hold that the jury should be instructed to allow full damages (except, perhaps, for pain suffered before the policeman's kick) if they find that a defendant "aggravated a previous injury to the spleen" in that way.

Second. The spleen had been ruptured before, and a policeman's kick caused no additional hospitalization or disability that would not have occurred anyway, but it did cause additional pain. That factual hypothesis probably calls for a different instruction to the jury.

What is a trial judge supposed to do when advocates tender only imperfect instructions that are correct as to some of the unidentified factual premises to which the jury might apply them but incorrect as to others among the many unidentified factual premises that evidence might support? This is a question not easily answered in the context of an ongoing trial in a court with a backlog of other cases awaiting trial. Of course, a trial court may find a solution that avoids a new trial, because on procedural grounds parties are precluded from later complaining on grounds that they did not disclose to the trial court before its ruling. Nevertheless, the adversary system is not fully serving its objective of contributing to a result as close to our ideal of justice as is humanly possible when the advocates leave middle ground and unstated premises unexplained in such a context as this. For the advocates as well as the trial judge, however, the problem is not easily resolved. The advocates, as well as the judge, are confronted with uncertainties of meaning of precedents bearing upon the issue before the court, and even when both advocates perceive and fully understand the ambiguities of their requests for instruction, both may have reason to believe their clients' respective interests are at least as well served by leaving the ambiguity as by objecting to instructions and requesting a clarification that might be either favorable or unfavorable, depending on how the issue is finally resolved, either in the trial court or on appeal.

CHAPTER 4

VALUES IN REASONED DECISIONMAKING

A. Introduction

A reasoned decision depends on premises. Some of the premises of a judge's decision are factual. Others are legal.

A legal premise is based on a rule of law. All rules of law are value-laden. They affect interests, and all interests are valued by someone in the community. Different persons and different groups value interests differently.

Every rule of law weighs against some interests and in favor of others. This is so whether or not the effect of the rule on any particular interest is acknowledged and whether or not the reasoned choice of the lawmaker adverts to that effect.

Judges are professional decisionmakers, committed to representing community interests and the community's value system. That value system is in part expressed in authoritative sources -- including constitutional provisions, statutes, and precedents. The authoritative sources do not answer all questions a judge may need to answer to decide a particular dispute, however, and the judge is thus required to make a choice, even though a reasoned choice, that is inevitably value-laden.

A judge's professional obligation extends as well to providing an explanation of the decision. To explain a decision, a judge states reasons. A statement of reasons for a decision discloses something about premises. Disclosure of premises, however, is a matter of degree.

INTRODUCTION   Sec. A

Because of inherent characteristics of law and the legal system, as well as limitations upon human insight and expression, no opinion (and no critique of an opinion) can ever be a full and clear explanation of all the premises and all of their value implications. A statement of reasons, including any judicial opinion, discloses only more or less clearly, and in more or less detail, some of the value consequences of the decision. Others are entirely unexpressed.

No analysis of interests and values at stake in a particular decision will ever be complete. This is so even when a judge is attempting to take explicit account of the direct and indirect effects of a proposed ruling. It is so even when a judge considers effects not only upon the interests and values explicitly argued by the parties but also upon the interests of others not represented before the court, and more generally public interests likely to be affected by the ruling. Limitations upon human perception, insight, and foresight will prevent the judge's utmost effort from being completely successful. Even so, we recognize a difference between a reasoned choice and an arbitrary choice, and we expect a judge's value-laden choice to be a reasoned choice.[1]

The impossibility of perceiving and understanding all interests at stake and forecasting all the effects of a ruling upon those interests means that disclosure of value implications of a judicial decision is, at best, a matter of degree. Nevertheless, it is useful for judges and their critics to recognize the value-laden nature of all judicial decisionmaking and to do some probing of premises to expose value implications. Consider, as examples, two illustrative cases in which the appropriate outcome is quite debatable and one can quickly identify clashing interests at stake.[2]

---

[1] See generally Chapter 1, supra.

[2] The hypothetical cases and much of the text of this chapter are taken almost verbatim from Keeton, Entitlement and Obligation, 46 U. Cin. L. Rev. 1 (1977) [cited hereinafter as "Entitlement and Obligation"]. I gratefully acknowledge the gracious permission of the School and the Law Review that I retain the copyright, in order to permit use of the article such as I make in this book.

Ch. 4   VALUES IN REASONED DECISIONMAKING

Case 4.1
The Adult Vaccine Victim[3]

Citizen, a 39-year-old person in good health, is persuaded to participate in a program of mass immunization by polio vaccine containing a live virus. The manufacturer of the vaccine and some of the public officials and community leaders who actively participate in the public persuasion are aware of a risk that a very few of the persons innoculated (some say no more than one in a million) will contract the disease from the vaccine and that some of these will be persons older than the age group likely to contract polio in the absence of an immunization program. This information is only partly publicized and does not reach Citizen, who contracts the disease from the vaccine and is permanently disabled. Citizen sues the manufacturer for damages. In the trial court, the jury finds that the manufacturer was not negligent but that the product (including the packaging and its incomplete warning of risks) was "defective" and "unreasonably dangerous" as those concepts are defined for them by the trial judge,[4] who

---

[3]This case is adapted from <u>Davis</u> v. <u>Wyeth Laboratories, Inc.</u>, 399 F.2d 121 (9th Cir. 1968). See also <u>Reyes</u> v. <u>Wyeth Laboratories, Inc.</u>, 498 F.2d 1264 (5th Cir. 1974), <u>cert. denied</u>, 419 U.S. 1096 (1974).

[4]The trial judge, if following the <u>Restatement (Second) of Torts</u> 402A (1965), might tell the jury:

> One who sells any product in a defective condition unreasonably dangerous to the user or consumer ... is subject to liability for physical harm thereby caused to the ultimate user ... if "(a) the seller is in the business of selling the product, and (b) the product reaches the ultimate user without substantial change."
>
> A "defective condition ... is ... a condition not contemplated by the ultimate consumer, which will be unreasonably dangerous to him." (<u>Id.</u> Comment g.)
>
> A product is not in defective condition "when it is safe for normal handling and consumption." (<u>Id.</u>

INTRODUCTION   Sec. A

is acting in the absence of any precedent directly on point in the jurisdiction of trial. Under the theory of strict liability for harm caused by a defective product, the trial judge enters a judgment against the manufacturer for damages, including compensation for economic loss and for pain and suffering. You are a judge of the appellate court of last resort. Other members of the court are equally divided. Will you affirm?

Case 4.2
Gypsy Moths and Honeybees[5]

Just before dawn on a Friday in June, a town Public Works Director, alerted by reports that gypsy moths are hatching and fortified with an up-to-the-minute forecast of weather favorable for spraying, gives the order to a helicopter contractor to spray. The Public Works Director is trying for the third straight year to control the moths that denude oak forests in the town and scatter their ugly, crunchy eggshells underfoot. A helicopter whirs over the town, putting down

---

Comment h.)

This rule of liability applies only when the defective condition of the product makes it unreasonably dangerous to the user. Many products cannot be made entirely safe for all consumption, and any food or drug necessarily involves some risk of harm, if only from over-consumption.

Some products, including some vaccines, are unavoidably unsafe though socially useful because of the disease or other adversity against which they are aimed. Such a product, properly prepared and accompanied by proper directions and warnings, is not defective, nor is it <u>unreasonably</u> dangerous. (<u>Id.</u> Comment k.) But if marketed without proper directions and warnings, it may be found to be defective and unreasonably dangerous.

[5]This case is adapted from a report in <u>The Boston Globe</u>, July 17, 1976, at 3.

a mist of pesticide in solution with oil. The copter crew is one hour into the five-hour assignment of spraying the 17,000 acres of woods and heavily treed residential areas of the town when six beekeepers rouse the Mayor to demand that the Mayor order the spraying stopped immediately.

"They've already killed thousands of our bees, and they'll kill every bee in town if they keep at it five hours."

"Our losses will run above $30,000."

"We should have been notified, at the least. There are ways to keep bees in."

"There's a human problem, too, and a moral question of the right not to be sprayed. It's dangerous."

The Mayor calls the Public Works Director, who reports:

"The crux of the gypsy moth infestation may be the 2,000 acre wildlife sanctuary in the windward corner of the town, which is owned by a trust. That area was not sprayed last year because the trustees objected.

"If we don't spray now, it will be too late. Besides, you can't satisfy everybody. I received as many complaints last year from people whose trees were not sprayed because of their proximity to the conservation land as from the beekeepers and environmentalists. We had to go back and spray infested trees at a cost considerably more than the $3.11 per acre we pay for aerial spraying.

"The decision about the time to spray depends on when the moths start hatching and what the weather is. The beekeepers knew we were planning to spray this year, and they never told me they wanted me to call them at 5:00 a.m."

The Mayor asks your advice on three

questions. In answering the first two of these questions -- about the town's liability -- assume that the judges and factfinders who decide them will be as wise and just as you are and will answer exactly as you think they ought to answer.

(1) Will the town be held liable to the beekeepers for the losses they have already suffered?

(2) Will the town be held liable for the additional losses the beekeepers will suffer if the spraying continues?

(3) Should the Mayor order the spraying stopped?

In Case 4.1, the decisionmaker is an appellate court. That is a role likely to be familiar to the readers of this book, even if less than fully understood and less than rigidly defined in the sources of authority to which we may look. The premises of decision are partly determinable from statutes and precedents and partly left to discovery or creation as may be needed for decision of the case at hand.

In Case 4.2, the decisionmaker is a Mayor. The premises of decision are partly like those for Case 4.1 and partly even less settled, leaving the decisionmaker even more leeway and discretion to weigh equities, claims of entitlement, claims of public good, and realities of practical politics. The Mayor is as surely accountable for decisionmaking as is an appellate court, and may as surely resort to "reasons" to explain to the municipal electorate. The Mayor, however, is not subject to the same kind of obligation of reasoned explanation as applies to the court.

One difference is that, given the wider leeway for a discretionary decision, the Mayor's explanation to the electorate may say very little about legal premises. The crux of the decision is at another point, somewhere in the wide range for discretion. In contrast, the court's decision must be guided, to far greater extent than the Mayor's decision, by legal premises.

To make a decision in Case 4.1, an appellate court (or a judge as decisionmaker) must choose the premises of decision. In choosing legal premises, the judge is making a value-laden choice.

Imposing the loss in Case 4.1 on the Vaccine Victim, however the choice to do so may be explained, will be perceived in some segments of the community as requiring the victim to make an enormous personal sacrifice for the benefit of the community. Imposing the loss instead on the manufacturer, however the choice to do so may be explained, will be perceived in some segments of the community as requiring the manufacturer to bear a burden that ought to be placed elsewhere. The circumstances of the case present the court with the hard choice between one or the other of these two outcomes, unless the court is to be innovative in a way quite beyond ordinary methods of judicial decisionmaking.

How explicit do we expect the court to be, in a case like Case 4.1, about the value implications of the choice it makes, whichever way its decision goes?

Do we expect the court to be explicit about economic implications, at least those for the the parties before the court? Perhaps as well for their insurers? And as well for all others in the same classes or group of persons as the plaintiff and defendant, whose interests may be deeply affected by the <u>stare decisis</u> effect of the decision?

Do we expect the court to be explicit about whether it concludes that the outcome of its analysis of economic implications has more or less weight in the court's lawmaking choice than the outcome of its analysis of other interests? And, as to interests that, at least more readily if not with ease, are susceptible of economic or mathematical assessment, how explicit should a court be about its views as to how the burden of costs of harm will be borne initially? About how they will thereafter be reallocated? About how the risks of future harm will be managed in light of the precedent set by the court's decision? About what impact these effects will have, in turn, upon the availability and cost of products and services, and about whether those effects will be consistent with community interests and values of all kinds?

B. Probing Premises for Value Implications

When pressed about a chosen legal premise, the judge may cite a statement of that premise in an authoritative precedent (or a statute or constitutional provision). Or the judge may derive the chosen premise, with the aid of logic, from a more basic assumption -- another premise -- for which the judge cites an authoritative precedent.

When citing or deriving premises from authoritative declarations of law, a judge ordinarily does not explore the value implications of the rules of law cited. Even if those implications were quite fully explored by the lawmaker whose authoritative declaration is cited, they need not and ordinarily are not restated each time the authoritative declaration is invoked.

If, instead of simply invoking an authoritative declaration perceived to be directly in point, a judge is citing it and reasoning by analogy from it, the judge may consider it appropriate to explore value implications of the different rules examined for the purpose of selecting the closest analogy. It is also possible, however, to compare different issues and the rules of law resolving them by comparing the characteristics of the different circumstances that present the different issues for decision, without adverting explicitly to the value implications of each of the different rules of law.

For example, the attorney for a plaintiff claiming injury from an explosion and fire after a highway crash of a truck transporting gasoline may cite precedents supporting strict liability for injuries resulting from use of explosives in construction, arguing that the court should, by analogy, apply strict liability to transporting gasoline on the highways. Opposing counsel may cite precedents establishing negligence, rather than strict liability, as the prevailing rule in highway accident cases, arguing that the court should apply that rule to this highway accident. The arguments of counsel and the reasoning of the court may proceed with comparisons exclusively focused on the factual similarities and differences between the case before the court and the cases invoked respectively by opposing counsel. Proceeding in this way, they may never focus the discussion explicitly on the similarities and differences among clashing interests of the parties to the claims arising in these different contexts and on possibly different evaluations of the weight of each of those interests in these different contexts. Thus, a judge, in making and explaining the choice to invoke strict liability, or instead decide the case under negligence law, may identify analogies that are used as premises of reasoning and may even, when pressed by counsel, identify premises of premises (for example, reasons stated for the rule adopted in each of the judicial opinions in cases selected as most closely analogous on the facts), while yet not discussing value implications explicitly.

When examining premises of premises -- either with or without attention as well to their value implications -- if pressed far enough the judge will eventually identify one or more premises that are neither stated in authoritative precedents nor derived by logic alone from them. The judge may then say that the issue to be decided was not directly answered by any precedent, and that the judge examined all the precedents deciding issues that seemed possibly analogous, identified the one most closely analogous, and either used or adapted the rule of that precedent as a premise for this decision.

One may proceed through such an exercise of step-by-step probing for more basic premises without ever being explicit about the value implications of any of the premises stated. There will come a point in such probing, however, at which either a value-laden choice is made without reasoned explanation or else the explanation turns to explicit consideration of the clashing interests that are affected by the choice and why, in the community's value system, one of those interests must yield to another because it is not possible to protect both unqualifiedly. Thus, as probing of premises goes deeper, it tends to have at least something to say about value-laden choice.

When we are pressed harder and harder to explain all the premises of a decision, we are likely to exhaust patience long before exhausting all insight about all value implications of premises. But the deeper truth is that even with unlimited patience, and 20-20 insight and foresight, we could not escape the reality that the value implications of choice can never be fully explained by reason, and some element of unexplained value-laden choice remains as part of even the most carefully reasoned decision.

Consider three of the fundamental truths that help to account for the limited degree of success of even the most thoughtful effort of judges (and of their critics) in exposing all the value-laden premises of a reasoned decision.

First is the fact that law is always developing.[1] Law

---

[1] See Chapter 1, Section B3, and Chapter 2, Section E2, supra.

does not contain enough authoritative declarations to answer all questions that may arise. More law must be created, by choice.

Second is the fact that the authoritative declarations that do exist are themselves founded on premises. To understand those authoritative declarations fully -- and regardless of whether they appear in constitutions, or statutes, or judicial opinions, or elsewhere -- we must understand what were the premises of those declarations.

Third is the fact that some of the premises of many authoritative declarations are transitory by their nature. For example, an assertion of "crisis," or at least a compelling need, is likely to be a part of the legislative history of a statute. Years or even decades later the circumstances characterized as a crisis or a compelling need may no longer exist. Another example is that premises of a lawmaking choice may be based on circumstances of a given state of scientific and social development that is materially changed by some invention, such as an engine powered by steam or by internal combustion. The phenomenon of transitory premises of lawmaking is pervasive.[2]

Explanations of value-laden choices made by a professional who is committed to applying community values in decisionmaking serve both the purpose of certification that the judge's decisionmaking is within the professional tradition of reasoned decision, responsive to the judge's understanding of community values, and the purpose of exposing the decision to public review and criticism. A judge's reasoned explanation of value implications of the premises of decision contributes to the administration of justice, and to the community's commitment to the legal system as an effective instrument of justice, even if the premises of the judge's decision, and their value implications, turn out in the long run not to be acceptable to the community. Candid explanation of reasoned decisionmaking exposes debatable premises to reasoned reexamination in a larger forum and for a longer period of time.

---

[2]For additional comments on transitory premises, see Chapter 2, Section D2, supra, and Chapter 6, Section H, infra.

Ch. 4   VALUES IN REASONED DECISIONMAKING

C. Deductive and Informative Reasoning

There is a significant difference between, first, using reason to derive a decision from premises already accepted before the reasoning commences ("derivative" or "deductive" reasoning) and, second, using reason, before one among competing sets of premises is chosen, to illumine the choice that must be made among the competing sets of premises ("informative" reasoning).

Under both modes of using reason, the outcome is determined by a combination of choice and reason. Under the derivative mode, choice occurs first (in the selection of premises). Only then is reason used to derive the outcome. Under the informative mode, the choice among different sets of premises under consideration is deferred until reason has been used to increase the decisionmaker's understanding of the implications that each of the different sets of premises will have for other cases as well as for the present case. The choice made in this way is a better informed choice.

The foregoing description of this contrast states it as a contrast between two different uses of reason. From another perspective it may be seen as a contrast between two different ways of exercising choice.

The derivative mode is to choose first, making your choice among alternative sets of premises and only later using reason to derive results to which those premises lead. This is the options-choice-reason sequence. You identify options, choose one, and reason to the result. The informative way of exercising choice is to choose last -- only after you have used reason to work out the respective results of all the alternative sets of premises identified as options. This is the options-reason-choice sequence. You choose among premises with awareness of their results, after using reason to expose what those results will be.

The informative mode of using reason is, it would seem, always appropriate in addressing an issue of first impression. Moreover, it has an important place even in relation to an issue that is claimed to be controlled by authority (whether constitutional, statutory, decisional, contractual, or otherwise). In determining whether the claim that the issue is controlled by authority is well founded, or instead that authority is distinguishable and the issue is one of first impression, a court exercises choice. The choice may be limited and constrained, but choice it is, nevertheless. Also, to whatever extent there is choice, it can be illumined by the second mode of using reason -- that is, by tracing out the implications of the different options remaining open to the decisionmaker, however limited in number or constrained in scope those options may be.

I doubt that anyone is ever able to achieve that ultimate degree of abstention from consideration of results that is implicit in a purely derivative mode of proceeding from identifying options through choice and then reason to results. That is, I doubt that anyone ever exercises choice while wearing total blinders about the results implicit in the choice. Yet curiously, the Anglo-American tradition emphasizes the derivative mode (options-choice-reason) both in judicial opinion writing and in more generalized explanations of decisionmaking and opinion writing.

If, as I have suggested, no one achieves total abstention from consideration of the results of choice, the contrast between the derivative and informative modes of using reason is as a practical matter one of degree or emphasis. It is nevertheless a contrast of real consequence. That is, it makes a difference which mode a judge emphasizes in conceiving the judicial role.

Without doubt, concerns about judicial activism help to account for emphasis on derivative reasoning and relative neglect of informative reasoning in explanations of judicial behavior. Invoking in this way legitimate concerns about activism is, however, likely to mislead. It tends to disregard the inescapable reality of judicial lawmaking. That imagery of judicial process should have been discarded with the discredited view that judges should only find law and never make it. Making law inevitably involves choice, and informed choice is distinctly to be preferred over choice without regard for consequence.

This is not to say, however, that consequence is the sole basis for choice. It is not alone consequence (either the effect in the one case on trial or the effect of the decision as precedent) that is important; critically important also is the method of choosing that consequence. We are seeking justice through law -- evenhanded treatment of like cases, and different treatment of any two cases only on reasoned, defensible grounds of differentiation that are part of our system of law. This is an objective we cannot achieve without concern for evaluating the premises of decision as well as the outcome. Concern for evaluating premises leads us to another contrast, discussed in Part D, immediately below.

D. Individual Entitlement and Social Calculus

There is a contrast among value-laden premises of judicial decisions with respect to whether they accord overriding value to individual entitlements or instead depend on a social calculus.

Because the phrases "individual entitlement(s)" and "social calculus" may carry different connotations among readers, I pause to explain the sense in which I use each phrase. The contrast between them may be illustrated by stating a pair of questions. Do the basic premises of a particular decision declare or assume that an identified type of interest of individuals in the society has priority in our value system? Or do the premises instead depend upon a "social calculus" <u>that weighs all types of interests, individual and social, and does not accord overriding weight to any type of individual interest?</u> If, in a social calculus, infinite weight were accorded to some individual interest, of course that social calculus would produce the same outcome as an individual-entitlement mode of thought in which that same interest was protected to the same extent, regardless of social cost. For this reason, the qualification expressed in the emphasized part of the text above is essential to expression of the contrast suggested here. Throughout this discussion, the unqualified terms "individual-entitlement" and "social-calculus" are used in the sense indicated here. I have chosen the term "social-calculus" rather than "utilitarian" in the hope of avoiding confusion between the concept suggested here and any theory of utilitarianism that uses "utilitarian" in a sense different from this.

One of these contrasting modes of thought gives priority to the claims of each individual for protection of some special types of interests even though the sum of these types of interests may be outweighed by the sum of all other affected interests. The other mode of thought gives priority to the social good as determined by an overall social cost-benefit assessment. As we examine premises closely, we may conclude that this contrast is often one of degree -- one of orientation and emphasis rather than direct contradiction. Also, we may differ in our perceptions of the contrast or in preferences for different ways of describing it. I propose to use the terms "individual entitlement(s)" and "social calculus."[1]

In Case 4.2, if you would advise the Mayor to order the spraying stopped, would your advice be founded on an individual-entitlement premise favoring the six beekeepers? If so, is this premise akin (though perhaps rather remotely) to the underlying premises of the ancient learning preserved for us in the Six Carpenters' Case -- not doing is no trespass?[2] Not spraying is to be preferred to spraying, when spraying will interere with nature's allocation of interests and risks among individuals.

Or would your advice to the Mayor to respect the demand of the six beekeepers be founded not on a distinction between doing and not doing -- between act and omission -- but rather upon an individual-entitlement respect for interests of individuals, whether beekeepers or environmentalists, that places a limit on the rights of others? In other words, no one will be expected to sacrifice one's own entitlement to serve the greater sum of interests of others.

Or would your decision be based on unease about the reliability of any social calculus that might be advanced, and a belief that an individual-entitlement premise is more defensible in the face of such overpowering uncertainty about the consequences of relying on social-calculus premises?

If, on the other hand, you would advise the Mayor not to intervene, would you be thinking of that as a not-doing choice? Or would you be thinking of the Mayor as throwing the weight of the office on the side of action -- spraying, in this instance? If the latter, there is at least a rather strong probability that your choice was founded on social-calculus premises. This is especially likely if you also advised the Mayor that the town will not be (and should

---

[1] For more extended discussion of the contrast, see Entitlement and Obligation, 46 U. Cin. L. Rev. 1 (1977), especially at pp. 10-18.

[2] 77 Eng. Rep. 695 (K.B. 1610). The "not doing" was not paying for the wine and bread the six carpenters consumed. Thus, even though they entered the tavern under license given by law rather than by consent of the tavern keeper, they were not trespassers ab initio because they were not trespassers at all.

not be) liable to the beekeepers. The explanation is probably still social-calculus (though perhaps to a lesser degree of probability), even if you advised the Mayor that the town will be (and should be) liable to the beekeepers.

In Case 4.1 the interests at stake are more profound, and uncertainty about the possible premises of each of the possible decisions is more severe. If you favored strict liability of the manufacturer to the Vaccine Victim in Case 4.1, was your decision founded on a principle of individual autonomy -- on the value of the individual -- that overrides the social calculus and leads to recognition of individual rights that may subject the immunization program to enormous expense? Or were you only assigning great weight to individual interests within a social calculus, with the consequence that you would reach a different outcome if you considered that the resulting expense would be prohibitive (that is, would be so high that the vaccination program could not be maintained simply because of its cost)? Or would you reach a different result if, though costs of compensation would not be prohibitively high, so many individuals, regardless of cost, would choose to assert rights of nonparticipation that the program of vaccination would be rendered ineffective if such rights are recognized?

If you favored nonliability of the manufacturer, did you do so to protect individual claims of freedom from risks of disease that would exist in the absence of an immunization program? Were you recognizing entitlements to protection against a threat of death or disablement from risks of nonvaccination of others because you valued that protection more than what you saw as lower-order claims of freedom from risks of vaccination?

If you favored strict liability of the manufacturer, was your preference based on a cost-benefit analysis taking account of all the economic interests at stake? Or on a cost-benefit analysis that places "economic" values on all interests at stake, including interests in such things as freedom of choice and freedom from "pain and suffering" as well as property interests and intangible economic interests? Would you still favor strict liability if a cost-benefit analysis made it appear that the cost would exceed the benefit unless damages for pain and suffering were wholly or partly excluded from the legally recognized cost by eliminating or limiting entitlement to such damages?

Or did you favor strict liability on a theory,

borrowing from Professor (now Dean) Calabresi, that we do not know the answer to the cost-benefit questions and manufacturers are in a better position than citizens to find out and then to make the appropriate "bribes" to others in the market place.[3]

If you favored nonliability of the manufacturer, was it because you thought that benefits of nonliability for supplying polio vaccine exceed costs? Or was it because regardless of how the analysis might come out for polio vaccine, you thought that, if a principle of strict liability were applied generally -- to polio vaccine (Case 4.1), swine flu vaccine, DPT vaccine (Case 2.1), and whatever else may come along, costs of the strict liability rule would outweigh benefits?

If you have not been ready to give a clear-cut answer to each one of the questions in this series, why not?

One possibility, I acknowledge, is that the questions are not adequately framed to present the issues clearly.

Another possibility is that you are torn between individual-entitlement premises and social-calculus premises, unwilling to accept either to the exclusion of the other, searching for accommodations between them, and as a result, willingly or not, committed to an unending succession of occasions for deciding just how you'll strike the accommodation in each new case. If you are in this state of mind, you may also be troubled about accepting as a premise for decisionmaking any economic analysis or other argument based on a model, in which you are asked to disregard or suspend judgment about value implications that remain unstated and unexplained.[4]

---

[3] See G. Calabresi, The Costs of Accidents (1970); Calabresi & Hirschoff, Toward a Test for Strict Liability in Torts, 81 Yale L. J. 1055 (1972). See also R. Dworkin, Law's Empire (1986), especially ch. 8; R. Posner, Economic Analysis of Law (3d ed. 1986), especially chs. 2, 19, 20.

[4] One who takes this perspective may, of course, be less troubled about temporarily suspending consideration of value implications, if the proponent of that course of reasoning finally gets around to addressing the value implications of the economic analysis advanced. "Like any other form of scholarly inquiry, economic analysis is non-neutral, but it still helps to illuminate choices about legal approaches." Braucher,

To what extent was your choice, when you made it, a reasoned choice? To what extent value-laden fiat?[5] Having stepped back to reexamine Case 4.1 a bit more, have you changed your position on the outcome? If not, have you modified the way you would explain it?

To the extent that your decision was, or now is, a reasoned decision, what role is reason serving? Are you tracing out the consequences of what you accept as authoritative premises, and accepting the result because you accept those premises? Or are you tracing out the implications of competing premises among which you finally make a choice -- a better informed choice because of your use of reason in this way?[6] If you are not comfortable with a clear-cut answer to these questions, is it because you have an urge to preserve the flexibility to decide case by case, but you also recognize the need to be principled? Are you, then, committed to both fiat and reason and to both kinds of uses of reason?

E. Lawmaking Choices Affecting Who Pays

1. Introduction

Natural persons seldom pay damages.

Often natural persons who act on behalf of legal entities are not even formally accountable to third persons for the contractual obligations they incur on behalf of the entities they represent. For this reason, as well as practical reasons apart from legal accountability, natural persons pay a very small percentage of the dollars paid in damages to satisfy nontort claims and judgments. The

---

Toward a Broader Perspective on the Role of Economics in Legal Policy Analysis: A Retrospective and Agenda From Albert O. Hirschman, 13 Law & Social Inquiry 741, 771 (1988).

[5] See Sinram v. Pennsylvania Railroad, 61 F.2d 767 (2d Cir. 1932) (L. Hand, J.) (referring to tribunal's choice as "fiat"). Judge Hand was, however, focusing more upon a tribunal's discretionary choice in applying a "standard" such as legal cause than in choosing one legal rule in preference to another. See Chapter 3, Section E3, supra.

[6] See generally Chapter 1, Section D, supra.

percentage of numbers of all nontort claims that natural persons pay is no doubt higher than the percentage of <u>all dollars</u> that natural persons pay, especially when claims in family and other specialized courts are taken into account. The point remains that legal entities other than natural persons pay most of the <u>dollars</u> paid on <u>nontort</u> claims.

The disparity is even sharper with respect to dollars paid in <u>tort</u> damages. Probably over 99% of all dollars paid in tort damages are paid by liability insurers or by legal entities that, in view of market conditions for liability insurance, have chosen to be "self-insurers" as to the relevant risks of liability. That is, even though in some instances quite reluctantly, they have chosen the course of "risk-retention" rather than either "risk-transference" through liability insurance or "risk avoidance" by changes in their ways of doing business.

The percentage of dollars paid by liability insurers compared with the percentage paid by self-insurers has varied from time to time. In comparison with 20 years earlier, probably liability insurers pay substantially less in the 1990s and self-insurers pay substantially more, because of expansions of the scope of tort liability and the fear of more expansions. These changes in law have made liability insurers more cautious and less willing to insure some kinds of liability risks. Some observers have declared that these developments in tort law have produced not only a "crisis" as to cost but also a "crisis" as to availability of liability insurance. These are subjects of large scope, not addressed here. One purpose here, however, is to call attention to the need to consider the bearing of these matters on lawmaking choices.

Lawmaking choices have a significant impact on who pays, regardless of whether this impact is explicitly considered by the courts making the choices. It has often occurred in tort lawmaking, and especially tort lawmaking in courts, that issues are discussed and choices are explained as if the defendant or defendants named in the action would bear the burden of paying any judgment for compensatory or punitive damages. Failure to consider the effects of liability insurance or other circumstances affecting where the burden is likely in fact to fall is an instance of the larger phenomenon of unstated and unexplored value

Ch. 4   VALUES IN REASONED DECISIONMAKING

implications of lawmaking choices.[1]

Lawmaking choices may have dramatic implications not only with respect to who bears the burden of payment in a case in which a lawmaking decision is made by a court, or in the earliest cases implementing a lawmaking choice by a legislature, but also with respect to transactions and relationships that are reshaped as arrangements are developed for bearing that burden in the future. An example is the development of "claims made" liability insurance coverage as liability insurers chose to withdraw from covering a part of the risk-sharing and risk-distribution arrangements that had long existed under "occurrence" liability insurance policies. The trend toward "claims made" policy forms has been especially pronounced in relation to the liability of professionals. This is one of the instances in which liability insurers have reduced the scope of the risks they choose to insure. Most insurers no longer cover the full scope of the "long-tail" risks of professionals. Major parts of those risks are "retained" by the professionals, who bear the risks of uncertain future rates for annually renewed claims-made policies that they will need to carry even after retiring from professional practice.[2]

Consider another illustration of decisionmaking of a kind that often has more significance because of its potential effect upon the interests of others than because of its effect on the interests of the parties before the court. This illustration is the development in the 1960s and later decades of the law of "constitutional torts." Much of the significance of this body of law concerns who pays. As a matter of practical reality, for example, police officers seldom pay the judgments rendered against them in actions brought pursuant to the federal Civil Rights Act, 42 U.S.C. §1983, or state counterparts of that Act. Either as a result of collective bargaining between police officers and town officials, or as a result of municipal governmental choice even where collective bargaining has not occurred, municipalities commonly either obtain liability insurance coverage for the benefit of police officers or enter into indemnity arrangements under which the municipalities pay. Of course, significant issues of public policy are presented with respect to liability insurance or indemnity arrangements

---

[1] See Sections A and B, this Chapter, supra.

[2] See R. Keeton & A. Widiss, Insurance Law §5.10(d) (1988).

that extend to liability of an officer premised on a state-of-mind test -- for example, a test involving "intent," or "reckless disregard," or "deliberate indifference" as to a consequence such as injury from excessive force or failure to provide emergency medical attention to a person in custody. In some instances, state legislatures have enacted legal tests for determining the scope of allowable commitment of public resources to meeting the burden of paying for harms caused in ways that result in liability of government employees under theories of constitutional tort. Under such legislation, indemnity from public resources may be prohibited as to harms caused intentionally. Does the prohibition extend to consequences of "reckless disregard" or "deliberate indifference"?

2. Burdens, Costs, and Incomplete Decisionmaking

All decisionmaking in the administration of justice is incomplete in a very broad sense. No court, or legislature, or any other decisionmaker can foresee and provide for all the cases that human events will present. Decisionmaking in the administration of justice is incomplete in this broad sense not by choice but by necessity.

In a second, less global sense, incomplete decisionmaking is the essence of the common law process. Judges are expected to decide the case at hand with the benefit of competing arguments sharply focused and honed by advocates whose accountability both as officers of the system and as professional representatives of their respective clients creates strong incentives for quality and thoroughness. A decision is precedent for the future and, with decreasing weight as analogy becomes more attenuated, for issues different from, but related to, those decided. It is part of the wisdom of the system that the court not be seen, either by itself or by others, as responsible for developing an overall solution not only for the case at hand but as well for all related issues. From a larger perspective that takes account of interests beyond those adequately represented by the parties to the action, inherently this is a process of decisionmaking that always remains incomplete. On each day of decision this process leaves much to be decided on other days, by the same or other tribunals as the turn of events may determine.

It is generally recognized, of course, that this pattern of incomplete decisionmaking has disadvantages as well as advantages in the quest for justice. In 20th century America, we have witnessed increasing demands for enactment of statutes that deal with a problem more comprehensively than case-by-case judicial decisionmaking can do. Nevertheless, it is still one of the basic premises of our legal system that the advantages of the common law process outweigh its disadvantages in relation to the great bulk of the issues of justice.

No entitlement is effectively recognized unless some obligation or set of obligations to fulfill it is also recognized. The point is illustrated by a formal declaration of procedural entitlement to a "speedy" trial before a jury. Who will bear the burden of obligation to fulfill that entitlement? Unless enough judges are appointed and enough resources are raised by taxes and earmarked to cover that part of the expenses of jury trials that are to be paid out of public funds, the enforceable entitlement is to a less speedy jury trial than the formally declared entitlement promised.

Within an operating legal system, it is probably true as a practical matter that no decision of entitlement lacks impact upon obligation, and no decision of obligation lacks impact upon entitlement. It does not follow, however, that claims of entitlement and burdens of obligation must be determined simultaneously. Experience indicates that often the principal determinations of entitlement and obligation occur in separate decisions, at different times, and by different decisionmakers. The implications of such separation plainly can be very significant.

At first glance it might appear that the tendency toward separation of decisions of entitlement and obligation -- illustrated above by procedural entitlements to speedy trial before a jury -- is inapplicable to claims of damages between a single plaintiff and a single defendant. The judgment, if one of entitlement of the plaintiff, is also one of obligation of the defendant. But even in an action for damages, it ordinarily happens that only some of the total set of issues of entitlement and obligation are addressed. What, for example, are the assumed premises with respect to how the loss will be borne or spread if the plaintiff's claim in a tort action is denied? If the claim is granted? We cannot identify the premises of obligation -- the premises of the total arrangement for bearing the burden of compensation through tort judgments -- without looking well beyond the impact on the defendant in the tort action.

Frequently the individual tort judgment is only one among the whole set of decisions made by courts, legislatures, and other decisionmakers to determine the obligations created to fulfill the entitlement recognized in the tort judgment. Liability insurance, government subsidies, and tax incentives are illustrations of the point. Also, in some instances the response of nongovernmental decisionmakers, expressed through market forces, may have even greater significance than the sum of governmental decisions.

Trends of law reform tend to focus attention to some extent upon pairing of obligation and entitlement. The tendency is less powerful, however, in relation to judicial lawmaking than in relation to legislation. Some developments of contract law illustrate the point.

In a context in which over 99% of contractual transactions in our society are contracts of adhesion, courts have increasingly recognized claims for relief inconsistent with those rules of classic contract law that were premised on a bargain between equals. One scholar has characterized the development as the death of contract, generally.[3] And when we examine the specialized field of insurance contracts, we find not only diminishing use of agency doctrines associated with contract but also striking expansion of the defense of unconscionability and striking development of a doctrine of honoring reasonable expectations even though they are contrary to what a painstaking study of the contractual documents would have disclosed.[4]

Burdens have been more explicitly discussed, along with benefits, in debates over compensation systems -- complexes of legislation and judicial lawmaking, and tort and insurance doctrines and arrangements -- as recognized entitlements have been expanded through most of the 20th century, and at an accelerated pace after midcentury.

Developments of substantive law during the 20th century have more often expanded than contracted recognized claims of entitlement. In the 1970s and 1980s, however,

---

[3] G. Gilmore, Death of Contract (1974).

[4] See, e.g., Smith v. Westland Life Ins. Co., 15 Cal. 3d 311, 539 P.2d 433, 123 Cal. Rptr. 649 (1975); C & J Fertilizer, Inc. v. Allied Mut. Ins. Co., 727 N.W.2d 169 (Iowa 1975); R. Keeton & A. Widiss, Insurance Law §6.3 (1988).

pressures for a reversal of this trend have increased. They have contributed not only to an annual legislative agenda for law reform but also to substantial recasting of briefs and arguments presented to courts.

Probing analysis of burden sharing will in some instances disclose a conflict of interest between a plaintiff in the case before the court and persons likely to be plaintiffs, presenting like claims, in the long-term future; or between a defendant before the court and persons likely to be defendants in similar cases in the future. This point is illustrated in the development of a body of law on "coordination of benefits" -- a phrase that began to appear in proposals for legislative reform in the 1960s.

The "collateral source" rule of tort law denies to a tort defendant any reduction of the measure of damages by reason of benefits received by the plaintiff from a collateral source, such as an accident insurance policy. Legislative reform proposals, even before the 1960s, in some instances introduced cost-saving provisions that abrogated the collateral source rule and reduced the plaintiff's measure of damages to "net" loss after deduction of benefits received from other sources. In the 1960s the phrase "coordination of benefits" came to be applied to provisions of this kind.

In the 1970s some statutes implementing such proposals were enacted, and in the 1980s some courts came to recognize a broader public policy interest in coordination of benefits, implicitly manifested in a body of legislation that included a number of mandates for application of the principle in particular contexts.[5] The public policy argument for coordination of benefits is founded on the premise that the entity first paying a tort judgment tends to develop a way of passing the burden along through insurance or through pricing of products, so the burden eventually falls on a large segment of the public (for example, purchasers of a product, or premium payers for a type of insurance, or even taxpayers of a given type of tax). When that happens, the burden is eventually higher because of transaction costs than if coordination of benefits were required.

The relative merit of arguments for and against

---

[5] See Cody v. Connecticut General Life Ins. Co., 387 Mass. 142, 148-51, 439 N.E.2d 234, 238-40 (1982).

coordination of benefits is a major topic of substantive law, and it is not examined here. The point underscored here is that these arguments were rarely examined in judicial opinions of earlier vintage than the 1970s, and even in the 1970s and 1980s were seldom considered as a basis for a lawmaking choice. When explored, they may lead to a reduced measure of recovery for the plaintiff in a particular case before the court (either by the court's implementation of a legislature's mandate, or by a court's own lawmaking choice), on the premise that the community generally, including individuals who in the future may have claims like that the plaintiff is asserting, will pay enough less in prices for products and premiums for insurance to more than outweigh the value of duplicative benefits such as the "collateral source" rule of tort law allows.

Dispute over the merits of "coordination of benefits" is, of course, merely one illustration of the broader dispute over the practical impact of a lawmaking choice as viewed from a long-term perspective that takes account not only of the immediate burden of obligation but as well how that burden is likely to be passed along and distributed.

Reform efforts in legislatures, even more so than in courts, whether aimed at expanding or instead at reducing the scope of liability of actors and enterprises, tend to focus some attention at least upon obligation as well as entitlement. Thus, legislative decisions to expand or reduce substantive entitlements, made in response to reform proposals, tend to be paired with some consideration of matching obligations. Nevertheless, the matching is incomplete. Legislative enactments as well as judicial decisions in cases in the courts may say little about where the burdens of obligation to fulfill entitlements will fall. As noted before, many tort judgments are paid initially by liability insurers. Of those that remain, most are paid by "target" defendants, who have a capacity to "self-insure" -- a capacity, like that of liability insurers, to cause the burden to be spread among a much larger group. In this context, basic premises of decisions of obligation are, or at least should be, as much concerned with where the burden of obligation will fall after distribution as with where it is placed by the initial decision of obligation. This is so regardless of whether that decision is made in a single case or is declared for a large body of disputes by a statute.

To some extent, legislatures and courts have consciously, deliberately addressed issues of allocation and distribution of the burdens of obligation. Legislatures of every state have enacted financial responsibility laws, and many have enacted other tort and insurance laws explicitly designed to cause the burden of obligation to be shifted from the nominal tortfeasor and distributed through insurance premiums to a much larger group. Also, in the 20th century, courts have refashioned doctrines of respondeat superior in ways that disclose premises rather different from those of earlier times. Among the apparent premises of the refashioned doctrines are some that depend on principles of distribution and allocation of burdens among the larger group who purchase the services or the goods of the enterprise.

The point remains, however, that important issues of obligation are often left unaddressed not only when courts are deciding whether or not to declare entitlements but also when legislatures are making such decisions.

CHAPTER 5

A JUDGE'S WRITING AND SPEAKING

A. Introduction

This chapter is addressed to you, whether or not you are or ever expect to be a judge. Thinking about how you, if a judge, would officially explain your decisions will help you better understand not only judging but as well other things you need to know to counsel and represent clients in relation to any transactions that may ever lead to a dispute before a judge.

Thinking about how you would officially explain a decision, orally in court or more formally in writing, is especially useful because the necessity of explaining disciplines choice. The point is illustrated by a common experience that is reported to happen over and over again. The judges of a court, sitting as a panel in a case, agree in conference on a disposition and assign one of the judges to draft the opinion. After working on the draft, the assigned judge reports to other judges of the panel, "It won't write." The discipline of working through the reasoned explanation of the outcome persuades the judge (and often other members of the panel as well) to reach a different disposition. This may happen because deeper probing leads to the conclusion that authoritative sources of law that the judges are professionally committed to applying constrain the court to reach that different disposition. It may happen, also, because deeper probing of unstated premises of the tentative panel decision persuades the court that this case is materially different from those it previously thought controlling -- it presents an issue of first impression that is better decided contrary to the initial impulse.

An advocate whose purpose is to persuade the court to reach a decision favoring the client the advocate represents is wise to take this point into account. Even if an advocate's brief and oral argument have moved the court, by whatever means, to the view advanced by the advocate, if the advocate has failed to show the court how to write it that way, all may be lost as the court makes that effort and encounters difficulties the advocate has not addressed. Thus, at some time in the preparation of every case, the advocate needs to think about the case from the perspective of the professional commitment of all the judges who will sit on the case to a reasoned explanation of the outcome, candidly explained.

The advocate needs to think about demonstrating by example how a reasoned explanation might read. Of course, the advocate may choose to argue for a more favorable outcome than the judges are likely to accept, and may or may not choose to advance as an alternative a somewhat less favorable outcome that would be better for the client than the outcome advanced by the opponent. The central point is that, for whatever position or alternative positions the advocate advances, the advocate should at least consider proposing a reasoned explanation that a judge could comfortably adopt as professionally appropriate, and not just an argument cast in more strident rhetoric.

Also, even if you never expect to be performing either in the role of judge or in the role of advocate, and your interest is solely to have a better understanding of judging in the legal system, it will be useful to examine judging through the eyes of a judge who is committed to writing a reasoned explanation of a hard choice.

With these points in view, this chapter is addressed to you as a judge, even if you occupy that role only hypothetically. Also, for reasons stated in Chapter 1,[1] you are asked to place yourself hypothetically in the role of a trial judge.

Throughout this book, and again in the present chapter, I have emphasized the values of candor. So, in the spirit of candor, I must tell you that I speak about guidelines for writing as a confirmed sinner -- but a well-meaning sinner. These guidelines state a genuine aim, even though in the real world of overloaded dockets it is often hard for a judge to find time to make drafts shorter,

---

[1]Chapter 1, Section B, _supra_.

simpler, and clearer.

Even so, the decisions trial judges make about when and how much to write, and how to go about it, are important parts of judging.

B. When and How Much to Write

Here are some recommendations about when and how much to write.

Write briefly in most matters. Write orders on the margins of motions often. Write very brief memoranda (for example, one to five pages) when a little more explanation is needed. Do say enough that the parties and their lawyers can understand why you decided as you did. Rarely write more than a brief memorandum in <u>denying</u> motions to dismiss, for summary judgment, and for change of venue. (Denial of a challenge to jurisdiction over person will in some cases warrant more.)

State findings and conclusions orally from the bench when possible.

Write opinions rarely. Write a full memorandum or opinion only when the issue is close and you need to explain why you have rejected arguments advanced by the loser(s). Write with the purpose of publishing only if you are deciding some issue(s) of first impression and your opinion (1) is likely to help lawyers and other judges save time in research or analysis, or (2) expresses some view not adequately represented in available materials. When you write with this purpose, take more time to edit thoroughly.

C. How the Decision is Reasoned

Reason substantively. Be careful that labels and legal jargon are tools, not impediments and not substitutes for substantive reasons.[1]

---

[1] For further comments on labels and meanings, <u>see</u> Chapter 3, Section A, <u>supra</u>.

Be clear about your use of reason and choice. Reconsider if your first draft uses "deductive" reasoning only -- that is, if it cites authority and the conclusions derived from the cited authority, without explaining why you chose that source of authority rather than another that might have pointed to a different result. More likely than not, your actual thought processes included "informative" reasoning -- that is, you examined different sources of authority (having contrasting implications for this case) and made an "informed choice" about which source applies to this case. If so, revise your draft to disclose your process of reasoning to your informed choice.[2]

Any computer is better at deductive reasoning than we human beings can ever be. Barring a power failure or a hardware failure of some kind, the computer never commits a logical fallacy. It never reaches an illogical conclusion. Instead, what it does is relentlessly tell you the logical result of the premises you feed into it. Computers do not make logical mistakes. Programmers and users -- human beings -- make the mistakes (or commit the sins of deliberately introducing a "virus" into the software). And usually the mistakes are not truly mistakes of logic. They are more often mistakes of choice that occur when you select the premises that you feed into the computer.[3]

In short, we will never do as well as computers in purely deductive reasoning.

But informative reasoning is another matter altogether. Even the most advanced development of so-called artificial intelligence in the computer-use field falls short of measuring up to the performance of a good judge at informative reasoning -- at reasoned choice.

Be respectful of the lawmakers (whether legislators, judges, or others) who have preceded you in the vineyard in which you are working. Treat their output reasonably and respectfully. If they have used an ambiguous phrase,[4] or even one that is literally unambiguous but plainly ill-

---

[2]*See* Chapter 1, Sections A and D, and Chapter 4, Section C, *supra*.

[3]*See* Chapter 4, Sections B and D, *supra*.

[4]An example is "intentional act." *See* Chapter 6, Section E, *infra*.

fitting in context,[5] read their entire cmmunication and construe it in a commonsense way that gives effect to their manifested meaning. Avoid the ultimate disrespect of presuming that the authority you cite (constitution, statute, judicial opinion, rule of procedure, etc.) explicitly or implicitly stated a particular mandate that you must follow, even though you are able to discover no justification for that mandate. If you are tempted on first draft to come out that way, reexamine your own analysis.

If it is an easy decision because one source of authority plainly applies and provides a clear mandate, write it that way. In this kind of case deductive reasoning is the central message. If the case is not that easy, probably you will have used informative reasoning. If so, be candid about it.

When deciding an issue of first impression, be cautious about embracing a rule that involves still more decision points than have been established by previous authority. Be especially cautious about adopting "evaluative standards" that depend on "weighing" or "balancing" many "factors," or even the "totality of the circumstances." Choosing (or creating) and applying such an evaluative standard may seem less attractive as a reasoned disposition of the case at hand after you have explored the implications for the future should your decision be allowed to stand as precedent.[6]

---

[5] [I]t is true that the words used, even in their literal sense, are the primary, and ordinarily the most reliable, source of interpreting the meaning of any writing: be it a statute, a contract, or anything else. But it is one of the surest indexes of a mature and developed jurisprudence not to make a fortress out of the dictionary; but to remember that statutes always have some purpose or object to accomplish, whose sympathetic and imaginative discovery is the surest guide to their meaning.

Cabell v. Markham, 148 F.2d 737, 739 (2d Cir.) (L. Hand, J.), aff'd, 326 U.S. 404 (1945).

[6]See Chapter 3, Section C3, supra.

Ch. 5   A JUDGE'S WRITING AND SPEAKING

D. Interpreting Communications: Problems of Manifested Meaning and Intent

There is a sense in which this Section D should simply be a subheading under Section C. That is, Section D is simply an important illustration of points made in Section C about how a decision is reasoned. I have made it a separate Section D because it is probably the most frequently recurring illustration of the difficulty of achieving 100% compliance with the guidelines stated in Section C.

The suggestions that follow apply to interpreting all kinds of communications in all kinds of documents and in all oral forms.

Identify the issue clearly. When examining printed or written words (or oral communications) to decide a disputed issue, be clear about whether you are applying a state-of-mind test (such as intent) or instead an objective test of manifested meaning (such as "manifested intent of contracting parties").[1]

---

[1] Usually the purpose of examining the communication is to determine manifested meaning, not intent -- to determine what the contracting parties (or the statutory drafters) said, not what they thought. Cf. Frigaliment Importing Co. Ltd. v. B.N.S. International Sales Corp., 190 F. Supp. 116 (S.D.N.Y. 1960) (Friendly, Circuit Judge, sitting as trial judge in a nonjury trial):

> The issue is, what is chicken? Plaintiff says "chicken" means a young chicken, suitable for broiling and frying. Defendant says "chicken" means any bird of that genus that meets contract specifications on weight and quality, including what it calls "stewing chicken" and plaintiff pejoratively terms "fowl". Dictionaries give both meanings, as well as some others not relevant here. To support it, plaintiff sends a number of volleys over the net; defendant essays to return them and adds a few serves of its own. Assuming that both parties were acting in good faith, the case nicely illustrates Holmes' remark "that the making of a contract depends not on the agreement of two minds in one intention, but on the agreement of two sets of external signs -- not on the parties' having meant the same thing but on their having said the same thing." The Path of the Law, in Collected Legal Papers, p. 178. I have concluded that plaintiff has not sustained its

Avoid the fictions of attributing intent to an entity such as a corporation or a legislature. A natural person may have a state of mind in a truly factual sense; an entity cannot. It is at least distracting and perhaps misleading to less careful readers to write about a "corporation's intent" or a "legislature's intent."[2] It is usually best not to use "legislative intent," because of the risk it will be misunderstood. If you do use it, be careful that the way you use it conveys the meaning of "manifested intent" rather than a state of mind.

Here, too, be respectful of authority.[3]

If you must fill gaps in manifested meaning of some communication (statute, contract, other document, or conversation) to decide the case, be candid about what you are doing and how and why you fill the gaps in the way you do.[4]

E. Combining Substance With Style

These suggestions are about combining substance with style.

Write a judicious opinion, not a brief. State the question to be decided neutrally. If the issue is close and difficult, say so. Identify the best argument or arguments against your decision and explain why you reject them. State, but do not overstate, the positive reasons your decision is either required by authority (constitution, statute, precedent, etc.) or is a sound resolution of an issue of first impression.

---

      burden of persuasion that the contract used "chicken"
      in the narrower sense.

(Emphasis in original).

[2] See Chapter 3, Section B4, supra, and Chapter 6, Sections B and G, infra.

[3] See Section C, this Chapter, supra.

[4] See also Chapter 6, Sections B and C, infra.

Be candid. Avoid legal fictions, if possible. If you conclude that precedent requires you to invoke a legal fiction, explain what you are doing and why.

Be clear.

Make it a _reasoned_ opinion.[1]

Use English. Use the Anglo-Saxon word if it clearly states your meaning. If you need to use legal jargon to explain connections with precedent, do so. But say it in English, too.

Take pride in simplicity, but not at the expense of clarity. If the idea is complex, say so, and explain it as clearly and crisply as you can. If the idea is simple and forthright, say it that way and move on. Shorter is usually better, but not if it hides rather than exposes meaning.

Revise your first draft, especially if you intend it to be published. Write shorter sentences, even if more of them. That is, break the long sentences into two or more. Shorten the opinion. Organize it. Make it march. Sacrifice even some gems of thought if they are diversions from the march. Resist diversions even in footnotes. If you can do so without interfering with the march, let the opinion sing a little.[2] But if you choose to add touches of elegance, be sure the opinion still marches in step and sings in tune.

F. The Jury Charge

Tailor your jury charge to the case on trial. Tell the jury all they need to know about the law to help them do their job, but nothing more. Do not burden them with explanations of points of law that are not relevant to the disputes of fact they must decide. If you use any legal jargon, be sure to explain its meaning clearly.

If the case is complex, and it is impossible to explain the needed law in a short charge, consider one or

---

[1] See Section C, this Chapter, _supra_.

[2] I gratefully acknowledge that I have borrowed this advice from Professor Archibald Cox's lectures on brief writing.

both of two means of helping the jury understand their job: (1) Use a separate interrogatory for each issue or set of related issues they must decide, and tailor your instructions to explain the interrogatories. (2) Send the charge to the jury in writing as well as delivering it orally.

G. Conclusion

Guidelines are useful, even if you are realistic enough to know that you will not succeed in measuring up to them always.

For example, if you have a set of chambers guidelines, and you tell your law clerks to observe them, and you openly invite them to point out any instances in which they think your own drafts may have departed from them, your departures will be fewer, and more clearly intentional.

I hope you have sensed that this chapter measures up to at least one of the recommended guidelines for writing. It is short.

CHAPTER 6

JUDGING STATUTES

A. Introduction

A fundamental characteristic of judging in late-20th century America is that very few court cases depend solely on common law grounds. Legislatures have enacted so many statutes on so many subjects that in most cases at least one party invokes at least one statute. Year by year, as more statutes are enacted, the percentage of judicial decisionmaking that involves statutes increases. It seems clear this trend will continue, with the consequence that judging statutes will become an even larger and more significant part of the work of judges than it has been in the past.

A second fundamental characteristic of the legal system that bears on the subject treated in this chapter is that a high percentage of the enacted statutes fit a classic pattern. They change but do not reduce the agenda for the courts. In few of the cases coming to decision before a court do the relevant statutes provide clear, direct answers to the questions of law the court must decide in order to determine what judgment to enter.

In time past, the law of torts was quintessentially common law. It seems appropriate, then, to use a tort case for the first illustration in this chapter.

Case 6.1
Rich, Cabbie, and Luce

Rich is in town for a big event. Having lingered in a bar a bit too long, he hails a cab and says "Step on it! I'll pay the fine if your're stopped!" Cabbie, spurred by

INTRODUCTION   Sec. A

visions of a big tip, speeds through a traffic light just after it has turned red and crashes into Luce, driving along without having his seat belt and shoulder harness fastened. Luce is thrown out of his car and is severely injured. Cabbie is less severely injured. Rich is relaxed and is uninjured.

Luce sues Cabbie and Rich. Cabbie claims against Luce and Rich. At trial the factfindings are as follows:

Damages sustained by Luce......$1 million
Damages sustained by Cabbie....$90 thousand
Allocated percentages of responsibility:
    Rich 20%
    Cabbie 70%
    Luce .... 10% (only for not fastening belts)

The state in which these events occur has no statute as to wearing seat belts, has a comparative negligence statute enacted in the 1970s, and has a statute on joint and divisible liability enacted in the 1980s, which reads in part as follows:

> A. He who conspires with another person to commit an intentional or willful act is answerable, jointly, with that person, for the damage caused by such act.
>
> B. If liability is not joint pursuant to paragraph A, ...[1] then liability caused by two or more persons shall be joint only to the extent necessary for the person suffering injury, death, or loss to recover fifty percent of his recoverable damages; [2] however when the amount of the injured person's recovery has been reduced in accordance with the comparative fault statute of the state, a judgment debtor shall not be liable for more than the degree of the judgment debtor's fault to a

judgment creditor to whom a greater degree of fault has been attributed. [3] All parties shall enjoy their respective rights of indemnity and contribution. [4] Except as described in paragraph A of this Article, or as otherwise provided by law, and hereinabove, the liability shall be several only and a joint tortfeasor shall not be jointly liable with any other person for damages attributable to the fault of such other person, including the person suffering injury, death, or loss, regardless of such other person's insolvency, ability to pay, degree of fault, or immunity by statute or otherwise.[1]

What judgment should be entered?

Case 6.2
After Luce's Settlement

Assume all facts to be the same as in Case 6.1, plus the following:

During trial, Luce settled with Cabbie for the full payment of the $25,000 limit of Cabbie's liability insurance policy.

What judgment should be entered?[2]

---

[1] This hypothetical statute is adapted from one enacted in Louisiana in the 1980s. La. Civ. Code Art. 2324. This draft, however, changes the distinctive Louisiana terminology of "solidary" liability to the terminology common in other states, of "joint" liability. The numerals in brackets in paragraph B -- [1], [2], [3], [4] -- have been inserted for ease of reference.

[2] In addition to the two problem cases stated in the text, I will refer occasionally to two other problem cases on which I have expressed

B. Determining Manifested Meaning

In Chapters 1 and 5 I have suggested that a judge's search for manifested meaning is aided by recognition of some fundamental characteristics of all texts (including oral as well as written communications). These are characteristics of all communications, regardless of context -- regardless of whether the text under examination is a statute, a contract, or a precedent. Those common characteristics of

---

views elsewhere. They are presented in this note as Cases 6.3 and 6.4.

Case 6.3
Wrongful Death and Punitive Damages

When a state's wrongful death act says nothing explicitly about punitive damages, may punitive damages be awarded in an action brought by or on behalf of survivors following the death of a 12-year-old pedestrian struck by a bus?

This problem, adapted from Mattyasovsky v. West Towns Bus Co., 61 Ill.2d 31, 330 N.E.2d 509 (1973), is discussed in Keeton, Statutes, Gaps, and Values in Tort Law, 44 J. Air L. & Com. 1 (1978).

Case 6.4
Electronic Eavesdropping

Assume a state statute on electronic eavesdropping, patterned after the federal statute.

Assume a tape recording, made by the mother of a 12-year-old child, to which the 12-year-old child acquiesces when told by the mother that she will ground him and cut off his allowance if he objects. The conversation recorded is between the child and a schoolmate about the schoolmate's distribution of cocaine. Is it an illegal recording? Is the schoolmate entitled to an order of suppression?

My views on a somewhat similar problem of interpretation of the federal statute are expressed in United States v. Vest, 639 F. Supp. 899 (D. Mass. 1986), aff'd, 813 F.2d 477 (1st Cir. 1987). Relevant parts of the federal statute are quoted in that opinion.

texts are restated below, in a form applying to statutes.[1]

One. Even when well-drafted, statutes leave vital questions unanswered. No phrase, no sentence, no paragraph, no section, no chapter, no code answers all the questions that will come before the courts in disputes about its application to human experience.

Two. When poorly-drafted, as is all to often the case, statutes present hosts of unanswered questions.

Three. Some of the unanswered questions are central to very broad areas of law that are affected by statutes but cannot be fully controlled by statutory mandates because of the human limitations of even the best legislators (and judges and commentators too, for that matter) in trying to foresee and provide answers for all questions that will arise. For example, what is the meaning of "in restraint of trade" or "unfair competition" in an anti-trust statute, or "right of privacy" in a Civil Rights Act, or "deceptive act or practice" in a consumer protection act, or "pattern of racketeering activity" in a RICO statute?

Before I state the fourth point, I pause to note that it is a more debatable proposition than any of the first three. To say the least, it is more common for lawyers in briefs and judges in opinions to say things that, taken literally, are inconsistent with this fourth point than with any of the first three.

Four. The search is for manifested meaning -- not unmanifested intent. Expressed another way, the search is for the objectively manifested meaning, not for somebody's unexpressed state of mind.[2]

In summary, judges of individual cases, when resolving disputes about the application of statutes to the cases before them, must faithfully administer statutory directives. Yet, try as they may, judges cannot find answers in the relevant statutes to all of the case disputes they must resolve.

---

[1] This statement of common characteristics of statutory texts is adapted from Keeton, *Statutes, Gaps, and Values in Tort Law*, 44 J. Air L. & Com. 1, 4-9 (1978).

[2] *See also* Chapter 5, Section D, *supra*.

How do and should judges respond to this dilemma?

What principles and rules of general application can we fashion for judges to use in this search?

C. Guidelines for Deciding Issues Regarding Statutory Meaning

I propose the following set of guidelines[1] for determining whether a statute has answered a particular question that is essential to deciding a case before the court and, if not, how the court should go about deciding that case:

One. If the statute addressed the issue at hand and answered it, apply the mandate of the statute (absent unconstitutionality).

Two. If the issue at hand is one beyond that core area of issues that the statute addressed and answered, defer to the statute's manifestations of principle and policy as far as they can be ascertained and are relevant to the issue at hand.

Three. Subject to the first two propositions, aim for resolving the issue at hand so as to produce the best total set of rules, including those within the core area of the statute and other cognate rules of law, whatever their source. Defer to the statute's manifestations of principle and policy, as far as they can be ascertained. Accept the inapplicable statutory mandate as a datum. Accept inapplicable directives appearing in other statutes and judicial precedents as data. Aim for a decision on this issue that will produce an evenhanded system for this issue and all the cognate issues that are answered in statutes and precedents.

Four. In determining whether a statute addressed the issue at hand, dispense with contrary-to-fact presumptions about the legislative process; be realistic and be candid. Use legislative history as data; avoid proceeding as if

---

[1] For an earlier version of these guidelines, see R. Keeton, Venturing to Do Justice 94-95 (1969). Materials presenting varied views on this subject appear in R. Aldisert, The Judicial Process 170-235 (1976).

legislative history were a statutory mandate. At most, declarations in legislative history are obiter dicta of the legislative process. If it is necessary to resort to legislative history, Guidelines Two and Three apply, not Guideline One. Also, do not treat failure to enact a mandate as if it were enacting a mandate. "Not speaking" to an issue is not "speaking" to that issue. Rarely, failure to enact legislation is a significant datum, and Guidelines Two and Three then apply. But never is it a mandate as in Guideline One.

D. The Contrast Between Intent and Objectively Manifested Meaning

If you have any doubts, or disagreement with me, about any of the four guidelines for determining the meaning of statutes and applying the statutes to particular cases, surely they are more likely to concern the second, third, or fourth. So, not only because the first precedes in logical order but also because I hope by discussing it to prepare you for what I wish to say on the others, I discuss it first.

In Section B4 above, and in the title of this Section D, I have used the phrase "objectively manifested meaning." In explaining why, I will be reflecting some of the frustrations of my more recent experience -- that is, experience as a trial judge -- which came after the initial formulation of the four guidelines stated in Section C.

As a trial judge, I am constantly confronted with arguments of trial lawyers asserting, either expressly or impliedly, that we should be thinking about the intent -- the state of mind -- of "somebody" or "some body." That is, they argue we should be thinking about intent of some natural person -- "somebody" in that sense -- or intent of some legal entity, some legally constituted body that is not a natural person -- such as a state legislature (or even a court that filed an opinion that is cited as precedent).

The first, fundamental difficulty with an argument about what the legislature intended is that, although a natural person may have a state of mind, such as intent, an entity that is not a natural person has no state of mind in any strictly factual sense.[1] Thus, we have moved to legal fiction when we talk about a legislature's intent.

Distinguish "legislative intent" from "legislature's intent." Except for the risk of its being misunderstood to mean a state of mind, "legislative intent" is a less distracting usage. In Chapter 5 I have urged judges to use it cautiously in writing opinions, because of the risk of being misunderstood. Nevertheless, properly used and understood, "legislative intent" may be a synonym for objectively manifested meaning of the statute. Professor Lon Fuller, among others, made essentially this point in calling attention to the fact that when one reads a document such as a statute (or a contract, or a judicial opinion), one may sense in it not only explicit mandates (or agreements) but also an underlying objective or purpose that serves to inform the reader about how the different provisions fit together and why they were put together in one document.

Reading a document to determine "legislative intent" or "contractual intent" in this sense is synonymous with searching for objectively manifested meaning.[2]

Coming back to the main point, then, and repeating it, I suggest that the first problem with speaking about a "legislature's intent" is that -- unless it is meant to be a synonym for "objectively manifested meaning," and for "legislative intent" in the sense I have just explained -- it is a legal fiction. Only a natural person can have a state of mind such as intent. No legal entity such as a legislature can have an "intent" in a strictly factual sense.

Second, arguments about what the legislature intended fail to take account of the governor's participation in the legislative process. A legislature does not ordinarily legislate alone, except by overriding a veto. The usual legislative entity consists of the legislature and the governor, acting together. Again, one may defensibly speak of "legislative intent" in the sense of objectively manifested meaning of what the legislature and governor do together. But it is fictional and misleading to speak of the "legislature's intent."

---

[1] As to "entity state-of-mind" more generally, see Chapter 3, Section B4, supra.

[2] See additional comments in Chapter 5, Section D, supra.

Third, even when in the legal system we are concerned with the meaning of something written, stated, or approved by a natural person, only very rarely are we concerned with that person's state of mind -- that person's intent. In contract law, for example, the rule that deals with two ships "Peerless" is an exception. In contrast, the general rule is that we search for "objectively manifested intent" -- an objective standard -- not "intent," the subjective standard. Thus, the legal system with only the rarest exceptions, such as the two-ships-"Peerless" rule, focuses not upon a writer's or speaker's intent but upon objectively manifested meaning. Indeed, the legal system often declines even to receive evidence of the person's secretly held state of mind, which may or may not be consistent with what the person said or did.

This fundamental characteristic of the way the law treats written documents -- including statutes as well as contracts -- helps to explain why Guideline Four cautions that statements in legislative history are the obiter dicta of the legislative process -- more like obiter dicta in judicial opinions than like holdings. The issue is what is the _objectively_ _manifested_ meaning of the statute. What some individuals or even a legislative committee said in discussing the proposed legislation is not a part of the mandate. In search of the mandate we look first and foremost to the objectively manifested meaning of the statute itself.

E. A Proposed Analysis of Cases 6.1 and 6.5

As an introduction to discussing Case 6.1, I wish to make it plain at the outset that I will not even purport to conclude what is the true meaning of the hypothetical statute, or of the Louisiana statute after which it was fashioned. The meaning of Louisiana statutes is for Louisiana judges to say. The meaning of the hypothetical state statute is for the hypothetical judges of the hypothetical state to say. I can only tell you what I predict (without having had the benefit of the arguments of advocates, which I genuinely value) the deciding judges will construe the statute to mean when it comes before them for decision.

In Case 6.1, a central problem of obscurity about manifested meaning is presented by the phrase, in paragraph

ANALYSIS OF CASES 6.1 AND 6.5   Sec. E

A of the statute, "an intentional or willful act."

By 1987, however, when the Louisiana legislature was using this phrase, it was acting in a context of several precedents -- decisions of the Supreme Court of Louisiana -- interpreting a different but quite similar phrase -- "an intentional act" -- as it appeared in a section of the workers' compensation chapter of the Louisiana statutes, R.S. 23:1032, as amended in 1976, declaring:

> Nothing in this Chapter [regarding immunity of the employer from tort liability for injury to an employee] shall affect the liability of the employer, or any officer, director, stockholder, partner, or employee of such employer or principal to a fine or penalty under any other statute or the liability, civil or criminal, resulting from an intentional act.

In Citizen v. Daigle,[1] citing Bazley v. Tortorich,[2] the Supreme Court of Louisiana held that

> "intentional act" should be interpreted according to the generally accepted meaning of intentional tort in the field of civil liability. The Bazley decision rejected plaintiff's argument that intentional act should be equated with "voluntary act" and formulated the following definition to be applied under the statute:
>
> > "The meaning of intent in this context is that the defendant either desired to bring about the physical results of his act or believed that they were substantially certain to follow from what he did." 397 So.2d at 482.
>
> Applying the statute as interpreted in Bazley to the facts of this case [Citizen v. Daigle], we hold that Cormier's shooting of plaintiff

---

[1] 418 So.2d 598 (La. 1982).

[2] 397 So.2d 475 (La. 1981).

[when Cormier pointed what he thought to be an unloaded, inoperative gun at plaintiff and pulled the trigger] was not an "intentional act" as contemplated by R.S. 23:1032.[3]

I am in no position to be critical of these decisions, even if I were inclined to be -- as I am not -- because they are quite compatible with what I have written as a co-author of Prosser & Keeton on Torts.[4] Even so, I do acknowledge that I understand the views and the sense of frustration of the dissenting justices in Citizen v. Daigle. The meaning of the statute in relation to the case before the court was not clearly manifested. The phrase "intentional act" was ambiguous. If not literally always ambiguous, that phrase is at least virtually always ambiguous. I urge judges never, never to use it, except of course when quoting a statute or precedent that uses it.

The reason it is ambiguous (a reason you will find stated in §8 of Prosser & Keeton)[5] is that every act is intentional in the sense that it involves a voluntary muscular movement, and the phrase "intentional act" fails to communicate to the reader what consequence of the act must have been intended by the actor in order for the act to be "intentional" in the statutory sense.

> Much of the confusion surrounding application of the legal requirement of intent arises from lack of a clear understanding of the relationship among act, intent, and motive.
>
> ... An involuntary muscular movement of a sleeping or otherwise incapacitated person will not support liability. But an "act," as that term is ordinarily used, is a voluntary contraction of the muscles, and nothing more. An act is to be distinguished from its consequences.... When "act" is used in this sense, it is tautological to speak of a "voluntary act," and self-contradictory to

---

[3] 418 So.2d at 203.

[4] §8 (5th ed. 1984).

[5] Id. at pp. 34-35.

speak of an "involuntary act," since every act is voluntary. Nevertheless, the phrases "voluntary act" and "involuntary act" do appear in legal prose. Moreover, differences may be deeper than merely a choice of terminology; one who uses the phrase "voluntary act" may be using "act" to mean something different from a mere voluntary contraction of the muscles; sometimes the phrase "voluntary act" is used to mean something closer to the concept of intent (as defined in the Restatement and in common usage), which focuses not upon the mere "act" (in the narrower sense, defined in the Restatement and in common usage) but upon volition in relation to consequences as well as volition in relation to the muscular contraction....[6]

Of course, what was said about the phrase "voluntary act" in this passage from Prosser & Keeton, published three years before the 1987 Act was passed by the Louisiana legislature, is equally applicable to the phrase "intentional act." Clearly, the Louisiana legislature in using this phrase was focusing upon "volition in relation to consequences as well as volition in relation to the muscular contraction." That much is easy to discern. The more difficult question is this: As to <u>what consequences</u>, or <u>what kinds of consequences</u>, must volition be proved in order to prove an "intentional act" in the sense of that phrase as used in this statute? To show an "intentional act" of Rich, for example, is it enough to show that, when Rich acted -- by saying "Step on it! I'll pay the fine if you're stopped!" -- Rich knew that Cabbie would violate several traffic laws regulating speed, right of way, and observance of traffic controls such as red lights and stop signs? Also, to show an "intentional act" of Cabbie, is it enough to show that, when he sped he knew it was substantially certain that he was violating traffic laws aimed at protecting against the risk of bodily harm in traffic accidents? Or, in order to prove an "intentional act" of Cabbie in the statutory sense, must it be shown that at some point when Cabbie still had a choice Cabbie knew, when then acting, that it was not merely a risk but instead a substantial certainty that he would injure the

---

[6]Prosser & Keeton, <u>Torts</u> §8, pp. 34-35 (5th ed. 1984) (footnotes omitted).

person he saw entering the intersection that he (Cabbie) was also entering at high speed against a red light? If this last among the possible meanings is determined to be the manifested meaning of this statutory phrase "intentional act," almost certainly the evidence in circumstances like those of Case 6.1 will be insufficient to support a finding that either Rich or Cabbie committed an "intentional act" that was a cause of harm to Luce.

"Intent" is a state of mind that focuses not on the act itself but upon some consequence of the act. When we use "intent," we must answer a question -- "Intent to cause what consequence?" -- in order to communicate unambiguously our meaning.

It happens to be a fact of life, however, that not everybody is that careful about the use of language. So, when a legislature uses the phrase "intentional act," judges have to do their best to determine manifested meaning. Judges are not free to throw up their hands in despair. They must decide the case at hand.

Nor are judges free to capitalize on the ambiguity of the statutory phrase and decide the case the way they like, as if they had no statutory directive. Instead, they must search for manifested meaning by reading the phrase in the context of the entire statute, and perhaps even with aid from legislative history if there is anything relevant in that source.

Having done that, the Supreme Court of Louisiana, quite wisely I believe, concluded that "intentional act" in the workers compensation statute referred to an act intended (roughly speaking, and for present purposes we need not attempt to be more precise) to cause physical harm to the employee.

Also among the precedents that were part of the context for the 1987 enactment was a case interpreting the phrase "bodily injury ... which is either expected or intended from the standpoint of the Insured," as it appears in homeowners liability insurance policies. In Pique v. Saia,[7] the Louisiana court held that the policy language

---

[7] 450 So.2d 654 (La. 1984). A judge of another court who is trying to predict how the Louisiana Supreme Court will interpret the Louisiana statute enacted in 1987 may be interested in what that court said, some

ANALYSIS OF CASES 6.1 AND 6.5 — Sec. E

excluding coverage for "bodily injury ... which is either expected or intended from the standpoint of the Insured" did not preclude coverage for injury to a police officer caused by an insured who "pushed himself away from a fence" while in a scuffle with police officers who were placing him under arrest, causing the whole group to fall on a concrete driveway, which in turn caused an elbow injury to one of the

---

years after the statute was enacted, in Breland v. Schilling, 550 So.2d 609 (La. 1989) (a homeowner's policy that excludes coverage for "bodily injury or property damage which is either expected or intended from the standpoint of the Insured" covers policyholder's liability to plaintiff third baseman whom policyholder struck in the jaw, causing unusually severe fractures, after third baseman dropped, tossed, or threw softball on policyholder as he lay prone near third base, having been tagged out). The court stated:

> This clause does not by its precise terms exclude coverage for bodily injury caused by the insured's intentional act.... The phrase "bodily injury ... which is expected or intended," emphasizes that an excluded injury is one which the insured _intended_, not one which the insured _caused_, however intentional the injury-producing act. The next phrase, "from the standpoint of the Insured," emphasizes again that it is the insured's subjective intention and expectation which delimit the scope of the exclusion....
>
> . . .
>
> We hold, therefore, that when minor bodily injury is intended and such results, the injury is barred from coverage. When serious bodily injury is intended, and such results, the injury is also barred from coverage. When a severe injury of a given sort is intended, and a severe injury of any sort occurs, then coverage is also barred. But when minor injury is intended, and a substantially greater or more severe injury results, whether by chance, coincidence, accident, or whatever, coverage for the more severe injury is not barred....

Id. at 611-14 (emphasis in original). The court's holding in Breland is, I believe, consistent with the interpretation I have proposed for the statute in Case 6.1. The reader is advised, however, that passages of the opinion not quoted here include comments about the interpretation of the Restatement (Second) of Torts that are contrary to views I have expressed above, in this section.

Ch. 6   JUDGING STATUTES

police officers.

With these and other precedents as part of the body of law in existence when the 1987 Act was passed, what conclusions should judges reach as to the manifested meaning of the phrase "intentional or willful act" in paragraph A of the statute quoted in Case 6.1?

First, I submit, the evidence probably would not support a finding that either Rich or Cabbie intended to hit or harm Luce (and even more probably, if we examined the record of a case tried as we might expect such a case to have been tried, we would conclude the factfinder had not made a finding that either Rich or Cabbie intended to hit or to harm Luce). In these circumstances, neither committed an "intentional act" within the meaning of paragraph A, as I have surmised that phrase will be interpreted by a court that must construe the statute to decide a case.

Second, however, we must face an issue not directly governed by the precedents. What is the meaning of "willful act"? "Willful," like "intentional," is ordinarily used in a sense referring to a state of mind. Also, that state of mind focuses on consequences rather than on the act itself. The troublesome question is: "Willful" in relation to what consequences of the act? Is an act willful only if it is also intended to cause harm? Is "willful," connected with "intentional" by "or," simply a synonym for "intentional"? If not, does "willful" mean "intentional plus"? Or may an act be "willful" even though not "intentional"? Each of these is a possible interpretation. Is it significant that the connective is "or," not "and"? It is often questionable, in context, to place heavy weight on the choice beween "or" and "and" as a connective. In any event, in whatever way one resolves all these questions, other questions remain. For example, is it enough to prove "intent to cause harm," or, in order to prove an "intentional or willful act," must one also prove that the act was accompanied by bad motive rather than, for example, that it was an act done because the actor believed he or she was being attacked (a circumstance in which the actor is protected by the privilege of self-defense unless his or her belief was unreasonable). Or, would it be enough to prove either "intent to cause harm" alone without bad motive, or knowledge of a risk of harm (perhaps even great risk) plus bad motive? Still another reasonable argument is that one proves that an act was "willful" as that term is used in this statute by proving no more than that the actor knew when acting that the act would create a grave risk, though not a substantial certainty, of harm to another (without either "intent to cause harm" or "bad motive"). If this last suggestion among all the possible meanings is determined to be the manifested meaning of the statute, then at least Cabbie and perhaps Rich as well may be found to have done a "willful act" that was a cause of the injury to Luce.

Third, if the last of these possible meanings -- a very expansive interpretation of "willful" -- is accepted, we must consider whether the evidence will support a finding that Rich and Cabbie "conspired" with each other to do a "willful act" that caused harm to Luce. This might have seemed a more difficult hurdle a generation back than today. The context in which the 1987 Act was passed includes an extensive history of criminal law developments expanding the scope of conspiracy as one might have understood it from reading earlier cases only. Nevertheless, on this issue also, there is room for debate about manifested meaning of the statute.

Thus, we have debatable questions of the manifested meaning of at least two statutory phrases -- "conspire with another person" and "intentional or willful act" -- and it may be that on facts like those in Case 6.1 it will be determined that Rich and Luce had each "conspire[d] with another person to commit an intentional or willful act" causing "damage" to Luce. Thus paragraph A would apply and both would be liable jointly for at least $900,000. The answer as to the remaining $100,000 depends on whether the finding of 10% responsibility against Luce because of his failure to fasten the seat belt and shoulder harness has any legal effect. I return to that issue shortly,[8] after first addressing other matters.

If this expansive interpretation of "intentional or willful act" is determined not to be the manifested meaning of the statute, it seems likely that paragraph A will be held inapplicable to a case like Case 6.1. What then?

First, consider Luce's claim against Rich. One may observe that it is unlikely that anything substantially more than a judgment for Cabbie's policy limits can ever be collected against Cabbie. Assume that to be $25,000. Also, assume a judgment for $1 million is collectible against Rich.

---

[8] See the comments following Case 6.5, in this section, infra.

Paragraph B[1] manifests a meaning, does it not, that after Luce collects $25,000 against Cabbie, the most Luce can collect against Rich is $475,000, thus bringing the total to 50% of Luce's total damages?

Paragraph B[2] does not apply to reduce Luce's claim against Rich because Rich's "degree of fault" is greater than that of Luce. Nor do parts B[3] and B[4] apply to this claim.

Second, consider Cabbie's claims. Cabbie's claim against Luce fails because Luce's only negligence was in failing to fasten his seat belt and shoulder harness. That may have been a cause of some of Luce's injuries but surely was not a cause of injury to Cabbie. Cabbie's claim against Luce fails.

As to Cabbie's claim against Rich, Cabbie has been found responsible for the greater degree of fault -- Cabbie 70%, Rich 20%, with Luce's 10% being irrelevant. Thus, even if we have a form of comparative negligence statute that permits a recovery, Rich is liable for no greater percentage of the $90,000 damages than Rich's degree of fault. If we disregard Luce's 10% -- as I submit we should -- Rich is liable for two-ninths of $90,000, or $20,000. If you disagree with disregarding the 10% finding against Luce, you probably also would hold that it was incorrect for the trial court not to require that the jury make findings, if the case was tried to a jury (or for the trial court to make findings, if tried nonjury), of degrees of fault between Rich and Cabbie that would add up to 100%. Why not instead just convert to a base or denominator of 100% the two findings that add up to 90%, which is what we do in assigning 2/9 to Rich and 7/9 to Cabbie?

Third, what effect should we give to the 10% finding against Luce because of Luce's not fastening the seat belt and shoulder harness? For decades, courts have been reluctant to treat failure to fasten a seat belt as a relevant breach of duty of reasonable care. But a growing body of precedents does so.[9]

---

[9] See, e.g., Lowe v. Estate Motors Ltd., 428 Mich. 439, 410 N.W.2d 706 (1987); Insurance Co. of North America v. Pasakarnis, 451 So.2d 447 (Fla. 1984); Spier v. Barker, 35 N.Y.2d 444, 363 N.Y.S.2d 916, 323 N.E.2d 164 (1974).

ANALYSIS OF CASES 6.1 AND 6.5 — Sec. E

Another problem about allocating damages based on fault is whether this should be done on a percentage basis or instead in a different way that asks the factfinder to determine what part, if any, of the damages found would have been avoided if the plaintiff had been wearing the seat belt and harness. This set of problems is mostly uncharted terrain. If you are a federal trial judge confronted with such a problem, you must do your best to predict what the court of last resort of the state whose law you are applying will decide when issues like these are presented.

I reiterate, to emphasize the point, that regardless of how fervently we might wish that everyone would use words in a way that conforms with the most common usage in the legal system -- as an aid to clarity of communication and understanding -- that will never happen. A judge, committed to determining meaning of a passage in a statute or in a precedent as faithfully as possible to the meaning manifested in that passage, taken in its context, is not free to take the circumstances of ambiguity as an opportunity to fill the gap in communication the way the judge personally would prefer it to be filled rather than the way most likely to be compatible with the entire communication in which the gap appears.

This Louisiana statute is a classic illustration of a statute as to which there is a clear mandate for a change in the law from what it had been before, but a gap in the specification of just how far that change goes -- a gap in the specification needed to decide the case before the court. Thus, Guideline One does not apply to Case 6.1, and we must turn to the kinds of inquiries suggested in Guidelines Two, Three, and Four.

I write not lightly or in jest but quite seriously when I say that I would prefer not to try to answer these debatable issues about interpretation of the words "conspires with another" and "intentional or willful act" in this statute without first having the benefit of adversary arguments by professional advocates representing the parties in a live case or controversy -- and preferably members of the bar of the state whose statute is at issue, because they are more likely than members of the bar of another state to be familiar with all the nuances of the context for the legislation.

To make more specific and concrete my suggestions

about using Guidelines Two, Three, and Four, however, I will suggest one among the lines of inquiry that might be explored by the advocates.

I referred earlier to the clarity of this statute in one respect -- in mandating a change with respect to "joint" (or, in Louisiana, "in solido") liability. Plainly the statute manifests a mandate to reduce to some extent the scope of "joint" liability for the total harm of which the tortfeasor's act is one among two or more contributing causes.

Before this statute was enacted, the law imposed "joint and several" liability in some rather different kinds of circumstances, including, among others, the following distinct categories.

(1) Concerted action (e.g., two assailants beating and robbing the plaintiff).[10]

(2) Concurring causes, each of which alone would have been sufficient to cause the entire harm of which a plaintiff complains (e.g., two fires that come together before burning plaintiff's house).[11]

(3) Single indivisible result (e.g., two cars colliding, and one veering off to strike the pedestrian plaintiff).[12]

(4) Arguably divisible results (e.g., traffic victim is taken to hospital, where malpractice occurs during treatment).[13]

Perhaps we would all agree that the statute of Case 6.1 means to reduce (to the extent required to assure collection of no more than 50% of the total damages) one tortfeasor's "joint" liability for the allocable share of an

---

[10] Prosser & Keeton, §46.

[11] Id., §41, pp. 266-67.

[12] Id., §52, at pp. 347-48.

[13] Id., §44 at p. 309. See also id., §52 at pp. 348-53.

insolvent second tortfeasor, at least in relation to most cases like those in categories (3) and (4). We may have more unease, and difference of opinion, about whether the statute means that a reckless tortfeasor is to receive this protection when the case is of the type in categories (3) and (4), however. Also, we may have differences among us about what the statute means for cases in category (2), and about whether some cases, even in category (1), are governed by paragraph B and not by paragraph A of the statute.

To which of these categories of cases -- and to differences within a category, such as the difference between merely negligent and reckless acts -- does the argument that apparently appealed to the legislature have most compelling force -- the argument of unfairness of imposing the entire risk of financial irresponsibility of a third-party contributor upon the defendant rather than the plaintiff?

Consider another case.

Case 6.5
Toxic Waste Disposal

Tortfeasor T1 (who continues to have large assets) hires Tortfeasor T2 (who has virtually no assets) to dispose of toxic waste at a location where it seeps onto plaintiff's adjacent property, making the property virtually worthless as well as creating difficult-to-appraise risks of bodily harm to plaintiff and plaintiff's family.

How does the statute, quoted in Case 6.1, affect this case?

Here the plaintiff is the classic innocent victim, and we may doubt that the statute means that the rule of joint liability is to be different for this case from what it has been. The words "willful act" in the statute provide a stronger base for this result than the words "intentional ... act," but an argument may be advanced that a factfinder might find that at least harm to property, if not harm to person, was also within the scope of intended consequences on the ground that both defendants, acting in concert, knew that it was substantially certain that the toxic waste would seep onto adjacent property.

The argument for inclusion within the statutory objective underlying paragraph A certainly has more force in relation to conduct like that of T1 and T2 in Case 6.5 than to conduct like that of Rich and Cabbie in Case 6.2. Where is the line to be drawn? The statute does not provide a clear answer. It has a gap in this respect. Courts must supply the answer.

For another perspective, I ask you, in considering the scope of liability of each among co-actors in cases like that of Rich, Cabbie, and Luce, and like that of toxic waste disposers (T1 and T2), to think also of the risk of financial irresponsibility of Cabbie and T2 as a peril, along with perils of physical harm to person and property. In relation to that peril -- that risk of nonphysical economic "damage" -- did Rich "conspire" with "Cabbie" to commit "an intentional or willful act"?

To stimulate your thoughts on that subject, I call attention to a passage that may seem familiar. Before I quote it, let me add that it was written by an author who used the phrase "voluntary act," but explained it as choice in relation only to the act and emphasized that even choosing to engage in a coordinated series of acts or conduct is not the equivalent of intending all the evil consequences that may flow from that series of acts. Here is the passage.

> It is not, however, without significance, that certain wrongs are described in language importing intent. The harm in such cases is most frequently done intentionally, and, if intent to cause a certain harm is shown, there is no need to prove knowledge of facts which made it likely that harm would follow. Moreover, it is often much easier to prove intent directly, than to prove the knowledge which would make it unnecessary.
>
> The cases in which a man is treated as the responsible cause of a given harm, on the one hand, extend beyond those in which his conduct was chosen in actual contemplation of that result, and in which, therefore, he may be said to have chosen to cause that harm; and, on the other hand, they do not extend to all instances where the damages would not have happened but for some remote election on his part. Generally speaking, the choice will be

found to have extended further than a simple act, and to have co-ordinated acts into conduct. Very commonly it will have extended further still, to some external consequence. But generally, also, it will be found to have stopped short of the consequence complained of.

The question in each case is whether the actual choice, or, in other words, the actually contemplated result, was near enough to the remoter result complained of to throw the peril of it upon the actor.

The speaker-author: Oliver Wendell Holmes, Jr., in The Common Law, Lecture IV, "Fraud, Malice, and Intent -- the Theory of Torts."[14]

Did Holmes use the phrase "intent to cause a certain harm" as meaning "purpose to cause a certain harm"? Did he use "prove intent directly" to mean "prove intent by showing purpose"? Did he use "prove the knowledge that would make it unnecessary" to prove intent directly to mean that the factfinder may (or must?) infer purpose to cause a certain harm when knowledge that the harm will be caused by the act is proved?

The second paragraph of the quoted passage makes the point that legal tests of accountability (that is, tests that determine whether one "is treated as the [legally] responsible cause of a given harm") extend liability beyond "those [cases] in which his conduct was chosen in actual contemplation of that result, and in which, therefore, he may be said [in fact, and not merely by legal fiction] to have chosen to cause that harm...." Also, it makes the point that in human experience an actor's

> choice will be found [in fact] to have extended further than [choosing] a simple act, and to have [extended to making a choice focusing upon] co-ordinat[ing] acts into conduct. Very commonly [the choice] will have extended further still, to some external consequence.

---

[14]At pp. 152, 159 (1881 ed.).

Do you agree that this restatement of Holmes' position, with the bracketed phrases inserted, is consistent with the manifested meaning of this passage extracted from his seminal lectures preserved for us in The Common Law?

The final point of the quoted paragraph is that even when the test for determining legal responsibility depends on a choice that extends to contemplation of "some external consequence," however, generally the actor's contemplation of consequences "will be found [in part] to have stopped short of the consequence complained of." Stated another way, the point is, as I interpret it, that even when legal accountability of an actor is based on the actor's choice in relationship to consequences of the action, the scope of liability extends beyond the consequences in contemplation at the time of the choice.

Bringing these ideas to bear upon Case 6.5, one may reasonably argue that "willful act" as that term is used in the statute is reasonably interpreted as having a meaning that embraces the "choice" of T1 to engage T2 to dispose of toxic waste, if the factfinder finds that T1 had in contemplation, at the least, that T2 would deposit the waste where it would be likely to cause harm to the property of others and that the owners of the harmed property would have only a worthless cause of action against T2 because of T2's financial irresponsibility.

In relation to Case 6.5 as well as Case 6.1, the statute of the hypothetical state (along with Louisiana's Act of 1987) has given us a mandate to move somewhat a bright line drawn through an area shading from one extreme to another -- a bright line separating (a) those cases in which the peril of financial irresponsibility of a co-actor is thrown upon an actor who, along with the co-actor, contributed to harm, from (b) those cases in which this peril of financial irresponsibility is thrown upon the victim. But the statute has left it to the courts to determine whether particular cases like those discussed here fall on one or the other side of the new location of this bright line. Explaining this point another way, we may say that the common law said there shall be a bright line, the statute says the bright line shall be moved from the point where the common law placed it, and guided by the legislatively manifested objectives regarding where the bright line is to be relocated, the courts will determine exactly where to place it, doing so with the benefits of the common law method of case-by-case adjudication after adversary presentations by

F. A Proposed Analysis of Case 6.2

Before the statute quoted in Case 6.1 came into effect, it appeared that a settlement like that of Cabbie with Luce would have discharged Cabbie's allocated percentage of the damages -- that is 70% of $1 million, or $700,000. This conclusion is facially supported by Judge Rubin's very lucid opinion in Diggs v. Hood.[1] In that case the court's manifestation of its meaning about all the issues before the court is admirably clear.

Thus Luce, in settling with Cabbie for $25,000, "settled his claim against [Cabbie] for less than it was worth,"[2] and cannot successfully complain about the fact that he now recovers only $200,000 rather than $500,000 against Rich.

One may wonder, however, whether the quotation I just used from Judge Rubin's opinion is fairly and correctly used when used in the way I just used it. Judge Rubin and the panel members with whom he sat apparently had before them thoroughly solvent tortfeasors, with neither of whom a plaintiff would be expected to have considered settling for $25,000 a good claim (as plaintiff assessed it) involving potential damages of $1 million or more. It was in that context that they spoke of a settlement of a claim for "less than it was worth." When, instead, a claim against Cabbie is in practical terms worth only $25,000 rather than $700,000 simply because no judgment above $25,000 can be collected, will the same rule apply? That seems to me to be a debatable issue of manifested meaning of the statute and the precedent.

One added point is that if this debatable issue is resolved in a way that reduces Luce's claim against Rich from $500,000 to $200,000, Luce may have a reasonably promising legal malpractice claim, for the $300,000 difference, against any attorney who represented Luce in that matter and failed to call attention to the risk of this very adverse consequence of the settlement with Cabbie.

---

[1] 772 F.2d 190 (5th Cir. 1985).

[2] 772 F.2d at 196.

G. Suggestions About How to Search for Manifested Meaning

The suggestions that follow may seem familiar. They simply apply in the present context ideas that have been developed in other parts of this book.

One. Try to formulate the question at issue neutrally.

Two. Be candid. Avoid legal fiction. Legal fictions may on occasion be useful. Always they carry risks of misunderstanding, both by the user and by the reader. Usually these risks far outweigh any benefits from use of legal fictions. These risks are especially severe when the fiction of a "legislature's intent" is used.

Three. Make your analysis by substance, not by labels.

Four. Be cautious about using "deductive" reasoning only. Always consider whether you should be using "informative" reasoning as well. When the circumstances call for applying Guideline One, deductive reasoning may be the judge's duty and only option. But when the circumstances call for using Guidelines Two, Three, and Four, informative reasoning is in order.

Five. Be cautious, also, about "informative reasoning." When using informative reasoning, think about the nature of the decision points you are creating for counselors, trial lawyers, and trial judges to use in their work. Be cautious about creating a multitude of decision points. Be especially cautious about adopting legal tests that require of trial lawyers and trial judges the application of an "evaluative standard" that depends on "weighing" many "factors."[1]

Six. Be respectful of the lawmakers who have preceded us in the particular vineyard in which we are working. Resist all temptations to pay the ultimate disrespect to the legislature and governor of presuming that they implicitly (having not done so explicitly) answered the question at issue in a way that creates distinctions that no member of the court can find any way to defend in reason and policy. Done in the name of respect, that is the ultimate disrespect

---

[1] *See also* Chapter 3, Sections A2 and C3, and Chapter 5, Section C, *supra*.

of presuming they acted "irrationally."[2]

H. Transitory Premises and Outmoded Statutes

Times change. A rule of law good for one time and set of circumstances may be quite out of place at another time, in changed circumstances. It has long been part of the common law tradiiton that when the factual premises of a judge-made rule of law no longer exist, the rule loses its force. When a legal rule becomes outmoded in light of scientific, social, or economic developments, a court is free to declare that legal rule no longer in effect.[1] Debates have arisen over how we should describe the exercise of this judicial power? Is the court "overruling" precedent? Or is it merely declaring the precedent no longer applicable in present circumstances? In any event, whatever one's preference may be as to how to describe this kind of judicial action, the legitimacy of the exercise of this power is now quite generally acknowledged with respect to allegedly outmoded judge-made law.

What is the scope of a court's legitimate power with respect to allegedly outmoded statutes? Who has authority to declare that the factual premises of a statutory rule of law no longer exist and that the statute has become outmoded?

Certainly a legislature may do so. First, it may do so by enacting another statute. Second, it may do so prospectively, either at the time of original enactment or

---

[2]Expressed another way the point is this: Distinguish between fictional or formal respect and respect in fact. By fictional respect I mean that form of respect in which we attribute to legislators (or judges who decided a precedent) answers to questions that, on candid analysis, we are more likely to conclude they did not consider at all, or if they did, did not try to answer. If we formally declare respect by assuming answers that we cannot think of any way to defend <u>rationally</u>, that is in fact rather disrespectful. It is assuming they gave an indefensible answer -- or at least one we cannot think of any way of defending.

For additional comments on what we mean by "rationally," <u>see</u> Chapter 1, Section 2D, <u>supra</u>.

[1]<u>See</u> Chapter 2, Section D2, <u>supra</u>.

by a later amendment, through a "sunset" provision (one that says the statute ceases to be effective on a specified date, unless the legislature acts again before that date).

If the legislature does not explicitly provide for termination of the effect of a statute, may a court at some later time declare that a statutory mandate is no longer effective? Or, as Professor Dworkin suggests, may a court declare that the statute has "since become" one with less effect, or different effect?[2] If a court may properly say at some time that a statute is somewhat outmoded and now has less effect, why may it not also at some later time declare the statute totally outmoded and of no effect? Is it only the legislature that has authority to declare a statute outmoded, partially or totally, by amending or repealing it, or by enacting a sunset provision, either initially or at some later time? Or do courts as well have some authority to determine that factual premises of statutory lawmaking are no longer valid? May a court, for example, apply its doctrine of "scrutiny" of the "rational basis" for a statute as of the date of the court's decision rather than as of the date of the enactment? When the legislature has not enacted a bright-line test for "sunset" or for "repeal," is legislation nevertheless subject to an implicit test for termination that is evaluative rather than bright-line in nature? The imagery of "sunset" may be even more apt for such an evaluative test than for a bright-line test that fixes a chronological moment for termination. May legislation have an inherent sunset because some essential factual premise is as surely transitory as the colors of a memorable sunset?

It might be argued, for example, that a court should declare that an ordinance prohibiting the sounding of an automobile horn near a horse and buggy is no longer legally enforceable -- because an essential factual premise for enactment of the ordinance no longer exists. The crisis -- or, less stridently described, the need -- that prompted its enactment no longer exists. Some legal systems recognize a doctrine of desuetude as at least a partial answer to this problem. Desuetude is, however, a doctrine of questionable

---

[2] R. Dworkin, Law's Empire, 348-50 (1986) (imaginary judge of superhuman intellect "does not amend out-of-date statutes" but "recognizes what the old statutes have since become").

applicability in American law.[3]

Professor (now Dean) Guido Calabresi has urged that courts should develop some better method than is now generally recognized as appropriate judicial method to deal with growing numbers of outmoded statutes.[4] Along with Judge Frank Coffin,[5] I have some concern about some of the details of Dean Calabresi's proposal on grounds of incompatibility with the judge's obligation to perform within the constraints of the judge's role as representative of the community's interest in enforcement of the community's law -- not the judge's own personal preference. Nevertheless, I believe, as I understand Judge Coffin does, Dean Calabresi's more general point is valid -- that, while maintaining fidelity to role, courts could and should do more than has thus far been done in developing principled methods of legal protection against enforcement of outmoded statutes. Moreover -- and quite consistently with Dean Calabresi's thesis as I understand it -- one may view the problem of outmoded statutes as fundamentally associated with the more pervasive phenomenon of transitory premises of lawmaking, whether the lawmaking is that of the legislative and executive branches or instead that of the third branch.

Developing principled methods for dealing with transitory premises of lawmaking would be better, for example, than depending on the discretion of prosecutors not to initiate criminal proceedings to enforce horse-and-buggy ordinances. Also, it would be better than using the less-than-candid method that Professsor Gilmore has called "misconstruing" the statutory text to accomplish needed change. Professor Gilmore observed that in the earlier part of this century (during the period of extreme reluctance of judges to acknowledge their lawmaking power), judges were more likely either (a) to use the always-available "technique of statutory misconstruction," or (b) to use a "new technique ... of 'constitutionalizing' the issues," than to assert a judicial power "to nullify statutes on other than

---

[3] See United States v. Elliott, 266 F. Supp. 318, 325-26 (S.D.N.Y. 1967) (comparing civil and common-law traditions and holding that nonuse alone does not abrogate statute).

[4] C. Calabresi, A Common Law for the Age of Statutes, 81-181 (1982).

[5] Book Review, 91 Yale L. J. 827, 841 (1982) (reviewing G. Calabresi, A Common Law for the Age of Statutes).

constitutional grounds."[6]

Of course, deliberately misconstruing a statute is a violation of the judge's professional commitment. If there is good reason, within the bounds of professional commitment, to disregard a statute because its enactment plainly depended on premises that have become outmoded, the values of candor support open acknowledgement of that fact as the reasoned explanation of the decision.

Focusing directly on the transitory nature of premises of statutes, another thoughtful commentator, addressing this problem in the context of a constitutional challenge to a legislature's fixing rates, asserted:

> The reasonableness of legislation, not that of legislators, is and ought to be the constitutional issue. The reasonableness of the means chosen by the legislature to effectuate a legitimate end may depend not only upon legislative facts that were brought to the legislature's attention at the time it acted but also upon legislative facts in existence at that time that were not brought to its attention and legislative facts that came into existence afterwards because of changed conditions. Legislative facts assumed by the legislature to be true may also be shown to be false. So long as the notion of substantive due process is not entirely abandoned, those challenging legislative action should be able to adduce any legislative facts that support their claim or dispute the validity of the legislative facts relied upon by the legislature. This position could help to validate, as well as invalidate, legislation.[7]

---

[6] Gilmore, Putting Senator Davies in Context, 4 Vt. L. Rev. 233, 239-40 (1979). See also Davies, A Response to Statutory Obsolescence: The Nonprimacy of Statutes Act, 4 Vt. L. Rev. 203 (1979); Calabresi, The Nonprimacy of Statutes Act: A Comment, 4 Vt. L. Rev. 247 (1979).

[7] Auerbach, The Anatomy of an Unusual Economic Substantive Due Process Case: Workers' Compensation Insurers Rating Association v. State, 68 Minn. L. Rev. 545, 585 (1984).

In support of his position, he called attention to Justice Holmes' opinion for the Court in <u>Chastleton Corp.</u> v. <u>Sinclair</u>.[8] Rent control in the District of Columbia was attacked as violating the Due Process Clause of the Fifth Amendment on the ground that the war-created emergency that justified rent control in 1919 had ended by 1922, despite a congressional declaration to the contrary. The opinion declares:

> We repeat what was stated in <u>Block v. Hirsh</u>, 256 U.S. 135, 154, as to the respect due to a declaration of this kind by the legislature so far as it relates to present facts. But even as to them a Court is not at liberty to shut its eyes to an obvious mistake, when the validity of the law depends upon the truth of what is declared.... And still more obviously so far as this declaration looks to the future it can be no more than prophecy and is liable to be controlled by events. A law depending upon the existence of an emergency or other certain state of facts to uphold it may cease to operate if the emergency ceases or the facts change even though valid when passed.[9]

In that case, Justice Holmes' opinion refers to "facts that we judicially know" as compelling the Court "to say that <u>the law has ceased to operate</u>."[10] Would he not use that same expression to make the point that a judicial precedent "has ceased to operate" when an essential premise fact on which it was based is no longer true? Even if "judicial notice" were understood to be limited to facts not reasonably disputable -- a suggestion that is subject to challenge[11] -- the Court has not so limited challenges to the legislative-fact premises on which a statute is said to survive "rational basis" scrutiny. For example, Professor

---

[8] 264 U.S. 543 (1924).

[9] <u>Id.</u> at 547-48.

[10] <u>Id.</u> at 549 (emphasis added). Consider why Justice Holmes used the italicized phrase rather than saying "the statute now has no rational basis."

[11] <u>See</u> Chapter 2, Section C, <u>supra</u>, and <u>Premise Facts</u>, 73 Minn. L. Rev. at 29-31.

Auerbach[12] calls attention to the fact that in <u>Carolene Products</u> the Court stated:

> [A] statute would deny due process which precluded the disproof in judicial proceedings of all facts which would show or tend to show that a statute depriving the suitor of life, liberty or property had a rational basis.
>
> . . . .
>
> Where the existence of a rational basis for legislation whose constitutionality is attacked depends upon facts beyond the sphere of judicial notice, such facts may properly be made the subject of judicial inquiry, <u>Borden's Farm Products Co. v. Baldwin</u>, 293 U.S. 194, and the constitutionality of a statute predicated upon the existence of a particular state of facts may be challenged by showing to the court that those facts have ceased to exist. <u>Chastleton Corporation v. Sinclair</u>, 264 U.S. 543.[13]

The relationship between transitory premises of statutes and durability of the statutory mandates is one deserving further exploration, and especially so in view of the increasing extent to which deciding cases involves judging statutes, because of the regular volume of legislation enacted each year.

---

[12] 68 Minn. L. Rev. at 588-89.

[13] <u>United States</u> v. <u>Carolene Products Co.</u>, 304 U.S. 144, 152-53 (1938). Professor Auerbach calls attention also to <u>Kassel</u> v. <u>Consolidated Freightways Corp.</u>, 450 U.S. 662 (1981), as a more recent instance in which the Court "agreed that evidence bearing on the constitutional issue could be introduced at a trial and would not be restricted to evidence before the legislature at the time it enacted the challenged legislation." 68 Minn. L. Rev. at 589.

PART THREE

CASE DEVELOPMENT AND DISPOSITION

CHAPTER 7

JUDGING IN PRETRIAL PROCEEDINGS

A. Judging Under Rules of Procedure

   1. Objectives of Rules of Procedure

The central objective of rules of procedure in the judicial system is stated crisply in Rule 1 of the Federal Rules of Civil Procedure: "[These rules] shall be construed to secure the just, speedy, and inexpensive determination of every action."[1]

Rules of procedure should facilitate disposition on the merits. They should help us reach, promptly and inexpensively, dispositions that are just in the sense that disputes of law and disputes of fact are resolved as fairly as possible, given the realities that decisions of both law and fact must be made by human actors, with all their strengths and failings.[2]

---

[1] Fed. R. Civ. P. 1.

[2] For a more extended statement of implications of this objective, see Keeton, The Function of Local Rules and the Tension with Uniformity, 50 U. Pitt. L. Rev. 853 (1989) (hereinafter cited as The Function of

Another way of expressing that part of the aim concerned with resolving disputes of law is to say rules of procedure should facilitate fair resolution of disputes over the substantive law to be applied in the case. They should help us reach decisions that are reasoned from premises that are declared by substantive law to be legitimate premises.[3]

2. Questions Not Answered by Rules

Rules of procedure share with statutes, contracts, and other forms of writings the characteristic of incompleteness.[4] Even though court-sponsored national and state rules are ordinarily drafted with the greatest of care by distinguished committees and with exceptionally able staff support, still they fail -- as every document does -- to supply answers to all the questions that arise as they are applied.

An illustration is the uncertain meaning of the provisions of Rule 16 bearing upon settlement initiatives of trial judges. The text of the relevant part of Rule 16 is reproduced in the margin.[5] What does Rule 16 say and mean,

---

Local Rules).

[3] Concerning the obligation of "reasoned" decisionmaking more generally, see Chapter 1, Sections A and D, supra.

[4] Concerning this characteristic of incompleteness generally, see Chapter 1, Section B3, and Chapter 6, Section C, supra.

[5] Rule 16. Pretrial Conferences; Scheduling; Management

> (a) Pretrial Conferences; Objectives. In any action, the court may in its discretion direct the attorneys for the parties and any unrepresented parties to appear before it for a conference or conferences before trial for such purposes as
>   (1) expediting the disposition of the action;
>   (2) establishing early and continuing control so that the case will not be protracted because of lack of management;
>   (3) discouraging wasteful pretrial activities;

about

> whether a trial judge (or magistrate) should, should not, or may at the judge's (or magistrate's) discretion, enter either 1) an order that the parties participate in a nonbinding summary jury trial, or 2) an order that the chief executives of the plaintiff

---

>> (4) improving the quality of the trial through more thorough preparation, and;[sic]
>> (5) facilitating the settlement of
> the case.
> . . . .
>
> (c) Subjects to be Discussed at Pretrial Conferences. The participants at any conference under this rule may consider and take action with respect to . . .
>
>> (7) the possibility of settlement or the use of extrajudicial procedures to resolve the dispute;
> . . . .
>
> At least one of the attorneys for each party participating in any conference before trial shall have authority to enter into stipulations and to make admissions regarding all matters that the participants may reasonably anticipate may be discussed.
> . . . .
>
> (f) Sanctions. If a party or party's attorney fails to obey a scheduling or pretrial order, or if no appearance is made on behalf of a party at a scheduling or pretrial conference, or if a party or party's attorney is substantially unprepared to participate in the conference, or if a party or party's attorney fails to participate in good faith, the judge, upon motion or the judge's own initiative, may make such orders with regard thereto as are just, and among others any of the orders provided in Rule 37(b)(2)(B), (C), (D). In lieu of or in addition to any other sanction, the judge shall require the party or the attorney representing the party or both to pay the reasonable expenses incurred because of any noncompliance with this rule, including attorney's fees, unless the judge finds that the noncompliance was substantially justified or that other circumstances make an award of expenses unjust.

corporation and the defendant corporation attend a Rule 16(b) scheduling conference (or some other pretrial conference), along with their lawyers, a) to discuss settlement and b) if no settlement is reached at the conference, to consider a stipulation for a "summary jury trial" or a "conditional summary trial," or some other alternative to traditional jury or nonjury trial, under the judge's supervision?[6]

Do you think the Rule either answers these questions explicitly, or gives you adequate guidance to predict the answers courts will give?

Plainly Rule 16 as initially drafted did not address these questions. The 1983 amendments strongly encouraged judicial intervention to promote settlement. They were enabling in the sense of legitimizing such efforts, even if less than explicit about details. In the 1930s, the minds of drafters were focused on more fundamental reforms. They were not thinking about settlement strategies and methods of alternative dispute resolution. In the 1970s and 1980s, these matters were on the minds of most drafters and critics. Even so, drafters did not provide answers to all the questions we might ask.[7]

The questions not answered by the rules must be answered by a court when the answers are essential to determination of some dispute before the court. The guidelines a court may appropriately use in determining the answers are essentially like those discussed in Chapter 6, Judging Statutes.

B. Rule and Discretion in Trial Procedure

Rules constrain discretion. Rules of practice and procedure -- national, state, and local -- are intrusions on the exercise of discretion by the trial judge in the

---

[6] The Function of Local Rules, 50 U. Pitt. L. Rev. 856-57 (footnotes omitted).

[7] For proposed answers to some of the questions Rule 16 leaves unanswered, see Chapter 8, Section A, infra.

individual case.[1] Every rule that prohibits or compels something limits the exercise of discretion to some extent. Of course, any rule of law, substantive or procedural, has this characteristic. Thus, a lawmaker who is fashioning a rule of procedure appropriately considers whether it is better to force all proceedings into one mold (for example, to require that a trial judge hold a settlement conference for every case within 120 days after it is filed) or instead to leave flexibility for the trial judge in the individual case to tailor proceedings to the distinctive circumstances of that case.[2]

The tension between rule and discretion illustrated in rules of civil procedure is less dramatic and significant than, for example, clashes over rule and discretion in criminal sentencing. Even so, the tension is relevant to procedural rulemaking.

Controversy over Rule 16 illustrates the point. Rule 16 was amended in 1983 with the explicit purpose of limiting discretion of district judges by directing that they intervene actively and early in managing discovery and trial preparation.[3] Rule 16 requires the judge to take time for a scheduling conference in every case, unless a local rule excepts cases of its category. Thus, the rule overrides a judge's belief from experience in the district in which the judge sits that the overall objective of Rule 1 -- just, speedy, and inexpensive determination of all the cases -- will be better advanced by being more selective about

---

[1] The term "rule" as ordinarily used when one speaks of a clash between "rule" and "discretion" means a kind of legal proposition, either substantive or procedural, that gives relatively firm and unqualified guidance as distinguished from a kind of proposition, such as a "standard" (see Chapter 3, Section A2, supra), which gives more leeway for a discretionary choice by the decisionmaker who is applying the legal proposition in a particular case. Thus, this meaning of "rule" is not identical with that of the term "rule" in the phrase "rule of procedure." For example, a "rule of procedure" may grant broad discretion to the decisionmaker. I use the term "rule" in both senses in this section, in conformity with both these common usages. I hope, however, that I have been sensitive enough to this possible ambiguity that the context of each use will make the intended meaning clear.

[2] See The Function of Local Rules, 50 U. Pitt. L. Rev. at 864-74.

[3] Id. at 865.

intervention.

C. Incentive Structures and Professional Conduct

The real incentive structure that rules tend to create in current circumstances may be an incentive structure not intended by drafters.

One significant reason this is so is that premises for the drafting of rules, like premises of other forms of lawmaking, are often transitory.[1] To understand both the drafters' apparent purposes in drafting the Federal Rules of Civil Procedure and the incentive structure actually created by rules as they will function in the 1990s and thereafter, we need to think about some characteristics of the profession and the courts in the 1930s and the 1990s.

Respect for authority, both in the courtroom and elsewhere, was more pronounced and more pervasive in the 1930s than it is in the 1990s. Also, we may infer that in the 1930s drafters of rules of procedure believed that clearly prescribing a mandate for discovery upon demand would accomplish the desired change. They counted on lawyers, as officers of the court, to respect the formal mandate and in general to cooperate in making it effective.

To an extent their expectations were justified. They predicted that more discovery would lead to more and better settlements, and to trials with fewer surprises. And so it did, to a degree.

Tradition was strong, however, and lawyers only slowly came to a practice of making discovery demands of the scope and sweep authorized by the new rules. Nevertheless, discovery demands did increase as the bar became accustomed to practice under the new rules. Unfortunately, resistance grew as well. More and more time of lawyers, judges, and magistrates was spent on discovery disputes.

The incentive structure actually in operation in the 1990s is affected, of course, by other practical forces as well as the terms of the rules themselves. Among those forces are the perceived attitudes of judges and magistrates

---

[1] See Chapter 2, Section D2, and Chapter 6, Section H, supra.

about discovery disputes. Why make concessions to a contentious opposing counsel, for the purpose of settling a discovery dispute without a hearing, if you believe a judge or magistrate is ready and willing to take the time to hear you whenever a dispute arises, and perhaps will even welcome the opportunity for a hearing that keeps the judge or magistrate in touch with the case and counsel? If two opposing lawyers both believe the judge or magistrate will be willing -- even eager -- to hear them, neither is likely to make concessions to resolve the dispute before hearing. Each lawyer prefers, during all the communications between them before they see the judge or magistrate, to hold out not only on everything that really matters but also on a few other things as to which concessions can be graciously made at the hearing.

Even if the lawyers come to realize that judges and magistrates with growing backlogs of cases are less patient than before, the incentive structure not to make concessions before hearing may remain intact. One reason is that an expectation grows that impatient judges and magistrates, rather than hearing them fully, will take the shortcut of slicing somewhere in the middle -- somewhere between the parties' rather extreme positions. Taking the time to understand the controversy better is a commitment of a scarce resource -- hearing time -- that the judge or magistrate may be reluctant to make. If lawyers expect judges and magistrates to take quickly some middleground position, then lawyers feel a pressure to preserve their extreme positions in order not to move the middleground over to the advantage of the adversary.

When lawyers tend to behave in ways that are responsive to this incentive structure, should judges and magistrates try to control the resulting contentiousness by invoking rules of professional conduct -- reminding the lawyers that they are officers of the court, and invoking sanctions if mere reminders are ineffective? Two practical considerations, among others, weigh heavily against doing so. First, anything that is in the nature of disciplining counsel is likely to be seen by the judge as one of the most onerous and unpleasant responsibilities of judging -- only a little less onerous than the responsibility of making sentencing decisions in criminal cases. Second, holding the hearings essential to fair and reasoned decisionmaking on sanctions is very time consuming. Given backlogs and time pressures under which most judges function, the judge is likely to be concerned that other cases will suffer still more delays if any substantial part of the judge's time is committed to imposing sanctions on counsel for unduly contentious behavior in discovery disputes.

Given these practical considerations, trial judges are likely to feel the need to search for alternatives to the incentive structure of the formal rules -- to search for better ways of managing pretrial proceedings than merely invoking the formal rules and holding hearings as numerous and as lengthy as may be necessary to resolve all discovery disputes.

D. Discretionary Judicial Management of Pretrial Proceedings

A trial judge may change the incentive structure described in the preceding section by, first, openly declaring that during pretrial proceedings he or she expects lawyers to proceed with discovery and trial preparation responsibly and without judicial intervention and, second, giving notice of intent to invoke a sanction designed to create incentives to cooperate.[1] Probably the sanction that is most effective for changing the incentive structure in this way is nonmonetary in form. It is the sanction of adopting as a judicial order the position of the attorney whose posture just before hearing is less unreasonable than the opponent's. That is, the judge hears the controversy only long enough to determine which side has been more unreasonable up to the point that the hearing commenced, and adopts the other side's position as the court's order resolving the discovery dispute.

Both to promote fairness and to achieve the desired change of incentive structure, a judge may announce the intent to impose this sanction (unless very compelling circumstances require a different order) in the Rule 16 scheduling conference, or at the first hint of contentiousness over discovery. The draft order presented in Form 7.A, immediately below, illustrates a way in which this kind of court intervention may occur in that minority of cases on a trial judge's docket in which counterproductive contentiousness develops between opposing counsel.

---

[1] See _The Function of Local Rules_, 50 U. Pitt. L. Rev. 868-69.

Form 7.A
Memorandum and Order Regarding Discovery

Discovery disputes have arisen in this case. On the basis of an examination of matters on file, the court is concerned that this may be an instance in which counsel on both sides are taking positions that do not comply with either the letter or the spirit of the Federal Rules of Civil Procedure. An excessive discovery demand, knowingly made, violates Rule 11 and Rule 26(g). An inadequate response, knowingly made, violates Rule 11, Rules 26(g), and other rules as well. For example:

(a) Fed. R. Civ. P. 33(a) requires that a party "furnish such information as is available to the party." That you may have an objection to interrogatories as excessively burdensome is not an excuse for your responding with nothing but objections or a motion for a protective order. You must forthwith furnish such information responsive to the interrogatories as is available through reasonable efforts. Failure to do so in this court is regarded as sufficient ground for imposition of sanctions.

(b) Fed. R. Civ. P. 34(b) provides that "[i]f objection is made to part of an item or category, the part shall be specified." It is implicit, if not explicit, that production or allowance of inspection "will be permitted as requested" except as to the part or parts to which stated objections apply. Thus, the fact that a demand for production is objectionable in part is not an excuse for producing nothing. Failure to produce documents or parts of documents to which no objection applies is in this court regarded as sufficient ground for imposition of sanctions.

(c) Fed. R. Civ. P. 36(a) provides that "when good faith requires that a party ... deny only a part of the matter of which an admission is requested, the party shall specify so much of it as is true and qualify or deny the remainder." Thus, an objection that goes only to some part or parts of requests for admission is not an excuse for failure to respond to all other parts to which the ground of objection is not applicable. Failure to respond with such admissions is in this court regarded as sufficient ground for imposition of sanctions.

(d) Fed. R. Civ. P. 26(g) provides that a party's attorney must sign each discovery request, response, or objection. The signature constitutes a certification that to the best of the attorney's knowledge, information, and belief formed after a reasonable inquiry, the discovery request, response, or objection is: "(1) consistent with these rules and warranted by existing law or a good faith argument for the extension, modification, or reversal of existing law; (2) not interposed for any improper purpose, such as to harass or to cause unnecessary delay or needless increase in the cost of litigation; and (3) not unreasonable or unduly burdensome or expensive ...." Certification in violation of Rule 26(g) is sufficient ground for imposition of sanctions.

The court will not serve, or acquiesce in a magistrate's serving, as a mediator for settlement of disputes over discovery in which each party takes unreasonable positions with the purpose of conceding what is plainly due under the rules only when before the court or magistrate. If counsel make excessive demands or insufficient responses after this cautionary order by the court, an order may be entered providing for more stringent controls over discovery, including the following:

(1) Having determined that both sides have been unreasonable, the court may impose an appropriate sanction, pursuant to Fed. R. Civ. P. 26(g) and 37. An appropriate sanction in this case may include an order in which the court declines to undertake the burdensome task of working out some compromise position that is a reasonable accommodation within the

range counsel should have agreed upon; the court may instead determine only which side has been more unreasonable and, as a sanction for misconduct, enter an order that discovery proceed in accordance with the other side's position.

(2) The court may award attorney fees against a party, or against counsel.

(3) The court may order that no client be charged for any of the time of counsel on either side spent on the discovery dispute in which counsel on both sides were taking unreasonable positions.

ORDER

For the foregoing reasons, it is ORDERED:

The parties are allowed 30 days from this date to resolve all outstanding discovery disputes or modify their respective positions to come into compliance with the Federal Rules of Civil Procedure, including Rule 11, Rule 26(g), and other rules relating to discovery. A hearing is scheduled for _____ _____ at _____m., to be held only if the parties have not succeeded in resolving all discovery disputes.

United States District Judge

I interpret the applicable rules as permitting this sanction. It is a sanction properly tailored to the need. In appropriate cases, a court may add attorney fees to this nonmonetary sanction. An award of attorney fees alone, however, does not give the parties anything close to the same strength of incentive as this kind of sanction does to be at least a little less unreasonable than the other side in the position maintained just before the hearing commences. As the parties modify their positions, each attempting to achieve the objective of being less unreasonable than the other, the distance between their originally extreme positions narrows. They may even decide it is better to settle the dispute than to take the final difference to the court for a ruling.

Ch. 7   JUDGING IN PRETRIAL PROCEEDINGS

E. **Judicial Intervention to Promote Disposition Without Trial**

Trial judges often participte in settlement negotiations. They may also encourage the parties to consider some alternative form of trial -- a possibility discussed in Chapter 8. In addition they may encourage parties to consider some form of "alternative dispute resolution" either outside the court or under court auspices. Two illustrations are presented here, in Forms 7.B and 7.C.

Form 7.B
Stipulation and Order
for
Summary Jury Trial
_____, 19__

I. <u>Statement of Aim</u>

The aim of this Stipulation and Order is to facilitate settlement of this controversy before trial and at reduced cost to the parties and the court in both time and other resources.

II. <u>Stipulations</u>

1. A Summary Jury Trial (SJT) will be held on _____, 19__, commencing at ____ a.m.

2. Unless excused by order of court, each party (or a representative having full settlement authority) shall attend the SJT, and may but is not required to attend the jury selection at ____ a.m.

[3. Do the parties wish to make other stipulations?]

III. <u>Order Regulating Summary Jury Trial</u>

1. The parties may, by stipulation, elect to have a Master (compensated by the parties) or a Magistrate, preside over the SJT. Absent such a stipulation, the judge before whom the case is pending will preside over the trial.

2. For a two-party case, ten jurors will be called. If none or only one is disqualified for cause after brief voir dire, each party will be allowed two peremptory challenges. Otherwise, each party will be allowed one peremptory challenge. The jury will consist of not less than five and not more than six persons. (If a case involves more parties, and additional peremptories are warranted, additional jurors will be called).

3. Unless excused by order of court, no later than three court days before the SJT counsel shall submit (jointly if they can agree, otherwise separately) proposed verdict form(s) and instructions to the jury (not more than 800 words, unless for good cause shown the court has authorized longer instructions). Counsel may obtain from the clerk copies of illustrative verdict form(s) and instructions prepared for use in other cases.

4(a). Before trial, counsel shall pre-mark all exhibits that are to be offered and advise each other in detail of any objections to admissibility of any of the proposed exhibits. All proposed exhibits to which no objections are made will be received at once immediately after the jury is selected and may be used or referred to at any time during the SJT.

(b). Except as provided in (c), all evidence and arguments shall be presented through the attorneys for the parties. The attorneys may summarize and comment on the evidence and may summarize or quote directly from depositions, interrogatories, requests for admissions, documentary evidence and sworn statements of potential witnesses. However, no witness' testimony may be referred to unless the reference is based upon one of the products of the various discovery procedures, or upon a written, sworn statement of the witness, or upon sworn affidavit of counsel that the witness would be called at trial and will not sign an affidavit, and that counsel has been told the substance of the witness' proposed testimony by the witness.

(c). By written notice to opposing counsel delivered at least two weeks before the SJT is held, a party may elect to use a portion of that party's allotted time in direct or cross-examination of one or more witnesses. The notice must identify the witness or witnesses who will be examined and must disclose, with reasonable specificity, the subject matter and expected length of the examination of each witness. When such an election has been made by one party, the period within which an opposing party may make a similar election closes either two weeks before trial or one week after the initial notice was delivered, whichever is later.

5. Plaintiff's counsel will proceed first, for fifty minutes. Defense counsel will then proceed, for one hour. Plaintiff's counsel will then have ten minutes for rebuttal. The verdict form(s) and the court's instructions to the jury will be given to the jury in writing, immediately after jury selection (before the presentations of counsel) unless the court orders otherwise.

6. The jury will be encouraged to return a unanimous verdict but will be instructed to return two or more separate verdicts, according to the views of different jurors, if they have not reached consensus after thirty minutes of deliberation. With the consent of all parties and all jurors and approval of the court, the attorneys may discuss the case with the jurors in court immediately after the verdict is received.

7. The proceedings will not be officially recorded. The parties may, by agreement, arrange for a court reporter.

8. The verdict(s) of the jury are advisory, being intended as an aid to the parties in their evaluation of the case for settlement, and will not have any binding effect unless the parties so agree.

9. The parties shall confer after verdict with the aim of reaching a settlement, and of course may confer for that purpose at any earlier time. The court will participate in the conference of the parties if the parties jointly request court participation.

10. This procedure is adapted from that described by Honorable Thomas D. Lambros, United States District Court, Northern

District of Ohio, in <u>The Summary Jury Trial and Other Alternative Methods of Dispute Resolution</u>, 103 F.R.D. 461 (1984). The parties are invited to propose any modifications that might make this procedure more useful in any way to the parties in this case.

_____
United States District Judge

Form 7.C
Stipulation and Order
for
Conditional Summary Trial
_____, 19__

The parties to the above-entitled action hereby stipulate and agree to the entry of the following as an Order of the Court, calling for the parties to engage in a Conditional Summary Trial as scheduled by the court and under the terms and conditions set forth below.

I.   Aim and Agreement of the Parties
This Order establishes a procedure aimed at aiding the parties to reach an early disposition of this case at reduced cost to the parties and to the public. This Order is entered with the full agreement of the parties.

II. Terms and Conditions
The following are the terms and conditions under which the Conditional Summary Trial shall proceed:

(1) The Presiding Officer shall be the judge to whom this case was drawn. The parties stipulate that no challenge, based upon the judge's having so served, will be raised by either party as to the judge's serving as the presiding judge at trial or with reference to any other matter in this case.

(2) Each party shall, not less than (20) days before the commencement of the Conditional Summary Trial, file with the court a written designation setting forth the name and title of a person having the full authority of that party to make a binding agreement to settle, and that person shall attend all sessions of the Conditional Summary Trial. Such person shall be a full-time employee of the Party and/or its affiliates, subsidiaries, or parent corporation. (That individual is hereinafter referred to as the "Representative.")

(3) The Conditional Summary Trial shall be held at a time scheduled by the court. The court has tentatively set _____, 199__, as the dates for conducting the Conditional Summary Trial.

(4) Not less than twenty (20) days before the commencement of the Conditional Summary Trial, the parties shall exchange lists of witnesses whose testimony they in good faith believe they may present through live testimony or by deposition or by affidavit, and the parties shall exchange lists of exhibits which they in good faith believe they will present at the Conditional Summary Trial. Within five (5) days thereafter, the parties shall exchange additional lists of any witnesses they may present (whether by way of live testimony or by deposition or by affidavit) and lists of additional documents they may present.

(5) During the Conditional Summary Trial, or in a pre-trial memorandum filed before it commences, each party shall make a full disclosure of all of its claims or defenses. A party is not required to disclose all of its evidence in support of its claims or defenses. Except for good cause shown, no party may hereafter raise a claim or defense not asserted during or before the Conditional Summary Trial.

(6) Each Representative will serve with the Presiding Officer as a member of the hearing panel. The Representatives may, as they prefer, consult with each other privately or in the presence of the Presiding Officer. Any disposition of the case on which they agree shall be incorporated into an Agreed Judgment subject to the court's approving it as a lawful disposition. If the Representatives cannot agree on a disposition within twenty-four (24) hours after the hearing is closed, each Representative (with freedom to consult with counsel) shall, within forty-eight (48) hours after the hearing is closed, file a proposed disposition. Within

seventy-two (72) hours after the hearing is closed, the Presiding Officer shall file a decision selecting whichever Representative's proposed disposition is, in the judgment of the Presiding Officer, the more appropriate disposition as between the two. The Presiding Officer is limited to choosing one or the other of these proposed dispositions. The disposition selected by the Presiding Officer shall be incorporated in a Judgment by Acquiescence unless opposition in writing, accompanied by a bond to secure performance of the payment of the $250,000 penalty herein provided [this figure may appropriately be the parties' estimates of the cost of trial], is filed within thirty (30) days after receipt of a copy of the Presiding Officer's report. If the outcome of trial (i.e., the final judgment, including such pre-judgment interest, costs and attorneys' fees as may be allowed by the court) is not more favorable to the objecting party than the disposition in the Presiding Officer's report, a penalty in the amount of two hundred fifty thousand dollars ($250,000) shall be assessed against the objecting party and added to or subtracted from the judgment otherwise due (and, if the subtraction is greater than the judgment otherwise due, shall result in a net judgment in the amount by which the $250,000 penalty exceeds the judgment otherwise due).

(7) Each party will have a total of five and one-half (5-1/2) hours for presentation, rebuttal, and summation of its case. The Presiding Officer and Representatives shall have one (1) hour for questioning of witnesses and counsel. The order of proceedings will be as follows:
    (a) plaintiff's affirmative case;
    (b) defendant's rebuttal of plaintiffs' case and affirmative defenses;
    (c) plaintiff's rebuttal;
    (d) questioning of witnesses or counsel by the Presiding Officer or Representatives;
    (e) defendant's summation; and
    (f) plaintiff's summation.

The time may be used for testimony as each party may choose, whether in narrative form (by witnesses or counsel), testimony in question-and-answer form (including cross-examination of a witness or an employee or agent testifying on behalf of an adverse party), affidavits, depositions, videotapes, introduction of documents or graphic and/or written summaries, and arguments on the facts and on the law, allocated as the party chooses. Each party shall have the right to the extent permitted by law to subpoena witnesses. Neither of the Representatives shall present evidence at the Conditional Summary Trial. Live testimony by witnesses shall be under oath. The Conditional Summary Trial shall not be deemed a hearing or proceeding under F.R. Evid. 804 for the purpose of establishing the admissibility of evidence at subsequent hearings or proceedings.

(8) Objections that proffered evidence is inadmissible may be stated and argued in the time period allocated to the objecting party. The failure to make an objection shall not be a waiver of the right to make that objection at trial, should a trial be held. Questions to an adverse party, if calling for discoverable information, shall be answered regardless of admissibility. The Presiding Officer will rule upon any assertions of privilege or nondiscoverability. The time required for the hearing and determination of disputes over privilege or nondiscoverability will not be charged against either party. Any rulings on objections and assertions of privilege or nondiscoverability are for purposes of this hearing only and shall not constitute rulings upon or waivers in relation to those matters in a subsequent proceeding or hearing of this action.

(9) During the deliberations of the Presiding Officer and the Representatives, the Presiding Officer shall give his or her thoughts as to how he or she would resolve any issues in dispute.

PROMOTING DISPOSITION WITHOUT TRIAL   Sec. E

(10) If the Representatives arrive at a settlement at any time during the Conditional Summary Trial, the court shall enter an Order incorporating the terms of such settlement.

(11) Any testimony given by any person at the Conditional Summary Trial shall not be admissible for any purpose at the trial of this action, nor shall such testimony be used for impeachment purposes at trial with the following exception: if testimony given by any person at the Conditional Summary Trial is contrary to testimony given by that person in the course of pre-trial discovery in this action, a party may file a motion with this court seeking leave to use that testimony from the Conditional Summary Trial for impeachment purposes at trial; the court, after hearing, will in its discretion determine whether leave should be granted in the interests of justice.

(12) Nothing in this Order shall prohibit the parties from availing themselves of the benefits of the provisions of Rule 68 of the Federal Rules of Civil Procedure nor shall it prevent or diminish any award of attorneys' fees.

(13) Neither party, without the assent of the other party, shall disclose to the Presiding Officer any demand or offer still outstanding or previously made.

/s/	/s/
Attorney for Plaintiff(s)	Attorney for Defendant(s)

_____
United States District Judge

F. Choices Committing Judicial and Party Resources
    to a Particular Case[1]

   1. **A Problem** of Limited Public and Private Resources

   For every case on a court's docket, some judge at some time in the life of the case, by action or inaction, makes at least one decision to commit scarce public resources (judge time and support services) and party resources (attorney and party time and support services) to one rather than others among all the available techniques for disposition of that case.

   The judge who takes no action in this respect has effectively made a decision to commit judge time to what we might call the hands-off technique. I use "hands-off" here not in any pejorative sense but just as a shorthand way of describing a decision not to use any form of intervention aimed at encouraging disposition short of full-scale discovery and full-length trial. Instead, the judge just stands ready to decide all pre-trial disputes that are presented to the court and at some point in the history of the case sets a credible date for trial. I do not mean "hands-off" to imply not even setting a trial date until requested to do so. That technique is so out of favor today that I do not discuss it here.

   Electing to use the hands-off technique, as I have defined it, commits to a case the judge time and other public and private resources that will be used if the case does not settle without judicial intervention. One way of roughly quantifying this commitment is to estimate the hours of judicial time the case will require if not settled and multiply by a fraction expressing the probability the case will not settle. Party resources expended will tend to be proportional in general, though not precisely. For a simplified example, put aside for a moment the time that may be spent in proceedings before trial. Just consider trial time. If, for example, for a given case you estimate a one-fifth probability of a 50-hour trial, the quantified commitment you make by deciding not to intervene is 50 hours x .20, or 10 hours of judge time. For convenience, let us

---

[1]This section is drawn from a paper prepared for a Federal Judicial Center Conference on the Judicial Role in Settlement, September 9-10, 1985. See D.M. Provine, Settlement Strategies for Federal District Judges (Federal Judicial Center 1986).

refer to this figure as the <u>judge-time quotient for trial</u> associated with the hands-off technique.

The judge who decides instead to intervene for the purpose of encouraging settlement makes another kind of commitment. You can roughly quantify this commitment also.

For illustration, suppose you estimate that by holding a one-hour settlement conference you can raise the settlement probability of this case from .80 to .82; thus, by using one hour of judge time immediately, you reduce the probability of trial time to .18 x 50, or 9 hours rather than 10. You have exactly broken even. The judge-time quotient for the case is still 10 hours (1 + 9).

Suppose you estimate that by committing 4 hours of your time to a summary jury trial of this case, you can raise the settlement probability to .88; thus you reduce the probability of trial time to .12 x 50, or 6 hours rather than 10. But having spent 4 hours doing so, you have again broken even (4 + 6 = 10).

Suppose you estimate that by committing 12 hours of your time to a conditional summary trial, a technique described in Form 7.C,[2] you can raise the settlement probability to .95; thus you reduce the probability of trial time to .05 x 50, or 2.5 hours. But having spent 12 hours doing it, you have suffered a net loss of 4.5 hours of judge time (12 + 2.5 = 14.5). This illustration alone is enough to tell you that conditional summary trial is not worth using unless the full trial would be long -- perhaps 150 hours or more.

Also, even a summary jury trial of 4 hours is of questionable value by this quantification measure if the full trial would be, let us say, no more than 20 or 25 hours.

The basic point, stated another way, is that a very high percentage of the cases on court dockets will settle anyway -- whether the trial judge intervenes or not. Think about a category of cases as to which you estimate that the probability is that 80% of the cases in that category will settle without judicial intervention. Judicial intervention in the cases in that category is worthwhile only if either (1) intervention will raise the probability of settlement

---

[2]Section E, this Chapter, <u>supra</u>.

enough above .80 to make up for the time committed to the effort, or (2) intervention will achieve some other benefit.

These illustrations are, of course, oversimplified. Judges make their decisions to intervene or not to do so for reasons beyond those reflected in these simple comparative quantifications.

Judges intervene in the hope that doing so causes more settlements, or better settlements, or earlier settlements, or settlements at lower cost in private resources. Still, the judge-time cost of the judicial intervention is justified if and only if it is outweighed by benefits in one or more of these ways. If, instead, the judge time that is spent in this effort is not more than balanced by the benefits of achieving somewhat more, better, earlier, or lower-process-cost settlements, the judge, though well meaning, will have caused some waste of scarce public resources, and private resources as well, that we can ill afford.

2. A Sequence of Choices

A trial judge faces not a single choice of this kind about allocation and use of scarce resources but a sequence of choices.

First: Should the judge intervene at all? This is a choice that must be made primarily on the basis of identifying the characteristics of the case that place it in one or another among the different broad categories of cases on the court docket.

Second: If choosing to intervene, should the judge do so by calling first for a conference?

Third: If so, shall the judge invite the parties as well as the lawyers?

Fourth: After considering all the additional characteristics of the case, learned through the conference, shall the judge use one or more additional techniques of judicial intervention to promote settlement of the case?

Fifth: If so, which one or more among the whole array, when, and in what order?

Is it possible to improve decisionmaking about techniques of judicial involvement in dispute resolution by making some quantitative comparisons of the commitment of public and private resources that are implicit, if not explicit, in the choices? How do we think in quantified terms about whether a particular case will settle? That is, how do we arrive at an estimate that it is 80% or 82% or 88% or 95% probable that a particular case will settle?

One rational way of going about this is to identify the characteristics of the case that place it within one or another of different categories of cases as to which we have information. That information might be -- though rarely is in fact -- a body of "credible" data about how many cases out of 100 cases in each of different categories settle. For example, more or less carefully gathered data might tell us that on the docket of court X, for the cases filed in years Y-1 through Y-10, by the time, years later, when all cases filed in those years had reached disposition, it turned out that

95% of motor vehicle cases settled

90% of products liability cases settled

85% of breach of contract cases settled

80% of discrimination cases settled

50% of prisoner complaints filed under 42 U.S.C. § 1983 (and not decided on dispositive motions) settled

85% of all other "triable" cases settled. ("Triable" cases, as the term is used here, do not include those that in no event would go to trial -- *e.g.*, those involving judicial review on an administrative record.)

I hasten to disclose that the percentage figures I have chosen here for illustration are not based on any data of which I am aware. Substitute your own figures and your own category descriptions if these make you uncomfortable. If you do not have any credible data about settlement experience for case categories on a court docket, you will be compelled just to make the best educated guesses you can make in order to think in any kind of quantitative terms about whether the choices about using or not using various techniques of judicial intervention represent wise decisions from the perspective of commitment of the court's scarce resource of judge time.

To think sensibly about these questions, in quantitative terms, we must differentiate among categories of cases. For example, if the court adopts court-annexed arbitration for motor vehicle cases only, and data show that only 4% of all cases in the court-annexed arbitration program go to trial but 15% of all other "triable" cases on the court's docket go to trial, we might infer that court-annexed arbitration was an unqualified success -- until someone pointed out that even in years before court-annexed arbitration was adopted, motor vehicle cases were substantially more likely to settle than any other category of cases on the docket.

I do not suggest that the illustrative figures are accurate for any particular court at any particular time. Certainly, also, I do not speak against court-annexed arbitration. Indeed, I think of it as one of many techniques of intervention to which a judge ought to give serious consideration when making comparative evaluations.

The point I am suggesting is this: To think about the percentage probability that a particular case will settle without intervention (that is, using the hands-off technique only), and the different percentage probability that the same case will settle if we use court-annexed arbitration, and the different percentage probability if we use summary jury trial or some other technique, we need to identify the characteristics of the case that enable us to place it in one of the several categories for each of which we have different estimates of hands-off judge-time quotients.

This is only the beginning of our thought process, but a very critical first step.

3. Decisions Based on Incomplete Information

Calculations of judge-time quotients for different techniques of judicial intervention in a particular case (or category of like cases) may help us think about what technique or techniques we should apply in particular cases. Of course, under the GIGO principle (Garbage-In, Garbage-Out), the judge-time quotients that we calculate are no better than the estimates we use in making them -- the estimate of probability of settlement absent intervention, the estimate of increased probability of settlement with each kind of intervention, and the estimate of length of trial if the case is not settled. Our empirical base for making these estimates is rather shaky, but most trial lawyers and trial judges nevertheless have a fair amount of confidence in their own estimates about matters such as these, based on their own experience. Indeed, trial lawyers and trial judges make decisions daily in reliance upon estimates of this kind.

It may be useful, nevertheless, to examine some hypotheses that bear upon the reliability of such estimates. It may be well at least to consider these hypotheses when evaluating other techniques in comparison with the hands-off technique of case managment. Failure to take these hypotheses into account may lead to unreliable estimates.

First, a credible trial setting is a powerful influence on the <u>timing</u> of settlement, but it has little to do with the <u>probability</u> of settlement, except as stated in the next hypothesis.

Second, for any particular category of cases, the longer the delay between the filing of the case and a credible trial setting, the higher is the percentage of cases settled. The costs of delay weigh heavily in the settlement calculus.

Third, the costs of delay often have differential impact on the parties. They affect not only the percentage of cases settled but also the terms of settlement.

Fourth, claims of success or failure of particular techniques of intervention to encourage settlement are seldom supportable by empirical evidence, because the data we have do not tell us enough about the different characteristics of cases and different treatment of like cases to support reasoned inferences of causal connections between treatments and results.

Fifth, nevertheless, we make virtually all of life's major decisions without empirical support for our premises of decision. It makes sense to do so in this instance also, but only after thinking about comparative costs and benefits of acting in different ways.

Perhaps some explanation of the fourth and fifth hypotheses is needed. A claim of success for a particular technique of intervention is not very credible unless it takes account of the fact that most cases were destined for settlement anyway. A settlement is not caused by, and should not be credited to, a particular judicial intervention if it would have happened anyway. Of course, intervention may affect timing (and thus cause benefits of earlier settlement) even if it does not increase the likelihood of settlement. That is a benefit certainly worthy of inclusion in our calculus.

It is very difficult to design and carry out an empirical study that credibly evaluates costs and benefits of a particular technique of intervention in comparison with the hands-off method, or any other particular method. For this reason, we must expect that we will have to continue to make these important choices about judicial intervention mostly on the basis of hunches and unproved hypotheses. It may be useful, however, at least to think about the relevant comparisons quantitatively, even if we do not have data to demonstrate that our quantifying estimates are correct.

Another cautionary note is in order. The estimates thus far used have been greatly oversimplified. First, they omitted consideration of all costs and benefits other than judge time saved or used. Second, they calculated the judge-time quotient for trial only and omitted consideration of judge time that to some degree of probability will or will not be used in proceedings before trial. To help us think about judge-time quotients for proceedings before trial as well as judge-time quotients for trial, perhaps it will be helpful to construct an analytic grid, at least for judge-time quotients if not for other costs (such as support services in clerk time, law clerk time, secretarial time, jury time, and jury fees and expenses).

Form 7.D, presented below for your consideration, is a Grid for Evaluating Techniques of Judicial Involvement in Dispute Resolution.

This is not a device that will enable you to determine empirically what choice you should make in a particular case, if you were the judge. It is intended as an aid to thinking about the factors you might wish to consider in deciding what to do in a particular case about choosing or not choosing to use one or more among techniques of judicial involvement in dispute resolution other than trial.

It is simply a way of putting into mathematical form, for those who find it helpful to do so, a commonsense way of thinking about whether it is wise to use scarce judge time to intervene in a case to encourage settlement and, if so, how best to go about it.

This grid does not take account of cases decided on dispositive motions (such as motions to dismiss and motions for summary judgment). For categories of cases in which such motions have a significant impact on the percentage of cases that go to trial, a more complex grid could be constructed and might be useful.

Think of the grid that appears here as a form with blanks in all the spaces where a number appears, and a blank in the caption following "Type of Case." The number that appears in each blank is either inserted as an estimate or calculated from some other estimate or set of estimates. The illustration used here is a case within a sub-category of product liability cases. It is a case of a relatively uncomplicated type, and the estimate is that it will take about 50 hours for a trial. At the moment the judge can first examine the file, cases of this type appear less likely to settle than, let us say, an ordinary motor vehicle tort case. The estimate used here is 80% probability of settlement under the hands-off technique (.20 likelihood of trial).

The grid presented here compares just four among the many alternatives one might consider in various cases.

Ch. 7   JUDGING IN PRETRIAL PROCEEDINGS

Form 7.D

**A Grid for Evaluating Techniques
of Judicial Involvement in Dispute Resolution
Type of Case: Products Liability**

Techniques of Judicial Involvement in Dispute Resolution	Judge-Time for Proceedings Before Trial (in hours)	Judge-Time Quotient for Trial (in hours)	Judge-Time for Technique of Intervention (in hours)	Total Predicted Judge-Time (in hours)
A. <u>Hands Off</u>	4	.20x50 10	0	14
B. <u>Settlement Conference</u>				
1) Just Before Trial Date	4	.18x50 9	1	14
2) At Rule 16 Conference	.95x4 3.8	.19x50 9.5	1	14.3
3) At Both Times	.95x4 3.8	.16x50 8	2	13.8
C. <u>Summary Jury Trial</u>				
1) Just Before Trial Date	4	.10x50 5	4	13
2) After Limited Discovery	.6x4 2.4	.11x50 5.5	4	11.9
D. <u>Conditional Summary Trial</u>				
1) Just Before Trial	4	.05x50 2.5	12	18.5
2) After Limited Discovery	.6x4 2.4	.06x50 3	12	17.4

This grid compares only the commitment of public resources as measured roughly by judge time incident to use of different techniques of judicial involvement. Judicial choices regarding intervention depend also on many other factors. One of those factors already noted is the impact of the choice upon the private resources of the parties that will be (or probably will be) committed to resolving the dispute. Will the impact of those resource costs fall equally or unequally on the parties, and with what potential effect on the fairness of ultimate resolution of this dispute? Also, what impact will the choice have -- in ways apart from costs in private resources -- upon the quality of the final resolution of the dispute? On its fairness? On the ways, if at all, it may affect ongoing relationships? On the ways, if at all, it may have other ongoing consequences?

This grid, and these comments, are focused on techniques of judicial intervention aimed at disposition before a trial begins. A similar method of evaluation may be used in thinking about proposed techniques of reducing the length and cost of trials, which are discussed in Chapter 8.

4. A Qualitative Perspective

The choices judges make about techniques of judicial involvement in dispute resolution have significant potential economic consequences. They result in wise or wasteful use of public and private resources.

Even more significant is the potential impact of these choices on the quality of justice. The aim of "just, speedy, and inexpensive" dispositions expresses three interdependent elements. Delay and cost -- two of those elements -- in current circumstances are significant not merely in themselves but also because they are two of the most intractable impediments to the third element of the tripartite aim -- the quality of justice. I will say more about this relationship of delay and costs to quality of disposition in Chapter 8.[3]

In all courts that have any backlog of cases, choices regarding judicial intervention to encourage settlement significantly affect the court's success or failure in

---

[3]Chapter 8, Section A, infra.

fulfilling the promise of the legal system to make available prompt as well as fair adjudication of all disputes before the court. Use of judicial time in techniques that <u>do not</u> increase the likelihood of settlement enough to outweigh the judicial time committed to them is not in the public interest. It is in the public interest, however, to commit judicial time to techniques that increase the likelihood of settlement enough to outweigh the judicial time committed to them, if those techniques are also designed and conducted in ways that do not impair the quality of the disposition of the dispute.

CHAPTER 8

CONDUCTING JURY AND NONJURY TRIALS

A. Incentive Structures and Judicial Management Revisited

Two themes presented in Chapter 7, in the context of problems of judging during pretrial proceedings, are relevant also to judging at trial. One is a theme regarding incentive structures for professional conduct of advocates.[1] The other is a theme regarding what has been called managerial judging.[2]

Associated with the larger storm of controversy over Rules of Procedure generally and Rule 16 in particular are some whirlwinds (perhaps even tornadoes) of controversy over the kind of judicial behavior that has been labeled managerial judging. Rule 16 itself focuses mostly on judicial control over pretrial development of cases.

---

[1] See Chapter 7, Section C, supra.

[2] See Chapter 7, Sections D, E, and F, supra. The additional comments on managerial judging in the remainder of this section are reproduced, with little modification, from my remarks at a symposium on the Federal Rules of Civil Procedure, later published in Time Limits as Incentives in an Adversary System, 137 U. Pa. L. Rev. 2053-58 (1989), copyright © University of Pennsylvania. I am grateful to the copyright owners for their gracious permission for the present use of these comments. My remarks at the symposium were comments on the thoughtful and perceptive paper prepared by Professor David L. Shapiro and later published under the title, Federal Rules, Local Rules, and State Rules: Uniformity, Divergence, and Emerging Procedural Patterns, 137 U. Pa. L. Rev. 1999 (1989).

With a few notable exceptions (including the thoughtful contributions of John Langbein),[3] pronouncements in praise or criticism of managerial judging have focused less on trial than on pretrial. Here, I propose to place the emphasis on trial, and how one's views about judicial control, initiative, management, or whatever you may wish to call it, will bear upon what happens in the trial. I do so in the belief that the expectations of judges and lawyers about the nature of the anticipated trial (if the case turns out to be one of the 5% or so that go through trial) deeply affect what they do in Rule 16 conferences and, more generally, throughout pretrial development of the case.

Adversary trial was never meant to be the speediest form of trial. The aim, and the claim, has been and now is <u>first in quality of disposition</u>, not first in time.

Why, then, have the recent amendments to Rule 16 strongly encouraged, if not mandated, judicial intervention to promote disposition without trial? Have the framers of amendments changed Rule 1's triple focus on "just, speedy, and inexpensive determination of every action" to emphasize "speedy and inexpensive" even if that may cause outcomes to fall short of being "just" determinations?

Before we accept that interpretation, we should examine more closely the inherent incentives of different models of adversary trials.

It often happens in an adversary trial that one side has a greater incentive than the other to aim for conciseness and clarity. If those on both sides expect that the judge will passively observe while an advocate with an interest in complicating the trial and making it longer works at that strategy, the parties are likely to engage in long, complicated, and contentious discovery, followed in a small percentage of cases by long, complicated, and contentious trial. The advocate with an interest in complexity and length of trial also has an interest in testing the limits of tolerance of the judicial officer (judge, magistrate, or master) who oversees discovery and the judicial officer (whether the same or another) who conducts the trial.

---

[3] <u>See, e.g.</u>, Langbein, <u>The German Advantage in Civil Procedure</u>, 52 U. Chi. L. Rev. 823, 835-41 (1985) (discussing choice and use of experts in Germany).

Do rulemakers, or judges in the exercise of inherent or prescribed functions, have the power to fashion alternative models of trial, not just alternatives to trial? If so, should that power be exercised? If the answer is yes, shall we develop new models in which the judge's role is different? Should the trial judge be more firmly in control of the method, length, and expense of the trial?

Why do some disputants who can afford to do so rent a judge? Judge shopping may be an element in the motivation, but probably a minor element in most instances. What counts more is that the parties are choosing a different, more streamlined, shorter model of trial, with a different role for the judge and different roles for the advocates. The judge's role may be defined formally by the terms of a stipulation that the parties and the judge agree to, or it may be incident to the known tendencies of the judge who is "rented" by agreement of the disputants.

Why do the parties choose a shorter trial than the one that would occur before the judge to whom the legal system would assign their case if they just took it to court? We should be examining that question seriously. The market place may be telling us something about perceptions of quality as well as perceptions of cost.

Rule 16(a)(5) says explicitly that the trial court "may in its discretion" call a conference for the purpose of "facilitating the settlement of the case."

Rule 16(c)(7) says explicitly that "[t]he participants at any conference under this rule may consider and take action with respect to," among other things, the possibility of "use of extrajudicial procedures to resolve the dispute...."

Observe that the rule says nothing explicitly about <u>judicial</u> as distinguished from <u>extrajudicial</u> alternative dispute resolution procedures. Are trial judges supposed to read Rule 16 as implying if not expressing a prohibition against judicially supervised alternatives to traditional adversary trials?[4]

Professor Shapiro, after noting that an interest in

---

[4] <u>See</u> Chapter 7, Sections A and B, for additional comments on Rule 16 and its meaning.

a higher degree of uniformity of federal practice was an articulated purpose of the Federal Rules of Civil Procedure, observed that the rulemakers also "wanted to escape the rigidities and technicalities" of procedural codes.[5] "The key, then," he adds, "was an increase in flexibility."[6] Trial judges were to be liberated from, for example, some of the rigorous restraints of law, compared with equity, and allowed more discretion to get to the merits expeditiously and inexpensively.

Encouraged by the key objective of flexibility that Professor Shapiro has observed, and not entirely discouraged by his perception that rulemakers held back from giving trial judges "express power to act coercively in any way not authorized" by other sources of authority,[7] I am inclined to read Rule 16 as not prohibiting trial judges from calling a Rule 16 conference for the purpose of discussing with the lawyers and their clients a proposed stipulation and order for a shorter and more sharply focused form of trial than the traditional model adversary trial -- a somewhat different model of adversary trial in which the roles of the lawyers and the judge are defined in a way that gives the trial judge both power and responsibility to control excesses of traditional adversariness.

If you believe the factfinder on disputed evidence will have a better understanding of the genuine disputes of material fact after a crisp, focused presentation in a span of two days or two weeks than after a less focused presentation of two months, you may prefer a more streamlined model of adversary trial not merely on grounds of speed and lower cost but as well on grounds of the expected quality of the decisionmaking.

Another significant theme Professor Shapiro observed in federal rulemaking is a "general endorsement of the adversary system and of party control of litigation,"[8] but tempered by reducing some of the excesses of the traditional

---

[5] Shapiro, _Federal Rule 16: A Look at the Theory and Practice of Rulemaking_, 137 U. Pa. L. Rev. 1969, 1975.

[6] _Id._

[7] _Id._ at 1981.

[8] _Id._ at 1975.

adversary system, including especially surprise and concealment.

After some experimentation, under stipulations of the parties, with both a one-day dispositive summary jury trial of a case that would have taken a week or two to try in the traditional way and several two-day conditionally dispositive trials of cases that would have taken two months or longer to try, I have this observation to report:

The time constraints placed upon the advocates gave them powerful incentives to discard techniques of lengthy direct and cross-examination of witnesses involving questions that were meant more to argue the case than to develop the testimony of the witnesses. Instead, they quoted selected passages from documents, depositions, and affidavits as they used their precious time to weave the evidence and argument together into crisp, clear presentations of their respective positions. Within reasonable limits and under reasonable controls, a shorter model of adversary trial may be better in quality of disposition -- closer to the aim of a just determination -- as well as speedier and less expensive.

I doubt, however, that it is possible to design such a shorter, better focused trial, without changing the trial judge's role to one of somewhat more rigorous control over the process than that implicit in the role of the judge in the traditional adversary trial.

I doubt that the framers of Rule 16 in the 1930s or the framers of the 1983 amendment were thinking about this problem. Indeed, I believe that even the Federal Rules of Evidence, which surely are more centrally focused upon trial than are the Federal Rules of Civil Procedure, do not have much to say that is relevant to this subject. The traditional adversary trial is governed more by tradition than by rule.

Tradition has its limits as a restraining influence, however. An illustration will help to clarify the point. As will be developed later in this chapter, even though we have no Federal Rules of Proof, trial judges do in fact apply rules of proof as well as Rules of Evidence in conducting a trial. The rules of proof they apply as they make rulings on objections to particular questions depart a great deal more from uniformity than do the rulings of the same judges on objections based on Rules of Evidence. This fact illustrates the point that in particular instances tradition may yield to rules --- even the rules generated and regularly invoked by the single judge before whom a case is tried. Nevertheless, the fact remains that tradition is a powerful influence on professional conduct. The tradition of the adversary trial is powerful indeed.

Model changes may be harder to achieve when traditions must be changed than when only rules need be changed. But rules can make an important contribution. Rule 16 and the amendments, despite ambiguities and shortcomings, have advanced serious consideration of extrajudicial alternatives to traditional adversary trials. Whether meant to do so or not, they have also encouraged many judges and lawyers to think more seriously about judicially supervised alternatives. Perhaps the time has come for serious thought to changing rules in ways that will legitimate and encourage the development of judicially supervised alternatives to traditional adversary trials.

You may have observed that I just used the phrase "judicially supervised." Is "judicial supervision" of a trial a form of "managerial judging"?

"Managerial judging" evokes quite varied imagery. When a trial judge is identified by name in a law professor's article as a "managerial judge," he or she may be in doubt about whether the label is meant as a compliment or a criticism. Was the phrase meant to allude to "managing" prisons, hospitals, and schools, or "managing" pre-trial development of cases, or "managing" settlement negotiations, or "managing" trials? And what kind of managing? Intrusive and illicit -- that is, by implicit threats that the judge will do things within the judge's power, even though beyond the judge's authority, to coerce compliance with the judge's expressed wishes? Or, instead, benign, constructive, and entirely legitimate managing?

I have wondered whether I might suggest a more suitable phrase than "managerial judging" to describe the kind of behavior that would be appropriate in a judicially supervised alternative to traditional adversary trial. On one occasion when I was wondering, I reached for the handiest thesaurus and, under the entry for "Management," found three-quarters of a page of suggestive terms. How do you react to just a few of them? What about care and control; stewardship over the trial; superintendence; regimen? Or housekeeping; administration; bureaucracy? Direction and leadership? Or (bearing in mind the admiralty jurisdiction), pilotage? Or (bearing in mind aviation as well as admiralty jurisdiction), the steering instrument, the joy-stick? Or (going western, as my thesaurus did not), corralling? The judge as wrangler? Or (in imagery recently evoked by Judge Selya), guru?[9] Or (in other imagery), manipulator, one who maneuvers, and pulls the strings, keeps order, polices, regulates, has a way with the parties and lawyers? Or, one who channels? (Do you envision a clear, clean stream or a muddy gutter?) Here's one I like -- a shepherd.

Judge Weinstein remarked at a symposium on the Federal Rules of Civil Procedure[10] that federal judges might be encouraged to be sheep, led by academic shepherds. Would trial lawyers prefer academic shepherds to judicial shepherds, or perhaps no shepherds at all? Before answering this question, perhaps we should sharpen it. Will the answer lawyers give be different if they are asked not about their preferences in a particular case in which their roles in that case have already been assigned, but about their preferences in a system in which each lawyer will sometimes be on the side that has incentives to simplicity and brevity and at other times on the side that has incentives to complexity and length?

Given provisions for sanctions like those of Rule 16, zealous trial advocates may enter the courtroom thinking, "We are officers of the court, who may be disciplined by the stern judge for any violations of Rules 11, 16 and 26, among others."

Envision, as an alternative, zealous trial advocates who enter the courtroom thinking, "Our judge is our shepherd. She leadeth us to a speedy and just determination of our case."

If we are not content just to call good judicial behavior "judging," shall we call it shepherding the case, speedily and inexpensively, to the fold of justice?

More to the point, shall we revise our rules to legitimate and encourage more of that kind of judging,

---

[9] See In re San Juan Dupont Plaza Hotel Fire Litigation, 859 F.2d 1007, 1010 (1st Cir. 1988).

[10] See Symposium: The 50th Anniversary of the Federal Rules of Civil Procedure, 1938-1988, 137 U. Pa. L. Rev. 1873 (1989).

whatever it may be called?

B. Tailored Trials

An illustration of a way in which a jury trial may be tailored consistently with the use of time limits as incentives within adversary trials is presented here in Form 8.A.[1]

---

[1] I acknowledge that in drafting this form I borrowed from Judge Pierre N. Leval, who of course is not to be held accountable for flaws in my implementation of his idea.

Form 8.A
Stipulation and Order
for
Tailored Jury Trial
_____, 19__

I. <u>Statement of Aim</u>

The aim of this Stipulation and Order is to create a set of procedures tailored to fit the distinctive characteristics of this case and "to secure the just, speedy, and inexpensive determination of [this] action," Fed. R. Civ. P. 1. The parties and the court intend

(a) that "the mode and order of interrogating witnesses and presenting evidence" be such as will "(1) make the interrogation and presentation effective for the ascertainment of truth, (2) avoid needless consumption of time, and (3) protect witnesses from harassment or undue embarrassment," Fed. R. Evid. 611(a),

(b) that "interim summations" by counsel be allowed from time to time as the presentation of evidence proceeds, in order to promote jury understanding of the evidence and the contentions of the parties, and

(c) that, with the consent of the parties or upon motion and hearing pursuant to Fed. R. Civ. P. 42(b), the court may order phasing of the trial "in furtherance of convenience" or when "conducive to expedition and economy," <u>id.</u>, and may receive a separate verdict on one or more separate issues before other issues are tried to the same jury.

II. Stipulations

1. Recognizing the right of each party to insist that "the testimony of witnesses shall be taken orally in open court," Fed. R. Civ. P. 43(a), the parties waive this right to the extent stated in this Stipulation and Order and agree that in this case direct examination of each witness shall be presented by affidavit, unless as to a particular witness an exception is allowed by the court pursuant to the provisions of this Stipulation and Order.

2. The parties agree that the time allowed to each party, for proceedings within each of the categories listed, shall be as stated in this paragraph, subject to any modification ordered by the court upon a showing of good cause. Within each of the three categories of time allowances, a party may allocate the allowed time as it sees fit.

	Plaintiff(s)	Group One Defendant(s)	Group Two Defendant(s)
A. Total for Opening Statements and All Summations (including Interim Summations)	___ hours	___ hours	___ hours
B. Total for Examination and Cross-Examination of All Witnesses	___ hours	___ hours	___ hours
C. Total for Making and Arguing Motions and Objections Orally	___ hours	___ hours	___ hours
SUM	___ hours	___ hours	___ hours

Total for the Case ___ hours, exclusive of time for the court's instructions to the jury, which may be given in part as the case proceeds ("interim instructions").

[Do the parties wish to propose any other stipulations? Following are examples for consideration.]

3. At any time more than 30 days before the trial begins either party may serve upon another party [or parties] [and file with the clerk] an offer of judgment. If within 10 days after the service of the offer a party upon whom the offer is served accepts by written notice served on the offeror, the clerk shall enter judgment accordingly. An offer not accepted within this time is no longer open, and evidence of an offer not accepted is not admissible at trial. If the offer is not accepted and the judgment finally entered is not more favorable to the offeree, the offeree shall be liable to the offeror for stipulated damages for the costs of trial, in the sum of _____ thousand dollars, which shall be included in the final judgment as an addition to or offset of the amount otherwise due (or as a net amount due if the offset exceeds the amount of a judgment otherwise to be entered against the offeror).

4. A jury of [8] will be selected. No alternates will be selected. The parties stipulate that if the court finds it necessary to excuse one or more jurors for cause after trial has commenced, the trial may proceed through deliberations to verdict as long as at least 5 qualified jurors remain.

5. If the deliberating jury consists of 5 persons, the verdict must be unanimous; if 6, a 5-1 verdict will be accepted; if 7, a 6-1 verdict; if 8, a 6-2 verdict.

III. <u>Order Regulating Trial</u>

A. <u>Jury Selection</u>

1. At least 2 court days before trial commences, counsel jointly (or each separately) shall file for use by the court during voir dire a list identifying parties, lawyers, and witnesses. The lists shall be

over-inclusive rather than under-inclusive in case of any doubt, in order to avoid risks of loss of jurors during trial because of acquaintance with a person whose possible relationship to the case was not made known during voir dire.

2. [If para. 4 is included in the Stipulations.] The plaintiff group will have 3 peremptory challenges and each of the two defendant groups will have 2 peremptory challenges. A panel of 15 will be seated and questioned by the court (including any voir dire questions proposed by the parties, either in advance or during voir dire, and found acceptable by the court). Whenever a panel member is excused for cause, another person will be called by the clerk to fill the vacant seat, and the voir dire will proceed. At the conclusion of voir dire, after 15 not subject to challenge for cause are seated, the court will invite each of the 15 panel members to speak about his or her personal background and experience (including such things as occupation, marital status, spouse occupation (if any), children, hobbies, reading interests). The parties will then deliver to the clerk in writing, simultaneously, their peremptory challenges. The first 8, in order of seating, who are not challenged will be the jury.

IV. Proposed Jury Instructions

A. Instructions to be Given Before Testimony Begins

1. Before testimony begins, the court will instruct the jury on the functions and roles of the jury and of counsel in the case, and on the jury's obligations to decide the case solely on the evidence presented, to refrain from discussing the case (with each other or anyone else), and to avoid contact with the parties and with published or broadcast accounts of the trial.

2. Preliminary instructions on the law

applicable to the claims and defenses in the case, or on other matters, may be given. The court will advise the parties of its tentative decision on this matter before opening statements, and will offer the parties an opportunity to be heard. Any requests for preliminary instructions shall be filed with the court at least 2 court days before trial commences.

3. The court may give interim instructions upon a determination of a need to do so to aid jury understanding. Requests by the parties for such instructions are invited, and the parties are encouraged to propose the content of requested instructions in written drafts.

B. <u>Final Jury Instructions</u>

1. The final charge will be given orally and furnished to the jury in writing. It will consist of the following components: (a) general instructions to guide the jury throughout its deliberations; (b) special interrogatories requesting the jury's findings on specific questions of fact and explanatory instructions on the law bearing specially upon the questions submitted in the special interrogatories; and (c) limiting instructions, including instructions as to evidence received against less than all the parties in the action. No general verdict will be requested.

(a) General Instructions: A draft of the court's proposed general instructions will be distributed. Any objections or proposed amendments must have been filed on or before _____.

(b) Special Interrogatories and Explanatory Instructions on the Law: Initial requests for special interrogatories and explanatory instructions on the law shall be filed on or before _____.

(c) Limiting Instructions: If the occasion for a limiting instruction can be anticipated, parties will be expected to have their requests prepared in advance in writing. If any evidence is received for a limited purpose, a party seeking the benefit of a limiting instruction in the court's final instructions will have the burden of assuring that a copy of the court's oral instruction is delivered to the clerk for inclusion in the final charge, and in the case of documentary evidence, for attachment to the exhibit. A form that may be used with exhibits is attached to this order as "Exhibit A."

C. Jury Deliberation: Unless a stipulation to the contrary is filed, only the first six jurors selected will deliberate (unless only 5 remain, in which case they will deliberate) and the verdict must be unanimous. The court encourages the parties to stipulate that all jurors selected and still serving when the case is submitted be the deliberating jury.

V. Procedure at Trial

A. <u>Opening Statements</u>

1. Opening statement by the plaintiff(s) will occur before any evidence is received.

2. Opening statement by each defendant will also occur before any evidence is received, unless the defendant has elected otherwise by notice filed and served at least one week before trial commences.

B. <u>Evidence</u>

1. Each party shall give advance notice to the court and the other parties, before jury selection, of the identity of all witnesses whose testimony (by affidavit, by deposition, or by oral testimony in trial) it

may offer during trial. At least two court days before it seeks to use the testimony of any witness, or on shorter notice for good cause shown, it shall advise the court and all other parties of its intent to use the testimony of the witness on the specified day. Except for good cause shown, no party shall be allowed to use the testimony of a witness other than the witnesses already listed on the filings with the court before trial commences. Except for good cause shown, no party shall introduce during direct examination documentary evidence other than those exhibits already listed with the court and furnished to the other parties before trial commences. These provisions with regard to documentary evidence shall not apply to cross-examination.

2. Absent a showing of good cause, the court will not exercise its discretion under Fed. R. Evid. 611(b) to allow the subject matter of the cross-examination to extend beyond the subject matter of the direct examination and matters affecting the credibility of the witness. A showing of good cause will also be required if the subject matter of the redirect is to be allowed to extend beyond matters covered on cross-examination. That a witness has come from outside the district or will be unavailable later in the trial may be found to constitute good cause to allow a party to treat him or her as its witness during what would otherwise be cross-examination, and to extend the examination beyond the scope of direct.

3. Use of Depositions at Trial:

Except for good cause shown no deposition testimony shall be introduced as direct examination, or during oral direct examination, other than those pages or portions thereof noted in previous filings with the court. This limitation shall not apply to the use of deposition testimony in cross-examination.

4. Stipulations may be read at any time, unless otherwise ordered in a particular instance upon a showing of good cause.

5. At least one-half hour before commencement of trial each day, counsel shall furnish the court reporter with a copy of any document from which counsel intends to read that day, except depositions to be read by two people in question and answer form. Documents to be used during cross-examination are excepted.

6. Whenever a single person is reading deposition testimony, in order to enable jurors and the reporter to understand clearly, the reader will say "Question" before each question is read and "Answer" before each answer is read.

7. All documents or other non-testimonial evidence that will be admitted at least in part without objection are to be pre-marked as exhibits using a numbering system. To effect the pre-marking, each of the parties will assign consecutive numbers to these documents, as follows: Plaintiff(s), 1-500; Group One Defendant(s), 501-999; Group Two Defendant(s), 1001-1,500.

A lettering system is to be used by each of the parties to pre-mark, for identification purposes, each piece of non-testimonial evidence it will offer to which objection has been made by the party against whom the document is sought to be admitted. The clerk will supply the parties with stickers to be used in pre-marking documents and other non-testimonial evidence, either as exhibits or for identification purposes.

C. <u>Objections, Motions to Strike, and Conferences Out of the Hearing of the Jury</u>

1. Counsel have the court's permission at all times to interrupt proceedings merely

to object or move to strike. Counsel need not state the ground(s) of objection unless the court asks for the ground(s), but (unless the court orders otherwise in a specific instance) counsel may without invitation by the court state the ground(s) merely by reference to a Rule designated by number, among the Federal Rules of Evidence. Also, unless otherwise ordered (as may be done, for example, when the court interrupts to sustain an objection because there are obvious, valid grounds), counsel may state the grounds in customary legal jargon (*e.g.*, "hearsay," "irrelevant," "lack of essential foundation"). Counsel are not to go beyond a bare statement of the ground(s); supporting or opposing arguments will not be stated in the hearing of the jury without the court's permission.

2. Conferences out of the hearing of the jury will be held to a minimum. <u>They will never occur at the beginning of a court day unless that timing is unavoidable.</u> When the court has directed jurors to be present at a designated hour, counsel asking for a conference out of the hearing of the jury at that hour will be required to show good cause why the need should not have been anticipated so the jury could have been released early the preceding day and why the conference cannot be deferred until the end of the current day, or at least until the next recess.

3. Short conferences out of the hearing of the jury may be held at the side bar farthest from the jury box. The jury will be sent to the jury room if a more extended conference out of their hearing is required.

D. <u>Schedule</u>

1. The court will aim for conducting this trial ____ a.m. to ____ p.m. Monday-Friday.

2. There will be no trial of this case on the following days: [Holidays and other days specially committed].

E. Sequestration of Witnesses

No person who is expected to testify as a witness in this civil action shall be present in the courtroom during the presentation of evidence (or have access to a transcript or summary of that evidence) except as follows:

1. As to the subject of their expert testimony, professional persons engaged by a party or by the party's counsel for the purpose of offering expert testimony.

2. One representative of each party designated by counsel to the court in advance of the trial as that party's representative.

A person who has testified and who is not expected to testify again for any party may be present in the courtroom after his or her testimony has been completed, but that person shall not state or summarize his or her own testimony or the testimony of others to prospective witnesses.

Except as provided in paragraph 1, counsel shall not state or summarize the testimony of others to prospective witnesses and shall not permit a prospective witness to read transcripts or summaries of previous testimony of other witnesses.

F. Miscellaneous Matters

1. Documents filed in court during trial: A party filing a document in court rather than in the Clerk's Office must file, with the original, a copy of the first page. Each document will be given a docket number by the clerk.

TAILORED TRIALS — Sec. B

2. All discovery is concluded.

3. Jurors will be permitted to take notes. Instructions will be given in the form of Exhibit B.

4. Drafts (not final) of interrogatories to the jury and the Charge will be distributed soon after requests of counsel have been filed (in accordance with Part IV-B above) and have been considered by the court.

United States District Judge

EXHIBIT A

EXHIBIT MARKING SLIP

The attached document or object is Exhibit No. _____.

Instructions to the Jury:

You may consider this document or object as evidence only with repsect to any party whose name is checked below. You may not consider this document or object as evidence with respect to any party whose name is not checked. If any limited purpose is set forth below then you may only consider this document or object for that limited purpose. If no limited purpose is set forth below, then you may consider this document or object for all purposes.

Party	Limited Purpose
_____ Plaintiff(s) _____	_____
_____	_____
	_____
Group One Defendant(s) _____	_____
_____	_____
	_____
Group Two Defendant(s) _____	_____
_____	_____
	_____

TAILORED TRIALS   Sec. B

EXHIBIT B

<u>INSTRUCTIONS TO JURORS ON NOTE-TAKING</u>

Members of the Jury:

You have the permission of the court to take notes during the evidence, the summations of attorneys at the conclusion of the evidence, and during my instructions to you on the law.

In many courts -- probably in most -- jurors are not permitted to take notes. The reasons are concerned with fear that taking notes may cause the jury, as a whole, to be less effective in serving as a completely fair and impartial factfinder. Because of the potential usefulness of taking notes, you will be permitted to take notes in this trial. However, for the purpose of protecting against the possible disadvantages that have led many courts to order that notes not be taken, I will instruct you to observe the following limitations:

1. <u>Note-taking is permitted, not required</u>. Each of you may take notes. No one is required to take notes.

2. <u>Take notes sparingly</u>. Do not try to summarize all of the testimony. Notes are for the purpose of refreshing memory. They are particularly helpful when dealing with measurements, times, distances, identities, and relationships.

3. <u>Be brief</u>. Over-indulgence in note-taking may be distracting. You, the jurors, must pass on the credibility of witnesses; hence, you must observe the demeanor and appearance of each person on the witness stand to assist you in passing on his or her credibility. Note-taking must not distract you from that task. If you wish to make a note, you need not sacrifice the opportunity to make important observations. You may make your note after having made the

observation itself. Keep in mind that when you ultimately make a decision in a case you will rely principally upon your eyes, your ears, and your mind, not upon your fingers.

4. <u>Your notes are for your own private use only. Do not use your notes, or any other juror's notes, as authority to persuade fellow jurors</u>. In your deliberations, give no more and no less weight to the views of a fellow juror just because that juror did or did not take notes. Your notes are not official transcripts. They are personal memory aids, just like the notes of the judge and the notes of the lawyers. Notes are valuable as a stimulant to your memory. On the other hand, you might make an error in observing, and you might make a mistake in recording what you have seen or heard. You are not, therefore, to use your notes as authority to persuade fellow jurors of what the evidence was during the trial.

5. <u>Do not take your notes away from court</u>. At the end of each day, please place your notes in the envelope which has been provided to you. A court officer will be directed to take the envelopes to a safe place and return them at the beginning of the next session on this case, unopened. At the conclusion of the case, after you have used your notes in deliberations, they will be collected and destroyed, to protect the secrecy of your deliberations.

United States District Judge

Form 8.B illustrates a way in which a <u>nonjury</u> trial may be tailored consistently with the use of time limits as incentives within adversary trials -- or with limits formally stated in some other way but having an impact similar to time limits.[2] Form 8.B also illustrates a way in which pretrial submission of proposed findings and conclusions may sharpen the focus of the trial, reduce its length, and enable the judge to make a prompt and well-informed decision soon after the evidence is closed.

---

[2] I acknowledge that in drafting this form I borrowed from former Judge Charles Renfrew, who of course is not to be held accountable for flaws in my implementation of his idea.

Ch. 8 CONDUCTING TRIALS

Form 8.B
Stipulation and Order
for
Tailored Non-Jury Trial
_____, 19__

I. Stipulations

1. Recognizing the right of each party to insist that "the testimony of witnesses shall be taken orally in open court," Fed. R. Civ. P. 43(a), the parties waive this right to the extent stated in this Stipulation and Order and agree that in this case direct examination of each witness shall be presented by affidavit, unless as to a particular witness an exception is allowed by the court pursuant to the provisions of this Stipulation and Order.

2. (Are there other special provisions the parties wish to adopt?)

II. Order Regulating Non-Jury Trial

A. Trial Date

This case is scheduled for non-jury trial commencing at _____a.m., _____, ____.

B. Clarification of Issues and Pre-Trial Filings

1. Aims. With the aims of promoting the court's and counsel's understanding of legal and factual issues and using efficiently the public and private resources committed to resolving this dispute, the court (1) will require that proposed findings and conclusions and affidavits to be used in lieu of oral direct examination be filed before trial commences, and (2) will aim for deciding the case immediately after oral argument at the conclusion of trial.

2. Initial Proposals. On or before _____ [6 weeks before trial date], counsel for the party having the burden of

proof on any claim or defense shall serve on other counsel (but not file with the clerk) three copies of Proposed Findings of Fact and Conclusions of Law. The statement shall list each finding and each conclusion in a separate numbered paragraph. Counsel are encouraged to be concise and to propose only the findings and conclusions that are essential to a claim or defense under the legal theory or theories advanced. (If two or more parties in a multi-party case have common positions, their counsel are urged to make and serve Proposals and Marked Responses jointly as far as possible.)

    3. <u>Marked Responses and Additional Proposals</u>.

    a. On or before _____ [4 weeks before trial date], counsel receiving Proposed Findings and Conclusions pursuant to paragraph 2 shall file with the clerk and serve on other counsel a copy of the Proposed Findings and Conclusions, marked as follows:

    (1) Only those parts of the proposed findings the accuracy of which is genuinely in dispute and only those parts of the conclusions of law that are contested shall be underlined.

    (2) Portions of the proposed findings the admissibility of which is contested shall be bracketed.

    (3) On the margin of the first page shall be typed or written the name of the party on whose behalf the Marked Response is filed, followed by the signature of counsel in accordance with Fed. R. Civ. P. 11.

    b. Counsel receiving Proposed Findings and Conclusions pursuant to paragraph 2, though not required to do so, may also at the time specified above, part 3-a, serve on other counsel three copies of Proposed Additional or Substitute Findings and Conclusions.

 c. Counsel receiving Proposed Additional or Substitute Findings and Conclusions shall, on or before _____ _____ [3 weeks before trial date], file with the clerk and serve on other counsel a Marked Response to the Proposed Additional or Substitute Findings and Conclusions.

 4. <u>Lists of Witnesses, Depositions and Exhibits</u>. Not later than _____ [2 weeks before trial date], each party shall file the following:

 a. A list of all prospective witnesses, together with the affidavits of each witness whose direct testimony is to be received by affidavit.

 b. A list of depositions to be used at trial as part of the party's case in chief, identifying pages or portions to be used. Depositions (or parts thereof) to be used only for impeachment or in cross-examination need not be listed.

 c. A list of exhibits to be introduced without objection, <u>identified by a single sequence of numbers</u>, regardless of which party is the proponent of an exhibit. Unless otherwise ordered, plaintiff's exhibits shall commence with Exhibit 1 and defendant's exhibits with Exhibit 501. (Consultation among counsel shall have occurred well in advance of the filing date to determine whether objections will be made to proffered exhibits.)

 d. A list of marked items to be offered at trial, as to which an opposing party has reserved the right to object, <u>identified by a sequence of capital letters and the party designation</u> (<u>e.g.</u>, Pl's A, B, C ...; D's A, B, C ...). A party reserving the right to object must file in writing, on the date stated above in this paragraph, a statement of the grounds of objection.

5. <u>Notice of Intent to Cross-Examine</u>. Not later than _____ [one week before trial date], counsel who wishes to cross-examine any witness whose direct testimony is to be received by affidavit shall give written notice to opposing counsel identifying the witness(es) to be cross-examined.

C. <u>Procedure at Trial</u>

1. <u>Use of Proposed Findings</u>. All parts of proposed findings neither underlined nor bracketed on the copy filed with the clerk before the trial begins will be received in evidence at the beginning of trial as uncontested. No other proof on uncontested matters will be required or accepted. Objections to the admissibility of bracketed, non-underlined parts of the proposed findings will be heard when such parts are offered, unless otherwise ordered. When the relevance or materiality of evidence offered at the trial is questioned, counsel offering the evidence shall be prepared to identify for the court the contested fact issue to which the offered evidence is relevant and material.

2. <u>Testimony</u>. Except as provided in part d below, all direct examination of witnesses at trial shall be presented by affidavit.

a. An affidavit of a witness, constituting the direct examination, must be in admissible form. That is, each statement in the affidavit must be in form such that if the witness were making the statement orally at trial, in response to a question, it would be admissible under the Federal Rules of Evidence. Statements that would be objectionable as conclusions, or objectionable because of lack of essential foundation evidence, should be avoided. <u>Cf.</u> Fed. R. Civ.

P. 56(e). To facilitate use at trial, the affidavit shall be prepared in numbered paragraphs, each of reasonable length.

b. When an affidavit is offered in evidence, opposing counsel may present objections. If the court sustains objection to any part of the affidavit, the proponent of the evidence may call the witness to the stand to attempt to cure or avoid grounds of objection and elicit evidence to replace that stricken on objection. This may be done as a completion of the direct examination before cross-examination commences. The court may place limitations on the opportunity for such curative additions to the direct testimony if counsel has inexcusably presented an affidavit not in compliance with part 2-a above.

c. If notice has been given by opposing counsel in accordance with II-B-5 above, the witness must be present for cross-examination and redirect examination.

d. In the following circumstances a party may use a deposition or call a witness for oral examination:

    (1) If notice is given in accordance with paragraph II-B-4-b above, the deposition of a witness may be used whenever Fed. R. Civ. P. 32 authorizes its use.

    (2) An opposing party and anyone having authority to represent that party as officer, director, or managing agent -- cf. Fed. R. Civ. P. 32(a)(2) -- may be called for oral examination at trial if notice has been given in accordance with paragraph II-B-5 above.

    (3) For good cause shown and upon motion filed on or before ____ _____ [2 weeks before

trial] (or filed thereafter but with good cause shown for late filing), all or part of the direct examination of any witness may be by oral examination at trial. The court may, even if no motion is filed, call a witness for oral examination to aid the court's fact finding; if this is done, the parties will be heard as to whether one or more other witnesses should also be called to assure fair opportunity to develop claims and defenses.

3. <u>Use of Depositions at Trial</u>. Except for good cause shown no deposition testimony shall be introduced in a case in chief other than those pages or portions as to which notice was given pursuant to II-B-4-b above. This limitation shall not apply to the use of deposition testimony for impeachment or in cross-examination.

4. <u>Stipulations</u>. Stipulations may be read at any time except during the testimony of a witness.

5. <u>Documents.</u> At least one-half hour before commencement of trial each day, counsel shall furnish the court reporter with a copy of any document from which counsel intends to read that day, except depositions to be read by two people in question and answer form. Documents to be used during cross-examination are excepted.

6. <u>Motions and Other Papers Filed During Trial</u>. A party filing a paper in court rather than in the Clerk's Office must file, with the original, a copy of the first page. Each filing will be given a docket number by the clerk.

D. <u>Phased Trial</u>

If the number and nature of claims and

defenses in the case makes phased trial useful, the court is prepared to consider separation of the trial into two or more phases. For example, a central issue or issues may be tried first, with a recess to follow in order to allow the parties to reassess their positions after decision in that phase of trial, thus making more effective use of the resources of the parties and the court. If such a phased trial is to be used, the schedule stated in this order will be used for Phase I and a new order will schedule any subsequent phase(s).

_____
United States District Judge

These illustrative forms of stipulations and orders regarding jury and nonjury trials suggest only a few among many ways in which the parties, their lawyers, and a trial judge may by cooperative effort tailor an adversary trial to serve the interests of the parties, as well as public interests, better than a lengthier and more traditionally contentious trial is likely to do. To some extent stipulations and orders like Forms 8.A and 8.B enable the parties to achieve a fair hearing at less expense with minimal likelihood of an outcome materially different from what it probably would have been at twice the expense or more. It is surely true also, however, that parties and their attorneys can do even more by additional stipulations that use more stringent time limits and other incentives to focus less on tangential issues and more upon the central issues of a dispute.

These forms of stipulations and orders illustrate also some among many contrasts between jury and nonjury trials, especially in relation to potential flexibility for adapting to the distinctive circumstances of a particular case. Mutually acceptable variations from the traditional model are more easily fashioned for nonjury than for jury trial.

For example, it is ordinarily easier in a nonjury case to conceive a practical plan for limiting the first phase to one or more potentially dispositive issues that can be tried in a limited span of court time and with limited cost in pretrial preparation. Also, the submission of testimony by affidavits or by deposition transcripts to be read by the decisionmaker out of court is more likely to be mutually acceptable in a nonjury trial. Moreover, proposed findings and conclusions can be exchanged between the parties and marked up to focus disputes of both fact and law, thus assuring that contrasting positions are made clearer to the decisionmaker than they are likely to be when the proposed findings and conclusions are separately filed days or weeks after trial (or even months later, as they sometimes are when counsel in a lengthy nonjury trial wish to wait until they have trial transcripts in hand before submitting their proposals).

From a trial judge's point of view, deciding a case as soon after the evidence closes as it is possible to think through the issues involved is likely to produce decisionmaking that is not only more efficient but also better in quality. Delay in disposition and the necessity of considering and ruling on matters presented in many other cases before working through the details of a reasoned decision in this case not only make the process of deciding more time consuming but also increase the difficulty of reaching the best decision.

The development of an alternative form of nonjury trial such as is illustrated in the Stipulation and Order for Tailored Nonjury Trial has changed the comparison between jury and nonjury trial in another respect. Absent such an alternative form of nonjury trial, the time from filing to disposition of a case in the trial court depends less on whether it is a jury or nonjury case than on the nature of the issues, the number of witnesses, and other such matters that bear upon the length of pretrial preparation and the length of trial testimony. In contrast, the availability of an alternative form of nonjury trial that requires less in-court trial time is likely to enable a busy court to reach the case, hear it, and decide it months (or in a very busy court, years) before it otherwise would have done so. A judge who is concerned about fair allocation of court time among cases, with priority to older cases except when good cause for preference is shown, is more likely to find time early for a two-day or two-week trial than for one that will take two months or longer.

C. Judging Proof

Even the judge least inclined to any form of "managerial judging"[1] must become an active decisionmaker when proof is being offered by the parties. In a nonjury trial, and ordinarily to a still greater extent in a jury trial, advocates will make objections to evidence. The adoption of formal Rules of Evidence for the federal and for many state courts has provided more structure and guidance for decisionmaking in this aspect of trials than existed before. Many debatable issues remain for the trial judge to decide, however.

The added structure provided by formal rules of evidence may not have decreased the effective scope of the trial judge's discretion. A rule such as Federal Rule 403 formally declares that the judge is to weigh probative value

---

[1]Concerning "managerial judging," see Chapter 7, Sections D, E, and F, and Chapter 8, Section A, supra.

of proffered evidence against other factors, including the likelihood of unfair prejudice and increased length of trial. Appellate courts review a trial judge's Rule 403 rulings under a deferential standard. Moreover, even if concluding that the trial court erred in an evidence ruling, an appellate court may invoke the harmless error principle.

This book does not focus on issues that arise in the application of the formal rules of evidence. It does, however, in this section focus on another aspect of the evidentiary phase of trials. In ruling on what we commonly call "objections to evidence," the trial judge is in fact applying some part of a set of rules about proof that are less formal and less clear than the Rules of Evidence. Indeed, the rules of proof that trial judges enforce vary significantly both among trial courts and among trial judges within a single trial court. These variations and the need for trial lawyers to be alert to them are often noted in trial advocacy instruction. They are seldom addressed elsewhere. Increasing pressures upon the legal system arising from increasing delay and expense create a need for reexamining the operating rules about proof, whether formal or informal.

As distinguished from a rule of evidence, which in most instances concerns admissibility, a "rule of proof," as I am using the phrase, concerns the way in which proof is presented or opposed.

An example of a "rule of proof" in this sense appears in the Stipulation and Order for Tailored Jury Trial presented in an earlier section.[2] In Part V-C of Form 8.A, paragraph 1 establishes some rules regarding the conduct of counsel during the offering of proof that are probably somewhat more restrictive than most trial judges enforce in most trials. For example, counsel may not fully explain their objections in the presence of the jury without advance approval by the court. Rules of this kind are rules that a judge may invoke, even when not stated in a formal Order Regulating Trial. A judge is even more likely to invoke them if counsel become especially contentious. The rules stated in Form 8.A allow an objecting attorney to state the ground(s) of objection in the presence of the jury, but only in customary legal jargon (such as "hearsay," "irrelevant," "lack of essential foundation"). They do not allow argument

---

[2]Section B of this Chapter, supra.

in the presence of the jury unless the court has determined that the proceedings can occur without risk that arguments formally addressed to the court are being inappropriately used for improper argument to the jury.

Other examples of rules of proof concern the manner and form of asking questions on direct and cross-examination. Rules regarding leading questions are in essence rules of proof as I use the term here. To some extent such rules appear formally in rules of evidence. Those formal rules leave so much discretion to the trial judge, however, that the trial lawyers, before trying a case in a court where they have not previously appeared, commonly make inquiries about the judge's practices and tendencies regarding such things as allowing leading questions without a formal showing of hostility or adverse interest.

Moreover, there are other rules of behavior and practice during the presentation of evidence of which there is no hint in formal rules of evidence. One trial judge requires counsel, when questioning a witness, to stand at a podium at a location fixed by the judge. A second allows counsel to move around the courtroom and to approach the witness without requesting permission of the court. A third allows counsel the same freedom with the exception that counsel is never to come close to the witness with raised voice or hostile manner.

Rules of proof may help to set the spirit of the trial as a fair and impartial proceeding aimed at disposition on the merits. The trial judge may allow and even encourage informality of counsel in ways that do not undermine that spirit or show disrespect for the court and the administration of justice according to the court's rulings, and do not show lack of civility toward other counsel, the jury, the parties, and the witnesses. The same trial judge may invoke stricter rules of courtroom behavior when one or more of the attorneys in a case have taken what the judge peceives to be unfair advantage of the allowance of informality.

Beyond rather general guidelines for conduct such as these, trial judges are likely to settle into common patterns of ruling on recurring issues having a closer bearing on the substantive content as well as the form of questions used by counsel in direct and cross-examination. For example, a trial judge may forbid a question that asks one witness to comment directly on the credibility of another witness, especially when the question is framed so a direct answer appears to be a charge that the other witness is lying and not just mistaken. If that is the judge's consistent practice, the effect is essentially the same as enforcing a "rule of proof" that one witness shall not be asked to comment directly on the credibility of another witness. It is, however, ordinarily an informally developed rule of which counsel must learn by inquiry or observation.

Rules of proof tend to be at least as difficult as rules of evidence to formulate precisely -- perhaps even more so. Even the judge whose rule it is may not be alert to the full dimensions of the rule in practice, with all its exceptions and qualifications. As a result, the judge may be less consistent in applying such an informal rule of proof than in applying a rule of evidence.

Another broad area of development of a set of informal rules of proof that vary from court to court and judge to judge concerns expert testimony.

One aspect of varied practice regarding the testimony of experts has been openly discussed, at least in trial advocacy training if not in more basic research and writing. Some trial judges expect counsel to establish an expert witness's qualifications and then state to the court that counsel "tenders" (or "offers") the witness as an expert in a stated field. Under this practice, the formulation of the statement of the field may become a debatable issue of both law and trial advocacy. Other trial judges -- and I am among them -- decline to rule on such a "tender." Ordinarily the only need for a ruling arises if there is a dispute between counsel about whether the witness is qualified to answer some particular question or questions. The court is better able to understand the issue and rule upon it properly when counsel is ready to ask a particular question about which there is dispute. The "tender" at an earlier time is in essence a request for an anticipatory ruling, when the issue is less clearly focused and the proposed ruling is more abstract in nature. Moreover, it is likely to be a needless ruling. In most trials, when an objection is made to a particular question of an expert, it is far more likely to relate to other matters than to qualifications of the witness to answer the question.

More significant is another kind of variation from court to court and judge to judge in relation to expert testimony. The Federal Rules of Evidence and similar rules in many states no longer require disclosure of the basis for an expert opinion before the opinion is stated in the presence of the jury. Might the judge nevertheless require disclosure, and should the judge do so, when the objection is that counsel believes that when disclosure is demanded, as may be done by the cross-examiner, the witness will not be able to offer any basis for the opinion that the court could determine to be one that reasonable jurors, correctly understanding the relevant law, could credit? Trial judges differ both in their basic views about this question and about the informal rules of proof that they apply when expert testimony is challenged on this ground. Also, relatively little guidance has developed in appellate opinions.[3]

When the traditions of adversary trial are undergoing changes and the conduct of the adversaries may become somewhat more varied and more contentious than has been customary, it is to be expected that even greater variations will develop with respect to the informal rules of proof in use in different courts and before different judges of the same court.

The nature and quality of these informal rules of proof is a matter deserving more attention, and more explicit consideration by the bench, the bar, and the academy.

D. Charges and Verdict Forms

A good charge to the jury is crisp and clear in style, precise and correct in content.

Matters of style have been addressed briefly in another Chapter.[1]

Content depends, of course, upon the issues of the particular case. Some generalizations about developing all kinds of tests for legal accountability have been developed in Chapter 3. A central point stated there is that sources of authority to which a trial judge and the trial lawyers in the case look for guidance seldom contain formulations of the

---

[3] See Keeton, Premise Facts, 73 Minn. L. Rev. 1, 51-54, 67-69 (1988).

[1] Chapter 5, supra.

tests for legal accountability suitable for use in explaining the applicable law to the jury. Usually the trial judge, aided by the requests and objections of the trial lawyers, must tailor tests of legal accountability to the circumstances of the particular case.

When the legal issues in the case are controlled by precedents and the particular case raises no unsettled issue, form books and the judge's own file of previous charges in similar cases may serve well as models from which the judge works in tailoring either a spontaneously delivered oral charge or a more carefully crafted written charge. It is especially likely that this method of tailoring the charge will be adequate for a tort or criminal trial that fits well within a common type.

In cases that are complex or for some other reason do not fit within a common pattern, tailoring a good charge to the jury is more difficult and requires more attention. Also it is too much to expect of a jury that they listen to a lengthy oral charge, understand it, remember all the instructions on all the different issues in the case, and then return a general verdict that correctly reflects their reasoned application of the entire charge to all the disputed and material fact questions in the case. It is more sensible in complex cases (1) to use special interrogatories, (2) to tailor instructions so they explain the interrogatories, one by one or in groups when that can be done crisply and clearly, (3) when possible to ask all the questions that need be answered under any contention of any party, so the appellate court may be able to order a different judgment rather than ordering a new trial if reversing one or more of the trial court's rulings on questions of law, and (4) to deliver the entire charge to the jury in writing as well as delivering it orally.

Especially is this so if precedents have not settled some potentially dispositive legal issue in the case -- that is, some issue that, if decided in one way by the court, will alone determine the outcome of the case. An illustration is the trial of state-law claims against state and municipal police officers for alleged arrest without probable cause, use of excessive force both in arrest and in transportation and detention before release on bail, and malicious prosecution, and federal law claims of associated violation of constitutional rights for which a remedy is available under 42 U.S.C. §1983.

Form 8.C, below, is an illustration of a verdict form used in a trial in late 1987. Names have been changed, and the case number is hypothetical. This verdict form submitted each question that any party asked to have submitted. Counsel deliberately did not request submission of every question that might arguably have been relevant under every legal contention not clearly foreclosed by the available precedents. They wisely chose not to ask the court to submit questions that for tactical reasons they would not have wished to ask the jury to answer. For this reason, it is very likely that this precise verdict form should not be used in any other case. It was tailored to this case, to the status of precedents at the time it was tried, and to fact questions that needed to be answered to preserve each of the legal issues that existing precedents at the time left unanswered. Partly for this very reason it serves well as an example of the way a verdict form may be tailored to the circumstances of the individual case and yet may be useful as a vehicle for suggesting ideas that the lawyers and the judge in another case may need to consider in drafting the verdict form for their case.

CHARGES AND VERDICT FORMS   Sec. D

Form 8.C

```
_____
                           )
ROBERT KELLOGG,            )
    Plaintiff              )
                           )
    v.                     )    CIVIL ACTION
                           )    NO. 88-2345-K
GRANT SUTCLIFF, et al.,    )
    Defendants             )
_____)
```

Verdict in Phase I of Trial

1(a). Did two or more of the defendants, acting together,
    arrest the plaintiff, Robert Kellogg, on or about June 10, 1986, without probable cause to believe that he (Kellogg) had committed one or more of the offenses with which he was charged?

Answer by placing a check mark in the blank that states your finding.

       _____YES   _____NO

If YES, place a check mark in the blank beside the name of each defendant who did so.

_____Grant Sutcliff
_____Julian Carrington
_____Matthew Phelps

1(b). Did one of the defendants, acting alone, or two or more of the defendants, but acting separately,
    arrest the plaintiff, Robert Kellogg, on or about June 10, 1986, without probable cause to believe that he (Kellogg) had committed one or more of the offenses with which he was charged?

Answer by placing a check mark in the blank that states your finding.

       _____YES   _____NO

Ch. 8   CONDUCTING TRIALS

If YES, place a check mark in the blank beside the name of each defendant who did so.

_____Grant Sutcliff
_____Julian Carrington
_____Matthew Phelps

If you have answered YES to any part of Questions 1(a) or 1(b), answer Question 1(c). If you have answered NO to all parts of Questions 1(a) and 1(b), skip Question 1(c).

    1(c). Did the defendant, in arresting the plaintiff, Robert W. Kellogg, without probable cause, act with the state of mind of believing in good faith that he had probable cause to arrest? Answer by placing a check mark in the blank beside YES or the blank beside NO as to each defendant, to state your finding.

As to defendant Grant Sutcliff:
    _____YES   _____NO
As to defendant Julian Carrington:
    _____YES   _____NO
As to defendant Matthew Phelps:
    _____YES   _____NO

    2(a). Did two or more of the defendants, acting together,
on or about June 10, 1986, use more force than they reasonably believed necessary in arresting, transporting the plaintiff (Kellogg) to the police barracks at Saugus, Massachusetts, and holding him there?

Answer by placing a check mark in the blank that states your finding.

            _____YES   _____NO
If YES, place a check mark in the blank beside the name of each defendant who did so.

_____Grant Sutcliff
_____Julian Carrington
_____Matthew Phelps

CHARGES AND VERDICT FORMS   Sec. D

2(b). Did one of the defendants, acting alone, or two or more of the defendants, but acting separately,
    on or about June 10, 1986, use more force than they reasonably believed necessary in arresting, transporting the plaintiff (Kellogg) to the police barracks at Saugus, Massachusetts, and holding him there?

Answer by placing a check mark in the blank that states your finding.

    _____YES   _____NO

If YES, place a check mark in the blank beside the name of each defendant who did so.

    _____Grant Sutcliff
    _____Julian Carrington
    _____Matthew Phelps

If you have answered YES to any part of Questions 2(a) or 2(b), answer Questions 2(c) and 2(d). If you have answered NO to all parts of Questions 2(a) and 2(b), skip Questions 2(c) and 2(d).

2(c). Was the defendant's use of excessive force such a flagrant abuse of official power as to shock the conscience of the community? Answer by placing a check mark in the blank beside YES or the blank beside NO as to each defendant, to state your finding.

As to defendant Grant Sutcliff:
    _____YES   _____NO
As to defendant Julian Carrington:
    _____YES   _____NO
As to defendant Matthew Phelps:
    _____YES   _____NO

2(d). Did any defendant, in using excessive force to arrest the plaintiff, Robert Kellogg, act with the purpose of causing harm to Robert Kellogg, and not as a result of a good faith mistake? Answer by placing a check mark in the blank beside YES

Ch. 8   CONDUCTING TRIALS

or the blank beside NO as to each defendant, to state your finding.

As to defendant Grant Sutcliff:
    _____YES   _____NO
As to defendant Julian Carrington:
    _____YES   _____NO
As to defendant Matthew Phelps:
    _____YES   _____NO

    3(a). Did two or more of the defendants, acting together,
> on or after June 10, 1986, make one or more false charges against the plaintiff (Kellogg), knowing the charge or charges to be false, and knowingly give false testimony before the grand jury, thus maliciously bringing about indictment and prosecution of the plaintiff (Kellogg) upon a charge or charges they knew to be false?

Answer by placing a check mark in the blank that states your finding.

        _____YES   _____NO

If YES, place a check mark in the blank beside the name of each defendant who did so.

_____Grant Sutcliff
_____Julian Carrington
_____Matthew Phelps

    3(b). Did one of the defendants, acting alone, or two or more of the defendants, but acting separately,
> on or after June 10, 1986, make one or more false charges against the plaintiff (Kellogg), knowing the charge or charges to be false, and knowingly give false testimony before the grand jury, thus maliciously bringing about indictment and prosecution of the plaintiff (Kellogg) upon a charge or charges they knew to be false?

CHARGES AND VERDICT FORMS   Sec. D

Answer by placing a check mark in the blank that states your finding.

_____YES   _____NO

If YES, place a check mark in the blank beside the name of each defendant who did so.

_____Grant Sutcliff
_____Matthew Phelps

The name of the defendant Julian Carrington is omitted from this question because it concerns a defendant's "acting separately," and it is undisputed that defendant Carrington did not give testimony before the grand jury.

If you have answered YES to any part of Questions 3(a) or 3(b), answer Questions 3(c) and 3(d). If you have answered NO to all parts of Questions 3(a) and 3(b), skip Questions 3(c) and 3(d).

3(c). Was any defendant's action in making false charges against plaintiff, Robert Kellogg, such a flagrant abuse of official power as to shock the conscience of the community? Answer by placing a check mark in the blank beside YES or the blank beside NO as to each defendant, to state your finding.

As to defendant Grant Sutcliff:
_____YES   _____NO
As to defendant Julian Carrington:
_____YES   _____NO
As to defendant Matthew Phelps:
_____YES   _____NO

3(d). Did any defendant in making false charges against plaintiff, Robert Kellogg, act with the purpose of causing harm to Robert Kellogg, and not as a result of a good faith mistake? Answer by placing a check mark in the blank beside YES or the blank beside NO as to each defendant, to state your finding.

As to defendant Grant Sutcliff:
_____YES   _____NO
As to defendant Julian Carrington:
_____YES   _____NO
As to defendant Matthew Phelps:
_____YES   _____NO

_____   _____
Date   Foreperson

E. Post-Trial Proceedings

Post-trial proceedings are typically anticlimactic. Also, they can be extremely troublesome if the trial judge and trial lawyers have given inadequate attention before and during trial to issues that may arise after trial.

Claims for pre-judgment or pre-verdict interest illustrate the point. In a trial of claims for breach of contract and fraud, if the evidence regarding damages depends in some way on generalized estimates of the net effect of streams of expense and income, but without specific calculations that identify dates of sustaining losses, the calculation may in effect, even if not explicitly in form, include an equivalent of interest. When such a method of proving damages is used, it may be difficult or even impossible to calculate pre-judgment interest as allowed by a statute. If prejudgment interest is allowed on the entire award, the effect is to allow interest twice on the losses for which an equivalent of interest has already been included in the estimated damages. Also, if a statute provides for simple rather than compounded prejudgment interest, the allowance of prejudgment interest on the full estimate of damages would be erroneous because of the inclusion of some interest on interest. In short, counsel and the trial judge should be thinking about the prejudgment interest issue as the case is prepared and tried --- not for the first time after verdict in a jury trial or findings of fact in a nonjury trial.

Claims for attorney fees are another common source of potentially extended and contentious post-trial proceedings.

In cases that involve multiple parties and multiple claims, counterclaims, and cross-claims, the terms of the appropriate judgment may be both complex and disputable.

Form 8.D is an example of a judgment fashioned after extensive written submissions, when counsel were unable to agree on the form of the judgment even after the court had ruled on all the proposed findings and conclusions submitted in a nonjury trial. Provisions were needed concerning recovery over by one against another of two or more parties against whom judgment was to be entered jointly and severally. The point is illustrated in Form 8.D, below. This circumstance illustrates the additional point that in some cases it will be impossible, at the time of entering the judgment, to calculate precisely all the future liabilities of the parties. Some of those future consequences depend on how a party with a right of recovery over against two or more others proceeds to collect by execution or otherwise. In Form 8.D, names have been changed and the case number is hypothetical.

Form 8.D

```
_____
                              )
JOSEPH DEE,                   )
     Plaintiff                )
                              )
v.                            )    CIVIL ACTION
                              )    NO. 83-2222-K
MICHAEL STEVENS,              )
     Defendant                )
                              )
_____)

_____
                              )
AMERICAN PENSION BENEFITS     )
CORP.,                        )
     Plaintiff                )
                              )
v.                            )    CIVIL ACTION
                              )    NO. 86-3333-K
MICHAEL STEVENS,              )
JONATHAN HALL, CHARLES HALL,  )
JOSEPH DEE, JAMES DALY, and   )
CATHERINE STEVENS, Executrix  )
of the Estate of JOHN STEVENS,)
     Defendants               )
_____)
```

Judgment
June 16, 1989

On the findings and conclusions stated in the Opinion of June 8, 1988, in the hearings of July 5, 1988 and September 3, 1988, in the Memorandum of February 2, 1989 except as modified by the concessions of American Pension Benefits Corporation, and in the Memorandum of June 16, 1989, and upon the submissions of counsel subsequent to February 2, 1989, it is ORDERED:

In Civil Action No. 86-3333-K

Judgment for plaintiff American Pension Benefits Corporation on Claim 1 against defendant Charles Hall in the amount of $113,542.64, plus interest in the amount of $83,979.93, which is interest at contract rates to date of judgment.

Judgment for plaintiff American Pension Benefits Corporation on Claim 2 against defendants Michael Stevens, Catherine Stevens as Executrix of the Estate of John Stevens, James Daly, Joseph Dee, and Jonathan Hall, jointly and severally, in the amount of $113,542.64, plus interest in the amount of $83,979.93, which is interest at contract rates to date of judgment.

Judgment for plaintiff American Pension Benefits Corporation on Claim 5 against defendant Michael Stevens in the amount of $113,542.64, plus interest in the amount of $83,979.93, which is interest at contract rates to date of judgment.

Judgment for plaintiff American Pension Benefits Corporation against defendants Charles Hall, Michael Stevens, Catherine Stevens as Executrix of the Estate of John Stevens, James Daly, Joseph Dee, and Jonathan Hall, jointly and severally, in the amount of $48,500 as attorney fees and costs.

The judgment shall bear interest (upon the principal sum of $113,542.64, upon the sum determined as interest on that amount to date of judgment, and upon the sum awarded as attorney fees and costs) at the federal judgment rate of 8.85% from date of judgment until paid.

The liability of all persons against whom judgment is here rendered is joint and several, and the total amount collectible by American Pension Benefits Corporation shall not exceed $113,542.64, plus interest of $83,979.93 to date of judgment, plus $48,500 as attorney fees and costs, plus interest from date of judgment until paid. Each of the persons against whom judgment is here rendered has a right of contribution in accordance with the law of Massachusetts against each other person against whom judgment is here rendered. All amounts collected by American Pension

Benefits Corporation on this judgment shall be applied first to principal and pre-judgment interest (recovered for the benefit of the Pension Plan), and post-judgment interest thereon. Only after full satisfaction of those parts of this judgment shall amounts collected be applied toward satisfaction of the award to American Pension Benefits Corporation for attorney fees and costs and post-judgment interest thereon.

<u>In Civil Action No. 83-2222-K</u>

Judgment for plaintiff Joseph Dee on his Claim 2 against defendant Michael Stevens in the amount necessary to indemnify Joseph Dee against loss under the judgment in Civil Action No. 86-3333-K. Any amount due and unpaid under this judgment shall bear interest at the federal judgment rate of 8.85% from the date due until paid.

<u>In Both Actions</u>:

All other claims, counterclaims, and cross-claims are dismissed.

_____
United States District Judge

E N D   of   T E X T

COURSE SUPPLEMENT ON JUDGING

TABLE OF CONTENTS

Course Description..261
Plan of Assignments...262

Part One

An Introduction to Judicial Decisionmaking

Reading Cases in Part One...................................263

Chapter 1. Commitments and Perspectives....................265
    Daniels v. Williams, 474 U.S. 327, 106 S. Ct. 662,
            88 L.Ed.2d 662 (1986).............265
    Verdict Form for a Claim Against Prison Officers
    for Use of Excessive Force.............................275
    DeShaney v. Winnebago County Department
    of Social Services, ___ U.S. ___, 109 S. Ct. 998,
            103 L.Ed.2d 249 (1989)............279
    Salinas v. Roadway Express, Inc., 735 F.2d 1574
            (5th Cir. 1984)...................302
    Zobel v. Williams, 457 U.S. 55, 102 Ct. 2309,
            72 L.Ed.2d 672 (1982) 312

Chapter 2. Law and Facts in the
           Administration of Justice....................342
    Shackil v. Lederle Laboratories,
            561 A.2d 511 (N.J. 1989)..........342
    In Re Asbestos Litigation, 829 F.2d 1233
            (3d Cir. 1987), cert. denied,
            108 S. Ct. 1586 (1988)............395
    Langan v. Valicopters, Inc., 88 Wn.2d 885,
            567 P.2d 218 (1977)...............446

Part Two

Making and Explaining Lawmaking Choices

Reading Cases in Part Two..................................456

Chapter 3. Fashioning Standards
            for Deciding Cases............................458
  Hustler Magazine v. Falwell, 85 U.S. 46,
            108 S. Ct. 876,
            99 L.Ed.2d 141 (1988).............458
  Sandstrom v. Montana, 442 U.S. 510,
            99 S. Ct. 2450,
            61 L.Ed.2d 39 (1979).............470
  Computer-Aided Exercises on Intent in Tort Law........488
  Oxford Shipping Co. v. New Hampshire Trading Corp.,
            691 F.2d 1 (1st Cir. 1982)........527
  United States v. Bank of New England,
            821 F.2d 844 (1st Cir. 1987)......538
  New England Tractor-Trailer Training of
  Connecticut, Inc. v. Globe Newspaper Co.,
            395 Mass. 471,
            480 N.E.2d 1005 (1985)...........562
  Bishop v. E.A. Strout Realty Agency,
            182 F.2d 503 (4th Cir. 1950)......574
  Chamberlain v. Mathis, 151 Ariz. 551,
            729 P.2d 905 (1986)...............580
  McKee v. American Home Products Corp., 782 P.2d 1045,
            113 Wash.2d 701 (1989)...........594
  Wards Cove Packing Co., Inc. v. Atonio,
            ___ U.S. ___, 109 S. Ct. 2115,
            104 L.Ed.2d 9 (1989)..............626

Chapter 4. Values in Reasoned Decisionmaking............662
  Davis v. Wyeth Laboratories, Inc.,
            399 F.2d 121 (9th Cir. 1968)......662
A Note on Reconsidering Cases in Chapters 1-3............681
Liability Insurance Materials............................682

Chapter 5. A Judge's Writing and Speaking...............686
Exercise 5.1...686
Exercise 5.2...692
Exercise 5.3...692

Chapter 6. Judging Statutes.............................693
  Kavadas v. Lorenzen,
            448 N.W.2d 219 (N.D. 1989)........693

<u>Gulden</u> v. <u>Crown Zellerbach Corp.</u>,
            890 F.2d 195 (9th Cir. 1989)......702

Chapter 7. Judging in Pretrial Proceedings..............709
   <u>Heileman Brewing Co.</u> v. <u>Joseph Oat Corp.</u>,
            871 F.d 648
                (7th Cir. 1989) (en banc).........709
Exercise7.1..749

Chapter 8. Conducting Jury and Nonjury Trials...........750
   <u>Bull</u> v. <u>McCuskey</u>, 96 Nev. 706,
            615 P.2d 957 (1980)...............750
   <u>Rossel</u> v. <u>Volkswagen</u>, 147 Ariz. 160,
            709 P.2d 517 (1985)...............757

Exercise 8.1...777

Course Description
(For a Course Based on These Materials)

<u>Judging</u>. This course is about the nature of judging within a legal system. The aim is to explore implications of a commitment by judges, and by other professionals of the system, to reasoned decisions, candidly explained. Part One introduces basic principles of making and explaining reasoned choices that decide disputes of "law" and disputes of "fact." Choices are examined as exercises of power guided by sources of authority to which the judge, and all others who participate in efforts to influence the judge's decision, are committed as professionals. Part Two focuses upon lawmaking choices, their value implications and ways of explaining the choices made. These matters are examined in the contexts of (1) creating and tailoring tests for legal accountability (including rules and standards of culpability, accountability, and immunity), (2) using duty and causation to measure the scope of accountability, (3) creating and tailoring procedural burdens of production or persuasion that decide marginal cases, (4) drafting opinions, and (5) judging statutes. Part Three concerns problems of case development and disposition that judges encounter as they guide cases through pretrial preparation and trial. Problems of trial examined in the course include methods of proof of facts and methods of adapting procedures to the different circumstances of individual cases in all kinds of trials -- jury and nonjury, civil and criminal. A central premise of this course is that, whether or not you are a judge or ever expect to be one, it makes a difference (both to your professional development and to the quality of the legal system) how well you understand judging in our legal system and what you believe about commitment to professionalism and method in judging.

Plan of Assignments
for a Course
(13 weeks of classes)

Week	Assigned Reading in Text	Assigned Reading in Course Supplement
1	Chapter 1 (pp. 1-27)	Introduction and Chapter 1 pp. 263-341
2	§§2A-2D (pp. 28-49)	In Chapter 2, pp. 342-94
3	§§2E-2H (pp. 50-65)	In Chapter 2, pp. 395-455
4	§§3A, 3B (pp. 66-89)	In Part Two, pp. 456-526
5	§§3C, 3D (pp. 90-98)	In Chapter 3, pp. 527-93
6	§§3E, 3F (pp. 99-111)	In Chapter 3, pp. 594-661
7	Chapter 4 (pp. 112-36)	Chapter 4, pp. 662-85
8	Chapter 5 (pp. 137-45)	Chapter 5, pp. 686-92
9	§§6A-6D (pp. 146-53)	In Chapter 6, pp. 693-701
10	§§6E-6H (pp. 154-76)	In Chapter 6, pp. 702-08
11	Chapter 7 (pp. 177-208)	Chapter 7, pp. 709-49
12	§§8A-8C (pp. 209-43)	In Chapter 8, pp. 750-76
13	§§8D, 8E (pp. 244-56)	In Chapter 8, pp, 777-803

PART ONE

AN INTRODUCTION TO JUDICIAL DECISIONMAKING

1. Reading Cases in Part One

As you read each judicial opinion reproduced in Part One of this Course Supplement consider, in addition to the substantive law issues, the following additional questions:

From what sources do judges obtain their factual and legal premises for reasoned decisionmaking?

What is a judge's role in lawmaking?

How and to what extent are the roles different for trial and appellate judges?

What do and should judges believe about the extent to which they are constrained and guided by a professional responsibility of "reasoned decisionmaking"?

What previously unanswered questions of law were decided in this case? What other, related questions were left to be answered, in the first instance, by a trial judge when applying the new law fashioned in this case?

2. The Varied Length of Reading Assignments in Different Parts and Chapters

The length (in pages) of reading assignments in Part One (Chapters 1 and 2) and in Chapter 3 (the first chapter of Part Two) is far greater than in later chapters. The principal reason for this disparity is that the editor expects that you will find it useful -- indeed almost imperative -- to read again some of the cases you previously

Supp. Part One   **INTRODUCTION**
                   TO DECISIONMAKING

read in earlier chapters as you study materials in the later chapters. A second reason is the editor's hope that you will find it more and more useful to have time for reflection about the materials, and about the relationships among materials in different chapters, as the course proceeds.

If you have ever wished for a course in which reading assignments became shorter near the end of the term, this may be it.

Special Note
on the
Form of Judicial Opinions
in the
Course Supplement

Judicial opinions in this Supplement have been reproduced by a computerized process from the text used in WESTLAW.

Among the advantages of this process were two of special weight: first, that an easy-to-read type face compatible with that in the remainder of this book could be used without rekeying all of the text and, second, that the paging of reporters could be shown for convenience of reference. In the text of an opinion as reproduced, the beginning of a page in the United States Reports is shown in boldface by a single asterisk followed by the page number; the beginning of a page in the Supreme Court Reporter is shown by a double asterisk followed by the page number.

Some disadvantages of this process were accepted as a trade off. One is that the italicizing (or underlining) of case names is not reproduced. The editor and publisher hope you will not find this a distraction. A second disadvantage is that brackets in the original are converted to parentheses here. Thus, for example, brackets around insertions in a quotation appear here as parentheses. Also, as a convenience for readers who may wish to use them, we have reproduced the West numbers (inserted at the beginning of different parts of the opinion as references to key number headnotes), but in parentheses rather than brackets.

CHAPTER 1

COMMITMENTS AND PERSPECTIVES

DANIELS v. WILLIAMS
474 U.S. 327, 106 S.Ct. 662 (1986)

Argued Nov. 6, 1985.
Decided Jan. 21, 1986.

PRISONS: inmate had no remedy under the Fourteenth Amendment for negligence of jailer.

Inmate brought civil rights actions against deputy sheriff to recover for injuries allegedly sustained when he slipped and fell on a pillow left on jail stairs by deputy sheriff. The United States District Court for the Eastern District of Virginia granted deputy's motion for summary judgment, and inmate appealed. The Court of Appeals, Fourth Circuit, 720 F.2d 792, affirmed. On petition for rehearing, the Court of Appeals, 748 F.2d 229, again affirmed. After granting certiorari, the Supreme Court, Justice Rehnquist, J., held that due process clause is not implicated by a state official's negligent act causing unintended loss of or injury to life, liberty, or property.

Affirmed.

Justice Marshall concurred in the result.

Justice Blackmun concurred in judgment and filed opinion.

Justice Stevens concurred in judgment and filed opinion, 106 S.Ct. 677.

DANIELS V. WILLIAMS

*327 **662 Syllabus[1]

Petitioner brought an action in Federal District Court under 42 U.S.C. section 1983, seeking to recover damages for injuries allegedly sustained when, while an inmate in a Richmond, Virginia, jail he slipped on a pillow negligently left on a stairway by respondent sheriff's deputy. Petitioner contends that such negligence deprived him of his "liberty" interest in freedom from bodily injury "without due process of law" within the meaning of the Due Process Clause of the Fourteenth Amendment. The District Court granted respondent's motion for summary judgment, and the Court of Appeals affirmed.

Held: The Due Process Clause is not implicated by a state official's negligent act causing unintended loss of or injury to life, liberty, or property. Pp. 663-67.

(a) The Due Process Clause was intended to secure an individual from an abuse of power by government officials. Far from an **663 abuse of power, lack of due care, such as respondent's alleged negligence here, suggests no more than a failure to measure up to the conduct of a reasonable person. To hold that injury caused by such conduct is a deprivation within the meaning of the Due Process Clause would trivialize the centuries-old principle of due process of law. Parratt v. Taylor, 451 U.S. 527, 101 S.Ct. 1908, 68 L.Ed.2d 420 (1981) overruled to the extent that it states otherwise. Pp. 663-66.

(b) The Constitution does not purport to supplant traditional tort law in laying down rules of conduct to regulate liability for injuries that attend living together in society. While the Due Process Clause speaks to some facets of the relationship between jailers and inmates, its protections are not triggered by lack of due care by the jailers. Jailers may owe a special duty of care under state tort law to those in their custody, but the Due Process Clause does not embrace such a tort law concept. Pp. 665-67. 748 F.2d 229, affirmed.

---

[1] The syllabus constitutes no part of the opinion of the Court but has been prepared by the Reporter of Decisions for the convenience of the reader. See United States v. Detroit Lumber Co., 200 U.S. 321, 337, 26 S.Ct. 282, 287, 50 L.Ed. 499.

REHNQUIST, J., delivered the opinion of the Court, in which BURGER, C.J., and BRENNAN, WHITE, POWELL, and O'CONNOR, JJ., joined. MARSHALL, J., concurred in the result. BLACKMUN and STEVENS, JJ., filed opinions concurring in the judgment.

*328 Justice REHNQUIST delivered the opinion of the Court.

(1) In Parratt v. Taylor, 451 U.S. 527, 101 S.Ct. 1908, 68 L.Ed.2d 420 (1981), a state prisoner sued under 42 U.S.C. section 1983, claiming that prison officials had negligently deprived him of his property without due process of law. After deciding that section 1983 contains no independent state-of-mind requirement, we concluded that although petitioner had been "deprived" of property within the meaning of the Due Process Clause of the Fourteenth Amendment, the State's postdeprivation tort remedy provided the process that was due. Petitioner's claim in this case, which also rests on an alleged Fourteenth Amendment "deprivation" caused by the negligent conduct of a prison official, leads us to reconsider our statement in Parratt that "the alleged loss, even though negligently caused, amounted to a deprivation." Id., at 536-537, 101 S.Ct., at 1913. We conclude that the Due Process Clause is simply not implicated by a negligent act of an official causing unintended loss of or injury to life, liberty or property.

In this section 1983 action, petitioner seeks to recover damages for back and ankle injuries allegedly sustained when he fell on a prison stairway. He claims that, while an inmate at the city jail in Richmond, Virginia, he slipped on a pillow negligently left on the stairs by respondent, a correctional deputy stationed at the jail. Respondent's negligence, the argument runs, "deprived" petitioner of his "liberty" interest in freedom from bodily injury, see Ingraham v. Wright, 430 U.S. 651, 673, 97 S.Ct. 1401, 1413, 51 L.Ed.2d 711 (1977); because respondent maintains that he is entitled to the defense of sovereign immunity in a state tort suit, petitioner is without an "adequate" state remedy, cf. Hudson v. Palmer, 468 U.S. ---, ----, 104 S.Ct. 3194, 3204-3205, 82 L.Ed.2d 393 (1984). Accordingly, the deprivation of liberty was without "due process of law."

*329 The District Court granted respondent's motion for summary judgment. A panel of the Court of Appeals for the Fourth Circuit affirmed, concluding that even if respondent could make out an immunity defense in state court, petitioner would not be deprived of a meaningful opportunity to present his case. 720 F.2d 792 (1983). On rehearing, the en banc

Court of Appeals affirmed the judgment of the District Court, but under reasoning different from that of the panel. 748 F.2d **664 229 (1984). First, a 5-4 majority ruled that negligent infliction of bodily injury, unlike the negligent loss of property in Parratt, does not constitute a deprivation of any interest protected by the Due Process Clause. The majority therefore believed that the postdeprivation process mandated by Parratt for property losses was not required. Second, the en banc court unanimously decided that even if a prisoner is entitled to some remedy for personal injuries attributable to the negligence of state officials, Parratt would bar petitioner's claim if the State provided an adequate postdeprivation remedy. Finally, a 6-3 majority concluded that petitioner had an adequate remedy in state court, even though respondent asserted that he would rely on sovereign immunity as a defense in a state suit. The majority apparently believed that respondent's sovereign immunity defense would fail under Virginia law.

Because of the inconsistent approaches taken by lower courts in determining when tortious conduct by state officials rises to the level of a constitutional tort, see Jackson v. City of Joliet, 465 U.S. 1049, 1050, 104 S.Ct. 1325, 1325, 79 L.Ed.2d 720 (1984) (WHITE, J., dissenting from denial of certiorari) (collecting cases), and the apparent lack of adequate guidance from this Court, we granted certiorari. 469 U.S. ----, 105 S.Ct. 2673, 86 L.Ed.2d 692 (1985). We now affirm.

In Parratt v. Taylor, we granted certiorari, as we had twice before, "to decide whether mere negligence will support a claim for relief under section 1983." 451 U.S., at 532, 101 S.Ct., at 1911. After examining the language, legislative history and prior interpretations of the statute, we concluded that section 1983, unlike *330 its criminal counterpart, 18 U.S.C. section 242, contains no state-of-mind requirement independent of that necessary to state a violation of the underlying constitutional right. Id., at 534-535, 101 S.Ct., at 1912. We adhere to that conclusion. But in any given section 1983 suit, the plaintiff must still prove a violation of the underlying constitutional right; and depending on the right, merely negligent conduct may not be enough to state a claim. See, e.g., Arlington Heights v. Metropolitan Housing Dev. Corp., 429 U.S. 252, 97 S.Ct. 555, 50 L.Ed.2d 450 (1977) (invidious discriminatory purpose required for claim of racial discrimination under the Equal Protection Clause); Estelle v. Gamble, 429 U.S. 97, 105, 97

S.Ct. 285, 291, 50 L.Ed.2d 251 (1976) ("deliberate indifference" to prisoner's serious illness or injury sufficient to constitute cruel and unusual punishment under the Eighth Amendment).

(2) In Parratt, before concluding that Nebraska's tort remedy provided all the process that was due, we said that the loss of the prisoner's hobby kit, "even though negligently caused, amounted to a deprivation (under the Due Process Clause)." 451 U.S., at 536-537, 101 S.Ct., at 1913. Justice POWELL, concurring in the result, criticized the majority for "pass(ing) over" this important question of the state of mind required to constitute a "deprivation" of property. Id., at 547, 101 S.Ct., at 1919. He argued that negligent acts by state officials, though causing loss of property, are not actionable under the Due Process Clause. To Justice POWELL, mere negligence could not "wor(k) a deprivation in the constitutional sense." Id., at 548, 101 S.Ct., at 1919 (emphasis in original). Not only does the word "deprive" in the Due Process Clause connote more than a negligent act, but we should not "open the federal courts to lawsuits where there has been no affirmative abuse of power." Id., at 548-549, 101 S.Ct., at 1919-1920; see also id., at 545, 101 S.Ct., at 1917 (Stewart, J., concurring) ("To hold that this kind of loss is a deprivation of property within the meaning of the Fourteenth Amendment seems not only to trivialize, but grossly to distort the meaning and intent of the Constitution"). Upon reflection, we agree and overrule Parratt to the extent that it states that mere lack of due care by a state *331 official may "deprive" an individual of life, liberty or property under the Fourteenth Amendment.

**665 The Due Process Clause of the Fourteenth Amendment provides: "(N)or shall any State deprive any person of life, liberty, or property, without due process of law." Historically, this guarantee of due process has been applied to deliberate decisions of government officials to deprive a person of life, liberty or property. E.g., Davidson v. New Orleans, 96 U.S. 97, 24 L.Ed. 616 (1878) (assessment of real estate); Rochin v. California, 342 U.S. 165, 72 S.Ct. 205, 96 L.Ed. 183 (1952) (stomach-pumping); Bell v. Burson, 402 U.S. 535, 91 S.Ct. 1586, 29 L.Ed.2d 90 (1971) (suspension of driver's license); Ingraham v. Wright, 430 U.S. 651, 97 S.Ct. 1401, 51 L.Ed.2d 711 (1977) (paddling student); Hudson v. Palmer, supra (intentional destruction of inmate's property). No decision of this Court before Parratt supported the view that negligent conduct by a state official, even though causing injury, constitutes a deprivation under the Due Process Clause. This history reflects the traditional and common-sense notion that the Due Process Clause, like its forebear in the Magna Carta, see Corwin, The Doctrine of Due Process of Law Before the Civil War, 24 Harv.L.Rev. 366, 368 (1911), was "'intended to secure the individual from the arbitrary exercise of the powers of government,'" Hurtado v. California, 110 U.S. 516, 527, 4 S.Ct. 111, 116, 28 L.Ed. 232 (1884) (quoting Bank of Columbia v. Okely, 4 Wheat. (17 U.S.) 235, 244, 4 L.Ed. 559 (1819)). See also Wolff v. McDonnell, 418 U.S. 539, 558, 94 S.Ct. 2963, 2975, 41 L.Ed.2d 935 (1974) ("The touchstone of due process is protection of the individual against arbitrary action of government, Dent v. West Virginia, 129 U.S. 114, 123, 9 S.Ct. 231, 233, 32 L.Ed. 623 (1889)."); Parratt, supra, 541 U.S., at 549, 101 S.Ct., at 1920 (POWELL, J., concurring in result). By requiring the government to follow appropriate procedures when its agents decide to "deprive any person of life, liberty, or property," the Due Process Clause promotes fairness in such decisions. And by barring certain government actions regardless of the fairness of the procedures used to implement them, e.g., Rochin, supra, it serves to prevent governmental power from being "used for purposes of oppression," Murray's Lessee v. *332 Hoboken Land & Improvement Co., 18 How. (59 U.S.) 272, 277, 15 L.Ed. 372 (1856) (discussing Due Process Clause of Fifth Amendment).

(3) We think that the actions of prison custodians in leaving a pillow on the prison stairs, or mislaying an inmate's property, are quite remote from the concerns just discussed. Far from an abuse of power, lack of due care suggests no more than a failure to measure up to the conduct of a reasonable person. To hold that injury caused by such conduct is a deprivation within the meaning of the Fourteenth Amendment would trivialize the centuries-old principle of due process of law.

The Fourteenth Amendment is a part of a constitution generally designed to allocate governing authority among the branches of the Federal Government and between that Government and the States, and to secure certain individual rights against both State and Federal Government. When dealing with a claim that such a document creates a right in prisoners to sue a government official because he negligently created an unsafe condition in the prison, we bear in mind Chief Justice Marshall's admonition that "we must never forget, that it is <u>a constitution</u> we are expounding," McCulloch v. Maryland, 4 Wheat. (17 U.S.) 316, 407, 4 L.Ed.

579 (1819) (emphasis in original). Our Constitution deals with the large concerns of the governors and the governed, but it does not purport to supplant traditional tort law in laying down rules of conduct to regulate liability for injuries that attend living together in society. We have previously rejected reasoning that "would make of the Fourteenth Amendment a font of tort law to be superimposed upon whatever systems may already be administered by the States," Paul v. Davis, 424 U.S. 693, 701, 96 S.Ct. 1155, 1160, 47 L.Ed.2d 405 (1976), **666 quoted in Parratt v. Taylor, 451 U.S., at 544, 101 S.Ct., at 1917.

The only tie between the facts of this case and anything governmental in nature is the fact that respondent was a sheriff's deputy at the Richmond city jail and petitioner was an inmate confined in that jail. But while the Due Process Clause of the Fourteenth Amendment obviously speaks to *333 some facets of this relationship, see, e.g., Wolff v. McDonnell, 418 U.S. 539, 94 S.Ct. 2963, 41 L.Ed.2d 935 (1974), we do not believe its protections are triggered by lack of due care by prison officials. "Medical malpractice does not become a constitutional violation merely because the victim is a prisoner," Estelle v. Gamble, 429 U.S. 97, 106, 97 S.Ct. 285, 292, 50 L.Ed.2d 251 (1976), and "false imprisonment does not become a violation of the Fourteenth Amendment merely because the defendant is a state official." Baker v. McCollan, 443 U.S. 137, 146, 99 S.Ct. 2689, 2695, 61 L.Ed.2d 433 (1979). Where a government official's act causing injury to life, liberty or property is merely negligent, "no procedure for compensation is <u>constitutionally</u> required." Parratt, 451 U.S., at 548, 101 S.Ct., at 1919 (POWELL, J., concurring in result) (emphasis added.)[1]

That injuries inflicted by governmental negligence are not addressed by the United States Constitution is not to say that they may not raise significant legal concerns and lead to the creation of protectible legal interests. The enactment of tort claim statutes, for example, reflects the view that injuries caused by such negligence should generally

---

[1] Accordingly, we need not decide whether, as petitioner contends, the possibility of a sovereign immunity defense in a Virginia tort suit would render that remedy "inadequate" under Parratt and Hudson v. Palmer, 468 U.S. ----, 104 S.Ct. 3194, 82 L.Ed.2d 393 (1984).

be redressed.[2] It is no reflection on either the breadth of the United States Constitution or the importance of traditional tort law to say that they do not address the same concerns.

In support of his claim that negligent conduct can give rise to a due process "deprivation," petitioner makes several arguments, none of which we find persuasive. He states, for example, that "it is almost certain that some negligence claims are within section 1983," and cites as an example the failure of a State to comply with the procedural requirements of Wolff v. McDonnell, supra, before depriving an inmate of good-time credit. We think the relevant action of the prison *334 officials in that situation is their deliberate decision to deprive the inmate of good-time credit, not their hypothetically negligent failure to accord him the procedural protections of the Due Process Clause. But we need not rule out the possibility that there are other constitutional provisions that would be violated by mere lack of care in order to hold, as we do, that such conduct does not implicate the Due Process Clause of the Fourteenth Amendment.

Petitioner also suggests that artful litigants, undeterred by a requirement that they plead more than mere negligence, will often be able to allege sufficient facts to support a claim of intentional deprivation. In the instant case, for example, petitioner notes that he could have alleged that the pillow was left on the stairs with the intention of harming him. This invitation to "artful" pleading, petitioner contends, would engender sticky (and needless) disputes over what is fairly pleaded. What's more, requiring complainants to allege something more than negligence would raise serious questions about what "more" than negligence--intent, recklessness or "gross negligence"--is required,[3] and indeed about what these elusive terms mean. **667 See Reply Brief for Petitioner 9 ("what terms like willful, wanton, reckless

---

[2] See, e.g., the Virginia Tort Claims Act, Va.Code section 8.01-195.1 et seq. (1984), which applies only to actions accruing on or after July 1, 1982, and hence is inapplicable to this case.

[3] Despite his claim about what he might have pleaded, petitioner concedes that respondent was at most negligent. Accordingly, this case affords us no occasion to consider whether something less than intentional conduct, such as recklessness or "gross negligence," is enough to trigger the protections of the Due Process Clause.

or gross negligence mean" has "left the finest scholars puzzled"). But even if accurate, petitioner's observations do not carry the day. In the first place, many branches of the law abound in nice distinctions that may be troublesome but have been thought nonetheless necessary:

"I do not think we need trouble ourselves with the thought that my view depends upon differences of degree. The whole law does so as soon as it is civilized." *335 LeRoy Fibre Co. v. Chicago, M. & St. P.R. Co., 232 U.S. 340, 354, 34 S.Ct. 415, 418, 58 L.Ed. 631 (1914) (Holmes, J., partially concurring).

More important, the difference between one end of the spectrum--negligence--and the other--intent--is abundantly clear. See O. Holmes, The Common Law 3 (1923). In any event, we decline to trivialize the Due Process Clause in an effort to simplify constitutional litigation.

Finally, citing South v. Maryland, 18 How. (59 U.S.) 396, 15 L.Ed. 433 (1856), petitioner argues that respondent's conduct, even if merely negligent, breached a sheriff's "special duty of care" for those in his custody. Reply Brief for Petitioner 14. The Due Process Clause, petitioner notes, "was intended to give Americans at least the protection against governmental power that they had enjoyed as Englishmen against the power of the crown." Ingraham v. Wright, 430 U.S., at 672-673, 97 S.Ct., at 1413. And South v. Maryland suggests that one such protection was the right to recover against a sheriff for breach of his ministerial duty to provide for the safety of prisoners in his custody. 18 How., at 402-403. Due Process demands that the State protect those whom it incarcerates by exercising reasonable care to assure their safety and by compensating them for negligently inflicted injury.

We disagree. We read South v. Maryland, supra, an action brought under federal diversity jurisdiction on a Maryland sheriff's bond, as stating no more than what this Court thought to be the principles of common law and Maryland law applicable to that case; it is not cast at all in terms of constitutional law, and indeed could not have been, since at the time it was rendered there was no due process clause applicable to the States. Petitioner's citation to Ingraham v. Wright does not support the notion that all common-law duties owed by government actors were somehow constitutionalized by the Fourteenth Amendment. Jailers may owe a special duty of care to those in their custody under state tort law, see Restatement (Second) of Torts section 314A(4) (1965), but for the reasons previously stated we reject the contention that the *336 Due Process Clause of the Fourteenth Amendment embraces such a tort law concept. Petitioner alleges that he was injured by the negligence of respondent, a custodial official at the city jail. Whatever other provisions of state law or general jurisprudence he may rightly invoke, the Fourteenth Amendment to the United States Constitution does not afford him a remedy.

Affirmed.

Justice MARSHALL concurs in the result.

Justice BLACKMUN, concurring in the judgment.

I concur in the result. See my opinion in dissent in Davidson v. Cannon, --- U.S. ----, 106 S.Ct. 668, 88 L.Ed.2d ---- (1986).

Supp. Ch. 1

Verdict Form for a Claim Against Prison Officers for Use of Excessive Force

Reproduced below is a verdict form (with hypothetical names inserted) used in a case tried in a United States District Court in 1988. (The Charge to the Jury, explaining this verdict form, is reproduced in Chapter 8 of this Course Supplement, <u>infra</u>.)

Plaintiff asserted (a) that he was improperly charged with an infraction of disciplinary rules of the prison, (b) that prison officials improperly ordered that, as punishment, he should not have a television set in his cell, and (c) that prison officers on an "extraction team" used excessive force in taking the television set against his protest.

1. Suppose the jury answers YES to Question 1(a), places check marks in all blanks in that question beside names, answers $50,000 to Question 1(b), answers NO to Question 2(a), and NO to Question 3(a) and all parts of Question 4. What judgment should the court enter?

2. You are law clerk to a judge trying another, quite similar case. If requested to do so by the plaintiff, should the trial court submit an additional interrogatory asking the jury whether they find that one or more of the defendants recklessly used excessive force?

ANTHONY DION,)
  Plaintiff)
)
v.)
) CIVIL ACTION
) NO. 90-3030
MICHAEL KATZ, <u>et al.</u>,)
  Defendants)

Verdict

<u>PART I -- Initial Restraint</u>

1(a). While the extraction team was in Anthony

275

Supp. Ch. 1   VERDICT FORM

Dion's cell on September 24, 1984, did one or more of the defendants use excessive force?

     _____YES   _____NO

If YES, place a check mark in the blank beside the name of each defendant who did so.

_____Herbert Mason, Lieutenant Correction Officer
_____James Watson, Correction Officer
_____Christopher Donlan, Correction Officer
_____Pasquale Perry, Correction Officer
_____James Ackroyd, Correction Officer
_____Mark Marino, Correction Officer

If NO, skip to Question 3. If YES, answer Questions 1(b) and 2.

  1(b). What amount of money, if any, do you find is required to fairly and reasonably compensate Anthony Dion for harm or injury caused by the use of excessive force. Answer in dollars or NONE.
      $_____

  2(a). While the extraction team was in Anthony Dion's cell on September 24, 1984, did one or more of the defendants maliciously and sadistically use force on Anthony Dion for the very purpose of causing harm?

     _____YES   _____NO

If YES, place a check mark in the blank beside the name of each defendant who did so.

_____Herbert Mason, Lieutenant Correction Officer
_____James Watson, Correction Officer
_____Christopher Donlan, Correction Officer
_____Pasquale Perry, Correction Officer
_____James Ackroyd, Correction Officer
_____Mark Marino, Correction Officer

If YES, answer Questions 2(b) and then go to Question 3. If NO, skip Question 2(b) and go to Question 3.

  2(b). What amount of money, if any, in addition to any amount you find in answer to Question 1(b), do you award against any defendant who you find maliciously and sadistically used force, to compensate for any additional

VERDICT FORM   Supp. Ch. 1

harm or injury caused by the malicious or sadistic use of
force. Answer by placing a check mark in the blank that
names the person against whom you make the award and answer
in dollars in the other blank beside that name; place a check
beside NO if you make no award against the person named.

Herbert Mason, Lieutenant Correction Officer
_____YES in the amount of $_____.   _____NO

James Watson, Correction Officer
_____YES in the amount of $_____.   _____NO

Christopher Donlan, Correction Officer
_____YES in the amount of $_____.   _____NO

Pasquale Perry, Correction Officer
_____YES in the amount of $_____.   _____NO

James Ackroyd, Correction Officer
_____YES in the amount of $_____.   _____NO

Mark Marino, Correction Officer
_____YES in the amount of $_____.   _____NO

PART II -- Four-Point Restraint

     3(a).   Did defendant Michael Katz, by keeping
Anthony Dion in four-point restraints for a period of time
during September 24, 1984 and September 25, 1984, use
excessive force or cause excessive force to be used?

                  _____YES   _____NO

If NO, skip to Question ___. If YES, answer Questions 3(b)
and 4.

     3(b).   Was a prison disturbance in existence when
defendant Michael Katz used excessive force or caused
excessive force to be used by keeping Anthony Dion in
four-point restraints?

                  _____YES   _____NO

If NO, skip to Question 4. If YES, answer Question 3(c)
before going on to Question 4.

     3(c).   By keeping Anthony Dion in four-point

Supp. Ch. 1   **VERDICT FORM**

restraints for a period on September 24, 1984, and September 25, 1984, did defendant Michael Katz maliciously and sadistically use force or cause force to be used on Anthony Dion for the very purpose of causing harm?

    _____YES   _____NO

If NO, skip to Question 4. If YES, answer Question 3(d) before going to Question 4.

  3(d). Do you award Anthony Dion compensatory damages against defendant Michael Katz for the acts you found in answering Question 3(c).

_____YES in the amount of $_____.   _____NO

PART III -- Punitive Damages

If you have answered YES to either Question 1(a) or Question 3(c) and have awarded at least some compensatory damages to Anthony Dion, answer Question 4. Otherwise skip Question 4.

  4. Do you award Anthony Dion punitive damages against one or more of the defendants? (Answer by placing a check mark in the blank that states your finding and, if your finding is YES, by specifying the amount in dollars.)

Herbert Mason, Lieutenant Correction Officer
_____YES in the amount of $_____.   _____NO

James Watson, Correction Officer
_____YES in the amount of $_____.   _____NO

Christopher Donlan, Correction Officer
_____YES in the amount of $_____.   _____NO

Pasquale Perry, Correction Officer
_____YES in the amount of $_____.   _____NO

James Ackroyd, Correction Officer
_____YES in the amount of $_____.   _____NO

Mark Marino, Correction Officer
_____YES in the amount of $_____.   _____NO

_____   _____
Date   Foreperson

DeSHANEY
v.
WINNEBAGO COUNTY DEPARTMENT OF SOCIAL SERVICES
109 S.Ct. 998 (1989)

Argued Nov. 2, 1988.
Decided Feb. 22, 1989.

CHILD ABUSE: state had no constitutional duty to protect child.

Mother of child who had been beaten by father brought civil rights action against social workers and local officials who had received complaints that the child was being abused by his father but had not removed him from his father's custody. The United States District Court for the Eastern District of Wisconsin, John W. Reynolds, J., entered summary judgment in favor of defendant, and mother appealed. The Court of Appeals for the Seventh Circuit, 812 F.2d 298, affirmed, and certiorari was granted. The Supreme Court, Chief Justice Rehnquist, held that State had no constitutional duty to protect child from his father after receiving reports of possible abuse.

Affirmed.

Justice Brennan dissented and filed an opinion in which Justice Marshall and Justice Blackmun joined.

Justice Blackmun dissented and filed an opinion.

*999 Syllabus[1]

Petitioner is a child who was subjected to a series of beatings by his father, with *1000 whom he lived. Respondents, a county department of social services and

---

[1] NOTE: Where it is feasible, a syllabus (headnote) will be released, as is being done in connection with this case, at the time the opinion is issued. The syllabus constitutes no part of the opinion of the Court but has been prepared by the Reporter of Decisions for the convenience of the reader. See United States v. Detroit Lumber Co., 200 U.S. 321, 337, 26 S.Ct. 282, 287, 50 L.Ed. 499.

several of its social workers, received complaints that petitioner was being abused by his father and took various steps to protect him; they did not, however, act to remove petitioner from his father's custody. Petitioner's father finally beat him so severely that he suffered permanent brain damage and was rendered profoundly retarded. Petitioner and his mother sued respondents under 42 U.S.C. section 1983, alleging that respondents had deprived petitioner of his liberty interest in bodily integrity, in violation of his rights under the substantive component of the Fourteenth Amendment's Due Process Clause, by failing to intervene to protect him against his father's violence. The District Court granted summary judgment for respondents, and the Court of Appeals affirmed.

Held: Respondents' failure to provide petitioner with adequate protection against his father's violence did not violate his rights under the substantive component of the Due Process Clause. Pp. 1002-1007.

(a) A State's failure to protect an individual against private violence generally does not constitute a violation of the Due Process Clause, because the Due Process Clause imposes no duty on the State to provide members of the general public with adequate protective services. The Clause is phrased as a limitation on the State's power to act, not as a guarantee of certain minimal levels of safety and security; while it forbids the State itself to deprive individuals of life, liberty, and property without due process of law, its language cannot fairly be read to impose an affirmative obligation on the State to ensure that those interests do not come to harm through other means. Pp. 1002-1004.

(b) There is no merit to petitioner's contention that the State's knowledge of his danger and expressions of willingness to protect him against that danger established a "special relationship" giving rise to an affirmative constitutional duty to protect. While certain "special relationships" created or assumed by the State with respect to particular individuals may give rise to an affirmative duty, enforceable through the Due Process Clause, to provide adequate protection, see Estelle v. Gamble, 429 U.S. 97, 97 S.Ct. 285, 50 L.Ed.2d 251; Youngberg v. Romeo, 457 U.S. 307, 102 S.Ct. 2452, 73 L.Ed.2d 28, the affirmative duty to protect arises not from the State's knowledge of the individual's predicament or from its expressions of intent to help him, but from the limitations which it has imposed on his freedom to act on his own behalf, through imprisonment, institutionalization, or other similar restraint of personal liberty. No such duty existed here, for the harms petitioner suffered did not occur while the State was holding him in its custody, but while he was in the custody of his natural father, who was in no sense a state actor. While the State may have been aware of the dangers that he faced, it played no part in their creation, nor did it do anything to render him more vulnerable to them. Under these circumstances, the Due Process Clause did not impose upon the State an affirmative duty to provide petitioner with adequate protection. Pp. 1004-1006.

(c) It may well be that by voluntarily undertaking to provide petitioner with protection against a danger it played no part in creating, the State acquired a duty under state tort law to provide him with adequate protection against that danger. But the Due Process Clause does not transform every tort committed by a state actor into a constitutional violation. Pp. 1006-1007.

812 F.2d 298 (CA7 1987) affirmed.

REHNQUIST, C.J., delivered the opinion of the Court, in which WHITE, STEVENS, O'CONNOR, SCALIA, and KENNEDY, JJ., joined. BRENNAN, J., filed a dissenting opinion, in which MARSHALL and BLACKMUN, JJ., joined. BLACKMUN, J., filed a dissenting opinion.

*1001 Chief Justice REHNQUIST delivered the opinion of the Court.

Petitioner is a boy who was beaten and permanently injured by his father, with whom he lived. The respondents are social workers and other local officials who received complaints that petitioner was being abused by his father and had reason to believe that this was the case, but nonetheless did not act to remove petitioner from his father's custody. Petitioner sued respondents claiming that their failure to act deprived him of his liberty in violation of the Due Process Clause of the Fourteenth Amendment to the United States Constitution. We hold that it did not.

I

The facts of this case are undeniably tragic. Petitioner Joshua DeShaney was born in 1979. In 1980, a Wyoming court granted his parents a divorce and awarded custody of Joshua to his father, Randy DeShaney. The father shortly thereafter moved to Neenah, a city located in Winnebago County, Wisconsin, taking the infant Joshua with him. There he entered into a second marriage, which also ended in divorce.

The Winnebago County authorities first learned that Joshua DeShaney might be a victim of child abuse in January 1982, when his father's second wife complained to the police, at the time of their divorce, that he had previously "hit the boy causing marks and (was) a prime case for child abuse." App. 152-153. The Winnebago County Department of Social Services (DSS) interviewed the father, but he denied the accusations, and DSS did not pursue them further. In January 1983, Joshua was admitted to a local hospital with multiple bruises and abrasions. The examining physician suspected child abuse and notified DSS, which immediately obtained an order from a Wisconsin juvenile court placing Joshua in the temporary custody of the hospital. Three days later, the county convened an ad hoc "Child Protection Team"--consisting of a pediatrician, a psychologist, a police detective, the county's lawyer, several DSS caseworkers, and various hospital personnel--to consider Joshua's situation. At this meeting, the Team decided that there was insufficient evidence of child abuse to retain Joshua in the custody of the court. The Team did, however, decide to recommend several measures to protect Joshua, including enrolling him in a preschool program, providing his father with certain counselling services, and encouraging his father's girlfriend to move out of the home. Randy DeShaney entered into a voluntary agreement with DSS in which he promised to cooperate with them in accomplishing these goals.

Based on the recommendation of the Child Protection Team, the juvenile court dismissed the child protection case and returned Joshua to the custody of his father. A month later, emergency room personnel called the DSS caseworker handling Joshua's case to report that he had once again been treated for suspicious injuries. The caseworker concluded that there was no basis for action. For the next six months, the caseworker made monthly visits to the DeShaney home, during which she observed a number of suspicious injuries on Joshua's head; she also noticed that he had not been enrolled in school and that the girlfriend had not moved out. The caseworker dutifully recorded these incidents in her files, along with her continuing suspicions that someone in the DeShaney household was physically abusing Joshua, but she did nothing more. In November 1983, the emergency room notified DSS that Joshua had been treated once again for injuries that they believed to be caused by child abuse. On the caseworker's next two *1002 visits to the DeShaney home, she was told that Joshua was too ill to see her. Still DSS took no action.

In March 1984, Randy DeShaney beat 4-year-old Joshua so severely that he fell into a life-threatening coma. Emergency brain surgery revealed a series of hemorrhages caused by traumatic injuries to the head inflicted over a long period of time. Joshua did not die, but he suffered brain damage so severe that he is expected to spend the rest of his life confined to an institution for the profoundly retarded. Randy DeShaney was subsequently tried and convicted of child abuse.

Joshua and his mother brought this action under 42 U.S.C. section 1983 in the United States District Court for the Eastern District of Wisconsin against respondents Winnebago County, its Department of Social Services, and various individual employees of the Department. The complaint alleged that respondents had deprived Joshua of his liberty without due process of law, in violation of his rights under the Fourteenth Amendment, by failing to intervene to protect him against a risk of violence at his father's hands of which they knew or should have known. The District Court granted summary judgment for respondents.

The Court of Appeals for the Seventh Circuit affirmed, 812 F.2d 298 (1987), holding that petitioners had not made out an actionable section 1983 claim for two alternative reasons. First, the court held that the Due Process Clause of the Fourteenth Amendment does not require a state or local governmental entity to protect its citizens from "private violence, or other mishaps not attributable to the conduct of its employees." Id., at 301. In so holding, the court specifically rejected the position endorsed by a divided panel of the Third Circuit in Estate of Bailey by Oare v. County of York, 768 F.2d 503, 510-511 (CA3 1985), and by dicta in Jensen v. Conrad, 747 F.2d 185, 190-194 (CA4 1984), cert. denied, 470 U.S. 1052, 105 S.Ct. 1754, 84 L.Ed.2d 818 (1985), that once the State learns that a particular child is in danger of abuse from third parties and actually undertakes to protect him from that danger, a "special relationship" arises between it and the child which imposes an affirmative constitutional duty to provide adequate protection. 812 F.2d, at 303-304. Second, the court held, in reliance on our decision in Martinez v. California, 444 U.S. 277, 285, 100 S.Ct. 553, 559, 62 L.Ed.2d 481 (1980), that the causal connection between respondents' conduct and Joshua's injuries was too attenuated to establish a deprivation of constitutional rights actionable under section 1983. 812 F.2d, at 301-303. The court therefore found it unnecessary to reach the question whether respondents' conduct evinced the "state of mind" necessary to make out a due process claim after Daniels v. Williams, 474 U.S. 327, 106 S.Ct. 662, 88 L.Ed.2d 662 (1986), and Davidson v. Cannon, 474 U.S. 344, 106 S.Ct. 668, 88 L.Ed.2d 677 (1986). 812 F.2d, at 302.

Because of the inconsistent approaches taken by the lower courts in determining when, if ever, the failure of a state or local governmental entity or its agents to provide an individual with adequate protective services constitutes a violation of the individual's due process rights, see Archie v. City of Racine, 847 F.2d 1211, 1220-1223, and n. 10 (CA7 1988) (en banc) (collecting cases), cert. pending, No. 88-576, and the importance of the issue to the administration of state and local governments, we granted certiorari. 485 U.S. ----, 108 S.Ct. 1218, 99 L.Ed.2d 419 (1988). We now affirm.

II

(1) The Due Process Clause of the Fourteenth Amendment provides that "(n)o State shall ... deprive any person of life, liberty, or property, without due process of law." Petitioners contend that the State[1] *1003 deprived Joshua of his liberty interest in "free(dom) from ... unjustified intrusions on personal security," see Ingraham v. Wright, 430 U.S. 651, 673, 97 S.Ct. 1401, 1413, 51 L.Ed.2d 711 (1977), by failing to provide him with adequate protection against his father's violence. The claim is one invoking the substantive rather than procedural component of the Due Process Clause; petitioners do not claim that the State denied Joshua protection without according him appropriate procedural safeguards, see Morrissey v. Brewer, 408 U.S. 471, 481, 92 S.Ct. 2593, 2600, 33 L.Ed.2d 484 (1972), but that it was categorically obligated to protect him in these circumstances, see Youngberg v. Romeo, 457 U.S. 307, 309, 102

---

[1] As used here, the term "State" refers generically to state and local governmental entities and their agents.

S.Ct. 2452, 2454, 73 L.Ed.2d 28 (1982).[2]

(2-5) But nothing in the language of the Due Process Clause itself requires the State to protect the life, liberty, and property of its citizens against invasion by private actors. The Clause is phrased as a limitation on the State's power to act, not as a guarantee of certain minimal levels of safety and security. It forbids the State itself to deprive individuals of life, liberty, or property without "due process of law," but its language cannot fairly be extended to impose an affirmative obligation on the State to ensure that those interests do not come to harm through other means. Nor does history support such an expansive reading of the constitutional text. Like its counterpart in the Fifth Amendment, the Due Process Clause of the Fourteenth Amendment was intended to prevent government "from abusing (its) power, or employing it as an instrument of oppression," Davidson v. Cannon, supra, at 348, 106 S.Ct., at 670; see also Daniels v. Williams, supra, at 331, 106 S.Ct., at 665 ("'"to secure the individual from the arbitrary exercise of the powers of government,"'" and "to prevent governmental power from being 'used for purposes of oppression'") (internal citations omitted); Parratt v. Taylor, 451 U.S. 527, 549, 101 S.Ct. 1908, 1919, 68 L.Ed.2d 420 (1981) (Powell, J., concurring in result) (to prevent the "affirmative abuse of power"). Its purpose was to protect the people from the State, not to ensure that the State protected them from each other. The Framers were content to leave the extent of governmental obligation in the latter area to the democratic political processes.

---

[2] Petitioners also argue that the Wisconsin child protection statutes gave Joshua an "entitlement" to receive protective services in accordance with the terms of the statute, an entitlement which would enjoy due process protection against state deprivation under our decision in Board of Regents v. Roth, 408 U.S. 564, 92 S.Ct. 2701, 33 L.Ed.2d 548 (1972). Brief for Petitioners 24-29. But this argument is made for the first time in petitioners' brief to this Court: it was not pleaded in the complaint, argued to the Court of Appeals as a ground for reversing the District Court, or raised in the petition for certiorari. We therefore decline to consider it here. See Youngberg v. Romeo, 457 U.S., at 316, n. 19, 102 S.Ct., at 2458, n. 19; Dothard v. Rawlinson, 433 U.S. 321, 323, n. 1, 97 S.Ct. 2720, 2724, n. 1, 53 L.Ed.2d 786 (1977); Duignan v. United States, 274 U.S. 195, 200, 47 S.Ct. 566, 568, 71 L.Ed. 996 (1927); Old Jordan Mining & Milling Co. v. Societe Anonyme des Mines, 164 U.S. 261, 264-265, 17 S.Ct. 113, 114-115, 41 L.Ed. 427 (1896).

(6, 7) Consistent with these principles, our cases have recognized that the Due Process Clauses generally confer no affirmative right to governmental aid, even where such aid may be necessary to secure life, liberty, or property interests of which the government itself may not deprive the individual. See, e.g., Harris v. McRae, 448 U.S. 297, 317-318, 100 S.Ct. 2671, 2688-2689, 65 L.Ed.2d 784 (1980) (no obligation to fund abortions or other medical services) (discussing Due Process Clause of Fifth Amendment); Lindsey v. Normet, 405 U.S. 56, 74, 92 S.Ct. 862, 874, 31 L.Ed.2d 36 (1972) (no obligation to provide adequate housing) (discussing Due Process Clause of Fourteenth Amendment); see also Youngberg v. Romeo, supra, 457 U.S., at 317, 102 S.Ct., at 2458 ("As a general matter, a State is under no constitutional duty to provide substantive services for those within its border"). As we said in Harris v. McRae, "(a)lthough the liberty protected *1004 by the Due Process Clause affords protection against unwarranted government interference, ... it does not confer an entitlement to such (governmental aid) as may be necessary to realize all the advantages of that freedom." 448 U.S., at 317-318, 100 S.Ct., at 2688-2689 (emphasis added). If the Due Process Clause does not require the State to provide its citizens with particular protective services, it follows that the State cannot be held liable under the Clause for injuries that could have been averted had it chosen to provide them.[3] As a general matter, then, we conclude that a State's failure to protect an individual against private violence simply does not constitute a violation of the Due Process Clause.

Petitioners contend, however, that even if the Due Process Clause imposes no affirmative obligation on the State to provide the general public with adequate protective services, such a duty may arise out of certain "special relationships" created or assumed by the State with respect to particular individuals. Brief for Petitioners 13-18. Petitioners argue that such a "special relationship" existed here because the State knew that Joshua faced a special danger of abuse at his father's hands, and specifically proclaimed, by word and by deed, its intention to protect him against that danger. Id.,

---

[3] The State may not, of course, selectively deny its protective services to certain disfavored minorities without violating the Equal Protection Clause. See Yick Wo v. Hopkins, 118 U.S. 356, 6 S.Ct. 1064, 30 L.Ed. 220 (1886). But no such argument has been made here.

at 18-20. Having actually undertaken to protect Joshua from this danger--which petitioners concede the State played no part in creating--the State acquired an affirmative "duty," enforceable through the Due Process Clause, to do so in a reasonably competent fashion. Its failure to discharge that duty, so the argument goes, was an abuse of governmental power that so "shocks the conscience," Rochin v. California, 342 U.S. 165, 172, 72 S.Ct. 205, 209, 96 L.Ed. 183 (1952), as to constitute a substantive due process violation. Brief for Petitioners 20.[4]

---

[4] The genesis of this notion appears to lie in a statement in our opinion in Martinez v. California, 444 U.S. 277, 100 S.Ct. 553, 62 L.Ed.2d 481 (1980). In that case, we were asked to decide, inter alia, whether state officials could be held liable under the Due Process Clause of the Fourteenth Amendment for the death of a private citizen at the hands of a parolee. Rather than squarely confronting the question presented here--whether the Due Process Clause imposed upon the State an affirmative duty to protect--we affirmed the dismissal of the claim on the narrower ground that the causal connection between the state officials' decision to release the parolee from prison and the murder was too attenuated to establish a "deprivation" of constitutional rights within the meaning of section 1983. Id., at 284-285, 100 S.Ct., at 558-559. But we went on to say:

"(T)he parole board was not aware that appellants' decedent, as distinguished from the public at large, faced any special danger. We need not and do not decide that a parole officer could never be deemed to 'deprive' someone of life by action taken in connection with the release of a prisoner on parole. But we do hold that at least under the particular circumstances of this parole decision, appellants' decedent's death is too remote a consequence of the parole officers' action to hold them responsible under the federal civil rights law." Id., at 285, 100 S.Ct., at 559 (footnote omitted).

Several of the Courts of Appeals have read this language as implying that once the State learns that a third party poses a special danger to an identified victim, and indicates its willingness to protect the victim against that danger, a "special relationship" arises between State and victim, giving rise to an affirmative duty, enforceable through the Due Process Clause, to render adequate protection. See Estate of Bailey by Oare v. County of York, 768 F.2d 503, 510-511 (CA3 1985); Jensen v. Conrad, 747 F.2d 185, 190-194, and n. 11 (CA4 1984) (dicta), cert. denied, 470 U.S. 1052, 105 S.Ct. 1754, 84 L.Ed.2d 818 (1985); Balistreri v. Pacifica Police Dept., 855 F.2d 1421, 1425-1426 (CA9 1988). But see, in addition to the opinion of the Seventh Circuit below, Estate of Gilmore v. Buckley, 787 F.2d 714, 720-723 (CA1), cert. denied, 479 U.S.

(8) We reject this argument. It is true that in certain limited circumstances the Constitution imposes upon the State affirmative *1005 duties of care and protection with respect to particular individuals. In Estelle v. Gamble, 429 U.S. 97, 97 S.Ct. 285, 50 L.Ed.2d 251 (1976), we recognized that the Eighth Amendment's prohibition against cruel and unusual punishment, made applicable to the States through the Fourteenth Amendment's Due Process Clause, Robinson v. California, 370 U.S. 660, 82 S.Ct. 1417, 8 L.Ed.2d 758 (1962), requires the State to provide adequate medical care to incarcerated prisoners. 429 U.S., at 103-104, 97 S.Ct., at 290-291.[5] We reasoned that because the prisoner is unable "'by reason of the deprivation of his liberty (to) care for himself,'" it is only "'just'" that the State be required to care for him. Ibid., quoting Spicer v. Williamson, 191 N.C. 487, 490, 132 S.E. 291, 293 (1926).

In Youngberg v. Romeo, 457 U.S. 307, 102 S.Ct. 2452, 73 L.Ed.2d 28 (1982), we extended this analysis beyond the Eighth Amendment setting,[6] holding that the substantive

---

882, 107 S.Ct. 270, 93 L.Ed.2d 247 (1986); Harpole v. Arkansas Dept. of Human Services, 820 F.2d 923, 926-927 (CA8 1987); Wideman v. Shallowford Community Hosp., Inc., 826 F.2d 1030, 1034-1037 (CA11 1987).

[5] To make out an Eighth Amendment claim based on the failure to provide adequate medical care, a prisoner must show that the state defendants exhibited "deliberate indifference" to his "serious" medical needs; the mere negligent or inadvertent failure to provide adequate care is not enough. Estelle v. Gamble, 429 U.S., at 105-106, 97 S.Ct., at 291-292. In Whitley v. Albers, 475 U.S. 312, 106 S.Ct. 1078, 89 L.Ed.2d 251 (1986), we suggested that a similar state of mind is required to make out a substantive due process claim in the prison setting. Id., at 326-327, 106 S.Ct., at 1088.

[6] The Eighth Amendment applies "only after the State has complied with the constitutional guarantees traditionally associated with criminal prosecutions.... (T)he State does not acquire the power to punish with which the Eighth Amendment is concerned until after it has secured a formal adjudication of guilt in accordance with due process of law." Ingraham v. Wright, 430 U.S. 651, 671-672, n. 40, 97 S.Ct. 1401, 1412-1413, n. 40, 51 L.Ed.2d 711 (1977); see also Revere v. Massachusetts General Hospital, 463 U.S. 239, 244, 103 S.Ct. 2979, 2983, 77 L.Ed.2d 605 (1983); Bell v. Wolfish, 441 U.S. 520, 535, n. 16, 99

component of the Fourteenth Amendment's Due Process Clause requires the State to provide involuntarily committed mental patients with such services as are necessary to ensure their "reasonable safety" from themselves and others. Id., at 314-325, 102 S.Ct., at 2457-2463; see id., at 315, 324, 102 S.Ct., at 2457, 2462 (dicta indicating that the State is also obligated to provide such individuals with "adequate food, shelter, clothing, and medical care"). As we explained, "(i)f it is cruel and unusual punishment to hold convicted criminals in unsafe conditions, it must be unconstitutional (under the Due Process Clause) to confine the involuntarily committed--who may not be punished at all--in unsafe conditions." Id., at 315-316, 102 S.Ct., at 2457-2458; see also Revere v. Massachusetts General Hospital, 463 U.S. 239, 244, 103 S.Ct. 2979, 2983, 77 L.Ed.2d 605 (1983) (holding that the Due Process Clause requires the responsible government or governmental agency to provide medical care to suspects in police custody who have been injured while being apprehended by the police).

(9) But these cases afford petitioners no help. Taken together, they stand only for the proposition that when the State takes a person into its custody and holds him there against his will, the Constitution imposes upon it a corresponding duty to assume some responsibility for his safety and general well-being. See Youngberg v. Romeo, supra, 457 U.S., at 317, 102 S.Ct., at 2458 ("When a person is institutionalized--and wholly dependent on the State(,) ... a duty to provide certain services and care does exist").[7] The rationale for this principle is simple enough: when the State by the affirmative exercise of its power so restrains an individual's liberty that it renders him unable to care for himself, and at the same time fails to provide for his basic human needs--e.g., food, clothing, shelter, medical care, and reasonable safety it *1006 transgresses the substantive limits on state action set by the Eighth Amendment and the Due Process Clause. See Estelle v. Gamble, 429 U.S., at 103-104, 97 S.Ct., at 290-291; Youngberg v.

S.Ct. 1861, 1872, n. 16, 60 L.Ed.2d 447 (1979).

[7] Even in this situation, we have recognized that the State "has considerable discretion in determining the nature and scope of its responsibilities." Youngberg v. Romeo, 457 U.S., at 317, 102 S.Ct., at 2458.

Romeo, supra, 457 U.S., at 315-316, 102 S.Ct., at 2457-2458. The affirmative duty to protect arises not from the State's knowledge of the individual's predicament or from its expressions of intent to help him, but from the limitation which it has imposed on his freedom to act on his own behalf. See Estelle v. Gamble, 429 U.S., at 103, 97 S.Ct., at 290 ("An inmate must rely on prison authorities to treat his medical needs; if the authorities fail to do so, those needs will not be met"). In the substantive due process analysis, it is the State's affirmative act of restraining the individual's freedom to act on his own behalf--through incarceration, institutionalization, or other similar restraint of personal liberty--which is the "deprivation of liberty" triggering the protections of the Due Process Clause, not its failure to act to protect his liberty interests against harms inflicted by other means.[8]

(10) The Estelle-Youngberg analysis simply has no applicability in the present case. Petitioners concede that the harms Joshua suffered did not occur while he was in the State's custody, but while he was in the custody of his natural father, who was in no sense a state actor.[9] While

---

[8] Of course, the protections of the Due Process Clause, both substantive and procedural, may be triggered when the State, by the affirmative acts of its agents, subjects an involuntarily confined individual to deprivations of liberty which are not among those generally authorized by his confinement. See, e.g., Whitley v. Albers, supra, 475 U.S. at 326-327, 106 S.Ct., at 1088 (shooting inmate); Youngberg v. Romeo, supra, 457 U.S. at 316, 102 S.Ct., at 2458 (shackling involuntarily committed mental patient); Hughes v. Rowe, 449 U.S. 5, 11, 101 S.Ct. 173, 177, 66 L.Ed.2d 163 (1980) (removing inmate from general prison population and confining him to administrative segregation); Vitek v. Jones, 445 U.S. 480, 491-494, 100 S.Ct. 1254, 1262-1264, 63 L.Ed.2d 552 (1980) (transferring inmate to mental health facility).

[9] Complaint 16, App. 6 ("At relevant times to and until March 8, 1984 (the date of the final beating), Joshua DeShaney was in the custody and control of Defendant Randy DeShaney"). Had the State by the affirmative exercise of its power removed Joshua from free society and placed him in a foster home operated by its agents, we might have a situation sufficiently analogous to incarceration or institutionalization to give rise to an affirmative duty to protect. Indeed, several Courts of Appeals have held, by analogy to Estelle and Youngberg, that the State may be held liable under the Due Process Clause for failing to protect children in foster homes from mistreatment at the hands of their foster

the State may have been aware of the dangers that Joshua faced in the free world, it played no part in their creation, nor did it do anything to render him any more vulnerable to them. That the State once took temporary custody of Joshua does not alter the analysis, for when it returned him to his father's custody, it placed him in no worse position than that in which he would have been had it not acted at all; the State does not become the permanent guarantor of an individual's safety by having once offered him shelter. Under these circumstances, the State had no constitutional duty to protect Joshua.

(11) It may well be that, by voluntarily undertaking to protect Joshua against a danger it concededly played no part in creating, the State acquired a duty under state tort law to provide him with adequate protection against that danger. See Restatement (Second) of Torts section 323 (1965) (one who undertakes to render services to another may in some circumstances be held liable for doing so in a negligent fashion); see generally W. Keeton, D. Dobbs, R. Keeton, & D. Owen, Prosser and Keeton on the Law of Torts section 56 (5th ed. 1984) (discussing "special relationships" which may give rise to affirmative duties to act under *1007 the common law of tort). But the claim here is based on the Due Process Clause of the Fourteenth Amendment, which, as we have said many times, does not transform every tort committed by a state actor into a constitutional violation. See Daniels v. Williams, 474 U.S., at 335-336, 106 S.Ct., at 678-679; Parratt v. Taylor, 451 U.S., at 544, 101 S.Ct., at 1917; Martinez v. California, 444 U.S. 277, 285, 100 S.Ct. 553, 559, 62 L.Ed.2d 481 (1980); Baker v. McCollan, 443 U.S. 137, 146, 99 S.Ct. 2689, 26, 61 L.Ed.2d 433 (1979); Paul v. Davis, 424 U.S. 693, 701, 96 S.Ct. 1155, 1160, 47 L.Ed.2d 405 (1976). A State may, through its courts and legislatures, impose such affirmative duties of care and protection upon its agents as it wishes. But not "all common-law duties owed by government actors were ... constitutionalized by the Fourteenth Amendment." Daniels v. Williams, supra, 474 U.S.

---

parents. See Doe v. New York City Dept. of Social Services, 649 F.2d 134, 141-142 (CA2 1981), after remand, 709 F.2d 782, cert. denied sub nom. Catholic Home Bureau v. Doe, 464 U.S. 864, 104 S.Ct. 195, 78 L.Ed.2d 171 (1983); Taylor ex rel. Walker v. Ledbetter, 818 F.2d 791, 794-797 (CA11 1987) (en banc), cert. pending sub nom. Ledbetter v. Taylor, No. 87-521. We express no view on the validity of this analogy, however, as it is not before us in the present case.

at 335, 106 S.Ct., at 678. Because, as explained above, the State had no constitutional duty to protect Joshua against his father's violence, its failure to do so--though calamitous in hindsight--simply does not constitute a violation of the Due Process Clause.[10]

Judges and lawyers, like other humans, are moved by natural sympathy in a case like this to find a way for Joshua and his mother to receive adequate compensation for the grievous harm inflicted upon them. But before yielding to that impulse, it is well to remember once again that the harm was inflicted not by the State of Wisconsin, but by Joshua's father. The most that can be said of the state functionaries in this case is that they stood by and did nothing when suspicious circumstances dictated a more active role for them. In defense of them it must also be said that had they moved too soon to take custody of the son away from the father, they would likely have been met with charges of improperly intruding into the parent-child relationship, charges based on the same Due Process Clause that forms the basis for the present charge of failure to provide adequate protection.

The people of Wisconsin may well prefer a system of liability which would place upon the State and its officials the responsibility for failure to act in situations such as the present one. They may create such a system, if they do not have it already, by changing the tort law of the State in accordance with the regular law-making process. But they should not have it thrust upon them by this Court's expansion of the Due Process Clause of the Fourteenth Amendment.

AFFIRMED.

---

[10] Because we conclude that the Due Process Clause did not require the State to protect Joshua from his father, we need not address respondents' alternative argument that the individual state actors lacked the requisite "state of mind" to make out a due process violation. See Daniels v. Williams, 474 U.S., at 334, n. 3, 106 S.Ct., at 677, n. 3. Similarly, we have no occasion to consider whether the individual respondents might be entitled to a qualified immunity defense, see Anderson v. Creighton, 483 U.S. 635, 107 S.Ct. 3034, 97 L.Ed.2d 523 (1987), or whether the allegations in the complaint are sufficient to support a section 1983 claim against the county and its Department of Social Services under Monell v. New York City Dept. of Social Services, 436 U.S. 658, 98 S.Ct. 2018, 56 L.Ed.2d 611 (1978), and its progeny.

Justice BRENNAN, with whom Justice MARSHALL and Justice BLACKMUN join, dissenting.

"The most that can be said of the state functionaries in this case," the Court today concludes, "is that they stood by and did nothing when suspicious circumstances dictated a more active role for them." Ante, at 1007. Because I believe that this description of respondents' conduct tells only part of the story and that, accordingly, the Constitution itself "dictated a more active role" for respondents in the circumstances presented here, I cannot agree that respondents had no constitutional duty to help Joshua DeShaney.

It may well be, as the Court decides, ante, at 1003-1004, that the Due Process Clause as construed by our prior cases creates no general right to basic governmental *1008 services. That, however, is not the question presented here; indeed, that question was not raised in the complaint, urged on appeal, presented in the petition for certiorari, or addressed in the briefs on the merits. No one, in short, has asked the Court to proclaim that, as a general matter, the Constitution safeguards positive as well as negative liberties.

This is more than a quibble over dicta; it is a point about perspective, having substantive ramifications. In a constitutional setting that distinguishes sharply between action and inaction, one's characterization of the misconduct alleged under section 1983 may effectively decide the case. Thus, by leading off with a discussion (and rejection) of the idea that the Constitution imposes on the States an affirmative duty to take basic care of their citizens, the Court foreshadows--perhaps even preordains--its conclusion that no duty existed even on the specific facts before us. This initial discussion establishes the baseline from which the Court assesses the DeShaneys' claim that, when a State has--"by word and by deed," ante, at 1004--announced an intention to protect a certain class of citizens and has before it facts that would trigger that protection under the applicable state law, the Constitution imposes upon the State an affirmative duty of protection.

The Court's baseline is the absence of positive rights in the Constitution and a concomitant suspicion of any claim that seems to depend on such rights. From this perspective, the DeShaneys' claim is first and foremost about inaction (the failure, here, of respondents to take steps to protect

Joshua), and only tangentially about action (the establishment of a state program specifically designed to help children like Joshua). And from this perspective, holding these Wisconsin officials liable--where the only difference between this case and one involving a general claim to protective services is Wisconsin's establishment and operation of a program to protect children--would seem to punish an effort that we should seek to promote.

I would begin from the opposite direction. I would focus first on the action that Wisconsin has taken with respect to Joshua and children like him, rather than on the actions that the State failed to take. Such a method is not new to this Court. Both Estelle v. Gamble, 429 U.S. 97, 97 S.Ct. 285, 50 L.Ed.2d 251 (1976), and Youngberg v. Romeo, 457 U.S. 307, 102 S.Ct. 2452, 73 L.Ed.2d 28 (1982), began by emphasizing that the States had confined J.W. Gamble to prison and Nicholas Romeo to a psychiatric hospital. This initial action rendered these people helpless to help themselves or to seek help from persons unconnected to the government. See Estelle, supra, 429 U.S. at 104, 97 S.Ct., at 291 ("(I)t is but just that the public be required to care for the prisoner, who cannot by reason of the deprivation of his liberty, care for himself"); Youngberg, supra, 457 U.S. at 317, 102 S.Ct., at 2458 ("When a person is institutionalized--and wholly dependent on the State--it is conceded by petitioners that a duty to provide certain services and care does exist"). Cases from the lower courts also recognize that a State's actions can be decisive in assessing the constitutional significance of subsequent inaction. For these purposes, moreover, actual physical restraint is not the only State action that has been considered relevant. See, e.g., White v. Rochford, 592 F.2d 381 (CA7 1979) (police officers violated due process when, after arresting the guardian of three young children, they abandoned the children on a busy stretch of highway at night).

Because of the Court's initial fixation on the general principle that the Constitution does not establish positive rights, it is unable to appreciate our recognition in Estelle and Youngberg that this principle does not hold true in all circumstances. Thus, in the Court's view, Youngberg can be explained (and dismissed) in the following way: "In the substantive due process analysis, it is the State's affirmative act of restraining the individual's freedom to act on his own behalf--through incarceration, institutionalization, *1009 or other similar restraint of personal liberty--which is the 'deprivation of liberty' triggering the protections of the Due Process Clause, not its failure to act to protect his liberty interests against harms inflicted by other means." Ante, at 1006. This restatement of Youngberg's holding should come as a surprise when one recalls our explicit observation in that case that Romeo did not challenge his commitment to the hospital, but instead "argue(d) that he ha(d) a constitutionally protected liberty interest in safety, freedom of movement, and training within the institution; and that petitioners infringed these rights <u>by failing to provide</u> constitutionally required conditions of confinement." 457 U.S., at 315, 102 S.Ct., at 2457 (emphasis added). I do not mean to suggest that "the State's affirmative act of restraining the individual's freedom to act on his own behalf," ante, at 1006, was irrelevant in Youngberg; rather, I emphasize that this conduct would have led to no injury, and consequently no cause of action under section 1983, unless the State then had failed to take steps to protect Romeo from himself and from others. In addition, the Court's exclusive attention to State-imposed restraints of "the individual's freedom to act on his own behalf," ante, at 1006, suggests that it was the State that rendered Romeo unable to care for himself, whereas in fact--with an I.Q. of between 8 and 10, and the mental capacity of an 18-month-old child, 457 U.S., at 309, 102 S.Ct., at 2454--he had been quite incapable of taking care of himself long before the State stepped into his life. Thus, the fact of hospitalization was critical in Youngberg not because it rendered Romeo helpless to help himself, but because it separated him from other sources of aid that, we held, the State was obligated to replace. Unlike the Court, therefore, I am unable to see in Youngberg a neat and decisive divide between action and inaction.

Moreover, to the Court, the only fact that seems to count as an "affirmative act of restraining the individual's freedom to act on his own behalf" is direct physical control. Ante, at 1006 (listing only "incarceration, institutionalization, (and) other similar restraint of personal liberty" in describing relevant "affirmative acts"). I would not, however, give Youngberg and Estelle such a stingy scope. I would recognize, as the Court apparently cannot, that "the State's knowledge of (an) individual's predicament (and) its expressions of intent to help him" can amount to a "limitation of his freedom to act on his own behalf" or to obtain help from others. Ante, at 1006. Thus, I would read Youngberg and Estelle to stand for the much more generous proposition that, if a State cuts off private sources of aid and then refuses aid itself, it cannot wash its hands of the harm that results from its inaction.

Youngberg and Estelle are not alone in sounding this theme. In striking down a filing fee as applied to divorce cases brought by indigents, see Boddie v. Connecticut, 401 U.S. 371, 91 S.Ct. 780, 28 L.Ed.2d 113 (1971), and in deciding that a local government could not entirely foreclose the opportunity to speak in a public forum, see, e.g., Schneider v. State, 308 U.S. 147, 60 S.Ct. 146, 84 L.Ed. 155 (1939); Hague v. CIO, 307 U.S. 496, 59 S.Ct. 954, 83 L.Ed. 1423 (1939); United States v. Grace, 461 U.S. 171, 103 S.Ct. 1702, 75 L.Ed.2d 736 (1983), we have acknowledged that a State's actions--such as the monopolization of a particular path of relief--may impose upon the State certain positive duties. Similarly, Shelley v. Kraemer, 334 U.S. 1, 68 S.Ct. 836, 92 L.Ed. 1161 (1948), and Burton v. Wilmington Parking Authority, 365 U.S. 715, 81 S.Ct. 856, 6 L.Ed.2d 45 (1961), suggest that a State may be found complicit in an injury even if it did not create the situation that caused the harm.

Arising as they do from constitutional contexts different from the one involved here, cases like Boddie and Burton are instructive rather than decisive in the case before us. But they set a tone equally well established in precedent as, and contradictory *1010 to, the one the Court sets by situating the DeShaneys' complaint within the class of cases epitomized by the Court's decision in Harris v. McRae, 448 U.S. 297, 100 S.Ct. 2671, 65 L.Ed.2d 784 (1980). The cases that I have cited tell us that Goldberg v. Kelly, 397 U.S. 254, 90 S.Ct. 1011, 25 L.Ed.2d 287 (1970) (recognizing entitlement to welfare under state law), can stand side by side with Dandridge v. Williams, 397 U.S. 471, 484, 90 S.Ct. 1153, 1161, 25 L.Ed.2d 491 (1970) (implicitly rejecting idea that welfare is a fundamental right), and that Goss v. Lopez, 419 U.S. 565, 573, 95 S.Ct. 729, 735, 42 L.Ed.2d 725 (1975) (entitlement to public education under state law), is perfectly consistent with San Antonio Independent School Dist. v. Rodriguez, 411 U.S. 1, 29-39, 93 S.Ct. 1278, 1294-1300, 36 L.Ed.2d 16 (1973) (no fundamental right to education). To put the point more directly, these cases signal that a State's prior actions may be decisive in analyzing the constitutional significance of its inaction. I thus would locate the DeShaneys' claims within the framework of cases like Youngberg and Estelle, and more generally, Boddie and Schneider, by considering the actions that Wisconsin took with respect to Joshua.

Wisconsin has established a child-welfare system specifically designed to help children like Joshua. Wisconsin law places upon the local departments of social services such as respondent (DSS or Department) a duty to investigate reported instances of child abuse. See Wis.Stat.Ann. section 48.981(3) (1987 and Supp.1988-1989). While other governmental bodies and private persons are largely responsible for the reporting of possible cases of child abuse, see section 48.981(2), Wisconsin law channels all such reports to the local departments of social services for evaluation and, if necessary, further action. section 48.981(3). Even when it is the sheriff's office or police department that receives a report of suspected child abuse, that report is referred to local social services departments for action, see section 48.981(3)(a); the only exception to this occurs when the reporter fears for the child's immediate safety. section 48.981(3)(b). In this way, Wisconsin law invites--indeed, directs--citizens and other governmental entities to depend on local departments of social services such as respondent to protect children from abuse.

The specific facts before us bear out this view of Wisconsin's system of protecting children. Each time someone voiced a suspicion that Joshua was being abused, that information was relayed to the Department for investigation and possible action. When Randy DeShaney's second wife told the police that he had "'hit the boy causing marks and (was) a prime case for child abuse,'" the police referred her complaint to DSS. Ante, at 1001. When, on three separate occasions, emergency room personnel noticed suspicious injuries on Joshua's body, they went to DSS with this information. Ante, at 1001-1002. When neighbors informed the police that they had seen or heard Joshua's father or his father's lover beating or otherwise abusing Joshua, the police brought these reports to the attention of DSS. App. 144-145. And when respondent Kemmeter, through these reports and through her own observations in the course of nearly 20 visits to the DeShaney home, Id., at 104, compiled growing evidence that Joshua was being abused, that information stayed within the Department--chronicled by the social worker in detail that seems almost eerie in light of her failure to act upon it. (As to the extent of the social worker's involvement in and knowledge of Joshua's predicament, her reaction to the news of Joshua's last and most devastating injuries is illuminating: "I just knew the phone would ring some day and Joshua would be dead." 812 F.2d 298, 300 (CA7 1987).)

Even more telling than these examples is the Department's control over the decision whether to take steps to protect a particular child from suspected abuse. While many different people contributed information and advice to this decision, it was up to the people at DSS to make the ultimate *1011 decision (subject to the approval of the local government's Corporation Counsel) whether to disturb the family's current arrangements. App. 41, 58. When Joshua first appeared at a local hospital with injuries signaling physical abuse, for example, it was DSS that made the decision to take him into temporary custody for the purpose of studying his situation--and it was DSS, acting in conjunction with the Corporation Counsel, that returned him to his father. Ante, at 1001. Unfortunately for Joshua DeShaney, the buck effectively stopped with the Department.

In these circumstances, a private citizen, or even a person working in a government agency other than DSS, would doubtless feel that her job was done as soon as she had reported her suspicions of child abuse to DSS. Through its child-welfare program, in other words, the State of Wisconsin has relieved ordinary citizens and governmental bodies other than the Department of any sense of obligation to do anything more than report their suspicions of child abuse to DSS. If DSS ignores or dismisses these suspicions, no one will step in to fill the gap. Wisconsin's child-protection program thus effectively confined Joshua DeShaney within the walls of Randy DeShaney's violent home until such time as DSS took action to remove him. Conceivably, then, children like Joshua are made worse off by the existence of this program when the persons and entities charged with carrying it out fail to do their jobs.

It simply belies reality, therefore, to contend that the State "stood by and did nothing" with respect to Joshua. Ante, at 1007. Through its child-protection program, the State actively intervened in Joshua's life and, by virtue of this intervention, acquired ever more certain knowledge that Joshua was in grave danger. These circumstances, in my view, plant this case solidly within the tradition of cases like Youngberg and Estelle.

It will be meager comfort to Joshua and his mother to know that, if the State had "selectively den(ied) its protective services" to them because they were "disfavored minorities," ante, at 1004, n. 3, their section 1983 suit might have stood on sturdier ground. Because of the posture of this case, we do not know why respondents did not take steps to protect

Joshua; the Court, however, tells us that their reason is irrelevant so long as their inaction was not the product of invidious discrimination. Presumably, then, if respondents decided not to help Joshua because his name began with a "j," or because he was born in the spring, or because they did not care enough about him even to formulate an intent to discriminate against him based on an arbitrary reason, respondents would not be liable to the DeShaneys because they were not the ones who dealt the blows that destroyed Joshua's life.

I do not suggest that such irrationality was at work in this case; I emphasize only that we do not know whether or not it was. I would allow Joshua and his mother the opportunity to show that respondents' failure to help him arose, not out of the sound exercise of professional judgment that we recognized in Youngberg as sufficient to preclude liability, see 457 U.S., at 322-323, 102 S.Ct., at 2461-2462, but from the kind of arbitrariness that we have in the past condemned. See, e.g., Daniels v. Williams, 474 U.S. 327, 331, 106 S.Ct. 662, 665, 88 L.Ed.2d 662 (1986) (purpose of Due Process Clause was "to secure the individual from the arbitrary exercise of the powers of government" (citations omitted)); West Coast Hotel Co. v. Parrish, 300 U.S. 379, 399, 57 S.Ct. 578, 585, 81 L.Ed. 703 (1937) (to sustain State action, the Court need only decide that it is not "arbitrary or capricious"); Euclid v. Ambler Realty Co., 272 U.S. 365, 389, 47 S.Ct. 114, 118, 71 L.Ed. 303 (1926) (State action invalid where it "passes the bounds of reason and assumes the character of a merely arbitrary fiat," quoting Purity Extract & Tonic Co. v. Lynch, 226 U.S. 192, 204, 33 S.Ct. 44, 47, 57 L.Ed. 184 (1912)).

*1012 Youngberg's deference to a decisionmaker's professional judgment ensures that once a caseworker has decided, on the basis of her professional training and experience, that one course of protection is preferable for a given child, or even that no special protection is required, she will not be found liable for the harm that follows. (In this way, Youngberg's vision of substantive due process serves a purpose similar to that served by adherence to procedural norms, namely, requiring that a State actor stop and think before she acts in a way that may lead to a loss of liberty.) Moreover, that the Due Process Clause is not violated by merely negligent conduct, see Daniels, supra, and Davidson v. Cannon, 474 U.S. 344, 106 S.Ct. 668, 88 L.Ed.2d 677 (1986), means that a social worker who simply makes a mistake of judgment under what are admittedly complex and difficult conditions will not find herself liable in damages under section 1983.

As the Court today reminds us, "the Due Process Clause of the Fourteenth Amendment was intended to prevent government 'from abusing (its) power, or employing it as an instrument of oppression.'" Ante, at 1003, quoting Davidson, 474 U.S., at 348, 106 S.Ct., at 670. My disagreement with the Court arises from its failure to see that inaction can be every bit as abusive of power as action, that oppression can result when a State undertakes a vital duty and then ignores it. Today's opinion construes the Due Process Clause to permit a State to displace private sources of protection and then, at the critical moment, to shrug its shoulders and turn away from the harm that it has promised to try to prevent. Because I cannot agree that our Constitution is indifferent to such indifference, I respectfully dissent.

Justice BLACKMUN, dissenting.

Today, the Court purports to be the dispassionate oracle of the law, unmoved by "natural sympathy." Ante, at 1007. But, in this pretense, the Court itself retreats into a sterile formalism which prevents it from recognizing either the facts of the case before it or the legal norms that should apply to those facts. As Justice BRENNAN demonstrates, the facts here involve not mere passivity, but active state intervention in the life of Joshua DeShaney-- intervention that triggered a fundamental duty to aid the boy once the State learned of the severe danger to which he was exposed.

The Court fails to recognize this duty because it attempts to draw a sharp and rigid line between action and inaction. But such formalistic reasoning has no place in the interpretation of the broad and stirring clauses of the Fourteenth Amendment. Indeed, I submit that these clauses were designed, at least in part, to undo the formalistic legal reasoning that infected antebellum jurisprudence, which the late Professor Robert Cover analyzed so effectively in his significant work entitled Justice Accused (1975).

Like the antebellum judges who denied relief to fugitive slaves, see id., at 119-121, the Court today claims that its decision, however harsh, is compelled by existing legal doctrine. On the contrary, the question presented by this case is an open one, and our Fourteenth Amendment precedents may be read more broadly or narrowly depending upon how one chooses to read them. Faced with the choice, I would adopt a "sympathetic" reading, one which comports with dictates of fundamental justice and recognizes that compassion need not be exiled from the province of judging. Cf. A. Stone, Law, Psychiatry, and Morality 262 (1984) ("We will make mistakes if we go forward, but doing nothing can be the worst mistake. What is required of us is moral ambition. Until our composite sketch becomes a true portrait of humanity we must live with our uncertainty; we will grope, we will struggle, and our compassion may be our only guide and comfort").

Poor Joshua! Victim of repeated attacks by an irresponsible, bullying, cowardly, and intemperate father, and abandoned by respondents who placed him in a dangerous *1013 predicament and who knew or learned what was going on, and yet did essentially nothing except, as the Court revealingly observes, ante, at 1001, "dutifully recorded these incidents in (their) files." It is a sad commentary upon American life, and constitutional principles--so full of late of patriotic fervor and proud proclamations about "liberty and justice for all," that this child, Joshua DeShaney, now is assigned to live out the remainder of his life profoundly retarded. Joshua and his mother, as petitioners here, deserve--but now are denied by this Court--the opportunity to have the facts of their case considered in the light of the constitutional protection that 42 U.S.C. section 1983 is meant to provide.

Supp. Ch. 1

SALINAS v. ROADWAY EXPRESS, INC.

United States Court of Appeals, Fifth Circuit.
July 16, 1984.
735 F.2d 1574

CIVIL RIGHTS: findings inadequate as basis for class membership cutoff date in employment discrimination action.

Black and Mexican-American truck drivers brought class action employment discrimination suit against trucking company, alleging that company violated Title VII by favoring white employees for higher paying position of road driver while nonwhites were relegated to lower paying position of city driver. The United States District Court for the Western District of Texas, Manuel H. Real, J. (sitting by designation), held that a prima facie case of employment discrimination was established, but that such activity by company ceased on January 1, 1968, and awarded retroactive seniority to ten class members and attorneys' fees to class counsel, but denied back pay. Drivers appealed and trucking company cross-appealed. The Court of Appeals, Johnson, Circuit Judge, held that: (1) remand was required to establish factual basis for district court's finding that January 1, 1968 constituted class membership cutoff date; (2) trial court erred in denying back pay on ground that evidence failed to demonstrate in any quantifiable way a means by which back pay could be awarded; (3) court erred in excluding class members who took no overt action to secure a road job, as such members should have been afforded an opportunity to demonstrate a present willingness to transfer to road jobs; (4) as particular driver could not have pursued his own Title VII action by reason of dismissal of prior action with prejudice, court was correct in not allowing him to intervene; and (5) dual seniority system effective under collective bargaining agreement between company and union was bona fide and nondiscriminatory.

Vacated and remanded.

*1576 Before GEE, RANDALL, and JOHNSON, Circuit Judges.

JOHNSON, Circuit Judge:

On September 17, 1971, black and Mexican-American truck drivers brought a class action employment discrimination suit in the Western District of Texas against their employer, Roadway Express, Inc. (Roadway), and their union representatives seeking equitable relief and back pay. The plaintiffs alleged that defendant Roadway had violated Title VII of the Civil Rights Act of 1964, 42 U.S.C. section 2000e et seq., by favoring white employees for the higher paying position of road driver while nonwhites were relegated to the lower paying position of city driver. The employees also contended that the union had violated the Act by agreeing with the employer to establish and maintain a dual seniority system in the collective bargaining agreement for city and road drivers which perpetuated past discriminatory practices. See 42 U.S.C. section 1981. Three other class actions involving similar issues, a substantially similar class, and virtually the same defendants were subsequently consolidated with the instant action for coordinated pretrial proceedings. The district court thereafter dismissed the other actions but allowed two of the named plaintiffs to intervene in this suit. The motions of George Salazar and Chester Torry to intervene as named plaintiffs were denied by the court.

Following a period of over five years in which the parties engaged in extensive discovery, the action was tried before the district court in April 1977. The trial judge bifurcated the proceedings into Phases I (liability) and II (remedy). At the conclusion of the Phase I proceedings, the court found that the plaintiffs had demonstrated a prima facie case of employment discrimination by Roadway; but, that such activity by the employer ceased on January 1, 1968. In Phase II, the court awarded retroactive seniority to ten class members and attorneys' fees to class counsel, but denied back pay. The court also concluded that the dual seniority system effective under the collective bargaining agreement is bona fide and nondiscriminatory. On appeal, the plaintiff class contends that the district court erred in: (1) finding that Roadway ceased discriminatory practices on January 1, 1968; (2) denying back pay; (3) its determination of seniority dates; (4) limiting relief to only those class members who did some overt act evidencing an intent to secure a road job; and (5) refusing to allow *1577 George Salazar to intervene. Plaintiff Thomas Salinas also challenges the court's holding that the dual seniority system is lawful. Chester Torry contends that the court erred in refusing to allow him to intervene. On cross-appeal, Roadway maintains that the court erred in not granting its motion for judgment as to all liability. We vacate the judgment of the district court for failure to comply with Fed.R.Civ.P. 52(a) and remand.

Roadway is the largest common carrier of general commodity freight in the United States, operating terminals in thirty-three states. For the purposes of collective bargaining, Roadway drivers are represented by the International Brotherhood of Teamsters (Teamsters). The Southern Conference of Teamsters is a delegate body of the Teamsters composed of representatives of the affiliated local unions in ten southern states. There are separate collective bargaining contracts between Roadway and the union concerning city and road drivers which establish different terms and conditions of employment, including seniority lists, rates of pay, and levels and types of fringe benefits. Thomas Salinas, as named plaintiff, brought suit on behalf of the class of black and Mexican-American city truck drivers in the Southern Conference. The certified class consisted of:

> All persons who have been reported by Roadway Express, Inc. to the Equal Employment Opportunity Commission as Negroes, Mexican Americans and Spanish Surnamed Americans, who do or did city driving for Roadway Express, Inc. at any time from November 21, 1968, until the present time, within the territory covered by the Southern Conference of Teamsters Supplemental Agreement to the National Master Freight Agreement (Arkansas, Louisiana, Oklahoma, Texas, Florida, Georgia, Mississippi, Tennessee and the City of Asheville, North Carolina).

Record Vol. III at 1614. In substance, the plaintiffs alleged that prior to the filing of their lawsuit in 1971, Roadway discriminated against blacks, Mexican-Americans, and Spanish-surnamed Americans in its hiring practices, and that Roadway's "no transfer" policy, coupled with the union's dual seniority system, perpetuated the effects of the discriminatory hiring practices even after the practices ceased.[1]

---

[1] Virtually the same attacks were made against Roadway's employment practices in a previous Title VII action. In Bing v. Roadway Express, Inc., 444 F.2d 687, 688 (5th Cir.1971) (Bing I), a class action brought by black city drivers in Roadway's Atlanta, Georgia, terminal, this Court detailed Roadway's "no transfer" policy:

Roadway ... has intentionally discouraged transfers between the collective bargaining units--particularly between the road driver unit and the city driver unit--through the application of a "no transfer' rule. The rule, in effect, requires an employee who desires to transfer

Class Membership Cutoff Date

The district court found that through statistical proof, as well as through individual testimony and exhibits, the plaintiffs had demonstrated a system-wide pattern and practice of racial discrimination by Roadway relative to the filling of road driving positions. The court also found: "However, the credible, believable evidence demonstrated that such activity by Roadway Express, Inc., ceased on January 1, 1968." Record Vol. X at 55. The plaintiffs maintain that the court's determination of the cutoff date for class membership was arbitrary.

The court's finding that Roadway ceased its unlawful activity on January 1, 1968, raises cause for concern in that it appears to be contradicted by other findings by the court. For instance, the court found that Roadway never employed a black road driver in the Southern Conference until May 5, 1969, and that no Mexican-American was employed in that position until March 11, 1972. Other of the court's findings also indicate that minorities were dissuaded *1578 from applying for road driving positions at least through May 1971. The reason that January 1, 1968, was selected as the cutoff date for class membership cannot be discerned from the district court's findings of fact and conclusions of law. Plaintiffs note that at a hearing on the court's proposed judgment, the trial judge indicated that he chose that date because class member Willie Luckett received a road driver application on that date in response to a letter that he had written to Roadway. See Record Vol. XII at 34-35. In its findings of fact, however, the court found that Luckett did not receive a letter from Roadway detailing the procedure for applying for a road job until March 19, 1971. Even more confusing is the fact that the court granted retroactive seniority to three class members who became city drivers

---

to another job to resign his present position and thereby forfeit the employment rights accrued under it. He must then apply for the new position as if he were a stranger to the Company, with no assurance from Roadway prior to resigning his job that he will be hired for the new position.

The Bing I Court found the conclusion inescapable that the no-transfer policy indeed had the effect of perpetuating Roadway's past discriminatory hiring policy. 444 F.2d at 690.

after January 1, 1968. It should also be noted that, in their proposed notices to class members, both Roadway and the plaintiffs recited that the class included minority employees who did or were doing city driving from November 1, 1968, until the time of suit.

(1, 2) This Court reviews the district court's findings under the clearly erroneous standard. In doing so, we cannot be left to speculate as to the factual basis for the district court's conclusion. This Court cannot determine whether the district court's selection of the January 1, 1968, cutoff date was clearly erroneous when the district court has made no more than conclusory findings. We must therefore vacate the judgment of the district court for failure to comply with Fed.R.Civ.P. 52(a)[2] and remand for findings which indicate, with specificity, the factual basis for the district court's determination of the cutoff date for class membership. See Redditt v. Mississippi Extended Care Centers, Inc., 718 F.2d 1381, 1386 (5th Cir.1983). In an effort to guide the court upon remand, we note that this Court has recognized the desirability of establishing a cutoff date for class membership in a Title VII suit in order to facilitate the disposition of the case. Sagers v. Yellow Freight System, Inc., 529 F.2d 721 (5th Cir.1976). In Sagers, this Court held that the district court did not err in establishing a cutoff date where there was ample unrefuted statistical evidence to support a finding that discrimination persisted at least until the cutoff date, and both the company and the plaintiff could agree on the date. 529 F.2d at 735. On remand, the district court is free to modify its ultimate conclusion concerning the cutoff date, or it may adhere to its original conclusion. It is stressed, however, that it is encumbent upon the court to clearly express the factual basis for its determination.

Denial of Back Pay Relief

(3-5) Plaintiffs next challenge the district court's refusal to grant relief in the form of back pay. The district court found that "(t)he evidence adduced at trial failed to demonstrate in any quantifiable way a means by

---

[2] Fed.R.Civ.P. 52(a) provides that "(i)n all actions tried upon the facts without a jury ... the court shall find the facts specially and state separately its conclusions of law thereon...."

which back pay could be awarded...." Record Vol. X at 56. The court also found that there were no equitable reasons to award back pay. Difficulty in calculating the precise amount of back pay does not defeat the right itself. Pettway v. American Cast Iron Pipe Co., 494 F.2d 211, 260 (5th Cir.1974) cert. denied, 439 U.S. 1115, 99 S.Ct. 1020, 59 L.Ed.2d 74 (1979). Indeed, "in computing a back pay award two principles are lucid: (1) unrealistic exactitude is not required, (2) uncertainties in determining what an employee would have earned but for discrimination, should be resolved against the discriminating employer." Id. at 260-61 (footnotes omitted). Moreover, when a class sustains an economic loss from discriminatory employment practices, there is a presumption in favor of back pay. United States v. United States Steel Corp., 520 F.2d 1043, 1053-54 (5th Cir.1975) cert. denied, 429 U.S. 817, 97 S.Ct. 61, 50 L.Ed.2d 77 (1976). Thus, back pay should be denied "only for reasons which, if generally applied, would not frustrate the central statutory purposes of eradicating discrimination *1579 throughout the economy and making persons whole for injuries suffered through past discrimination." Albemarle Paper Co. v. Moody, 422 U.S. 405, 421, 95 S.Ct. 2362, 2373, 45 L.Ed.2d 280 (1975). During the remedy phase of the trial, plaintiffs offered the testimony of an expert witness who compared the wages of city and road drivers between 1968 and 1974 and computed a differential of average wages between the two positions from 1969 to 1974. The expert also testified that it was possible to do individual calculations. This evidence stands in stark contrast to the district court's findings. Upon remand, the back pay issue should be reconsidered by the court.

Rightful Place Seniority

(6) Plaintiffs also maintain that the district court erred in its determination of seniority dates. In cases of this type, the calculation of rightful place seniority is predicated upon the date that an individual class member qualified for road employment and such a position became available. Sagers, 529 F.2d at 734; see also Rodriguez v. East Texas Motor Freight, 505 F.2d 40 (5th Cir.1974); Bing v. Roadway Express, Inc., 485 F.2d 441 (5th Cir.1973) (Bing II). In the instant case, the district court granted road terminal seniority to ten class members retroactive to March 19, 1971. March 19, 1971, is presumably the date that the first vacancy occurred after January 1, 1968. Upon remand, the district court should recalculate the seniority date of each individual plaintiff found to be entitled to relief

utilizing the formula enunciated in Sagers. See 529 F.2d at 734.

Proof of Willingness to Transfer

(7) The plaintiff class maintains that the district court erred in granting relief only to those ten class members who the court determined were ready, willing, and able to accept employment as over-the-road drivers. The court expressly found that only those ten individuals made informal inquiry concerning road jobs, expressed an interest in obtaining road jobs, and took some overt action to secure road jobs. In International Brotherhood of Teamsters v. United States, 431 U.S. 324, 365-66, 97 S.Ct. 1843, 1870, 52 L.Ed.2d 396 (1977), the Court acknowledged that "(w)hen a person's desire for a job is not translated into a formal application solely because of his unwillingness to engage in a futile gesture he is as much a victim of discrimination as is he who goes through the motions of submitting an application." Indeed, the best indication of whether a city driver desired to transfer to a road job in the past is reflected in whether he presently desires to transfer. See Rodriguez, 505 F.2d at 64. It was therefore error for the district court to out of hand exclude class members who took no overt action to secure a road job. Upon remand, the court should afford an opportunity to class members excluded from relief to demonstrate their present willingness to transfer to road jobs.

George Salazar

(8) The plaintiff class contends that George Salazar should have been allowed to intervene as a named plaintiff because he had filed a charge with the Equal Employment Opportunity Commission (EEOC) on April 15, 1966, and had obtained a right-to-sue letter. After Salazar received the right-to-sue letter, however, he failed to timely institute the required civil action. When Salazar did eventually file suit, his action was dismissed with prejudice by the district court, and he did not appeal the dismissal. In order to qualify as a named plaintiff in the instant action, Salazar must have been in a position to pursue his own Title VII action. See Hodge v. McLean Trucking Co., 607 F.2d 1118, 1120-21 (5th Cir.1979). Since Salazar could not have pursued his own Title VII action, the court was correct in not allowing him to intervene.

Chester Torry

(9) On November 17, 1971, Chester Torry filed an EEOC charge in Memphis against Roadway. Upon receiving a right-to-sue letter, he timely filed a class action suit in the Western District of Tennessee in December 1976. In February 1977, Roadway *1580 moved for a protective order on the grounds that Torry was included in the class as defined by the court in the instant action. Torry thereafter made a motion to intervene in this action, which the district court denied. The relief fashioned by the district court in its final judgment was limited to drivers in the Houston, Dallas, and San Antonio terminals. On appeal, Torry contends that the district court apparently excluded the Memphis class members because it believed that the consent decree in United States v. Roadway Express, Inc., 2 Empl.Prac.Dec. (CCH) 10,295 (N.D.Ohio 1970), was res judicata as to their claims.

In May 1968, the United States Attorney General brought suit against Roadway in federal court in the Northern District of Ohio alleging that Roadway was engaged in a system-wide pattern and practice of denying employment opportunities to blacks. After extensive litigation and negotiations, a consent decree was entered by the district court on September 1, 1970. The Teamsters, though never formally made a party to the litigation, also participated in the formulation of the consent decree. The decree enjoined Roadway from:

> (a) engaging in any act or practice whereby Negroes are denied equal employment opportunities because of race or color including the right to be hired, promoted, upgraded or assigned, and continued in employment;
>
> (b) failing or refusing to hire, promote, upgrade or reassign any individual, terminating any individual's status as an employee or applicant for employment because of his race or color;
>
> (c) engaging in any act or practice which has the purpose or effect of discriminating against any individual because of his race or color.

United States v. Roadway, 2 Empl.Prac.Dec. at 10,295. The decree also permitted all city drivers at Baltimore/Washington and Dallas, regardless of race, to request consideration for transfer to a road driver position between October 1 and October 30, 1970. The decree further directed Roadway to offer to thirty-two named individuals, who had unsuccessfully sought to apply for over-the-road positions at Memphis in January 1968, over-the-road positions if they were qualified, as vacancies occurred.

Torry maintains that for purposes of res judicata and collateral estoppel, he and the Memphis class are not bound by the prior action by the Attorney General because they were neither parties to it, nor have interests such as to be in privity with the Attorney General. Although Torry was employed by Roadway as a city driver on September 1, 1970, the date of the consent decree, he and the class of black city drivers that he purports to represent were not granted any relief as a result of the decree because the decree made no provision for black city drivers who desired to transfer to road driving positions after January 1968. Thus, his action sought an extension of the relief granted in United States v. Roadway, and was not precluded by the consent decree. See Rodriguez, 505 F.2d at 65; Williamson v. Bethlehem Steel Corp., 468 F.2d 1201 (2d Cir.1972), cert. denied, 411 U.S. 931, 93 S.Ct. 1893, 36 L.Ed.2d 390 (1973). On remand, the district court should proceed to the merits of Torry's claim.

Dual Seniority System

(10) Plaintiff Salinas challenges the court's conclusion that the dual seniority system effective under the collective bargaining agreement between Roadway and the union is bona fide and nondiscriminatory. The identical seniority system was reviewed by the Supreme Court in Teamsters. There, the Court held that "an otherwise neutral, legitimate seniority system does not become unlawful under Title VII simply because it may perpetuate pre-Act discrimination. Congress did not intend to make it illegal for employees with vested seniority rights to continue to exercise those rights, even at the expense of pre-Act discriminatees." 431 U.S. at 353-54, 97 S.Ct. at 1864. We therefore reject Salinas' contention.

Timeliness of Plaintiffs' Action

On cross-appeal, Roadway contends that it was entitled to judgment as to all liability because a discrimination charge by a class *1581 member was not timely filed with the EEOC. Thomas Salinas filed a charge of discrimination with the EEOC in February 1971. He received a right-to-sue letter in September 1971 and filed suit in district court shortly thereafter. Because the district court found that Roadway ceased its discriminatory practices on January 1, 1968, Roadway reasons that under United Air Lines v. Evans, 431 U.S. 553, 97 S.Ct. 1885, 52 L.Ed.2d 571 (1977), plaintiffs' suit was untimely because the EEOC charge was not filed within 180 days of the end of discrimination. In Evans, the Supreme Court held that the operation of United's seniority system was not unlawful under Title VII even though it perpetuated post-Act discrimination, because the discrimination had not been the subject of a timely complaint by the discriminatee. 431 U.S. at 558, 97 S.Ct. at 1889. Roadway's contention that plaintiffs' action was untimely is inextricably tied to the district court's finding that discrimination by Roadway ceased on January 1, 1968. Because we vacate and remand the district court's judgment for more complete findings, we do not reach defendant's argument.

The judgment of the district court is vacated and the cause remanded for proceedings not inconsistent with this opinion.

VACATED AND REMANDED.

Supp. Ch. 1

ZOBEL v. WILLIAMS
102 S.Ct. 2309, 457 U.S. 55, 72 L.Ed.2d 672

Argued Oct. 7, 1981.
Decided June 14, 1982.

ALASKA DIVIDEND DISTRIBUTION: EQUAL PROTECTION

Suit was brought by Alaska residents challenging dividend distribution plan as violative of their right to equal protection guarantees and their constitutional right to migrate to Alaska, to establish residency there and thereafter enjoy full rights of Alaska citizenship on same terms as all other citizens. The Superior Court, Third Judicial District, Anchorage, Ralph E. Moody, J., granted summary judgment in plaintiffs' favor, holding that plan violated rights of interstate travel and equal protection, and appeal was taken. The Alaska Supreme Court, 619 P.2d 448, reversed and upheld statute, and probable jurisdiction was noted. The United States Supreme Court, Chief Justice Burger, held that only apparent justification for retrospective aspect of Alaska's dividend distribution program, favoring established residents over new residents, was constitutionally unacceptable, and thus Alaska's dividend distribution plan violated equal protection guarantees.

Reversed and remanded.

Justice Brennan filed a concurring opinion in which Justices Marshall, Blackmun and Powell joined.

Justice O'Connor, filed an opinion concurring in the judgment.

Justice Rehnquist filed a dissenting opinion.

**2310 Syllabus[1]

*55 After Alaska amended its Constitution to establish a Permanent Fund into which the State must deposit at least 25% of its mineral income each year, the state legislature in

---

[1] The syllabus constitutes no part of the opinion of the Court but has been prepared by the Reporter of Decisions for the convenience of the reader. See United States v. Detroit Lumber Co., 200 U.S. 321, 337, 26 S.Ct. 282, 287, 50 L.Ed. 499.

1980 enacted a dividend program to distribute annually a portion of the Fund's earnings directly to the State's adult residents. Under the plan, each adult resident receives one dividend unit for each year of residency subsequent to 1959, the first year of Alaska's statehood. Appellants, residents of Alaska since 1978, brought an action in an Alaska state court challenging the statutory dividend distribution plan as violative of, inter alia, their right to equal protection guarantees. The trial court granted summary judgment in appellants' favor, but the Alaska Supreme Court reversed and upheld the statute.

Held : The Alaska dividend distribution plan violates the guarantees of the Equal Protection Clause of the Fourteenth Amendment. Pp. 2311-2315.

(a) Rather than imposing any threshold waiting period for entitlement to dividend benefits or establishing a test of bona fides of state residence, the dividend statute creates fixed, permanent distinctions between an ever-increasing number of classes of concededly bona fide residents based on how long they have lived in the State. Sosna v. Iowa, 419 U.S. 393, 95 S.Ct. 553, 42 L.Ed.2d 532; Memorial Hospital v. Maricopa County, 415 U.S. 250, 94 S.Ct. 1076, 39 L.Ed.2d 306; Dunn v. Blumstein, 405 U.S. 330, 92 S.Ct. 995, 31 L.Ed.2d 274; and Shapiro v. Thompson, 394 U.S. 618, 89 S.Ct. 1322, 22 L.Ed.2d 600, distinguished. When a state distributes benefits unequally, the distinctions it makes are subject to scrutiny under the Equal Protection Clause, and generally a law will survive that scrutiny if the distinctions rationally further a legitimate state purpose. Pp. 2311-2313.

(b) Alaska has shown no valid state interests that are rationally served by the distinctions it makes between citizens who established residence before 1959 and those who have become residents since then. Neither the State's claimed interest in creating a financial incentive for individuals to establish and maintain residence in Alaska nor its claimed interest in assuring prudent management of the Permanent Fund is rationally related to such distinctions. And the State's interest in rewarding citizens for past contributions is not a legitimate state purpose. Alaska's reasoning could open the door to state apportionment of other rights, benefits, and services according to length of residency, and would *56 permit the states to divide citizens into expanding numbers of permanent classes. Such a result would be clearly impermissible. Pp. 2313-2315.

619 P.2d 448, reversed and remanded.

Chief Justice BURGER delivered the opinion of the Court.

The question presented on this appeal is whether a statutory scheme by which a State distributes income derived from its natural resources to the adult citizens of the State in varying amounts, based on the length of each citizen's residence, violates the equal protection rights of newer state citizens. The Alaska Supreme Court sustained the constitutionality of the statute. **2311 619 P.2d 448 (1980). We stayed the distribution of dividend funds, 449 U.S. 989, 101 S.Ct. 524, 66 L.Ed.2d 286 (1980), and noted probable jurisdiction, 450 U.S. 908, 101 S.Ct. 1344, 67 L.Ed.2d 331 (1981). We reverse.

I

The 1967 discovery of large oil reserves on state-owned land in the Prudhoe Bay area of Alaska resulted in a windfall to the State. The State, which had a total budget of $124 million in 1969, before the oil revenues began to flow into the state coffers, received $3.7 billion in petroleum revenues during the 1981 fiscal year.[1] This income will continue, and *57 most likely grow for some years in the future. Recognizing that its mineral reserves, although large, are finite and that the resulting income will not continue in perpetuity, the State took steps to assure that its current good fortune will bring long-range benefits. To accomplish this, Alaska in 1976 adopted a constitutional amendment establishing the Permanent Fund into which the State must deposit at least 25% of its mineral income each year. Alaska Const., Art. IX, section 15. The amendment prohibits the legislature from appropriating any of the principal of the Fund but permits use of the Fund's earnings

---

[1] Alaska Dept. of Revenue, Revenue Sources FY 1981-1983 (Sept.1981). (Includes General Fund unrestricted petroleum revenues of $3.3 billion and petroleum revenues directly deposited in the Permanent Fund in the amount of $400 million. An additional $900 million was transferred from the General Fund to the Permanent Fund in the 1981 fiscal year.) The 1980 census reports that Alaska's adult population is 270,265; per capita 1981 oil revenues amount to $13,632 for each adult resident. Petroleum revenues now amount to 89% of the State's total government revenue. Ibid.

for general governmental purposes.

In 1980, the legislature enacted a dividend program to distribute annually a portion of the Fund's earnings directly to the State's adult residents. Under the plan, each citizen 18 years of age or older receives one dividend unit for each year of residency subsequent to 1959, the first year of statehood. The statute fixed the value of each dividend unit at $50 for the 1979 fiscal year; a one-year resident thus would receive one unit, or $50, while a resident of Alaska since it became a State in 1959 would receive 21 units, or $1,050. The value of a dividend unit will vary each year depending on the income of the Permanent Fund and the amount of that income the State allocates for other purposes. The State now estimates that the 1985 fiscal year dividend will be nearly four times as large as that for 1979.

Appellants, residents of Alaska since 1978, brought this suit in 1980 challenging the dividend distribution plan as violative of their right to equal protection guarantees and their constitutional right to migrate to Alaska, to establish residency there and thereafter to enjoy the full rights of Alaska *58 citizenship on the same terms as all other citizens of the State. The Superior Court for Alaska's Third Judicial District granted summary judgment in appellants' favor, holding that the plan violated the rights of interstate travel and equal protection. A divided Alaska Supreme Court reversed and upheld the statute.[2]

II

The Alaska dividend distribution law is quite unlike the durational residency requirements we examined in Sosna v. Iowa, 419 U.S. 393, 95 S.Ct. 553, 42 L.Ed.2d 532 **2312

---

[2] The infusion of Permanent Fund earnings into state general revenues also led the Alaska Legislature to enact a statute giving residents a one-third exemption from state income taxes for each year of residence; this operated to exempt entirely anyone with three or more years of residency. The Alaska Supreme Court, again by a 3-2 vote, held that this statute violated the State Constitution's equal protection clause. Williams v. Zobel, 619 P.2d 422 (1980). Chief Justice Rabinowitz, the only justice in the majority in both cases, found that the tax exemption statute, but not the dividend distribution plan, could "be perceived as a penalty imposed on a person who chooses to exercise his or her right to move into Alaska." 619 P.2d, at 458.

(1975); Memorial Hospital v. Maricopa County, 415 U.S. 250, 94 S.Ct. 1076, 39 L.Ed.2d 306 (1974); Dunn v. Blumstein, 405 U.S. 330, 92 S.Ct. 995, 31 L.Ed.2d 274 (1972); and Shapiro v. Thompson, 394 U.S. 618, 89 S.Ct. 1322, 22 L.Ed.2d 600 (1969). Those cases involved laws which required new residents to reside in the State a fixed minimum period to be eligible for certain benefits available on an equal basis to all other residents.[3] The asserted purpose of the durational residency requirements was to assure that only persons who had established bona fide residence received rights and benefits provided for residents.

The Alaska statute does not impose any threshold waiting period on those seeking dividend benefits; persons with less *59 than a full year of residency are entitled to share in the distribution. Alaska Stat.Ann. section 43.23.010 (Supp.1981).[4] Nor does the statute purport to establish a test of the bona fides of state residence. Instead, the dividend statute creates fixed, permanent distinctions between an ever-increasing number of perpetual classes of concededly bona fide residents, based on how long they have

---

[3] In the durational residency cases, we examined state laws which imposed waiting periods on access to divorce courts, Sosna v. Iowa; eligibility for free nonemergency medical care, Memorial Hospital v. Maricopa County; voting rights, Dunn v. Blumstein; and welfare assistance, Shapiro v. Thompson.

[4] Section 43.23.010(b) provides:

"For each year, an individual is eligible to receive payment of the permanent fund dividends for which he is entitled under this section if he

"(1) is at least 18 years of age; and

"(2) is a state resident during all or part of the year for which the permanent fund dividend is paid."

The remainder of section 43.23.010 establishes the number of dividend units residents are entitled to receive and the method of payment. Section 43.23.010(f) provides that a resident entitled to benefits under subsection (b) who was a resident for less than a full year is entitled to a dividend prorated on the basis of the number of months of state residence.

been in the State.

(1) Appellants established residence in Alaska two years before the dividend law was passed. The distinction they complain of is not one which the State makes between those who arrived in Alaska after the enactment of the dividend distribution law and those who were residents prior to its enactment. Appellants instead challenge the distinctions made within the class of persons who were residents when the dividend scheme was enacted in 1980. The distinctions appellants attack include the preference given to persons who were residents when Alaska became a State in 1959 over all those who have arrived since then, as well as the distinctions made between all bona fide residents who settled in Alaska at different times during the 1959 to 1980 period.[5]

(2-4) *60 When a state distributes benefits unequally, the distinctions it makes are subject to scrutiny under the Equal Protection Clause of the Fourteenth Amendment.[6] **2313

---

[5] The Alaska statute does not simply make distinctions between native-born Alaskans and those who migrate to Alaska from other states; it does not discriminate only against those who have recently exercised the right to travel, as did the statute involved in Shapiro v. Thompson, 394 U.S. 618, 89 S.Ct. 1322, 22 L.Ed.2d 600 (1969). The Alaska statute also discriminates among long-time residents and even native-born residents. For example, a person born in Alaska in 1962 would have received $100 less than someone who was born in the State in 1960. Of course the native Alaskan born in 1962 would also receive $100 less than the person who moved to the State in 1960.

The statute does not involve the kind of discrimination which the Privileges and Immunities Clause of Art. IV was designed to prevent. That Clause "was designed to insure to a citizen of State A who ventures into State B the same privileges which the citizens of State B enjoy." Toomer v. Witsell, 334 U.S. 385, 395, 68 S.Ct. 1156, 1161, 92 L.Ed. 1460 (1948). The Clause is thus not applicable to this case.

[6] The Alaska courts considered whether the dividend distribution law violated appellants' constitutional right to travel. The right to travel and to move from one state to another has long been accepted, yet both the nature and the source of that right have remained obscure. See Jones v. Helms, 452 U.S. 412, 417-419, and nn.12 and 13, 101 S.Ct. 2434, 2439-2440, and nn.12 and 13, 69 L.Ed.2d 118 (1981); Shapiro v. Thompson, supra, at 629-631, 89 S.Ct., at 1328-1329; United States v. Guest, 383 U.S. 745, 757-759, 86 S.Ct. 1170, 1177-1178, 16 L.Ed.2d 239 (1966). See

Generally, a law will survive that scrutiny if the distinction it makes rationally furthers a legitimate state purpose. Some particularly invidious distinctions are subject to more rigorous scrutiny. Apellants claim that the distinctions made by the Alaska law should be subjected to the higher level of scrutiny applied to the durational residency requirements in Shapiro v. Thompson, supra, and Memorial Hospital v. Maricopa County, supra. The State, on the other hand, asserts that the law need only meet the minimum rationality test. In any event, if the statutory scheme cannot pass even the minimal *61 test proposed by the State, we need not decide whether any enhanced scrutiny is called for.

A

(5) The State advanced and the Alaska Supreme Court accepted three purposes justifying the distinctions made by the dividend program: (a) creation of a financial incentive for individuals to establish and maintain residence in Alaska; (b) encouragement of prudent management of the Permanent Fund; and (c) apportionment of benefits in recognition of undefined "contributions of various kinds, both tangible and intangible, which residents have made during their years of residency," 619 P.2d at 458.[7]

---

also Z. Chafee, Three Human Rights in the Constitution of 1787, pp. 188-193 (1956). In addition to protecting persons against the erection of actual barriers to interstate movement, the right to travel, when applied to residency requirements, protects new residents of a state from being disadvantaged because of their recent migration or from otherwise being treated differently from longer term residents. In reality, right to travel analysis refers to little more than a particular application of equal protection analysis. Right to travel cases have examined, in equal protection terms, state distinctions between newcomers and longer term residents. See Memorial Hospital v. Maricopa County, 415 U.S. 250, 94 S.Ct. 1076, 39 L.Ed.2d 306 (1974); Dunn v. Blumstein, 405 U.S. 330, 92 S.Ct. 995, 31 L.Ed.2d 274 (1972); Shapiro v. Thompson, supra. This case also involves distinctions between residents based on when they arrived in the State and is therefore also subject to equal protection analysis.

[7] These purposes were enumerated in the first section of the Act creating the dividend distribution plan, 1980 Alaska Sess.Laws, ch. 21, section 1(b):

As the Alaska Supreme Court apparently realized, the first two state objectives--creating a financial incentive for individuals to establish and maintain Alaska residence, and assuring prudent management of the Permanent Fund and the State's natural and mineral resources--are not rationally related to the distinctions Alaska seeks to make between newer residents and those who have been in the State since 1959.[8] *62 Assuming, arguendo, that granting increased dividend benefits for each year of continued Alaska residence might give some residents an incentive to stay in the State in order to reap increased dividend benefits in the future, the State's interest is not in any way served by granting greater dividends to persons for their residency during the 21 years prior to the enactment. **2314 [9]

"(b) The purposes of this Act are

"(1) to provide a mechanism for equitable distribution to the people of Alaska of at least a portion of the state's energy wealth derived from the development and production of the natural resources belonging to them as Alaskans;

"(2) to encourage persons to maintain their residence in Alaska and to reduce population turnover in the state; and

"(3) to encourage increased awareness and involvement by the residents of the state in the management and expenditure of the Alaska permanent fund (art. IX, sec. 15, state constitution)."

Thus we need not speculate as to the objectives of the legislature.

[8] In response to the argument that the objectives of stabilizing population and encouraging prudent management of the Permanent Fund and of the State's natural resources did not justify the application of the dividend program to the years 1959 to 1980, the Alaska Supreme Court maintained that the retrospective aspect of the program was justified by the objective of rewarding state citizens for past contributions. 619 P.2d, at 461-462, n.37. See also dissenting opinion of Justice Dimond, id., at 469-471.

[9] In fact, newcomers seem more likely to become dissatisfied and to leave the State than well-established residents; it would thus seem that the State would give a larger, rather than a smaller, dividend to new residents if it wanted to discourage emigration. The separation of

Nor does the State's purpose of furthering the prudent management of the Permanent Fund and the State's resources support retrospective application of its plan to the date of statehood. On this score the State's contention is straightforward:

"(A)s population increases, each individual share in the income stream is diluted. The income must be divided equally among increasingly large numbers of people. If residents believed that twenty years from now they would be required to share permanent fund income on a per capita basis with the large population that Alaska will no doubt have by then, the temptation would be great to urge the legislature to provide immediately for the highest possible percentage return on the investments of the permanent fund principal, which would require investments in riskier ventures." Id., at 462.

The State similarly argues that equal per capita distribution would encourage rapacious development of natural resources. *63 Ibid. Even if we assume that the state interest is served by increasing the dividend for each year of residency beginning with the date of enactment, is it rationally served by granting greater dividends in varying amounts to those who resided in Alaska during the 21 years prior to enactment? We think not.

The last of the State's objectives--to reward citizens for past contributions--alone was relied upon by the Alaska Supreme Court to support the retrospective application of the law to 1959. However, that objective is not a legitimate state purpose. A similar "past contributions" argument was made and rejected in Shapiro v. Thompson, 394 U.S., at 632-633, 89 S.Ct., at 1330:

"Appellants argue further that the challenged classification may be sustained as an attempt to distinguish between new and old residents on the basis of the

---

residents into classes hardly seems a likely way to persuade new Alaskans that the State welcomes them and wants them to stay.

Of course, the State's objective of reducing population turnover cannot be interpreted as an attempt to inhibit migration into the State without encountering insurmountable constitutional difficulties. See Shapiro v. Thompson, 394 U.S., at 629, 89 S.Ct., at 1328.

contributions they have made to the community through the payment of taxes.... Appellants' reasoning would permit ... the State to apportion all benefits and services according to the past tax (or intangible) contributions of its citizens. <u>The Equal Protection Clause prohibits such an apportionment of state services</u>." (Emphasis added.)

Similarly, in Vlandis v. Kline, 412 U.S. 441, 93 S.Ct. 2230, 37 L.Ed.2d 63 (1973), we noted that "apportion(ment of) tuition rates on the basis of old and new residency ... would give rise to grave problems under the Equal Protection Clause of the Fourteenth Amendment." Id., at 449-450, and n.6, 93 S.Ct., at 2234-2235, and n.6.[10]

*64 If the states can make the amount of a cash dividend depend on length of residence, what would preclude varying university tuition on a sliding scale based on years of residence--or even limiting access **2315 to finite public facilities, eligibility for student loans, for civil service jobs, or for government contracts by length of domicile? Could states impose different taxes based on length of residence? Alaska's reasoning could open the door to state apportionment of other rights, benefits, and services according to length of residency.[11] It would permit the

---

[10] Even if the objective of rewarding past contributions were valid, it would be ironic to apply that rationale here. As Representative Randolph noted during debate in the state legislature on the dividend statute:

"The pipeline is the entity that has allowed us all this latitude to do all the things we're considering doing, not only today but throughout the session. And without ... newcomers, we couldn't have built that pipeline. Without their skill, without their ability, without their money, the pipeline wouldn't be there. So I get a little bit tired of-- and I've got a hunch an awful lot of people who have been here five or six or seven or ten years, whatever we knock off as newcomers, get a little bit tired of being chastized and penalized and discriminated against for having not been born here or not have been here 30 or 40 or 50 years."

[11] Apportionment would thus be prohibited only when it involves "fundamental rights" and services deemed to involve "basic necessities of life." See Memorial Hospital v. Maricopa County, 415 U.S., at 259, 94 S.Ct., at 1082.

states to divide citizens into expanding numbers of permanent classes.[12] Such a result would be clearly impermissible.[13]

B

We need not consider whether the State could enact the dividend program prospectively only. Invalidation of a portion of a statute does not necessarily render the whole invalid unless it is evident that the legislature would not have enacted the legislation without the invalid portion. Buckley v. *65 Valeo, 424 U.S. 1, 108, 96 S.Ct. 612, 677, 46 L.Ed.2d 659 (1976); United States v. Jackson, 390 U.S. 570, 585, 88 S.Ct. 1209, 1218, 20 L.Ed.2d 138 (1968); Champlin Refining Co. v. Corporation Comm'n of Oklahoma, 286 U.S. 210, 234, 52 S.Ct. 559, 564, 76 L.Ed. 1062 (1932). Here, we need not speculate as to the intent of the Alaska Legislature; the legislation expressly provides that invalidation of any portion of the statute renders the whole invalid:

"Sec. 4. If any provision enacted in sec. 2 of this Act (which included the dividend distribution plan in its entirety) is held to be invalid by the final judgment, decision or order of a court of competent jurisdiction, then that provision is nonseverable, and all provisions enacted in sec. 2 of this Act are invalid and of no force or effect." 1980 Alaska Sess. Laws, ch. 21, section 4.

---

[12] "Such a power in the States could produce nothing but discord and mutual irritation, and they very clearly do not possess it." Passenger Cases, 7 How. 283, 492, 12 L.Ed. 702 (1849) (Taney, C.J., dissenting).

[13] Starns v. Malkerson, 326 F.Supp. 234 (Minn.1970), summarily aff'd, 401 U.S. 985, 91 S.Ct. 1231, 28 L.Ed.2d 527 (1971), cannot be read as a contrary decision of this Court. First, summary affirmance by this Court is not to be read as an adoption of the reasoning supporting the judgment under review. Fusari v. Steinberg, 419 U.S. 379, 391, 95 S.Ct. 533, 540, 42 L.Ed.2d 521 (1975) (concurring opinion). See also Colorado Springs Amusements, Ltd. v. Rizzo, 428 U.S. 913, 920-921, 96 S.Ct. 3228, 3232, 49 L.Ed.2d 1222 (1976) (BRENNAN, J., dissenting); Edelman v. Jordan, 415 U.S. 651, 671, 94 S.Ct. 1347, 1359, 39 L.Ed.2d 662 (1974). Moreover, as we pointed out in Vlandis v. Kline, 412 U.S. 441, 452-453, n.9, 93 S.Ct. 2230, 2236-2237, n.9, 37 L.Ed.2d 63 (1973), we considered the Minnesota one-year residency requirement examined in Starns a test of bona fide residence, not a return on prior contributions to the commonwealth.

However, it is of course for the Alaska courts to pass on the severability clause of the statute.

III

The only apparent justification for the retrospective aspect of the program, "favoring established residents over new residents," is constitutionally unacceptable. Vlandis v. Kline, supra, at 450, 93 S.Ct., at 2235. In our view Alaska has shown no valid state interests which are rationally served by the distinction it makes between citizens who established residence before 1959 and those who have become residents since then.

We hold that the Alaska dividend distribution plan violates the guarantees of the Equal Protection Clause of the Fourteenth Amendment. Accordingly, the judgment of the Alaska Supreme Court is reversed, and the case is remanded for further proceedings not inconsistent with this opinion.

Reversed and remanded.

Justice BRENNAN, with whom Justice MARSHALL, Justice BLACKMUN, and Justice POWELL join, concurring.

I join the opinion of the Court, and agree with its conclusion that the retrospective aspects of Alaska's dividend-distribution **2316 law are not rationally related to a legitimate *66 state purpose. I write separately only to emphasize that the pervasive discrimination embodied in the Alaska distribution scheme gives rise to constitutional concerns of somewhat larger proportions than may be evident on a cursory reading of the Court's opinion. In my view, these concerns might well preclude even the prospective operation of Alaska's scheme.

I

I agree with Justice O'CONNOR that these more fundamental defects in the Alaska dividend-distribution law are, in part, reflected in what has come to be called the "right to travel."[1] That right--or, more precisely, the federal

---

[1] What is notably at stake in this case, and what clearly must be taken into account in determining the constitutionality of this legislative scheme, is the national interest in a fluid system of

interest in free interstate migration--is clearly, though indirectly, affected by the Alaska dividend-distribution law, and this threat to free interstate migration provides an independent rationale for holding that law unconstitutional. At the outset, however, I note that the frequent attempts to assign the right to travel some textual source in the Constitution seem to me to have proved both inconclusive and unnecessary. Justice O'CONNOR plausibly argues, post, at 2322-2323, that the right predates the Constitution and was carried forward in the Privileges and Immunities *67 Clause of Art. IV. But equally plausible, I think, is the argument that the right resides in the Commerce Clause, see Edwards v. California, 314 U.S. 160, 173, 62 S.Ct. 164, 166, 86 L.Ed. 119 (1941), or in the Privileges and Immunities Clause of the Fourteenth Amendment, see id., at 177-178, 62 S.Ct., at 168-169 (Douglas, J., concurring). In any event, in light of the unquestioned historic recognition of the principle of free interstate migration, and of its role in the development of the Nation, we need not feel impelled to "ascribe the source of this right to travel interstate to a particular constitutional provision." Shapiro v. Thompson, 394 U.S. 618, 630, 89 S.Ct. 1322, 1329, 22 L.Ed.2d 600 (1969). It suffices that:

"'The constitutional right to travel from one State to another ... occupies a position fundamental to the concept of our Federal Union. It is a right that has been firmly established and repeatedly recognized.

"'...(T)he right finds no explicit mention in the Constitution. The reason, it has been suggested, is that a right so elementary was conceived from the beginning to be a necessary concomitant of the stronger Union the Constitution created. In any event, freedom to travel throughout the United States has long been recognized as a

---

interstate movement. It may be that national interests are not always easily translated into individual rights, but where the "right to travel" is involved, our cases leave no doubt that it will trigger intensified equal protection scrutiny. See, e.g., Memorial Hospital v. Maricopa County, 415 U.S. 250, 94 S.Ct. 1076, 39 L.Ed.2d 306 (1974); Dunn v. Blumstein, 405 U.S. 330, 92 S.Ct. 995, 31 L.Ed.2d 274 (1972); Shapiro v. Thompson, 394 U.S. 618, 89 S.Ct. 1322, 22 L.Ed.2d 600 (1969). As the Court notes, the "right to travel" is implicated not only by "actual barriers to interstate movement," but also by "state distinctions between newcomers and longer term residents." Ante, at 2312, n.6.

basic right under the Constitution.'" Id., at 630-631, 89 S.Ct., at 1329, quoting United States v. Guest, 383 U.S. 745, 757-758, 86 S.Ct. 1170, 1177-1178, 16 L.Ed.2d 239 (1966).

As is clear from our cases, the right to travel achieves its most forceful expression in the context of equal protection analysis. But if, finding no citable passage in the Constitution to assign as its source, some might be led to question the independent vitality of the principle of free interstate migration, I find its unmistakable essence in that document that transformed a loose confederation of States into one Nation. A scheme of the sort adopted by Alaska is inconsistent with the federal structure even in its prospective operation.

**2317 A State clearly may undertake to enhance the advantages of industry, economy, and resources that make it a desirable place in which to live. In addition, a State may make residence within its boundaries more attractive by offering direct benefits to its citizens in the form of public services, lower taxes than other States offer, or direct distributions of its *68 munificence. Through these means, one State may attract citizens of other States to join the numbers of its citizenry. That is a healthy form of rivalry: It inheres in the very idea of maintaining the States as independent sovereigns within a larger framework, and it is fully--indeed, necessarily--consistent with the Framers' further idea of joining these independent sovereigns into a single Nation. But a State cannot compound its offer of direct benefits in the inventive manner exemplified by the Alaska distribution scheme: For if each State were free to reward its citizens incrementally for their years of residence, so that a citizen leaving one State would thereby forfeit his accrued seniority, only to have to begin building such seniority again in his new State of residence, then the mobility so essential to the economic progress of our Nation, and so commonly accepted as a fundamental aspect of our social order, would not long survive.

II

The Court today reaffirms the important principle that, at least with respect to a durational-residency discrimination, a State's desire "to reward citizens for past contributions" is clearly "not a legitimate state purpose." Ante, at 2314. I do not think it "odd," post, at 2319, that the Court disclaims reliance on the "right to travel" as the source of this limitation on state power. In my view, the acknowledged illegitimacy of that state purpose has a different heritage--it reflects not the structure of the Federal Union but the idea of constitutionally protected equality. See Shapiro v. Thompson, supra, at 632-633, 89 S.Ct., at 1330 ("The Equal Protection Clause prohibits such an apportionment of state services"); Vlandis v. Kline, 412 U.S. 441, 450, n.6, 93 S.Ct. 2230, 2235, n.6, 37 L.Ed.2d 63 (1973). The Constitution places the recently naturalized immigrant from a foreign land on an equal footing with those citizens of a State who are able to trace their lineage back for many generations within the State's borders. The 18-year-old native resident of a State is as much a citizen as the 55-year-old native resident. But *69 the Alaska plan discriminates against the recently naturalized citizen, in favor of the Alaska citizen of longer duration; it discriminates against the 18-year-old native resident, in favor of all residents of longer duration. If the Alaska plan were limited to discriminations such as these, and did not purport to apply to migrants from sister States, interstate travel would not be noticeably burdened--yet those discriminations would surely be constitutionally suspect.

The Fourteenth Amendment guarantees the equal protection of the law to anyone who may be within the territorial jurisdiction of a State. That Amendment does not suggest by its terms that equal treatment might be denied a person depending upon how long that person has been within the jurisdiction of the State. The Fourteenth Amendment does, however, expressly recognize one elementary basis for distinguishing between persons who may be within a State's jurisdiction at any particular time--by setting forth the requirements for state citizenship. But it is significant that the Citizenship Clause of the Fourteenth Amendment expressly equates citizenship only with simple residence.[2] That **2318 Clause does not provide for, and does not allow

---

[2] "(A) citizen of the United States can, of his own volition, become a citizen of any State of the Union by a bona fide residence therein, with the same rights as other citizens of that State." Slaughter-House Cases, 16 Wall. 36, 80, 21 L.Ed. 394 (1873). See id., at 112-113 (Bradley, J., dissenting) ("A citizen of the United States has a perfect constitutional right to go to and reside in any State he chooses, and to claim citizenship therein, and an equality of rights with every other citizen").

for, degrees of citizenship based on length of residence.[3] And the Equal Protection Clause would not tolerate such distinctions. *70 In short, as much as the right to travel, equality of citizenship is of the essence in our Republic. As the Court notes, States may not "divide citizens into expanding numbers of permanent classes." Ante, at 2315.

It is, of course, elementary that the Constitution does not bar the States from making reasoned distinctions between citizens: Insofar as those distinctions are rationally related to the legitimate ends of the State they present no constitutional difficulty, as our equal protection jurisprudence attests. But we have never suggested that duration of residence vel non provides a valid justification for discrimination. To the contrary, discrimination on the basis of residence must be supported by a valid state interest independent of the discrimination itself. To be sure, allegiance and attachment may be rationally measured by length of residence--length of residence may, for example, be used to test the bona fides of citizenship--and allegiance and attachment may bear some rational relationship to a very limited number of legitimate state purposes. Cf. Chimento v. Stark, 353 F.Supp. 1211 (NH), summarily aff'd, 414 U.S. 802, 94 S.Ct. 125, 38 L.Ed.2d 39 (1973) (7-year citizenship requirement to run for Governor); U.S.Const., Art. I, section 2, cl. 2, section 3, cl. 3; Art. II, section 1, cl. 5. But those instances in which length of residence could provide a legitimate basis for distinguishing one citizen from another are rare.

Permissible discriminations between persons must bear a rational relationship to their relevant characteristics. While some imprecision is unavoidable in the process of legislative classification, the ideal of equal protection requires attention to individual merit, to individual need. In almost all instances, the business of the State is not with the past, but with the present: to remedy continuing

---

[3] The American aversion to aristocracy developed long before the Fourteenth Amendment and is, of course, reflected elsewhere in the Constitution. See Art. I, section 9, cl. 8 ("No Title of Nobility shall be granted by the United States"). See also Virginia Declaration of Rights (1776), in R. Rutland, The Birth of the Bill of Rights, App. A (1955) ("no man, or set of men, are entitled to exclusive or separate emoluments or privileges from the community, but in consideration of publick services").

injustices, to fill current needs, to build on the present in order to better the future. The past actions of individuals may be relevant in assessing their present needs; past actions may also be relevant in predicting current ability and future performance. In addition, *71 to a limited extent, recognition and reward of past public service have independent utility for the State, for such recognition may encourage other people to engage in comparably meritorious service. But even the idea of rewarding past public service offers scarce support for the "past contribution" justification for durational-residence classifications since length of residence has only the most tenuous relation to the actual service of individuals to the State.

Thus, the past-contribution rationale proves much too little to provide a rational predicate for discrimination on the basis of length of residence. But it also proves far too much, for "it would permit the State to apportion all benefits and services according to the past ... contributions of its citizens." Shapiro v. Thompson, 394 U.S., at 632-633, 89 S.Ct., at 1330. In effect, then, the past-contribution rationale is so far-reaching in its potential application, and the relationship between residence and contribution to the State so vague and insupportable, that it amounts to little more than a restatement of the criterion for discrimination that it purports to justify. But while duration of residence has minimal utility as a measure of things that are, in fact, constitutionally relevant, resort to duration of residence as the basis for a distribution of state largesse does closely track the constitutionally untenable position that the longer one's residence, the worthier one is of the State's favor. In my view, it is **2319 difficult to escape from the recognition that underlying any scheme of classification on the basis of duration of residence, we shall almost invariably find the unstated premise that "some citizens are more equal than others." We rejected that premise and, I believe, implicitly rejected most forms of discrimination based upon length of residence, when we adopted the Equal Protection Clause.

Justice O'CONNOR, concurring in the judgment.

The Court strikes Alaska's distribution scheme, purporting to rely solely upon the Equal Protection Clause of the Fourteenth *72 Amendment. The phrase "right to travel" appears only fleetingly in the Court's analysis, dismissed with an observation that "right to travel analysis refers to little more than a particular application of equal protection analysis." Ante, at 2312, n.6. The Court's reluctance to rely explicitly on a right to travel is odd, because its holding depends on the assumption that Alaska's desire "to reward citizens for past contributions is not a legitimate state purpose." Ante, at 2314. Nothing in the Equal Protection Clause itself, however, declares this objective illegitimate. Instead, as a full reading of Shapiro v. Thompson, 394 U.S. 618, 89 S.Ct. 1322, 22 L.Ed.2d 600 (1969), and Vlandis v. Kline, 412 U.S. 441, 93 S.Ct. 2230, 37 L.Ed.2d 63 (1973), reveals, the Court has rejected this objective only when its implementation would abridge an interest in interstate travel or migration.

I respectfully suggest, therefore, that the Court misdirects its criticism when it labels Alaska's objective illegitimate. A desire to compensate citizens for their prior contributions is neither inherently invidious nor irrational. Under some circumstances, the objective may be wholly reasonable.[1] Even a generalized desire to reward citizens for past endurance, particularly in a State where years of hardship only recently have produced prosperity, is not innately improper. The difficulty is that plans enacted to further this objective necessarily treat new residents of a State less favorably than the *73 longer term residents who have past contributions to "reward." This inequality, as the Court repeatedly has recognized, conflicts with the constitutional purpose of maintaining a Union rather than a mere "league of States." See Paul v. Virginia, 8 Wall. 168, 180, 19 L.Ed. 357 (1869). The Court's task, therefore, should be (1) to articulate this constitutional principle,

---

[1] A State, for example, might choose to divide its largesse among all persons who previously have contributed their time to volunteer community organizations. If the State graded its dividends according to the number of years devoted to prior community service, it could be said that the State intended "to reward citizens for past contributions." Alternatively, a State might enact a tax credit for citizens who contribute to the State's ecology by building alternative fuel sources or establishing recycling plants. If the State made this credit retroactive, to benefit those citizens who launched these improvements before they became fashionable, the State once again would be rewarding past contributions. The Court's opinion would dismiss these objectives as wholly illegitimate. I would recognize them as valid goals and inquire only whether their implementation infringed any constitutionally protected interest.

explaining its textual sources, and (2) to test the strength of Alaska's objective against the constitutional imperative. By choosing instead to declare Alaska's purpose wholly illegitimate, the Court establishes an uncertain jurisprudence. What makes Alaska's purpose illegitimate? Is the purpose illegitimate under all circumstances? What other state interests are wholly illegitimate? Will an "illegitimate" purpose survive review if it becomes "important" or "compelling"?[2] These ambiguities **2320 in the Court's analysis prompt me to develop my own approach to Alaska's scheme.

Alaska's distribution plan distinguishes between long-term residents and recent arrivals. Stripped to its essentials, the plan denies non-Alaskans settling in the State the same privileges afforded longer term residents. The Privileges and Immunities Clause of Art. IV, which guarantees "(t)he Citizens of each State ... all Privileges and Immunities of Citizens in the several States," addresses just this type of discrimination.[3] Accordingly, I would measure Alaska's *74

---

[2] The Court's conclusion that Alaska's scheme lacks a rational basis masks a puzzling aspect of its analysis. By refusing to extend any legitimacy to Alaska's objective, the Court implies that a program designed to reward prior contributions will never survive equal protection scrutiny. For example, the programs described in n.1, supra, could not survive the Court's analysis even if the State demonstrated a compelling interest in rewarding volunteer activity or promoting conservation measures. The Court's opinion, although purporting to apply a deferential standard of review, actually insures that any governmental program depending upon a "past contributions" rationale will violate the Equal Protection Clause.

[3] While the Clause refers to "Citizens," this Court has found that "the terms 'citizen' and 'resident' are 'essentially interchangeable' ... for purposes of analysis of most cases under the Privileges and Immunities Clause." Hicklin v. Orbeck, 437 U.S. 518, 524, n.8, 98 S.Ct. 2482, 2486, n.8, 57 L.Ed.2d 397 (1978) (quoting Austin v. New Hampshire, 420 U.S. 656, 662, n.8, 95 S.Ct. 1191, 1195, n.8, 43 L.Ed.2d 530 (1975)). This opinion, therefore, will refer to "nonresidents" of Alaska, as well as to "noncitizens" of that State.

It is settled that the Privileges and Immunities Clause does not protect corporations. See Paul v. Virginia, 8 Wall. 168, 19 L.Ed. 357 (1869). The word "Citizens" suggests that the Clause also excludes aliens. See, e.g., id., at 177 (dictum); L. Tribe, American

scheme against the principles implementing the Privileges and Immunities Clause. In addition to resolving the particular problems raised by Alaska's scheme, this analysis supplies a needed foundation for many of the "right to travel" claims discussed in the Court's prior opinions.

I

Our opinions teach that Art. IV's Privileges and Immunities Clause "was designed to insure to a citizen of State A who ventures into State B the same privileges which the citizens of State B enjoy." Toomer v. Witsell, 334 U.S. 385, 395, 68 S.Ct. 1156, 1161, 92 L.Ed. 1460 (1948). The Clause protects a nonresident who enters a State to work, Hicklin v. Orbeck, 437 U.S. 518, 98 S.Ct. 2482, 57 L.Ed.2d 397 (1978), to hunt commercial game, Toomer, supra, or to procure medical services, Doe v. Bolton, 410 U.S. 179, 93 S.Ct. 739, 35 L.Ed.2d 201 (1973).[4] A fortiori, the Privileges and Immunities Clause should protect the "citizen of State A who ventures into State B" to settle there and establish a home.

In this case, Alaska forces nonresidents settling in the State to accept a status inferior to that of oldtimers. In its first year of operation, the distribution scheme would have given $1,050 to an Alaskan who had lived in the State since *75 statehood. A resident of 10 years would have received $500, while a one-year resident would have received only $50. In effect, therefore, the State told its citizens: "Your status depends upon the date on which you established residence here. Those of you who migrated to the State cannot share its bounty on the same basis as those who were here before you." Surely this scheme imposes one of the "disabilities of alienage" prohibited by Art. IV's Privileges and Immunities Clause. See Paul v. Virginia, supra, at 180.

Constitutional Law section 6-33, p. 411, n.18 (1978). Any prohibition of discrimination aimed at aliens or corporations must derive from other constitutional provisions.

[4] See generally Ward v. Maryland, 12 Wall. 418, 430, 20 L.Ed. 449 (1871) (The Clause "plainly and unmistakably secures and protects the right of a citizen of one State to pass into any other State of the Union for the purpose of engaging in lawful commerce, trade, or business, without molestation; to acquire personal property; (and) to take and hold real estate...").

It could be argued that Alaska's scheme does not trigger the Privileges and Immunities Clause because it discriminates among classes of residents, rather than between residents and nonresidents. This argument, however, misinterprets the force of Alaska's distribution system. Alaska's scheme classifies citizens on the basis of their former residential status, imposing a relative burden on those who migrated to the State after 1959. Residents who arrived in Alaska after that date have a less valuable citizenship right than do the oldtimers who preceded them. Citizens who arrive in the State tomorrow will receive an even smaller claim on Alaska's resources. The fact that this discrimination unfolds **2321 after the nonresident establishes residency does not insulate Alaska's scheme from scrutiny under the Privileges and Immunities Clause. Each group of citizens who migrated to Alaska in the past, or chooses to move there in the future, lives in the State on less favorable terms than those who arrived earlier. The circumstance that some of the disfavored citizens already live in Alaska does not negate the fact that "the citizen of State A who ventures into (Alaska)" to establish a home labors under a continuous disability.[5]

*76 If the Privileges and Immunities Clause applies to Alaska's distribution system, then our prior opinions describe the proper standard of review. In Baldwin v. Montana Fish and Game Comm'n, 436 U.S. 371, 98 S.Ct. 1852, 56 L.Ed.2d 354 (1978), we held that States must treat

---

[5] See Note, A Constitutional Analysis of State Bar Residency Requirements under the Interstate Privileges and Immunities Clause of Article IV, 92 Harv.L.Rev. 1461, 1464-1465, n.17 (1979) (labeling contrary argument "technical").

As the Court points out, ante, at 2312, n.5, Alaska's plan differentiates even among native Alaskans, by tying their benefits to date of birth. If the scheme merely distributed benefits on the basis of age, without reference to the date beneficiaries established residence in Alaska, I doubt it would violate the Privileges and Immunities Clause. Under those circumstances, a 25-year-old Texan establishing residence in Alaska would acquire the same privileges of citizenship held by a 25-year-old native Alaskan. The scheme would not treat the citizen who moves to the State differently from citizens who already reside there. The Court does not explain whether it would find such an age-based scheme objectionable.

residents and nonresidents "without unnecessary distinctions" when the nonresident seeks to "engage in an essential activity or exercise a basic right." Id., at 387, 98 S.Ct., at 1862. On the other hand, if the nonresident engages in conduct that is not "fundamental" because it does not "bea(r) upon the vitality of the Nation as a single entity," the Privileges and Immunities Clause affords no protection. Id., at 387, 383, 98 S.Ct., at 1862, 1860.

Once the Court ascertains that discrimination burdens an "essential activity," it will test the constitutionality of the discrimination under a two-part test. First, there must be "'something to indicate that non-citizens constitute a peculiar source of the evil at which the statute is aimed.'" Hicklin v. Orbeck, supra, at 525-526, 98 S.Ct., at 2487 (quoting Toomer v. Witsell, supra, at 398, 68 S.Ct., at 1163). Second, the Court must find a "substantial relationship" between the evil and the discrimination practiced against the noncitizens. 437 U.S., at 527, 98 S.Ct., at 2488.

Certainly the right infringed in this case is "fundamental." Alaska's statute burdens those nonresidents who choose to settle in the State.[6] It is difficult to imagine a right more *77 essential to the Nation as a whole than the right to establish residence in a new State. Just as our federal system permits the States to experiment with different social and economic programs, New State Ice Co. v. Liebmann, 285 U.S. 262, 311, 52 S.Ct. 371, 386, 76 L.Ed. 747 (1932) (Brandeis, J., dissenting), it allows the individual to settle in the State offering those programs best tailored to his or her tastes.[7] Alaska's encumbrance on the right of

---

[6] The "burden" imposed on nonresidents is relative to the benefits enjoyed by residents. It is immaterial, for purposes of the Privileges and Immunities Clause, that the nonresident may enjoy a benefit in the new State that he lacked completely in his former State. The Clause addresses only differences in treatment; it does not judge the quality of treatment a State affords citizens and noncitizens.

[7] See also Baldwin v. G.A.F. Seelig, Inc., 294 U.S. 511, 523, 55 S.Ct. 497, 500, 79 L.Ed. 1032 (1935) (the Constitution "was framed upon the theory that the peoples of the several states must sink or swim together, and that in the long run prosperity and salvation are in union and not division"); Paul v. Virginia, 8 Wall., at 180 ("Indeed, without some provision of the kind removing from the citizens of each State the

nonresidents to settle in that State, therefore, must satisfy the dual standard identified in Hicklin.

Alaska has not shown that its new residents are the "peculiar source" of any evil **2322 addressed by its disbursement scheme. The State does not argue that recent arrivals constitute a particular source of its population turnover problem. Indeed, the State urges that it has a special interest in persuading young adults, who have grown to maturity in the State, to remain there. Brief for Appellees 35, n.24. Nor is there any evidence that new residents, rather than old, will foolishly deplete the State's mineral and financial resources. Finally, although Alaska argues that its scheme compensates residents for their prior tangible and intangible contributions to the State, nonresidents are hardly a peculiar source of the "evil" of partaking in current largesse without having made prior contributions. A multitude of native Alaskans—including children and paupers—may have failed to contribute to the State in the past. Yet the State does not dock paupers *78 for their prior failures to contribute, and it awards every person over the age of 18 dividends equal to the number of years that person has lived in the State.

Even if new residents were the peculiar source of these evils, Alaska has not chosen a cure that bears a "substantial relationship" to the malady. As the dissenting judges below observed, Alaska's scheme gives the largest dividends to residents who have lived longest in the State. The dividends awarded to new residents may be too small to encourage them to stay in Alaska. The size of these dividends appears to give new residents only a weak interest in prudent management of the State's resources. As a reward for prior contributions, finally, Alaska's scheme is quite ill-suited. While the phrase "substantial relationship" does not require mathematical precision, it demands at least some recognition of the fact that persons who have migrated to Alaska may have

---

disabilities of alienage in the other States, and giving them equality of privilege with citizens of those States, the Republic would have constituted little more than a league of States; it would not have constituted the Union which now exists"); Edwards v. California, 314 U.S. 160, 173, 62 S.Ct. 164, 166, 86 L.Ed. 119 (1941) (Constitution prohibits "attempts on the part of any single State to isolate itself from difficulties common to all of them by restraining the transportation of persons and property across its borders").

contributed significantly more to the State, both before and after their arrival, than have some natives.

For these reasons, I conclude that Alaska's disbursement scheme violates Art. IV's Privileges and Immunities Clause. I thus reach the same destination as the Court, but along a course that more precisely identifies the evils of the challenged statute.

II

The analysis outlined above might apply to many cases in which a litigant asserts a right to travel or migrate interstate.[8] To historians, this would come as no surprise. Article *79 IV's Privileges and Immunities Clause has enjoyed a long association with the rights to travel and migrate interstate.

The Clause derives from Art. IV of the Articles of Confederation. The latter expressly recognized a right of "free ingress and regress to and from any other State," in addition to guaranteeing "the free inhabitants of each of these states ... (the) privileges and immunities of free citizens in the several States."[9] While the Framers **2323

---

[8] Any durational residency requirement, for example, treats nonresidents who have exercised their right to settle in a State differently from longer term residents. This is not to say, however, that all such requirements would fail scrutiny under the Privileges and Immunities Clause. The durational residency requirement upheld in Sosna v. Iowa, 419 U.S. 393, 95 S.Ct. 553, 42 L.Ed.2d 532 (1975) (one year to obtain divorce), for example, would have survived under the analysis outlined above. In Sosna the State showed that nonresidents were a peculiar source of the evil addressed by its durational residency requirement. Those persons could misrepresent their attachment to Iowa and obtain divorces that would be susceptible to collateral attack in other States. Iowa adopted a reasonable response to this problem by requiring nonresidents to demonstrate their bona fide residency for one year before obtaining a divorce. I am confident that the analysis developed in Hicklin v. Orbeck, 437 U.S. 518, 98 S.Ct. 2482, 57 L.Ed.2d 397 (1978), will adequately identify other legitimate durational residency requirements.

[9] Even before adoption of the Articles, a few of the Colonies explicitly protected freedom of movement. The Rhode Island Charter gave members of that Colony the right "to passe and repasse with freedome,

of our Constitution omitted the reference to "free ingress and regress," they retained the general guaranty of "privileges and immunities." Charles Pinckney, who drafted the current version of Art. IV, told the Convention that this Article was "formed exactly upon the principles of the 4th article of the present Confederation." 3 M. Farrand, Records of the Federal Convention of 1787, p. 112 (1934). Commentators, therefore, have assumed *80 that the Framers omitted the express guaranty merely because it was redundant, not because they wished to excise the right from the Constitution.[10]

---

into and through the rest of the English Collonies, upon their lawful and civill occasions." Z. Chafee, Three Human Rights in the Constitution of 1787, p. 177 (1956). The Massachusetts Body of Liberties provided: "Every man of or within this Jurisdiction shall have free libertie, not with standing any Civill power, to remove both himself and his familie at their pleasure out of the same, provided there be no legall impediment to the contrarie." Id., at 178. Massachusetts showed some of the same liberality to foreigners entering the Colony:

"If any people of other Nations professing the true Christian Religion shall flee to us from the Tiranny or oppression of their persecutors, or from famyne, warres, or the like necessary and compulsarie cause, They shall be entertayned and succoured among us, according to that power and prudence god shall give us." Ibid.

These attitudes contrasted with the more restrictive views prevailing in 17th-century Europe. See generally id., at 163-171.

[10] See, e.g., id., at 185; Note, The Right to Travel and Exclusionary Zoning, 26 Hastings L.J. 849, 858-859 (1975); Comment, The Right to Travel: In Search of a Constitutional Source, 55 Neb.L.Rev. 117, 119-120, n. 14 (1975); Comment, A Strict Scrutiny of the Right to Travel, 22 UCLA L.Rev. 1129, 1130, n.7 (1975).

See also Austin v. New Hampshire, 420 U.S., at 661, 95 S.Ct., at 1195 (footnotes omitted) (Article IV of the Articles of Confederation was "carried over into the comity article of the Constitution in briefer form but with no change of substance or intent, unless it was to strengthen the force of the Clause in fashioning a single nation"); United States v. Wheeler, 254 U.S. 281, 294, 41 S.Ct. 133, 134, 65 L.Ed. 270 (1920) ("the text of Article IV, section 2, of the Constitution, makes manifest that it was drawn with reference to the corresponding clause of the Articles of Confederation and was intended to perpetuate its limitations; and ... that view has been so conclusively settled as to leave no room

Early opinions by the Justices of this Court also traced a right to travel or migrate interstate to Art. IV's Privileges and Immunities Clause. In Corfield v. Coryell, 6 F.Cas. 546, 552 (No. 3,230) (CC ED Pa.1823), for example, Justice Washington explained that the Clause protects the "right of a citizen of one state to pass through, or to reside in any other state." Similarly, in Paul v. Virginia, 8 Wall., at 180, the Court found that one of the "undoubt(ed)" effects of the Clause was to give "the citizens of each State ... the right of free ingress into other States, and egress from them...." See also Ward v. Maryland, 12 Wall. 418, 430, 20 L.Ed. 449 (1871). Finally, in United States v. Wheeler, 254 U.S. 281, 297-298, 41 S.Ct. 133, 135, 65 L.Ed. 270 (1920), the Court found that the Clause fused two distinct concepts: (1) "the right of citizens of the States to reside peacefully in, and to have free ingress into and egress from" their own States, and (2) the right to exercise the same privileges in other States.

History, therefore, supports assessment of Alaska's scheme, as well as other infringements of the right to travel, under the Privileges and Immunities Clause. This Clause *81 may not address every conceivable type of discrimination that the Court previously has denominated a burden on interstate travel. I believe, however, that application of the Privileges and Immunities Clause to controversies involving the "right to travel" would at least begin the task of reuniting this elusive right with the constitutional principles it embodies. Because I believe that Alaska's distribution scheme violates the Privileges and Immunities Clause of Art. IV, I concur in the Court's judgment insofar as it reverses the judgment of the Alaska Supreme Court.

Justice REHNQUIST, dissenting.

Alaska's dividend distribution scheme represents one State's effort to apportion unique economic benefits among its citizens. Although the wealth received from the oil deposits of Prudhoe Bay may be quite unlike the economic resources enjoyed by most States, Alaska's distribution of that wealth is in substance no different from any other State's allocation of economic benefits. The distribution scheme being in the nature of economic regulation, I am at

---

for controversy").

a loss to see the rationality behind the Court's invalidation of it as a denial of equal protection. This Court has long held that state economic regulations are presumptively valid, and violate the Fourteenth Amendment only in the rarest of circumstances:

"When local economic regulation is challenged solely as violating the Equal **2324 Protection Clause, this Court consistently defers to legislative determinations as to the desirability of particular statutory discriminations. See, e.g., Lehnhausen v. Lake Shore Auto Parts Co., 410 U.S. 356 (93 S.Ct. 1001, 35 L.Ed.2d 351) (1973). Unless a classification trammels fundamental personal rights or is drawn upon inherently suspect distinctions such as race, religion, or alienage, our decisions presume the constitutionality of the statutory discriminations and require only that the classification challenged be rationally related to a legitimate state interest. States are accorded wide latitude in the regulation *82 of their local economies under their police powers, and rational distinctions may be made with substantially less than mathematical exactitude." New Orleans v. Dukes, 427 U.S. 297, 303, 96 S.Ct. 2513, 2516, 49 L.Ed.2d 511 (1976). See also Minnesota v. Clover Leaf Creamery Co., 449 U.S. 456, 101 S.Ct. 715, 66 L.Ed.2d 659 (1981); United States Railroad Retirement Board v. Fritz, 449 U.S. 166, 101 S.Ct. 453, 66 L.Ed.2d 368 (1980); Hughes v. Alexandria Scrap Corp., 426 U.S. 794, 96 S.Ct. 2488, 49 L.Ed.2d 220 (1976).

Despite the highly deferential approach which we invariably have taken toward state economic regulations, the Court today finds the retroactive aspect of the Alaska distribution scheme violative of the Fourteenth Amendment. The Court concludes that the State's first two justifications are not rationally related to the retroactive portion of the distribution scheme, and that the third justification—the reward of citizens for their past contributions—is not a legitimate state objective. But the illegitimacy of a State's recognizing the past contributions of its citizens has been established by the Court only in certain cases considering an infringement of the right to travel,[1] and the

---

[1] The Court relies upon Shapiro v. Thompson, 394 U.S. 618, 89 S.Ct. 1322, 22 L.Ed.2d 600 (1969), and Vlandis v. Kline, 412 U.S. 441, 93 S.Ct. 2230, 37 L.Ed.2d 63 (1973), in holding that Alaska may not justify its dividend distribution scheme by a desire to reward its citizens for their past contributions. In Shapiro, however, the Court found that the

majority itself rightly declines to apply *83 the strict scrutiny analysis of those right-to-travel cases. See ante, at 2312-2313. The distribution scheme at issue in this case impedes no person's right to travel to and settle in Alaska; if anything, the prospect of receiving annual cash dividends would encourage immigration to Alaska. The State's third justification cannot, therefore, be dismissed simply by quoting language about its legitimacy from right-to-travel cases which have no relevance to the question before us.

So understood, this case clearly passes equal protection muster. There can be no doubt that the state legislature acted rationally when it concluded that dividends retroactive to the year of statehood would "recognize the 'contributions of various kinds, both tangible and intangible,' which residents have made during their years of state residency." 619 P.2d 448, 458 (Alaska 1980). Nor can there be any doubt that Alaska, perhaps more than any other State in the Union, has good reason for recognizing such contributions.[2]

---

classification at issue "touche(d) on the fundamental right of interstate movement" and therefore could be justified only if it promoted a "compelling state interest." 394 U.S., at 638, 89 S.Ct., at 1333 (emphasis in original). Similarly, Vlandis concerned the right to move to and establish residency in Connecticut, and noted only in dicta that rewarding citizens for their past contributions was an impermissible state objective. See 412 U.S., at 449-450, and n. 6, 93 S.Ct., at 2234-2235, and n.6.

Although I have expressed my disagreement with this holding even in the right-to-travel cases, see Memorial Hospital v. Maricopa County, 415 U.S. 250, 286-287, 94 S.Ct. 1076, 1095-1096, 39 L.Ed.2d 306 (1974) (REHNQUIST, J., dissenting); Vlandis v. Kline, supra, at 468-469, 93 S.Ct., at 2244 (same), there is no need to rely upon that dissenting position here. The majority does not analyze this as a right-to-travel case. Compare ante, at 2312-2313, with Memorial Hospital v. Maricopa County, supra, at 261-262, 94 S.Ct., at 1083-1084, and Shapiro v. Thompson, supra, at 634, 638, 89 S.Ct., at 1331, 1333.

[2] As the Alaska Supreme Court noted, those who have lived in Alaska from the year of its statehood have borne unusual expenses and hardships:

"'A government such as the one embodied in the Alaska constitution, ... with its complete range of governmental services, was expensive for a State with limited sources of taxation. Alaska could only boast a couple of pulp mills.... The State's business enterprises were small and

Because *84 the distribution **2325 scheme is thus rationally based, I dissent from its invalidation under the guise of equal protection analysis.[3] In striking down the Alaskan scheme, the Court seems momentarily to have forgotten "the principle that the Fourteenth Amendment gives the federal courts no power to impose upon the States their views of what

---

catered mostly to local needs. In addition, Alaska's population was modest and hardly amounted to more than that of a medium-sized city in the continental United States.

"'Accordingly, revenues were small. Yet, the demands were great. The State government had to provide all the governmental services and social overhead required by modern American society. For instance, it would have been relatively simple to build a few roads, furnish normal police protection, and establish the customary school facilities. But nothing was normal in Alaska; it was and remains a land of superlatives. Subarctic engineering is relatively new, but the State would have to face the problem of permafrost conditions that frequently cause the roadtop to buckle and heave. Police protection would have to be provided for an area one-fifth the size of the forty-eight United States but with very few roads available. Flying would become a way of life for law enforcement officials as well as other Alaskans--an expensive way of life. "Bush schools" scattered along the Aleutian chain, through the Yukon Valley, and on the Seaward Peninsula and the islands of southeastern Alaska were expensive to maintain. It was not until the discovery of oil on a large scale that the picture changed.'" 619 P.2d, at 462, n.37 (quoting C. Naske, An Interpretive History of Alaskan Statehood 169-170 (1973)).

[3] I also disagree with the suggestion of Justice O'CONNOR that the Alaska distribution scheme contravenes the Privileges and Immunities Clause of Art. IV of the Constitution. That Clause assures that nonresidents of a State shall enjoy the same privileges and immunities as residents enjoy: "It was designed to insure to a citizen of State A who ventures into State B the same privileges which the citizens of State B enjoy." Toomer v. Witsell, 334 U.S. 385, 395, 68 S.Ct. 1156, 1161, 92 L.Ed. 1460 (1948). We long ago held that the Clause has no application to a citizen of the State whose laws are complained of. "The constitutional provision there alluded to did not create those rights, which it called privileges and immunities of citizens of the States. It threw around them in that clause no security for the citizen of the State in which they were claimed or exercised. Nor did it profess to control the power of the State governments over the rights of its own citizens." Slaughter-House Cases, 16 Wall. 36, 77, 21 L.Ed. 394 (1873).

constitutes wise economic or social policy." Dandridge v. Williams, 397 U.S. 471, 486, 90 S.Ct. 1153, 1162, 25 L.Ed.2d 491 (1970).

CHAPTER 2

LAW AND FACTS IN THE ADMINISTRATION OF JUSTICE

SHACKIL v. LEDERLE LABORATORIES

Supreme Court of New Jersey.
561 A.2d 511, 116 N.J. 155

Argued Sept. 13, 1988.
Decided July 31, 1989.

SYNOPSIS

Child and her parents filed negligence, breach of warranty, misrepresentation, and strict liability action against manufacturers of combined diphtheria-pertussis-tetanus vaccine, after child who was inoculated allegedly suffered seizure disorder that resulted in chronic encephalopathy and severe retardation. The Superior Court, Law Division, Passaic County, dismissed. On appeal, the Superior Court, Appellate Division, 219 N.J.Super. 601, 530 A.2d 1287, reversed and remanded. After grant of leave to appeal, the Supreme Court, Clifford, J., held that risk-modified market-share liability would not be adopted in DPT vaccine manufacturing context.

Reversed; judgment for manufacturers reinstated.

O'Hern, J., filed dissenting opinion in which Handler, J., joined.

*512 The opinion of the Court was delivered by

CLIFFORD, J.

This is a medical-malpractice and products-liability action

arising out of the 1972 inoculation of the infant plaintiff with a combined diphtheria-pertussis-tetanus vaccine, commonly known as DPT vaccine. Despite extensive discovery, plaintiffs were unable to identify the manufacturer of the DPT vaccine administered to the infant plaintiff. The issue is whether, in the context of childhood vaccinations, New Jersey should substitute for the element of causation-in-fact a theory of "market share" liability, thereby shifting to defendant manufacturers the burden of proof on the issue of causation.

We conclude that the imposition of a theory of collective liability in this case would frustrate overarching public-policy and public-health considerations by threatening the continued availability of needed drugs and impairing the prospects of the development of safer vaccines. Moreover, we are satisfied that an alternative compensation scheme established by Congress, entitled the National Childhood Vaccine Injury Act of 1986, 42 U.S.C.A. sections 300aa-1 to -34 (West Supp.1988), will fulfill in large measure the goal of providing compensatory relief to vaccine-injured plaintiffs.

We therefore reverse the judgment of the Appellate Division and reinstate summary judgment in favor of defendant manufacturers.

I

Underlying this appeal is a profound human tragedy. On October 24, 1972, two days before her second birthday, plaintiff Deanna Marrero was given a final "booster" shot of a DPT vaccine by Dr. Feld, *513 defendant pediatrician. Plaintiff Clara Morgan Shackil, the child's mother, noticed that within twenty-four hours of the inoculation Deanna displayed symptoms of extreme pain. The rapid deterioration of her condition resulted in the loss of her then-acquired verbal, motor, and mental capacities. Deanna, now eighteen years of age, has been diagnosed as having chronic encephalopathy and severe retardation. She is institutionalized and requires constant care.

In April 1985, thirteen years after the inoculation that allegedly caused plaintiff's condition, Deanna Marrero and her parents brought suit against Dr. Feld and Lederle Laboratories, one of the manufacturers of DPT during 1971-72. The complaint asserted theories of negligence, breach of warranty, misrepresentation, and strict liability based on design defect. Plaintiffs' delay in filing suit was occasioned by the fact that it was not until 1984 that Mrs. Shackil became aware of the linkage between brain damage and the pertussis portion of the DPT vaccine.

Largely because of the extensive time that had elapsed between the inoculation and the lawsuit, plaintiffs were unable to establish that Lederle Laboratories in fact manufactured the vaccine that caused Deanna's injuries. The pediatrician, Dr. Feld, retained no records that would have revealed the brand name of the vaccine administered, and his pharmacist is no longer alive. In his deposition, Dr. Feld testified that he had used Lederle's vaccine "for the most part"; however, he also indicated that on occasion he had used DPT vaccines manufactured by Eli Lilly, Wyeth Laboratories, Parke-Davis, and Pitman-Moore. Dr. Feld did not mention the name of National Drug Company, the only remaining manufacturer of DPT at the time of Deanna's inoculation.

Plaintiffs amended their complaint to include the additional manufacturers referred to in Dr. Feld's deposition but not National Drug Company. After several months of discovery, however, plaintiffs were still unable to identify the manufacturer of the vaccine administered to Deanna. Consequently, defendants Lederle, Eli Lilly, Wyeth, and Parke-Davis moved for summary judgment based on plaintiffs' failure to satisfy an essential element of a prima facie case--the identity of the manufacturer and distributor of the DPT dosage.

Relying on Namm v. Charles E. Frosst & Co., 178 N.J.Super. 19, 427 A.2d 1121 (App.Div.1981), the trial court granted defendant manufacturers' motions for summary judgment and entered orders dismissing the complaints as to those defendants. The Appellate Division granted leave to appeal and reversed. Shackil v. Lederle Laboratories, 219 N.J.Super. 601, 530 A.2d 1287 (1987).

In the Appellate Division the case produced three opinions, two leading to a reversal and remand, and one to an affirmance. The lead opinion explained that although the trial court was correct in relying on Namm to dismiss the complaint, the Appellate Division's role was "to determine what the Supreme Court would do if faced with the problem before us." 219 N.J.Super. at 621, 530 A.2d 1287. The lead opinion held that the rejection of collective liability theories, "which have been developed in states with views of tort law similar to our own(,) would be an unwarranted deviation from what we believe to be a course already charted by our Supreme Court." Ibid.

The lead opinion examined and summarized the current theories of concert of action, alternative liability, enterprise liability, and market-share liability, id. at 622-30, 530 A.2d 1287, as do we, infra at 514-515. According to the lead opinion a "risk-modified market share" approach was most aptly suited to the circumstances of this case. Under that approach

> (a) plaintiff should first demonstrate that the specific manufacturer of a defective product proven to have caused the injury cannot be identified, and join the manufacturers of a substantial share of the relevant market, defined as all who could have distributed the product to the plaintiff. Once this has been accomplished, the burden is placed on the defendants to exculpate themselves by *514 proving either non-participation, possession of a reduced market share or that their product engendered a lower risk. Our aim should be to determine the percentage of the potential risk to the plaintiff caused by each manufacturer of the product, and in this respect our resolution of this issue departs somewhat from a pure market share analysis. (Id. at 630-31, 530 A.2d 1287.)

Under the lead opinion, on remand the trial court was to impose risk-modified market-share liability as a substitute for the causation-in-fact requirement "only if the standards to which plaintiffs seek to hold defendants have not been preempted by federal regulation, and if plaintiffs otherwise demonstrate that the product, with its recognized utility, was indeed defective, given the existing technology when it was manufactured and distributed." Id. at 634, 530 A.2d 1287 (citing Feldman v. Lederle Laboratories, 97 N.J. 429, 452, 479 A.2d 374 (1984)).

A second opinion, concurring in the judgment of remand and not foreclosing the availability of market-share liability, agreed that reliance on Namm, supra, 178 N.J.Super. 19, 427 A.2d 1121, would be misplaced, and that a remand would appropriately "permit development of an adequate record from which the Supreme Court can review the matter in the context of specific factfinding." 219 N.J.Super. at 640-41, 530 A.2d 1287. The concurring member added that the remand should determine as well whether the recently-enacted products-liability legislation, N.J.S.A. 2A:58C-1 to -7, applied to the case, and if not, whether any policies embodied in the new legislation were nonetheless relevant to the analysis.

The dissenting member of the Appellate Division panel reasoned that in the absence of "amendatory legislation," an intermediate appellate court should not depart from "traditional concepts and basic principles," 219 N.J.Super. at 642, 530 A.2d 1287, but should leave such a decision to a court of last resort. Moreover, the dissenter below concluded that the collective-liability theory adopted by the lead opinion was not administratively sound and would "add to the cost of the end product and discourage the production of needed drugs and commodities." Id. at 643, 530 A.2d 1287. Finally, any decision supporting collective liability in this case was inappropriate in light of the legislature's recent enactment of a products-liability statute, and placed the legislature in "the position of having to react to what may well be unwarranted judicial fiat." Id. at 643, 530 A.2d 1287.

We granted leave to appeal, 109 N.J. 519, 520, 537 A.2d 1304 (1987), and have permitted the participation of various amici. Our primary focus is on whether plaintiffs have demonstrated that a theory of market-share liability should be applied to the facts of this case to allow plaintiffs' claims against defendant manufacturers to proceed. Because this appeal emanates from a motion for summary judgment, we must construe the pleadings and papers in the light most favorable to the nonmoving party, in this case the plaintiffs. E.g., Ruvolo v. American Casualty Co., 39 N.J. 490, 499, 189 A.2d 204 (1963); Judson v. Peoples Bank & Trust Co. of Westfield, 17 N.J. 67, 75, 110 A.2d 24 (1954). Therefore, we will assume that the vaccines manufactured by defendants were defectively designed and that Deanna's injuries were directly caused by a DPT inoculation and not from a hereditary immunological or neurological disorder, issues that would potentially surface at later stages of this litigation. See, e.g., Niemiera v. Schneider, 114 N.J. 550, 554, 555 A.2d 1112 (1989) (noting possibility of independent cause of plaintiffs' injuries, unrelated to DPT inoculation); Feldman v. Lederle Laboratories, supra, 97 N.J. at 429, 479 A.2d 374 (whether a prescription drug is "unavoidably unsafe," and therefore subject to section 402A of the Restatement (Second) of Torts comment k protection, is to be determined on a case-by-case basis).

II

At the center of this appeal is the traditional element of causation-in-fact, "that reasonable connection between the act or omission of the defendant and the damages *515 which plaintiff has suffered." W. Keeton, D. Dobbs, R. Keeton & D. Owen, Prosser & Keeton on the Law of Torts section 41 at 263 (5th ed. 1984) (hereinafter Prosser & Keeton). The purpose of the causation-in-fact requirement, besides assigning blameworthiness to culpable parties, is to limit the scope of potential liability and thereby encourage useful activity that would otherwise be deterred if there were excessive exposure to liability. Fischer, "Products Liability--An Analysis of Market Share Liability," 34 Vand.L.Rev. 1623, 1628-29 (1981) (citing W. Prosser, Handbook of the Law of Torts 237, 239 (4th ed. 1971)). Although proof of causation-in-fact is ordinarily an indispensable ingredient of a prima facie case, exceptions have nevertheless arisen that have allowed plaintiffs to shift to defendant or a group of defendants the burden of proof on the causation issue. Those exceptions include "concert of action," with its offspring, "enterprise liability"; alternative liability; and market-share liability. In fact, the theory that we are urged to adopt in this case, modified market-share liability, is essentially an extension of the alternative-liability theory. The concert-of-action exception nevertheless warrants brief comment.

(1) The theory of "concert of action" derives from the criminal concept of aiding and abetting. Ryan v. Eli Lilly & Co., 514 F.Supp. 1004, 1015 (D.S.C.1981). It allocates responsibility among parties who "in pursuance of a common plan or design to commit a tortious act, actively take part in it, or further it by cooperation or request, or * * * lend aid or encouragement to the wrongdoers, or ratify and adopt the wrongdoer's acts done for their benefit * * *." Prosser & Keeton, supra, section 46 at 323. The clearest example of "concerted action" liability is the drag race in which two drivers agree to race and one collides with and injures a third party. Both drivers are jointly and severally liable for the injury to the third party even though only one driver inflicted the harm. Restatement (Second) of Torts section 876 at 315 (1982). Some courts have applied the theory of "concert of action" in the context of DES, a synthetic drug that was prescribed for pregnant women to prevent miscarriage and was later proven to be linked to cellular abnormalities. See, e.g., Abel v. Eli Lilly & Co., 418 Mich. 311, 336-39,

343 N.W.2d 164, 176 (holding all DES manufacturers jointly and severally liable if unable to exculpate themselves), cert. den. sub nom. E.R. Squibb & Sons v. Abel, 469 U.S. 833, 105 S.Ct. 123, 83 L.Ed.2d 65 (1984); Bichler v. Eli Lilly & Co., 55 N.Y.2d 571, 450 N.Y.S.2d 776, 436 N.E.2d 182 (1982) (because DES manufacturer made no motion to dismiss the complaint for failure to state a cause of action, "concerted action" theory became controlling law of case), overruled, Hymowitz v. Eli Lilly & Co., 73 N.Y.2d 487, 541 N.Y.S.2d 941, 945, 539 N.E.2d 1069, 1073 (N.Y.1989). But see Ryan v. Eli Lilly & Co., supra, 514 F.Supp. 1004 (rejecting application of concert-of-action theory of liability against DES manufacturers). Moreover, an extension of this theory, called "enterprise liability," was developed in the context of the blasting-cap industry in Hall v. E.I. du Pont de Nemours & Co., 345 F.Supp. 353 (E.D.N.Y.1972). As explained in the lead opinion below, "(t)he enterprise or industry-wide liability theory imposes liability on all members of an industry (that) has produced a product causing a particular harm. The defendants then have the opportunity to exculpate themselves." 219 N.J.Super. at 624, 530 A.2d 1287. In Hall the court allowed a relaxation of the traditional burden of proving causation because defendants, six blasting-cap manufacturers and their industry trade association "exercise(d) actual collective control over a particular risk-creating product * * *." 345 F.Supp. at 376.

Without embarking on an analysis of the merits in or the inherent problems of applying concert-of-action theory to prescription drugs, we are persuaded that the theory is not applicable to this case. There are no allegations that the manufacturers of DPT had a "tacit understanding" or "common plan" to produce a defective product or not to conduct adequate tests on the vaccine. Indeed, unlike the producers of DES, for example, each of the manufacturers involved in this case made the DPT vaccine *516 by a different process, protected by patent or trade secret. Each process was separately licensed by the Food and Drug Administration (FDA) under established guidelines for the production of the vaccine. 21 C.F.R. section 620.1 to 620.6 (1988); see, e.g., Jones by Jones v. Lederle Laboratories, 695 F.Supp. 700, 703-04 (E.D.N.Y.1988). In addition, each lot of the DPT vaccine was separately tested by the office of Biologics Research and Reviews, a division of the FDA. 21 C.F.R. 620.6 (1988). Application of "concert of action" to this case "would (therefore) expand the doctrine far beyond its intended scope and would render virtually any manufacturer liable for the defective products of an entire industry, even if it could be demonstrated that the product which caused the injury was not made by the defendant." Sindell v. Abbott Laboratories, 26 Cal.3d 588, 605, 163 Cal.Rptr. 132, 141, 607 P.2d 924, 933 cert. den., 449 U.S. 912, 101 S.Ct. 286, 66 L.Ed.2d 140 (1980); accord Hymowitz v. Eli Lilly & Co., supra, 73 N.Y.2d 487, 541 N.Y.S.2d at 945, 539 N.E.2d at 1073; Martin v. Abbott Laboratories, 102 Wash.2d 581, 598, 689 P.2d 368, 379 (1984).

A second exception to the causation-in-fact requirement, termed "alternative liability," was developed by the California Supreme Court in Summers v. Tice, 33 Cal.2d 80, 199 P.2d 1 (1948). The opinion in that case is essentially the starting point for any analysis of market-share liability. In Summers, two hunters fired their guns in the direction of plaintiff, whose eye was severely injured as a result of one of the gunshots. At trial, plaintiff established that both defendants were negligent; however, plaintiff was unable to identify which shot hit him. The trial court nevertheless concluded that the negligence of both defendants was the legal cause of the injury and that therefore both were responsible for the result. On appeal, the Supreme Court of California upheld the trial court's relaxation of the causation-in-fact requirement, reasoning that because both defendants were negligent in respect of the plaintiff, it would be unjust to require the victim to isolate the guilty defendant. Id. at 88, 199 P.2d at 3. Consequently, the burden was shifted to each defendant to exculpate himself, on the failure of which he would incur liability for the entire damages. See, e.g., Restatement (Second) of Torts section 433B(3) (1965) (codifying theory in Summers).

(2) "Alternative liability" is not applicable where not all of the culpable defendants have been joined in the action. See Sindell v. Abbott Laboratories, supra, 26 Cal.3d at 602, 163 Cal.Rptr. at 139, 607 P.2d at 931. That impediment to "alternative liability" has not deterred courts from fashioning a separate theory, denominated "market share liability," which embodies the concept of "alternative liability" while eliminating the necessity of joining all possible tortfeasors and the requirement of contemporaneous negligent acts. The seminal market-share case is Sindell v. Abbott Laboratories, supra, 26 Cal.3d 588, 163 Cal.Rptr. 132, 607 P.2d 924, a class-action suit based on design defect, brought against the manufacturers of the drug DES for injuries sustained in utero. Because of the latent nature of the injury and the fact that the drug was produced by

approximately two hundred manufacturers from a generic formula that was prescribed interchangeably, plaintiffs were unable to identify the manufacturer who actually produced the injury-causing product. The California Supreme Court held that the inability to identify a defendant was not fatal to plaintiff's cause of action, provided plaintiff join as defendants a "substantial share" of manufacturers who produced or supplied "the DES which her mother might have taken." Id. at 612, 163 Cal.Rptr. 145, 607 P.2d at 937. The burden would then shift to the defendant manufacturers to demonstrate that they could not have produced the DES ingested by plaintiff's mother. Any manufacturer that could not exculpate itself would be held liable "for the proportion of the judgment represented by its share of the market" of DES. Ibid.

Two important policy considerations supported the Sindell court's decision to apply market-share liability. The first, "most persuasive" consideration was the one addressed in Summers:

*517 (A)s between an innocent plaintiff and negligent defendants, the latter should bear the cost of the injury. Here, as in Summers, plaintiff is not at fault in failing to provide evidence of causation, and although the absence of such evidence is not attributable to the defendants either, their conduct in marketing a drug the effects of which are delayed for many years played a significant role in creating the unavailability of proof. (Id. at 610-11, 163 Cal.Rptr. at 144, 607 P.2d at 936.)

The second consideration was that a DES manufacturer was in a better position to insure against the risk of injury; "thus, holding it liable for defects and failure to warn of harmful effects will provide an incentive to product safety." Id. at 611, 163 Cal.Rptr. at 144, 607 P.2d at 936.

The market-share theory announced in Sindell was subsequently adopted, with modifications, by three states' highest courts. See Hymowitz v. Eli Lilly & Co., supra, 73 N.Y.2d 487, 541 N.Y.S.2d 941, 539 N.E.2d 1069 (N.Y.1989) (adopting market-share theory of liability in which DES defendants are liable in proportion to their share in national market irrespective of proof that they did not cause the injury); Martin v. Abbott Laboratories, supra, 102 Wash.2d 581, 689 P.2d 368 (adopting "modified market share" liability, in which plaintiff must join only one defendant who produced or marketed injury-causing product; burden is then shifted to defendant to prove its percentage share of market and thereby lower presumptive equal share of market); Collins v. Eli Lilly & Co., 116 Wis.2d 166, 342 N.W.2d 37 (adopting modified market-share theory of liability in which each DES defendant is liable in proportion to its "respective contribution" to the result, as measured by various factors), cert. den., 469 U.S. 826, 105 S.Ct. 107, 83 L.Ed.2d 51 (1984); see also Smith v. Eli Lilly & Co., 173 Ill.App.3d 1, 122 Ill.Dec. 835, 527 N.E.2d 333 (1988) (adopting theory of liability enunciated in Martin, supra, in context of DES). But see Mulcahy v. Eli Lilly & Co., 386 N.W.2d 67, 76 (Iowa 1986) (rejecting market share theory in DES context on policy grounds and categorizing approach as more appropriately within the legislative domain); Zafft v. Eli Lilly & Co., 676 S.W.2d 241, 247 (Mo.1984) (rejecting market-share-liability approach in DES context on grounds that the theory would discourage desired pharmaceutical research and development and would provide little incentive to produce safer products). In addition, two federal courts have made the "bold foray( ) into terra incognita," Tidler v. Eli Lilly & Co., 851 F.2d 418 (D.C.Cir.1988), and allowed DES diversity claims to proceed under the market-share theory. See McCormack v. Abbott Laboratories, 617 F.Supp. 1521 (D.Mass.1985) (allowing DES claim to proceed under Massachusetts law); McElhaney v. Eli Lilly & Co., 564 F.Supp. 265, 269-71 (D.S.D.1983) (holding that because under South Dakota law plaintiff is not required to identify which of defendant-DES manufacturers produced injury-causing product, burden on causation issue is shifted to defendants). But see Tidler v. Eli Lilly & Co., supra, 851 F.2d 418 (refusing to apply market-share liability to DES manufacturers under the laws of Maryland and District of Columbia because neither state recognizes "non-identification" theories); Mizell v. Eli Lilly & Co., 526 F.Supp. 589 (D.S.C.1981) (holding that the application of Sindell market-share liability against DES manufacturers would violate public policy of South Carolina).

Despite its limited acceptance, the Sindell decision left several issues unanswered. See, e.g., Sindell, supra, 26 Cal.3d at 615, 163 Cal.Rptr. at 147, 607 P.2d at 939 (Richardson, J., dissenting) (noting absence of any guidance regarding "substantial share" of the relevant market). Among them was the question of whether market-share liability was intended to apply to claims other than DES. That issue has frequently arisen in the context of asbestos litigation, where in most cases market-share liability is held inapplicable for public-policy reasons, see, e.g., Thompson v. Johns-Manville Corp., 714 F.2d 581 (5th Cir.1983) (refusing to apply "market share" liability in diversity case because it represents "radical departure( ) from traditional *518 theories of tort liability," id. at 583), and because

> products containing asbestos are not uniformly harmful--many products contain different degrees of asbestos. Thus "the total risk created by any manufacturer would be a function of both its share of the market and the relative harmfulness of its products"; but a company's market share could not be adjusted for the latter relation. (Starling v. Seaboard Coast Line R.R. Co., 533 F.Supp. 183, 191 (S.D.Ga.1982) (citation omitted).).

See also Mullen v. Armstrong World Indus. Inc., 200 Cal.App.3d 250, 246 Cal.Rptr. 32 (Ct.App.1988) (rejecting the application of "market share" liability against the manufacturers of asbestos products because of diverse nature of products); Goldman v. Johns-Manville Sales Corp., 33 Ohio St.3d 40, 514 N.E.2d 691 (1987) (refusing to apply Sindell to asbestos products on grounds that there was a difference between risks associated with asbestos and that it would be inherently unfair to hold companies accountable for market share); cf. Blackston v. Shook & Fletcher Insulation Co., 764 F.2d 1480 (11th Cir.1985) (holding that "significant policy reasons" favor retention of proximate cause as an essential element of cause of action in asbestos litigation).

At present, there are three reported cases addressing the question of whether to apply a theory of market-share liability to a vaccine case. Of these three only one involves the theory urged in this case, that is, that the vaccine is defectively designed. Thus, in Senn v. Merrell-Dow Pharmaceuticals, Inc., 305 Or. 256, 751 P.2d 215 (1988), the Oregon Supreme Court rejected a theory of market-share liability against two DPT manufacturers in the context of a design-defect claim on grounds that the "adoption of any theory of alternative liability requires a profound change in fundamental tort principles," which was perceived as more properly in the domain of the legislature. Id. at 271, 751 P.2d 223.

The other two cases involve the imposition of market-share liability in respect of a vaccine based on a manufacturing defect, a theory not relied on in this case. Nevertheless, those cases warrant our attention. In Sheffield v. Eli Lilly

& Co., supra, 144 Cal.App.3d 583, 192 Cal.Rptr. 870, plaintiff's claim against the manufacturers of the Salk polio vaccine was summarily dismissed for failure to identify the defendant who had supplied the injury-causing vaccine. Plaintiffs appealed, urging the application of market-share liability.

The California Court of Appeals held that the rationale of Sindell was inapplicable for several reasons. First, the alleged defect related to the method in which the vaccine was processed (the "infectivity potential of the virus" had not been destroyed) and not to the design of the product, as was the case in Sindell. Id. at 594, 192 Cal.Rptr. at 876. The court explained:

> Here, unlike Sindell, the injuries did not result from the use of a drug generally defective when used for the purpose it was marketed, but because some manufacturer made and distributed a defective product. The product that allegedly injured plaintiffs was itself not a unit of a total generic pharmaceutical product but a deviant defective vaccine. (Ibid.)

The court reasoned that it would be unfair to hold four innocent manufacturers responsible for an injury caused by the one tortfeasor who manufactured the defective dosage. Id. at 599, 192 Cal.Rptr. at 880; cf. Brown v. Superior Court of California, 44 Cal.3d 1049, 245 Cal.Rptr. 412, 751 P.2d 470 (1988) (holding that market-share theory of liability was inapplicable to fraud and breach-of-warranty claims).

The second reason why Sindell was inapplicable to the polio-vaccine context of Sheffield was that the "delay in discovering the alleged causation was in no way related to the nature of the defective product or any other act or omission of the unknown tortfeasor," again unlike Sindell, where the "delay was occasioned because the potential for harm was latent and did not manifest itself for many years." Id. 144 Cal.App.3d at 594, 192 Cal.Rptr. at 877.

Finally, the Sheffield court was of the view that an application of Sindell to the *519 facts of the case would subvert the important public policy of encouraging swift production and marketing of new pharmaceutical products. Id. at 597-98, 192 Cal.Rptr. at 878-79. Specifically, the court noted that if market-share liability had been generally prevalent during the development of the poliomyelitis vaccine, manufacturers would have been reluctant to proceed with the distribution of the vaccine, and consequently thousands of polio sufferers would not have been saved by the Salk vaccine program. Id. at 599, 192 Cal.Rptr. at 880.

If Sheffield clarifies the question of whether market-share liability is applicable to vaccines that are defective because of manufacturing flaws, then the decision in Morris v. Parke, Davis & Co., 667 F.Supp. 1332, (C.D.Cal.1987) beclouds it. In Morris, a federal district court in California reasoned that Sheffield's prohibition against the application of market-share liability was limited to only one type of manufacturing defect: that involving one unit that deviates from ostensibly identical units. Id. at 1341. Sheffield was inapplicable, according to the Morris court, to manufacturing defects shared by an industry "resulting from common (perhaps for reasons of economy) substandard means of production, storage and transportation or marketing." Id. at 1342. The court then went on to impose market-share liability on the manufacturers of DPT vaccines insofar as their vaccines contained this second type of manufacturing defect.

The court in Morris therefore focused only on the first point made in Sheffield: that market share liability was inappropriate for a manufacturing defect case. As a consequence, the court managed to elude the other two grounds on which Sheffield was premised: the fact that the delay in discovering the defect was unrelated to the nature of DPT, and the important public policy considerations attendant on expanding liability to needed pharmaceutical products. See Sheffield v. Eli Lilly & Co., supra, 144 Cal.App.3d at 594, 192 Cal.Rptr. at 876-77.

Moreover, we are not convinced that the Morris court was correct in classifying the defect as stemming from the manufacturing process. See Cepeda v. Cumberland Eng'g Co., Inc., 76 N.J. 152, 169, 386 A.2d 816 (1978) (pointing up the distinction between manufacturing defects and defects of design). Although the court in Morris later stated that it was "irrelevant * * * whether the defect which caused the plaintiff's injuries is common to the products of all the defendant manufacturers because it was a design defect or because it was a manufacturing defect (shared by an industry)," 667 F.Supp. at 1342, that statement is at odds with the court's earlier pronouncement that plaintiff's design-defect claims had been dismissed on grounds that comment k of the Restatement (Second) of Torts section 402A was applicable. Id. at 1334 n. 1. As such, the analysis in Morris lacks persuasive force.

We digress from a general overview of collective-liability precedent briefly to examine New Jersey case law. With the exception of the Appellate Division lead opinion in this case, there is no New Jersey decision that has expressly adopted concert of action, alternative liability, or market-share liability in the context of a products-liability action. Although in Ferrigno v. Eli Lilly & Co., 175 N.J.Super. 551, 420 A.2d 1305 (Law Div.1980), a trial court held that alternative liability based on a percentage-share apportionment was permissible in DES cases, the complaint was subsequently dismissed following the Appellate Division's opinion in Namm v. Charles E. Frosst & Co., supra, 178 N.J.Super. 19, 427 A.2d 1121, which refused to adopt a theory of collective liability in a DES action.

The parties to this appeal appear to accept the proposition that this Court impliedly adopted a theory of alternative liability in NOPCO Chemical Div. v. Blaw-Knox Co., 59 N.J. 274, 281 A.2d 793 (1971), and Anderson v. Somberg, 67 N.J. 291, 338 A.2d 1, cert. den., 423 U.S. 929, 96 S.Ct. 279, 46 L.Ed.2d 258 (1975), by allowing recovery without proof of a precise causative agent. In NOPCO, supra, 59 N.J. 274, 281 A.2d 793, a transportation-bailment *520 case, a commercial drying machine was delivered in damaged condition to plaintiff's place of business, and plaintiff sued the manufacturer, the carriers, and bailees "who successively, but unconnectedly, handled (the machine) until it reached its final destination." Id. at 278, 281 A.2d 793 (emphasis added). However, because of the complex nature of the transportation and bailment chain, plaintiff was unable to establish which defendant was handling the machine when it was damaged. The absence of "identification" evidence resulted in dismissal of plaintiff's case at trial. That ruling was affirmed by a divided Appellate Division panel. This Court reversed, holding that plaintiff could make out a prima facie case by proving "the nature of the damage, the identity of the respective defendants who handled (the machine), and the general capacities in which they did so." Id. at 284, 281 A.2d 793. Because the defendants separately owed plaintiff a duty of care and had superior knowledge of the occurrence, this Court concluded that it was appropriate to impose on the defendants the burden of going forward with evidence demonstrating their "particular part in the overall transaction in explanation or exoneration of (their) conduct with relation to the damage." Ibid. Plaintiff retained the ultimate burden of persuasion in respect of each defendant.

A situation somewhat analogous to NOPCO was presented in Anderson v. Somberg, supra, 67 N.J. 291, 338 A.2d 1, in which plaintiff, during the course of his surgery, was injured by a defective medical instrument but was unable to establish, as among the hospital, the doctor, and the instrument's manufacturer or distributor, exactly where culpability should lie. A plurality of this Court devised a sharply limited exception to the traditional rule that plaintiff carry the entire burden of proof in establishing liability. The exception provided that

> where an unconscious or helpless patient suffers an admitted mishap not reasonably foreseeable and unrelated to the scope of the surgery (such as cases where foreign objects are left in the body of the patient), those who had custody of the patient, and who owed him a duty of care as to medical treatment, or not to furnish a defective instrument for use in such treatment can be called to account for their default. They must prove their nonculpability, or else risk liability for the injuries suffered. (Id. at 298, 338 A.2d 1.)

Unlike the approach taken in NOPCO, the plurality shifted to defendants not merely the burden of going forward with explanatory evidence but also the burden of persuasion on the liability question, ruling that the Appellate Division had correctly determined that "since at least one of the defendants could not sustain his burden of proof, at least one of them would be liable." Ibid. That approach, which could conceivably be characterized as one of "alternative liability," has not been duplicated in any New Jersey case since Anderson. It is limited to one factual context.

Although the plurality opinion in Anderson relaxed the burden of persuasion in respect of the element of causation, it did not eliminate the requirement that some "reasonable connection" be established between the defendant and the ultimate harm. Prosser & Keeton, supra, section 41 at 263; see, e.g., Thompson v. Johns-Manville Corp., supra, 714 F.2d at 583. Significantly, plaintiff in Anderson sued all who might have been liable for his injury, as defined by all those who participated in the chain of events leading up to the injury. 67 N.J. at 304, 338 A.2d 1; see NOPCO, supra, 59 N.J. 274, 281 A.2d 793. Indeed, one of the justifications for shifting the burden of persuasion was that the defendants had engaged in conduct that "activated legal obligations by _each_ of them to plaintiff." Anderson, supra, 67 N.J. at 298, 338 A.2d 1 (emphasis added). In sum, the decision in Anderson, even were it construed to apply outside of its factual context, does not support the adoption of market-share liability, which would eliminate the requirement of proof of any connection between defendant and the actual injury. Hence, there is no trend in this *521 jurisdiction toward wholesale adoption of market-share liability.

III

(3) With the foregoing in mind, we proceed to the question of whether New Jersey should expand current principles of tort law to adopt risk-modified market-share liability in the DPT context. Preliminarily, we must address the issue of whether DPT is a "generic product" that is uniformly harmful and therefore amenable to a market-share analysis. However, the central consideration on which our decision is essentially premised is whether as a matter of sound public policy this Court should modify traditional tort theory to allow plaintiffs' design-defect claims to proceed. In examining this second question, we look to the general policies that formed the basis of the Sindell decision as well as the specific policy considerations that would accompany an expansion of tort law in the context of vaccines.

A determination of whether DPT is "uniformly harmful" must rest on a full understanding of the product involved in this appeal. DPT is a biological product made from three separate components: diphtheria toxoid, tetanus toxoid, and pertussis vaccine, each of which stimulates the production of antibodies that protect the body against those childhood diseases. Two major kinds of preparations used to produce immunity are the toxoid type (diphtheria and tetanus), and the whole-cell type (pertussis). Toxoid preparations contain small amounts of the toxins produced by certain bacteria, chemically treated to stimulate immunity without causing disease symptoms. The diphtheria and tetanus portions of the DPT vaccine are therefore not the source of any harmful side-effects. Instead, it is the pertussis portion of the DPT vaccine, made from a whole-cell type of preparation, that harbors the alleged defect.

Apparently because of the complex nature of the pertussis organism, the poisonous substances produced by the bacteria have been difficult to isolate. Consequently, the vaccine that was developed, still in use today, is made from a whole-cell type of vaccine preparation in which whole cells have simply been isolated and inactivated. This type of vaccine preparation is cruder than the toxoid-type preparation, and has been accompanied by adverse reactions varying from local to systemic. The injury alleged in this case--acute encephalopathy--represents a severe injury that is estimated to occur once in every 110,000 doses of the vaccine. Staff of the House Subcomm. on Health and the Environment of the House Comm. on Energy and Commerce, 99th Cong., 2d Sess., Report on Childhood Immunizations 25 (Comm. Print 1986) (hereinafter Comm. Print).

Two other methods of vaccinating against pertussis should be mentioned. The first alternative method, which was on the market under the trade name Tri-Solgen at the time of Deanna's inoculation, is a "split-cell" or "soluble" vaccine, in which cells of the pertussis have been split or fragmented by a chemical process. It is unclear whether that method removed the poisonous substances from the organism, or what portions of the pertussis cell remained in the vaccine. However, according to one of the clinicians who conducted early tests on the product, Tri-Solgen produced a "high degree of antibody response and markedly lower incidence of systemic and local reactions." Weihl, "Extracted Pertussis Antigen," 106 American Journal of Diseases of Children 210-15 (1963).

According to plaintiffs, however, Tri-Solgen too was defectively designed inasmuch as the vaccine did not completely eradicate the dangerous toxins inherent in pertussis. Plaintiffs refer us to another method of pertussis vaccination, developed by the Japanese, in which all of the toxins have allegedly been eliminated. This "acellular" method of pertussis vaccination has been in widespread use in Japan since 1981 but is not licensed in the United States. Its overall safety and clinical efficacy have not been formally reported.

At the time of Deanna's inoculation, five DPT manufacturers were producing a whole-cell pertussis vaccine, whereas one, Eli Lilly, was producing a split-cell vaccine. *522 The products were clearly not identical because Eli Lilly's Tri-Solgen engendered a lower risk of harm. Nevertheless, the Appellate Division lead opinion swept all producers into one market share, placing the burden on Eli Lilly to prove that its product was less dangerous. Although we reserve decision on the general appropriateness of including products with differing degrees of risk in a market-share analysis, we are wary of the inclusion, in the lead opinion below, of Tri-Solgen inasmuch as the product may have represented the "state of the art" in vaccine design at the time of the inoculation. See, e.g., N.J.S.A. 2A:58C-3(a)(1) (providing that "state of the art" is an absolute defense in products-liability actions).

We are not persuaded, however, that the remaining whole-cell vaccines were also inappropriate for market-share analysis solely because they were made from a biological, as opposed to a chemical, formula. Although the vaccines were separately patented or carried separate trade names, there is sufficient evidence that pediatricians used the whole-cell products interchangeably. One notable study, conducted on vaccines produced by Wyeth, Connaught, Lederle, and Parke-Davis, concluded that there was no significant difference in the rates of more serious reactions by vaccine manufacturers. Baraff, Cody, Cherry, "DPT-Associated Reactions: An Analysis by Injection Site, Manufacturers, Prior Reactions and Dose," 73 Pediatrics 31 (Jan. 1984). Indeed, any differences that were observed were for less-serious reactions and appeared to be related to differences in vaccine lots rather than in the specific vaccines. Ibid.

We turn, then, from the arguments that have been premised on technical distinctions between DES and DPT to the thrust of this appeal: the public-policy and public-health considerations that would accompany the imposition of market-share liability in this context.

IV

This Court has adopted the basic tenet that "(t)he torts process, like the law itself, is a human institution designed to accomplish certain social objectives." People Express Airlines, Inc. v. Consolidated Rail Corp., 100 N.J. 246, 254, 495 A.2d 107 (1985). One of the primary objectives is to ensure "that innocent victims have avenues of legal redress, absent a contrary, overriding public policy." Id. at 254-55, 495 A.2d 107. Thus, implicit in any decision to broaden liability in order to provide compensation is a judgment that the goals of public policy will likewise be served. See, e.g., Kelly v. Gwinnell, 96 N.J. 538, 545, 476 A.2d 1219 (1984) (imposition of social-host liability is consistent with overall social goal of reducing drunken driving); Henningsen v. Bloomfield Motors, Inc., 32 N.J. 358, 161 A.2d 69 (1960) ("society's interests can only be protected by eliminating the requirement of privity between the maker and his dealers and the reasonably expected ultimate consumer"). In this case, however, we are presented with a difficult circumstance in which societal goals, in encouraging the use and development of needed drugs, would be thwarted by the imposition of unlimited liability on manufacturers in order to provide compensation to those injured by their products.

We deem it a matter of paramount importance that this case involves a vaccine--a product regarded as essential to the public welfare. Before the vaccine's appearance, the disease pertussis claimed the lives of thousands of children in the United States each year and left many others with severe injuries, including spastic paralysis, mental retardation, and other neurological disorders. Comm. Print, supra, at 9. In one epidemic alone, pertussis was responsible for as many as 7,518 deaths, afflicting a total of 265,269 children. Id. at 10. As a result of national immunization efforts sponsored by the federal government and begun in the early 1950s after the development of the vaccine, the country showed a ninety-nine percent reduction in the number of reported cases per 100,000 population during the years 1943 to 1976, and an even more dramatic reduction in the number of deaths. Hinman and Koplan, "Pertussis and Pertussis Vaccine: Reanalysis of Benefits, Risks and *523 Costs," 251 J.A.M.A. 3109-13 (1984). Indeed, Congress has noted that the

> (v)accination of children against deadly disabling, but preventable(,) infectious diseases has been one of the most spectacularly effective public health initiatives this country has ever undertaken. (H.R.Rep. No. 908, 99th Cong., 2d Sess, 4, reprinted in 1986 U.S.Code Cong. & Admin.News 6344, 6345.)

Those efforts notwithstanding, pertussis, not having been entirely eradicated, continues to pose a threat to the health of this country's children. Cherry, "The Epidemiology of Pertussis and Pertussis Immunization in the United Kingdom and the United States: A Comparative Study," 14:2 Current Problems in Pediatrics 67 (February 1984). Where there has been a reduced level of pertussis immunization, such as in Great Britain and Japan, major epidemics of the disease have recurred. Id. at 69. Hence, the federal government continues actively to finance and monitor immunization efforts through the National Institutes of Health, the Food and Drug Administration, and the Center for Disease Control. New Jersey has assisted in this effort, as have the majority of states, by mandating that all school children be immunized before beginning their elementary-school education. N.J.A.C. 8:57-4:10. Nevertheless, a recent study from the Children's Defense Fund indicates that DPT immunization rates have fallen sharply since 1980, particularly among non-white infants. CDF, The Health of America's Children xi, 62-64 (1989).

Recent trends in the production and distribution of DPT have threatened the supply of the vaccine, with a predictable effect on the nation's immunization efforts.

These trends include rapidly increasing prices for vaccines, a decline in the number of organizations involved in the production and distribution of vaccines which in turn may lead to interruptions in the supply of vaccines, and an increasing number of product liability lawsuits against vaccine manufacturers which allege injuries due to vaccines. (Comm. Print, supra, at 59.)

There are now only two commercial entities willing to produce the DPT vaccine, id. at 68, as contrasted with five in 1984. The overwhelming reason for the decrease in the number of manufacturers is the "extreme liability exposure, (the) cost of litigation and the difficulty of continuing to obtain adequate insurance." Vaccine Injury Compensation: Hearing Before Subcomm. on Health and the Environment of the House Comm. on Energy and Commerce, 98th Cong., 2d Sess. 295 (Sept. 10 1984) (Statement of Daniel Shaw, Jr., Vice-President for Medical Affairs, Wyeth Laboratories). As a consequence of this withdrawal phenomenon, the remaining firms must concentrate their efforts on expanding production to meet the nation's supply needs as opposed to focusing on research and development. Comm. Print, supra, at 67-70. The market's fragility has been reflected in the exorbitant increase in price of the DPT vaccine from eleven cents a dose in 1984 to $11.40 a dose in 1986 (eight dollars of which goes to insurance costs). Brown v. Superior Court, supra, 44 Cal.3d at 1064-65, 245 Cal.Rptr. at 421, 751 P.2d at 479.

In addition to the policy of ensuring the continued use of this essential drug is the more immediate need to develop a safer alternative vaccine. The creation of an alternative-vaccine design is a slow and complex process that demands the consolidated efforts of scientists, researchers, government agencies, and manufacturers. More importantly, it involves significant expense, shouldered almost entirely by vaccine manufacturers. Comm. Print, supra, at 89. Although research is already underway on an acellular vaccine, similar to that developed in Japan, id. at 38, it is estimated that research will be costly; a dose of the vaccine will cost approximately ten times more than the vaccine currently produced by the whole-cell method. Ibid; Anderson, "The Problems Associated With a Development in Clinical Testing of an Improved Pertussis Vaccine," 20 Adv. App. Microbio. 43, 52 (1976), cited in Burke, "DPT Vaccine Controversy: An Assessment of the Liabilities of Manufacturers and Administering Physicians *524 Under Several Legal Theories," 17 Seton Hall L. J. Rev. 541, 548 (1987).

It is against this backdrop that we are asked to expand the scope of liability to which vaccine manufacturers may be held, irrespective of whether they actually produced the injury-causing product. We are told that this expansion represents the "trend" in modern tort law--an assertion that fails to take into account that "(i)t is not, however, the trend, but the social policy underlying it, that should guide the development of the common law." Frame v. Kothari, 115 N.J. 638, 653, 560 A.2d 675, 683 (1989) (Wilentz, C.J., and Garibaldi, J., concurring) (citing B. Cardozo, The Paradoxes of Legal Science (1928), reprinted in Selected Writings of Benjamin Nathan Cardozo 251, 284 (M. Hall ed. 1947). It is apparent that DPT manufacturers would have difficulty sustaining the increased cost attendant on the imposition of market-share liability while simultaneously covering ascending research costs in order to halt the unfortunate sequence of events that spawned this appeal, as well as continuing to meet current production needs. So much is clear from the extensive Congressional research on this subject, see Hearings, supra, at 1-350 (Sept. 19, 1984, & Dec. 19, 1984); Comm. Print., supra, at 1-103, which has spawned the development of a new system of vaccine-injury compensation, National Childhood Vaccine Injury Act of 1986, 42 U.S.C.A. sections 300aa-1 to -34 (West Supp.1988) (the Act). Of broader concern is the effect of market-share liability on the development of other experimental drugs, such as a vaccine against the spread of acquired-immune-deficiency syndrome (AIDS). See McKenna, "The Impact of Product Liability Law on the Development of a Vaccine Against the AIDS Virus," 55 U. Chi. L. Rev. 943 n. 4 (1988).

The overriding public policy of encouraging the development of necessary drugs is not unfamiliar to products-liability law. It is encompassed within comment k of the Restatement (Second) of Torts 402A, which provides that the producers of unavoidably unsafe products (products, including vaccines, that in the current state of human knowledge are incapable of being made safe for their intended and ordinary use) are not strictly liable for the unfortunate consequences attending their use. To merit that protection the product must be properly prepared and accompanied by proper directions and warnings. The exemption is premised on the ground that it would be "against the public interest" to apply strict liability to unavoidably dangerous products because of "the very serious tendency to stifle medical research and testing." White v. Wyeth Laboratories, 40 Ohio St.3d 390, 533 N.E.2d 748 (1988); see Brown v. Superior Court, supra, 44 Cal.3d at 1058, 245 Cal.Rptr. at 416, 751 P.2d at 479. The policies underlying the exemption are supportive of today's decision. See Payton v. Abbott Laboratories, 386 Mass. 540, 562-563, 437 N.E.2d 171, 184 (1982) (rejecting application of "market share" theory inasmuch as "(p)ublic policy favors the development and marketing of new and more efficacious drugs.").

Mindful of the desirability of providing compensatory relief to vaccine-injured persons, we look to the recent comprehensive efforts of Congress. After extensive research and hearings on the subject of the unique problems presented by childhood vaccine injuries, see, e.g., Hearings, supra; Comm. Print supra, Congress devised a no-fault compensation scheme, entitled the National Childhood Vaccine Injury Act of 1986, 42 U.S.C.A. sections 300aa-1 to -34, "under which awards can be made to vaccine-injured persons quickly, easily, and with certainty and generosity." H. Rep. No. 908, 99th Cong., 2d Sess., at 3 (1986), reprinted in "1986 U.S.Code Cong. & Admin.News" 6344 (hereinafter House Report). See generally 38 L. Frumer & M. Freedman, Products Liability section 51.02 (1988) (providing extensive analysis of the Act); Schwartz & Mahshigian, "National Childhood Vaccine Injury Act of 1986: An Ad Hoc Remedy or a Window for the Future?" 48 Ohio St.L.J. 367 (1987) (examining vaccine-liability crisis and the Act's remedies); Note, "The National Childhood Vaccine Injury Act of 1986: A Solution to the Vaccine Liability Crisis?" 63 Wash. L. Rev. 149 (1988) (addressing the "role of the tort system in the *525 vaccine liability crisis" and the probable success of the Act in resolving that crisis).

The Act provides that a person who has suffered illness, injury, or death need only submit a petition to the United States Claims Court alleging that the injury is vaccine-related. A presumption of vaccine-relatedness arises when the injury suffered is listed in the Vaccine Injury

Table, contained in 42 U.S.C.A. section 300aa-14, and when the first symptoms of the injury occurred within the time period set forth in the Table. A special master then reviews the claim and the evidence, and prepares findings of fact and conclusions of law on whether compensation is appropriate, and, if so, the amount of the award. 42 U.S.C.A. section 300aa-12(c).

For those injured by a vaccine administered before October 1, 1988, the award is to represent "actual unreimbursable expenses" incurred from the date of the judgment awarding such expenses, and "reasonable projected unreimbursable expenses" including rehabilitation costs and costs incurred for custodial care. 42 U.S.C.A. section 300aa-15(a)(1)(A) & (c). The only significant limitation is that the amount for pain and suffering, lost earnings, and attorneys fees may not exceed $30,000. 42 U.S.C.A. section 300aa-15(b). If the petitioner filed a civil action before the effective date of the compensation program and chose to withdraw from the action in order to file a petition, however, the Court of Claims may award costs and expenses incurred in the civil action, including the reasonable value of the attorney's time if suit was filed under a contingent-fee arrangement. 42 U.S.C.A. section 300aa-15(e)(2).

The Act is funded by a "Manufacturers Excise Tax on Childhood Vaccines." House Report at 34, reprinted in "1986 U.S.Code Cong. & Admin. News" 6375. The tax is "set to generate sufficient annual income for the (National Vaccine Injury Compensation Trust) Fund to cover all costs of compensation * * *." Ibid. To assure funding during the nascent stages of the Act, Congress has authorized and appropriated advances to the Fund. "Departments of Labor, Health and Human Services, and Education and Related Agencies Appropriations Act," 1989, Pub.L. No. 100-436, 102 Stat. 1680 (1988). Specifically, for payments of claims associated with post-Act administrations of vaccines, Congress has appropriated, for fiscal year 1989 alone, "such sums as may be necessary"; for those claims associated with pre-Act administrations, Congress has appropriated "such sums as may be necessary, not to exceed eighty million dollars." Ibid. Therefore, as we understand it, Congress has appropriated, for pre-Act vaccine injuries, up to eighty million dollars for fiscal year 1989 as an advance or "front" money to the Fund, so that there will be funds on hand immediately for the payment of claims. Those dollars came from general revenues. The scheme contemplates that once the excise tax gets up to speed and generates enough money to keep the Act funded, the

Fund will pay back, with interest, the amount it "borrowed" from the general revenues. We are therefore satisfied that the Act currently enjoys sufficient funding; moreover, it is clear that Congress has exercised the foresight to maintain that status in the future.

The goal of Congress was to afford a remedy for plaintiffs who would otherwise engage in protracted litigation against a vaccine manufacturer with the consequent risk of being denied recovery because of failure to prove the prima facie elements of a tort-law cause of action. The compensation scheme contained in the Act therefore does away with the traditional tort-law requirements of proof with respect to causation, injury, negligence, and defect. House Report, supra, at 12, reprinted in "1986 U.S.Code Cong. & Admin.News" at 6353. As the legislative history to the Act notes,

> (c)urrently, vaccine-injured persons can seek recovery for their damages only through the civil tort system or through a settlement arrangement with the vaccine manufacturer. Over time, neither approach has proven satisfactory. Lawsuits and settlement negotiations can take months and even years to complete. Transaction costs—including attorneys' fees and court payments—are high. And *526 in the end, no recovery may be available. Yet futures have been destroyed and mounting expenses must be met. (House Report, supra, at 6, reprinted in "1986 U.S.Code Cong. & Admin.News" at 6347.)

Thus, by eliminating traditional elements of proof that often prove fatal to a tort-law claim, the compensation scheme contained in the Act went "beyond even the most (expansive) ruling issued by a court in a vaccine case." Id. at 26, reprinted in "1986 U.S.Code Cong. & Admin.News" at 6367. It could even be argued that in one sense the Act embodies a theory of collective liability, inasmuch as it does not require identification of a manufacturer; moreover, it allocates the cost of vaccine-related accidents among all manufacturers by imposing a tax on each dose of vaccine produced.

In addition to serving the goal of compensation, the Act was also intended to protect the unstable vaccine market by maintaining an adequate number of vaccine manufacturers. The legislative history observes that

> (t)he loss of any of the existing manufacturers of

childhood vaccines at this time could create a genuine public health hazard in this country. Currently there (are) only * * * two manufacturers of the DPT vaccine * * *. (T)he withdrawal of even a single manufacturer would present the very real possibility of vaccine shortages, and, in turn, increasing numbers of unimmunized children, and perhaps, a resurgence of preventable diseases. (Id. at 7, reprinted in "1986 U.S.Code Cong. & Admin.News" at 6348.)

Consequently, the compensation scheme embodied in the Act is structured so that all victims who are injured after 1988 must first prosecute a claim under the Act before pursuing a separate cause of action under tort law. 42 U.S.C.A. section 300aa-11. Although victims injured before 1988 have the option of filing a claim under the Act, all victims regardless of the date of injury are precluded from receiving a subsequent award in a civil trial if they have agreed to accept a compensation award under the Act. In that way the compensation scheme is "intended to lessen the number of lawsuits against manufacturers." Id. at 12, reprinted in "1986 U.S.Code Cong. & Admin.News" at 6353.

In this case plaintiffs had the option of withdrawing their state tort-law claim without prejudice and filing a claim for compensation under the Act. The relevant section is 42 U.S.C.A. section 300aa-11(a)(5)(A), which provides:

> A plaintiff who on the effective date of this subpart has pending a civil action for damages for a vaccine-related injury or death may, at any time within 2 years after the effective date of this subpart or before judgment, whichever occurs first, elect to withdraw such action without prejudice and file a petition under subsection (b) of this section for such injury and death.

See, e.g., Foyle by McMillan v. Lederle Laboratories, 674 F.Supp. 530, 533 (E.D.N.C.1987) (noting "withdrawal" provision of the Act). Given the expedient procedures for filing a claim under the Act and the near certainty of an award, as contrasted with the arduous process of convincing a state appeals court to dispense with the requirement of causation-in-fact, the first option would appear to have been plaintiffs' more prudent course of action. Indeed, under the Act, attorneys consulted about a vaccine-related injury are required to inform their clients of the availability of compensation under the Act. 42 U.S.C.A. section 300aa-10(b).

Instead of pursuing that remedy under the Act, however, plaintiffs have chosen the more hazardous and cumbersome route of attempting to reshape tort-law theory to encompass their claim. They remind us that if we affirm the order of summary judgment, and thereby disallow collective liability in this instance, they will then be precluded from filing a claim under the Act. See 42 U.S.C.A. section 300aa-11(a)(5)(A) & (B). But that predicament, admittedly harsh, was a risk of which they were well aware and one that they willingly encountered. It therefore cannot form the basis of a determination by this Court to allow *527 market-share liability or any modification thereof. The aim of the Act has always been to make vaccine liability more predictable by attracting claimants like these plaintiffs, whose legal position is tenuous, before they received a final determination by a court of law. No statutory purpose would be served if all potential claimants were permitted to cast the die first in a lawsuit and then turn to the Act in the event they were denied relief.

In sum, the existence of the Act is critical in this case for several reasons. First, it illustrates the complex nature of the problem underlying this appeal, which cannot be resolved simply by expanding tort-law theory. Second, it made available a means of compensatory relief for this plaintiff, which, although potentially smaller than a jury award might have been, was nonetheless certain. Finally, it satisfies the tort goal of encouraging safer products, inasmuch as the Act establishes a national program for the research and development of safer vaccines.

(4) Not to be confused with this analysis is the separate question of whether the Act preempts state tort-law claims for design defect. See Hurley v. Lederle Laboratories, 851 F.2d 1536 (5th Cir.1988); Abbot v. American Cyanamid, 844 F.2d 1108 (4th Cir.1988); Foyle by McMillan v. Lederle Laboratories, supra, 674 F.Supp. at 533 (E.D.N.C.1987); Martinkovic v. Wyeth Laboratories, 669 F.Supp. 212 (N.D.Ill.1987); Graham v. Wyeth Laboratories, 666 F.Supp. 1483 (D.Kan.1987); Patten v. Lederle Laboratories, 655 F.Supp. 745 (D.Utah 1987); Note, "DPT Vaccine-Related Injury Actions: Federal Preemption Reconsidered," 41 Rutgers L. Rev. 373 (1988). The preemption issue appears to be well settled: the National Childhood Vaccine Injury Act does not expressly or impliedly preempt traditional state tort-law claims. Hurley, supra, 851 F.2d at 1539-40; Abbot, supra, 844 F.2d at 1112-13. (The Act does, however, limit state

tort claims based on an injury arising after the effective date of compensation program to the extent that it codifies comment k of the Restatement (Second) of Torts, 42 U.S.C.A. section 300aa-22(b)(1), and creates a presumption that a vaccine's warning was valid if it complied with FDA requirements. 42 U.S.C.A. section 300aa-22(b)(2).) The fact that there is no preemption does not dissuade us from our result, because the issue in this case is not whether to allow a currently-viable claim to proceed, but whether to expand existing precedent in the face of a federal statute whose main goals--the development of an alternative approach to compensation and the protection of an unstable vaccine market--are in conflict with such an expansion.

In addition to the National Childhood Vaccine Injury Act, another piece of remedial legislation must be briefly acknowledged. The legislature recently passed a series of statutes, N.J.S.A. 2A:58C-1 to -7, in an effort to "establish clear rules" in respect of various product-liability issues, as well as clarify "specific matters as to which the decisions of the courts in New Jersey have created uncertainty." Senate Judiciary Committee Statement, No. 2805, L.1987, c. 197. Although there is no provision in those enactments governing the question of collective liability, they evince an intent to limit the expansion of products-liability law by creating absolute defenses and rebuttable presumptions of nonliability. See N.J.S.A. 2A:58C-3(a)(1) (adopting "state of the art" as complete defense in design defect claims); N.J.S.A. 2A:58C-3(a)(2) (providing that a product is not defectively designed if inherent characteristics of the product are known to ordinary person who uses it or consumes it with knowledge common to class of persons for whom product was intended); N.J.S.A. 2A:58C-3(a)(3) (adopting comment k of the Restatement (Second) of Torts, which provides that a manufacturer or seller is not liable for a design defect if harm results from unavoidably unsafe aspect and product is accompanied by proper warning); N.J.S.A. 2A:58C-4 (establishing presumption of adequate warning if warning approved or prescribed by FDA). In this manner, the legislature sought to "balance () the interests of the public and the individual with a view towards economic reality." Shackil, supra, 219 N.J.Super. *528 at 543, 530 A.2d 1287. We perceive our decision today as consistent with that goal.

IV

Rather than approach our decision from the perspective of

an analytical criticism of the market-share approach, we have chosen to posit today's ruling on the regressive effect that collective liability would have on the social policy of encouraging vaccine production and research. Our dissenting colleagues argue (1) that our analysis is not compatible with the procedural posture of this appeal, post at 541, (2) that our result is based on public-policy considerations more relevant to the issue of "duty" than of "causation," post at 529, 536, and (3) that our analysis has mistakenly applied considerations of the "unavoidably unsafe" nature of the product to the more general market-share question, post at 529. We address these points separately.

Plaintiffs' brief accompanying their motion for leave to appeal from the trial court's summary dismissal of their action alleges two errors: first, that there was a genuine issue of material fact regarding identification of a culpable defendant; second, "that defendants' motion for summary judgment should not have been granted because a concert of action, alternative liability, or enterprise theory of liability (was) applicable on the facts of the case." On appeal the lead opinion in the Appellate Division went right past the first issue-understandably, given that opinion's approach-and found that in respect of the second issue a "risk-modified market share" theory was applicable, thereby shifting proof of causation-in-fact to defendants. The applicability of market-share theory was subsequently briefed and argued by all parties and amici in defendants' interlocutory appeal to this Court. There was no motion by plaintiffs seeking to have us address any other issue. It is therefore puzzling that the dissent should contend that "(i)t is terribly unfair to deprive this tragically disabled child of any remedy whatsoever for her catastrophic injuries on the basis of theories of law never presented to the Law Division * * *." Post at 541. In fact the court below treated the precise issue that plaintiffs raised-the applicability of collective liability to the circumstances of this case-and this Court has sought to give comprehensive treatment to the issues-all of the issues-raised here.

(5) A separate procedural infraction perceived by the dissent is the premising of our decision on an insufficient factual record. Post 541. The dissent would have us remand this case to the trial court to permit plaintiffs to demonstrate "that the nature of this product and industry is such that market-share liability is an appropriate principle of causation to apply to the breaches of duty asserted." Id. at 541. Stated another way, our colleagues would allow a

jury to determine the issue of an "unavoidably dangerous" design defect before the action could be dismissed on the basis of absence of proof of causation.

The difficulty with that approach is that it would place a fundamental public-policy decision, one to the analysis of which this Court is peculiarly well-suited, in a jury's hands to consider under the guise of an "unavoidably dangerous" design-defect analysis, which the dissent assumes embodies the same considerations as those that address the question of dispensing with the element of causation-in-fact. It clearly does not. The only commonality that exists between the current analysis and the "unavoidably dangerous" exception contained in comment k of the Restatement (Second) of Torts section 402A is that they are premised on the similar policy of encouraging the production of safe and efficacious drugs. Neither the language of comment k nor its underlying spirit would support the dissent's maneuver of placing the cart before the horse by calling for a decision on the issue of defect before the issue of causation.

In addition, the dissent argues that our result is based on public-policy considerations "more relevant to the question of 'duty' than to the 'causation' question before us today." Post at 529. The contention is that "(w)hile causation questions are primarily concerned with the difficulty of *529 proving, discovering, or even conceptualizing physical causal relationships, the tortious conduct question concerns even more profound notions of duty and moral responsibility." Post at 536. One need look no further than the early decisions in Summers and Sindell, which expanded principles of causation, to counter that assertion. In both cases, the underlying rationale was that as a matter of general policy, it was fairer to place the cost of injury on the negligent defendants than on an innocent plaintiff. Sindell, supra 26 Cal.3d at 610-11, 163 Cal.Rptr. at 144, 607 P.2d at 936; Summers, supra, 33 Cal.2d at 88, 199 P.2d at 3-4. An additional policy consideration was that the imposition of liability would provide an incentive to produce safer products. Sindell, supra, 26 Cal.3d at 610-11, 163 Cal.Rptr. at 144, 607 P.2d at 936. None of those justifications was based more on "causation," as opposed to "duty," principles; instead, the courts' focus was in furthering the general goals of tort law: morality, justice, fairness, and compensation to victims. An attempt to compartmentalize those goals into "causation" and "duty" issues is inventive but unconvincing.

Although we agree with the dissent's observation that New Jersey's approach to tort law "has been flexible to adapt traditional limitations on causation and recovery to the evolving needs of a complex society," post at 535, a more significant countervailing consideration informs today's decision: the imposition of market-share liability in this case would cut against the societal goals of maintaining an adequate supply of life-saving vaccines and of developing safer alternatives to current methods of vaccinations. Our aim is not to insulate vaccine manufacturers from liability, but to acknowledge a painful reality-that the excessive exposure to liability that imposition of this novel theory would produce would inevitably discourage highly useful activity.

V

The foregoing discussion should make clear that our opinion is confined solely to the context of vaccines. It should not be read as forecasting an inhospitable response to the theory of market-share liability in an appropriate context, perhaps one in which its application would be consistent with public policy and where no other remedy would be available. This case, the Court's first exposure to market-share liability, may therefore come to represent the exception rather than the rule.

Reversed. The judgment for defendant manufacturers is reinstated. No costs.

O'HERN, J., dissenting.

This is a case not so much about "market-share" liability as it is about the social utility of childhood vaccines that pose an infinitesimal but ever-present risk of catastrophic side effects. Like most parents, I had no idea of the potential side effects of the whooping-cough vaccine when it was administered to my own children. Knowing its possible consequences today, as an informed parent, I am certain that I would accept the risk as one in the best interests of the child. I have a sense that the product may be unavoidably unsafe. I would have no sense of outrage if, after weighing all of these risks, a child of mine suffered a severe side effect. Of course, I would welcome a no-fault remedy such as is found in the National Childhood Vaccine Injury Act, 42 U.S.C.A. sections 300aa-1 to -34, but I might not expect the tort-liability system to compensate me or my child for the known potential of loss.

It is this intuitive feeling about the worth of the DPT vaccines, rather than a sense of injustice about the market share theory itself, that drives the Court to reject a "market-share" theory of liability in cases of multiple tortfeasors. Thus, I believe the Court has inverted its priorities. It has rejected the market-share theory by addressing the "unavoidably-unsafe" issue. While the latter defense may be valid in this case, it is not appropriate to resolve that issue on this summary judgment motion. The majority has decided the market-share question on policy grounds more relevant to the question of "duty" than to the "causation" question before us today. In doing so it has deprived the plaintiffs of *530 the opportunity to investigate and present argument concerning the disputed policy question decided by the majority. In addition, by applying the "unavoidably-unsafe" policy questions to the more general market-share question the Court has precluded recovery even for failure-to-warn and negligence theories-a result not warranted even if one were to accept the majority's policy analysis. See Brown v. Superior Court of California, 44 Cal.3d 1049, 245 Cal.Rptr. 412, 751 P.2d 470 (1988) (holding prescription drug manufacturers not strictly liable for resulting injuries, but still subject to manufacturing defect, negligence, and failure-to-warn claims).

I

A.

What is market-share liability? And why do people say such bad things about it? At first glance, the doctrine appears to offend our notions of causation: How can you hold me responsible for something if you cannot prove I did it? Glenn O. Robinson, in his analysis of the issue, "Multiple Causation in Tort Law: Reflections on the DES Cases," 68 Va.L.Rev. 713 (1982), suggests that the doctrine is nothing more than a familiar application of tort law's way of dealing with multiple tortfeasors. When multiple tortfeasors have caused an injury, the plaintiff is ordinarily relieved of the burden of proving which of them has caused the injury. The usual example is the case of two people who have set fires, either of which would have destroyed a farm field. Neither is excused from his or her conduct by saying "I caused you no injury. The other fire would have destroyed your farm anyway." Restatement (Second) of Torts section 432(2) & comment d, illustrations 3, 4 (1965). Another example is the concert-of-action theory. This liability theory holds defendants liable when, in pursuing a common scheme, any of them breaches a duty owed to a third person regardless of who causes the injury. See Andreassen v. Esposito, 90 N.J.Super. 170, 216 A.2d 607 (App.Div.1966) (participant in illegal drag race liable for injuries caused by other driver), certif. denied, 46 N.J. 605, 218 A.2d 644 (1966); see W. Prosser, Law of Torts 291-93 (4th ed. 1971); Restatement (Second) of Torts section 876 (1977) (adopting the concert-of-action theory).

"Alternative liability" imposes liability on two or more actors all of whom breached a duty of care but it is not clear which party's breach caused the injury. The most famous case involving alternative liability is Summers v. Tice, 33 Cal.2d 80, 199 P.2d 1 (1948). Because two hunters were both negligent in shooting in the plaintiff's direction, and it could not be proven which gun was the source of the plaintiff's eye and lip injuries, the court shifted the burden to each defendant to exculpate himself or be liable for the entire damages. Id. at 89, 199 P.2d at 5. If Summers is the classic statement of alternative liability, then the elements of the doctrine are: (1) plaintiff is unable to identify which defendant caused the injury; (2) all potentially liable injured parties are joined as defendants; (3) each defendant breached a duty of care owed to plaintiff; and (4) defendants are in a far better position to offer evidence of causation than plaintiff is.

The Restatement (Second) of Torts section 433B(3) (1965) has adopted the doctrine, saying:

> Where the conduct of two or more actors is tortious, and it is proved that harm has been caused to the plaintiff by only one of them, but there is uncertainty as to which one has caused it, the burden is upon each such actor to prove that he has not caused the harm.

Comment h to this subsection, often quoted by litigants' counsel, says, in relevant part, that although

> (t)he cases thus far decided in which the rule * * * has been applied all have been cases in which all of the actors involved have been joined as defendants. * * * It is possible that cases may arise in which some modification of the rule stated may be necessary because of complications arising from the fact that one of the actors involved is not or cannot be joined as a defendant

* * * or because of substantial differences in the character of *531 the conduct of the actors or the risks which they have created.

See Annotation, "Liability of several persons guilty of acts one of which alone caused injury, in absence of showing as to whose act was the cause," 5 A.L.R.2d 98 (1949).

The Summers alternative-liability principles were applied to an industry to impose "enterprise liability" in Hall v. E.I. Du Pont De Nemours & Co., Inc., 345 F.Supp. 353 (E.D.N.Y.1972). Thirteen children were injured in twelve unrelated accidents by unmarked blasting caps that the children found and detonated. Plaintiffs could not identify the particular manufacturers, so they sued "substantially the entire blasting cap industry and its trade association * * *." Id. at 386. That court permitted the plaintiffs to establish liability based on a variety of theories all recognizing that the development of "explicit or implicit safety standards, codes, and practices which are widely adhered to in an entire industry * * * could support a finding of joint control of risk and a shift of the burden of proving causation to the defendants" where individual defendant-manufacturers cannot be identified. Id. at 374.

In the touchstone case of "market-share" liability, Sindell v. Abbott Laboratories, 26 Cal.3d 588, 607 P.2d 924, 163 Cal.Rptr. 132, cert. denied, 449 U.S. 912, 101 S.Ct. 285, 286, 66 L.Ed.2d 140 (1980), the California Supreme Court rejected all three of the above theories of liability: (1) concert of action was unsupported by the facts of DES's development; (2) pure alternative liability was not allowed because not all of the possibly-responsible parties were in the suit; and (3) enterprise liability did not apply because (a) the DES industry was so large, (b) unlike in Hall, supra, 345 F.Supp. 353, there was no allegation that the defendants had developed common safety standards through a trade association, and (c) adherence to industry standard was mandated, at least in part, by the government. Id. 26 Cal.3d at 601-610, 607P.2d at 930-35, 163 Cal.Rptr. at 139-143.

The Sindell Court proposed a new theory. The policy reasons were clearly expressed:

> In our contemporary complex industrialized society, advances in science and technology create fungible goods which may harm consumers and which cannot be traced to any specific producer. The response of the courts can

be either to adhere rigidly to prior doctrine, denying recovery to those injured by such products, or to fashion remedies to meet these changing needs. * * *

The most persuasive reason for finding plaintiff states a cause of action is that advanced in Summers: as between an innocent plaintiff and negligent defendants, the latter should bear the cost of the injury. (Id. at 610-611, 607 P.2d at 936, 163 Cal.Rptr. at 144.)

The Sindell doctrine is that "(i)f plaintiff joins in the action the manufacturers of a substantial share of the (product allegedly causing injury) which her mother might have taken, * * * the burden of proof (shifts) to defendants to demonstrate that they could not have made the substance which injured plaintiff * * *." Id. at 611, 607 P.2d at 937, 163 Cal.Rptr. at 145. The difference from alternative liability is that the plaintiff is not required to have before the court each and every manufacturer of the product. However, by the requirement of the substantial share of the market you increase the "likelihood that this comparative handful of producers manufactured the (product) which caused plaintiff's injuries." Ibid, 607 P.2d at 937, 163 Cal.Rptr. at 145.

As we know, the Wisconsin Supreme Court has mapped out a variant on these theories of liability in Collins v. Eli Lilly Co., 116 Wis.2d 166, 342 N.W.2d 37, cert. denied, 469 U.S. 826, 105 S.Ct. 107, 83 L.Ed.2d 51 (1984). As in Sindell, the Wisconsin Court rejected the concert-of-action, alternative-, and enterprise-liability theories. The Wisconsin Court went on to recognize "the fundamental fairness of Sindell's shifting the burden of proof to the defendants," but concluded that the "unalloyed market share theory does not constitute *532 the most desirable course to follow in DES cases because the theory, while conceptually attractive, is limited in practical applicability." Id. at 188-189, 342 N.W.2d at 48. According to that court, "defining the market and apportioning market share (is) a near impossible task if it is to be done fairly and accurately," and "a second 'mini-trial' to determine market share" would be a "waste of judicial resources." Id. 188-192, 342 N.W.2d at 48-49. The court reasoned that each company "contributed to the risk of injury" even if all of them did not act in concert.

We conclude that it is better to have drug companies

or consumers share the cost of the injury than to place the burden solely on the innocent plaintiff. Finally, the cost of damages awards will act as an incentive for drug companies to test adequately the drugs they place on the market for general medical use. This incentive is especially important in the case of mass-marketed drugs because consumers and their physicians in most instances rely upon advice given by the supplier and the scientific community and, consequently, are virtually helpless to protect themselves from serious injuries caused by deleterious drugs. (Id. at 190-194, 342 N.W.2d at 49-50 (footnote omitted).)

Therefore, the Wisconsin Court ruled that plaintiff could proceed initially against one defendant and must prove the following: (1) the plaintiff's mother took the product; (2) the product caused the plaintiff's injury; (3) the defendant-producer marketed the type of product that claimant took, i.e., the color, shape, size, etc.; and (4) the manufacturer's conduct in producing the product constituted beach of duty to the plaintiff. Id. at 193-194, 342 N.W.2d at 50.

Plaintiff can recover all damages from the one defendant. Ibid, 342 N.W.2d at 50. Plaintiff may, of course, sue as many companies as may be possibly liable and the companies may implead others. Id. at 194-196, 342 N.W.2d at 51. Once the prima facie case is proven, the burden of proof shifts to the defendant to prove it did not produce or market the DES at the relevant time or in the relevant market. Id. at 197-198, 342 N.W.2d at 52. It is up to each to establish that its DES could not have reached plaintiff's mother. Assigning liability and apportioning damages is then done under the Wisconsin comparative-negligence statute. Id. at 197-199, 342 N.W.2d at 52-53.

In the final and the most significant case, a recent decision of the New York Court of Appeals adopted a form of market-share liability with the significant qualification that it would not excuse manufacturers who could show that their product did not injure the plaintiff. Hymowitz v. Eli Lilly and Company, 73 N.Y.2d 487, 539 N.E.2d 1069, 541 N.Y.S.2d 941 (1989).

(F)or essentially practical reasons, we adopt a market share theory using a national market. We are aware that that (sic) the adoption of a national market will likely result in a disproportion between the liability of individual manufacturers and the actual injuries each manufacturer caused in this state. * * * Thus our market share theory cannot be founded upon the belief that, over the run of cases, liability will approximate causation in this State * * *. Nor does the use of a national market provide a reasonable link between liability and the risk created by a defendant to a particular plaintiff * * *. Instead, we choose to apportion liability so as to correspond to the overall culpability of each defendant, measured by the amount of risk of injury each defendant created to the public at large. Use of a national market is a fair method, we believe, of apportioning defendants' liabilities according to their total culpability in marketing DES for use during pregnancy. Under the circumstances, this is an equitable way to provide plaintiffs with the relief they deserve, while also rationally distributing the responsibility for plaintiffs' injuries among defendants.

* * *

Nevertheless, because liability here is based on the overall risk produced, and not causation in a single case, there should be no exculpation of a defendant who, although a member of the market *533 producing DES for pregnancy use, appears not to have caused a particular plaintiff's injury. * * *

Finally, we hold that the liability of DES producers is several only, and should not be inflated when all participants in the market are not before the court in a particular case. We understand that, as a practical matter, this will prevent some plaintiffs from recovering 100% of their damages. However, we eschewed exculpation to prevent the fortuitous avoidance of liability, and thus, equitably, we decline to unleash the same forces to increase a defendant's liability beyond its fair share of responsibility. (Id. 73 N.Y.2d at 512-513, 541 N.Y.S.2d at 950, 539 N.E.2d at 1078 (citations and footnote omitted).)

Although perhaps the most controversial of the market-share decisions, its holding results in the scheme that is most similar to the almost universally-praised federal Vaccine Act.

As noted, Professor Robinson conceives of such alternative liability rules, and especially the Sindell rule, as being variants on the Summers principle. See Robinson, supra, 68 Va. L. Rev. 713. He notes, however, that because in Summers there was a one in two probability that either defendant was responsible for the shot that injured the plaintiff, the result is much more acceptable from an intuitive basis. Id. at 724. In contrast, in the DES cases the odds on any given producer "could be less than 1 in 300." Ibid. If, for example,

> 90% of the market is divided equally, under the Summers rule of joint and several liability each of the manufacturers risks 100% liability based on a 15% probability that it caused the injury. * * *
>
> In recognition of this disparity, the Sindell case adopted a rule that reduces the disproportion between potential liability and the probability that a defendant caused the injury by imposing liability on producers only according to their respective market shares in the sale of DES. (Id. at 725.)

The Sindell court also imposed a requirement that a "substantial share" of the market be joined, but Robinson finds this aspect unpersuasive and inconsistent with the opinion's underlying logic. See id. at 725-26.

With these qualifications, Robinson notes that

> (i)n fact, the departure from traditional doctrine is not so large as may appear. * * * Sindell itself is essentially an application of Summers v. Tice, modified to include a rule of contribution. To be sure, the application of Summers to an entire industry, as distinguished from two hunters, stretches that precedent, at least as it has been construed heretofore. Yet it does no violence to the underlying principle of Summers, rationalized either in terms of shifting the burden of proof on causation or in terms of a substantive liability rule. Indeed, this application of Summers is conservative insofar as it incorporates a rule of contribution limiting each tortfeasor's liability commensurate with its particular contribution to the aggregate risk created by the product. (Id. at 768.)

B.

Recognition of a market-share theory of liability would be entirely consistent with New Jersey's history and traditions.

Judge Carton's provocative dissent in Nopco Chem. Co. v. Blaw-Knox Co., 113 N.J.Super. 19, 24, 272 A.2d 549 (App.Div.), rev'd, 59 N.J. 274, 281 A.2d 793 (1971), foreshadows the growth of our law. There, one or more of multiple defendants handling a commercial product during its journey from the factory to the purchaser were responsible for its damaged condition. Ibid. Plaintiff could not prove which of the defendants had caused the damage. Thus, all defendants argued that they were entitled to a dismissal of plaintiff's claims. Ibid. Judge Carton reasoned:

> The law does not compel such a "lame and impotent conclusion." Reason and ordinary common sense dictate that * * * existing procedures be adapted or a new remedy be devised which will *534 cause those parties most likely to possess knowledge of the occurrence to come forward with the facts peculiarly within their possession. To me it seems indefensible that the court should stand idly by and lend itself to such an obvious thwarting of justice. (Ibid.)

His dissent carried the day in the New Jersey Supreme Court, which held that "(w)e are firmly of the view that the complexity of the situation should not leave plaintiff remediless or require it to sue each defendant separately and successively at its peril simply because there is no precise precedent in this State." Nopco Chem. Div. v. Blaw-Knox Co., 59 N.J. 274, 282, 281 A.2d 793 (1971).

So too, in Anderson v. Somberg, 67 N.J. 291, 338 A.2d 1 cert. denied, 423 U.S. 929, 96 S.Ct. 279, 46 L.Ed.2d 258 (1975), a multiple-defendant, surgical-injury case, this Court adopted a form of alternative liability. The Anderson plurality held that the plaintiff must recover from at least one of the defendants since no theory for the cause of the instrument's breaking in the plaintiff's spinal canal "was within reasonable contemplation save for the possible negligence of (the doctor) in using the instrument, or * * * (a) defect * * * attributable to a dereliction of duty by the manufacturer, the distributor, the hospital, or all of them." Id. at 296, 338 A.2d 1. A Nopco -like shift in the burden of production was insufficient. Rather, the burden of proof shifted as well. Id. at 300, 338 A.2d 1. Since at least one defendant must inevitably fail to meet the burden, a verdict must be returned for the plaintiff. Ibid. In concurring, Justice Jacobs voted to affirm on the basis of the Appellate Division majority opinion which held that the jury should have been instructed to return a verdict against at least one of the defendants because the contrary verdict represented a miscarriage of justice. Id. at 305, 338 A.2d 1. The dissent argued that the suit became "trial by lot, or by chance." Id. at 312, 338 A.2d 1.

But the Anderson judgment has stood the test of time. When one of multiple tortfeasors has most probably caused plaintiff's injury, the law does not permit those tortfeasors to exonerate themselves by insisting that the plaintiff's inability to prove which of them caused the injury is a total bar in law to recovery.

In New Jersey, we have confronted several other situations in which causation is difficult, if not impossible, to prove within traditional standards, and have always rejected a complete bar to redress for wrongful conduct. As the majority has rightly noted:

> The torts process, like the law itself, is a human institution designed to accomplish certain social objectives. One objective is to ensure that innocent victims have avenues of legal redress, absent a contrary, overriding public policy. * * *
>
> * * * (W)e strive to ensure that the application of negligence doctrine advances the fundamental purpose of tort law and does not unnecessarily or arbitrarily foreclose redress based on formalisms or technicalisms. (People Express Airlines, Inc. v. Consolidated Rail Corp., 100 N.J. 246, 254-55, 495 A.2d 107 (1985).)

Of course, causation-in-fact is far more than a technicalism. But the principle of causation is not an end of the legal system, but rather the means by which the legal system achieves its purposes. Thus, in Evers v. Dollinger, 95 N.J. 399, 471 A.2d 405 (1984), we recognized that under the circumstances, it would be impossible for the plaintiff to prove that if her physician had acted non-negligently, she would more likely than not have avoided the spread and recurrence of cancer. However, rather than insulate from liability tortious conduct that may have caused injury, we permitted recovery if the plaintiff could demonstrate within a reasonable degree of medical probability that if the physician had acted non-negligently, there was a substantial chance that her condition might have been avoided. We recognized the same standard in Hake v. Manchester Township, 98 N.J. 302, 486 A.2d 836 (1985), permitting recovery if the plaintiff could show that there was a substantial chance that the decedent could have survived if rescue had been attempted. We have also relieved plaintiffs of the *535 burden of proving the causal connection between negligence and damages when a health-care provider has negligently contributed to a condition. Fosgate v. Corona, 66 N.J. 268, 272-73, 330 A.2d 355 (1974).

Our approach has been flexible to adapt traditional limitations on causation and recovery to the evolving needs of a complex society. In our recent decision in Ayers v. Jackson Township, 106 N.J. 557, 525 A.2d 287 (1987), we eliminated the requirement that a defendant be shown to have caused physical injury as a predicate to recovery. No party could prove that the defendant's tortious conduct had proximately caused the plaintiff's medical injury except for an unquantifiable enhanced risk of future disease. However, each party could prove exposure to risk-causing substance and the need for medical surveillance to permit early discovery and treatment of any disease that might develop. In the absence of proof of actual physical injury, we allowed a limited and modified recovery of damages. The opinion recognized the economic reality of risk of injury to human health, and imposed legal consequences.

In each of those cases we were confronted with parties who had breached a duty of care, a victim ostensibly injured as a result of that breach of duty, and a seemingly unprovable causal connection. Yet, rather than permit a whole class of tortious acts and injuries to be unremediable, we recognized a standard of causation appropriate to the circumstances.

In the case of generic drugs, marketed in such a manner as to make them essentially undistinguishable to the party bearing the risk of injury, market-share liability is just such an appropriate principle of liability. Professor Landes and Judge Posner, who advanced the theory that the role of the law is to foster the most economic advantages for society, suggested that "the idea of causation becomes a result rather than the premise of the economic analysis of accidents." Landes & Posner, "Tort Law as a Regulatory Regime for Catastrophic Personal Injuries," 13 Journal of Legal Studies 417 (1984). Within that context I believe that the proportionate market-share theory of liability poses the fairest solution to to the problem. It is a resolution described by the amici curiae Merck & Co., Inc., Abbott Laboratories, and The Upjohn Company as "the least unfair" of the non-identification liability theories.

II

A.

The majority has not expressed any disagreement with the conceptual underpinnings of market-share liability. See ante at 528. Rather, the majority states that "the thrust of this appeal: (is) the public-policy and public-health considerations that would accompany the imposition of market-share liability in this context." Ante at 522. It thus appears that it has no objection to the market-share concept of causation, but is solely, and perhaps justifiably, concerned that the imposition of any liability for this clearly beneficial vaccine will be detrimental to society's interest in the availability of essential pharmaceutical products. While this is undoubtedly a valid concern, even if it properly related to the causation question before us today, surely we have an insufficient record on which to decide the question. Recall that the Law Division addressed one and only one question: whether New Jersey would recognize alternative liability for defective products under any state of facts. Moreover, the majority's premise does not necessitate its conclusion. Put another way, it is obvious that none of the majority's expressed concerns would be affected by a sudden discovery by the parties of the actual manufacturer of the DPT dose in this case. Thus, under the majority's ruling a manufacturer must bear the same risks of liability that the majority seeks to insulate the industry from, except to the extent that the company can issue a product that would be for any reason difficult to distinguish from that of other manufacturers.

The majority rejects the market-share theory of causation for this product based on its perception that DPT is a beneficial drug and that any liability will threaten its supply and the efforts to develop a safer *536 alternative. In New Jersey, we have been particularly candid to recognize proximate causation as an expression of legal policy. See Brown v. United States Stove Co., 98 N.J. 155, 173, 484 A.2d 1234 (1984); Caputzal v. The Lindsay Co., 48 N.J. 69, 77-78, 222 A.2d 513 (1966). Nevertheless, the "legal policy" has always addressed the concerns underlying the reasons for a "causation" limitation on liability, i.e., "whether conduct can be considered sufficiently causally connected to accidental harm so as to justify the imposition of liability * * *." Brown, supra, 98 N.J. at 173, 484 A.2d 1234. Courts have had to conform the causation requirement to the needs of a changing society, recognizing that although the intentional battery may be the "classic" tort, such simple connections between conduct and result are increasingly less discernible.

The question of whether conduct should be considered tortious (here, whether a product should be considered safe) is also a policy question, but the policy issues are different from those presented for the causation issue. While causation questions are primarily concerned with the difficulty of proving, discovering, or even conceptualizing physical causal relationships, the tortious conduct question concerns even more profound notions of duty and moral responsibility. See Kelly v. Gwinnell, 96 N.J. 538, 476 A.2d 1219 (1984). Traditionally, a finding of tortious conduct required a conclusion that the actor acted in some way that society has recognized as immoral or wrong. See Brown v. Kendall, 60 Mass. (6 Cush.) 292 (1850). Modern concepts of strict liability have departed from the culpability requirement in favor of more pragmatic concepts, e.g., Michalko v. Cooke Color and Chem. Corp., 91 N.J. 386, 451 A.2d 179 (1982), but the notion that a person must have acted "badly" still pervades the doctrine. Thus a manufacturer will not be held responsible for injuries caused by a product unless the plaintiff can prove that the product was "defective." O'Brien v. Muskin Corp., 94 N.J. 169, 179-80, 463 A.2d 298 (1983) ("The necessity of proving a defect in the product as part of the plaintiff's prima facie case distinguishes strict from absolute liability, and thus prevents the manufacturer from also becoming the insurer of a product.").

In Feldman v. Lederle Laboratories, 97 N.J. 429, 479 A.2d 374 (1984), this Court was presented with the argument that all prescription drugs that are unsafe should be immunized from strict liability under comment k to section 402A of the Restatement (Second) of Torts. Id. at 441. Public policy, it was argued, demanded that prescription drugs be considered immune from strict liability because they were unavoidably unsafe. Ibid. We rejected such a wholesale argument:

> (W)e see no reason to hold as a matter of law and policy that all prescription drugs that are unsafe are unavoidably so. Drugs, like any other products, may contain defects that could have been avoided by better manufacturing or design. Whether a drug is unavoidably unsafe should be decided on a case-by-case basis; we perceive no justification for giving all prescription drug manufacturers a blanket immunity from strict

liability manufacturing and design defects claims under comment k.

Moreover, even if a prescription drug were unavoidably unsafe, the comment k immunity would not eliminate strict liability for failure to provide a proper warning. (Id. at 447, 479 A.2d 374.)

Plaintiffs in this case have asserted that safer DPT vaccines were available. They have also asserted, among other claims, that the warnings were inadequate and that the companies were negligent in their decision to market the whole-cell DPT virus. Under Feldman, these causes of action would be permitted to go forward even if the vaccine were unavoidably unsafe. Similarly, even the decision in Brown v. Superior Court, supra, 44 Cal.3d 1049, 1069-70 n. 12, 751 P.2d 470, 483 n. 12, 245 Cal.Rptr. 412, 424 n. 12, which rejected Feldman's case-by-case approach to the unavoidably-unsafe question and instead imposed a blanket unavoidably-unsafe immunity for all prescription drugs, would permit these other causes of action to proceed. Finally, although the federal Act *537 prohibits recovery in civil actions for injuries from vaccines administered after the effective date of the Act, if the side-effect was unavoidable, it permits suits claiming a failure-to-warn and improper manufacture in appropriate circumstances. 42 U.S.C.A. section 300aa-22(b)(1). By contrast, this Court has applied the policy considerations underlying the unavoidably-unsafe determination to impose a much more sweeping immunity.

The Court is quite explicit in limiting its rejection of market-share liability to contexts in which the relevant public policy considerations are present. Nevertheless, the decision gives no real guidance respecting its scope. Does it apply to all vaccines or just children's vaccines? Or is it applicable to all drugs that, in hindsight, we think are important? Perhaps it is applicable to all drugs that the drug manufacturer might have thought at the time distributed were important. Other courts refusing to impose strict liability on prescription-drug manufacturers have extended their holdings to drugs like DES, thalidomide, and even accutane. See Brown, supra, 44 Cal.3d at 1067-68, 751 P.2d at 481, 245 Cal.Rptr. at 422-423. Is this Court saying that the children who developed severe birth defects due to their mothers' ingestion of accutane to clear their complexion would also not be able to recover, lest the drug companies be hesitant to release new drugs? How are "important" drugs defined: complexion?, nausea?, fertility? Obviously we need not in every case define the holding applicable to other factual contexts, but if the purpose of our holding is for manufacturers to be encouraged to release important drugs, how can they find out in advance which ones the Court will consider important? They will always be operating at the risk the Court is trying to insulate them from. See Brown, supra, 44 Cal.3d at 1068-69, 751 P.2d at 482, 245 Cal.Rptr. at 423.

B.

Perhaps the scope would be more discernible if the policy arguments themselves were more clear. For example, the majority refuses to impose any liability on DPT manufacturers because it feels that this result will encourage the development of safer drugs. Ordinarily the presumption is the opposite:

> Imposing liability on defendants for their negligent conduct discourages others from similar tortious behavior, fosters safer products to aid our daily tasks, vindicates reasonable conduct that has regard for the safety of others, and, ultimately, shifts the risk of loss and associated costs of dangerous activities to those who should be and are best able to bear them. (People Express, supra, 100 N.J. at 255, 495 A.2d 107.)

See also Michalko, supra, 91 N.J. at 401 n. 4, 451 A.2d 179 ("imposing strict liability would induce providers of services to invest in safety, leading to greater protection for their customers and reduced accident costs."); Beshada v. Johns-Manville Products Corp., 90 N.J. 191, 207, 447 A.2d 539 (1982) ("By imposing on manufacturers the costs of failure to discover hazards, we create an incentive for them to invest more actively in safety research.").[1] Although I might understand the temptation to avoid strict liability for beneficial drugs, see, Brown, supra, 44 Cal.3d at 1069-70 n.

---

[1] Congress, as well, appears to have reached a conclusion contrary to that of the Court. See Schwartz & Mahshigian, "National Childhood Vaccine Injury Act of 1986: An Ad Hoc Remedy or a Window for the Future?," 48 Ohio St.L.J. 387, 395 (1987) ("Congress may have decided to retain the tort system for vaccine injury claims, at the expense of greater predictability, as a means of providing incentives for the manufacture of safe vaccines.").

12, 751 P.2d at 483 n. 12, 245 Cal.Rptr. at 424 n. 12, I do not see how this applies to a failure-to-warn or negligence claim where all that is called for is for the company to act reasonably. For the unavoidable procedural posture of this case, a procedural posture that the defendants have created, is that they have admitted that each manufactured and distributed a prescription drug that contains a common defect, that each failed to warn users of the dangers of the drug, that there are safer alternative designs for the drug, and, finally, that each acted negligently in the manufacture and *538 marketing of the drug. This summary judgment action requires those admissions.

Furthermore, generally the logic that a manufacturer should not be held strictly liable for prescription drugs has been applied only where the drug could not be made safer. In Feldman, supra, we said: "(W)e see no reason to hold as a matter of law and policy that all prescription drugs that are unsafe are unavoidably so. Drugs, like any other products, may contain defects that could have been avoided by better manufacturing or design." 97 N.J. at 447. By contrast, in this case, the drug companies argued that the fact that there was a safer product should exempt them from liability since the market-share analysis would be too difficult. Although I could perhaps understand reducing, or even exempting, the safer product from its market share of liability, I cannot understand why we would insulate the companies making the less-safe products. Plaintiff asserts that some of the companies continued to manufacture, market, and try to outsell the ostensibly-safer vaccine, Tri-Solgen, even after they had concluded that Tri-Solgen was safer than their product.[2] I fail to see why any manufacturer should feel compelled to make a safer vaccine when in this case we find

---

[2] Lederle's recently-released internal correspondence "stated that the test results demonstrated that Lederle's product had a significantly higher reaction rate than Lilly's non-cellular vaccine." Burke, "DPT Vaccine Controversy: An Assessment of the Liabilities of Manufacturers and Administering Physicians Under Several Legal Theories," 17 Seton Hall L.Rev. 541, 569 (1987). Further clinical evaluations were planned by Lederle, but they were never completed. Frankly, I rather suspect that these qualitative differences in the DPT vaccines would be winnowed out in the trial process. The reaction rate that we are talking about here is the catastrophic reaction rate, not those who suffer greater or lesser degrees of discomfort and distress. It is the catastrophic common defect that must be shown to be qualitatively different.

public policy to demand their exemption from liability even though the plaintiff alleges, and therefore we must assume, that the defendants knowingly continued to market and manufacture a product they knew to be less safe, and that they refused to inform physicians of the additional risk.

The majority's attempt to influence the future behavior of DPT manufacturers is misdirected insofar as the federal Act will most certainly be the sole motivating force for their actions. Under the federal Act, a party injured by a vaccine administered after October 1, 1988, the effective date of the Act, is effectively prohibited from filing a civil action until after his or her other claim under the Act has been adjudicated. 42 U.S.C.A. section 300aa-11(a)(2, 3). The party can file suit at that time only if it waives any compensation awarded under the Act. 42 U.S.C.A. section 300aa-21. Given the recent State legislation cited by the majority, ante at 527-28, making such product-liability actions difficult to win, as well as the federal legislation precluding liability in civil actions for some claims arising from injuries caused by a vaccine administered after the effective date of the federal Act, 42 U.S.C.A. section 300aa-22, it is unlikely that many claimants will risk their award to pursue a civil action, and even more unlikely that anyone denied compensation under the federal Act will be able to succeed in a civil action. Thus, any fear of liability that may affect a manufacturer's decision to attempt to develop a safer product, or conversely to cease production, would be virtually unaffected by the majority's decision today. In addition, in an effort to assure continuing vaccine availability and development of safer vaccines, the Act devotes substantial resources to the coordination of public and private efforts towards developing safer vaccines and programs to administer them. 42 U.S.C.A. sections 300aa-2, -3.

The final policy argument that needs to be examined is the extent to which liability expenses are the cause of the price increases. The problem appears very complex. One commentator has stated that "unlike some other products, the incidence of serious injury with children's vaccines is very low. Thus, a vaccine compensation system can be self-funding by adding a very small excise tax to the price of vaccines." Schwartz & Mahshigian, supra, 48 Ohio St. L.J. at 393 (footnote omitted). If injuries are so rare, perhaps the claim that price increases are due to liability costs *539 should be more critically examined. However, even if one accepts the Court's "findings" that the price per dose increased in two years from 11%4a to $11.40, $8.00 for insurance, ante at 523, that still amounts to a twenty-seven-fold increase in non-insurance-related costs corresponding to the development of a market with only two suppliers. Moreover, since the liability exposure has been greatly reduced by the federal Act, presumably the insurance costs have reduced accordingly. Although the majority claims that its holding is consistent with the federal Act, it is clear that Congress, which spent much more time and money examining the issue, decided that it would be inappropriate to deny compensation, recognizing that an appropriately-limited liability would not threaten the industry.

III

This brings me to the most troublesome aspect of the majority's opinion: its adjudication of the available remedies under the federal act and willingness to fault the plaintiff for asserting her rights. In reading the majority opinion I get a sense that the Court feels that in pursuing a tort recovery the plaintiff is somehow seeking a windfall or something more than she deserved. Nevertheless, the federal Act specifically prohibits states from "establish(ing) or enforc(ing) a law which prohibits an individual from bringing a civil action against a vaccine manufacturer for damages for a vaccine-related injury or death if such civil action is not barred by this part." 42 U.S.C.A. section 300aa-22(e). Surely Congress did not intend state courts to accomplish the same effect by molding state common law to deny recovery in reliance on the general availability of a federal remedy.

In addition to the fact that the plaintiff should not be penalized for exercising her right under the federal act to pursue her tort remedy, at the time this suit was filed, the federal act had not yet been enacted. Therefore, plaintiff could not be sure whether she would be eligible to recover under it. Moreover, even now it is unclear whether any remedy plaintiff would be "entitled" to would actually be sufficiently funded. Finally, although the plaintiff is permitted to withdraw her State tort suit and pursue the federal remedy, she will not be allowed to do so if this case is dismissed. Before the Court limits tort recovery under New Jersey partially on the basis of an alternative remedy, we should be certain that such remedy is, in fact, both sufficient and available.

Defendants maintain that Deanna Marrero is eligible to receive compensation under the program. Under the Act, vaccine injury victims are divided into three groups:

(a) those who both were injured by a vaccine administered before October 1, 1988, the effective date of the Act, and filed a civil suit prior to that date, 42 U.S.C.A. section 300aa-11(a)(4, 5);

(b) those injured by a vaccine administered before October 1, 1988, who had not filed a civil suit prior to that date. 42 U.S.C.A. section 300aa-11(a)(6);

(c) those injured by a vaccine administered after October 1, 1988. 42 U.S.C.A. section 300aa-11(a)(3).

Those in the first category, such as Deanna Marrero, may continue any pending lawsuit, but will become ineligible for compensation under the Act unless damages were denied or their suit dismissed with prejudice prior to October 1, 1988, 42 U.S.C.A. section 300aa-11(a)(4), or the plaintiff voluntarily withdraws the pending suit prior to October 1, 1990. 42 U.S.C.A. section 300aa-11(a)(5). The second group may file a civil suit, but are then ineligible to file a claim under the Act. 42 U.S.C.A. section 300aa-11(a)(6). The third group must complete the Act's compensation proceeding and reject its judgment before pursuing a civil claim. 42 U.S.C.A. section 300aa-11(a)(2, 3). No party may file a claim under the Act if damages have been awarded for a vaccine-related injury under a judgment or settlement of a civil action. 42 U.S.C.A. section 300aa-11(a)(7).

The Act also creates an affirmative defense of sorts. In order to award compensation, the special master or the court must find that there is not a preponderance of the evidence that the injury was caused by factors unrelated to the administration of *540 the vaccine. 42 U.S.C.A. 300aa-13(a)(1)(B). The majority of courts reviewing both the provisions and legislative history of the Act have concluded that "Congress contemplated that civil tort remedies for vaccine-related injuries have been available, are now available, and will continue to be available under certain circumstances, even after the effective date of the Act." Patten v. Lederle Laboratories, 655 F.Supp. 745, 749 (D.Utah 1987). Thus, we should not deny our State remedy due to the availability of a federal remedy when the Act creating that federal remedy contemplates the continuing availability of State remedies.

Moreover, although this suit was filed on April 19, 1985, the Act was not passed until November 14, 1986. Thus no alternative federal remedy was available at the time the suit was filed. The Act is partially funded by a Vaccine Injury Compensation Trust Fund funded by an excise tax on vaccines. 26 U.S.C.A. section 9510. Compensation for persons injured by vaccines administered after the effective date of the Act will be awarded from this Trust Fund. 42 U.S.C.A. section 300aa-15(i)(2). Compensation for persons injured by vaccines administered before the effective date of the Act, like Deanna Marrero, is made from appropriations. 42 U.S.C.A. section 300aa-15(i)(1).

Congress has authorized appropriations for this purpose of $80 million for this year and the same amount for each of the next three fiscal years, but these appropriations were not authorized until December 22, 1987, two and one-half years after this suit was filed. 42 U.S.C.A. section 300aa-15(j). Congress is currently considering additional appropriations measures to fund this aspect of the program. Nevertheless, there is a serious debate over whether such appropriations are or will be sufficient to give the statutory award to all persons injured prior to the Act. Furthermore, authorization of an appropriation is only one step in a long process before the money is actually appropriated. Many forces along the way can lead to reduction or elimination of the funding. The majority points to the one-time appropriation of $80 million out of the $320 million authorized as evidence of the certainty of funding. I am not so sure that the need for a B-2 bomber may not take precedence in other years over vaccine funding. The Act also places an overall cap of 3500 on the number of claims that can be filed for injuries due to vaccines administered prior to the Act. 42 U.S.C.A. section 300aa-11(b)(1)(B). In short, the remedy may or may not ever be there.

Finally, this plaintiff will be ineligible for compensation under the Act if summary judgment is granted. The Act precludes the filing of a claim where the injured party has received damages pursuant to a settlement. 42 U.S.C.A. section 300aa-11(a)(7). Although plaintiff had settled her claim with her doctor, such settlement was withdrawn prior to court approval in recognition that such settlement would preclude a later claim under the Act. However, plaintiff will also be unable to file a claim unless she voluntarily withdraws her State court action by October 1, 1990, and prior to judgment. 42 U.S.C.A. section 300aa-11(a)(5). Therefore, by refusing to recognize market-share liability as a valid theory in this case, we are precluding plaintiff from withdrawing her suit prior to judgment and effectively extinguishing both her state and federal recovery. While such a result might be appropriate were we to conclude that market-share liability was somehow conceptually lacking, and therefore inappropriate in New Jersey, the result is wholly unfair under the majority's rationale. Although I believe that the Act represents a tremendous advance in the development of an effective reparation system for vaccine-related injuries, unfortunately under the majority's ruling the Act will not apply to the current cause of action.

From my perspective, the most critical and significant provision of the Act is that it creates the Vaccine Injury Compensation Trust Fund with money collected from an excise tax on vaccines. 26 U.S.C.A. section 9510. In other words, the industry as a whole shares the risk of financial compensation for injuries after October 1, 1988, attributable to individual manufacturers. See 42 U.S.C.A. section 300aa-15(i)(2). I think that we would do well to mold our tort law to this model. I agree that punitive damages are *541 inappropriate in this setting of market-share responsibility and that proportional several liability is the fairest solution. We should be candid to recognize, in the face of the enormous medical, legal, and social ramifications of childhood-vaccine injuries, that the goal of the legal system should be to steer a course toward the result that will yield the greatest benefits to human health. That principle involves a candid recognition of the limitations of tort liability to deal fully with the problem while at the same time seeking the maximum prevention of human disease and the maximum fairness in the alleviation of human suffering.

IV

I am usually the last person ever to insist on strict adherence to the Civil Rules of Procedure. But there is something deeply flawed about the way this case has proceeded. It is terribly unfair to deprive this tragically disabled child of any remedy whatsoever for her catastrophic injuries on the basis of theories of law never presented to the Law Division and on the basis of an alternative federal remedy that was not in existence when her case was argued in the Law Division and not even funded when her case was argued in our Court.

I have no idea of the extent to which Deanna can understand these proceedings, but surely she would see the law as the cruelest of hoaxes: dismissing her state common-law claim because she had a federal remedy while with the same stroke of the pen extinguishing that federal remedy because she had elected to ask us if there was a state remedy for her catastrophic injuries. The most that we should do in this situation is to give a declaration of what a claimant's rights are, not to ask a twelve-year-old girl to play a game of blind man's bluff with our legal system.

I would hold that New Jersey should recognize market-share liability in an appropriate case. I see no reason why plaintiff should not be permitted to demonstrate that the nature of this product and industry is such that market-share liability is an appropriate principle of causation to apply to the breaches of duty asserted. Were we to reject "market-share" on this record, we would be out of step with both California and New York. If those two great states can mold their law to the needs of their citizens without dislocation of public markets, I fail to see how the industry could not abide the needs of New Jersey's citizens. The policy questions surrounding the necessity of this drug will not be ignored, but will be addressed if the defendants raise the defense that the product is unavoidably unsafe.

I would remand the case, then, to the Law Division, as the Appellate Division did, to resolve whether DPT is an unavoidably unsafe product and, if not, whether there is a sufficiently common defect in the products marketed to invoke a Sindell-style market-share liability in New Jersey. This is no mean challenge. Deanna will face an enormous uphill struggle in asserting her claims. I have no doubt that we should abide by the recently-enacted guidance of our products-liability act, N.J.S.A. 2A:58C-4, that a failure-to-warn claim in the case of prescription drugs should be measured by compliance with the FDA's required warnings. Congress has enacted the same principle as one of national policy for all injuries due to vaccines administered after the effective date of the Act. 42 U.S.C.A. section 300aa-22(b)(2). And I genuinely doubt that she will be able to establish that there was indeed an equally effective and safer alternative vaccine.[3] The FDA has refused to re-license Tri-Solgen, and the so-called Japanese acellular vaccine is nowhere near availability for marketing. Finally, the proof of actual medical causation will remain as elusive as ever. See Niemiera v. Schneider, 114 N.J. 550, 555 A.2d 1112 (1989) (plaintiff's injuries were assertedly attributable to causes other than DPT). By contrast, if she elects to withdraw her suit and is eligible under the federal Act, *542 she will enjoy a presumption that the vaccine caused her injuries. See 42 U.S.C.A. section 300aa-13.

Armed with foreknowledge of the legal principles that will be applied, her counsel can then exercise judgment on whether or not this vaccine can be proven not to be unavoidably unsafe within the meaning of our law and to contain a common defect such that the imposition of market-share liability is warranted. Under the federal Act her attorney is obligated to inform her that compensation may be available under the federal program. 42 U.S.C.A. section 300aa-10(b). Fully informed of her chances of recovery under both our State tort law and the federal Act, she might elect to seek, if eligible, the federal vaccine remedy. She deserves this chance.

I cannot play a shell game of remedies with a disabled child. No member of the Appellate Division genuinely believed that the New Jersey Supreme Court would not recognize a form of market-share liability. Each differed as to either the form of alternative liability or whether the decision could be made only by "either the Supreme Court or the Legislature." 219 N.J.Super. at 642, 530 A.2d 1287. No judge or lawyer did predict or could have predicted that the New Jersey Supreme Court would find that market-share liability was indeed an acceptable principle of New Jersey tort law ("This case * * * may therefore come to represent the exception rather than the rule.") Ante at 529, but a principle that could not be invoked when there was an alternative federal remedy.

---

[3] The data overwhelmingly support the efficacy of DPT if administered with proper warnings. See S.Rep. No. 483, 99th Cong., 2d Sess. 3 (1986) (Morbidity and mortality have dramatically decreased due to child immunization programs, e.g., in the case of DPT the number of cases decreased from 265,269 in 1934 to 2,000 in 1982, and the number of deaths declined from 7,500 in 1934 to 4 in 1982.)

Deanna Marrero has suffered enough. She ought not to have had to guess under which hand of the law she might find some surcease of her suffering. She ought at least to have been given a chance to know the rules before she had to make the choice.

For reversal-Justices CLIFFORD, POLLOCK, GARIBALDI and STEIN-4.

For affirmance-Justices HANDLER and O'HERN-2.

In re ASBESTOS LITIGATION

United States Court of Appeals, Third Circuit
829 F.2d 1233

Argued Feb. 24, 1987.
Decided Sept. 22, 1987.
As Amended Sept. 28 and Oct. 8, 1987.
Rehearings and Rehearings En Banc Denied Nov. 2, 1987.

EQUAL PROTECTION: common law as announced by state's highest court is "law" for equal protection purposes.

After consolidating all pending asbestos cases for argument, the United States District Court for the District of New Jersey, sitting en banc, 628 F.Supp. 774, certified question to the Court of Appeals. The Court of Appeals, Weis, Circuit Judge, held that: (1) common-law precedent announced by state's highest court is "law" within meaning of equal protection clause; but (2) New Jersey common law that "state-of-the-art" defense is not available to asbestos manufacturers in products liability action although it is available to drug manufacturers in products liability action does not deprive the asbestos manufacturers of equal protection; and (3) denial of "state-of-the-art" defense to asbestos manufacturers did not deprive them of due process.

Question answered in the negative.

Becker, Circuit Judge, filed a concurring opinion.

James Hunter, III, Circuit Judge, filed a dissenting opinion.

Before WEIS, BECKER and HUNTER, Circuit Judges.

OPINION OF THE COURT

WEIS, Circuit Judge.

(1) The district court has certified to us the question whether decisions of the New Jersey Supreme Court violate the Equal Protection Clause in abolishing the state-of-the-art defense in asbestos personal injury cases. We determine that a common law precedent announced by a state's highest court is "law" within the meaning of the Equal Protection Clause.

Using the rational basis standard, we conclude that the state court rulings survive the constitutional challenge.

The district court of New Jersey consolidated all of its pending asbestos cases for argument and disposition of the defendants' attack on the state supreme court's bar against "state-of-the-art" evidence in those personal injury cases. Sitting in banc, the district court rejected the defendants' contention that they were denied equal protection and certified the question to us under 28 U.S.C. section 1292(b). We accepted the interlocutory appeal.

Asbestos litigation poses a serious problem for American tort law, which traditionally has provided for a "one-on-one" adjudication of claims.[1] The formidable number of asbestos suits has prompted efforts to adapt the procedural framework of the existing tort system with its inefficiencies, high costs, and inconsistent judgments to the pressing demands of this massive litigation. See In re School Asbestos Litigation, 789 F.2d 996, 1000-01 (3d Cir.1986).

More than 30,000 asbestos personal injury claims were filed nationwide by 1986, and an additional 180,000 claims are projected to be on court dockets by the year 2010. Id. at 1000. Because no federal statute governs the substantive law applicable to these claims, they are controlled by the tort laws of the various states under theories of negligence, warranty, or strict liability. The courts in New Jersey, both state and federal, have been confronted by a particularly heavy concentration of these cases.

New Jersey common law recognizes the doctrine of strict liability in products liability claims. The supreme court of the state first adopted that theory in Henningsen v. Bloomfield Motors, 32 N.J. 358, 161 A.2d 69 (1960), and later decisions expanded its scope. See Restatement (Second) of Torts section 402A. Freund v. Cellofilm Properties, Inc., 87 N.J. 229, 432 A.2d 925 (1981); Suter v. San Angelo

---

[1] A similar difficulty arose in the Agent Orange litigation, where the mass tort claims challenged the capacity of traditional rules to deal effectively with numerous suits involving multiple plaintiffs and defendants. There, too, the practical realities of case management coupled with the complexities of the claims imposed substantial hardships on existing tort procedures. See In re: "Agent Orange" Product Liability Litigation, 506 F. Supp. 737, 782-87 (E.D.N.Y.1979).

Foundry & Machine Co., 81 N.J. 150, 406 A.2d 140 (1979); Santor v. A & M Karagheusian, 44 N.J. 52, 207 A.2d 305 (1965).

In 1982, the Supreme Court of New Jersey issued a controversial decision in Beshada v. Johns-Manville Products Corp., 90 N.J. 191, 447 A.2d 539 (1982). The plaintiffs there claimed damages based on the defendants' failure to warn of the dangers of asbestos. In response, the defendants asserted the "state-of-the-art" defense--that at the relevant times they did not know, nor could have known, of the danger of their products.

The state supreme court ruled that "culpability is irrelevant" in products liability cases because "(s)trict liability focuses on the product, not the fault of the manufacturer." Id. 447 A.2d at 546. Accordingly, *1236 a rule excluding the state-of-the-art defense would be consistent with the underlying policies of strict liability and would further its goals of risk spreading, accident avoidance, and simplification of the fact-finding process. The court reasoned that if the expenses arising from these claims were allocated to the costs of production, the manufacturers would be encouraged to improve product safety. Elimination of the defense would also ease the costly and time-consuming burden of proving "scientific knowability" and avert juror confusion about the differences between negligence and strict liability. Id. 447 A.2d at 547-49. The Beshada opinion was not limited to asbestos cases, but applied to all products liability suits.

Two years later, the same court allowed drug manufacturers to assert the state-of-the-art defense, concluding that producers of pharmaceuticals have a duty to warn about dangers of which they know or should know based on reasonably obtainable or available knowledge. Feldman v. Lederle Laboratories, 97 N.J. 429, 452, 479 A.2d 374, 386 (1984). Despite this shift in position, however, Feldman did not overrule Beshada; the court chose instead to explicitly restrict the earlier case to "the circumstances giving rise to its holding." Id.

One month later, a defendant asbestos manufacturer relied on Feldman and sought permission to introduce state-of-the-art evidence in a suit then pending in the state court. The trial court denied the motion on the ground that New Jersey law prohibited asbestos manufacturers from asserting the defense. In the Matter of Asbestos Litigation

Venued in Middlesex County, No. L-52237-81 (N.J.Super.Ct., Law Div.), aff'd, 99 N.J. 201, 491 A.2d 700 (1984). The state supreme court summarily affirmed, stating: "(h)aving recognized that Beshada (citation omitted) applies to all pending asbestos cases, the ... Order of the Superior Court ... is summarily affirmed." In the Matter of Asbestos Litigation Venued in Middlesex County, 99 N.J. 201, 491 A.2d 700 (1984).

The present appeal arises out of this unsettled background. In various personal injury cases brought in the district court, defendant asbestos manufacturers attempted to introduce evidence on the state-of-the-art defense. They alleged that Beshada's preclusion of that defense had the effect of treating them discriminatorily and less favorably than all other manufacturers. To avoid inconsistent rulings, the district court considered the matter in banc and entered an order applicable to all of its pending asbestos cases. In re Asbestos Litigation, 628 F.Supp. 774 (D.N.J.1986).

A majority of the district judges decided that the defendants' request should be denied. In their view, legitimate concerns of case management, economics, as well as social welfare policy affecting exposed plaintiffs justified preclusion of the state-of-the-art defense. Id. at 779. Noting that strict liability in workmen's compensation had withstood similar equal protection attacks, id. at 779 n. 3, and finding a rational relationship between the Beshada ruling and its goals, the judges rejected the constitutional challenge.

A minority of the judges dissented on the grounds that the state supreme court had neither clearly articulated its rationale for eliminating the defense nor substantiated its expectations that the anticipated benefits would result.[2]

On appeal to this court, defendants contend that the New Jersey Supreme Court's decisions unconstitutionally discriminate among categories of civil litigants because no rational basis for the classification can be posited. Defendants also maintain that by failing to give adequate reason for its action, the state court violated the Due

---

[2] See In re Asbestos Litigation, 628 F. Supp. 774 (D.N.J.1986) (en banc), Judge Bissell wrote the opinion for the majority of eight judges and Chief Judge Fisher wrote for the six dissenting judges.

Process Clause of the Fourteenth Amendment.

Plaintiffs assert that the rational basis test is the appropriate standard for reviewing this equal protection challenge and that *1237 the wisdom of the state common law rule is not at issue.

First, we observe the somewhat unusual posture in which this case reaches us. The attack on the ruling, or more accurately the series of rulings, of the state supreme court did not come to the district court as a direct appeal.

(2) A United States District Court may not entertain an appeal from judgments of the highest court of a state. Only the United States Supreme Court may exercise such review, and then only in cases within its jurisdiction. See District of Columbia Court of Appeals v. Feldman, 460 U.S. 462, 482, 103 S.Ct. 1303, 1314, 75 L.Ed.2d 206 (1983); Rooker v. Fidelity Trust, 263 U.S. 413, 416, 44 S.Ct. 149, 150, 68 L.Ed. 362 (1923). The parties to the cases at hand constitute different groups than those in the challenged state court litigation, and hence neither res judicata nor law of the case principles apply. Defendants here have no avenue to attack the precedential effect of the New Jersey judgment governing their case except through objections to rulings in these cases filed in federal court.

The question presented to the district court, and now to us, is a variation on the theme of Erie R.R. Co. v. Tompkins, 304 U.S. 64, 58 S.Ct. 817, 82 L.Ed. 1188 (1938), that is, whether the New Jersey decisions are binding even if their tenor is not in harmony with the federal constitution.

Erie requires that, in diversity cases, federal courts apply the substantive law produced by the state legislature or the highest court of the state. The Erie doctrine envisions a federal district court in diversity functioning as would a state trial court in similar circumstances.

There is, however, a fundamental difference between the two judicial systems that affects the application of the appropriate law. The state trial court is bound by its judicial hierarchical organization to follow the state supreme court's rulings on constitutionality despite possible doubt about the correctness of the decisions. In the absence of binding federal precedent, the state trial court should defer to the highest court of the state. The federal district court, however, takes as its authority on federal constitutional issues decisions of the United States Courts of Appeals and the United States Supreme Court, rather than those of the state supreme court.

The case before us differs from that where state court action usually is subjected to federal scrutiny--the habeas corpus petition. In that setting, a district court reviews the very same case adjudicated by a state appellate court. Here, however, the district court acts in the first instance on a case never before a state tribunal, yet governed by that state's precedent.

(3) The threshold issue, thus, is whether Erie controls in circumstances where state law violates the federal constitution. Because the United States District Courts have the primary obligation to interpret and apply federal law, undoubtedly they can, and must, abjure Erie if its application would conflict with the United States Constitution.

This case presents several other curious features. Defendants do not contest being included within the scope of the Beshada doctrine along with other manufacturers. Rather, they complain that they were not excluded from it as were the other manufacturers in Feldman. Essentially, they do not argue that the strict liability holding of Beshada is constitutionally defective, whatever its other failings may be, but that asbestos manufacturers have been singled out for discriminatory treatment compared to other producers. Phrased differently, they protest the failure of the New Jersey Supreme Court to reverse Beshada in its entirety, rather than only partially.

In addition, unlike the usual equal protection case that challenges a legislative enactment, this attack is directed at the common law as announced by a state's highest court.

I.

History shows that state supreme court holdings were not always included within the meaning of "laws" to which equal protection applies. The oft-cited case of Swift *1238 v. Tyson, 41 U.S. 1 (16 Pet), 10 L.Ed. 865 (1842), illustrates the original judicial interpretation. Section 34 of the Judiciary Act of 1789 provided that the "laws of the several states ... shall be regarded as rules of decision." Initially, the Supreme Court interpreted "laws" narrowly to include only statutory enactments and to exclude decisional law. In Swift v. Tyson, Justice Story commented, "(i)n the ordinary use of language it will hardly be contended that the decisions of Courts constitute laws. They are, at most, only evidence of what the laws are, and are not of themselves laws.... The laws of a state are more usually understood to mean the rules and enactments promulgated by the legislative authority thereof, or long established local customs having the force of laws." 41 U.S. at 18.

In overruling Swift v. Tyson, Erie did not specifically address the meaning of "laws" in the equal protection context, but did expand the meaning to encompass, as rules of decision, both statutory law and decisional law. Justice Brandeis wrote that "whether the law of the State shall be declared by its Legislature in a statute or by its highest court in a decision is not a matter of federal concern." 304 U.S. at 78, 58 S.Ct. at 822.

Since that time, the Supreme Court has continued to use the word "laws" in its broader sense, reflecting to a degree the influence of Legal Realism and its conclusion that courts do, in fact, "make" law. In Illinois v. City of Milwaukee, 406 U.S. 91, 100, 92 S.Ct. 1385, 1391, 31 L.Ed.2d 712 (1972), the Court saw "no reason not to give 'laws' its natural meaning" and concluded that "section 1331 (federal question) jurisdiction will support claims founded upon federal common law as well as those of a statutory origin."

In Romero v. International Terminal Operating Co., 358 U.S. 354, 79 S.Ct. 468, 3 L.Ed.2d 368 (1959), Justice Brennan spoke for four members of the Court who reached the issue and agreed that "laws" embraced federal common law. Referring to Erie, he explained that the Court had recognized there that the statutory word "laws" includes court decisions, and that rules of substantive law are "as fully 'laws' of the United States as if they had been enacted by Congress." Id. at 393, 79 S.Ct. at 491. See also Maine v. Thiboutot, 448 U.S. 1, 4, 100 S.Ct. 2502, 2504, 65 L.Ed.2d 555 (1980); Kuhn v. Fairmont Coal Co., 215 U.S. 349, 370, 30 S.Ct. 140, 147, 54 L.Ed. 228 (1909) (Holmes, J., dissenting).

(4) Whatever may have been the reaction of the courts in earlier times, we are persuaded that the district court properly considered the common law of New Jersey to be within the scope of the Equal Protection Clause.

II.

(5) Because equal protection claims may be reviewed under a number of standards which differ in intensity, we find it necessary to select the proper test for use in this case. As a general rule, classifications that neither regulate suspect classes nor burden fundamental rights must be sustained if they are rationally related to a legitimate governmental interest. See Empire Kosher Poultry, Inc. v. Hallowell, 816 F.2d 907 (3d Cir.1987); Price v. Cohen, 715 F.2d 87, 92, 94 (3d Cir.1983), cert. denied, 465 U.S. 1032, 104 S.Ct. 1300, 79 L.Ed.2d 700 (1984); Jamieson v. Robinson, 641 F.2d 138, 142 (3d Cir.1981).

(6) The matter at issue here, the right of a manufacturer to invoke the state-of-the-art defense, is not fundamental under the Constitution nor is it a suspect classification. The Supreme Court has observed that "despite the fact that 'otherwise settled expectations' may be upset," a state may modify or abolish a cause of action at common law. Duke Power Co. v. Carolina Envtl. Study Group, 438 U.S. 59, 88 n. 32, 98 S.Ct. 2620, 2638 n. 32, 57 L.Ed.2d 595 (1978), quoting Usery v. Turner Elkhorn Mining Co., 428 U.S. 1, 16, 96 S.Ct. 2882, 2892, 49 L.Ed.2d 752 (1976).

In Duke Power, the Court upheld the constitutionality of the Price-Anderson Act, even though it carved out the private nuclear power industry for federal treatment in tort liability where usually state common *1239 law would govern. That case approved a statutory ceiling on recoverable damages because the statute provided a "reasonably just" substitute for state law remedies. 438 U.S. at 93-94, 98 S.Ct. at 2641. In response to objections raised by potential plaintiff-victims, the Court cited Munn v. Illinois, 94 U.S. (4 Otto) 113, 134, 24 L.Ed. 77 (1876), for the principle that "(a) person has no property, no vested interest, in any rule of the common law." The Munn Court had no doubt that "the law itself, as a rule of conduct, may be changed at the will or whim of the legislature unless prevented by constitutional limitations." Id.

In Silver v. Silver, 280 U.S. 117, 50 S.Ct. 57, 74 L.Ed. 221 (1929), the Court rejected an equal protection attack on a state statute denying recovery of damages by a gratuitous passenger against the driver of an automobile. The Court observed that "the Constitution does not forbid the creation of new rights, or the abolition of old ones recognized by the common law, to attain a possible legislative object." Id. at 122, 50 S.Ct. at 58. See also Corey v. Jones, 650 F.2d 803 (5th Cir.1981).

Other legislative alterations in the tort field have also withstood constitutional challenge. Of particular interest are the drastic changes in the traditional negligence standard for liability. The no-fault workmen's compensation program is one illustration of such treatment. See Lower Vein Coal Co. v. Industrial Bd., 255 U.S. 144, 41 S.Ct. 252, 65 L.Ed. 555 (1921); New York Central R.R. v. White, 243 U.S. 188, 37 S.Ct. 247, 61 L.Ed. 667 (1917). Legislation that treats medical malpractice suits differently than other negligence claims provides another example. See Woods v. Holy Cross Hosp., 591 F.2d 1164 (5th Cir.1979); Fein v. Permanente Med. Group, 38 Cal.3d 137, 695 P.2d 665 (1985); Florida Patient's Compensation Fund v. Von Stetina, 474 So.2d 783 (Fla.1985); Johnson v. St. Vincent Hosp., Inc., 273 Ind. 374, 404 N.E.2d 585 (1980); State ex rel. Strykowski v. Wilkie, 81 Wis.2d 491, 261 N.W.2d 434 (1978).

(7) In short, the nature of the right to assert a particular defense in a tort action is not among those characterized as "fundamental." It is not included in the field of human rights that touches on personal liberty, an area of special concern to the courts. Nothing inherent in the right to a tort defense lends itself to demand more scrupulous review than the other social and economic matters traditionally examined under the rational relationship test. See G.D. Searle & Co. v. Cohn, 455 U.S. 404, 102 S.Ct. 1137, 71 L.Ed.2d 250 (1982); United States R.R. Retirement Bd. v. Fritz, 449 U.S. 166, 101 S.Ct. 453, 66 L.Ed.2d 368 (1980); Massachusetts Bd. of Retirement v. Murgia, 427 U.S. 307, 96 S.Ct. 2562, 49 L.Ed.2d 520 (1976); Ortwein v. Schwab, 410 U.S. 656, 93 S.Ct. 1172, 35 L.Ed.2d 572 (1973).

It is by now well established that in confronting a problem in the area of economic and social welfare, a state does not violate the Equal Protection Clause merely because the classifications drawn by its laws are imperfect. "If the classification has some 'reasonable basis,' it does not offend the Constitution simply because the classification 'is not made with mathematical nicety or because in practice it results in some inequality.'" Dandridge v. Williams, 397 U.S. 471, 485, 90 S.Ct. 1153, 1161, 25 L.Ed.2d 491 (1970). See also New Orleans v. Dukes, 427 U.S. 297, 96 S.Ct. 2513, 49 L.Ed.2d 511 (1976).

Having determined that the nature of the right asserted here does not place it in a category requiring heightened scrutiny, we must now consider whether the judicial rather than legislative origin of the alleged infringement mandates a more searching review. As noted earlier, classifications subject to the Equal Protection Clause generally originate in the legislature. In the case before us, the dissenting district judges observed that where judicial action creates the classification, the "efficacy of the checks and balances inherent in 'the democratic process' is substantially reduced." 628 F.Supp. at 780 (Fisher, C.J., dissenting). For that reason, they concluded that a more critical equal protection test should be applied here.

*1240 The presumption of validity attaching to state legislation is based to some extent on the proposition that improvident decisions will be rectified eventually by the democratic process. Vance v. Bradley, 440 U.S. 93, 97, 99 S.Ct. 939, 942, 59 L.Ed.2d 171 (1979). However, we are not persuaded that this consideration carries any particular weight in the present circumstances.

The common law ruling by the New Jersey Supreme Court is susceptible to prompt and uncomplicated reversal by the state legislature if it deems fit. That procedure is not in the least more complex than if the precedent promulgated by the state supreme court had been enacted as a statute by the legislature. It is important to remember that speedy statutory revision remains available to correct any imprudent state court common law precedent. In fact, a bill intended to overrule Beshada was introduced in the New Jersey legislature. This bill never emerged from the Committee on Judiciary to which it was referred, consequently aborting the legislative effort to restore the state-of-the-art defense in products liability litigation to pre-Beshada status. S. 1465, 201st N.J. Leg., 1st Sess. (1984).

The democratic process is as readily accessible to overrule a common law precedent created by the state's highest court as it is to repeal a statutory enactment. We recognize that in a democracy the legislature may be the more appropriate branch to draw classifications based on public policy. As a popularly elected body, the legislature is in a position to tap the thinking of its constituency and has the resources to secure data generally not available to the courts.

Nevertheless, particularly in the tort field, the common law tradition remains strong. States exercise considerable latitude to accomplish fundamental shifts in policy by judicial action as well as by legislation. For example, the abolition of contributory negligence as a complete defense and the substitution of comparative negligence has been effected in some states by the courts, see, e.g., Hoffman v. Jones, 280 So.2d 431 (Fla.Sup.1973), while in other jurisdictions by the legislature. See, e.g., 42 Pa.Cons.Stat.Ann. section 7102 (Purdon 1982); N.J.Stat.Ann. section 2A:15-5.1 (West Supp.1986).

(8) We are not convinced that either the nature of the subject matter or the procedure utilized in arriving at the challenged ruling constitutes sufficient grounds for requiring a stricter standard of review for common law decisions subjected to equal protection attacks.

One other element present here--case management--tips the scale in favor of the state court ruling. The Beshada court gave prime consideration to this concern, a subject in which the expertise of a court substantially outweighs that of a legislature and deserves due deference.

Taking the significant elements entering into the state court's ruling and balancing them against the valid competency concerns of court and legislature, we discern no measurable imbalance that weakens the presumption of regularity attaching to the state's choice of alternatives. Considering the social, economic, and administrative nature of the issues before the state court, we cannot say that its action in deciding the state-of-the-art defense question warrants strict scrutiny. We therefore conclude that the rational basis test is applicable to the classification drawn by the Beshada and Feldman courts.

III.

(9) We now turn to a closer examination of the challenged state decisions.

Beshada was an appeal of six consolidated asbestos personal injury cases. As noted earlier, the New Jersey Supreme Court's opinion did not limit its discussion or holding to asbestos manufacturers, but spoke of strict liability in general. The court reasoned that the phrase "duty to warn" was misleading because it implied negligence concepts irrelevant to the concerns of strict liability.

According to the court, the correct focus was whether the product was defective for lack of a warning. If so, the proper aim of the litigation was to compensate the victims. *1241 Ultimately, the court concluded that even if a manufacturer had no knowledge of a condition that required a warning, as between the innocent victims of a defective product and the distributors of that product, the latter should bear any unforeseen costs.

Academic criticism of Beshada has been harsh. See generally The Passage of Time: The Implications for Product Liability, 58 N.Y.U.L.Rev. 733 (1983). One commentator termed the decision "unjustifiable on grounds of logic and public policy." Schwartz, The Post-Sale Duty to Warn: Two Unfortunate Forks in the Road to a Reasonable Doctrine, 58 N.Y.U.L.Rev. 892, 902 (1983). Another said, "(b)y and large I regard the decision as indefensible.... If our only goal is compensation, we should not handle products liability cases through the tort system." Epstein, Commentary, 58 N.Y.U. L.Rev. 930, 933 (1983).

Deans Page and Wade, whose works were favorably cited in Beshada, also criticized the decision. Dean Wade remarked that "(t)he Pennsylvania and New Jersey courts appear to be straining too hard in their efforts to develop a different standard of product actionability for strict liability actions.... (B)ecause of the way in which insurance premiums are set ... these tests may render a disservice to both product suppliers and consumers throughout the country." Wade, On Effect in Product Liability of Knowledge Unavailable Prior to Marketing, 58 N.Y.U.L.Rev. 734, 744 (1983). Dean Page described the policy reasons articulated in Beshada as "weak justification(s) for a narrower rule of strict liability." Page, Generic Product Risks: The Case Against Comment K and for Strict Tort Liability, 58 N.Y.U.L.Rev. 853, 879 (1983).

The failure to warn issue next came before the New Jersey court in the 1984 Feldman case. There, the court reversed its former position and said, "(g)enerally, the state-of-the-art ... and available knowledge are relevant factors" and "generally conduct should be measured by knowledge at the time the manufacturer distributed the product." 479 A.2d at 386.

Feldman acknowledged Beshada only by saying, "we do not overrule Beshada," but proceeded to "restrict (it) to the circumstances giving rise to its holding." Id. 479 A.2d at 388. The opinion further noted "in passing, that, although not argued and determined in Beshada, there were or may have been data and other information generally available, aside from scientific knowledge, that arguably could have alerted the manufacturer at an early stage in the distribution of its product to the dangers associated with its use." Id.

At another point, the Feldman court concluded that Beshada would not demand a contrary conclusion in "the typical design defect or warning case." Id. 479 A.2d at 387. The court also refused to agree that Beshada held "generally or in all cases ... that in a warning context knowledge of the unknowable is irrelevant in determining the applicability of strict liability." Id.

These imprecise statements and the unequivocal ruling in Middlesex Asbestos Litigation that Beshada applies to pending asbestos cases leads us to the following assessment: (1) in New Jersey, Beshada does apply to asbestos cases but not to all products liability cases; and (2) Feldman does not govern asbestos cases, but does not necessarily apply to all other products liability cases.

New Jersey, therefore, does treat asbestos cases differently than other products liability cases. However, we do not know if this disparate treatment applies exclusively to asbestos cases. In addition to the expressed justifications of risk-spreading, accident avoidance, and simplification of the fact-finding process, Feldman provides yet another underlying reason for precluding the state-of-the-art defense in the asbestos setting. The opinion suggests that these manufacturers knew the dangers of asbestos and, consequently, the state-of-the-art defense could not be sustained.[3]

*1242 This theory is expressed more clearly in Fischer v. Johns-Manville Corp., 103 N.J. 643, 512 A.2d 466 (1986), an opinion handed down after the state supreme court refused to apply Feldman to asbestos cases. Fischer determined that one manufacturer did know the hazards of asbestos by the 1930s and that other manufacturers could have gained similar knowledge through articles published at that time in scientific journals. Feldman had earlier held that "a reasonably prudent manufacturer will be deemed to know of reliable information generally available or reasonably obtainable in the industry." 479 A.2d at 387.

---

[3] See Asbestos Litigation Reporter, 13,800-01 (Jan. 2, 1987) for documentary evidence of the knowledge of asbestos diseases available in 1930.

Although it may be said that Fischer embodies post-hoc justification for Beshada, the latter had cited Hardy v. Johns-Manville Sales Corp., 509 F.Supp. 1353 (E.D.Tex.1981), one of a series of cases within the Fifth Circuit reflecting varying judicial responses to the state-of-the-art defense in asbestos litigation even before Beshada appeared on the scene. See e.g. Hardy v. Johns-Manville Sales Corp. ("Hardy II") 681 F.2d 334 (5th Cir.1982); Migues v. Fibreboard Corp., 662 F.2d 1182 (5th Cir.1982); Borel v. Fibreboard Paper Products Corp., 493 F.2d 1076 (5th Cir.1973); Hardy v. Johns-Manville Sales Corp. ("Hardy I"), 509 F.Supp. 1353 (E.D.Tex.1981); Flatt v. Johns-Manville Sales Corp., 488 F.Supp. 836 (E.D.Tex.1980); Mooney v. Fibreboard Corp., 485 F.Supp. 242 (E.D.Tex.1980).[4]

Some federal courts believed that because asbestos plaintiffs so frequently litigated the state-of-the-art issue, they were entitled to use offensive collateral estoppel to preclude further repetition. Hardy I, 509 F.Supp. at 1361; Flatt v. Johns-Manville Sales Corp., 488 F.Supp. at 841. The Court of Appeals, however, determined that to use collateral estoppel in this context would be to "elevate judicial expedience over considerations of justice and fair play." Hardy II, 681 F.2d at 348.

In Hardy I, the district court applied collateral estoppel based on an omnibus order derived from the earlier Court of Appeals decision in Borel to preclude relitigation of the state-of-the-art defense. The trial court construed Borel to establish that, as a matter of law, the plaintiffs need not prove the defendants knew or should have known of the dangerous propensities of their products.

The Court of Appeals, however, concluded that the district court had tried to reach a result that the binding substantive law of the forum state had not yet reached. Consequently, because necessary procedural prerequisites were absent and because doubts existed as to the accuracy of the underlying findings, the Court of Appeals refused to give preclusive effect to the issue of the state-of-the-art

---

[4] The Court of Appeals for the Fourth Circuit has also discussed the subject. See also Spartanburg County School Dist. Seven v. National Gypsum Co., 805 F.2d 1148 (4th Cir.1986); Reed v. Tiffin Motor Homes, Inc., 697 F.2d 1192 (4th Cir.1982).

defense.[5]

We do not overlook the fact that exposure to asbestos may vary in degree depending on whether an individual works in a plant that manufactures asbestos products or simply drives an automobile equipped with asbestos brake linings. Nevertheless, Beshada's broad language, when applied to the concrete facts of asbestos litigation and read together with Fischer, is not completely divorced from reality, despite its abstract appearance of assessing culpability for failure to know and warn of the unknowable.

In the case at hand, the dissenting district judges have mounted powerful arguments to sustain the equal protection challenge. Ultimately these arguments are grounded in the wisdom and correctness of Beshada and its progeny, an appraisal not within the function of the federal courts when called upon to assess equal protection attacks on state law. This restraint is especially appropriate when the reviewing court employs the rational basis standard, a test that does not permit federal courts to strike down classifications because they *1243 are unwise or inartfully drawn. United States R.R. Retirement Bd. v. Fritz, 449 U.S. 166, 101 S.Ct. 453, 66 L.Ed.2d 368 (1980); Delaware River Basin Comm'n v. Bucks County Water & Sewer Auth., 641 F.2d 1087 (3d Cir.1981).

Moreover, we must not overlook the importance of allocating the burden of proof. In equal protection cases, those who challenge state law must convince the court that the factual assumptions on which the classification is apparently based could not reasonably be conceived as true by the governmental decision maker. See Vance v. Bradley, 440 U.S. at 110, 99 S.Ct. at 949. See also Malmed v. Thornburgh, 621 F.2d 565, 571 (3d Cir.), cert. denied, 449 U.S. 955, 101 S.Ct. 361, 66 L.Ed.2d 219 (1980). We cannot say that the asbestos manufacturers have met that burden.

Nor may we ignore the federalism concerns that color this controversy. These considerations are invoked by long-standing acceptance of the notion that tort law, much like

---

[5] For a detailed analysis of the difficulties of applying collateral estoppel to asbestos litigation, see Green, The Inability of Offensive Collateral Estoppel to Fulfill Its Promise: An Examination of Estoppel in Asbestos Litigation, 70 Iowa L.Rev. 141 (1984).

the law of domestic relations, belongs almost exclusively to the states. Although that principle alone would not require a federal court to stay its hand when a violation of equal protection occurs, we must recognize that the states possess a high degree of competence as well as a traditional claim of independence in this field.

From that perspective, too, it is unrealistic to ignore the fact that the doctrine of strict products liability advocated by the Restatement (Second) of Torts section 402A and adopted by New Jersey is in itself a classification that imposes discriminatory liability on a particular group of defendants. At the turn of the century, the common law held manufacturers and defendant-distributors of defective products liable in most instances only if proved negligent. State court decisions, however, developed tort law to wipe out the reasonable conduct defense and to establish liability without fault not only for manufacturers of defective products, but also for the utterly fault-free retailer. Nevertheless, no equal protection challenge has successfully undermined that doctrine.[6]

In refining and narrowing the section 402A theory, Beshada eliminates one more defense to the liability of asbestos defendants. Because the court's reasoning may be applicable to other defendants in similar circumstances, the justification advanced both directly and indirectly by the New Jersey court may be regarded as weak and ill-advised. We cannot, however, conclude that the state court's position is irrational. The concepts of risk-spreading and compensation for victims by manufacturers of unreasonably dangerous products are cornerstones of section 402A, and they may be consistently applied to asbestos as well as to other products.

Although not in itself a determinative factor in the elimination of a substantive defense, the desirability of simplifying the fact-finding process and thus making it easier for victims to recover has been recognized by the law. Workmen's compensation programs and no-fault auto insurance

---

[6] See Gogol v. Johns-Manville Sales Corp., 595 F. Supp. 971, 974-75 (D.N.J.1984), another asbestos case, where the court addressed a similar equal protection question. Recognizing that tort law makes numerous distinctions between classes of litigants, the court found no constitutional violation.

plans share that common goal. Under workmen's compensation laws, both the employer and the employee yield common law rights in exchange for a plan of prompt, fixed payments controlled by an administrative agency. Nevertheless, the Supreme Court made it clear in Duke Power that the lack of a quid pro quo is not a prerequisite to approval of modification of traditional common law tort doctrine. 438 U.S. at 88, 98 S.Ct. at 2638.

Administrative convenience standing alone is not an adequate ground for the elimination of a substantive defense. Medora v. Colautti, 602 F.2d 1149, 1153 n. 9 (3d Cir.1979). However, we cannot help but be conscious of the extraordinary size of the asbestos personal injury litigation. As we commented in In Re School District Asbestos Litigation, this unprecedented phenomenon in American tort law requires *1244 states be given some leeway in devising their own solutions.

In reaching its decision, the Beshada court considered the possibility that a jury might become confused by the testimony of experts who would "speculate as to what knowledge was feasible in a given year." Consequently, the court opined that it should "resist legal rules that will so greatly add to the costs both sides incur in trying a case." 477 A.2d at 548.

It might be questioned whether the defendants themselves worried about the potential cost of producing evidence necessary to reduce or eliminate their liability and whether they, in fact, welcomed the court's concern about their litigation expenses. Moreover, Beshada's interest in simplifying the trial of asbestos cases was substantially undercut by Fischer, where the state supreme court permitted personal injury plaintiffs to receive punitive damages on proof that the defendants had failed to comply with the state-of-the-art.[7] Notwithstanding the distinction between what was known and what was knowable, for all practical purposes what Beshada precluded from coming in the front door, Fischer allows in the back door. Thus, the goal of

---

[7] We note that this opinion invoked one of the grounds we reluctantly predicted would be used by state courts to permit punitive damages in asbestos personal injury cases. In re School Asbestos Litigation, 789 F.2d at 1004. The New Jersey court rationalized its decision in part by noting that because other states allowed the recovery of exemplary damages, New Jersey citizens should have similar rights.

simplifying asbestos litigation is eroded by the New Jersey decision to award punitive damages in these cases.

Although we find the Fischer case troubling, we once again acknowledge our limited function in reviewing cases of this type. We cannot overlook the fact that those plaintiffs who wish to avoid the cost of proving the foundation for an uncertain award of punitive damages still may take advantage of the simplified compensation claim Beshada makes available. While the use of that alternative may be conspicuous by its rarity, we have no empirical data that suggests it will never be employed.

IV.

(10) We further conclude that the due process challenge raised on appeal is not sustainable. Appellants have not been deprived of their due process right to be heard; they have only been denied one available defense. Because other defenses remain in their arsenal, they have not lost their ability to defend against the claims brought by asbestos victims. Nor can the contention that the New Jersey court's reasoning is unarticulated and irrational stand in light of the steady evolution over the last twenty years of the doctrine of strict products liability in that state's law. As our discussion of equal protection indicated, there are legitimate state interests here that have a reasonable basis, enabling the New Jersey law to survive scrutiny under the Due Process Clause.

V.

In summary, we conclude that common law decisions of state supreme courts are subject to equal protection scrutiny under the same rational basis standard applicable to legislative enactments. Decisions of the state supreme court that fall within the economic and social fields are to be evaluated under the rational relationship test. We further decide that the policies of risk-spreading, compensation for victims, and simplification of trials in the highly unusual circumstances of asbestos claims furnish an adequate, albeit minimal, basis for eliminating the state-of-the-art defense in these cases and preclude a successful equal protection challenge to the New Jersey Supreme Court decision abolishing that defense.

The district court has presented to us the question whether, in strict liability failure to warn cases in New

Jersey, the judicially imposed denial of the state-of-the-art defense to manufacturers of asbestos-containing products constitutes a violation of the Equal Protection Clause of the Fourteenth Amendment.

We answer in the negative.

*1245 BECKER, Circuit Judge, concurring.

I join in Parts I, II and IV of Judge Weis's opinion and concur wholly in the result. I also join in portions of Part III, in which Judge Weis explains why he finds a rational basis for New Jersey's distinguishing asbestos cases from prescription drug cases in terms of the state-of-the-art defense.[1] However, I do not believe that Judge Weis has identified with sufficient precision the New Jersey Supreme Court's reasons for making the distinction under review, a distinction I believe to be supported by a valid government objective and rational within our equal protection jurisprudence. Specifically, I believe that, on the basis of adjudicative facts determined in cases that had the full panoply of procedural protections, the New Jersey Supreme Court has determined a legislative fact--that the hazards of asbestos exposure were knowable to the industry at all relevant times. The subject of legislative factfinding is rarely discussed in the jurisprudence, and I write separately to explain why I think it validates the New Jersey Supreme Court's distinction.

Appellants complain that the New Jersey Supreme Court deprives manufacturers and distributors of asbestos-containing products of the state-of-the-art defense in products liabilityfailure to warn actions, which other manufacturers and distributors are entitled to assert in the same kind of lawsuits. Appellants urge that no rational theoretical basis exists for differentiating between these classes of litigants. Judge Weis in his opinion demonstrates that is not clear that all other manufacturers may take advantage of the state-of-the-art defense, although he agrees that New Jersey "does treat asbestos cases differently than other product liability cases." Weis Op., at 1241. I believe that we need not find constitutional infirmity even if we assume for the sake of argument appellants' worst case

---

[1] For the reasons I have not joined in the balance of Part III, see infra, at 1251-52.

scenario, i.e., that New Jersey singles out the asbestos industry.

I.

As I read the New Jersey Supreme Court's cases, the court does not deny asbestos defendants the state-of-the-art defense on theoretical grounds. Instead, I believe that the New Jersey court, via the Beshada-Feldman-Fischer trilogy, has determined a legislative fact--that, at all relevant times, asbestosis harms were knowable to the industry. That being the case, the New Jersey Supreme Court has reasonably decided to preclude endless relitigation of what was "knowable" to the asbestos industry.[2]

Believing that "Feldman provides yet another underlying reason for precluding the state-of-the-art defense in the asbestos setting," Judge Weis observes that "the (Feldman) opinion suggests that these manufacturers knew the dangers of asbestos and, consequently, the state-of-the-art defense could not be sustained." Maj. ap. at 1241 (footnote omitted). Although I agree with Judge Weis that the New Jersey Supreme Court has determined that the harms of asbestos were actually known to at least one asbestos manufacturer, I do not believe that it found in Feldman that the harms of asbestos were actually known to the industry. Rather, on the basis of what could have been known, that opinion determines constructive knowledge sufficient to defeat the state-of-the-art defense. *1246 It was not until Fischer v. Johns-Manville Corp., 103 N.J. 643, 512 A.2d 466 (1986), that the court found that at least one asbestos manufacturer actually knew of the harms.

---

[2] The state-of-the-art defense, as the name implies, does not merely rest on an inquiry concerning what a manufacturer knew. Rather, the defense is intended to limit liability to those dangers of which the seller "has knowledge, or by application of reasonable, developed human skill and foresight should have knowledge." Restatement (Second) of Torts, section 402A comment j. Implicit in the defense, therefore, is the obligation to investigate and keep abreast of recent developments-an obligation imposed under the aegis of "constructive knowledge(, which) may encompass virtually all information that is in the public domain." Green, The Inability of Offensive Collateral Estoppel to Fulfill Its Promise: An Examination of Estoppel in Asbestos Litigation, 70 Iowa L. Rev. 141, 190 n. 276. The relevant determination is thus not what was known, but what was knowable. See also infra at 1247.

The Beshada court did have before it the factual dispute concerning what was known. It found, however, that it need not resolve the "substantial factual dispute about what defendants knew and when they knew it," 447 A.2d at 542, referring both to a finding that "(k)nowledge of the danger (of asbestos) can be attributed to the industry as early as the mid-1930's...." Id. 447 A.2d at 542, (quoting Hardy v. Johns-Manville Sales Corp., 509 F.Supp. 1353, 1355 (E.D. Texas 1981)) and the contrary assertions of the asbestos industry.[3] Pertinent in Feldman is the exact manner that the court restricted the application of Beshada when it differentiated between asbestos products and other products in the context of the state-of-the-art defense:

> We do not overrule Beshada, but restrict Beshada to the circumstances giving rise to its holding. See, e.g., Friedman v. Podell, 21 N.J. 100, 105, 121 A.2d 17 (1956); Konrad v. Anheuser-Busch, Inc., 48 N.J.Super. 386, 388 (137 A.2d 633) (Law Div.1958) ("Cases state principles but decide facts, and it is only the decision on the facts that is binding precedent."). We note in passing, that, although not argued and determined in Beshada, there were or may have been data and other information generally available, aside from scientific knowledge, that arguably could have alerted the manufacturer at an early stage in the distribution of its product to the dangers associated with its use.

97 N.J. at 455, 479 A.2d 374. Thus, while the New Jersey Supreme Court in Beshada expressly did not decide "what defendants knew and when they knew it," 447 A.2d at 542, it also refrained from deciding that question in Feldman. In Feldman, it stated only that the manufacturers "arguably _could_ have (been) alerted ... at an early stage in the distribution of its product to the dangers associated with its use," 97 N.J. at 455, 479 A.2d 374 (emphasis supplied). Rather than finding actual knowledge, the Feldman opinion thus intimated its views on constructive knowledge, which is sufficient to defeat the state-of-the-art defense, based on facts brought to its attention in Beshada.

---

[3] Hardy, in turn, rests to a significant degree on Borel v. Fibreboard Paper Products Corp., 493 F.2d 1076 (5th Cir.1973), cert. denied, 419 U.S. 869, 95 S.Ct. 127, 42 L.Ed.2d 107 (1974).

In Fischer the New Jersey Supreme Court determined not only that asbestosis harms were knowable by the asbestos industry, but that those harms were actually known by at least one manufacturer. In that case, the court recited two single-spaced pages of facts that determined to its satisfaction that at least one company "did in fact have knowledge of the hazards of asbestos ... as early as the 1930's." 103 N.J. at 649, 512 A.2d 466 (quoting Fischer v. Johns-Manville Corporation, Bell Asbestos Mines, 193 N.J.Super. 113, at 117, 472 A.2d 577). For example, the court referred to "eleven scientific articles published between 1936 and 1941 documenting the grave pulmonary hazards of exposure to asbestos and discussing the measures which could be taken to protect workers." Id. at 650, 512 A.2d 466 (quoting 193 N.J.Super. at 118, 472 A.2d 577). On the more individualized level of worker exposure, a doctor testified that "from the beginning of his employment (in 1944) he saw persons with asbestosis 'on a regular and frequent basis' and frequently made recommendations that such employees receive job reclassifications which would remove them from continued exposure to asbestos dust." Id. at 651, 512 A.2d 466 (quoting 193 N.J.Super. at 120, 472 A.2d 577). As early as 1933, noted the court, asbestos workers were filing claims against at least one asbestos manufacturer. See id. at 650, 512 A.2d 466 (quoting 193 N.J.Super. at 118).

The state-of-the-art defense decides not what the defendant or another party knew--a fact relating to a particular party--but what was knowable--a fact about the state of the world. In Feldman, the court adverted to what was knowable, but *1247 in Fischer it made a concrete determination. By deciding that even one company in the industry--Johns-Manville--knew of asbestosis, the Supreme Court of New Jersey, culminating the trilogy, found that the harms were knowable to the industry as a whole.

To my mind, it was not inappropriate for the court to rely on this determination--or even a similar earlier determination, see, e.g., Hardy, cited in Beshada, 447 A.2d at 542--in finding legislative facts[4] when it determined that the rule of Beshada should continue to govern the asbestos industry. As Justice Holmes recognized long ago, "the court may ascertain as it sees fit any fact that is merely a ground

---

[4] For a definition of legislative facts and demonstration that knowability is a legislative fact, see infra at Part I. B.

for laying down a rule of law." Chastleton Corp. v. Sinclair, 264 U.S. 543, 548-49, 44 S.Ct. 405, 406, 68 L.Ed. 841 (1924). To forbid such recognition would force courts to fashion laws without reference to reality.

Judge Hunter, in dissent, acknowledges that one manufacturer was found to have known of asbestos' harms in Fischer, but he finds that case unhelpful for judging the rationality of the challenged differentiation between asbestos and non-asbestos defendants because it was decided after the differentiation was first drawn. See Dissent, at 1259, n. 5. I disagree. I believe that the New Jersey Supreme Court rested the differentiation on the views it intimated in Feldman, i.e., the legislative fact that asbestos' harms were knowable. This avenue was open to New Jersey's highest court despite the putative protestations of a federal court, see Hardy, or the lack of "a certain degree of consensus," id. As Professor Davis has opined,

> judge-made law would stop growing if judges, in thinking about questions of law and policy, were forbidden to take into account the facts they believe, as distinguished from facts which are "clearly * * * within the domain of the indisputable." Facts most needed in thinking about problems of law and policy have a way of being outside the domain of the clearly indisputable.

Fed.R.Evid. 201 advisory committee's note quoting Davis, A System of Judicial Notice Based on Fairness and Convenience, in Perspectives of Law 69, 82 (1964).

Leaving aside the argument that the court's pronouncement in Feldman amounted to such a legislative fact-finding, and assuming that that fact was not found until Fischer, I still do not believe that we should today pronounce it irrational. Labelling the differentiation irrational would be contrary New Jersey's current position regarding manufacturers' ability to have known. Moreover, it would involve this court in a meaningless ritual of striking down a differentiation that we know to be supportable, only for the state court to revive it as supported on the basis we have already identified. For similar reasons, Justice Stevens has warned about unduly emphasizing actual motivation for the differentiation under review in equal protection challenges of legislative enactments.

> Actual purpose is sometimes unknown. Moreover, undue emphasis on actual motivation may result in

identically worded statutes being held valid in one State and invalid in a neighboring State. I therefore believe that we must discover a correlation between the classification and either the actual purpose of the statute or a legitimate purpose that we may reasonably presume to have motivated an impartial legislature.

United States Railroad Retirement Bd. v. Fritz, 449 U.S. 453, 180-81, 101 S.Ct. 453, 462, 66 L.Ed.2d 368 (1980) (Stevens, J., concurring in the judgment). Because the legislative fact-findings of Fischer may reasonably be presumed to have motivated a hypothetical impartial court, we would have to affirm even had Feldman not preceded that case.

The determination of knowability implicates the standard to which the state is willing to hold a manufacturer of a product: not only must a manufacturer stay *1248 abreast of what has already been discovered about his product, but he must also diligently pursue information about its possible dangers before he introduces it for distribution throughout the marketplace. See supra at 1245 n. 2. As such, under the aegis of "constructive knowledge," the New Jersey Supreme Court has made a policy judgment concerning the diligence with which the manufacturers should have undertaken additional investigation. See Feldman, 479 A.2d at 386-87. Thus, regardless of whether a given manufacturer is found to have actually known of the harms, the New Jersey Supreme Court could find that the industry was chargeable with the knowledge that was attainable had the manufacturers undertaken the task of discovery. As Judge Weis indicates, the court in Feldman made clear that "a reasonably prudent manufacturer <u>will be deemed</u> to know of reliable information generally available or reasonably obtainable in the industry." 479 A.2d at 387 (emphasis supplied); see Weis Op., at 1242. Such a determination cannot be made without reference to facts concerning the availability of information to the asbestos industry as a whole. However, once this factual assessment had been made, the court was also justified in precluding the relitigation of the factual basis of the state-of-the-art defense.[5]

II.

---

[5] See, e.g., Forte Towers, Inc. v. City of Miami Beach, 360 So.2d 81, 82 (Fla.App.1978) (precluding relitigation of factual predicate).

Judge Hunter in dissent argues that, because the use of legislative facts concerning the knowability of asbestos harms does not satisfy the requirements of the collateral estoppel doctrine, it violates due process. I disagree. The above discussion demonstrates that, in choosing to allow the state-of-the-art defense for other industries, the New Jersey Supreme Court did not have to turn a blind eye to its belief that the harms of asbestos were knowable to the asbestos indutry as a whole. Common law courts could not fashion rules grounded in reality if they were obliged to proceed without aid of legislative facts. As is evident from other cases that have found legislative facts, legislative fact-finding by such a court need not conform to the requirements of collateral estoppel to pass due process muster. I therefore do not believe that the New Jersey Supreme Court can be held to have acted unconstitutionally in finding the legislative facts it did when fashioning the law at issue in this case.

In the New Jersey Supreme Court cases discussed above, the factual determination concerning the knowability of asbestos harms is a legislative fact. "Adjudicative facts are simply the facts of the particular case. Legislative facts, on the other hand, are those which have relevance to legal reasoning and the lawmaking process, whether in the formulation of a legal principle or ruling by a judge or court or in the enactment of a legislative body." Fed.R.Evid. 201(a) advisory committee's note. Under this dichotomy, the pertinent facts, which concern the nature of the asbestos industry as a whole and what it could have known, were properly treated by the court as legislative. As one commentator has noted,

> An industry-wide question calls for facts about the industry; facts about each company may be unhelpful and may even get in the way. If a court ... is making law to govern an industry of 100 companies, the useful facts are about the 100 companies as a group, not about each company. The facts about the group are legislative, even though they are the sum of adjudicative facts about each company.

3 K. Davis, Administrative Law Treatise section 15:5, at 152-53 (2d ed. 1980) (emphasis in original). The issue of the knowability of asbestos harms concerns not what a particular litigant knew, but rather what knowledge was in the realm of the possible for the industry as a whole. Because the knowability of the harms of asbestos may thus be

a legislative fact upon which a court can fashion a rule of law, it was not inappropriate for the New Jersey Supreme Court to base a legal rule upon these legislative facts. See generally Fed.R.Evid. 201(a) advisory committee's note; Morgan, Judicial Notice, 57 Harv.L.Rev. 269, 270-71 (1944).[6]

---

[6] Judge Hunter believes that the state-of-the-art determination concerning the knowability of asbestos' harms is an adjudicative fact. Arguing by analogy, he finds the issue similar to whether asbestosis and mesothelioma were caused by asbestos exposure in a particular case, held to be a matter of adjudicative fact in Laster v. Celotex, 587 F.Supp. 542 (S.D.Ohio 1984). The analogy fails, however, because the development of these diseases relates to the peculiar conditions under which a person is exposed-for example, whether the person smokes and the ambient air concentration of asbestos dust. See Laster, 587 F.Supp. at 543. In the context of what was knowable by the asbestos industry, however, the peculiarities of a specific manufacturer are irrelevant. See supra at 1245 n. 2, 1247-1248. What *may* have been known is the heart of the state-of-the-art inquiry; in the causation inquiry, by contrast, "judicial notice that the inhalation of asbestos *may* cause asbestosis under certain conditions would have no appreciable impact." Laster, 587 F.Supp. at 544 (emphasis in original).

In any event, if the knowability of asbestos' harms were purely an adjudicative fact, it could not be the subject of a legislative fact-finding. The contrary is true, however, for the Senate Committee on Labor and Public Welfare made a specific legislative finding concerning the knowability of asbestos' harms when deciding to enact the Occupational Safety and Health Act.

Asbestos is another material which continues to destroy the lives of workers. For 40 years it has been known that exposure to asbestos caused the severe lung scarring called asbestosis.

S.Rep. No. 1282, 91st Cong., 2d Sess., reprinted in 1970 U.S. Code Cong. and Admin. News, 91st Cong., 2d Sess. 5177, 5178.

Judge Hunter also argues that "culpable knowledge," like disease causation, is an ultimate fact that cannot be resolved on the basis of legislative facts. First, I am perplexed by the phrase "culpable knowledge," for the state-of-the-art inquiry does not look at what was known by the individual defendant, but what could have been known in the industry by the application of reasonable diligence. See supra at 1245 n. 2, 1247-1248. Second, I fail to understand why legislative fact-finding cannot resolve an ultimate issue; indeed, in the Supreme

Many courts and commentators have argued that a court should not rely on legislative facts without giving the parties an opportunity for comment upon them. See, e.g., Bulova Watch Co. v. K. Hattori & Co., 508 F.Supp. 1322, 1328-29 (E.D.N.Y.1981); 3 K. Davis, Administrative Law Treatise section 15:9; S. Saltzburg & K. Redden, Federal Rules of Evidence Manual 60 (4th ed. 1986) ("We do not claim Judges cannot rely on a broad range of facts to force the law forward. We suggest only that the parties should be permitted to participate in the march."). It is therefore noteworthy that the Beshada case was itself concerned with developing facts pertinent to the knowability of asbestos harms. Additionally, the Hardy and Borel cases, on which Beshada and Feldman appear to be predicated, as well as the Fischer case, were litigated with the full panoply of procedural protections. Moreover, the court in Beshada did not hear from only one member of the industry; rather, a broad cross-section of the industry was represented. See 447 A.2d at 541-42. Finally, the members of the asbestos industry had the opportunity to advocate a contrary conclusion in In re Asbestos Litigation Venued in Middlesex County, 99 N.J. 201, 491 A.2d 700 (1984), and again in Fischer. Hence, the affected industry has had relevant opportunities to respond to the New Jersey Supreme Court's determination of the pertinent legislative facts.

It is unclear whether Judge Hunter would find relevant to his due process point the legislative nature of the facts

---

Court cases Judge Hunter cites as finding legislative facts, those facts seem to relate only to ultimate issues. See Dissent at 1257; Church of Latter-Day Saints v. Amos, --- U.S. ----, 107 S.Ct. 2862, 2875, 97 L.Ed.2d 273 (1987) (O'Connor, J., concurring) (perception of endorsement of religion in Establishment Clause case); United States v. Leon, 468 U.S. 897, 918-21, 104 S.Ct. 3405, 3418-19, 82 L.Ed.2d 677 (1984) (deterrent effect of exclusionary rule); compare Hawkins, 358 U.S. at 77-78, 79 S.Ct. at 138 (allowing adverse spousal privilege because adverse testimony found to hurt marriage) with Trammel v. United States, 445 U.S. 40, 52, 100 S.Ct. 906, 913, 63 L.Ed.2d 186 (overruling Hawkins because "(w)hen one spouse is willing to testify against the other in a criminal proceeding their relationship is almost certainly in disrepair"). Finally, I disagree with the characterization of the state-of-the-art defense as the ultimate issue in a products liability case. It is no more or less ultimate a determinant of liability than, to take Judge Hunter's other example, causation.

relied on by the New Jersey Supreme Court. Because *1250 a legislative fact is not an individualized fact, however, the Constitution does not mandate that it be found through a process of individualized fact-finding.[7] Because legislative facts are the basis for a rule of law, they need not be relitigated in each succeeding case that invokes the rule and thereby indirectly relies on the legislative fact. It does not offend due process to craft the rule without allowing individualized process for redetermination of the legislative facts on which the rule is based. See, e.g., New York Times v. Sullivan, 376 U.S. 254, 278, 84 S.Ct. 710, 725, 11 L.Ed.2d 686 (1964) (finding state libel law unconstitutional because of "the pall of fear and timidity imposed upon those who would give voice to public criticism"); Hawkins v. United States, 358 U.S. 74, 78, 79 S.Ct. 136, 138, 3 L.Ed.2d 125 (1958) ("Adverse testimony given in criminal proceedings would, we think, be likely to destroy almost any marriage.").

Judge Hunter would apparently require a state Supreme Court to adhere to the strictures of collateral estoppel doctrine whenever it rests a rule of law upon a legislative fact that had been previously determined as an adjudicative fact in a prior court case. Such a rule would deprive courts of the ability to fashion rules with reference to the reason borne of experience. "The history of the common law shows a constant pattern of questions once treated as fact growing into matters of law after the courts have gained knowledge and experience concerning them." Korn, Law, Fact, and Science in the Courts, 66 Colum.L.Rev. 1080, 1105 (1966). Thus, for example, the decision to admit into evidence novel scientific testimony is first tested by individual adjudications before judicial recognition eliminates the need for a preliminary foundation. See United States v. Downing,

---

[7] Thus the Supreme Court long ago found a critical difference between Londoner v. Denver, 210 U.S. 373, 28 S.Ct. 708, 52 L.Ed. 1103 (1908), in which a small number of people were exceptionally affected upon individual grounds by a tax increase and therefore should have been afforded individual due process, and Bi-Metallic Inv. Co. v. State Bd. of Equalization, 239 U.S. 441, 36 S.Ct. 141, 60 L.Ed. 372 (1915), in which the court found that a general tax increase could be predicated without individualized fact-finding.

753 F.2d 1224, 1234 (3d Cir.1985).[8] Courts have even elevated the fact finding of a single jury verdict to the position of legislative fact on which to base a rule of law.[9] In all instances of adjudicative facts' elevation to legislative facts, the prior adjudications, with their full panoply of procedural protections, influence the court's view of reality. The legislative facts, in turn, influence the rule that is fashioned, and the due process clause does not require individualized determination or reconsideration of the legislative facts in all subsequent cases.

Finally, Judge Hunter goes beyond testing the New Jersey Supreme Court's determination against the due process clause of the fourteenth amendment. He also finds that, "(i)f judicial notice can be taken of such ultimate facts at all, it can only be within the strictures of Fed.R.Evid. 201." Dissent, at 1259; see also id. At 1260 (finding "does not satisfy the requirements of Fed.R.Evid. 201"). While I find the advisory committee's comments illuminating on the distinction between adjudicative and legislative facts, I do not believe that Rule 201 binds any state court. More important, Judge Hunter's point seems inapposite to the central issue. The question is not whether New Jersey wisely found legislative facts--I do not endorse the New Jersey Supreme Court's finding, for I do not pass on the wisdom of what it has done. Rather, for our purposes it is sufficient *1251 that New Jersey behaved rationally.[10] Because

---

[8] Specifically, although originally a subject to be re-established by expert testimony in every case, courts long ago came to give blood-grouping tests conclusive effect in paternity suits. See, e.g., Jordan v. Mace, 144 Me. 351, 69 A.2d 670 (1949); see generally Ross, The Value of Blood Tests as Evidence in Paternity Cases, 71 Harv. L.Rev. 466 (1958).

[9] See, e.g., Commonwealth v. Sullivan, 146 Mass. 142, 15 N.E. 491 (1888) (finding on the basis of a prior jury decision that, as a matter of law, a certain game was a regulated "lottery"), cited in Korn, Law, Fact, and Science in the Courts, 66 Colum. L.Rev. 1080, 1104 (1966).

[10]. As one commentator has noted in the context of legislative fact-finding by a legislative body:

Given the bent to test due process according to the information available to the legislature, the truth-content of the data is not

legislative facts underlie the New Jersey Supreme Court's decision to continue to withhold the state-of-the-art defense from asbestos manufacturers, the differentiation under review cannot be deemed irrational.

III.

I have not joined the balance of Part III of Judge Weis' opinion because I do not find a rational basis for New Jersey's distinction in any of the other justifications he advances. I briefly note my differences with the remainder of Judge Weis' Part III.

For the most part, the other rationales advanced by Judge Weis do not explain the New Jersey Supreme Court's distinction; rather, they imply that, because of the New Jersey Supreme Court's conceded hegemony over the development of that state's tort law, we must defer to whatever distinction the court draws. For example, he appears to regard the differentiation in and of itself as a matter of state policy in a matter of state expertise, which is said to deserve our deference. See, e.g., Weis Op., at 1243 ("Because the court's reasoning may be applicable to other defendants in similar circumstances, the justification advanced both directly and indirectly by the New Jersey court may be regarded as weak and ill-advised. We cannot, however, conclude that the state court's position is irrational."). Additionally, Judge Weis draws attention to "the federalism concerns that color this controversy"--concerns, I must note, that are ever present in Fourteenth Amendment challenges. Id., At 1243.

To determine the issue on the basis of such deference, however, assumes the answer to the equal protection inquiry. If we were to defer to the extent suggested by Judge Weis in all equal protection cases, no differentiation could be found irrational. Moreover, this extra dose of deference is duplicative. As Judge Weis so artfully demonstrates in Part

---

directly relevant. The question is whether sufficient data exists which could influence a reasonable legislature to act, not whether ultimately this data is true.

E. Cleary, McCormick on Evidence section 331, at 768 (2d ed. 1972) (footnote omitted); see also Burns Baking Co. v. Bryan, 264 U.S. 504, 517, 44 S.Ct. 412, 415, 68 L.Ed. 813 (1924) (Brandeis, J., dissenting).

II of his opinion, deference to legislative and state decisionmakers is part of the rationale behind the rational relation standard itself. To add greater deference would totally eviscerate that standard. This is clearly not the intended result of rational relation scrutiny. See, e.g., Cleburne v. Cleburne Living Center, 473 U.S. 432, 105 S.Ct. 3249, 87 L.Ed.2d 313 (1985) (finding city ordinance unconstitutional under rational relation equal protection scrutiny). Rather, the rational relation standard requires at least one justification for the challenged differentiation. It may be that the justification is to be judged by the lax standard enunciated in Vance v. Bradley, 440 U.S. 93, 111, 99 S.Ct. 939, 949, 59 L.Ed.2d 171 (1979) (reviewing court must be convinced "that the legislative facts on which the classification is apparently based could not reasonably be conceived to be true by the governmental decisionmakers"), but one such justification must nonetheless exist.

Additionally, although Judge Weis does not rely on administrative convenience simpliciter, he justifies the differentiation at least partially on that basis. I agree with Judge Weis to the extent that he holds that administrative convenience may play a role in prompting differentiation when an independent reason also supports it. As I have explained supra, I find that the New Jersey Supreme Court has reached the conclusion that that the state-of-the-art defense should not be available to the asbestos manufacturers because the harms of asbestos were knowable to the industry. Administrative convenience is thus a justification for the differentiation because state courts are not proscribed by the Equal Protection Clause from refusing to hear a defense *1252 that, as a matter of law, is doomed to fail. However, beyond such considerations, administrative convenience fails as a justification.

IV.

While states must be allowed to make their own policy judgments in matters such as tort law, they cannot use that discretion to arbitrarily discriminate against a class of litigants. Where a factual basis supports a differentiation, however, both the policy decision and the underlying factual determination deserves our deference.[11] In an equal protection case, those challenging the state law "must convince the court that the legislative facts on which the classification is apparently based could not reasonably be conceived to be true by the governmental decisionmaker." Vance v. Bradley, 440 U.S. 93, 111, 99 S.Ct. 939, 949, 59 L.Ed.2d 171 (1979), quoted in Minnesota v. Clover Leaf Creamery Co., 449 U.S. 456, 464, 101 S.Ct. 715, 724, 66 L.Ed.2d 659 (1981) (citing other cases). Because the court has found that at least one asbestos manufacturer had actual knowledge of the harms of asbestos at all relevant times, I do not believe that its determination of knowability "could not reasonably be conceived to be true by the governmental decisionmaker." I therefore concur in this aspect of Part III of Judge Weis's opinion.[12]

JAMES HUNTER, III, Circuit Judge, dissenting:

PRELIMINARY STATEMENT

In these diversity cases, we look to the law of New Jersey.

---

[11]. Because the determination of legislative facts is thus a component of fashioning a rule of law, the clearly erroneous standard of Rule 52(a) does not apply to review of a federal court's findings concerning legislative facts. See Lockhart v. McCree, 476 U.S. 162, 106 S.Ct. 1758, 1762 n. 3, 90 L.Ed.2d 137 (1986); see generally Dunagin v. City of Oxford, Miss., 718 F.2d 738, 748-49 n. 8 (5th Cir.1983) (en banc) (plurality opinion of Reavley, J.).

[12]. Another reason exists for deferring to a state supreme court's determination of legislative facts. Because a state court must make a decision concerning legislative facts despite imperfect information, its decision deserves deference. As Justice Blackmun's concurrence in United States v. Leon, 468 U.S. 897, 927, 104 S.Ct. 3405, 3423, 82 L.Ed.2d 677 (1984) (Blackmun, J., concurring), noted concerning the issues in that case,

I see no way to avoid making an empirical judgment of this sort and I am satisfied that the Court has made the correct one on the information before it. Like all courts, we face institutional limitations on our ability to gather information about "legislative facts...." Nonetheless, we cannot escape the responsibility to decide the question before us, however imperfect our information may be, and I am prepared to join the Court on the information now at hand.

New Jersey has embraced the full panoply of products liability law. See, e.g., Suter v. San Angelo Foundry & Mach. Co., 81 N.J. 150, 406 A.2d 140 (1979); Henningsen v. Bloomfield Motors, 32 N.J. 358, 161 A.2d 69 (1960). The "state-of-the-art" defense is normally available to defendants in products liability actions. This defense precludes liability where the manufacturer can prove that it did its work properly and produced the product in accordance with the practices and procedures appropriate to the product's known dangers. Today this court has ruled that the manufacturers of one product may not use the state-of-the-art defense. That product is asbestos. The court has said to asbestos manufacturers: there are too many asbestos cases, these cases have clogged up the court calendars, schedules and statistics; the proof of "state-of-the-art" is too time-consuming and concerned with too many variables; and, in any event, we do not think you could prove the defense even if we gave you the chance. Thus, one narrow class of defendants is deprived of a potentially exculpatory defense in the interest of expediency and calendar control. The manufacturers of all other products--including Agent Orange, the Dalkon Shield and DES--may use the defense, even if they are also clogging up the court calendar and causing statistical chaos. Only the asbestos industry is treated differently. This is just plain wrong and I dissent.

I.

It is beyond dispute that a classification that neither discriminates against a suspect *1253 class nor impinges upon a fundamental right does not violate the Equal Protection Clause if it is rationally related to a legitimate governmental purpose. See United States Railroad Retirement Bd. v. Fritz, 449 U.S. 166, 175, 101 S.Ct. 453, 459, 66 L.Ed.2d 368 (1980). While it is beyond our authority to strike down laws simply because we conclude that they are unwise or inartfully drawn, id., neither are we required to give our stamp of approval to classifications that are arbitrary or wholly insubstantial. See Delaware River Basin Commission v. Bucks County Water & Sewer Authority, 641 F.2d 1087, 1097 (3d Cir.1981) ("the rationality standard is not 'toothless'"). Whether or not the lawmakers' "governmental purpose" under review must be clearly articulated by the lawmakers in order to be deemed legitimate cannot be definitively answered by reference to Supreme Court precedent. Compare Fritz, 449 U.S. at 170, 101 S.Ct. at 456 with Fritz, 449 U.S. at 187, 101 S.Ct. at 466 (Brennan, J., dissenting) (citing Weinberger v. Wiesenfeld, 420 U.S. 636,

648 n. 16, 95 S.Ct. 1225, 1233 n. 16, 43 L.Ed.2d 514 (1975)). However, our own precedents teach us that "(s)o long as we are careful not to attribute to the legislature purposes which it cannot reasonably be understood to have entertained, we find that in examining the challenged provisions we may consider purposes advanced by counsel ... or suggested initially by ourselves." Delaware River Basin, 641 F.2d at 1092. Our job then, is to determine whether the common law doctrine challenged in this case is in furtherance of a legitimate state purpose put forward by the New Jersey Supreme Court, the appellees, the United States District Court for the District of New Jersey, or ourselves, and whether the common law rule fits closely enough with any of those purposes that it can be said to be rationally related to them. I conclude that New Jersey's common law rule creates a classification that is not rationally related to a legitimate governmental purpose, and therefore deprives asbestos manufacturers of the equal protection of the laws in violation of the Constitution of the United States. Before engaging in this constitutional analysis, I will review the line of cases in question.

II.

In Freund v. Cellofilm Properties, Inc., 87 N.J. 229, 432 A.2d 925 (1981), the New Jersey Supreme Court explained the difference between a failure to warn claim based on strict liability and a failure to warn claim based on negligence. Under either rubric, plaintiff will recover damages from the defendant if, given the dangerousness of the product, the manufacturer's failure to provide warnings was unreasonable. The failure to provide warnings will be found unreasonable if warnings would have made the product safer. Negligence and strict liability actions differ in the manner in which the manufacturer's knowledge of the product's dangerousness is determined. Where a negligence plaintiff must prove that the defendant knew or should have known of the dangerousness of the product, the defendant's knowledge of the product's dangers is presumed as a matter of law in the strict liability action. Thus, "negligence is conduct-oriented, asking whether defendant's actions were reasonable; strict liability is product-oriented, asking whether the product was reasonably safe for its foreseeable purposes." Beshada v. Johns-Manville Corp., 90 N.J. 191, 200, 447 A.2d 539, 544 (1982) (citing Freund, 87 N.J. at 238, 432 A.2d at 929).

In Beshada v. Johns-Manville Corp., the New Jersey Supreme Court decided that the state-of-the-art defense is inapplicable to a strict liability failure-to-warn claim. Through the state-of-the-art defense, defendants are able to introduce evidence of the technology available at the time the product was manufactured and distributed in order to prove that the state of scientific knowledge was such that they could not have known of the product's dangers when it was put into the stream of commerce. Id. 90 N.J. at 202, 447 A.2d at 545. The state-of-the-art defense is thus logically incompatible with Freund, which imputes knowledge to defendants as a matter of law. Moreover, because state-of-the-art is essentially a negligence defense, in that it *1254 seeks to explain why defendants are not culpable, it seems inappropriate in a strict liability case, in which culpability is irrelevant. Beshada, 90 N.J. at 204, 447 A.2d at 546. The court admitted that "the phrase 'duty to warn' is misleading, (because i)t implies negligence concepts with their attendant focus on the reasonableness of defendant's behavior." Id. Nevertheless, the court committed itself to strict liability in failure-to-warn cases, and firmly rejected the state-of-the-art defense.

In response to a torrent of criticism, the New Jersey Supreme Court departed from its stand against the state-of-the-art defense in Feldman v. Lederle Laboratories, 97 N.J. 429, 479 A.2d 374 (1984). In Feldman, the court concluded that strict liability for failure to warn was inherently illogical. "A warning that a product may have an unknowable danger warns one of nothing." Id. at 454, 479 A.2d at 387. The court did not eliminate the strict liability failure to warn cause of action, but chose instead to transform it. Where, in Freund and Beshada, strict liability actions were characterized by the imputation to defendant of knowledge of the product's dangerousness, in Feldman, they became characterized by the applicable burden of proof. "In strict liability warning cases the defendant should properly bear the burden of proving that the information was not reasonably available or obtainable and that it therefore lacked actual or constructive knowledge of the defect." Id. at 455-56, 479 A.2d at 388. The court refused to overrule Beshada, but did "restrict Beshada to the circumstances giving rise to its holding." Id.[1] It is in

---

[1] The meaning of this sentence is by no means clear on its face. Subsequent case law was has shown that "restricting Beshada to the circumstances giving rise to its holding" means that asbestos defendants are not permitted to use the state-of-the-art defense. See In re Asbestos Litigation Venued in Middlesex County, 99 N.J. 201, 491 A.2d 700

the context of this murky state of New Jersey "law" that we must address our problem.

III.

By "restrict(ing) Beshada to the circumstances giving rise to its holding," the New Jersey Supreme Court created the classification challenged here. My review of the Beshada-Feldman line of cases leads me to conclude that the challenged classification represents nothing more than an unprincipled, expedient, and ineffective response to widespread criticism of the Beshada doctrine combined with an unwillingness to give up the application of Beshada to asbestos manufacturers. If so, the Beshada-Feldman classification is undeniably arbitrary. Worse yet, I fear that the New Jersey Supreme Court's sole purpose may have been to inflict a special punishment on asbestos manufacturers. The Constitution does not permit the New Jersey courts to level either an arbitrary or a punitive sanction against asbestos manufacturers (or the manufacturer of any other product, for that matter). Proper analysis of this classification under the rational basis test should disclose to us whether the classification is impermissibly arbitrary or punitive. I will address each of the justifications for the common law rule advanced by Judge Weis and Judge Becker: the asbestos manufacturers' knowledge of the dangers of asbestos; case-management; and jury confusion.[2]

A.

Judge Weis and Judge Becker agree that the principal "legitimate state purpose" underlying the Beshada-Feldman

---

(1984). The restriction has not yet been applied to any other manufacturer, and there is no indication that it will be.

[2] In Beshada, the court articulated its reason for precluding the use of the state-of-the-art defense in all strict liability failure-to-warn cases. The court justified its ruling on the basis of traditional strict liability policy concerns: deep pockets, risk spreading and accident avoidance incentives. The articulation of purposes underlying the Beshada rule does not, however, provide any basis for the Feldman distinction, which limits the Beshada rule to one class of defendants alone.

doctrine is "the New Jersey Supreme Court('s reasonable decision) to preclude (the) endless relitigation of what was 'knowable' to the asbestos industry." Becker at 1245-46. According to Judge Weis, "(t)he (Feldman *1255) opinion suggests that (asbestos) manufacturers knew the dangers of asbestos and, consequently, the state-of-the-art defense (cannot) be sustained" by those manufacturers. Weis at 1241. Specifically, the New Jersey Supreme Court concluded in Feldman that "there were or may have been data or other information generally available, aside from scientific knowledge, that arguably could have alerted the manufacturer at an early stage ... to the dangers (of asbestos)." 97 N.J. at 456, 479 A.2d at 388. Thus, since the majority of this panel and the New Jersey Supreme Court claim to know for a certainty that all asbestos manufacturers either acted with full knowledge of the dangers of their product or could and should have obtained such knowledge, those manufacturers should not be permitted to litigate the knowledge question any further. I have trouble accepting this aim as a "legitimate state purpose" under the Equal Protection Clause, because I believe it violates the Due Process Clause of the Fourteenth Amendment. See U.S. Const. amend. XIV, Sec. 1 cl. 3.

This so-called legitimate state purpose can best be described as a de facto exercise of collateral estoppel without benefit of the procedural niceties. On the basis of the New Jersey Supreme Court's declaratory dicta in Feldman that asbestos manufacturers did indeed possess culpable knowledge at all relevant times, those manufacturers must be collaterally estopped from litigating the question of their knowledge ever again. Judge Weis feels that this "legitimate state purpose" is a creature somehow related to collateral estoppel, as his discussion of a series of fifth circuit opinions dealing with the procedural complexity of collateral estoppel in massive asbestos litigation demonstrates. His review of the line of cases culminating in the fifth circuit's opinion in Hardy v. Johns-Manville Sales Corp., ("Hardy II "), 681 F.2d 334 (5th Cir.1982), leads him to conclude that "Beshada 's broad language, when applied to the concrete facts of asbestos litigation and read together with Fischer (v. Johns-Manville Corp., 103 N.J. 643, 512 A.2d 466 (1986)), is not completely divorced from reality." Weis at 1242. I am not sure what this statement means, but it is clear that Judge Weis has concluded that, since plaintiffs have experienced difficulties in prevailing on their collateral estoppel motions heretofore, see, e.g., Hardy II, the courts may constitutionally grant all plaintiffs the benefit of collateral estoppel through application of their own wisdom rather than the traditional channels of legal process. I believe that Hardy II teaches a much different lesson than this. I read Hardy II as reiterating the well-worn legal principle that defendants will be collaterally estopped from relitigating factual issues where

> The party asserting the estoppel (can) show that: (1) the issue to be concluded is identical to that involved in the prior action; (2) in the prior action the issue was "actually litigated"; and (3) the determination made of the issue in the prior action (was) necessary and essential to the resulting judgment.

681 F.2d at 341. The grant of a collateral estoppel motion where these conditions are not met violates a party's right to due process. See Blonder-Tongue Laboratories, Inc. v. University of Illinois Found., 402 U.S. 313, 329, 91 S.Ct. 1434, 1443, 28 L.Ed.2d 788 (1971). A fortiori, Judge Weis' sua sponte grant of collateral estoppel to all future asbestos plaintiffs violates the Due Process Clause and thus cannot provide a legitimate state purpose under the rationality test. Indeed, "to use collateral estoppel in this context would be to 'elevate judicial expedience over considerations of justice and fair play.'" Weis at 1242 (quoting Hardy II, 681 F.2d at 348).

Judge Weis points out that, after its decision in Feldman, the New Jersey Supreme Court found that at least one asbestos manufacturer--Johns-Manville--did indeed have actual knowledge of the dangers of asbestos as early as the 1930's. See Fischer v. Johns-Manville Corp., 103 N.J. 643, 512 A.2d 466 (1986). I cannot understand how the subsequent adjudication of an unrelated party's culpable knowledge can render the Feldman court's attribution of knowability to all asbestos manufacturers *1256 by judicial fiat constitutional. This conclusion very simply does not satisfy the requirements of the collateral estoppel doctrine. It is a fundamental tenet of our procedural law that the court's factual findings in the Fischer case can only be used against Johns-Manville. "The requirement that a person against whom the conclusive effect of a judgment is invoked must be a party or a privy to the prior judgment ... has been repeatedly affirmed(.)" Hardy II, 681 F.2d at 338 (citations omitted). Accord Parklane Hosiery Co. v. Shore, 439 U.S. 322, 327 n. 7, 99 S.Ct. 645, 649 n. 7, 58 L.Ed.2d 552 (1979) ("It is a violation of due process for a judgment to be binding on a litigant who was not a party or a privy and therefore has never had an opportunity to be heard.") (citations omitted). Thus, with or without the Fischer court's adjudication of Johns-Manville's actual knowledge, the principle justification for the challenged classification asserted by Judge Weis is very simply not a legitimate state purpose for the New Jersey Supreme Court's discriminatory treatment of asbestos manufacturers.

B.

Judge Becker attempts to circumvent the collateral estoppel problem by characterizing the New Jersey Supreme Court's conclusion in Feldman "that the hazards of asbestos exposure were knowable to the industry at all relevant times," Becker at 1245, as a "legislative fact" of which the court may freely take judicial notice. I believe that Judge Becker's argument fails because it relies on a misapprehension of the nature of the legislative facts that may be judicially noticed under the common law of evidence. There are two kinds of fact of which courts may take judicial notice: "adjudicative" and "legislative."[3] "Adjudicative facts are simply the facts of the particular case." Fed.R.Evid. 201 advisory committee's note. "'Adjudicative facts,' ... are the ultimate facts in the case, plus those evidential facts that are sufficiently central to the controversy that they should be left to the jury unless clearly indisputable." 21 C. Wright & K. Graham, Federal Practice and Procedure section 5103, at 478 (1977). "Legislative facts, on the other hand, are those which have relevance to legal reasoning and the lawmaking process, whether in the formulation of a legal principle or ruling by a judge or court or in the enactment of a legislative body." Fed.R.Evid. 201 advisory committee's note.

My understanding of what constitutes a "legislative fact" seems to be at odds with Judge Becker's. In my view, legislative facts are those social, economic and philosophical facts upon which we rely to fashion just, appropriate and suitable rules of law. We derive these legislative facts from a common-sense assessment of how modern-day Americans live and view their world. Legislative

---

[3] The adjudicative fact-legislative fact dichotomy was first articulated by Professor Kenneth Culp Davis in 1942. See Davis, An Approach to Problems of Evidence in the Administrative Process, 55 Harv. L. Rev. 364, 404-07 (1942).

facts are broad conceptions or beliefs about the interaction of law and society that inform judicial policy-making. As such, these legislative facts may be truisms, or may be wholly incapable of proof or disproof. The United States Supreme Court regularly takes judicial notice of legislative facts to resolve cases involving major policy determinations in the areas of constitutional law and criminal procedure. See, e.g., Church of Latter-Day Saints v. Amos, --- U.S. ----, 107 S.Ct. 2862, 2875, 97 L.Ed.2d 273 (1987) (O'Connor, J., concurring) ("The determination of whether the objective observer will perceive an endorsement of religion 'is not a question of simple historical fact. Although evidentiary submissions may help answer it, the question is, like the question whether racial or sex-based classifications communicate an invidious message, in large part a legal question to be answered on the basis of judicial interpretation of social facts.'") (quoting Lynch v. Donnelly, 465 U.S. 668, 693-94, 104 S.Ct. 1355, 1369-70, 79 L.Ed.2d 604 (1984) (O'Connor, J., concurring)); United States v. Leon, 468 U.S. 897, 918-21, 104 S.Ct. 3405, 3418-19, 82 L.Ed.2d 677 (1984) (discussing the probable deterrent effect of the exclusionary *1257 rule on police officers); Detroit Edison Co. v. NLRB, 440 U.S. 301, 318, 99 S.Ct. 1123, 1132, 59 L.Ed.2d 333 (1979) ("The sensitivity of any human being to disclosure of information that may be taken to bear on his or her competence is sufficiently well known to be an appropriate subject of judicial notice." (footnote omitted)); Hawkins v. United States, 358 U.S. 74, 77-78, 79 S.Ct. 136, 138, 3 L.Ed.2d 125 (1958) ("The basic reason the law has refused to pit wife against husband or husband against wife in a trial where life or liberty is at stake was a belief that such a policy was necessary to foster family peace, not only for the benefit of husband, wife and children, but for the benefit of the public as well.... Adverse testimony given in criminal proceedings would, we think, be likely to destroy any marriage."); Brown v. Board of Education, 347 U.S. 483, 494, 74 S.Ct. 686, 691, 98 L.Ed. 873 (1954) ("To separate (Negro children) from others of similar age and qualifications solely because of their race generates a feeling of inferiority as to their status in the community that may affect their hearts and minds in a way unlikely ever to be undone.").

I realize, of course, that not all judicially noticed legislative facts involve the kinds of fundamental and glamorous policy questions central to the cases cited in the previous paragraph. Indeed, the observations made through the medium of judicial notice are just as likely to be obvious and mundane. See e.g., Kessler Inst. for Rehabilitation v. NLRB, 669 F.2d 138, 141 (3d Cir.1982) (court takes judicial notice of "the delays in the postal system which have been increasing over the years"); Neeld v. National Hockey League, 594 F.2d 1297, 1300 (9th Cir.1979) (court takes judicial notice of dangers posed by one-eyed hockey players to uphold rule barring such players from professional hockey teams). Furthermore, courts may take judicial notice of legislative facts for reasons totally unrelated to the development of policy. For example, courts regularly take judicial notice of legislative facts in order to determine whether or not particular activities come within specified statutory prohibitions. See, e.g., United States v. Gould, 536 F.2d 216, 220-21 (8th Cir.1976) (court takes judicial notice of fact that cocaine hydrochloride is derivative of the cocoa leaf in order to determine whether or not it is a Schedule II controlled substance). However, I have never heard of any case in which the resolution of an ultimate fact--e.g., the innocence or culpability of a products liability defendant--was reached through the judicial notice of legislative facts.

The asbestos manufacturers' actual or constructive knowledge of the potential harms of asbestos does not bear any resemblance to the legislative facts judicially noticed in the cases cited above or in any other case I have found. The knowledge question does not rest upon a generalized assumption or conclusion about the state of things in order to come to a rational policy decision; rather, it demands the resolution of a hard, cold, specific factual dispute that is central to the products liability litigation between the injured plaintiffs and defendant asbestos manufacturers before the court in each case. The question posed involves a determination of who knew what, when they knew it, and when they should have known it. To my way of thinking, this has every indicia of an adjudicative fact.

> When a court ... finds facts concerning the immediate parties--who did what, where, when, how, and with what motive or intent--the court ... is performing an adjudicative function, and the facts are conveniently called adjudicative facts....
>
> Stated in other terms, the adjudicative facts are those to which the law is applied in the process of adjudication. They are the facts that normally go to the jury in a jury case. They relate to the parties, their activities, their properties, their businesses.

Supp. Ch. 2   In re ASBESTOS LITIGATION

2 K. Davis, Administrative Law Treatise section 15.03, at 353 (1958) (quoted in Gould, 536 F.2d at 219).

Nor am I persuaded by Judge Becker's assertion in footnote 6 of the concurring opinion that "if the knowability of asbestos' harms were purely an adjudicative fact, it could not be the subject of a legislative *1258 fact-finding." Not every fact found by a legislature is necessarily legislative. Legislatures can and often do find facts that would undeniably be classified as "adjudicative" if they had been found in a judicial proceeding. For instance, in 1979 the House Select Committee on Assassinations found that

> A. Lee Harvey Oswald fired three shots at President John F. Kennedy. The second and third shots he fired struck the President. The third shot he fired killed the President.
>
> 1. President Kennedy was struck by two rifle shots fired from behind him.
>
> 2. The shots that struck President Kennedy from behind him were fired from the sixth floor window of the southeast corner of the Texas School Book Depository building.
>
> 3. Lee Harvey Oswald owned the rifle that was used to fire the shots from the sixth floor window of the southeast corner of the Texas School Book Depository building.
>
> 4. Lee Harvey Oswald, shortly before the assassination, had access to and was present on the sixth floor of the Texas School Book Depository building.
>
> 5. Lee Harvey Oswald's other actions tend to support the conclusion that he assassinated President Kennedy....

H.R.Rep. No. 1828, 95th Cong., 2d Sess. 1 (1979). Since these facts were found by a legislature, Judge Becker would characterize them as legislative facts. Thus, if Judge Becker's definition of "legislative fact" is correct, then we would have to reach the extraordinary conclusion that a court trying Lee Harvey Oswald for the murder of President Kennedy could take judicial notice of the "legislative fact" that Lee Harvey Oswald killed President Kennedy, and thereby the court could avoid the inconvenience of requiring the government to prove the ultimate fact in the case. It is beyond peradventure that such a use of judicial notice of "legislative facts" would constitute not only a denial of due process but also a violation of the bill of attainder clause. U.S. Const. art. I, section 10, cl. 1. Notwithstanding any legislative pronouncement on the matter and notwithstanding the firmness of the trial judge's belief of Oswald's guilt, the court could not deprive Oswald of his day in court simply because "he doesn't have a chance of winning, anyway." However, this is precisely the way that the Beshada-Feldman rule treats asbestos defendants. I believe that Judge Becker's attempt to characterize the knowability of asbestos harms as a "legislative fact" is misguided and does not justify our countenancing this pernicious rule.

My conclusion that the knowledge question requires the determination of an adjudicative rather than a legislative fact is buoyed by analogous decisions reached in two other asbestos cases. See Hardy II, 681 F.2d at 347-48; Laster v. Celotex Corp., 587 F.Supp. 542 (S.D.Ohio 1984). In Hardy and Laster, the courts were asked to take judicial notice of a fact closely related to the one before us--whether or not exposure to asbestos causes cancer, pleural mesothelioma or asbestosis. Without hesitation, both courts classified the fact to be noticed as an adjudicative fact. See Laster, 587 F.Supp. at 543 ("Clearly, the facts pertaining to whether asbestosis and mesothelioma are caused by exposure to asbestos are 'adjudicative facts' under Rule 201."). The causation issue clearly requires the resolution of an adjudicative (rather than a legislative) fact for the same reasons that the knowledge or knowability issue does. First, like the question of knowledge, the question of asbestos' role in the development of certain diseases "relate(s) to the (immediate) parties, their activities, (and) their businesses," and thus must be classified as an adjudicative fact. More importantly, disease causation and culpable knowledge are both ultimate facts in products liability litigation,[4] and cannot *1259 be properly resolved by

---

[4] In footnote 6 of the concurring opinion, Judge Becker urges that the knowability vel non of the harms of a particular product is not an ultimate fact in a strict liability-failure to warn case. I respectfully disagree. "'Ultimate' facts are those which the law makes the occasion for imposing its sanctions." The Evergreens v. Nunan, 141 F.2d 927, 928 (2d Cir.1944) (Hand, J.) "Ultimate facts" describe those specific historical or narrative facts which are decisive to the outcome of a particular case because their proof is absolutely necessary to establish

judicial notice of legislative facts.[5] See Korematsu v.

---

the elements of a claim or defense. See Winters v. Lavine, 574 F.2d 46, 57-58 n. 12 (2d Cir.1978). Clearly, the unknowability of harms associated with a particular product is the ultimate narrative or historic fact that a producer of that product must prove in order to establish the state-of-the-art defense.

[5] Judge Becker argues that adjudicative facts may be "elevated to legislative facts" and relied upon to shape judicial decisions in later litigation. See Becker at 1250. I express no opinion on this statement as a general matter. However, I find the proposition faulty as applied to the instant case for two reasons. First, prior to its development of the Beshada-Feldman classification, the New Jersey Supreme Court had never found as an adjudicative fact that any asbestos manufacturer had knowledge of the potential harms of asbestos. Admittedly, such a finding was made in Fischer, but that case was decided two years after Feldman, and could not have provided a basis for the Beshada-Feldman classification. To the extent that the New Jersey Supreme Court may have relied on the Borel-Hardy line of cases, such reliance is undercut by the fifth circuit's rejection in Hardy II of a lower court's effort to rely on facts adjudicated in previous cases by means of collateral estoppel or judicial notice. Furthermore, I do not think adjudicative facts can possibly be elevated to the level of legislative facts unless a certain degree of consensus has been reached in the earlier litigation. Otherwise, judges may be tempted to reach into an uncertain and confusing mass of conflicting decisions and--shunning the restraints imposed by the laws of evidence and collateral estoppel--pull out the result most to their liking. Such procedures run afoul of the proper presentation of proof in our adversary system. I hasten to remind Judge Becker that "(t)he doctrines of 'legislative facts' and 'judicial notice' are not talismans by which gaps in a litigant's evidentiary presentation may be repaired on appeal." City of New Brunswick v. Borough of Milltown, 686 F.2d 120, 131 n. 15 (3d Cir.1982), cert. denied, 459 U.S. 1201, 103 S.Ct. 1184, 75 L.Ed.2d 431 (1983).

For similar reasons, I think that the statement by Professor Davis quoted by Judge Becker on page 1247 of the concurrence does not support his judicial notice thesis. First of all, I do not believe that Professor Davis was thinking about the propriety of applying a fact adjudicated in one or a handful of products liability cases against an entire industry. I think his concern was with the ability of judicial and administrative tribunals to fashion regulatory rules on the basis of generalized observations about a specific industry. Second, I cannot believe that Professor Davis would approve of the development of an industry-wide "legislative fact" on the basis of a fact adjudicated about only one company in the industry. I am certain that he would require

United States, 584 F. Supp. 1406, 1415 (N.D.Cal.1984). If judicial notice can be taken of such ultimate facts at all, it can only be within the strictures of Fed.R.Evid. 201.

A court may only take judicial notice of an adjudicative fact where that fact is "generally known within the territorial jurisdiction of the trial court(; and) ... capable of accurate and ready determination by resort to sources whose accuracy cannot reasonably be questioned." Fed.R.Evid. 201. Even assuming that some potential hazards of asbestos were known in the 1930's, it is by no means "generally known" or indisputable that the various specific uses of asbestos (e.g., the use of asbestos to insulate automobile brake linings) were all known to be hazardous to *1260 workers or consumers as far back as the 1930's. The fifth circuit and the Southern District of Ohio were not even willing to take judicial notice of the fact that asbestos necessarily causes the various diseases with which it has been associated. According to the fifth circuit in Hardy II, "(t)he proposition that asbestos causes cancer, because it is inextricably linked to a host of disputed issues--... (including whether or not) this manufacturer (was) reasonably unaware of the asbestos hazards in 1964--is not at present so self-evident a proposition as to be subject to judicial notice." Hardy II, 681 F.2d at 347-48. Similarly, the issue of knowledge or knowability is "not at present so self-evident a proposition to be subject to judicial notice." Therefore, the issue of knowledge or knowability cannot properly be judicially noticed as an adjudicative fact under Fed.R.Evid. 201.

Fed.R.Evid. 201 also provides that "(a) party is entitled upon timely request to an opportunity to be heard as to the propriety of taking judicial notice and the tenor of the matter noticed." The parties in this case were not given such an opportunity. Judge Becker argues that "the affected industry (i.e., asbestos manufacturers) had relevant opportunities to respond to the New Jersey Supreme Court's determination of the pertinent legislative facts." Becker at 1249. The significant opportunities cited by Judge Becker include the industry's participation in two fifth circuit cases, Hardy and Borel, and in two cases decided by the New

---

some broader consensus about industry-wide knowledge before elevating an adjudicative fact about Johns-Manville to a legislative fact about all asbestos manufacturers.

Jersey Supreme Court after the Beshada-Feldman classification had been developed, Fischer and In re Asbestos Litigation Venued in Middlesex County, 99 N.J. 201, 491 A.2d 700 (1984). Judge Becker's conclusion is unprecedented. I have never heard of any case that has permitted a party's "opportunity to be heard" to be satisfied in subsequent litigation before the same court, or--even more incredibly--in prior litigation before an unrelated tribunal. Furthermore, even if Judge Becker's remarkable conclusion were to be accepted, it does not satisfy the requirements of Fed.R.Evid. 201, which requires the court to provide "an opportunity to be heard <u>as to the propriety of taking judicial notice</u>," Fed.R.Evid. 201 (emphasis added), not simply an opportunity to be heard on the merits. I find the New Jersey Supreme Court's failure to give the asbestos manufacturers an opportunity to be heard as to the propriety of taking judicial notice understandable, in light of the fact that they probably did not realize they were taking judicial notice (of either a legislative or an adjudicative fact) until so informed by Judge Becker.

In sum, Judge Becker has grasped the notion of legislative facts--a notion that this court has viewed with the greatest of skepticism, City of New Brunswick, 686 F.2d at 131--in an attempt to fix the broken shell of the Beshada decision and to patch-over New Jersey's violation of the Equal Protection and Due Process clauses. "All the King's horses...."

C.

Judge Weis observes that although "(a)dministrative convenience standing alone is not an adequate ground for the elimination of a substantive defense ... (the court) cannot help but be conscious of the extraordinary size of the asbestos personal injury litigation." Weis at 1243. While Judge Weis has rejected explicit reliance on the case management rationale as an independent justification for the Beshada-Feldman classification, he continues to believe that it buttresses the other justifications he has put forward. Because I find none of the other arguments advanced by Judge Weis or Judge Becker persuasive, I will examine the administrative convenience argument separately to determine whether it provides any support for the challenged classification. I find that it does not. The simple fact that elimination of a defense for one group saves time is not enough to justify discriminating between that group and another that is similarly situated. The case management rationale simply cannot provide a legitimate basis for depriving this one class of manufacturers of an exculpatory defense, particularly in light of the massive expenditure of court time and judicial energy required by DES, Dalkon Shield, Agent Orange *1261 and miscellaneous pharmaceutical and environmental disaster litigation. I do not mean to imply that the Fourteenth Amendment bars any effort to address a perceived crisis in a particular kind of litigation; legislatures all over the country have demonstrated that such crises can be dealt with constitutionally by developing means that are rationally related to the aim of averting them.

Judge Weis looks to the nationwide enactment of no-fault automobile insurance statutes to provide support by analogy for the Beshada-Feldman classification. Due to the extreme diversity of these statutes, I have limited myself to an examination of the laws of New Jersey and Pennsylvania to determine whether Judge Weis' reliance is justified. The New Jersey Automotive Reparation Act, N.J. Stat. Ann. 39:6A-8 (West 1973 & Supp.1986), "bars suit for bodily injury ... unless the injury either is permanent as opposed to 'soft-tissue,' or requires treatment with a cost or equivalent value of $200." Rybeck v. Rybeck, 141 N.J. Super. 481, 488, 358 A.2d 828, 832 (Law Div.1976). Similarly, the Pennsylvania No-fault Motor Vehicle Insurance Act, 40 Pa.Stat.Ann. section 1009.301(a)(5)(B) (repealed 1984) (Purdon Supp.1987), permitted only those victims whose medical expenses exceed $750 to sue in tort. Singer v. Sheppard, 464 Pa. 387, 403, 346 A.2d 897, 905 (1975). Both statutes were upheld in the face of numerous constitutional challenges, including the discriminatory deprivation of tort recovery for victims of lesser injuries. The state courts determined that such a distinction served a legitimate state purpose:

> (A)uto accident injury claims were reasonably seen by the Legislature to present a special problem requiring reform. It was that class of claims that created the calendar congestion, that ate up the investigative and administrative insurance dollar, that represented justice worst delayed, and that most invited compensation without fault determination.

Rybeck, 141 N.J. Super. at 498, 358 A.2d at 837. Further, the state courts were convinced that the discrimination against victims of minor injuries created a classification that was rationally related to the achievement of the legitimate state purpose. See Singer, 464 Pa. at 403, 346 A.2d at 905. So am I. Wresting the adjudication of minor injuries from state courts and assuring those victims of a certain and sure recovery through the insurance system is rationally related to the state's purpose of relieving an overburdened court docket. This method of case-management bears no resemblance to one that simply deprives one class of litigants of a potentially exculpatory defense. Any victim whose injuries reach the threshhold amount is entitled to go to court and present his negligence claim like any other tort plaintiff; and the defendant is entitled to use all common law defenses available. Thus, dockets are streamlined without either party losing any legal right.

According to Judge Weis, workers' compensation programs share with no-fault auto insurance plans "(the common goal) of simplifying the fact-finding process and thus making it easier for victims to recover." Weis at 1243. This is not my understanding of the goal of workers' compensation statutes. I had always learned that they were developed as a kind of social insurance based on the policy decision that the compensation of workers' injuries should be absorbed by the employer as a cost of doing business. See New York Cent. R. Co. v. White, 243 U.S. 188, 205, 37 S.Ct. 247, 253, 61 L.Ed. 667 (1917). Furthermore, I do not think that the classification created by the workers' compensation statutes even represents a useful analogy to the Beshada-Feldman classification. Workers' compensation statutes create a classification based on the ongoing relationship between the employer and the employee, not on the personal (or corporate) identities of those parties outside of that relationship. Manufacturers of asbestos owe no greater duty to their employees under these statutes than do purveyors of paper clips. Workers' compensation statutes are analogous to inter-familial tort immunity and guest-host statutes, but not *1262 to the discriminatory treatment of asbestos manufacturers challenged here.[6]

---

[6] Judge Weis' observation that "the doctrine of strict liability is in itself a classification that imposes discriminatory liability on a particular group of defendants," Weis at 1243, is similarly misleading. Restatement (Second) of Torts, section 402A (1965), sets out a special standard of strict liability to be used by consumers against retailers and manufacturers. This special standard is not discriminatorily applied to such defendants because of who they are, however, but because of what they do, i.e., put products into the stream of commerce. It is the activity, not the particular defendant, that triggers the application of strict liability. If the same defendant injures an individual through a means other than product manufacture and distribution, in a mundane

D.

The final "legitimate state purpose" advanced by Judge Weis is the reduction of jury confusion through the complete elimination of the state-of-the-art defense in asbestos cases. The Beshada court had observed that "vast confusion is virtually certain to arise from any attempt to deal in a trial setting with the concept of scientific knowability," Beshada, 90 N.J. at 207, 447 A.2d at 548, and that "discussion of state-of-the-art could easily confuse juries into believing that blame-worthiness is at issue." Id. This confusion does not stem from the nature of asbestos litigation, however, but from the interplay of the strict liability failure-to-warn action with the state-of-the-art defense. See Beshada, 90 N.J. at 204, 447 A.2d at 546. The likelihood of jury confusion provides a justification for one of two paths not taken by the New Jersey Supreme Court: (a) the elimination of a strict liability cause of action requiring the defendant to warn of the unknown and unknowable through the reversal of Freund and Beshada; or (b) the continued unavailability of the state-of-the-art defense to any defendant in a strict liability failure-to-warn action. The New Jersey Supreme Court balked and refused to make this difficult choice. The jury confusion rationale is, in my opinion, totally undermined by the New Jersey Supreme Court's recent decision in Fischer v. Johns-Manville Corp., 103 N.J. 643, 512 A.2d 466 (1986), holding that punitive damages were available to plaintiffs against asbestos defendants in strict liability failure-to-warn cases. The evidence introduced to determine a punitive damages award is the very same evidence--the state of scientific knowledge at the time of manufacture--that is relied upon in a state-of-the-art defense. Thus, if jury confusion is to be minimized by the exclusion of such evidence, the Fischer rule is sure to restore that confusion by the introduction of such evidence. I think the Fischer holding is fatal to the jury confusion

---

slip and fall action, for example, that defendant will be liable for negligence only. Differential regulation of different kinds of activities pervades tort law and all other areas of public and private law, from criminal law to conflict of interests. Furthermore, strict liability is not exclusively reserved for use against miscreant manufacturers and retailers, but is also available for use against participants in "abnormally dangerous activities." See Restatement (Second) of Torts section 520 (1977).

rationale.

CONCLUSION

My position by no means constitutes the establishment of tort law for New Jersey. It simply means that since New Jersey common law is subject to the operation of the Equal Protection Clause, that clause quite plainly works to bar New Jersey from depriving asbestos manufacturers alone of the state-of-the-art defense, a defense that is available to all other manufacturers in products liability cases. The Supreme Court of New Jersey simply cannot establish a law that violates the Federal Constitution. And this court cannot look the other way and ignore its duty to defend that Constitution.

My answer to the question presented is that the judicially imposed denial of the state-of-the-art defense to manufacturers of asbestos-containing products does constitute a violation of the Equal Protection Clause of the Constitution.

QUESTIONS:

1. Can you frame a proposed legal rule that would make the "knowability" of asbestos hazards an adjudicative fact in each case in which an asbestosis victim sues one or more asbestos manufacturers?

2. Can you frame a proposed legal rule that would make the "knowability" of asbestos hazards a premise fact to be decided by the state court of last resort, and once having been decided to be controlling not only for the case then decided but as well for all cases presented thereafter for adjudication?

Supp. Ch. 2

LANGAN
v.
VALICOPTERS, INC.

Supreme Court of Washington, En Banc. Aug. 4, 1977.
567 P.2d 218, 88 Wash.2d 855.

Organic farmers brought action for crop damage allegedly caused by aerial spraying of agricultural pesticides. The Superior Court, Yakima County, Blaine Hopp, Jr., J., entered judgment against defendants and they appealed. The Court of Appeals, Third Division, certified case to the Supreme Court which accepted certification. The Supreme Court, Dolliver, J., held that: (1) evidence supported finding that plaintiffs had suffered damage as result of crop spraying; (2) liability for damage caused by crop dusting or spraying is imposed on basis of strict liability, and (3) plaintiff farmer's testimony that helicopter flew over his house at low level while spray was turned on and administrative rule prohibiting pilots during spraying operations from flying directly over occupied structure except with permission of occupants, supported instruction on wanton misconduct.

Affirmed.

*219 DOLLIVER, Associate Justice.

This is an appeal from a judgment against appellants for damages resulting from their crop spraying activities. Patrick and Dorothy Langan, respondents, own a small (2 1/2 to 3 acre) farm in the Yakima Valley. The Langans are organic farmers: that is, they use no nonorganic fertilizers, insecticides or herbicides to aid them in their farming but rely on natural fertilizers and natural pest control agents. They had planned to can and sell their produce to organic food buyers.

Valicopters, Inc., is a Washington corporation which engages in the aerial application of agricultural pesticides. Gene Bepple, one of the owners of Valicopters, Inc., was the helicopter pilot at the time of the incident giving rise to this lawsuit. The Thalheimers, doing business as Thalheimer Farms, owned and farmed the land adjoining that of the respondents. It was their land that was being sprayed by Valicopters. Simplot Soilbuilders sold the agricultural chemical to Thalheimers for aerial application.

On June 3, 1973, Bepple sprayed for Colorado beetle

infestation on the Thalheimer farm with a chemical pesticide known as Thiodan. A small patch of the farm was sprayed with the chemical Guthion. While applying the pesticides to Thalheimers' property, Bepple traveled approximately 45 miles per hour while 6 to 8 feet off the ground with a 42-foot application boom extending from the sides of the helicopter. Patrick Langan testified that, during one spraying pass, the helicopter began spraying while it was over his property. This testimony was disputed. He further testified that the spray settled on the entire length of their tomato, bean, garlic, cucumber and Jerusalem artichoke rows.

The Langans and other organic farmers founded and are members of the Northwest Organic Food Producers' Association (NOFPA). The bylaws of NOFPA contain the following pertinent provisions:

> 7. No poisonous insecticides, repellents, herbicides, artificial fertilizers, stimulants or hormones may be used on food or in soil in which products are grown or animals are grazed. If any such item is applied by the grower to any committed acreage that has been previously committed and certified, the acreage will be withdrawn from certification and this farmer cannot be recertified without approval of the Executive Committee.

> 9. No member shall be allowed to market foods or advertise food as certified organically grown by NOFPA if laboratory tests on the finished crop indicates (sic) the presence of more than ten percent (10%) of the maximum pesticide residue tolerances allowable by the Food and Drug Administration. In the event the finished crop reflects a residue higher than the allowable tolerances set forth in this section, the member's seal for any such crop shall immediately be suspended and public notice made thereof.

NOFPA Bylaws, art. 4, §§ 7, 9.

A laboratory test conducted after the spraying indicated the presence of 1.4 parts per million by weight of Thiodan on the Langans' crop tissue. The United States ***220** Department of Health, Education and Welfare, Food and Drug Administration's tolerance for Thiodan on tomatoes and beans is 2.0 parts per million. Following the test results, the Board of Directors of NOFPA revoked the Langans' certification as organic food growers in conformance with bylaw No. 7. The Langans' entire property was decertified in conformance with the NOFPA rule which requires decertification when a portion of the land is contaminated.

Due to the decertification, the Langans did not grow their tomatoes and beans to fruition. Instead, they pulled them from the ground to prevent further contamination of the soil. The Langans had no contract to sell the contaminated tomatoes and beans commercially.

After a jury trial, a judgment in the amount of $5,500 was entered against appellants. They appealed to the Court of Appeals, Division Three. That court certified the case to this court and we accepted certification.

At the outset, it must be determined whether there was substantial evidence to support the jury's finding that respondents' damage occurred as a result of the spraying. Appellants contend that NOFPA erroneously interpreted its own bylaws. They argue that neither rule No. 7 nor rule No. 9 required immediate decertification of appellants' property and that the tomatoes and beans should have been tested for chemicals when those crops had fully matured. The bylaws of that organization are essentially a contract between NOFPA and its members. See Rodruck v. Sand Point Maintenance Comm'n, 48 Wash.2d 565, 295 P.2d 714 (1956). In construing a contract, the intention of the parties will be given great, if not controlling, weight. See Kennedy v. Weyerhaeuser Tbr. Co., 54 Wash.2d 766, 344 P.2d 1025 (1959).

A director of NOFPA testified that their interpretation of rule No. 7, coupled with the basic purpose of NOFPA (to insure consumers that the products are organically grown if they are sold under the organization's seal) required decertification of respondents' farm. The Langans apparently agreed with this interpretation and did not question the legitimacy of the decertification. This decertification, which prompted the Langans to pull the crops, provided substantial evidence for the jury to conclude that they suffered damage as a result of crop spraying.

The next issue is whether the trial court erred by instructing the jury that appellants would be strictly liable for damage that was proximately caused by their aerial spraying. The trial judge gave the following instruction:

> If you find that defendants' chemicals fell upon plaintiffs' crops, you are instructed that as a matter

of law the defendants are liable for such damage to plaintiffs' crops, if any, as you find was proximately caused by defendants' spray application.

Liability for damage caused by crop dusting or spraying generally is imposed on the basis of either negligence or strict liability. See generally Liability for Injury Caused by Spraying or Dusting of Crops, Annot., 37 A.L.R.2d 833 (1971). The courts in most jurisdictions that have held crop dusters liable have used the theory of negligence. See, e.g., Lundberg v. Bolon, 67 Ariz. 259, 194 P.2d 454 (1948); Hammond Ranch Corp. v. Dodson, 199 Ark. 846, 136 S.W.2d 484 (1940); Miles v. A. Arena & Co., 23 Cal.App.2d 680, 73 P.2d 1260 (1937); Binder v. Perkins, 213 Kan. 365, 516 P.2d 1012 (1973). However, other opinions which have ostensibly relied upon the principles of negligence have been criticized by legal writers because the reasoning is not clear or more nearly resembles strict liability. Comment, Crop Dusting: Two Theories of Liability?, 19 Hastings L.J. 476, 482-89 (1968); Note, Crop Dusting: Legal Problems in a New Industry, 6 Stan.L.Rev. 69, 75-80 (1953).

Three jurisdictions have held crop dusting to be an activity to which the principles of strict liability apply. Young v. Darter, 363 P.2d 829 (Okla.1961); Loe v. Lenhardt, 227 Or. 242, 362 P.2d 312 (1961); Gotreaux v. Gary, 232 La. 373, 94 So.2d 293 (1957) (applying civil law). In Loe v. Lenhardt, supra, *221 Justice Goodwin, writing for the majority, noted that the dangers of spraying agricultural chemicals by aircraft has been the subject of considerable legislative attention nationwide, citing the laws of 29 states. These laws, he concluded, were evidence of the dangerous character of aerial spraying. The court recognized the activity was one capable of inflicting damage notwithstanding the exercise of utmost care by the applicator, and that the damage was within the scope of the risk created by spraying an adjoining field. The court cited Bedell v. Goulter, 199 Or. 344, 362-63, 261 P.2d 842 (1953), a case involving strict liability for blasting, in which it stated:

> " * * * Basic to the problem is 'an adjustment of conflicting interests', ... of the right of the blaster, on the one hand, to pursue a lawful occupation and the right of an owner of land, on the other, to its peaceful enjoyment and possession. Where damage is sustained by the latter through the nonculpable activities of the former, who should bear the loss--the man who caused it

or a 'third person', as Judge Hand says, 'who has no relation to the explosion, other than that of injury'?"

Loe v. Lenhardt, supra 227 Or. at 253, 362 P.2d at 318.

In Washington, this court has adopted the Restatement (Second) of Torts §§ 519, 520 (Tent.Draft No. 10, 1964). Pacific Northwest Bell Tel. Co. v. Port of Seattle, 80 Wash.2d 59, 491 P.2d 1037 (1971); Siegler v. Kuhlman, 81 Wash.2d 448, 502 P.2d 1181 (1972). Section 519 of the Restatement provides:

> (1) One who carries on an abnormally dangerous activity is subject to liability for harm to the person, land or chattels of another resulting from the activity, although he has exercised the utmost care to prevent such harm.
>
> (2) Such strict liability is limited to the kind of harm, the risk of which makes the activity abnormally dangerous.

Section 520 lists the factors to be used when determining what constitutes an abnormally dangerous activity:

> In determining whether an activity is abnormally dangerous, the following factors are to be considered:
>
> (a) Whether the activity involves a high degree of risk of some harm to the person, land or chattels of others;
>
> (b) Whether the gravity of the harm which may result from it is likely to be great;
>
> (c) Whether the risk cannot be eliminated by the exercise of reasonable care;
>
> (d) Whether the activity is not a matter of common usage;
>
> (e) Whether the activity is inappropriate to the place where it is carried on; and
>
> (f) The value of the activity to the community.

Whether an activity is abnormally dangerous is a question of law for the court to decide. Siegler v. Kuhlman, supra ;

Restatement (Second) of Torts § 520, comment (1) (Tent.Draft No. 10, 1964). In making this determination, we have considered each of the factors listed in the Restatement, § 520. We note that not all of the elements listed in § 520 must weigh equally in favor of characterizing an activity as abnormally dangerous in order that we may so find it to be.

> In determining whether the danger is abnormal, the factors listed in Clauses (a) to (f) of this Section are all to be considered, and are all of importance. Any one of them is not necessarily sufficient of itself in a particular case, and ordinarily several of them will be required for strict liability. Because of the interplay of these various factors, it is not possible to reduce abnormally dangerous activities to any exact definition. The essential question is whether the risk created is so unusual, either because of its magnitude or because of the circumstances surrounding it, as to justify the imposition of strict liability for the harm which results from it, even though it is carried on with all reasonable care.

Restatement (Second) of Torts § 520, comment (f) (Tent.Draft No. 10, 1964). See, generally Peck, Negligence and Liability *222 Without Fault in Tort Law, 46 Wash.L.Rev. 225 (1971). However, in this case, each test of the Restatement is met.

§ 520(a): Whether the activity involves a high degree of risk of some harm to the person, land or chattels of others.

It is undisputed among the authorities cited to us that crop dusting involves an element of risk of harm. In Note, Crop Dusting: Legal Problems in a New Industry, 6 Stan.L.Rev. at 72-75, the author points out that the drift of chemicals is virtually unpredictable due to three "uncertain and uncontrollable factors: (1) the size of the dust or spray particles; (2) the air disturbances created by the (applicating aircraft); and (3) natural atmospheric forces." The author discusses these three factors in detail and notes:

> In the opinion of leading scientists who are working to alleviate the dangers of crop dusting, it is impossible to eliminate drift with present knowledge and equipment. Experience bears this out.

6 Stan.L.Rev. at 75. The author states further that the problem of drift is reduced but not eliminated by the use of helicopters. Subsequent commentators have made the same

observations about the uncontrollability of drift. See, e. g., Comment, Crop Dusting: Two Theories of Liability?, supra at 477-79. In this case, there is no evidence that it is possible to eliminate the risk of drift in crop spraying.

§ 520(b): Whether the gravity of the harm which may result from it is likely to be great.

Whether there will be great harm depends upon what adjoining property owners do with their land. For example, one property owner may grow wheat (a narrow-leafed crop) and his neighbor may grow peas (a broad-leafed crop). The wheat farmer may wish to spray his crop with the chemical herbicide (weed killer) 2,4-D, which kills only broad-leafed plants. If the 2,4-D drifts onto the pea farmer's property, his entire crop could be destroyed since peas are broad-leafed plants. Frear, Chemistry of Insecticides, Fungicides and Herbicides 316 (2d ed. 1948). The reported cases are illustrative of the many possible fact situations which indicate that neighboring property may be sensitive to and damaged by the spraying activity of an adjoining landowner. See Comment, Crop Dusting: Two Theories of Liability?, 19 Hastings L.J. 476, 479, n. 38. The cases cited in that note include the following situations: Gerrard Co. v. Fricker, 42 Ariz. 503, 27 P.2d 678 (1933) (bees killed by insecticide Dutox No. 20); Bynum Cooperage Co. v. Coulter, 219 Ark. 818, 244 S.W.2d 955 (1952) (cotton damaged by 2,4-D); McPherson v. Billington, 399 S.W.2d 186 (Tex.Civ.App.1965) (hogs killed by arsenical). The extent of damage can be very high. See, e. g., Crouse v. Wilbur-Ellis Co., 77 Ariz. 359, 272 P.2d 352 (1954) (plaintiff recovered $10,000 when his cantaloupe crop was damaged by insecticide containing sulphur); Sanders v. Beckwith, 79 Ariz. 67, 283 P.2d 235 (1955) (plaintiff recovered $10,000 when his dairy herd was injured by DDT and benzene hexachloride).

As the present case illustrates, it is economically damaging for an organic farmer who is a member of NOFPA to apply nonorganic materials to his crops because he would lose the association's certification. There was substantial evidence before the trial court that, once an organic farmer loses his certification, it is highly unlikely that he will be able to sell his crops on the regular commercial market due to his failure to enter into contracts with commercial produce buyers before the season begins, and, even if he could sell his crops to a commercial produce buyer, the farmer would be unable to command as high a price for his goods as he could on the organic market.

§ 520(c): Whether the risk cannot be eliminated by the exercise of reasonable care.

The same elements that produce a high degree of risk of harm, namely the uncontrollability of dust or spray drift (s 520(a) above), also cannot be eliminated by the exercise of reasonable care. See Note, Crop *223 Dusting: Legal Problems in a New Industry, supra at 75.

§ 520(d): Whether the activity is not a matter of common usage.

The Restatement (Second) of Torts, § 520(i) (Tent.Draft No. 10, 1964), observes "An activity is a matter of common usage if it is customarily carried on by the great mass of mankind, or by many people in the community." Although we recognize the prevalence of crop dusting and acknowledge that it is ordinarily done in large portions of the Yakima Valley, it is carried on by only a comparatively small number of persons (approximately 287 aircraft were used in 1975) and is not a matter of common usage.

§ 520(e): Whether the activity is inappropriate to the place where it is carried on.

Given the nature of organic farming, the use of pesticides adjacent to such an area must be considered an activity conducted in an inappropriate place.

s 520(f): The value of the activity to the community.

As a criterion for determining strict liability, this factor has received some criticism among legal writers. In 2 Harper & James, Law of Torts, Comment to § 14.4 (Supp. 1968), the authors suggest that § 520(f) is not a true element of strict liability: "The justification for strict liability, in other words, is that useful but dangerous activities must pay their own way." See also Note, Regulation and Liability in the Application of Pesticides, 49 Iowa L.Rev. 135, 144-45 (1963).

There is no doubt that pesticides are socially valuable in the control of insects, weeds and other pests. They may benefit society by increasing production. Whether strict liability or negligence principles should be applied amounts to a balancing of conflicting social interest the risk of harm versus the utility of the activity. In balancing these interests, we must ask who should bear the loss caused by the pesticides. See Note, Regulation and Liability in the Application of Pesticides, supra ; Prosser, Law of Torts § 59 (2d ed. 1955); Siegler v. Kuhlman, 81 Wash.2d 448, 502 P.2d 1181 (1972) (Rosellini, J., concurring).

In the present case, the Langans were eliminated from the organic food market for 1973 through no fault of their own. If crop dusting continues on the adjoining property, the Langans may never be able to sell their crops to organic food buyers. Appellants, on the other hand, will all profit from the continued application of pesticides. Under these circumstances, there can be an equitable balancing of social interests only if appellants are made to pay for the consequences of their acts.

We realize that farmers are statutorily bound to prevent the spread of insects, pests, noxious weeds and diseases. RCW 15.08.030 and RCW 17.10.140-.150. But the fulfillment of that duty does not mean the ability of an organic farmer to produce organic crops must be destroyed without compensation.

Thus, for the reasons mentioned above, we find that the trial court did not err by instructing the jury on strict liability.

It is next contended by all appellants that the trial court erred when it gave the following instruction on wanton misconduct:

> Wanton misconduct is the intentionally doing of an act which one has a duty to refrain from doing or the intentional failure to do an act which he has a duty to do, in reckless disregard of the consequences and under such surrounding circumstances and conditions that a reasonable man would know, or should know, that such conduct would, in a high degree of probability, result in substantial harm to another's property.

The respondents contend that sufficient evidence is provided by the testimony of Patrick Langan. He testified that the helicopter flew over himself and his house at a low level while the spray was turned on. Respondents claim that this was in violation of WAC 16-235-050, which provides:

*224 Aircraft pilots during spraying operations, are prohibited from turning and/or low flying ... (2) directly over an occupied structure such as a residence, ... except by permission of the person(s) whose occupied structure is involved.

Appellants simply claim that this evidence is insufficient to support the instruction given.

Each party is entitled to have his theory of the case presented to the jury if there is substantial evidence to support it. Hester v. Watson, 74 Wash.2d 924, 448 P.2d 320 (1968). We think Mr. Langan's testimony and the administrative rule amply support the giving of this instruction.

There is no reversible error; the judgment of the trial court is affirmed.

WRIGHT, C. J., ROSELLINI, HAMILTON, STAFFORD, UTTER, HOROWITZ and HICKS, JJ., and HENRY, J. Pro Tem., concur.

PART TWO

MAKING AND EXPLAINING LAWMAKING CHOICES

Reading Cases in Part Two to Understand Not Only the Decisions But Also the Decisionmaking

As the course description at the beginning of this Course Supplement discloses, you will be examining the role of courts in lawmaking choices among many varied legal tests of <u>culpability, accountability, and immunity</u>. In the editor's view (which, of course, you are invited to challenge), in every case in this Supplement the court made one or more choices that adopted, as law, a test of culpability, accountability, or immunity that had not previously been stated in authoritative sources such as constitutions, statutes, and precedents. Read the case to identify the lawmaking choice or choices the court made. At some point, you may wish to reread the cases in Chapters 1 and 2 with this perspective in mind.

As you read cases in Chapter 3, especially, consider each legal test for deciding cases that you understand the court to have adopted, and <u>describe the test precisely if you think the opinion clearly defines it</u>. Is it in part at least a state-of-mind test? If you think the opinion is ambiguous, describe each of the tests it might reasonably be interpreted as adopting. If a state-of-mind test is adopted, precisely what is the state of mind that is a prerequisite to accountability or immunity? If a test has objective elements, precisely what are they?

Who will apply the test in a particular controversy

on trial -- judge or jury? If jury, what precisely should the judge say to the jury to explain to them the question or questions "of fact" that they are to decide in applying the test to the case on trial? To help you think about what the judge should say to the jury, this Course Supplement includes some excerpts from jury charges. The content of a jury charge is subject to substantial variation at the discretion of the trial judge. Whether "typical" or not, however, these excerpts will serve as examples that you may evaluate in thinking about what a trial judge should say to a jury to explain a test of accountability or immunity.

What difference does it make for the outcome of future cases that the court adopted the test it chose rather than another that was proposed in dissenting opinions or by one or another of the advocates, or some other test you would propose? Will the court's lawmaking choice have substantial effect on the outcome of future cases? On who pays any judgments for damages, as well as who is declared liable?

Should a court consider any or all of these questions before it makes its lawmaking choice of one test of accountability or immunity rather than another?

Do you think of other questions that a court ought to consider before determining its lawmaking choice?

To what extent was the court candid, explicit, and clear about the reasons for the court's choice? If you were a judge of the court deciding the matter, would you have urged more, or less, or different reasoned explanation?

These few questions are suggestive. They are not meant to be exhaustive. Note, and be prepared to discuss, other questions that occur to you as you read these cases.

CHAPTER 3

FASHIONING STANDARDS FOR DECIDING CASES

**HUSTLER MAGAZINE
v.
FALWELL**
108 S.Ct. 876

Argued Dec. 2, 1987.
Decided Feb. 24, 1988.

TORTS: First and Fourteenth Amendments prohibited public figure from recovering damages for intentional infliction of emotional distress.

Public figure sued publishers of advertisement parody for libel, invasion of privacy, and intentional infliction of emotional distress. The United States District Court for the Western District of Virginia, James C. Turk, Chief Judge, dismissed invasion of privacy claim and entered judgment against publishers on emotional distress claim and against public figure on libel claim. Appeal and cross appeal were taken. The Fourth Circuit Court of Appeals, Chapman, Circuit Judge, 797 F.2d 1270, affirmed. Certiorari was granted. The Supreme Court, Chief Justice Rehnquist, held that First and Fourteenth Amendments prohibited public figure from recovering damages for tort of intentional infliction of emotional distress.

Reversed.

Justice White filed an opinion concurring in the judgment.

Justice Kennedy took no part in the consideration or decision of the case.

HUSTLER V. FALWELL

**877 Syllabus[1]

*46 Respondent, a nationally known minister and commentator on politics and public affairs, filed a diversity action in Federal District Court against petitioners, a nationally circulated magazine and its publisher, to recover damages for, inter alia, libel and intentional infliction of emotional distress arising from the publication of an advertisement "parody" which, among other things, portrayed respondent as having engaged in a drunken incestuous rendezvous with his mother in an outhouse. The jury found against respondent on the libel claim, specifically finding that the parody could not "reasonably be understood as describing actual facts or events," but ruled in his favor on the emotional distress claim, stating that he should be awarded compensatory and punitive damages. The Court of Appeals affirmed, rejecting petitioners' contention that the "actual malice" standard of New York Times Co. v. Sullivan, 376 U.S. 254, 84 S.Ct. 710, 11 L.Ed.2d 686 must be met before respondent can recover for emotional distress. Rejecting as irrelevant the contention that, because the jury found that the parody did not describe actual facts, the ad was an opinion protected by the First Amendment to the Federal Constitution, the court ruled that the issue was whether the ad's publication was sufficiently outrageous to constitute intentional infliction of emotional distress.

Held: In order to protect the free flow of ideas and opinions on matters of public interest and concern, the First and Fourteenth Amendments prohibit public figures and public officials from recovering damages for the tort of intentional infliction of emotional distress by reason of the publication of a caricature such as the ad parody at issue without showing in addition that the publication contains a false statement of fact which was made with "actual malice," i.e., with knowledge that the statement was false or with reckless disregard as to whether or not it was true. The State's interest in protecting public figures from emotional distress is not sufficient to deny First Amendment protection to speech that is patently offensive and is intended to inflict emotional injury when that speech could not reasonably have

---

[1] The syllabus constitutes no part of the opinion of the Court but has been prepared by the Reporter of Decisions for the convenience of the reader. See United States v. Detroit Lumber Co., 200 U.S. 321, 337, 26 S.Ct. 282, 287, 50 L.Ed. 499.

been interpreted as stating actual facts about the public figure involved. Here, respondent is clearly a "public figure" for First Amendment purposes, and the lower courts' finding that the ad parody was not reasonably believable must be accepted. "Outrageousness" *47 in the area of political and social discourse has an inherent subjectiveness about it which would allow a jury to impose liability on the basis of the jurors' tastes or views, or perhaps on the basis of their dislike of a particular expression, and cannot, consistently with the First Amendment, form a basis for the award of damages for conduct such as that involved here. Pp. 879-883.

797 F.2d 1270 (CA4 1986), reversed.

REHNQUIST, C.J., delivered the opinion of the Court, in which BRENNAN, MARSHALL, BLACKMUN, STEVENS, O'CONNOR, and SCALIA, JJ., joined. WHITE, J., filed an opinion concurring in the judgment. KENNEDY, J., took no part in the consideration or decision of the case.

Chief Justice REHNQUIST delivered the opinion of the Court.

Petitioner Hustler Magazine, Inc., is a magazine of nationwide circulation. Respondent Jerry Falwell, a nationally known minister who has been active as a commentator on politics and public affairs, sued petitioner and its publisher, petitioner Larry **878 Flynt, to recover damages for invasion of *48 privacy, libel, and intentional infliction of emotional distress. The District Court directed a verdict against respondent on the privacy claim, and submitted the other two claims to a jury. The jury found for petitioners on the defamation claim, but found for respondent on the claim for intentional infliction of emotional distress and awarded damages. We now consider whether this award is consistent with the First and Fourteenth Amendments of the United States Constitution.

The inside front cover of the November 1983 issue of Hustler Magazine featured a "parody" of an advertisement for Campari Liqueur that contained the name and picture of respondent and was entitled "Jerry Falwell talks about his first time." This parody was modeled after actual Campari ads that included interviews with various celebrities about their "first times." Although it was apparent by the end of each interview that this meant the first time they sampled Campari, the ads clearly played on the sexual double entendre of the general subject of "first times." Copying the form and layout of these Campari ads, Hustler's editors chose respondent as the featured celebrity and drafted an alleged "interview" with him in which he states that his "first time" was during a drunken incestuous rendezvous with his mother in an outhouse. The Hustler parody portrays respondent and his mother as drunk and immoral, and suggests that respondent is a hypocrite who preaches only when he is drunk. In small print at the bottom of the page, the ad contains the disclaimer, "ad parody--not to be taken seriously." The magazine's table of contents also lists the ad as "Fiction; Ad and Personality Parody."

Soon after the November issue of Hustler became available to the public, respondent brought this diversity action in the United States District Court for the Western District of Virginia against Hustler Magazine, Inc., Larry C. Flynt, and Flynt Distributing Co. Respondent stated in his complaint that publication of the ad parody in Hustler entitled *49 him to recover damages for libel, invasion of privacy, and intentional infliction of emotional distress. The case proceeded to trial.[1] At the close of the evidence, the District Court granted a directed verdict for petitioners on the invasion of privacy claim. The jury then found against respondent on the libel claim, specifically finding that the ad parody could not "reasonably be understood as describing actual facts about (respondent) or actual events in which (he) participated." App. to Pet. for Cert. C1. The jury ruled for respondent on the intentional infliction of emotional distress claim, however, and stated that he should be awarded $100,000 in compensatory damages, as well as $50,000 each in punitive damages from petitioners.[2] Petitioners' motion for judgment notwithstanding the verdict was denied.

On appeal, the United States Court of Appeals for the Fourth Circuit affirmed the judgment against petitioners. Falwell v. Flynt, 797 F.2d 1270 (CA4 1986). The court rejected petitioners' argument that the "actual malice" standard of New York Times Co. v. Sullivan, 376 U.S. 254, 84 S.Ct. 710, 11 L.Ed.2d 686 (1964), must be met before

---

[1] While the case was pending, the ad parody was published in Hustler magazine a second time.

[2] The jury found no liability on the part of Flynt Distributing Co., Inc. It is consequently not a party to this appeal.

respondent can recover for emotional distress. The court agreed that because respondent is concededly a public figure, petitioners are "entitled to the same level of first amendment protection in the claim for intentional infliction of emotional distress that they received in (respondent's) claim for libel." 797 F.2d, at 1274. But this does not mean that a literal application of the actual malice rule is appropriate in the context of an emotional distress claim. In the court's view, the New York Times decision emphasized the constitutional importance **879 not of the falsity of the statement or the defendant's disregard for the truth, but of the heightened level of culpability embodied in the requirement of "knowing ... or reckless" conduct. Here, the New York *50 Times standard is satisfied by the state-law requirement, and the jury's finding, that the defendants have acted intentionally or recklessly.³ The Court of Appeals then went on to reject the contention that because the jury found that the ad parody did not describe actual facts about respondent, the ad was an opinion that is protected by the First Amendment. As the court put it, this was "irrelevant," as the issue is "whether (the ad's) publication was sufficiently outrageous to constitute intentional infliction of emotional distress." Id., at 1276.⁴ Petitioners then filed a petition for rehearing en banc, but this was denied by a divided court. Given the importance of the constitutional issues involved, we granted certiorari.

This case presents us with a novel question involving First Amendment limitations upon a State's authority to protect its citizens from the intentional infliction of emotional distress. We must decide whether a public figure may recover damages for emotional harm caused by the publication of an ad parody offensive to him, and doubtless gross and repugnant in the eyes of most. Respondent would have us find that a

---

³ Under Virginia law, in an action for intentional infliction of emotional distress a plaintiff must show that the defendant's conduct (1) is intentional or reckless; (2) offends generally accepted standards of decency or morality; (3) is causally connected with the plaintiff's emotional distress; and (4) caused emotional distress that was severe. 797 F.2d, at 1275, n. 4 (citing Womack v. Eldridge, 215 Va. 338, 210 S.E.2d 145 (1974)).

⁴ The court below also rejected several other contentions that petitioners do not raise in this appeal.

State's interest in protecting public figures from emotional distress is sufficient to deny First Amendment protection to speech that is patently offensive and is intended to inflict emotional injury, even when that speech could not reasonably have been interpreted as stating actual facts about the public figure involved. This we decline to do.

At the heart of the First Amendment is the recognition of the fundamental importance of the free flow of ideas and opinions on matters of public interest and concern. "(T)he *51 freedom to speak one's mind is not only an aspect of individual liberty--and thus a good unto itself--but also is essential to the common quest for truth and the vitality of society as a whole." Bose Corp. v. Consumers Union of United States, Inc., 466 U.S. 485, 503-504, 104 S.Ct. 1949, 1961, 80 L.Ed.2d 502 (1984). We have therefore been particularly vigilant to ensure that individual expressions of ideas remain free from governmentally imposed sanctions. The First Amendment recognizes no such thing as a "false" idea. Gertz v. Robert Welch, Inc., 418 U.S. 323, 339, 94 S.Ct. 2997, 3007, 41 L.Ed.2d 789 (1974). As Justice Holmes wrote, "(W)hen men have realized that time has upset many fighting faiths, they may come to believe even more than they believe the very foundations of their own conduct that the ultimate good desired is better reached by free trade in ideas--that the best test of truth is the power of the thought to get itself accepted in the competition of the market...." Abrams v. United States, 250 U.S. 616, 630, 40 S.Ct. 17, 22, 63 L.Ed. 1173 (1919) (dissenting opinion).

The sort of robust political debate encouraged by the First Amendment is bound to produce speech that is critical of those who hold public office or those public figures who are "intimately involved in the resolution of important public questions or, by reason of their fame, shape events in areas of concern to society at large." Associated Press v. Walker, decided with Curtis Publishing Co. v. Butts, 388 U.S. 130, 164, 87 S.Ct. 1975, 1996, 18 L.Ed.2d 1094 (1967) (Warren, C.J., concurring in result). Justice Frankfurter put it succinctly in Baumgartner v. United States, **880 322 U.S. 665, 673-674, 64 S.Ct. 1240, 1245, 88 L.Ed. 1525 (1944), when he said that "(o)ne of the prerogatives of American citizenship is the right to criticize public men and measures." Such criticism, inevitably, will not always be reasoned or moderate; public figures as well as public officials will be subject to "vehement, caustic, and sometimes unpleasantly sharp attacks," New York Times, supra, 376 U.S., at 270, 84 S.Ct., at 721. "(T)he candidate who vaunts his spotless record and sterling integrity cannot convincingly cry 'Foul' when an opponent or an industrious reporter attempts *52 to demonstrate the contrary." Monitor Patriot Co. v. Roy, 401 U.S. 265, 274, 91 S.Ct. 621, 626, 28 L.Ed.2d 35 (1971).

Of course, this does not mean that any speech about a public figure is immune from sanction in the form of damages. Since New York Times Co. v. Sullivan, supra, we have consistently ruled that a public figure may hold a speaker liable for the damage to reputation caused by publication of a defamatory falsehood, but only if the statement was made "with knowledge that it was false or with reckless disregard of whether it was false or not." Id., 376 U.S., at 279-280, 84 S.Ct., at 726. False statements of fact are particularly valueless; they interfere with the truth-seeking function of the marketplace of ideas, and they cause damage to an individual's reputation that cannot easily be repaired by counterspeech, however persuasive or effective. See Gertz, 418 U.S., at 340, 344, n. 9, 94 S.Ct., at 3007, 3009, n. 9. But even though falsehoods have little value in and of themselves, they are "nevertheless inevitable in free debate," id., at 340, 94 S.Ct., at 3007, and a rule that would impose strict liability on a publisher for false factual assertions would have an undoubted "chilling" effect on speech relating to public figures that does have constitutional value. "Freedoms of expression require 'breathing space.'" Philadelphia Newspapers, Inc. v. Hepps, 475 U.S. 767, 772, 106 S.Ct. 1558, 1561, 89 L.Ed.2d 783 (1986) (quoting New York Times, 376 U.S., at 272, 84 S.Ct., at 721). This breathing space is provided by a constitutional rule that allows public figures to recover for libel or defamation only when they can prove both that the statement was false and that the statement was made with the requisite level of culpability.

Respondent argues, however, that a different standard should apply in this case because here the State seeks to prevent not reputational damage, but the severe emotional distress suffered by the person who is the subject of an offensive publication. Cf. Zacchini v. Scripps-Howard Broadcasting Co., 433 U.S. 562, 97 S.Ct. 2849, 53 L.Ed.2d 965 (1977) (ruling that the "actual malice" standard does not apply to the tort of appropriation of a right of publicity). In respondent's view, and in the view of the *53 Court of Appeals, so long as the utterance was intended to inflict emotional distress, was outrageous, and did in fact inflict serious emotional distress, it is of no constitutional import whether the statement was a fact or an opinion, or whether it was true or false. It is the intent to cause injury that is the gravamen of the tort, and the State's interest in preventing emotional harm simply outweighs whatever interest a speaker may have in speech of this type.

Generally speaking the law does not regard the intent to inflict emotional distress as one which should receive much solicitude, and it is quite understandable that most if not all jurisdictions have chosen to make it civilly culpable where the conduct in question is sufficiently "outrageous." But in the world of debate about public affairs, many things done with motives that are less than admirable are protected by the First Amendment. In Garrison v. Louisiana, 379 U.S. 64, 85 S.Ct. 209, 13 L.Ed.2d 125 (1964), we held that even when a speaker or writer is motivated by hatred or ill-will his expression was protected by the First Amendment:

"Debate on public issues will not be uninhibited if the speaker must run the risk that it will be proved in court that he spoke out of hatred; even if he did speak *881 out of hatred, utterances honestly believed contribute to the free interchange of ideas and the ascertainment of truth." Id., at 73, 85 S.Ct., at 215.

Thus while such a bad motive may be deemed controlling for purposes of tort liability in other areas of the law, we think the First Amendment prohibits such a result in the area of public debate about public figures.

Were we to hold otherwise, there can be little doubt that political cartoonists and satirists would be subjected to damages awards without any showing that their work falsely defamed its subject. Webster's defines a caricature as "the deliberately distorted picturing or imitating of a person, literary style, etc. by exaggerating features or mannerisms for satirical effect." Webster's New Unabridged Twentieth *54 Century Dictionary of the English Language 275 (2d ed. 1979). The appeal of the political cartoon or caricature is often based on exploration of unfortunate physical traits or politically embarrassing events--an exploration often calculated to injure the feelings of the subject of the portrayal. The art of the cartoonist is often not reasoned or evenhanded, but slashing and one-sided. One cartoonist expressed the nature of the art in these words:

"The political cartoon is a weapon of attack, of scorn and ridicule and satire; it is least effective when it tries to pat some politician on the back. It is usually as welcome as a bee sting and is always controversial in some quarters." Long, The Political Cartoon: Journalism's Strongest Weapon, The Quill, 56, 57 (Nov. 1962).

Several famous examples of this type of intentionally injurious speech were drawn by Thomas Nast, probably the greatest American cartoonist to date, who was associated for many years during the post-Civil War era with Harper's Weekly. In the pages of that publication Nast conducted a graphic vendetta against William M. "Boss" Tweed and his corrupt associates in New York City's "Tweed Ring." It has been described by one historian of the subject as "a sustained attack which in its passion and effectiveness stands alone in the history of American graphic art." M. Keller, The Art and Politics of Thomas Nast 177 (1968). Another writer explains that the success of the Nast cartoon was achieved "because of the emotional impact of its presentation. It continuously goes beyond the bounds of good taste and conventional manners." C. Press, The Political Cartoon 251 (1981).

Despite their sometimes caustic nature, from the early cartoon portraying George Washington as an ass down to the present day, graphic depictions and satirical cartoons have played a prominent role in public and political debate. Nast's castigation of the Tweed Ring, Walt McDougall's characterization of presidential candidate James G. Blaine's banquet with the millionaires at Delmonico's as "The Royal *55 Feast of Belshazzar," and numerous other efforts have undoubtedly had an effect on the course and outcome of contemporaneous debate. Lincoln's tall, gangling posture, Teddy Roosevelt's glasses and teeth, and Franklin D. Roosevelt's jutting jaw and cigarette holder have been memorialized by political cartoons with an effect that could not have been obtained by the photographer or the portrait artist. From the viewpoint of history it is clear that our political discourse would have been considerably poorer without them.

Respondent contends, however, that the caricature in question here was so "outrageous" as to distinguish it from more traditional political cartoons. There is no doubt that the caricature of respondent and his mother published in Hustler is at best a distant cousin of the political cartoons described above, and a rather poor relation at that. If it were possible by laying down a principled standard to separate the one from the other, public discourse would probably suffer little or no harm. But we doubt that there is any such standard, and we are quite sure that the pejorative description "outrageous" does not supply **882 one. "Outrageousness" in the area of political and social discourse has an inherent subjectiveness about it which would allow a jury to impose liability on the basis of the jurors' tastes or views, or perhaps on the basis of their dislike of a particular expression. An "outrageousness" standard thus runs afoul of our longstanding refusal to allow damages to be awarded because the speech in question may have an adverse emotional impact on the audience. See NAACP v. Claiborne Hardware Co., 458 U.S. 886, 910, 102 S.Ct. 3409, 3424, 73 L.Ed.2d 1215 (1982) ("Speech does not lose its protected character ... simply because it may embarrass others or coerce them into action"). And, as we stated in FCC v. Pacifica Foundation, 438 U.S. 726, 98 S.Ct. 3026, 57 L.Ed.2d 1073 (1978):

"(T)he fact that society may find speech offensive is not a sufficient reason for suppressing it. Indeed, if it is the speaker's opinion that gives offense, that consequence is a reason for according it constitutional protection. *56 For it is a central tenet of the First Amendment that the government must remain neutral in the marketplace of ideas." Id., at 745-746, 98 S.Ct., at 3038.

See also Street v. New York, 394 U.S. 576, 592, 89 S.Ct. 1354, 1366, 22 L.Ed.2d 572 (1969) ("It is firmly settled that ... the public expression of ideas may not be prohibited merely because the ideas are themselves offensive to some of their hearers").

Admittedly, these oft-repeated First Amendment principles, like other principles, are subject to limitations. We recognized in Pacifica Foundation, that speech that is "'vulgar,' 'offensive,' and 'shocking'" is "not entitled to absolute constitutional protection under all circumstances." 438 U.S., at 747, 98 S.Ct., at 3039. In Chaplinsky v. New Hampshire, 315 U.S. 568, 62 S.Ct. 766, 86 L.Ed. 1031 (1942), we held that a state could lawfully punish an individual for the use of insulting "'fighting' words--those which by their very utterance inflict injury or tend to incite an immediate breach of the peace." Id., at 571-572, 62 S.Ct., at 769. These limitations are but recognition of the observation in Dun & Bradstreet, Inc. v. Greenmoss Builders, Inc., 472 U.S. 749, 758, 105 S.Ct. 2939, 2945, 86 L.Ed.2d 593 (1985), that this Court has "long recognized that not all speech is of equal First Amendment importance." But the sort of expression involved in this case does not seem to us to be governed by any exception to the general First Amendment principles stated above.

We conclude that public figures and public officials may not recover for the tort of intentional infliction of emotional distress by reason of publications such as the one here at issue without showing in addition that the publication contains a false statement of fact which was made with "actual malice," i.e., with knowledge that the statement was false or with reckless disregard as to whether or not it was true. This is not merely a "blind application" of the New York Times standard, see Time, Inc. v. Hill, 385 U.S. 374, 390, 87 S.Ct. 534, 543, 17 L.Ed.2d 456 (1967), it reflects our considered judgment that such a standard is necessary to give adequate "breathing space" to the freedoms protected by the First Amendment.

*57 Here it is clear that respondent Falwell is a "public figure" for purposes of First Amendment law.[5] The jury found against respondent on his libel claim when it decided that the Hustler ad parody could not "reasonably be understood as describing actual facts about (respondent) or actual events in which (he) participated." App. to Pet. for Cert. C1. The Court of Appeals interpreted the jury's finding to be that the ad parody "was not reasonably believable," **883 797 F.2d, at 1278, and in accordance with our custom we accept this finding. Respondent is thus relegated to his claim for damages awarded by the jury for the intentional infliction of emotional distress by "outrageous" conduct. But for reasons heretofore stated this claim cannot, consistently with the First Amendment, form a basis for the award of damages when the conduct in question is the publication of a caricature such as the ad parody involved here. The judgment of the Court of Appeals is accordingly

Reversed.

Justice KENNEDY took no part in the consideration or

---

[5] Neither party disputes this conclusion. Respondent is the host of a nationally syndicated television show and was the founder and president of a political organization formerly known as the Moral Majority. He is also the founder of Liberty University in Lynchburg, Virginia, and is the author of several books and publications. Who's Who in America 849 (44th ed. 1986-1987).

decision of this case.

Justice WHITE, concurring in the judgment.

As I see it, the decision in New York Times v. Sullivan, 376 U.S. 254, 84 S.Ct. 710, 11 L.Ed.2d 686 (1964), has little to do with this case, for here the jury found that the ad contained no assertion of fact. But I agree with the Court that the judgment below, which penalized the publication of The parody, cannot be squared with the First Amendment.

Supp. Ch. 3

SANDSTROM
v.
State of MONTANA

**99 S.Ct. 2450, *442 U.S. 510, 61 L.Ed.2d 39

Argued April 18, 1979.
Decided June 18, 1979.

CRIMINAL LAW

Defendant was convicted in the Third District Court, Deer Lodge County, of deliberate homicide, and he appealed. The Montana Supreme Court, 176 Mont. 492, 580 P.2d 106, affirmed, and certiorari was granted. The Supreme Court, Mr. Justice Brennan, held that because the jury, which was instructed that the law presumes a person intends the ordinary consequences of his voluntary acts, may have interpreted the presumption as conclusive or as shifting the burden of persuasion, and because either interpretation would have violated the Fourteenth Amendment's requirement that the state prove every element of a criminal offense beyond a reasonable doubt, the instruction given was unconstitutional.

Reversed and remanded.

Mr. Justice Rehnquist, with whom Mr. Chief Justice Burger joined, filed a concurring opinion.

**2451 Syllabus[1]

*510 Based upon a confession and other evidence, petitioner was charged under a Montana **2452 statute with "deliberate homicide," in that he "purposely or knowingly" caused the victim's death. At trial, petitioner argued that, although he killed the victim, he did not do so "purposely or knowingly," and therefore was not guilty of deliberate

---

[1] The syllabus constitutes no part of the opinion of the Court but has been prepared by the Reporter of Decisions for the convenience of the reader. See United States v. Detroit Lumber Co., 200 U.S. 321, 337, 26 S.Ct. 282, 287, 50 L.Ed. 499.

homicide. The trial court instructed the jury that "(t)he law presumes that a person intends the ordinary consequences of his voluntary acts," over petitioner's objection that such instruction had the effect of shifting the burden of proof on the issue of purpose or knowledge. The jury found petitioner guilty, and the Montana Supreme Court affirmed, holding that although shifting the burden of proof to the defendant by means of a presumption is prohibited, allocation of "some burden of proof" to a defendant is permissible. Finding that under the instruction in question petitioner's sole burden was to produce "some " evidence that he did not intend the ordinary consequences of his voluntary acts, and not to disprove that he acted "purposely or knowingly," the Montana court held that the instruction did not violate due process standards.

Held: Because the jury may have interpreted the challenged presumption as conclusive, like the presumptions in Morissette v. United States, 342 U.S. 246, 72 S.Ct. 240, 96 L.Ed. 288, and United States v. United States Gypsum Co., 438 U.S. 422, 98 S.Ct. 2864, 57 L.Ed.2d 854, or as shifting the burden of persuasion, like that in Mullaney v. Wilbur, 421 U.S. 684, 95 S.Ct. 1881, 44 L.Ed.2d 508, and because either interpretation would have violated the Fourteenth Amendment's requirement that the State prove every element of a criminal offense beyond a reasonable doubt, the instruction is unconstitutional. Pp. 2454-2460.

(a) The effect of a presumption in a jury instruction is determined by the way in which a reasonable juror could have interpreted it, not by a state court's interpretation of its legal import. Pp. 2454-2455, 2456.

(b) Conclusive presumptions "conflict with the overriding presumption of innocence with which the law endows the accused and which extends to every element of the crime," Morissette, supra, at 275, 72 S.Ct. at 255, and they "invad(e the) factfinding function," United States Gypsum Co., supra, at 446, 98 S.Ct. at 2878, which in a criminal case the law assigns to the jury. The presumption announced to petitioner's jury may well have had exactly *511 these consequences, since upon finding proof of one element of the crime (causing death), and of facts insufficient to establish the second (the voluntariness and "ordinary consequences" of petitioner's action), the jury could have reasonably concluded that it was directed to find against petitioner on the element of intent. The State was thus not forced to prove "beyond a reasonable DOUBT ... EVERY FACT NECESSARY TO

CONSTITUTE the crime ... charged," in re Winship, 397 U.S. 358, 364, 90 S.Ct. 1068, 1072, 25 L.Ed.2d 368, and petitioner was deprived of his constitutional rights. Pp. 2458-2459.

(c) A presumption which, although not conclusive, had the effect of shifting the burden of persuasion to petitioner, would have suffered from similar infirmities. If the jury interpreted the presumption in this manner, it could have concluded that upon proof by the State of the slaying, and of additional facts not themselves establishing the element of intent, the burden was then shifted to petitioner to prove that he lacked the requisite mental state. Such a presumption was found constitutionally deficient in Mullaney, supra. Pp. 2459-2460.

(d) Without merit is the State's argument that since the jury could have interpreted the word "intends" in the instruction as referring only to petitioner's "purpose," and could have convicted petitioner solely for his "knowledge" without considering "purpose," it might not have relied upon the tainted presumption at all. First, it is not clear that a jury would have so interpreted "intends". More significantly, even if a jury could have ignored the **2453 presumption, it cannot be certain that this is what it did do, as its verdict was a general one. Pp. 2459-2460.

(e) Since whether the jury's reliance upon the instruction constituted, or could have ever constituted, harmless error are issues that were not considered by the Montana Supreme Court, this Court will not reach them as an initial matter. Pp. 2460-2461.

176 Mont. 492, 580 P.2d 106, reversed and remanded.

*512 Mr. Justice BRENNAN delivered the opinion of the Court.

The question presented is whether, in a case in which intent is an element of the crime charged, the jury instruction, "the law presumes that a person intends the ordinary consequences of his voluntary acts," violates the Fourteenth Amendment's requirement that the State prove every element of a criminal offense beyond a reasonable doubt.

I

On November 22, 1976, 18-year-old David Sandstrom confessed to the slaying of Annie Jessen. Based upon the confession and corroborating evidence, petitioner was charged on December 2 with "deliberate homicide," Mont.Code Ann. section 45-5-102 (1978), in that he "purposely or knowingly caused the death of Annie Jessen." App. 3.[1] At trial, Sandstrom's attorney informed the jury that, although his client admitted killing Jessen, he did not do so "purposely or knowingly," and was therefore not guilty of "deliberate homicide" but of a lesser crime. Id., at 6-8. The basic support for this contention was the testimony of two court-appointed mental health experts, each of whom described for the jury petitioner's mental state at the time of the incident. Sandstrom's attorney argued that this testimony demonstrated that petitioner, due to a personality disorder aggravated by alcohol consumption, did not kill Annie Jessen "purposely or knowingly."[2]

*513 The prosecution requested the trial judge to instruct the jury that "(t)he law presumes that a person intends the ordinary consequences of his voluntary acts." Petitioner's counsel objected, arguing that "the instruction has the effect of shifting the burden of proof on the issue of" purpose or knowledge to the defense, and that "that is

---

[1] The statute provides:

"45-5-101. Criminal homicide. (1) A person commits the offense of criminal homicide if he purposely, knowingly, or negligently causes the death of another human being.

"(2) Criminal homicide is deliberate homicide, mitigated deliberate homicide, or negligent homicide.

"45-5-102. Deliberate homicide. (1) Except as provided in 45-5-103(1), criminal homicide constitutes deliberate homicide if:

"(a) it is committed purposely or knowingly...."

[2] Petitioner initially filed a notice of intent to rely on "mental disease or defect excluding criminal responsibility" as a defense. That defense required evidence that defendant was "unable either to appreciate the criminality of his conduct or to conform his conduct to the requirements of law." Mont.Code Ann. section 46-14-101 (1978). The defense was withdrawn at trial, with the petitioner contending that, although he was not "unable" to form the requisite intent, he did not have it at the time of the killing.

impermissible under the Federal Constitution, due process of law." Id., at 34. He offered to provide a number of federal decisions in support of the objection, including this Court's holding in Mullaney v. Wilbur, 421 U.S. 684, 95 S.Ct. 1881, 44 L.Ed.2d 508 (1975), but was told by the judge: "You can give those to the Supreme Court. The objection is overruled." App. 34. The instruction was delivered, the jury found petitioner guilty of deliberate homicide, id., at 38, and petitioner was sentenced to 100 years in prison.

Sandstrom appealed to the Supreme Court of Montana, again contending that **2454 the instruction shifted to the defendant the burden of disproving an element of the crime charged, in violation of Mullaney v. Wilbur, supra, In re Winship, 397 U.S. 358, 90 S.Ct. 1068, 25 L.Ed.2d 368 (1970), and Patterson v. New York, 432 U.S. 197, 97 S.Ct. 2319, 53 L.Ed.2d 281 (1977). The Montana court conceded that these cases did prohibit shifting the burden of proof to the defendant by means of a presumption, but held that the cases "do not prohibit allocation of _some_ burden of proof to a defendant under certain circumstances." 176 Mont. 492, 497, 580 P.2d 106, 109 (1978). Since in the court's view, "(d)efendant's sole burden under instruction No. 5 was to produce _some_ evidence that he did not intend the ordinary consequences of his voluntary acts, not to disprove that he acted 'purposely' or 'knowingly,' ... the instruction does not violate due process *514 standards as defined by the United States or Montana Constitution ...." Ibid. (emphasis added).

Both federal and state courts have held, under a variety of rationales, that the giving of an instruction similar to that challenged here is fatal to the validity of a criminal conviction.[3] We granted certiorari, 439 U.S. 1067, 99 S.Ct.

---

[3] See Chappell v. United States, 270 F.2d 274 (CA9 1959); Bloch v. United States, 221 F.2d 786 (CA9 1955); Berkovitz v. United States, 213 F.2d 468 (CA5 1954); Wardlaw v. United States, 203 F.2d 884 (CA5 1953); State v. Warbritton, 211 Kan. 506, 506 P.2d 1152 (1973); Hall v. State, 49 Ala.App. 381, 272 So.2d 590, 593 (Crim.App.1973). See also United States v. Wharton, 139 U.S.App.D.C. 293, 433 F.2d 451 (1970). In addition, two United States Courts of Appeals have ordered their District Courts to delete the instruction in future cases. See United States v. Garrett, 574 F.2d 778 (CA3 1978); United States v. Chiantese, 560 F.2d 1244 (CA5 1977). The standard reference work for federal instructions, 1 E. Devitt & C. Blackmar, Federal Jury Practice and Instructions 405 (3d ed. 1977), describes the instruction as "clearly erroneous," and as

II

(1) The threshold inquiry in ascertaining the constitutional analysis applicable to this kind of jury instruction is to determine the nature of the presumption it describes. See Ulster County Court v. Allen, 442 U.S. 140, 157-163, 99 S.Ct. 2213, 2224-2227, 60 L.Ed.2d 777 (1979). That determination requires careful attention to the words actually spoken to the jury, see id., at 157-159, n. 16, 99 S.Ct., at 2225, for whether a defendant has been accorded his constitutional rights depends upon the way in which a reasonable juror could have interpreted the instruction.

(2) Respondent argues, first, that the instruction merely described a permissive inference--that is, it allowed but did not require the jury to draw conclusions about defendant's intent from his actions--and that such inferences are constitutional. Brief for Respondent 3, 15. These arguments need not detain us long, for even respondent admits that "it's possible" that *515 the jury believed they were required to apply the presumption. Tr. of Oral Arg. 28. Sandstrom's jurors were told that "(t)he law presumes that a person intends the ordinary consequences of his voluntary acts." They were not told that they had a choice, or that they might infer that conclusion; they were told only that the law presumed it. It is clear that a reasonable juror could easily have viewed such an instruction as mandatory. See generally United States v. Wharton, 139 U.S.App.D.C. 293, 298, 433 F.2d 451, 456 (1970); Green v. United States, 132 U.S.App.D.C. 98, 99, 405 F.2d 1368, 1369 (1968). See also Montana Rule of Evidence 301(a).[4]

In the alternative, respondent urges that, even if viewed as a mandatory presumption rather than as a permissive inference, the **2455 presumption did not conclusively

---

constituting "reversible error," id., at 448.

[4] "Rule 301. (a) Presumption defined. A presumption is an assumption of fact <u>that the law requires to be made</u> from another fact or group of facts found or otherwise established in the action or proceeding." (Emphasis added.)

establish intent but rather could be rebutted. On this view, the instruction required the jury, if satisfied as to the facts which trigger the presumption, to find intent unless the defendant offered evidence to the contrary. Moreover, according to the State, all the defendant had to do to rebut the presumption was produce "some" contrary evidence; he did not have to "prove" that he lacked the required mental state. Thus, "(a)t most, it placed a <u>burden of production</u> on the petitioner," but "did not shift to petitioner the <u>burden of persuasion</u> with respect to any element of the offense...." Brief for Respondent 3 (emphasis added). Again, respondent contends that presumptions with this limited effect pass constitutional muster.

We need not review respondent's constitutional argument on this point either, however, for we reject this characterization of the presumption as well. Respondent concedes there is a "risk" that the jury, once having found petitioner's act *516 voluntary, would interpret the instruction as automatically directing a finding of intent. Tr. of Oral Arg. 29. Moreover, the State also concedes that numerous courts "have differed as to the effect of the presumption when given as a jury instruction without further explanation as to its use by the jury," and that some have found it to shift more than the burden of production, and even to have conclusive effect. Brief for Respondent 17. Nonetheless, the State contends that the only authoritative reading of the effect of the presumption resides in the Supreme Court of Montana. And the State argues that by holding that "(d)efendant's sole burden under instruction No. 5 was to produce <u>some</u> evidence that he did not intend the ordinary consequences of his voluntary acts, not to disprove that he acted 'purposely' or 'knowingly,'" 176 Mont., at 497-498, 580 P.2d at 109 (emphasis added), the Montana Supreme Court decisively established that the presumption at most affected only the burden of going forward with evidence of intent--that is, the burden of production.[5]

---

[5] For purposes of argument, we accept respondent's definition of the production burden when applied to a defendant in a criminal case. We note, however, that the burden is often described quite differently when it rests upon the prosecution. See United States v. Vuitch, 402 U.S. 62, 72 n. 7, 91 S.Ct. 1294, 1299, 28 L.Ed.2d 601 (1971) ("evidence from which a jury could find a defendant guilty beyond a reasonable doubt"); C. McCormick, Evidence section 338, p. 790, and n. 33 (2d ed. 1972), p. 101, and n. 34.1 (Supp.1978). We also note that the effect of a failure to meet the production burden is significantly different for the

(3) The Supreme Court of Montana is, of course, the final authority on the legal weight to be given a presumption under Montana law, but it is not the final authority on the interpretation *517 which a jury could have given the instruction. If Montana intended its presumption to have only the effect described by its Supreme Court, then we are convinced that a reasonable juror could well have been misled by the instruction given, and could have believed that the presumption was not limited to requiring the defendant to satisfy only a burden of production. Petitioner's jury was told that "(t)he law presumes that a person intends the ordinary consequences of his voluntary acts." They were not told that the presumption could be rebutted, as the Montana Supreme Court held, by the defendant's simple presentation of "some" evidence; nor even that it could be rebutted at all. Given the common definition of "presume" as "to suppose to be true without proof," Webster's New Collegiate Dictionary 911 (1974), and given the lack of qualifying instructions as to the legal effect of the presumption, we cannot discount the possibility that the jury may have interpreted **2456 the instruction in either of two more stringent ways.

First, a reasonable jury could well have interpreted the presumption as "conclusive," that is, not technically as a presumption at all, but rather as an irrebuttable direction by the court to find intent once convinced of the facts triggering the presumption. Alternatively, the jury may have interpreted the instruction as a direction to find intent upon proof of the defendant's voluntary actions (and their "ordinary" consequences), unless the defendant proved the contrary by some quantum of proof which may well have been considerably greater than "some" evidence--thus effectively shifting the burden of persuasion on the element of intent. Numerous federal and state courts have warned that instructions of the type given here can be interpreted in

---

defendant and prosecution. When the prosecution fails to meet it, a directed verdict in favor of the defense results. Such a consequence is not possible upon a defendant's failure, however, as verdicts may not be directed against defendants in criminal cases. United States v. Martin Linen Supply Co., 430 U.S. 564, 572-573, 97 S.Ct. 1349, 1355, 51 L.Ed.2d 642 (1977); Carpenters v. United States, 330 U.S. 395, 408, 67 S.Ct. 775, 782, 91 L.Ed. 973 (1947); Mims v. United States, 375 F.2d 135, 148 (CA5 1967).

just these ways. See generally United States v. Wharton, 139 U.S.App.D.C. 293, 433 F.2d 451 (1970); Berkovitz v. United States, 213 F.2d 468 (CA5 1954); State v. Roberts, 88 Wash.2d 337, 341-342, 562 P.2d 1259, 1261-1262 (1977) (en banc); State v. War *518 211 Kan. 506, 509, 506 P.2d 1152, 1155 (1973); Hall v. State, 49 Ala.App. 381, 385, 272 So.2d 590, 593 (Crim.App.1973). See also United States v. Chiantese, 560 F.2d 1244, 1255 (CA5 1977). And although the Montana Supreme Court held to the contrary in this case, Montana's own Rules of Evidence expressly state that the presumption at issue here may be overcome only "by a preponderance of evidence contrary to the presumption." Montana Rule of Evidence 301(b)(2).[6] Such a requirement shifts not only the burden of production, but also the

---

[6] Montana Code Ann. section 26-1-602 (1978) states:

"'(D)isputable presumptions' ... may be controverted by other evidence. The following are of that kind:

* * *

"3. that a person intends the ordinary consequence of his voluntary act."

Montana Rule of Evidence 301 provides:

"(b)(2) All presumptions, other than conclusive presumptions, are disputable presumptions and may be controverted. <u>A disputable presumption may be overcome by a preponderance of evidence contrary to the presumption. Unless the presumption is overcome, the trier of fact must find the assumed fact in accordance with the presumption.</u>" (Emphasis added.)

See also Monaghan v. Standard Motor Co., 96 Mont. 165, 173-174, 29 P.2d 378, 379-380 (1934). At oral argument, the Attorney General of Montana agreed that "admittedly Montana law ... states that a presumption requires a person to overcome that presumption by a preponderance of evidence." Tr. of Oral Arg. 30.

We do not, of course, cite this Rule of Evidence to dispute the Montana Supreme Court's interpretation of its own law. It merely serves as evidence that a reasonable man--here, apparently, the drafter of Montana's own Rules of Evidence--could interpret the presumption at issue in this case as shifting to the defendant the burden of proving his innocence by a preponderance of the evidence.

ultimate burden of persuasion on the issue of intent.[7]

*519 We do not reject the possibility that some jurors may have interpreted the challenged instruction as permissive, or, if mandatory, as requiring only that the defendant come forward with "some" evidence in rebuttal. However, the fact that a reasonable juror could have given the presumption **2457 conclusive or persuasion-shifting effect means that we cannot discount the possibility that Sandstrom's jurors actually did proceed upon one or the other of these latter interpretations. And that means that unless these kinds of presumptions are constitutional, the instruction cannot be adjudged valid.[8] Ulster County Court v. Allen, 442 U.S., at 159-160, n. 17, 99 S.Ct., at 2226, and at 175-176, 99 S.Ct., at 2234 (POWELL, J., dissenting); Bachellar v. Maryland, 397 U.S. 564, 570-571, 90 S.Ct. 1312, 1315-1316, 25 L.Ed.2d 570 (1970); Leary v. United States, 395 U.S. 6, 31-32, 89 S.Ct. 1532, 1545-1546, 23 L.Ed.2d 57 (1969); Carpenters v. United States, 330 U.S. 395, 408-409, 67 S.Ct. 775, 782, 91 L.Ed. 973 (1947); Bollenbach v. United States, 326 U.S. 607, 611-614, 66 S.Ct. 402, 404-405, 90

---

[7] The potential for these interpretations of the presumption was not removed by the other instructions given at the trial. It is true that the jury was instructed generally that the accused was presumed innocent until proved guilty, and that the State had the burden of proving beyond a reasonable doubt, that the defendant caused the death of the deceased purposely or knowingly. App. 34-35; Brief for Respondent 21. But this is not rhetorically inconsistent with a conclusive or burden-shifting presumption. The jury could have interpreted the two sets of instructions as indicating that the presumption was a means by which proof beyond a reasonable doubt as to intent could be satisfied. For example, if the presumption were viewed as conclusive, the jury could have believed that, although intent must be proved beyond a reasonable doubt, proof of the voluntary slaying and its ordinary consequences constituted proof of intent beyond a reasonable doubt. Cf. Mullaney v. Wilbur, 421 U.S. 684, 703 n. 31, 95 S.Ct. 1881, 1892, 44 L.Ed.2d 508 (1975) ("These procedural devices require (in the case of a presumption) ... the trier of fact to conclude that the prosecution has met its burden of proof with respect to the presumed ... fact by having satisfactorily established other facts").

[8] Given our ultimate result in this case, we do not need to consider what kind of constitutional analysis would be appropriate for other kinds of presumptions.

L.Ed. 350 (1946). It is the line of cases urged by petitioner, and exemplified by **In re Winship**, 397 U.S. 358, 90 S.Ct. 1068, 25 L.Ed.2d 368 (1970), that provides the appropriate mode of constitutional analysis for these kinds of presumptions.[9]

*520 III

In Winship, this Court stated:

> "Lest there remain any doubt about the constitutional stature of the reasonable-doubt standard, we explicitly hold that the Due Process Clause protects the accused against conviction except

---

[9] Another line of our cases also deals with the validity of certain kinds of presumptions. See Ulster County Court v. Allen, 442 U.S. 140, 99 S.Ct. 2213, 60 L.Ed.2d 777 (1979); Barnes v. United States, 412 U.S. 837, 93 S.Ct. 2357, 37 L.Ed.2d 380 (1973); Turner v. United States, 396 U.S. 398, 90 S.Ct. 642, 24 L.Ed.2d 610 (1970); Leary v. United States, 395 U.S. 6, 89 S.Ct. 1532, 23 L.Ed.2d 57 (1969); United States v. Romano, 382 U.S. 136, 86 S.Ct. 279, 15 L.Ed.2d 210 (1965); United States v. Gainey, 380 U.S. 63, 85 S.Ct. 754, 13 L.Ed.2d 658 (1965); Roviaro v. United States, 353 U.S. 53, 77 S.Ct. 623, 1 L.Ed.2d 639 (1957); Tot v. United States, 319 U.S. 463, 63 S.Ct. 1241, 87 L.Ed. 1519 (1943). These cases did not, however, involve presumptions of the conclusive or persuasion-shifting variety. See Ulster County Court v. Allen, 442 U.S., at 157, and n. 16, 99 S.Ct., at 2224-2225, and n. 16; and at 169, 99 S.Ct., at 2231 (POWELL, J., dissenting); Mullaney v. Wilbur, supra, 421 U.S., at 703 n. 31, 95 S.Ct., at 1892 (1975); Leary v. United States, supra, 395 U.S., at 35, 89 S.Ct., at 1547; Roviaro v. United States, supra, 353 U.S., at 63, 77 S.Ct., at 629; C. McCormick, Evidence 831 (2d ed. 1972).

A line of even older cases urged upon us by respondent is equally inapplicable. In Agnew v. United States, 165 U.S. 36, 50, 17 S.Ct 235, 240, 41 L.Ed. 624 (1897), the trial court's instruction expressly stated that the presumption was not conclusive, and this Court found that other problems with the instruction were cured by the charge considered as a whole. The other proffered cases simply involved general comments by the Court upon the validity of presuming intent from action. See Radio Officers v. NLRB, 347 U.S. 17, 45, 74 S.Ct. 323, 338, 98 L.Ed. 455 (1954); Cramer v. United States, 325 U.S. 1, 31, 65 S.Ct. 918, 933, 89 L.Ed. 1441 (1945). See also Reynolds v. United States, 98 U.S. 145, 167, 25 L.Ed. 244 (1879) (religious objection to polygamy law not a defense).

upon proof beyond a reasonable doubt <u>of every fact</u> necessary to constitute the crime with which he is charged." Id., at 364, 90 S.Ct. at 1073 (emphasis added).

Accord, Patterson v. New York, 432 U.S., at 210, 97 S.Ct. at 2327. The petitioner here was charged with and convicted of deliberate homicide, committed purposely or knowingly, under Mont.Code Ann. section 45-5-102(a) (1978). See App. 3, 42. It is clear that under Montana law, whether the crime was committed purposely or knowingly is a fact necessary to constitute the crime of deliberate homicide.[10] Indeed, *521 it was the lone **2458 element of the offense at issue in Sandstrom's trial, as he confessed to causing the death of the victim, told the jury that knowledge and purpose were the only questions he was controverting, and introduced evidence solely on those points. App. 6-8. Moreover, it is conceded that proof of defendant's "intent" would be sufficient to establish this element.[11] Thus, the question before this Court is whether the challenged jury instruction had the effect of relieving the State of the burden of proof enunciated in Winship on the critical question of petitioner's state of mind. We conclude that under either

---

[10]. The statute is set out at n. 1, supra. In State v. McKenzie, 177 Mont. 280, 327-328, 581 P.2d 1205, 1232 (1978), the Montana Supreme Court stated:

"In Montana, a person commits the offense of deliberate homicide if he purposely or knowingly causes the death of another human being. Sections 94-5-102(1)(a), 94-5-101(1), R.C.M.1947. <u>The statutorily defined elements of the offense</u>, each of which the State must prove beyond a reasonable doubt, <u>are therefore causing the death of another human being with the knowledge</u> that you are causing <u>or with the purpose</u> to cause the death of that human being." (Emphasis added.)

Accord, State v. Collins, 178 Mont. 36, 45, 582 P.2d 1179, 1184 (1978) ("committing the homicide 'purposely or knowingly' is an element of deliberate homicide").

[11]. Respondent agrees that "intent" and "purpose" are roughly synonymous, see also Webster's New Collegiate Dictionary 601 (1974), but contests the relevance of "intent" to "knowledge." See Tr. of Oral Arg. 18; Brief for Respondent 8-9. This problem is discussed in Part IV, infra.

of the two possible interpretations of the instruction set out above, precisely that effect would result, and that the instruction therefore represents constitutional error.

(4) We consider first the validity of a conclusive presumption. This Court has considered such a presumption on at least two prior occasions. In Morissette v. United States, 342 U.S. 246, 72 S.Ct. 240, 96 L.Ed. 288 (1952), the defendant was charged with willful and knowing theft of Government property. Although his attorney argued that for his client to be found guilty, "'the taking must have been with felonious intent'," the trial judge ruled that "'(t)hat is presumed by his own act.'" Id., at 249, 72 S.Ct. at 243. After first concluding that intent was in fact an element of the crime charged, and after declaring that "(w)here intent of the accused *522 is an ingredient of the crime charged, its existence is ... a jury issue," Morissette held:

"It follows that the trial court may not withdraw or prejudge the issue by instruction that the law raises a presumption of intent from an act. It often is tempting to cast in terms of a 'presumption' a conclusion which a court thinks probable from given facts.... (But) (w)e think presumptive intent has no place in this case. A conclusive presumption which testimony could not overthroew would effectively eliminate intent as an ingredient of the offense. A presumption which would permit but not require the jury to assume intent from an isolated fact would prejudge a conclusion which the jury should reach of its own volition. A presumption which would permit the jury to make an assumption which all the evidence considered together does not logically establish would give to a proven fact an artificial and fictional effect. In either case, this presumption would conflict with the overriding presumption of innocence with which the law endows the accused and which extends to every element of the crime." Id., at 274-275, 72 S.Ct. at 255-256. (Emphasis added; footnote omitted.)

(5) Just last Term, in United States v. United States Gypsum Co., 438 U.S. 422, 98 S.Ct. 2864, 57 L.Ed.2d 854 (1978), we reaffirmed the holding of Morissette. In that case defendants, who were charged with criminal violations of the Sherman Act, challenged the following jury instruction:

"The law presumes that a person intends the necessary and natural consequences of his acts. Therefore, if the effect of the exchanges of pricing information was to raise, fix, maintain and stabilize prices, then the parties to them are presumed, as a matter of law, to have intended that result." 438 U.S., at 430, 98 S.Ct., at 2869.

*523 After again determining that the offense included the element of intent, we held:

"(A) defendant's state of mind or <u>intent is an element of a criminal offense which ... cannot be taken from the trier of fact through reliance on a legal presumption</u> of wrongful intent from proof of an effect on prices. Cf. Morissette v. United States....

**2459 "Although an effect on prices may well support an inference that the defendant had knowledge of the probability of such a consequence at the time he acted, the jury must remain free to consider additional evidence before accepting or rejecting the inference.... (U)ltimately the decision on the issue of intent must be left to the trier of fact alone. The instruction given invaded this factfinding function." Id., at 435, 446, 98 S.Ct. at 2872, 2878 (emphasis added).

See also Hickory v. United States, 160 U.S. 408, 422, 16 S.Ct. 327, 332, 40 L.Ed. 474 (1896).

As in Morissette and United States Gypsum Co., a conclusive presumption in this case would "conflict with the overriding presumption of innocence with which the law endows the accused and which extends to every element of the crime," and would "invade (the) factfinding function" which in a criminal case the law assigns solely to the jury. The instruction announced to David Sandstrom's jury may well have had exactly these consequences. Upon finding proof of one element of the crime (causing death), and of facts insufficient to establish the second (the voluntariness and "ordinary consequences" of defendant's action), Sandstrom's jurors could reasonably have concluded that they were directed to find against defendant on the element of intent. The State was thus not forced to prove "beyond a reasonable doubt ... every fact necessary to constitute the crime ... charged," 397 U.S., at 364, 90 S.Ct. at 1073, and defendant was deprived of his constitutional rights as explicated in Winship.

(6) *524 A presumption which, although not conclusive, had the effect of shifting the burden of persuasion to the

defendant, would have suffered from similar infirmities. If Sandstrom's jury interpreted the presumption in that manner, it could have concluded that upon proof by the State of the slaying, and of additional facts not themselves establishing the element of intent, the burden was shifted to the defendant to prove that he lacked the requisite mental state. Such a presumption was found constitutionally deficient in Mullaney v. Wilbur, 421 U.S. 684, 95 S.Ct. 1881, 44 L.Ed.2d 508 (1975). In Mullaney, the charge was murder, which under Maine law required proof not only of intent but of malice. The trial court charged the jury that "'malice aforethought is an essential and indispensable element of the crime of murder.'" Id., at 686, 95 S.Ct. at 1883. However, it also instructed that if the prosecution established that the homicide was both intentional and unlawful, malice aforethought was to be implied unless the defendant proved by a fair preponderance of the evidence that he acted in the heat of passion on sudden provocation. Ibid. As we recounted just two Terms ago in Patterson v. New York, "(t)his Court unanimously agreed with the Court of Appeals that Wilbur's due process rights had been invaded by the presumption casting upon him the burden of proving by a preponderance of the evidence that he had acted in the heat of passion upon sudden provocation." 432 U.S., at 214, 97 S.Ct. at 2329. And Patterson reaffirmed that "a State must prove every ingredient of an offense beyond a reasonable doubt, and ... may not shift the burden of proof to the defendant" by means of such a presumption. Id., at 215, 97 S.Ct. at 2330.

(7) Because David Sandstrom's jury may have interpreted the judge's instruction as constituting either a burden-shifting presumption like that in Mullaney, or a conclusive presumption like those in Morissette and United States Gypsum Co., and because either interpretation would have deprived defendant of his right to the due process of law, we hold the instruction given in this case unconstitutional.

*525 IV

(8) Respondent has proposed two alternative rationales for affirming petitioner's conviction, even if the presumption at issue in this case is unconstitutional. First, the State notes that the jury was instructed **2460 that deliberate

homicide may be committed "purposely or knowingly."[12] App. 35 (emphasis added). Since the jury was also instructed that a person "intends" the ordinary consequences of his voluntary acts, but was not provided with a definition of "intends," respondent argues that jurors could have interpreted the word as referring only to the defendant's "purpose." Thus, a jury which convicted Sandstrom solely for his "knowledge," and which interpreted "intends" as relevant only to "purpose", would not have needed to rely upon the tainted presumption at all.

We cannot accept respondent's argument. As an initial matter, we are not at all certain that a jury would interpret the word "intends" as bearing solely upon purpose. As we said in United States v. United States Gypsum Co., 438 U.S., at 445, 98 S.Ct. at 2877, "(t)he element of intent in the criminal law has traditionally *526 been viewed as a bifurcated concept embracing either the specific requirement of purpose or the more general one of knowledge or awareness." See also W. LaFave & A. Scott, Criminal Law 196 (1972).

But, more significantly, even if a jury could have ignored the presumption and found defendant guilty because he acted

---

[12]. The jurors were instructed:

"INSTRUCTION NO. 7

"'Knowingly' is defined as follows: A person acts knowingly with respect to conduct or to a circumstance described by a statute defining an offense when he is aware of his conduct or that the circumstance exists. A person acts knowingly with respect to the result of conduct described by a statute defining an offense when he is aware that it is highly probable that such result will be caused by his conduct. When knowledge of the existence of a particular fact is an element of an offense, such knowledge is established if a person is aware of a high probability of its existence. Equivalent terms such as 'knowing' or 'with knowledge' have the same meaning.

"INSTRUCTION NO. 8

"'Purposely' is defined as follows: A person acts purposely with respect to a result or to conduct described by a statute defining an offense if it is his conscious object to engage in that conduct or to cause that result." App. 35-36.

knowingly, we cannot be certain that this is what they did do.[13] As the jury's verdict was a general one, App. 38, we have no way of knowing that Sandstrom was not convicted on the basis of the unconstitutional instruction. And "(i)t has long been settled that when a case is submitted to the jury on alternative theories the unconstitutionality of any of the theories requires that the conviction be set aside. See, e. g., Stromberg v. California, 283 U.S. 359, 51 S.Ct. 532, 75 L.Ed. 1117 (1931)." Leary v. United States, 395 U.S., at 31-32, 89 S.Ct. at 1545-1546. See Ulster County Court v. Allen, 442 U.S., at 159-160, n. 17, 99 S.Ct., at 2226, and at 175-176, 99 S.Ct., at 2234 (POWELL, J., dissenting); Bachellar v. Maryland, 397 U.S., at 570-571, 90 S.Ct. at 1315-1316; Brotherhood of Carpenters v. United States, 330 U.S., at 408-409, 67 S.Ct. at 782; Bollenbach v. United States, 326 U.S., at 611-614, 66 S.Ct. at 404-405.

(9) Respondent's final argument is that even if the jury did rely upon the unconstitutional instruction, this constituted harmless error under Chapman v. California, 386 U.S. 18, 87 S.Ct. 824, 17 L.Ed.2d 705 (1967), because both defendant's confession and the psychiatrist's testimony demonstrated that Sandstrom possessed the requisite mental state. Brief for Respondent 4-13. In reply, it is said that petitioner confessed only to the slaying and not to his mental state, that the psychiatrist's testimony amply supported his defense, Brief for Petitioner 15-16, and that in any event an unconstitutional jury instruction on an element of the crime can never constitute harmless error, see generally *527 Carpenters v. United States, supra, 330 U.S., at 408-409, 67 S.Ct., at 782; Bollenbach v. United States, supra, 326 U.S., at 614, 615, 66 S.Ct., at 405-406. As **2461 none of these issues was considered by the Supreme Court of Montana, we decline to reach them as an initial matter here. See Moore v. Illinois, 434 U.S. 220, 232, 98 S.Ct. 458, 54 L.Ed.2d 424 (1977); Coleman v. Alabama, 399 U.S. 1, 11, 90 S.Ct. 1999, 2004, 26 L.Ed.2d 387 (1970). The Montana court will, of course, be free to consider them on remand if it so desires. Ibid. Accordingly, the judgment

---

[13]. Indeed, with respondent's interpretation of "intends" as going solely to "purpose," it would be surprising if the jury considered "knowledge" before it considered "purpose." With the assistance of the presumption, the latter would have been easier to find than the former, and there is no reason to believe the jury would have deliberately undertaken the more difficult task.

of the Supreme Court of Montana is reversed, and the case is remanded for further proceedings not inconsistent with this opinion.

It is so ordered.

Mr. Justice REHNQUIST, with whom THE CHIEF JUSTICE joins, concurring.

The Fourteenth Amendment to the United States Constitution prohibits any State from depriving a person of liberty without due process of law, and in Mullaney v. Wilbur, 421 U.S. 684, 95 S.Ct. 1881, 44 L.Ed.2d 508 (1975), this Court held that the Fourteenth Amendment's guarantees prohibit a State from shifting to the defendant the burden of disproving an element of the crime charged. I am loath to see this Court go into the business of parsing jury instructions given by state trial courts, for as we have consistently recognized, "a single instruction to a jury may not be judged in artificial isolation, but must be viewed in the context of the overall charge." Cupp v. Naughten, 414 U.S. 141, 146-147, 94 S.Ct. 396, 400, 38 L.Ed.2d 368 (1973). And surely if this charge had, in the words of the Court, "merely described a permissive inference," ante at 2454, it could not conceivably have run afoul of the constitutional decisions cited by the Court in its opinion. But a majority of my Brethren conclude that "it is clear that a reasonable juror could easily have viewed such an instruction as mandatory," ante, at 2454, and counsel for the State admitted in oral argument "that 'it's possible' that the jury believed they were required to apply the presumption." Ante, at 2454.

*528 While I continue to have doubts as to whether this particular jury was so attentively attuned to the instructions of the trial court that it divined the difference recognized by lawyers between "infer" and "presume," I defer to the judgment of the majority of the Court that this difference in meaning may have been critical in its effect on the jury. I therefore concur in the Court's opinion and judgment.

Supp. Ch. 3

Computer-Aided Exercises on Intent in Tort Law

Background Materials for "Intent", pages 489-526, are adapted, with permission of West Publishing Company, from <u>Computer-Aided and Workbook Exercises on Tort Law</u> (1976), and with the permission of West Publishing Company and the Center for Computer-Assisted Legal Instruction, from <u>Computer-Aided and Workbook Exercises on Insurance Law</u> (1990).

INTENT EXERCISES Supp. Ch. 3
Problem 1

An Exercise on the Use of Intent
in the Law of Torts

This is a set of background materials for a computer-aided exercise. You should proceed through parts I-V of these materials before you begin the exercise on a computer terminal.

Carry this set of materials with you since you will need to refer to it from time to time. These materials are also available on the computer, but it will slow you down if you have to ask the computer for them.

Part I

Introduction

In this exercise you will be asked to consider a fact situation involving potential claims of intentional tort and to apply the concept of intent, as defined in the Restatement (Second) of Torts (1965), in answering questions that a lawyer or a judge might be required to consider.

It will help you both in working through this exercise and in keeping in perspective the relationship between its subject matter and larger questions of tort and insurance law if you will keep in mind not only what it is designed to do for you but also what it is not designed to do. The purpose is to develop and strengthen your understanding of the Restatement concept of intent and your skill in applying it. It is not the purpose of this exercise to develop an evaluation of the Restatement concept, though of course you will be better prepared to go forward with such an evaluation when you have completed this exercise. Only when you have a good understanding of the concept and skill in applying it will you be able to envision the results this concept of intent produces in practical applications, and to get some sense of how difficult or easy the concept will be for judges, lawyers, and jurors to use. This is only part of the basis you will need for the evaluation, but certainly an essential part.

We often speak of intent as a fact. To describe or to think about intent, however, we use (whether consciously or not) some concept of intent -- some explicit or implicit definition. In this respect intent, like other concepts, is part of a system of classification that we use as an aid to reasoning. Classification is a means of breaking an unmanageable whole into what we hope will be manageable parts. "Intent" (or "intention," the two words ordinarily being used interchangeably) is one of the key ideas of classification used, and sometimes misused, in thinking about the law of torts and some aspects of the law of insurance.

Supp. Ch. 3   INTENT EXERCISES

It happens that "intent" is used in not one but many different senses. More often than not, writers and speakers do not state the sense in which they use the term, and this may result at least in imprecise communication and perhaps in imprecise thinking as well. By close study, however, we can often ascertain the sense from the context.

I suggest two hypotheses about the varied concepts of intent that are used in thinking, writing, and speaking about law. Test these hypotheses by your own observations as you proceed with your study. First, despite some variations in detail, there are rather strong tendencies of usage. By close observation we can distinguish between common and uncommon characteristics of concepts of intent in use. Second, there are contrasts in the tendencies of usage that correlate with contrasting contexts. I believe -- though others differ with this observation -- that there is some difference between the set of most common characteristics of the concept of intent used in tort cases and the set of most common characteristics of the concept of intent used in criminal cases. My suggestion is that judicial opinions in tort cases tend more than judicial opinions in criminal cases to apply a definition of intent that rigorously depends on the actor's state of mind and not at all on what the state of mind of some other person in the actor's position might have been. Check this suggestion against your own observations as you study torts and criminal law. If you agree that this contrast exists, consider what the explanation for it might be. The present exercise does not develop the contrast, but I hope it will prepare you to make the observations for yourself.

The <u>Restatement of Torts</u> purports to apply a single, consistent concept of intent throughout. The development of this carefully considered definition of intent is one of the contributions of the <u>Restatement</u> to better understanding of tort law. Since the drafters were attempting to "restate" the law of torts, they were aiming for a definition consistent with the most common usage in judicial opinions in tort cases, and it seems a fair assessment that they achieved this aim. Thus, in developing an understanding and an ability to apply the concept of intent as defined in the <u>Restatement</u> you will also be preparing yourself to understand the most common, though not the only, sense in which courts use the term in tort cases and in insurance cases.

It is likely that there will be one or more ways in which the <u>Restatement</u> concept of intent differs from what you would have expected, and that may affect your final evaluation of the concept. During this exercise, however, remember that the purpose is to develop your understanding and skill in applying the <u>Restatement</u> concept itself. I would like to encourage your natural interest in evaluating the concept. However, I ask you to try to keep that interest from interfering with your performance in understanding and applying the concept.

Although the <u>Restatement</u> falls short of eliminating all ambiguity and doubt in defining and explaining the concept of intent that it adopts, for most of the contexts in which you will have occasion to use this concept the <u>Restatement</u> takes a clear-cut position, free from uncertainty and leaving no room for reasonable differences of opinion about what it means. In those contexts that in my judgement are within this range of clear-cut meaning, I have arranged for the computer to evaluate your answers as "right" or "wrong," "full credit" or "no credit," rather than using a softened statement such as "I agree" or "I disagree." In contrast, in the exceptional contexts that seem to me to be areas of uncertain meaning, the computer is prepared to acknowledge and identify the uncertainty.

The foregoing comments have referred to the use of concepts of intent in judicial opinions. Another context of use of such concepts is the argument of counsel to the jury. For example, plaintiff's counsel might wish to present to the jury various sets of factfindings that would support a verdict for the plaintiff, arguing that the jury should return a verdict for the plaintiff if they find any of these sets of facts. The assertion that a particular set of factfindings is enough to support a verdict for the plaintiff is, of course, a proposition of law -- one that depends in some instances on a concept of intent. If counsel, during argument to the jury, asserts a proposition of law that is incorrect, opposing counsel may object and obtain an instruction by the court to the jury. Ordinarily the instruction given by the court will be one directing the jury to disregard counsel's statement about the law and take their instructions on the law solely from the court's charge to the jury, which in most jurisdictions is given after counsel have completed their summations.

The court's charge to the jury is an additional context in which propositions about what sets of factfindings are sufficient to sustain a verdict for one party or the other will appear.

Part II infra presents the <u>Restatement</u> concept of intent. Part III identifies common imperfections in using the <u>Restatement</u> concept of intent. Each of the statements of common imperfection is a statement that might appropriately be used by counsel as an objection to a proposition advanced by opposing counsel or by the trial judge. Thus, in most jurisdictions both the <u>Restatement</u> concept and the statements of imperfection in applying it are matters you might put to good use as counsel for one of the parties in the trial of a claim of intentional tort, or the trial of an insurance coverage dispute that depends in any way upon applying a concept of intent. Even if there are precedents for application of a different concept of intent in your jurisdiction you might want to urge a court to test those precedents against the <u>Restatement</u> concept.

Supp. Ch. 3   INTENT EXERCISES

Part II

Excerpts from
<u>Restatement (Second) of Torts</u> (1965)
Copyright 1965, reprinted with the permission
of the American Law Institute

§2. Act

The word "act" is used throughout the Restatement of this Subject to denote an external manifestation of the actor's will and does not include any of its results, even the most direct, immediate, and intended.

Comment:

a. <u>Necessity of volition</u>. There cannot be an act without volition. Therefore, a contraction of a person's muscles which is purely a reaction to some outside force, such as a knee jerk or the blinking of the eyelids in defense against an approaching missile, or the convulsive movements of an epileptic, are not acts of that person. So too, movements of the body during sleep when the will is in abeyance are not acts. Since some outward manifestation of the defendant's will is necessary to the existence of an act which can subject him to liability, it is not enough that a third person has utilized a part of the defendant's body as an instrument to carry out his own intention to cause harm to the plaintiff. In such case, as in the case of the knee jerk, the actor is the third person who has used the defendant's body as an instrument to accomplish some purpose of his own, or who has struck the defendant's leg so as to have caused the knee jerk.

b. <u>Freedom of actor's will</u>. If the actor's will is in fact manifested by some muscular contraction, including those which are necessary to the speaking of words, it is not necessary that his will operate freely and without pressure from outside circumstances. Indeed, the fact that the pressure is irresistible in the sense that it is one which reasonable men cannot be expected to resist, does not prevent its manifestation from being an act, although it may make the act excusable. A muscular reaction is always an act unless it is a purely reflexive reaction in which the mind and will have no share. Thus, if A, finding himself about to fall, stretches his hand out to seize some object, whether a fellow human being or a mere inanimate object, to save himself from falling, the stretching out of his hand and the grasping of the object is an act in the sense in which that word has heretofore been used, since the defendant's mind has grasped the situation and has dictated a muscular contraction which his rapidly formed judgment leads him to believe to be helpful to prevent his fall. While the decision is formed instantaneously, none the less the movement of the hand is a response to the will exerted by a mind which has already determined upon a distinct course of action. The exigency in which the defendant is placed, the necessity for a rapid decision, the fact that the decision corresponds to a universal tendency of mankind, may be enough to relieve the defendant from liability, but it is not enough to prevent his grasping of the object from being his act.

c. <u>Act and its consequences</u>. The word "act" includes only the external manifestation of the actor's will. It does not include any of the effects of such manifestation, no matter how direct, immediate, and intended. Thus, if the actor, having pointed a pistol at another, pulls the trigger, the act is the pulling of the trigger and not the impingement of the bullet upon the other's person. So too, if the actor intentionally strikes another, the act is only the movement of the actor's hand and not the contact with the other's body immediately established.

. . .

§8A. Intent

The word "intent" is used throughout the Restatement of this Subject to denote that the actor desires to cause consequences of his act, or that he believes that the consequences are substantially certain to result from it.

Comment:

a. "Intent," as it is used throughout the Restatement of Torts, has reference to the consequences of an act rather than the act itself. When an actor fires a gun in the midst of the Mojave Desert, he intends to pull the trigger; but when the bullet hits a person who is present in the desert without the actor's knowledge, he does not intend that result. "Intent" is limited, wherever it is used, to the consequences of the act.

b. All consequences which the actor desires to bring about are intended, as the word is used in this Restatement. Intent is not, however, limited to consequences which are desired. If the actor knows that the consequences are certain, or substantially certain, to result from his act, and still goes ahead, he is treated by the law as if he had in fact desired to produce the result. As the probability that the consequences will follow decreases, and becomes less than substantial certainty, the actor's conduct loses the character of intent, and becomes mere recklessness, as defined in §500. As the probability decreases further, and amounts only to a risk that the result will follow, it becomes ordinary negligence, as defined in §282. All three have their important place in the law of torts, but the liability attached to them will differ.

Supp. Ch. 3   INTENT EXERCISES

Illustrations:

1. A throws a bomb into B's office for the purpose of killing B. A knows that C, B's stenographer, is in the office. A has no desire to injure C, but knows that his act is substantially certain to do so. C is injured by the explosion. A is subject to liability to C for an intentional tort.

2. On a curve in a narrow highway A, without any desire to injure B, or belief that he is substantially certain to do so, recklessly drives his automobile in an attempt to pass B's car. As a result of this recklessness, A crashes into B's car, injuring B. A is subject to liability to B for his reckless conduct, but is not liable to B for any intentional tort.

. . .

§13. Battery: Harmful Contact

An actor is subject to liability to another for battery if:

(a) he acts intending to cause harmful or offensive contact with the person of the other or a third person, or an imminent apprehension of such a contact, and

(b) a harmful contact with the person of the other directly or indirectly results.

Comment:

c. As to the meaning of "intending" see §8A. If an act is done with the intention described in this Section, it is immaterial that the actor is not inspired by any personal hostility to the other, or a desire to injure him. Thus the fact that the defendant who intentionally inflicts bodily harm upon another does so as a practical joke, does not render him immune from liability so long as the other has not consented. This is true although the actor erroneously believes that the other will regard it as a joke, or that the other has, in fact, consented to it. One who plays dangerous practical jokes on others takes the risk that his victims may not appreciate the humor of his conduct and may not take it in good part. So too, a surgeon who performs an operation upon a patient who has refused to submit to it is not relieved from liability by the fact that he honestly and, indeed, justifiably believes that the operation is necessary to save the patient's life. Indeed, the fact that medical testimony shows that the patient would have died had the operation not been performed and that the operation has effected a complete cure is not enough to relieve the physician from liability. See §892A, Illustration 2.

. . .

§16. Character of Intent Necessary

(1) If an act is done with the intention of inflicting upon another an offensive but not a harmful bodily contact, or of putting another in apprehension of either a harmful or offensive bodily contact, and such act causes a bodily contact to the other, the actor is liable to the other for a battery although the act was not done with the intention of bringing about the resulting bodily harm.

(2) If an act is done with the intention of affecting a third person in the manner stated in Subsection (1), but causes a harmful bodily contact to another, the actor is liable to such other as fully as though he intended so to affect him.

Comment on Subsection (1):

a. In order that the actor shall be liable under the rule stated in this Section, it is not necessary that he intend to bring about the harmful contact which results from his act. It is enough that he intends to bring about an offensive contact or an apprehension of either a harmful or offensive contact, and that the bodily harm results as a legal consequence from such offensive contact or from such apprehension. The interest in freedom from either form of contact or from the apprehension of it is so far a part of the other's interest in his bodily security that the intention to inflict an offensive contact or to create an apprehension of either a harmful or offensive contact is sufficient to make the actor liable for a harmful contact resulting therefrom, even though such harmful contact was not intended.

Illustrations:

1. Intending an offensive contact, A lightly kicks B on the shin. The blow, although offensive, is so slight that it would normally cause no bodily harm. B is suffering from a diseased leg, of which A neither knows nor has reason to know. The slight blow so aggravates the diseased condition as to result in a prolonged and expensive illness, which finally leads to permanent harm to the leg. A is subject to liability to B for the bodily harm caused by his act.

2. A is playing golf. B, his caddie, is inattentive and A becomes angry. Intending to frighten but not to harm B, A aims a blow at him with a golf club which he stops some eight inches from B's head. Owing to the negligence of the club maker from whom A has just bought the club,

the rivet which should have secured the head is defective, though A could not have discovered the defect without removing the head. The head of the club flies off and strikes B in the eye, putting it out. A is subject to liability to B for the loss of his eye.

Comment on Subsection (2):

b. The intention which is necessary to make the actor liable under the rule stated in this Section is not necessarily an intention to cause a harmful or offensive contact or an apprehension of such contact to the plaintiff himself or otherwise to cause him bodily harm. It is enough that the actor intends to produce such an effect upon some other person and that his act so intended is the legal cause of a harmful contact to the other. It is not necessary that the actor know or have reason even to suspect that the other is in the vicinity of the third person whom the actor intends to affect and, therefore, that he should recognize that his act, though directed against the third person, involves a risk of causing bodily harm to the other so that the act would be negligent toward him.

Illustration:

3. A and B are trespassers upon C's land. C sees A but does not see B, nor does he know that B is in the neighborhood. C throws a stone at A. Immediately after C has done so, B raises his head above a wall behind which he has been hiding. The stone misses A but strikes B, putting out his eye. C is subject to liability to B.

. . .

§18. Battery: Offensive Contact

(1) An actor is subject to liability to another for battery if:
(a) he acts intending to cause a harmful or offensive contact with the person of the other or a third person, or an imminent apprehension of such a contact, and (b) an offensive contact with the person of the other directly or indirectly results.

(2) An act which is not done with the intention stated in Subsection (1,a) does not make the actor liable to the other for a mere offensive contact with the other's person although the act involves an unreasonable risk of inflicting it and, therefore, would be negligent or reckless if the risk threatened bodily harm.

Comment:

. . .

INTENT EXERCISES Supp. Ch. 3

Comment on Clause (a) of Subsection (1):

e. In order that the actor may be liable under the rule stated in this Section, it is necessary that an act be done for the purpose of bringing about a harmful or offensive contact or an apprehension of such contact to another or to a third person or with knowledge that such a result will, to a substantial certainty, be produced by his act. It is not enough to make the act intentional that the actor realize that it involves any degree of probability of a harmful or offensive contact or an apprehension of such contact, less than a substantial certainty that it will so result.

Comment on Clause (b) of Subsection (1):

f. <u>Effect of mistake</u>. As to what constitutes an effective consent to an offensive contact, see §§892-892D. As to the conditions under which a consent given by the other is not effective as a consent to prevent the actor from being liable, see §§892-892C. In order that a consent may be effective to preclude the actor's liability, it must be to the offensive contact which the actor inflicts upon the other. It is not enough that a consent be given to the act which causes it. The actor's liability is based upon the offensiveness of his contact with the other's person, and this in many instances depends upon the identity of him who inflicts it or the circumstances under which it is inflicted. There are many contacts which no reasonable man or woman would regard as offensive if brought about by particular persons or by persons standing in particular relations to him or her, but which everyone would regard as highly offensive if inflicted by other persons. Thus, there are many familiarities permissible between husband and wife which any decent married woman would feel not only offensive but degrading if attempted by a stranger, and even the most prudish of women feel no offense at examination by physicians which would be intolerable to them if made by a layman. In such a case, if the actor knows that the other's consent is given under a mistake as to any one of these factors, the consent affords him no protection.

. . .

g. <u>Necessity of intention</u>. The interest which one has in the inviolability of his person and, therefore, in freedom from unpermitted contacts which, while offensive to a reasonable sense of personal dignity cause no substantial or tangible bodily harm, is an interest of dignitary rather than of material value. As such, it is protected only against intentional invasion. The actor is not liable for an act which involves risk, no matter how great and unreasonable, that it will cause only an offensive contact, although his conduct if it involved a similar risk of invading a materially valuable interest would be actionable negligence or even recklessness. So too, the actor whose conduct is negligent or

Supp. Ch. 3   **INTENT EXERCISES**

reckless because of the risk involved of causing an invasion of some materially valuable interest does not become liable if it causes only an offensive contact.

Illustrations:

   3. A, without any intention of wetting anyone, throws water out of his window at night. He knows that B is walking down the street toward his house and that there is a strong probability, though not a certainty, that the water will wet B. A is not liable to B if a small quantity of water splashes in his face but does him no bodily harm.

   4. A throws dirty water from his window at B who is walking on a street below. A few drops fall on B's hand but do him no bodily harm. A is subject to liability to B.

   5. A drives an automobile through a city street. Being engrossed in conversation, he does not see B, a pedestrian, who, seeing A's car approaching, steps aside. The mudguard brushes B's coat and the wheels splash mud in B's face. A is not liable to B.

   6. A, while driving an automobile, sees B standing on the sidewalk. He drives his car through a muddy puddle for the purpose of splashing B. A few drops of muddy water splash on B's hand but neither does him bodily harm nor damage his clothing. A is subject to liability to B.

§20. Character of Intent Necessary

   (1) If an act is done with the intention of inflicting upon another a harmful bodily contact or of putting the other in apprehension of either a harmful or offensive bodily contact, and if it causes an offensive bodily contact to the other, the actor is subject to liability to the other although the act was not done with the intention of bringing about the resulting offensive contact.

   (2) If an act is done with the intention of affecting a third person in the manner stated in Subsection (1) but causes an offensive bodily contact to another, the actor is subject to liability to such other as fully as though he intended so to affect him.

Comment on Subsection (1):

   a. In order that an offensive contact may be actionable, it is not necessary that the actor intend to inflict an offensive contact. It is enough that he intends to inflict either an offensive or a harmful contact or bring about and apprehension of such contact.

Illustrations:

INTENT EXERCISES   Supp. Ch. 3

1. A aims a blow at B with a heavy stick. A bystander checks his arm so that the stick merely grazes B's body, doing no harm. A is subject to liability to B.

2. A, intending merely to frighten B, throws a bucketful of water at him. The water unexpectedly splashes in B's face. A is subject to liability to B.

. . .

Comment on Subsection (2):

b. _Intent to inflict offensive contact upon third person._ As in the case of an act which results in a harmful bodily contact, so here the actor is subject to liability not only where he intends to bring about harmful or offensive contact with the other or an apprehension on the part of the other of such a contact, but also where he intends to inflict such a contact or to create and apprehension of it on the part of a third person. The rule stated in this Section applies although the actor neither knows nor has reason to know that the other is in the vicinity of the third person and therefore neither recognizes nor as a reasonable man should recognize that his act creates any possibility of so affecting the other.

Illustration:

3. A intentionally throws a bucketful of water over B. C is known by A to be standing arm-in-arm with B. A neither knows nor has reason to know that D is in the vicinity of B. As A throws the water, D unexpectedly approaches B and the water drenches B, C, and D. A is subject to liability to all three.

Supp. Ch. 3   INTENT EXERCISES

Part III

Common Imperfections
in Applying the Concept of Intent

<u>A Structure for Thinking about Intent</u>. To get maximum benefit from this computer-aided exercise, you will need to have a good (though certainly not perfect) understanding of the <u>Restatement</u> concept of intent before you go to a computer terminal. This may require two or three hours of painstaking study, but experience indicates that in the end you will move more rapidly toward full understanding of the concept and its practical implications if you will take the time at the outset to understand six aspects of this concept that are the most common sources of error in applying it. This is, of course, not the only useful structure for thinking about the concept, but it is a structure well worth mastering.

The first step toward acquiring an understanding of the <u>Restatement</u> concept is to read the excerpts from the <u>Restatement</u> produced in Part II (pages 492-99 supra). You should read those pages now if you have not already done so.

The key idea of each of the parts of this six-part structure for thinking about the <u>Restatement</u> concept of intent is stated in the first sentence of one of the six numbered paragraphs, immediately below. The second sentence of each paragraph is in the form of a statement of what is wrong with an attempted application of the concept to some fact situation; thus, it is in a form that might be used by a trial lawyer as an objection to a proposed instruction to a jury.

INTENT EXERCISES
Numbered List of Common Imperfections

Supp. Ch. 3

1. STATE OF MIND. Intent, as defined by the <u>Restatement of Torts</u>, is a state of mind of the actor. The stated proposition is based on a standard other than the actor's state of mind.

2. SUBSTANTIAL CERTAINTY. Substantial certainty is the <u>Restatement</u> standard for belief-intent (or knowledge-intent). The stated proposition clearly departs from (or does not clearly adhere to) the <u>Restatement</u> standard of substantial certainty.

3. CONSEQUENCES. Intent concerns consequences of an act (or omission) and not the act itself. The stated proposition concerns consequences that clearly differ from (or do not clearly conform with) those that must be intended under the <u>Restatement</u> requirement for liability on the theory in issue.

4. ASSUMING THE DISPUTED. Assuming the accuracy of assertions of fact that may reasonably be disputed at trial is error. The stated proposition, unqualified, is incorrect because it depends on a factual assumption that may not be supported by the factfindings at trial.

5. SPECIFICITY OF PERSON. For claims of intentional tort against person, intent to cause requisite consequences to a third person rather than the claimant is sufficient, but (under one interpretation of inconclusive passages in the <u>Restatement</u>) intent to cause such consequences to some as yet undetermined person in a class or group is insufficient. The stated proposition would permit a finding of intentional tort on the latter basis.

6. SIMULTANEOUS WITH ACT. Liability for intentional tort depends on an intent existing simultaneously with the act (or omission) on which liability is based. The stated proposition would permit liability based on an act and intent occurring at different times.

The remainder of this part (pages 502-06) presents more detailed discussion and illustration of these six key ideas than you need master before beginning the exercise. I recommend that you read it through once before beginning the exercise and return to it later for closer study when the need arises.

Supp. Ch. 3   **INTENT EXERCISES**

    1. STATE OF MIND. Intent, as defined by the <u>Restatement</u>, is strictly descriptive, not normative. The purpose for which we inquire into an actor's intent is nearly always normative -- to enlighten our choices about what legal consequences should follow. But intent itself is factual, not normative. It is a state of mind. A factfinding that an actor had a stated intent is a finding that the described state of mind did exist in the actor's mind. A finding that such a state of mind should have existed, or that it would have existed in the mind of a reasonable person in the actor's position, is not a finding of intent.

    2. SUBSTANTIAL CERTAINTY. The <u>Restatement</u> concept of intent has two independent parts. The two-part distinction is between desire and belief. In this context, purpose and desire are used interchangeably. Also, belief and knowledge are used interchangeably.* An actor intends a particular consequence to flow from an act when in the actor's mind there is either (a) a desire (or purpose) to produce that consequence or (b) a belief (or knowledge) that the act is substantially certain to produce that consequence. It is customary in ordinary discourse to speak of a desired consequence as intended. It is less common to speak of an undesired consequence as intended, even when the actor believes (or knows) that the act is substantially certain to produce the consequence. Partly because of this deviation from customary usage, and partly because of the inherent difficulty of the concept wholly apart from customary usage, there is greater danger of error in applying the concept of belief-intent (or knowledge-intent) than in applying the concept of desire-intent (or purpose-intent). The most common mistake is substituting some other concept for the "substantial certainty" in the actor's mind that constitutes "believing" (or "knowing") as used in the <u>Restatement of Torts</u>. In qualifying "certainty" with the adjective "substantial," the drafters of the <u>Restatement</u> were acknowledging that absolute certainty is simply not a part of the human condition. They did not mean to dilute the concept of certainty so far as to make it equivalent merely to an exceptionally high probability. They were expressing a concept of "certainty" for all practical purposes. "Very highly probable" is not enough to constitute "substantial certainty" in this sense.

---

* No doubt there are contexts in which it is important to distinguish between knowledge and belief; in the context of applying the <u>Restatement</u> concept of intent, however, the focus is on "substantial certainty" in the mind of the actor, and not on whether that state of mind is in accord with external realities. The first edition of the <u>Restatement</u> used the term "know" (or a derivative), in this context, and the <u>Restatement (Second)</u> more often uses the term "believe" (or a derivative), but it seems clear that this change of terminology did not change the underlying concept of intent.

INTENT EXERCISES

3. CONSEQUENCES. Intent concerns consequences. We cannot fully describe a state of mind of intent without identifying the intended consequences -- without answering the question: intent to what? For each intentional tort, there is a distinctive set of consequences that are a part of the intent that is a requisite of liability on that theory. A very common mistake in applying the concept of intent is asserting that the intent requirement is met by a finding of intent to cause a set of consequences that differs from the set of consequences that must be intended under the requirement for liability on the theory in issue.

For the tort of battery, the consequences that are an essential part of an accurate statement of the requisite intent are, according to the Restatement, §13, "a harmful or offensive contact with the person of the other or a third person, or an imminent apprehension of such a contact." The intent required for battery is not present if the actor intends not to cause any contact and not to cause any "imminent apprehension" of contact but instead to cause apprehension of a contact some time later. Also, the intent required for battery is not present if the actor intends only to strike the plaintiff's dog, while not held by the plaintiff, but accidentally (for example, on the back swing) strikes the plaintiff instead.

In this six-part structure for thinking about intent, the issue of specificity of person (which is in essence one aspect of the broad question, what consequences must be intended) is considered in paragraph 5.

> Special Note: It is a defensible position that the Restatement is unclear with respect to whether, when a claim is based on intended contact, the plaintiff must prove that the defendant intended that the contact be harmful or offensive as well as intending that the contact occur. It is defensible also to carry forward this ambiguity in applying the Restatement concept of intent. However, it seems likely that a court squarely confronted with the issue would require the ambiguity to be resolved one way or the other. Though precedents are inconclusive, probably most courts would require intent that the contact be harmful or offensive in quality rather than requiring only that the defendant intended a contact that turned out to be harmful or offensive. (Unless otherwise directed you are to assume that there is no precedent directly on this point in your jurisdiction.)

4. ASSUMING THE DISPUTED. The mistake of assuming the accuracy of disputable facts is not distinctively associated with applying the concept of intent; it occurs often in other contexts as well. But no statement of the most common errors in application of the concept of intent would be complete without inclusion of this error.

5. SPECIFICITY OF PERSON. Both the Restatement and judicial decisions clearly support extension of the theory of battery to others than the intended victim when the defendant's intent was directed at a

particular victim. Nevertheless, the intent that is required for intentional torts against person, such as battery, is an intent directed at a person or persons. Thus, for battery, Restatement §13 requires an intent "to cause a harmful or offensive contact with the person of the other or a third person, or an imminent apprehension of such a contact." (Emphasis added.)

One may reasonably argue that policy justifications for liability under the theory of battery remain compelling as long as the defendant's intent was directed at personal contact, even though not with a particular person. On the other hand, fact situations raising this problem are usually situations in which the defendant acted not with the desire of causing such a contact but instead with some other desire and with knowledge that acting with that desire was substantially certain to cause such a contact. One may have doubts about treating a person who acts with knowledge, but no desire that the requisite type of contact occur, just as severely as we treat a person who acts with the desire that it occur. And such doubts may be exacerbated by attenuation of the concept of "intent against person" to include cases of intent to place a crowd of persons at risk with knowledge that someone, unidentifiable at the time of the act, will suffer a contact.

Compare two cases: first, a case in which the defendant, for the purpose of injuring the plaintiff, sets a bomb in plaintiff's car, with a trigger mechanism, hoping but not knowing whether the plaintiff will enter the car and trigger the bomb, or when; second, a case in which the defendant, a builder, is substantially certain that one or more workers will be injured during construction of a large building, and with this knowledge acts to cause the construction to go forward. One difference is that the defendant in the first case desired the contact and the defendant in the second did not. A second difference is that the intent of the defendant in the first case was directed at a particular person; in the second, the defendant's knowledge-intent concerned no particular person, but only the knowledge that some as yet unidentifiable person or persons among a large group would suffer the contact.

When the plaintiff in the first case triggers the bomb, a battery is consummated. In contrast, there is no precedent for holding that the second case is a battery, though it may be debated whether the explanation is lack of the requisite intent, or instead some other reason -- for example, a theory of privilege based on the social value of the defendant's activity.

Acceptance or rejection of a theory of battery in this context is likely to have little practical significance, in view of the likelihood of the same outcome regardless of whether the theory applied is battery (qualified by privilege) or instead a theory of liability for unintended consequences (recklessness, negligence, or strict liability). Attenuation of the concept of intent against person is more likely to have significant consequences in other areas of the law, including misrepresentation. Such attenuation is especially likely to be rejected when it bears upon the scope of insurance coverage.

Special Note: Although it is clear that one who acts with intent to cause a contact on a second person and with intent that it be harmful or offensive to that person is subject to liability for battery if instead the act causes a harmful or offensive contact upon a third person, the Restatement uses the phrase "contact with the person of the other or a third person" (emphasis added) and is inconclusive with respect to whether the same result follows if the intent was only that the members of a group be subjected to a risk of contact under circumstances making it substantially certain that someone among them, not identifiable in advance, would suffer the contact.

6. SIMULTANEOUS WITH ACT. An actor does not commit an intentional tort by carelessly creating a hazardous condition that is a trap for the unwary and thereafter, when circumstances are beyond the actor's control, forming the state of mind of desire or knowledge that the plaintiff will fall into the trap. In such circumstances the actor may be liable for negligence, but not battery.

The numbered list below is an exact repetition of the list as it appears on page 501 supra, except that illustrations (designated by the letters A, B, etc.) are added. The purpose of providing the list in both forms is to enable you to use the list as it appears (page 501) when that is most convenient, but also to enable you to use the list with illustrations when you wish to study a suspect proposition more closely.

Most of the statements and illustrations in this numbered list can fairly be called errors. Others are identified by the Special Notes (pp. 503, 505) as areas of uncertainty in the law and in the Restatement; in relation to these areas of uncertainty one might reasonably argue that the position identified here is defensible and that its assertion is not error.

Whenever you are using either the list alone (page 501) or the list with illustrations, infra, read with great care. Note that a single assertion may include more than one of this numbered list of imperfections. For example, consider the assertion that:

the defendant had the intent required for battery if a reasonable person in his position would have believed it very probable that the defendant's act would produce an offensive contact upon the plaintiff.

The statement has Imperfection 1 because it speaks of what would have been in the mind of a reasonable person in defendant's position; it does not concern the defendant's own state of mind. It also has Imperfection 2 because it uses the standard "very probable" rather than the standard "substantially certain."

INTENT EXERCISES — Supp. Ch. 3

Numbered List with Illustrations

1. STATE OF MIND. Intent, as defined by the <u>Restatement of Torts</u>, is a state of mind of the actor. The stated proposition is based on a standard other than the actor's state of mind.

   Illustrations: This imperfection occurs when--

   A. The stated proposition refers to a finding concerning what the defendant should have known would happen.

   B. The stated proposition depends on a finding of substantial certainty (or some other standard) from the point of view of some other observer and not the actor's own state of mind.

   C. The stated proposition asserts in effect that the law treats the actor as if having formed a state of mind that fulfills the definition of intent when in fact the actor may not have formed any such state of mind. A common version of this error is the assertion that the law "charges" the actor with knowledge of a fact, whether the actor knew the fact or not, when the circumstances are such that a reasonable person would have realized that fact. These circumstances might sustain a finding of negligence but they are not enough to sustain a finding of intent. (Whenever this mistake occurs, the mistake identified in paragraph B, immediately above, is also present.)

2. SUBSTANTIAL CERTAINTY. Substantial certainty is the <u>Restatement</u> standard for belief-intent (or knowledge-intent). The stated proposition clearly departs from (or does not clearly adhere to) the <u>Restatement</u> standard of substantial certainty.

   Illustrations: This imperfection occurs when --

   A. The reference to what was "believed" or "known" (or a derivative) does not require as near an approach to certainty as being "substantially certain" that a particular consequence will follow.

   B. The reference to what was "believed" or "known" (or a derivative) is expressed in language other than "being substantially certain" that a particular consequence will follow and it is unclear whether the language used has a meaning different from "being substantially certain."

3. CONSEQUENCES. Intent concerns consequences of an act (or omission)

Supp. Ch. 3   INTENT EXERCISES

and not the act itself. The stated proposition concerns consequences that clearly differ from (or do not clearly conform with) those that must be intended under the <u>Restatement</u> requirement for liability on the theory in issue.

   Illustrations: This imperfection occurs, in relation to a claim of battery when --

   A. The described consequence is one that the defendant might intend without intending either a personal contact or apprehension of such a contact. That is, the defendant might neither desire that a contact with person or apprehension of such a contact occur nor believe it to be substantially certain that such a contact or apprehension of such a contact will occur. (Whenever this mistake occurs, the imperfection identified in paragraph B, immediately below, is also present.)

   B. The described consequence might not be a "harmful or offensive" contact with person, or apprehension of a "harmful or offensive" contact with person.

   See the Special Note on page 503.

   C. The stated proposition purports to include all the different states of mind that would meet the requisites of battery (or all that would do so and also appear to be supportable by the evidence), but it omits one or more of the states of mind that would be sufficient.

   D. The stated proposition requires (that is, says the requisite intent cannot be established without) a finding not only of intent to produce a contact with person but also of intent that it be a "harmful or offensive" contact. (This position is not clearly established by precedents. See the Special Note on page 503. But, it is a defensible position and is one that counsel might choose to advance. For example, counsel for plaintiff in an action for battery might object to a charge having this characteristic and urge that plaintiff, having proved that defendant intended the contact in question, need not prove also that the defendant intended that the contact be "harmful or offensive.")

   4. ASSUMING THE DISPUTED. Assuming the accuracy of assertions of fact that may reasonably be disputed at trial is error. The stated proposition, unqualified, is incorrect because it depends on a factual assumption that may not be supported by the factfindings at trial.

Illustrations: This imperfection occurs when--

    A. The stated proposition makes and assertion of fact introduced by the word "because" (or a word of similar meaning in context, such as "since") but available information leaves open the possibility that the asserted fact will be in dispute at trial.

    B. An assertion, in the stated proposition, that the actor "must have had" a particular state of mind is an assertion of fact, but available information leaves open the possibility that the asserted fact will be in dispute at trial.

5. SPECIFICITY OF PERSON. For claims of intentional tort against person, intent to cause requisite consequences to a third person rather than the claimant is sufficient, but (under one interpretation of inconclusive passages in the <u>Restatement</u>) intent to cause such consequences to some as yet undetermined person in a class or group is insufficient. The stated proposition would permit a finding of intentional tort on the latter basis.

6. SIMULTANEOUS WITH ACT. Liability for intentional tort depends on an intent existing simultaneously with the act (or omission) on which liability is based. The stated proposition would permit liability based on an act and intent occurring at different times.

7. The stated proposition is erroneous in some respect not within paragraphs 1-6.

Part IV

Fact Situation: Jones v. Davis

You are an associate of a lawyer to whom Jones comes for advice and representation with respect to a potential claim for damages. Jones appears at the law office on crutches and with his left leg in a cast. He tells the following story:

About three weeks ago I was walking along a sidewalk in a business section of the city. A man dumped a pail of water at me from a scaffold beside an upper story window of an office building. I tried to dodge the water and tripped over a fire hydrant. I fell, and broke my leg. Some of the water hit me. A police officer who investigated told me that the man who dumped the water is a window washer by the name of Davis. He said Davis denied that he was trying to hit anybody and said he was just throwing away waste water.

INTENT EXERCISES   Supp. Ch. 3

Part V

Illustrative Question on Insurance Law Coverage:

One of your associates asserts the following proposition about the fact situation of <u>Jones v. Davis</u> (Part IV of the materials):

> If the jury finds that when Davis threw the water, it was apparent that some of the water would splash on Jones and that the contact would be offensive to Jones, then the liability insurance coverage carried by Davis will not apply to the tort claim of Jones against Davis.

Is this proposition correct, without qualification?

Answer YES, NO, RABYES, or RABNO.*

After answering turn to the next page.

*   RABYES means "reasonable arguments for both positions and I prefer YES."

   RABNO means "reasonable arguments for both positions and I prefer NO."

The correct answer is NO.

The stated proposition deviates from the <u>Restatement</u> concept of intent by committing error 1 (Illustration 1B) because it requires only a finding that "it was apparent" from some unstated point of view and not a finding that Davis had the state of mind of knowing or believing that the stated results would follow.

The stated proposition deviates from the <u>Restatement</u> concept of intent by committing error 2 (Illustration 2B) because it uses another concept ("apparent") rather than the <u>Restatement</u> concept of "being substantially certain." It is unclear whether "apparent" may convey a meaning short of "substantial certainty."

Because of error 1, it is clear that this jury finding does not defeat liability insurance coverage for the tort claims of Jones against Davis. This finding is insufficient to establish that the impact on Jones was not fortuitous (a point relevant to any contention of "implied exception" from liability insurance coverage) or that the impact was "expected or intended" from the point of view of Davis (a point relevant to any contention for applicability of a clause in the policy declaring that the policy does not apply "to bodily injury ... which is either expected or intended from the standpoint of the insured").

The significance of error 2 is more debatable in the insurance context than in the tort law context because the word "expected" as used in the policy clause may be held to have a meaning quite different from "intended." <u>See §5.4(d)</u> of R. Keeton & A. Widiss, <u>Insurance Law</u> (1988).

INTENT EXERCISES   Supp. Ch. 3

Illustrative Question on Tort Law: One of your associates asserts the following proposition about the fact situation of Jones v. Davis (Part IV of the materials):

When he threw the water, Davis had the requisite state of mind for battery on Jones if it was apparent that some of the water would splash on Jones and that the contact would be offensive to Jones.

Is this proposition correct, without qualification?

Answer YES, NO, RABYES, or RABNO.*

After answering, turn to the next page.

* See Page 511 for Instructions on Answering and an explanation of the meaning of RABYES or RABNO.

Supp. Ch. 3   **INTENT EXERCISES**

The correct answer is NO.

Turn to the next page.

INTENT EXERCISES   Supp. Ch. 3

Regardless of whether you answered **correctly**, consider the following question:

    Which one or more of the Common Imperfections (listed in Part III of the materials) occur in the proposition stated in the Illustrative Question? Answer with the number or numbers of the applicable items in the numbered list.

After answering, turn to the next page.

Supp. Ch. 3   INTENT EXERCISES

The correct answer is 1, 2.

The stated proposition commits error 1 (Illustration 1B) because it requires only a finding that "it was apparent" from some unstated point of view and not a finding that Davis had the state of mind of knowing or believing that the stated results would follow.

The stated proposition commits error 2 (Illustration 2B) because it uses another concept ("apparent") rather than the <u>Restatement</u> concept of "being substantially certain." It is unclear whether "apparent" may convey a meaning short of "substantial certainty."

If you gave a different answer and, after reconsideration, you still doubt or disagree with this answer, perhaps you should talk to a fellow student or your instructor before you start the computer exercise.

Special Note: It might also be suggested that paragraph 3 (Illustration 3D) of the list of Common Imperfections applies in this instance. The argument for this position is Position A below. Position B is the opposing position.

Position A: The proposition stated in this Illustration implies that it is necessary that Davis intend the offensive quality of the contact as well as intending the contact; as pointed out in Illustrations 3B and 3D, the <u>Restatement</u>, as well as precedent, leaves this issue in doubt.

Position B: The proposition stated in the Illustrative Question purports only to state that Davis did have the requisite state of mind if stated conditions did exist; it does not apply if these conditions did not exist. It does not say that these are the only conditions that would fulfill the requisites. To interpret the statement as Position A does is to substitute the words "if, but only if," for the word "if." When "if, but only if" appears in a context such as this, the proposition purports to include all the different states of mind that would meet the requisites of battery (or all that would do so and also appear to be supportable by the evidence). In contrast, when "if" alone appears, the proposition does not purport to be all-inclusive.

INTENT EXERCISES   Supp. Ch. 3

In support of Position A one might respond that even though literal interpretation supports Position B in the present instance, still the proposition in the Illustrative Question is imperfect because it is likely to lead one to infer that it was meant to be all-inclusive. The cogency of this response depends on the reasonableness of the inference that the stated proposition was meant to be all-inclusive, and this will vary with the context. However, throughout the present exercise you are asked to adopt Position B on this issue, wherever it arises. That is, construe a proposition that uses "if" alone as not intended to be all-inclusive.

Applying this construction makes paragraph 3 of the Common Imperfections inapplicable to the proposition stated in this Illustrative Question.

Supp. Ch. 3   INTENT EXERCISES

YOU NEED NOT READ MATERIALS BEYOND THIS POINT BEFORE STARTING PROBLEM 1 ON THE COMPUTER TERMINAL. YOU WILL BE DIRECTED TO RELEVANT PARTS OF THE REMAINING MATERIALS OF THIS PROBLEM AS YOU PROCEED WITH THE COMPUTER-AIDED EXERCISE.

Part VI

Other Materials

Excerpts from American Bar Association
Code of Professional Responsibility (1971)
(Footnotes are omitted from these excerpts.)

Canon 7

A lawyer should represent a client zealously within the bounds of the law.

. . .

EC7-23: The complexity of law often makes it difficult for a tribunal to be fully informed unless the pertinent law is presented by the lawyers in the cause. A tribunal that is fully informed on the applicable law is better able to make a fair and accurate determination of the matter before it. The adversary system contemplates that each lawyer will present and argue the existing law in the light most favorable to his client. Where a lawyer knows of legal authority in the controlling jurisdiction directly adverse to the position of his client, he should inform the tribunal of its existence unless his adversary has done so; but, having made such disclosure, he may challenge its soundness in whole or in part.

. . .

DR7-106   Trial Conduct

. . .

(B) In presenting a matter to a tribunal, a lawyer shall disclose:

INTENT EXERCISES

(1) Legal authority in the controlling jurisdiction known to him to be directly adverse to the position of his client and which is not disclosed by opposing counsel.

(2) Unless privileged or irrelevant, the identities of the clients he represents and of the persons who employed him.

Note: For this exercise, you are not asked to examine materials on this subject other than the ABA Code of 1971. You would, of course, wish to examine the Code or other provisions applicable in the court where you are appearing, should you face an issue of this kind in practice.

Supp. Ch. 3   INTENT EXERCISES

Part VII

Form for Questions on Proposed Charge

Question: At the trial of the case of Jones v. Davis, Jones testifies consistently with the story he told when he first came to your law office. A bystander, called as a witness for plaintiff, testifies that he was watching from across the street and saw Davis standing on the scaffold, about 30 feet above the sidewalk, looking down in the direction from which Jones was approaching, until Jones was close at which time Davis dumped the water. Davis testifies that he was just throwing away waste water, was not trying to hit anyone, and did not know anyone was walking below. Each witness testifies that Jones, Davis and the bystander were the only persons in the vicinity when this incident occurred. In a conference in chambers, the trial judge shows counsel a tentative charge instructing the jury as follows regarding the state of mind of defendant required for battery:

You will find that the defendant Davis had the state of mind required for battery if, but only if, you make one or more of the following findings of fact:

. . .

Your senior, who is leading trial counsel for plaintiff asks what, if any, objections you would recommend making to the proposed charge.

In answering this question, state first any objections that appear in Paragraphs 1-6 of the list of Common Imperfections. Begin each objection as a new paragraph, starting with the applicable symbol from the list of Common Imperfections, followed by a period. Then proceed with further explanation if you wish to make any.

After you have indicated each of the applicable objections from the first six paragraphs of the list of Common Imperfections, if there are any other objections you would recommend, state each in a separate paragraph. Begin the first such Paragraph "7". Begin the next "8". Etc.

In answering this question, please use the form 1B, 1C, 5 (if those are the applicable symbols), not merely 1, 5.

End of Materials for Problem 1

INTENT EXERCISES   Supp. Ch. 3

Problem 2

Computer-Generated Intent Exercises

The primary purposes of these exercises are, first, to give you an opportunity for practice in applying the Restatement of Torts concept of intent, which is presented and explained on pages 489-509 supra; second, to provide you with an evaluation of your performance; third, if you are having difficulties, to identify for you the parts of the discussion of Common Imperfections in Applying the Concept of Intent, pages 500-09, that you might usefully reexamine.

All of these exercises are based on one fact situation which follows:

Ben drove an automobile along a city street in the late afternoon. Randy, age six, being pursued by Pat, age ten, ran into the street in the middle of a block, in front of Ben's car. Pat threw a rock that went through the open window of Ben's car and struck Ben. Because he was distracted by being hit, Ben failed to stop his car until after it had struck Randy. Randy was severely injured.

The computer is prepared to submit to you a series of exercises in each of which you are asked to evaluate a statement about the intent requirement for battery as applied to potential claims arising from this fact situation.

After each statement is presented, you are asked whether it is correct without qualification. Answer YES or NO.

If you correctly answer YES, the computer so advises you. If you wish to continue to another exercise, you may do so by pressing the return key.

If you incorrectly answer NO, the computer advises you that the correct answer is YES. If, on reconsideration, you still disagree, you are invited to record your reasons for consideration by your instructor. If you wish to continue to another exercise, you may do so by pressing the return key.

If you incorrectly answer YES, the computer so advises you and then asks that you reexamine the statement and identify which one or more of the numbered paragraphs of the Common Imperfections in Applying the Concept of Intent (pages 500-09 supra) occur in the statement.

If you correctly answer NO, the computer so advises you and then asks you to identify the applicable Common Imperfections.

Supp. Ch. 3   **INTENT EXERCISES**

In the General Version of this problem you are asked to identify applicable imperfections by numbers only (e.g., 1, 2, 5).

In the Specific Version of this problem, when an error is like one of the Illustrations, you are asked to identify the applicable letter of the illustration as well as the number (e.g., 1B, 2A, 5).

Unless you elect otherwise, the first ten examples submitted to you will be in the General Version and the remainder in the Specific Version.

Under both versions, after you have answered, the computer advises you of your score on the question and also advises you what the full-credit answer is. In both the General and Specific Versions, the computer identifies applicable illustrations as well as numbered paragraphs, but identification of illustrations is not a part of the basis for scoring in the General Version.

The computer is prepared to submit more exercises as long as you think it useful to proceed.

An illustrative exercise appears on the next four pages. Work through this exercise before you go to a computer terminal.

INTENT EXERCISES   Supp. Ch. 3

Illustration

The following statement is one among the thousands of statements the computer may present to you for evaluation:

Pat had a state of mind sufficient to meet the requirement of intent for battery against Randy if Pat was aware of the circumstances when he threw the rock, and in those circumstances it was substantially certain that his act would cause a contact with the person of Randy and that the contact would be harmful.

Is this proposition correct, without qualification? Answer YES or NO.

After you have answered, please turn to the next page.

Supp. Ch. 3   INTENT EXERCISES

The correct answer is NO.

Please turn to the next page.

INTENT EXERCISES   **Supp. Ch. 3**

General Version

    List by number each of the Common Imperfections (page 501) occurring in the proposition that appears on page 523.

After you have answered, please turn to the next page.

Specific Version

    List by number (and by letter, if an illustration applies) each of the Common Imperfections (pages 502-09) occurring in the proposition that appears on page 523.

After you have answered, please turn to the next page.

Supp. Ch. 3   INTENT EXERCISES

[General Version] The full-credit answer is 1.

[Specific Version] The full-credit answer is 1B.

The phrase "it was substantially certain that" commits the error illustrated in paragraph 1B, page 507. That is, it depends on a finding of substantial certainty from the point of view of some other observer rather than depending on a finding that Pat's own state of mind was one of substantial certainty that his act would cause the stated consequence.

It might be suggested that imperfection 3D applies also. The answering argument is stated on pages 516-17, above. In these exercises, please follow the same instructions as in Problem 1, page 517, under which 3D is inapplicable in this instance.

If you do not fully understand this illustration, perhaps you should talk with a fellow student or your instructor before you begin this series of exercises on the computer.

End of Materials for Problem 2

OXFORD SHIPPING CO., LTD.
v.
NEW HAMPSHIRE TRADING CORP.

United States Court of Appeals, First Circuit.
697 F.2d 1

Argued Oct. 7, 1982.
Decided Dec. 28, 1982.
Rehearings Denied Jan. 20, 1983.

SHIPPING: damages resulting from seizure of vessel could be recovered from shipper by vessel owner.

Carrier brought action to recover damages resulting from seizure of vessel as a result of shipper's attempts to cheat purchaser of scrap metal which was being shipped on vessel. The United States District Court for the District of New Hampshire, Martin F. Loughlin, J., entered judgment in favor of defendant shipper, scrap dealer that sold scrap to shipper, president of scrap dealer, and agent retained to issue bills of lading and perform other tasks associated with loading and shipping scrap, and carrier appealed. The Court of Appeals, Breyer, Circuit Judge, held that damages resulting from seizure of vessel could be recovered from shipper and agent retained to issue bills of lading and perform other tasks associated with loading and shipping scrap.

Reversed and remanded.

2 Before PECK, Senior Circuit Judge, CAMPBELL and BREYER, Circuit Judges.

* Of the Sixth Circuit, sitting by designation.

BREYER, Circuit Judge.

Oxford Shipping Co., Ltd. ("Oxford"), is a subsidiary of a large Hong Kong commercial firm. Oxford's assets consist principally of one cargo ship, the "Eastern Saga." Oxford claims that it was hurt when its ship was seized by South Korean authorities as a result of a scheme to cheat a Korean firm, Yulsan. Yulsan had bought about 20,000 tons of scrap metal, which applicable bills of lading represented to be aboard the "Eastern Saga," but the ship actually contained only about 17,000 tons of metal.

Oxford brought suit to recover damages in New Hampshire federal district court. It sued Avon Trading Corporation ("Avon"), the shipper that used the "Eastern Saga" to transport the metal; New Hampshire Trading Corp. ("NHT"), a scrap dealer that sold scrap to Avon; Frederic Gendron, the president of NHT; and Tager Steamship Agency ("Tager"), an agent retained to issue bills of lading and perform other tasks associated with loading and shipping the scrap.

Since Oxford itself seems to have been innocent of wrongdoing (although the captain and crew of its ship may have known of the plot), while several of the defendants seem to have been guilty of conduct ranging from simple breach of fiduciary duty to what approaches criminal behavior, one might believe at first glance that it would be fairly easy for Oxford (the company and its shareholders) to recover for the harms suffered. The record reveals, however, a highly complicated set of legalistic arguments, made by the defendants' lawyers and by Oxford's lawyers in response, that led the district court to conclude that the defendants were entitled to judgment on all counts. Oxford appeals. Our review of the case convinces us that the law should, and does, correspond with one's elementary sense of justice: namely, as between Oxford and most of these defendants, the defendants rather than Oxford and its shareholders should pay for the damage caused.

*3 I

The complex set of facts underlying this litigation can be simplified as follows. Avon contracted in 1978 to sell roughly 20,000 tons of scrap metal to Yulsan. Avon subchartered the "Eastern Saga" from Transamerica Steamship Corp., which had previously subchartered the vessel from several other firms which in turn had chartered it from Oxford. The evidence before the district court indicated that Avon tried to cheat Yulsan by only loading some 17,000 tons of scrap on board. In particular, after buying an initial quantity of scrap elsewhere, Avon purchased roughly 7,000 tons of scrap from NHT, but represented the amount as over 10,000 tons. Avon used various false documents to conceal the fraud, including bills of lading issued by Tager that overstated the weight of the scrap by several thousand tons. In issuing the bills of lading, Tager relied upon a letter signed by NHT's Gendron concerning the scrap weight, but Gendron testified at trial that the letter was written by Avon officials and signed by him at their behest, and that he was not aware that it misrepresented the amount of scrap sold by NHT to Avon.

The captain and first officer of the "Eastern Saga," who were agents of Oxford, probably knew that the ship was carrying too little scrap, for they were approached by Avon officials at several points with schemes to cover up the shortfall by taking on water ballast and dumping it in South Korea while the ship was being unloaded. They refused to go along with the plot, but they do not appear to have informed either their superiors at Oxford or Yulsan itself of what was going on. When the ship reached South Korea the short-weighting was quickly discovered, and Yulsan had the "Eastern Saga" seized by South Korean port authorities. The fact that Yulsan had accepted the bills of lading, however, apparently triggered automatic payment through letters of credit, so Yulsan appears to have had to pay for the missing metal. Yulsan began litigation in South Korea against Oxford and other parties to recover the value of the shortfall, and Oxford was able to extract its ship in the interim only by posting a security bond worth approximately $200,000.

Oxford began its suit in federal district court to recover for various losses incurred by the seizure of its ship and for the potential liability created by Yulsan's claims against it. Oxford sought to recover from Avon, NHT, Gendron, and Tager for breach of contract, negligence, and fraudulent misrepresentation in connection with Avon's attempted fraud against Yulsan. After a four-day bench trial, the district court entered judgment against Oxford on every claim.

II

Claims against Avon

Oxford's claims against Avon rest primarily upon its contention that, in providing false information for the bills of lading, Avon breached its contractual obligations to Oxford. We believe that the district court properly characterized the claim as one arising under the Carriage of Goods by Sea Act, 46 U.S.C. sections 1300 et seq. ("COGSA"). COGSA provides in part that

> (t)he shipper shall be deemed to have guaranteed to the carrier the accuracy at the time of shipment of the marks, number, quantity, and weight (of the cargo), as furnished by him; and the shipper shall indemnify the carrier against all loss, damages, and expenses arising

or resulting from inaccuracies in such particulars.

46 U.S.C. section 1303(5). The facts make clear that Avon breached its duty to supply accurate information about the weight of the cargo. In fact, Avon deliberately overstated the weight. Yet the district court held that Avon need not indemnify Oxford for its "loss, damages, and expenses ... resulting from (those) inaccuracies" (other than Oxford's potential liability to Yulsan), because Oxford's officers on the "Eastern Saga" knew about Avon's fraud. This fact, in the court's view, "equitably estopped" Oxford from recovering.

*4 (1, 2) Although the factual findings of the district court concerning the knowledge of Oxford's officers are not clearly erroneous, Fed.R.Civ.P. 52(a), the court erred in its legal conclusion that those facts supported the application of equitable estoppel. As an initial matter, it is far from clear that the doctrine of equitable estoppel applies under section 1303(5); on its face, section 1303(5) imposes absolute liability on a shipper who supplies a carrier with inaccurate information about a cargo, without regard to the carrier's conduct. Moreover, even if it were assumed that the common law defense of equitable estoppel were incorporated into the statutory cause of action created by section 1303(5), the defense simply has no application here. Traditionally, the doctrine of equitable estoppel

> operates to preclude a party (who has made representations of fact through his words or conduct) '(f)rom asserting rights which might perhaps have otherwise existed ... as against another person, who has in good faith relied upon such conduct, and has been led thereby to change his position for the worse, and who on his part acquired some corresponding right ....'

Precious Metals Associates, Inc. v. Commodity Futures Trading Commission, 620 F.2d 900, 908 (1st Cir.1980), quoting 2 J. Pomeroy, Equity Jurisprudence section 804, at 1421-22 (3d ed. 1905); see, e.g., Lavin v. Marsh, 644 F.2d 1378 (9th Cir.1981). In this case, neither Oxford nor its agents made any representations to Avon concerning the cargo, nor did Avon rely on any representations in pursuing its fraudulent scheme, nor would it have had the requisite good faith had it done so. Insofar as Oxford's agents failed in their duty to inform Oxford (and Yulsan) about Avon's conduct, Avon was helped rather than hindered by their conduct.

(3, 4) The doctrine most on point here is not that of equitable estoppel, which we cannot find to have been applied in a case like this one, but the defense of "acquiescence." That defense bars an indemnitee from obtaining indemnification when the indemnitee knowingly acquiesces in the indemnitor's wrongful conduct. See, e.g., Missouri Pac. R.R. Co. v. Winburn Tile Mfg. Co., 461 F.2d 984, 989 (8th Cir.1972); Missouri Pac. R.R. Co. v. Arkansas Oak Flooring, 434 F.2d 575, 578-79 (8th Cir.1970). As is true of "equitable estoppel," we have found no case implying this defense under COGSA. In any event, we do not believe that the defense bars recovery by an innocent principal-indemnitee against a culpable agent-indemnitor merely because another of the principal's agents has knowledge of the indemnitor's wrongdoing. See Becker v. Central Telephone and Utilities Corp., 365 F.Supp. 984, 988-89 (D.S.D.1973) (acquiescence requires awareness of dangerous situation created by indemnitor, and "'awareness' denotes something more than imputed legal 'knowledge'"), vacated on other grounds sub nom. Becker v. Black & Veatch Consulting Engineers, 509 F.2d 42 (8th Cir.1974); cf. Standard Oil Co. of California v. Intrepid, Inc., 26 Cal.App.3d 135, 139-40, 102 Cal.Rptr. 604, 607-08 (1972) (negligence of ship owner precludes recovery from indemnitor only if ship owner's conduct prevented or substantially handicapped indemnitor in performing his duties).

(5, 6) Becker holds explicitly, and Standard Oil implicitly, that an indemnitee is not barred from recovery by mere imputed knowledge of an indemnitor's negligence. If so, so much the less should an indemnitee be barred by imputed knowledge of an intentional fraud. Cases barring recovery under the acquiescence doctrine frequently have involved some degree of joint fault between the indemnitor and the indemnitee. There is no degree of joint fault here, for the only failing outside of Avon's own intentional misconduct is the breach by Oxford's agents of a duty to inform that they owed to Oxford rather than to Yulsan. As between an innocent principal whose loss is caused in part by an unfaithful or negligent agent, and another agent who has injured the principal through willful misconduct, the latter rather than the former ought to bear the burden of the loss. This case does not present any special circumstances suggesting a contrary result. We therefore *5 hold that Oxford was not "equitably estopped" or barred by "acquiescence," and that it is entitled to recover from Avon under the indemnity provision of COGSA.

The district court dismissed Oxford's further negligence and fraud claims against Avon on the ground that COGSA preempted these common law bases of liability. While several lower court decisions support this conclusion, see Miller Export Corp. v. Hellenic Lines, Ltd., 534 F.Supp. 707, 710 (S.D.N.Y.1982); National Automotive Publications, Inc. v. United States Lines, Inc., 486 F.Supp. 1094, 1099 (S.D.N.Y.1980); B.F. McKernin & Co. v. United States Lines, Inc., 416 F.Supp. 1068, 1071 (S.D.N.Y.1976), we need neither accept nor reject these decisions. Since Oxford's COGSA claim is an adequate basis for the relief it seeks against Avon, we need not reach the issue.

III

Claims against NHT and Gendron

Oxford's claims against NHT and its president Gendron involve the same issues and concern the same conduct, namely Gendron's letter to Tager stating that NHT had loaded over 10,000 tons of scrap on the ship. As Gendron apparently knew, NHT had, in reality, loaded only some 7,400 tons.

Oxford based its claim primarily on the theory that NHT, through Gendron, had fraudulently misrepresented the weight of the cargo. The district court held that under New Hampshire law, a plaintiff must show an intent to deceive in order to recover for fraud. See Hanson v. Edgerly, 29 N.H. 343 (1854); Lord v. Colley, 6 N.H. 99 (1833). It found no such intent here. Gendron testified that the misleading letter was typed by an Avon official, that it was placed before him, and that he signed it without looking closely at it. Gendron testified that he did not know he was helping Avon perpetrate a fraud.

(7, 8) The district court credited enough of this testimony to find that Gendron lacked the requisite intent to deceive. The district court saw Gendron testify. Judgments of credibility are peculiarly within its province; they will not be disturbed by this court without a compelling showing of error, and no such showing has been made. See Fed.R.Civ.P. 52(a); Pepsi-Cola Metropolitan Bottling Co. v. Pleasure Island, Inc., 345 F.2d 617, 621 (1st Cir.1965). We therefore reject Oxford's efforts to have us overturn as clearly erroneous the court's finding that Gendron was "an innocent dupe"--difficult as it may be to join in that characterization on the basis of the paper record before us. Oxford might have found it easier to prove that Gendron simply acted recklessly, with conscious indifference to the truth of the statements to which he affixed his signature; such a showing might have been sufficient under New Hampshire law. See Manchester Bank v. Connecticut Bank and Trust Co., 497 F.Supp. 1304, 1316-17 (D.N.H.1980) (applying New Hampshire law); Saidel v. Union Assurance Society, 84 N.H. 232, 149 A. 78 (1930). However, Oxford did not pursue that theory of liability below, and we therefore do not consider it further (if Oxford is even raising it) on appeal. See Johnston v. Holiday Inns, Inc., 595 F.2d 890, 894 (1st Cir.1979).

(9) Oxford also attempted to recover from Gendron and NHT on a negligence count. The district court held that NHT, as a supplier to a shipper, owed no duty of care to Oxford, the carrier whose services the shipper hired. The district court's holding is supported by precedent. See Atlantic Overseas Corp. v. Feder, 452 F.Supp. 347, 351 (S.D.N.Y.) (freight forwarder), aff'd, 594 F.2d 851 (2d Cir.1978), cert. denied, 444 U.S. 829, 100 S.Ct. 55, 62 L.Ed.2d 37 (1979). In light of Oxford's failure to make any argument whatsoever on this point on appeal, we shall not disturb that holding.

IV

Claims against Tager

Oxford's claims against Tager, while asserted under headings of "contract," "negligence," and "fraudulent misrepresentation," come down to an assertion that Tager, in issuing false bills of lading, breached *6 a fiduciary duty that it owed to Oxford. In making a "contract" claim, Oxford essentially seeks to find an implied contractual term forbidding Tager from issuing a false bill of lading; in making its "tort" claim, it seeks to find a negligent act. The legal claim that Oxford asserts, however, is simply founded upon basic principles of the law of agency. Tager does not dispute that it was an agent of Oxford, hired to arrange for supplies and services for the "Eastern Saga," to prepare government documentation, to enter and clear the ship through customs, and to prepare bills of lading. As Oxford's agent Tager owed Oxford a "fiduciary" duty of care. See Restatement (Second) of Agency section 379.

The district court found that Tager had indeed breached its fiduciary obligations in two respects. First, Oxford's captain asked Tager to put in the bill of lading a statement that "weight, quantity and quality" were "unknown," but Tager failed to do so. The court found, however, that even if this clause had been inserted, Oxford would have remained liable and its ship still would have been seized. The court therefore concluded that no causal connection existed between the alleged breach and Oxford's injury. Because we find below that Oxford is entitled to recover against Tager on other grounds, it is unnecessary for us to determine whether the court's causation holding is erroneous.

Second, the court found that Tager breached its fiduciary obligations by failing accurately to determine how much scrap had been loaded before making out the bill of lading. The court went on to hold that Oxford nonetheless could not recover because of the "contributory negligence" of Oxford's captain and first officer--negligence that consisted of their failing to tell Oxford or Yulsan about the plot. We believe that, in this respect, the court erred.

(10) The legal question presented is simply whether an innocent principal (Oxford) is barred from collecting for damages caused by one set of negligent agents (Tager) because another set of agents has also been negligent (the captain and first officer)--in other words, whether one agent's contributory negligence is to be imputed to his principal to bar the principal from recovering from another negligent agent. The courts that have faced this question have divided in their responses. Compare Buhl v. Viera, 328 Mass. 201, 102 N.E.2d 774 (1954) (contributory negligence of one agent not imputed to bar recovery by principal against second agent); Brown v. Poritzky, 30 N.Y.2d 289, 283 N.E.2d 751, 332 N.Y.S.2d 872 (1972) (same); and Zulkee v. Wing, 20 Wis. 408 (1866) (same), with Insurance Co. of North America v. Anderson, 92 Idaho 114, 438 P.2d 265 (1968) (contributory negligence imputed), and Capitola v. Minneapolis, S.P. & S.S.M. Railroad Co., 258 Minn. 206, 103 N.W.2d 867 (1960) (same). We believe that the better reasoned cases are those that would allow recovery in these circumstances. We also believe that those are the cases that the New Hampshire Supreme Court would follow.

Our conclusion rests on our view that in the cases in which the contributory negligence of one agent has been held to bar an innocent principal from recovering against another, the courts have simply reasoned by analogy from a different situation without recognizing the difference. The different situation is that in which the principal seeks to recover from a third party, such as when Firm A seeks to recover from a driver of a car who negligently collides with Firm A's truck. In such circumstances, courts often have held that the contributory negligence of Firm A's driver, if sufficient to bar the driver's own recovery, is sufficient to bar recovery by Firm A as well. The servant's or agent's contributory negligence is "imputed" to the master or principal. See Restatement (Second) of Agency section 317 (principal-agent); Restatement (Second) of Torts section 486 (master-servant).

(11) This general rule of imputation presumably is grounded in the desire to require the principal to recover from his agent, rather than allowing him to pursue the third party as well. If so, that rationale is defeated rather than furthered if two negligent agents are allowed to impute each *7 other's negligence and bar recovery against either: instead of being remitted to his agents for relief, the principal is barred from recovering against them altogether. We have not found any other plausible rationale underlying the imputing of contributory negligence that would require imputation in this case. Given the basic legal rule that a principal can recover for damages caused by an agent's breach of his duties of trust and care, we see no reason why the principal should be barred by the fact that injuries were caused by two agents or two sets of agents. To allow each to set up that breach of duty of the other as a defense to the principal's claim is, in effect, to disallow the principal's recovery where more than one agent defaults in his duty. We see no rational basis for such a distinction.

Given the lack of a rational basis for imputing the agents' contributory negligence to the principal here, and the New Hampshire Supreme Court's flat statement that the "'waning defense of contributory negligence' should not be extended by imputation," Glidden v. Butler, 288 A.2d 695, 696, 112 N.H. 68 (1972), we believe that the New Hampshire courts would follow Buhl, Brown, and Zulkee here, and would not impute the captain's or first officer's negligence to Oxford to bar Oxford's recovery against its agent Tager. In light of this holding we need not reach Oxford's claim based on "fraudulent misrepresentation," for Oxford already had an adequate basis for recovering against Tager.

IV

Avon cross-appeals from the district court's judgment. Avon notes that the district court stated that "in the event Oxford is required to pay over (the amounts due Yulsan) as a result of the cargo shortage, it is entitled to indemnification in this amount from Avon." Avon claims that this sentence is an "advisory opinion" in violation of Article III of the Constitution.

Since the judgment appealed from was in Avon's favor, and since the statement made was in no sense necessary to that judgment, the statement was dictum. There is no known basis for an appeal from a dictum. In any event, our present opinion makes clear that Oxford could recover for the amounts at issue. Thus, we need not spend time trying to develop a theory that might support Avon's right to appeal, for, regardless, Avon would lose.

V

Because of the confused nature of the arguments on this appeal and the state of the record, we wish to make clear how the district court is to proceed on remand. The liability of Avon and Tager for damages has been established. The two defendants are jointly and severally liable for all of Oxford's damages. Cf. Mihoy v. Proulx, 113 N.H. 698, 313 A.2d 723 (1973); Tetreault v. Gould, 83 N.H. 99, 138 A. 544 (1927). Thus, the court need only determine the amount of damages.

It is not clear at this stage of the proceedings precisely what Oxford's damages consist of. Apparently, Oxford lost the use of its ship while it was being held in South Korea, and may have incurred other expenses as well. But, one expense that has not yet been incurred consists of money that might have to be paid by Oxford to Yulsan to reimburse Yulsan for its losses. Ordinarily, Oxford would not be entitled to indemnification or any other recovery for the anticipated amount of its liability to Yulsan until that liability is fixed by, for example, entry of a final judgment. See Mitsui Steamship Co. v. Jarka Corp. of Philadelphia, 218 F.Supp. 424 (E.D.Pa.1963). No such Korean judgment has yet been entered.

Although neither Avon nor any of the other appellees has raised the issue, we note that in A/S J. Ludwig Mowinckles Rederi v. Tidewater Construction Corp., 559 F.2d 928 (4th Cir.1977), the Fourth Circuit effectively dismissed an indemnification claim because no judgment or settlement had been reached in the litigation for which indemnification was sought. The court stressed, however, that "(w)hether an indemnification issue is ripe for adjudication depends *8 on the facts and circumstances under consideration," id. at 932, and it based its decision on the possibility that the parties seeking indemnification might not have any damage claim at all against the indemnitor if the other litigation concluded in their favor.

Here, because Oxford is conclusively entitled to recover for elements of damage that already have been fully incurred, the argument for dismissing Oxford's claims related to Yulsan's suit is less compelling. Instead, given the present posture of the case, the practical solution is for the district court to award damages at the present time for all other elements of damage proved by Oxford, and to defer entry of a damage award for Oxford's anticipated liability to Yulsan until that liability is finally established, if in fact it is. Cf. Moran Towing & Transportation Co. v. United States, 56 F.Supp. 104 (S.D.N.Y.1944) (case retained on docket but trial stayed until liability established). Whether the format and outcome of the South Korean litigation will give rise to any further issues concerning the appropriate relief in this forum is not a question that we address. The district court and the parties will be able to consider any such issues if and when they arise. To forestall unnecessary confusion, the clerk of this court shall forward a copy of this opinion to the South Korean court before which the related litigation is pending.

The judgment of the district court in favor of Avon Trading Corporation and Tager Steamship Authority is reversed. The cause is remanded for further proceedings consistent with this opinion.

Supp. Ch. 3

UNITED STATES OF AMERICA
v.
BANK OF NEW ENGLAND, N.A.

United States Court of Appeals, First Circuit.
821 F.2d 844

Argued March 4, 1987.
Decided June 10, 1987.

BANKING   bank had fair warning that customer's withdrawals of more than $10,000 in cash by using multiple checks, each one individually under $10,000, were reportable under Currency Transaction Reporting Act.

Bank was convicted of 31 violations of Currency Transaction Reporting Act by the United States District Court for the District of Massachusetts, Rya W. Zobel, J. Bank appealed. The Court of Appeals, Bownes, Circuit Judge, held that: (1) Currency Transaction Reporting Act and implementing regulations, defining "transaction in currency" to mean "the physical transfer of currency from one person to another," provided Bank with adequate warning that single, lump-sum transfer of cash exceeding $10,000 was reportable, regardless of number of checks customer used to obtain money, for purpose of due process requirement of fair warning; (2) definition of "pattern" was not impermissibly broad; (3) evidence proved that bank had had knowledge that customer's transactions came within Act; and (4) jury could have concluded that failure by bank personnel to, at least, inquire about reportability of transactions constituted flagrant indifference to obligations imposed by Act, for purpose of supporting finding of willfulness on part of bank.

Affirmed.

See also, D.C., 640 F.Supp. 36.

*846 Before BOWNES and SELYA, Circuit Judges, and PETTINE,[1] Senior District Judge.

---

[1] Of the District of Rhode Island, sitting by designation.

BOWNES, Circuit Judge.

The Bank of New England appeals a jury verdict convicting it of thirty-one violations of the Currency Transaction Reporting Act *847 (the Act).[1] 31 U.S.C. sections 5311-22 (1982).[2] Department of Treasury regulations promulgated under the Act require banks to file Currency Transaction Reports (CTRs) within fifteen days of customer currency transactions exceeding $10,000. 31 C.F.R. section 103.22

---

[1] The Act is also referred to as the Bank Secrecy Act.

[2] The Act provides in relevant part:

section 5313. Reports on domestic coins and currency transactions

(a) When a domestic financial institution is involved in a transaction for the payment, receipt, or transfer of United States coins or currency (or other monetary instruments the Secretary of the Treasury prescribes), in an amount, denomination, or amount and denomination, or under circumstances the Secretary prescribes by regulation, the institution and any other participant in the transaction the Secretary may prescribe shall file a report on the transaction at the time and in the way the Secretary prescribes. A participant acting for another person shall make the report as the agent or bailee of the person and identify the person for whom the transaction is being made.

section 5322. Criminal penalties

(a) A person willfully violating this subchapter or a regulation prescribed under this subchapter (except section 5315 of this title or a regulation prescribed under section 5315) shall be fined not more than $1,000, imprisoned for not more than one year, or both.

(b) A person willfully violating this subchapter or a regulation prescribed under this subchapter (except section 5315 of this title or a regulation prescribed under section 5315), while violating another law of the United States or as part of a pattern of illegal activity involving transactions of more than $100,000 in a 12-month period, shall be fined no more than $500,000, imprisoned for not more than 5 years, or both.

(1986).[3] The Act imposes felony liability when a bank willfully fails to file such reports "as part of a pattern of illegal activity involving transactions of more than $100,000 in a twelve-month period" 31 U.S.C. section 5322(b).

I. THE ISSUES

The Bank was found guilty of having failed to file CTRs on cash withdrawals made by James McDonough. It is undisputed that on thirty-one separate occasions between May 1983 and July 1984, McDonough withdrew from the Prudential Branch of the Bank more than $10,000 in cash by using multiple checks--each one individually under $10,000--presented simultaneously to a single bank teller. The Bank contends that such conduct did not trigger the Act's reporting requirements. It also urges that felony liability should not have been imposed because it did not engage in a pattern of illegal activity. In addition, the Bank avers that, if it did commit a felony violation, it did not commit thirty-one of them. The Bank also argues that the trial judge's instructions on willfulness were fatally flawed, and that, in any event, the evidence did not suffice to show that it willfully failed to file CTRs on McDonough's transactions. Finally, the Bank submits that during her charge to the jury, the trial judge erroneously alluded to evidence of the Bank's conduct after the dates specified in the indictment.

The Bank had been named in a federal grand jury indictment which was returned on October 15, 1985. Count One of the indictment alleged that between May 1983 and May 1985, James McDonough, the Bank, and Carol Orlandella and Patricia Murphy--both of whom were former head tellers with the Bank's Prudential Branch--unlawfully conspired to conceal from the IRS thirty-six of McDonough's currency transactions. The trial court directed a verdict of acquittal on this count.

---

[3] The regulations then in effect provided:

section 103.22 Reports of currency transactions

(a)(1) Each financial institution, other than a casino shall file a report of each deposit, withdrawal, exchange of currency or other payment or transfer, by, through, or to such financial institution, which involves a transaction in currency of more than $10,000.

Defendants Murphy and Orlandella were found not guilty of charges that they individually aided and abetted the failure to file CTRs on McDonough's transactions.

The bulk of the indictment alleged that the Bank, as principal, and McDonough, as an aider and abettor, willfully failed to file CTRs on thirty-six occasions between May 1983 and July 1984. Five counts were dismissed because, on those occasions, McDonough received cashier's checks from *848 the Bank, rather than currency. McDonough was acquitted of all charges against him. The Bank was found guilty on the thirty-one remaining counts. We affirm.

II. THE REPORTABILITY OF McDONOUGH'S TRANSACTIONS

The evidence at trial revealed that from 1978 through September 1984, McDonough was a regular customer at the Prudential Branch of the Bank of New England. McDonough visited that branch several times a month to withdraw large sums of cash from various corporate accounts. On thirty-one occasions from May 1983 through July 1984, McDonough requested a number of counter checks--blank checks which a teller encodes with the customer's account number--which he would then make payable to cash for sums varying between $5,000 and $9,000. On each of the charged occasions, McDonough simultaneously presented to a teller between two and four counter checks, none of which individually amounted to $10,000. Each check was recorded separately as an "item" on the Bank's settlement sheets. Once the checks were processed, McDonough would receive in a single transfer from the teller, one lump sum of cash which always amounted to over $10,000. On each of the charged occasions, the cash was withdrawn from one account. The Bank did not file CTRs on any of these transactions until May 1985, shortly after it received a grand jury subpoena.

The Bank contends that its conviction must be overturned because it did not engage in conduct that can be construed as violative of the Currency Transaction Reporting Act. It argues that the Act and its implementing regulations do not provide fair warning that a violation occurs if a financial institution fails to report a cash withdrawal in excess of $10,000 effected by a customer's use of multiple checks, each of which is less than $10,000. The Bank submits that since the Act fails to give sufficient notice that such conduct triggers the reporting requirements, its conviction violates fundamental norms of due process. It points out that the Constitution forbids the conviction of a defendant for conduct not clearly proscribed by penal statutes. United States v. Bass, 404 U.S. 336, 348, 92 S.Ct. 515, 522, 30 L.Ed.2d 488 (1971); Lanzetta v. New Jersey, 306 U.S. 451, 453, 59 S.Ct. 618, 619, 83 L.Ed. 888 (1939); United States v. Anzalone, 766 F.2d 676 (1st Cir.1985). The Bank asserts that to convict it for conduct not expressly prohibited by the Currency Transaction Reporting Act offends the basic constitutional canon that "the power of punishment is vested in the legislative, not in the judicial(,) department." United States v. Boston & Me. R.R., 380 U.S. 157, 160, 85 S.Ct. 868, 870, 13 L.Ed.2d 728 (1965) (quoting United States v. Wiltberger, 5 U.S. (5 Wheat.) 76, 5 L.Ed. 37 (1820)).

The Currency Transaction Reporting Act instructs the Treasury Department to promulgate regulations specifying the circumstances and currency amounts which trigger the Act's reporting requirements. 31 U.S.C. section 5313 (1982). The Treasury regulations, promulgated in 1972, provide: "Each financial institution ... shall file a report of each deposit, withdrawal, exchange of currency or other payment or transfer ... to such financial institution, which involves a transaction in currency of more than $10,000." 31 C.F.R. section 103.22 (1986). The question is whether the due process requirement of fair warning forbids us from reading this regulation as imposing a duty on banks to file reports on customers who withdraw more than $10,000 in cash at one time by using two to four checks instead of only one check.

The Treasury regulations define "transaction in currency" to mean a "transaction involving the physical transfer of currency from one person to another." 31 C.F.R. section 103.11 (1986). In the instant case, McDonough's practice was to visit the same branch of the same bank on only one occasion in a single day. He simultaneously would present to a single bank teller two to four checks, all made payable to cash, for varying amounts under $10,000 which, when added together, equalled a sum greater than $10,000. In return, the same bank teller would transfer to him in a single *849 motion a wad of cash totalling more than $10,000.

(1) We have no trouble categorizing such conduct as a single physical transfer of currency in excess of $10,000 from the Bank to McDonough. We, therefore, conclude that the language of the regulations itself gave the Bank fair warning that McDonough's transactions were reportable. This case does not, as the Bank suggests, involve a bank customer engaging in multiple currency transactions. McDonough engaged in thirty-one separate transactions, each exceeding

$10,000, which were effected by the use of multiple checks. The use of multiple checks during a single transfer of currency is not the same as multiple currency transactions. Thus, the Bank's citation to comments from agency officials, such as the IRS Assistant Commissioner for Criminal Investigation, about the reportability of multiple transactions is irrelevant. These comments have no bearing on the resolution of this case, but, instead, are addressed to situations in which a customer obtains over $10,000 via more than one physical transfer of currency.[4] E.g., United States v. Reinis, 794 F.2d 506 (9th Cir.1986) (cash withdrawal exceeding $10,000 effected by defendant's and his agents' purchase of several cashier's checks from the same bank in a single day but at different times, held not reportable since there was no single transfer of currency exceeding $10,000 to either defendant personally or any one of his agents); United States v. Dela Espriella, 781 F.2d 1432 (9th Cir.1986) (defendant who obtained more than $100,000 currency a day by sending several agents to 19 different bank locations to purchase cashier's checks for less than $10,000 each did not engage in a reportable transaction); United States v. Varbel, 780 F.2d 758 (9th Cir.1986) (no CTRs required to be filed on defendant who obtained $50,000 in three days by purchasing six cashier's checks, each under $10,000, from six different banks); United States v. Denmark, 779 F.2d 1559 (11th Cir.1986) (CTR need not be filed on defendant who purchased 14 checks for approximately $9,900 each from 14 different financial institutions); United States v. Cogswell, 637 F.Supp. 295 (N.D.Cal.1985) (no CTR required to be filed on defendant who

---

[4] For example, the Bank cites the following statement from the Comptroller General:

> The regulations were silent on the propriety of a customer's conducting multiple transactions to avoid reporting....
>
> ....
>
> ... Similarly, although the regulations required reporting for each single transaction above $10,000, they did not specifically prohibit dividing a large transaction into several smaller transactions to circumvent the reporting requirement.

Comptroller General, Report to Congress, Bank Secrecy Reporting Requirements Have Not Yet Met Expectations, Suggesting Need for Amendment, GGD-81-80, at 23-24 (1981)

purchased three different cashier's checks each slightly less than $10,000 at three different banks in a single day). Indeed, the IRS Assistant Commissioner for Criminal Investigation specifically discussed Varbel, Denemark, and Cogswell immediately after stating that the Treasury regulations do not require "that multiple currency transactions on the same day (each less than $10,000) that aggregate more than $10,000, be reported by a financial institution." Tax Evasion, Drug Trafficking and Money Laundering as They Involve Financial Institutions: Hearings Before The Subcomm. on Financial Institutions Supervision, Regulation and Insurance of the House Comm. on Banking, Finance and Urban Affairs, 99th Cong., 2d Sess. 181 (1986).

The instant case does not involve a defendant employing several agents to purchase a number of checks, each under $10,000, from the same bank in a single day. Nor does it involve a single defendant visiting different banks on the same day; or different branches of the same bank on the same or different days; or even different visits to the same branch of the same bank on the same day. The fact that such practices may be regarded as multiple transactions, and their reportability under the act may be uncertain, is of no moment here. It is undisputed that each of the violations charged in the indictment involved a single, lump-sum transfer of more than $10,000 to McDonough from the Bank's Prudential *850 Branch. McDonough's method of withdrawing more than $10,000 in cash can be regarded as multiple transactions only by disregarding the fact that he would make but one visit in a day to the same branch of the same bank where he would simultaneously present more than one check to one teller who would hand him in one motion a single sum of cash exceeding $10,000. McDonough could be said to have engaged in multiple transactions only by reading the regulations as attaching paramount importance to the number of checks presented by a customer. The regulations, however, impart primary significance to the amount of currency transferred, defining transaction as "the physical transfer of currency from one person to another." 31 C.F.R. section 103.11. On every occasion for which it was found guilty, the Bank transferred more than $10,000 to McDonough in a single act.

This case falls squarely within the Act's reporting requirements because it involves the physical transfer of more than $10,000 in currency from one bank in one day to a single customer during a single visit. A survey of the case law indicates that when a customer uses several checks, each of which is less than $10,000, in order to withdraw more than

$10,000 from the same bank on the same day, he has engaged in a reportable transaction. See United States v. Cure, 804 F.2d 625, 629 (11th Cir.1986) ("purchase of multiple cashier's checks in an aggregate amount of more than $10,000 from different branches of the same bank on the same day constitutes a single transaction in excess of $10,000"); United States v. Heyman, 794 F.2d 788, 792 (2d Cir.) (financial institution must report a customer deposit exceeding $10,000 which had been divided into small sums and in a single day deposited into different accounts held by the same customer in the same financial institution), cert. denied, --- U.S. ----, 107 S.Ct. 585, 93 L.Ed.2d 587 (1986); United States v. Giancola, 783 F.2d 1549 (11th Cir.) (bank must file CTRs on defendants who purchased over $10,000 in cashier's checks in a single day by structuring transactions in amounts of less than $10,000 at different branches of the same bank), cert. denied, --- U.S. ----, 107 S.Ct. 669, 93 L.Ed.2d 721 (1986); United States v. Tobon-Builes, 706 F.2d 1092 (11th Cir.1983) (defendant's conduct, whereby on ten occasions he entered bank and each time simultaneously purchased two cashier's checks for $9,000, "clearly came within the ambit of the financial institution reporting requirements"); United States v. Thompson, 603 F.2d 1200 (5th Cir.1979) (bank employee who divided $45,000 loan into five $9,000 notes and then simultaneously handed five bundles of $9,000 cash to borrower, properly convicted of failing to file a CTR on a $45,000 transaction).

As some of the cases cited hold, the reporting requirements may attach, even if a customer obtains $10,000 or more by visiting different branches of the same bank at various times in a single day. This is not the situation here; McDonough always obtained more than $10,000 cash by making one visit on a given day to the same branch of the same bank. We need not decide whether the current regulations can be read to impose a reporting obligation when a customer receives more than $10,000 currency by making numerous visits on the same day to different branches of the same bank. The Treasury Department, at the urging of other branches of government, recently has amended the current regulations so that they expressly obligate financial institutions to treat as a single reportable transaction, multiple currency transactions by a customer which total more than $10,000 in a single day.[5] This amendment is irrelevant to the matter *851 before us, since McDonough did not engage in multiple currency transactions.

The Bank relies heavily on our decision in United States v. Anzalone, 766 F.2d 676 (1st Cir.1985). In that case, we overturned a bank customer's conviction for violations of the Act. The defendant in Anzalone had purchased three checks on November 13, 1980, from the Haymarket Cooperative Bank. Each of the checks was less than $10,000, but in the aggregate they amounted to $25,000. Thereafter, the defendant purchased nine different checks on nine separate days, totalling $75,000. None of the checks individually, however, exceeded $10,000. We held that nothing in either the Act or its regulations obligated a bank customer to report cash withdrawals of $10,000 or more. 766 F.2d at 681-82. Anzalone also had been convicted of willfully aiding and abetting the Haymarket Bank's failure to file a CTR. We reversed that conviction, holding that "(t)he Bank, under the circumstances of this case, did not commit any crime by failing to report transactions as it lacked knowledge of their 'structured' nature." 766 F.2d at 683.

Anzalone held that the Treasury Regulations then in effect imposed no duty on a customer to inform a financial institution that he or she is structuring transactions to avoid the Act's reporting requirements. The case also held that the Haymarket Bank did not have to report transactions that it did not know were being structured to avoid the Act's

---

[5] The amendment reads as follows:

section 103.22 Reports of currency transactions.

(a)(1) Each financial institution other than a casino shall file a report of each deposit, withdrawal, exchange of currency or other payment, or transfer, by, through, or to such financial institution which involves a transaction in currency of more than $10,000.

Multiple currency transactions shall be treated as a single transaction if the financial institution has knowledge that they are by or on behalf of any person and result in either cash in or cash out totalling more than $10,000 during any one business day....

52 Fed.Reg. 11436 (April 8, 1987).

reporting requirements. Judge Aldrich concurred with this holding, but wrote separately to emphasize his view that the bank did have a duty to report the November 13, 1980, withdrawal in which Anzalone acquired three $8,500 checks from three separate tellers at two different branches of the Haymarket Bank. The government, however, chose to lump Anzalone's conduct on November 13 with his actions on the nine separate days thereafter, when he purchased nine different checks, totalling $75,000, each of which was slightly less than $10,000. Thus, the government's presentation of the case rendered it unnecessary for the court to decide whether Anzalone's November 13 transaction was reportable. Judge Aldrich, therefore, had no reason to diverge from the court's main holding. 766 F.2d at 683-84.

Anzalone involved the reportability of two kinds of transactions. First, it held that the Act does not require a bank to report multiple transactions undertaken on different days which aggregate to more than $10,000, if the bank does not know the transactions are being structured to avoid the Act's reporting requirements. 766 F.2d at 683. Second, Anzalone did not decide whether a customer engages in a reportable transaction when he obtains more than $10,000 by receiving a total of three transfers of currency from two branches of the same bank in a single day. Anzalone thus does not foreclose a holding that both these kind of transactions are reportable. But more importantly, the facts of the instant case are wholly distinguishable from either of these two situations. Anzalone, therefore, has no direct bearing on the issues before us.

On thirty-one occasions, James McDonough visited the same branch of the same bank at one time in a single day. He presented between two and four checks totalling more than $10,000 to one bank teller and received from the teller a single sum of cash in excess of $10,000. Since the regulations define transaction in currency to mean "the physical transfer of currency from one person to another," we hold that the Bank had adequate warning that a single, lump-sum transfer of cash exceeding $10,000 was reportable, regardless of the number of checks the customer uses to obtain the money.

III. THE IMPOSITION OF FELONY LIABILITY ON THE BANK

A. The "Pattern" Instruction

(2) 31 U.S.C. section 5322(b) provides in pertinent part:

(b) A person willfully violating this subchapter or a regulation prescribed under this subchapter (except section 5315 of this title or a regulation prescribed under section 5315), ... as part of a pattern of illegal activity involving transactions *852 of more than $100,000 in a 12-month period shall be fined....

The Bank claims that the jury was erroneously instructed on the definition of "a pattern of illegal activity" and that, therefore, a new trial is necessary. Before we examine the pattern instruction, we note that the Bank did not, despite the provisions of Federal Rule of Criminal Procedure 30, object to the instructed definition. This means that the instruction must stand unless it constituted plain error. United States v. Krowen, 809 F.2d 144, 150 (1st Cir.1987); United States v. Kakley, 741 F.2d 1, 3 (1st Cir.), cert. denied, 469 U.S. 887, 105 S.Ct. 261, 83 L.Ed.2d 197 (1984). Nor did the Bank submit a suggested definition of pattern in its requests for instructions.

The district court's instruction was:

Pattern simply means repeated transactions. One transaction is not a pattern; two may not be either, but if you get a series of transactions, that may then be a pattern. And in this context, what we're talking about is a pattern of repeated failures to file required reports on these transactions.

The Government must prove that the transactions involved more than $100,000 in a 12-month period. No one transaction has to be greater than $100,000, so long as the total of the transactions is in any 12-month period. It's a shifting period, so you can look at any period that you want. And if within that period, transactions of more than $100,000 occurred and there was a willful failure to file with respect to them, then this fourth element has been satisfied.

So, if you find that a series of transactions occurred that required the filing of reports and that the total of such transactions in any 12-month period involved more than $100,000, this element is satisfied, even if no one transaction itself exceeded 100,000 dollars. It is kind of a fillip on the multiple business. So, if you find that a reportable transaction occurred, that no report was filed, that transaction may be considered as part of the pattern if others occurred and if in any 12-month period the total was more than $100,000.

(3) The Bank attacks the instruction on two grounds: that the definition of pattern is impermissibly broad; and the court failed to distinguish between a pattern of conduct by the defendant McDonough and a pattern of activity by the Bank. We reject both contentions.

There are three cases construing "a pattern of illegal activity" under the Act. In United States v. Dickinson, 706 F.2d 88 (2d Cir.1983), the court appeared to adopt the following definition: "the pattern of illegal activity <u>must involve repeated violations</u> of the Act itself, related to each other and together involving more than $100,000." Id. at 91 (emphasis added). The court stated later: "The requirement that the violations be part of a pattern merely excludes cases where the violations are isolated events and not part of a common or systematic scheme." Id. at 92.

The Ninth Circuit in United States v. Beusch, 596 F.2d 871 (9th Cir.1979), discussed the meaning of pattern under 31 U.S.C. section 1059, the predecessor statute to section 5322(b):

> First, the plain language of subsection (2) of section 1059 indicates to us that a series of currency transfers which, by themselves, constitute only misdemeanors, may also constitute felonious activity if they (a) show a pattern of illegal activity, and (b) exceed $100,000 over a 12-month period. In contrast to subsection (1) of section 1059, which requires other illegal activity (i.e., activity not involving violations of the Bank Secrecy Act), subsection (2) evidences no similar requirements. <u>We infer, therefore, that a series of misdemeanor violations of the act may, by themselves, call forth the increased penalties of subsection (2)</u>.

Id. at 878 (emphasis added).

The most recent case we could find on the subject is United States v. Valdes-Guerra, 758 F.2d 1411 (11th Cir.1985). The court stated:

> While there is little caselaw construing the phrase "pattern of illegal activity," both circuits which have directly confronted *853 the issue have held that <u>a</u>

series of currency reporting violations which, by themselves, constitute only misdemeanors may also be felonious if they show a pattern of illegal activity and exceed $100,000.00 over a twelve-month period. United States v. Dickinson, 706 F.2d 88, 91-93 (2d Cir.1983); United States v. Beusch, 596 F.2d 871, 878-79 (9th Cir.1979). We agree with those courts that the legislative history of section 5322(b) evinces an intent not only to deal seriously with reporting violations undertaken in conjunction with violations of other federal laws, but also to punish as a felony violations undertaken in a repeated manner which "involve very large sums of money." H.R.Rep. No. 91-975, 91st Cong., 2d Sess. (1970), 1970 U.S. Code Cong. & Ad.News 4394, 4406. Congress intended that "serious violations under this title" could not "be shrugged off as a mere cost of doing business." Id. (emphasis added); Dickinson, 706 F.2d at 92.

Id. at 1414 (emphasis added).

(4) The common theme running through these three cases is that a pattern consists of repeated violations or a series of violations. The court's instruction clearly embodied this. While the instruction might have been more accurate if it defined pattern as repeated and related violations of the Act, the omission of the word related does not even come close to plain error. Under the evidence adduced, it was clear that the repeated failures by the Bank to report were directly related to the withdrawals by McDonough. These failures were not isolated events; they entailed repeated failures to file CTRs on similar transactions by the same customer. The similarity of the transactions, coupled with the frequency and regularity of their repetition, establish a related scheme.

(5) The contention that the instruction did not distinguish between a pattern by McDonough and another by the Bank is technically correct, but it ignores the rest of the charge in which the court repeatedly informed the jury that each defendant must be judged separately. The court also pointed out that it was the Bank that had the duty to report the transactions. To argue that the Bank must be divorced from McDonough is to ignore reality; McDonough made the withdrawals. The question for the jury was whether the Bank knowingly and willfully broke the law by failing to report them.

We have a final comment. When a defendant fails to specifically request an instruction on "a crucial and potentially complex issue of fact for a jury," Appellant's Brief at 24, and then fails to object to the instruction given, one of two conclusions can be drawn: that the defendant deliberately left the matter to the discretion of the trial judge; or it decided to play the waiting game in the hope of getting an appealable error without committing itself. Since we uphold the jury instruction, no more need be said.

B. Conviction of Thirty-One Felonies

This issue, which is an extension of the previous one, also involves the construction of 31 U.S.C. section 5322(b). At the time of indictment, the penalty for a violation of section 5322(b) was a fine of $500,000 andor imprisonment for not more than five years. Section 5322(a) made a violation a misdemeanor with a fine of not more than $1,000 andor imprisonment for not more than one year.[6] The question is whether each of the thirty-one violations that was "part of a pattern of illegal activity involving transactions of more than $100,000 in a 12-month period" may be separately prosecuted as a felony or whether a pattern of violations within a 12-month period constitutes only a single felony offense. The district court ruled that, if a pattern of illegal activity was proven, each violation constituted a felony. The Bank duly objected to this construction of the statute.

(6) Although the Bank argues that the ruling rewrote the statute in defiance of precedent, we find that the district court's *854 ruling comports with the plain language of the statute and its legislative history and has solid precedential support. The statute makes it a crime for a person to violate the subchapter "as part of a pattern of illegal activity." The words "as part" can only refer to a single violation. In order for subsection (b) to apply, there must be "a pattern of illegal activity involving transactions exceeding $100,000 in any 12-month period." A pattern, by any definition, must consist of more than one

---

[6] 31 U.S.C. section 5322(b) has since been amended to increase the maximum prison term to ten years. Section 5322(a) has been amended to provide for a fine of not more than $250,000 andor imprisonment for not more than five years, thus making any violation a felony.

failure to report. It is not the pattern that is proscribed, but the willful violation that is a part of the pattern. As the court noted in United States v. Kattan-Kassin, 696 F.2d 893 (11th Cir.1983), an absurd result can occur if the felony is limited to the pattern of violations: "after committing two violations involving more than $100,000, a violator would be immune from prosecution (under section 5322(b)) for the remainder of the twelve-month period, subject only to minor misdemeanor penalties." Id. at 896.

There can be no doubt that the legislative history of section 5322(b) and its predecessor, 31 U.S.C. section 1059, shows that Congress intended that the section be used to punish violators severely. See United States v. Valdes-Guerra, 758 F.2d at 1414; United States v. So, 755 F.2d 1350, 1355 (9th Cir.1985); United States v. Dickinson, 706 F.2d at 92; United States v. Kattan-Kassin, 696 F.2d at 897; United States v. Beusch, 596 F.2d at 879. Severe punishment can best be assured by treating as a separate felony each violation that is "part of a pattern of illegal activity involving transactions exceeding $100,000 in any 12-month period." 31 U.S.C. section 5322(b).

Although both the Ninth and Eleventh Circuits concur that Congress intended to punish severely those who repeatedly violate the Act's reporting requirements, they differ as to how best to implement that legislative intent. The Ninth Circuit does not regard any transaction as felonious until the $100,000 threshold has been reached, United States v. So, 755 F.2d at 1355; thereafter, every transaction is treated as a felony. The Eleventh Circuit, as we have already noted, treats every transaction as felonious if the $100,000 threshold is reached within a twelve-month period. Thus, under the Ninth Circuit's approach, there would be twenty-one felonies; under the Eleventh Circuit's approach, there would be thirty-one felonies. No matter which approach we adopt, the verdict stands since the fine levied against the Bank was far below that which could have been imposed under either approach. Both the Ninth Circuit and the Eleventh Circuit have advanced plausible constructions of the Act's felony provision. Because we are convinced that Congress wished to impose the severest possible penalty on repeated violators of the Act, we adopt the approach taken by the Eleventh Circuit in Kattan-Kassin: if a pattern of illegal activity involving transactions exceeding $100,000 is proven, each violation is a felony. We, therefore, affirm the district court's ruling and find no error in the jury instruction on this issue.

IV. WILLFULNESS OF THE BANK'S CONDUCT

A. The Trial Court's Instruction on Willfulness

(7, 8) Criminal liability under 31 U.S.C. section 5322 only attaches when a financial institution "willfully" violates the CTR filing requirement. A finding of willfulness under the Reporting Act must be supported by "proof of the defendant's knowledge of the reporting requirements and his specific intent to commit the crime." United States v. Hernando Ospina, 798 F.2d 1570, 1580 (11th Cir.1986); United States v. Eisenstein, 731 F.2d 1540, 1543 (11th Cir.1984). Willfulness can rarely be proven by direct evidence, since it is a state of mind; it is usually established by drawing reasonable inferences from the available facts. United States v. Wells, 766 F.2d 12, 20 (1st Cir.1985).

The Bank contends that the trial court's instructions on knowledge and specific intent effectively relieved the government of its responsibility to prove that the Bank acted willfully. The trial judge began her instructions on this element by outlining *855 generally the concepts of knowledge and willfulness:

> Knowingly simply means voluntarily and intentionally. It's designed to exclude a failure that is done by mistake or accident, or for some other innocent reason. Willfully means voluntarily, intentionally, and with a specific intent to disregard, to disobey the law, with a bad purpose to violate the law.

(9) The trial judge properly instructed the jury that it could infer knowledge if a defendant consciously avoided learning about the reporting requirements. The court then focused on the kind of proof that would establish the Bank's knowledge of its filing obligations. The judge instructed that the knowledge of individual employees acting within the scope of their employment is imputed to the Bank. She told the jury that "if any employee knew that multiple checks would require the filing of reports, the bank knew it, provided the employee knew it within the scope of his employment,...."

The trial judge then focused on the issue of "collective knowledge":

> In addition, however, you have to look at the bank as an institution. As such, its knowledge is the sum of the knowledge of all of the employees. That is, the bank's knowledge is the totality of what all of the employees know within the scope of their employment. So, if Employee A knows one facet of the currency reporting requirement, B knows another facet of it, and C a third facet of it, the bank knows them all. So if you find that an employee within the scope of his employment knew that CTRs had to be filed, even if multiple checks are used, the bank is deemed to know it. The bank is also deemed to know it if each of several employees knew a part of that requirement and the sum of what the separate employees knew amounted to knowledge that such a requirement existed.

After discussing the two modes of establishing knowledge—via either knowledge of one of its individual employees or the aggregate knowledge of all its employees—the trial judge turned to the issue of specific intent:

> There is a similar double business with respect to the concept of willfulness with respect to the bank. In deciding whether the bank acted willfully, again you have to look first at the conduct of all employees and officers, and, second, at what the bank did or did not do as an institution. The bank is deemed to have acted willfully if one of its employees in the scope of his employment acted willfully. So, if you find that an employee willfully failed to do what was necessary to file these reports, then that is deemed to be the act of the bank, and the bank is deemed to have willfully failed to file.
> ....
>
> Alternatively, the bank as an institution has certain responsibilities; as an organization, it has certain responsibilities. And you will have to determine whether the bank as an organization consciously avoided learning about and observing CTR requirements. The Government to prove the bank guilty on this theory, has to show that its failure to file was the result of some flagrant organizational indifference. In this connection, you should look at the evidence as to the bank's effort, if any, to inform its employees of the law; its effort to check on their compliance; its response to various bits of information that it got in August and September of '84 and February of '85; its

policies, and how it carried out its stated policies.
....

If you find that the Government has proven with respect to any transaction either that an employee within the scope of his employment willfully failed to file a required report or that the bank was flagrantly indifferent to its obligations, then you may find that the bank has willfully failed to file the required reports.

The Bank contends that the trial court's instructions regarding knowledge were defective *856 because they eliminated the requirement that it be proven that the Bank violated a known legal duty. It avers that the knowledge instruction invited the jury to convict the Bank for negligently maintaining a poor communications network that prevented the consolidation of the information held by its various employees. The Bank argues that it is error to find that a corporation possesses a particular item of knowledge if one part of the corporation has half the information making up the item, and another part of the entity has the other half.

(10, 11) A collective knowledge instruction is entirely appropriate in the context of corporate criminal liability. Riss & Company v. United States, 262 F.2d 245, 250 (8th Cir.1958); Inland Freight Lines v. United States, 191 F.2d 313, 315 (10th Cir.1951); Camacho v. Bowling, 562 F.Supp. 1012, 1025 (N.D.Ill.1983); United States v. T.I.M.E.-D.C., Inc., 381 F.Supp. 730, 738-39 (W.D.W.Va.1974); United States v. Sawyer Transport, Inc., 337 F.Supp. 29 (D.Minn.1971), aff'd, 463 F.2d 175 (8th Cir.1972). The acts of a corporation are, after all, simply the acts of all of its employees operating within the scope of their employment. The law on corporate criminal liability reflects this. See, e.g., United States v. Cincotta, 689 F.2d 238, 241, 242 (1st Cir.), cert. denied, 459 U.S. 991, 103 S.Ct. 347, 74 L.Ed.2d 387 (1982); United States v. Richmond, 700 F.2d 1183, 1195 n. 7 (11th Cir.1983). Similarly, the knowledge obtained by corporate employees acting within the scope of their employment is imputed to the corporation. Steere Tank Lines, Inc. v. United States, 330 F.2d 719, 722 (5th Cir.1964). Corporations compartmentalize knowledge, subdividing the elements of specific duties and operations into smaller components. The aggregate of those components constitutes the corporation's knowledge of a particular operation. It is irrelevant whether employees administering one component of an operation know the specific activities of employees administering another aspect of the operation:

> (A) corporation cannot plead innocence by asserting that the information obtained by several employees was not acquired by any one individual who then would have comprehended its full import. Rather the corporation is considered to have acquired the collective knowledge of its employees and is held responsible for their failure to act accordingly.

United States v. T.I.M.E.-D.C., Inc., 381 F.Supp. at 738. Since the Bank had the compartmentalized structure common to all large corporations, the court's collective knowledge instruction was not only proper but necessary.

(12) Nor do we find any defects in the trial court's instructions on specific intent. The court told the jury that the concept of willfulness entails a voluntary, intentional, and bad purpose to disobey the law. Her instructions on this element, when viewed as a whole, directed the jury not to convict for accidental, mistaken or inadvertent acts or omissions. It is urged that the court erroneously charged that willfulness could be found via flagrant indifference by the Bank toward its reporting obligations. With respect to federal regulatory statutes, the Supreme Court has endorsed defining willfulness, in both civil and criminal contexts, as "a disregard for the governing statute and an indifference to its requirements." Trans World Airlines, Inc. v. Thurston, 469 U.S. 111, 127 & n. 20, 105 S.Ct. 613, 625 & n. 20, 83 L.Ed.2d 523 (1985); United States v. Illinois Central R. Co., 303 U.S. 239, 58 S.Ct. 533, 82 L.Ed. 773 (1938); accord Stein Distributing Company v. Dept. of Treasury Bureau of Alcohol, Tobacco & Firearms, 779 F.2d 1407, 1413 (9th Cir.), cert. denied, --- U.S. ----, 106 S.Ct. 1963, 90 L.Ed.2d 649 (1986); United States v. Dye Construction, 510 F.2d 78, 82 (10th Cir.1975); F.X. Messina Construction Corp. v. Occupational Safety and Health Review Commission, 505 F.2d 701, 702 (1st Cir.1974); United States v. Tarver, 642 F.Supp. 1109 (D.Wyo.1986); United States v. T.I.M.E.-D.C., Inc., 381 F.Supp. at 740-41. Accordingly, we find *857 no error in the court's instruction on willfulness.

B. Evidence of Willfulness

The Bank asserts that the evidence did not suffice to show that it had willfully failed to comply with the Act's reporting requirements. We review the evidence in the light most favorable to the government. United States v. Medina, 761 F.2d 12, 16 n. 3 (1st Cir.1985); United States v. Tierney, 760 F.2d 382, 384 (1st Cir.), cert. denied, --- U.S. ----, 106 S.Ct. 131, 88 L.Ed.2d 108 (1985).

As already discussed, the language of the Treasury regulations itself gave notice that cash withdrawals over $10,000 were reportable, regardless of the number of checks used. Primary responsibility for CTR compliance in the Bank's branch offices was assigned to head tellers and branch managers. Head tellers Orlandella and Murphy, who knew of the nature of McDonough's transactions, also knew of the CTR filing obligations imposed by the Bank. The jury heard testimony from former bank teller Simona Wong, who stated that she knew McDonough's transactions were reportable, and that the source of her knowledge was head teller Murphy.

(13) Even if some Bank personnel mistakenly regarded McDonough as engaging in multiple transactions, there was convincing evidence that the Bank knew that his withdrawals were reportable. An internal memo sent in May 1983 by project coordinator Jayne Brady to all branch managers and head tellers stated that "'(r)eportable transactions are expanded to include multiple transactions which aggregate more than $10,000 in any _one day_.' This includes deposits or withdrawals by a customer to or from more than one account." (Emphasis in original.) The Prudential Branch Manual instructed that if Bank personnel know that a customer has engaged in multiple transactions totalling $10,000 or more, then such transactions should be regarded as a single transaction. In addition, since 1980, the instructions on the back of CTR forms have directed that reports be filed on multiple transactions which aggregate to over $10,000. Finally, a Bank auditor discussed with Orlandella and Murphy, the Bank's obligation to report a customer's multiple transactions in a single day which amount to more than $10,000. We do not suggest that these evidentiary items in themselves legally bound the Bank to report McDonough's transactions; it is the language of the regulations that impose such a duty. This evidence, however, proved that the Bank had ample knowledge that transactions like McDonough's came within the purview of the Act.

(14) Regarding the Bank's specific intent to violate the reporting obligation, Simona Wong testified that head teller Patricia Murphy knew that McDonough's transactions were reportable, but, on one occasion, deliberately chose not to

file a CTR on him because he was "a good customer." In addition, the jury heard testimony that bank employees regarded McDonough's transactions as unusual, speculated that he was a bookie, and suspected that he was structuring his transactions to avoid the Act's reporting requirements. An internal Bank memo, written after an investigation of the McDonough transactions, concluded that a "person managing the branch would have to have known that something strange was going on." Given the suspicions aroused by McDonough's banking practices and the abundance of information indicating that his transactions were reportable, the jury could have concluded that the failure by Bank personnel to, at least, inquire about the reportability of McDonough's transactions constituted flagrant indifference to the obligations imposed by the Act.

We hold that the evidence was sufficient for a finding of willfulness.

C. Instructions Pertaining to the Bank's Post-July 1984 Conduct

At trial, the government introduced evidence of the Bank's CTR compliance efforts after July 31, 1984, the last date on which the Bank was charged with failing to *858 file a CTR. On August 7, 1984, the Bank learned that McDonough's transactions were being investigated by law-enforcement agencies. In addition, the branch manager and head teller were told specifically that McDonough's transactions were reportable. The government introduced evidence of the Bank's conduct after July 1984, which could be found to show scant effort by the Bank to comply with its legal obligations, even after it had learned that McDonough had come under suspicion. The Bank's failure to file a CTR on McDonough's July 31, 1984, transaction was highlighted specifically. The government argued that when the Bank was told directly by law enforcement officers on August 7 that McDonough's transactions were reportable, it should have at least completed a CTR on the July 31 withdrawal, while it still had time to meet the statute's fifteen-day filing deadline. The government also pointed to the fact that between August 1984 and May 1985 there occurred a flurry of law-enforcement activity surrounding McDonough's transactions with the Bank. The Bank, however, did not make any effort to report McDonough's 1983 and 1984 transactions until May 1985, after it received a federal grand jury subpoena.

This evidence was admitted originally on the Count One

conspiracy charge which the trial court dismissed after all testimony had been taken. The Bank did not move to strike this evidence once the conspiracy charge was dismissed. During closing argument, the government urged that the post-July 1984 evidence manifested the Bank's disregard of its reporting duty, and thus inferentially illuminated its mental state during the time period charged in the indictment. The trial court instructed the jury that it could consider post-July 1984 conduct as probative of the Bank's intent to violate the Act. Specifically, the court told the jury that the evidence might shed light on whether the Bank had been flagrantly indifferent to its reporting obligations.

The Bank made a timely objection to this instruction. It argued that the Act's statutory and regulatory language prohibited a finding of willfulness based on evidence beyond the fifteen-day deadline for filing CTRs on reportable transactions. The Bank also avers that the judge's instructions invited the jury to convict it for acts not charged as violations in the indictment.

(15) A common sense reading of the statute and its regulations suggests that the fifteen-day filing deadline simply marks the commencement of the offense. Federal Rule of Evidence 404(b)[7] has been held to allow the admission of acts or conduct subsequent to the offense charged to prove intent to commit the alleged illegal act.[8] United States v.

---

[7] Federal Rule of Evidence 404(b) provides:

(b) Other crimes, wrongs, or acts. Evidence of other crimes, wrongs, or acts is not admissible to prove the character of a person in order to show that he acted in conformity therewith. It may, however, be admissible for other purposes, such as proof of motive, opportunity, intent, preparation, plan, knowledge, identity, or absence of mistake or accident.

[8] United States v. Bourque, 541 F.2d 290 (1st Cir.1976), relied on by the Bank, does not hold to the contrary. In Bourque, the issue was whether subsequent conduct by the defendant could be used to establish the actus reus--the failure to file a tax return on a prescribed date. In the instant case, the criminal act--the defendant's failure to file CTRs--is established. The issue is whether the Bank possessed the requisite mental state. Nothing in Bourque suggests that the prosecution is barred from using subsequent conduct to shed light on the defendant's

Whalely, 786 F.2d 1229, 1232-33 (4th Cir.1986); United States v. Hurley, 755 F.2d 788, 790 (11th Cir.1985); United States v. Arroyo-Angulo, 580 F.2d 1137, 1149 (2d Cir.), cert. denied, 439 U.S. 913, 99 S.Ct. 285, 58 L.Ed.2d 260 (1978); United States v. Gallo, 543 F.2d 361, 364-65 (D.C.Cir.1976). In prosecutions for willful failure to file tax returns, for example, the element of willfulness may be shown by conduct subsequent to the date on which the return was due. United States v. Sempos, 772 F.2d 1, 2 (1st Cir.1985); *859 United States v. Richards, 723 F.2d 646, 648-49 (8th Cir.1983); United States v. Serlin, 707 F.2d 953, 959 (7th Cir.1983). We note also that the Bank's defense at trial included claims that the nonreporting of these transactions occurred accidentally or by mistake. Rule 404(b) invites the admission of relevant instances of subsequent conduct to show "absence of mistake or accident." Because the Bank did not move to strike the evidence after Count One was dismissed, and since Rule 404(b) allows the admission of subsequent conduct to show a defendant's mental state at the time of the charged offense, we uphold the district court's instruction that post-July 1984 conduct was probative of the Bank's mental state.[9]

(16) We also reject the Bank's contention that the trial judge's reference to the post-July 1984 evidence in her instructions regarding willfulness invited the jury to convict for conduct not charged in the indictment. Viewing the instructions as a whole, we do not think that this reference prejudiced the Bank in any significant way. The trial judge instructed the jury that it should only consider the charges specified in the indictment. She stressed that the offenses charged were thirty-one failures to file CTRs within fifteen days of handling a reportable transaction. She stated that such failures must be willful. The trial judge mentioned the post-July 1984 evidence only once,

---

mens rea at the time of the commission of the criminal act.

[9] We reject the suggestion by amicus, the Massachusetts Bankers Association, that our endorsement of the trial court's instruction makes a continuing offense out of a failure to file a CTR within fifteen days of handling a reportable transaction. The act constituting the offense is established after fifteen days. Conduct beyond the fifteen-day filing period is not relevant to whether the offensive act was committed, but only to the mental state with which the act was committed.

specifying that the jury should consider this evidence in connection with the element of willfulness.

In United States v. Baskes, 649 F.2d 471 (7th Cir.1980), cert. denied, 450 U.S. 1000, 101 S.Ct. 1706, 68 L.Ed.2d 201 (1981), the defendant objected to the trial judge's instruction to the jury that subsequent act evidence could be considered to shed light on the defendant's intent to commit the charged offense. The defendant urged that "additional illegalities could be inferred from the (subsequent act) evidence and ... might confuse the issue and mislead the jury." Id. at 480. The Seventh Circuit upheld the charge, noting that the trial judge instructed the jury that it could only consider the evidence as it related to the defendant's intent. Id. at 481. It would have been preferable if the trial judge here had directly and specifically informed the jury that the post-July 1984 evidence could be considered only on the issue of the Bank's state of mind before July 1984. It is significant, however, that this evidence was mentioned only once, in direct connection with the instructions on the element of specific intent. The trial judge had already carefully instructed the jury to disregard the conspiracy charge against the defendants, which involved alleged criminal conduct by the Bank after July 1984. Moreover, the jury was given a redacted copy of the indictment which lacked any reference to conduct engaged in by the Bank after July 1984, and instructed only to consider the charges, "outlined by date," specified therein. Viewed as a whole, the instructions provided sufficient guidance to the jury that the post-July 1984 evidence was relevant only to the intent with which the Bank committed the offenses charged in the redacted indictment.

Affirmed.

Supp. Ch. 3

NEW ENGLAND TRACTOR-TRAILER TRAINING OF CONNECTICUT, INC.
v.
GLOBE NEWSPAPER COMPANY.

Supreme Judicial Court of Massachusetts, Suffolk.
480 N.E.2d 1005

Argued Dec. 5, 1984.
Decided July 24, 1985.

Truck driving schools brought defamation action against newspaper. The Suffolk Superior Court, Peter F. Brady, J., entered summary judgment for newspaper as against one school, and that school appealed. The Appeals Court reversed, 462 N.E.2d 1134, and the newspaper applied for further review. The Supreme Judicial Court, Liacos, J., held that affidavit of school president raised genuine issues of whether newspaper intended to refer to appealing school, rather than to its coplaintiff, and was so understood, and whether it was negligent in publishing articles which reasonably could be understood to refer to appealing school.

Reversed.

*1006 Before HENNESSEY, C.J., and LIACOS, ABRAMS, LYNCH and O'CONNOR, JJ.

LIACOS, Justice.

The plaintiff, New England Tractor-Trailer Training of Connecticut, Inc. (NETTT-Conn), and New England Tractor-Trailer Training of Mass., Inc. (NETTT-Mass), sued the Globe Newspaper Company (Globe) alleging that a series of articles published by the Globe on career training schools defamed NETTT-Mass and NETTT-Conn. The complaint was in two counts. Count one alleged defamation of NETTT-Mass, and count two alleged defamation of NETTT-Conn. The Globe filed a motion for summary judgment on count two and on part of count one. Both parties filed affidavits. A judge of the Superior Court in Suffolk County granted the Globe's motion. Subsequently, NETTT-Mass and the Globe stipulated to the dismissal with prejudice of count one of the complaint. NETTT-Conn appealed the allowance of summary judgment on count two. The Appeals Court reversed. 18 Mass.App. 906, 462 N.E.2d 1134 (1984). We granted the Globe's application for further appellate review. We reverse the trial judge's entry of summary judgment for the Globe on count two.

The record reveals the following facts. Commencing on March 25, 1974, the Globe published a series of articles pertaining to the private vocational training industry. NETTT-Conn claimed in its complaint that it was defamed by six of the articles in the series. The first article, published in the morning edition of the Globe on March 25, 1974, announced the Globe's investigation into private vocational schools and named no particular schools or types of schools. The second article, published in the evening edition of the Globe on March 25, 1974, and in the morning edition of the Globe on March 26, 1974, described the Globe's investigation in more detail and focused on a particular training school, ITT Tech. The third article, published on March 27, 1974, was entitled, "Home-study schools: Con game or wave of the future?", and again contained generalized comments about the private vocational training industry. It was complemented by four separate articles, also published in the same March 27, 1974, edition, describing four separate schools, none of which was NETTT-Conn.

On March 29, 1974, the Globe published a set of articles on the private vocational training industry including one entitled, "Dead-end trip on rattletrap trucks." This article described the "New England Tractor-Trailer School" and quoted Arlan Greenberg, who was described as "N.E. Tractor president." The school was referred to variously as "New England Tractor-Trailer School," "New England," "N.E. Tractor Trailer," and "N.E. Tractor." This article was highly critical of "New England Tractor-Trailer School." It stated, inter alia, that several instructors at the school had been teaching without required certificates; that the trucks were "run-down," "decrepit, sometimes unsafe"; that Arlan Greenberg, "N.E. Tractor president," "made a number of demonstrably false statements and misrepresentations about the school"; and that the school's contracts *1007 with its students "violate(d) the laws of at least two states." The last two articles, published on April 12, 1974, and June 6, 1974,[1] referred to "New England Tractor-Trailer School," and concerned investigations of the school by the Massachusetts Registry of Motor Vehicles, the office of the Attorney General of Massachusetts, and the New Hampshire Attorney General's Consumer Protection Division. These last two articles repeated many of the critical statements about "New

---

[1] The June 6, 1974, article was published in substantially the same form in both the morning and evening editions of the Globe.

England Tractor-Trailer School" which were contained in the March 29, 1974, article.

The plaintiff claims that it was defamed by these articles. The defendant, Globe, argues that the articles did not defame the plaintiff because they were not written "of and concerning" the plaintiff. Hanson v. Globe Newspaper Co., 159 Mass. 293, 294, 34 N.E. 462 (1893). The Globe argues that the articles published on March 25, 26, and 27, 1974, contained only generalized statements about the private vocational training industry or referred to particular schools, none of which was, or could be confused with, NETT-Conn. The Globe further argues that the articles published on March 29, April 12, and June 6, 1974, concerned NETT-Mass exclusively and were not of and concerning NETT-Conn. The plaintiff contests the Globe's assertions. It argues that while NETT-Conn and NETT-Mass are distinct corporations (the former incorporated under the laws of Connecticut, the latter under the laws of Massachusetts), they hold themselves out to be one school with two locations. The plaintiff argues that there is a genuine issue of material fact, i.e., whether the articles were of and concerning NETT-Conn, and that summary judgment should not have been granted for the Globe. Mass.R.Civ.P. 56(c), 365 Mass. 824 (1974).

(1) It is a fundamental principle of the law of defamation that a plaintiff must show, inter alia, that the allegedly defamatory words published by a defendant were of and concerning the plaintiff. New York Times Co. v. Sullivan, 376 U.S. 254, 288, 292, 84 S.Ct. 710, 730, 733, 11 L.Ed.2d 686 (1964). See Geisler v. Petrocelli, 616 F.2d 636, 639 (2d Cir.1980); Fetler v. Houghton Mifflin Co., 364 F.2d 650, 651 (2d Cir.1966); Restatement (Second) of Torts section 613 (1977). This requirement is described at length in Hanson v. Globe Newspaper Co., supra, ("In a suit for libel or slander, it is always necessary for the plaintiff to allege and prove that the words were spoken or written of and concerning the plaintiff"). The Globe argues that, since an affidavit of the author of these articles shows, without contradiction, that there was no subjective intent to defame NETT-Conn, it must prevail as matter of law. The Globe relies primarily on Hanson to sustain its position.

It is true that in Hanson v. Globe Newspaper Co., supra, the majority opinion adopted essentially a subjective test for the determination whether a defendant's words are of and concerning the plaintiff.² The court stated, "The defendant's meaning in regard both to the person to whom the words should be applied and the imputations against him is always to be ascertained." Id. 159 Mass. at 294-295, 34 N.E. 462. The central inquiry was aimed at discovering the subjective intent of the defendant because "(d)efamatory language is harmful only as it purports to be the expression of the thought of him who uses it," id. at 295, 34 N.E. 462, and the defendant's "meaning, to be ascertained in a proper way, is what gives character to his act, and makes it innocent or wrongful," id. at 296, 34 N.E. 462. Thus, "all the questions relate back to the ascertainment of (the defendant's) meaning." Id.³ Compare, however, the dissent

---

²In Hanson, the defendant newspaper published an article about the criminal activity of someone it identified as "H.P. Hanson, a real estate and insurance broker of South Boston." Id. at 294, 34 N.E. 462. The newspaper apparently intended to describe one "A.P.H. Hanson" who was a real estate and insurance broker of South Boston and who had been assessed a criminal fine. However, the plaintiff in Hanson was another man whose name actually was H.P. Hanson, and who was also a real estate and insurance broker of South Boston. The plaintiff sued for libel because the allegations of criminal activity were defamatory and untrue as to him. A judge of the Superior Court "found as a fact that the alleged libel declared on by the plaintiff was not published by the defendant of or concerning the plaintiff." Id. This court found that the evidence warranted that finding and that judgment for the defendant newspaper was warranted. Id. at 299, 34 N.E. 462.

³ Notwithstanding this strong language in favor of a purely subjective inquiry into the defendant's state of mind, the court posited a number of "questions" to ascertain the defendant's meaning which necessarily were objective in nature. The court stated that the speaker's meaning may "legitimately be ascertained ... from the language used ... the circumstances under which it was written and the facts to which it relates ... <u>so far as they can readily be ascertained by those who read the words</u>, and who attempt to find out the meaning of the author in regard to the person of whom they were written" (emphasis supplied). Id. The court also stated that it "may be doubtful" whether the defendant "should ever be permitted to state his undisclosed intention in regard to the person of whom the words are used." Id. at 297, 34 N.E. 462.

Moreover, the court also stated that if a defendant's language was "free from ambiguity in regard to the person referred to, and points clearly to a well known person, it would be held to have been published

of Holmes, J. (in which Morton and Barker, JJ., joined), id. at 299, 303, 34 N.E. 462: "Of course it does not matter that the defendant did not intend to injure the plaintiff, if that was the manifest tendency of his words."

Two points need be made about Hanson. First, Hanson bears close scrutiny today from the twin perspectives of tort law and constitutional law. Written nearly 100 years ago, it represents an historical view of tort law largely rejected by later cases, see infra at 1010, and it fails to accommodate the profound changes in defamation law brought about by New York Times Co. v. Sullivan, supra, and Gertz v. Robert Welch, Inc., 418 U.S. 323, 94 S.Ct. 2997, 41 L.Ed.2d 789 (1974). Second, the issue of negligent defamation of an entity in the position of NETTT-Conn was not before the court. Hanson, supra 159 Mass. at 299, 34 N.E. 462.

We believe that a purely subjective test for determining whether a defendant's words are of and concerning the plaintiff represents an outmoded historical conception of tort law. See 2 F. Harper & F. James, Torts section 16.2 (1956). As stated by Justice Holmes, an awkward person's "slips are no less troublesome to his neighbors than if they sprang from guilty neglect." O.W. Holmes, Jr., The Common Law 108 (1881). Tort law generally deems those injured by a person's unintentional slips deserving of compensation if the slips could have been avoided through the use of ordinary care.

(2, 3) A purely subjective test for determining whether a defendant's words are of and concerning the plaintiff unduly narrows the potential for liability in defamation cases and leaves deserving plaintiffs uncompensated. In determining

---

concerning that person, although the defendant should show that through some mistake of fact, not easily discoverable by the public, he had designated in his publication a person other than the one whom he intended to designate." Id. at 296, 34 N.E. 462. Thus, at some point--when the words unambiguously referred to a person not intended (and thus, presumably did not refer to the person intended)--the purely subjective inquiry could be replaced by a purely objective inquiry. For if the words were "free from ambiguity, the defendant (might) not be permitted to show that through ignorance or mistake he said something, either by way of designating the person, or making assertions about him, different from that which he intended to say." Id. at 296-297, 34 N.E. 462.

the proper test, however, we affirm the "profound national commitment to the principle that debate on public issues should be uninhibited, robust, and wide-open," New York Times Co. v. Sullivan, supra 376 U.S. at 270, 84 S.Ct. at 721, and the constitutional rule which follows that courts may not impose liability without fault in defamation cases. Gertz v. Robert Welch, Inc., supra 418 U.S. at 347, 94 S.Ct. at 3010. In Gertz, the Supreme Court of the United States held that "so long as they do not impose *1009 liability without fault, the States may define for themselves the appropriate standard of liability for a publisher or broadcaster of defamatory falsehood injurious to a private individual." Id. In Stone v. Essex County Newspapers, Inc., 367 Mass. 849, 855, 330 N.E.2d 161 (1975), we resolved the conflict between the "right of redress to one who suffers injury to his reputation by the publishing of a defamatory falsehood" and the "freedom of expression ... guaranteed by the First Amendment," by holding that "private ... persons may recover compensation on proof of negligent publication of a defamatory falsehood" (emphasis in original). Id. at 858, 330 N.E.2d 161. In the present case, we similarly hold that private persons or entities may recover compensation (assuming proof of all other elements of a claim for defamation) on proof that the defendant was negligent in publishing defamatory words which reasonably could be interpreted to refer to the plaintiff.[4]

---

[4] We assume that NETTT-Conn is a private entity, since no argument has been made to the contrary. See Stone v. Essex County Newspapers, Inc., supra at 858, 330 N.E.2d 161.

We note that the United States Supreme Court recently, in a plurality opinion, has cast some doubt on an aspect of the holding in Gertz v. Robert Welch, Inc., 418 U.S. 323, 94 S.Ct. 2997, 41 L.Ed.2d 789 (1974). In Dun & Bradstreet, Inc. v. Greenmoss Builders, Inc., --- U.S. ----, 105 S.Ct. 2939, 86 L.Ed.2d 593 (1985) (plurality opinion, Burger, C.J., and White, J., concurring in the judgment), five Justices appear to take the view that private parties need not prove actual malice in order to recover presumed or punitive damages if the libelous matter is not one "of public concern," id. at ----, 105 S.Ct. at 2948 (plurality opinion), "of general public importance," id. (Burger, C.J., concurring in the judgment), or "of public importance," id. at ----, 105 S.Ct. at 2954 (White, J., concurring in the judgment). The rationale of the plurality opinion was that "speech on matters of purely private concern is of less First Amendment concern." Id. at ----, 105 S.Ct. at 2946 (plurality opinion). Justice White's concurrence, in which he indicates his preference that Gertz be overruled, states that the Gertz requirement

To the extent that Hanson requires proof that the alleged defamatory matter was of and concerning the plaintiff, we adhere to that rule. However, to the extent that Hanson appears to require a plaintiff to prove that the defendant actually intended to refer to the plaintiff before liability may attach, we decline to follow it. Rather, we adopt the view that "(t)he question is not so much who was aimed at, as who was hit," Corrigan v. Bobbs-Merrill Co., 228 N.Y. 58, 63-64, 126 N.E. 260 (1920), with one all-important proviso. While the plaintiff need not prove that the defendant "aimed" at the plaintiff, he or she must prove that the defendant was negligent in writing or saying words which reasonably could be understood to "hit" the plaintiff. Davis v. R.K.O. Radio Pictures, Inc., 191 F.2d 901, 904 (8th Cir.1951) ("The issue (is) whether persons who knew or knew of the plaintiff could *reasonably* have understood the exhibited picture to refer to him" (emphasis in original)). Bee Publications, Inc. v. Cheektowaga Times, Inc., 107 A.D.2d 382, 485 N.Y.S.2d 885, 888 (1985) ("(W)here extrinsic facts are relied on to prove the reference to a plaintiff, he must show that the conclusion that the publication refers to him is reasonable and that the extrinsic facts upon which that *1010 conclusion is based were known to those who read or heard the publication"). See also Restatement (Second) of Torts section 564, at 165 (1977) ("A defamatory communication is made concerning the person to whom its recipient correctly,

---

that private parties prove "some kind of fault on the part of the defendant," id. at ----, 105 S.Ct. at 2954, also is inapplicable to private parties suing on matters of private concern. Justice White alone states this proposition, however, and we do not interpret the plurality opinion, with its two concurrences in the judgment, to so alter the Gertz holding. We do not decide whether the matters discussed in the Globe articles touched on matters of public concern. We view the fault requirement of Gertz to be intact regardless whether the private parties are suing on matters of public or private concern. In any case, we base our holding in the present case--that a private plaintiff must prove that the defendant was negligent in publishing defamatory words which reasonably could be interpreted to refer to the plaintiff--on our own common law. "Most liabilities in tort ... are founded on the infliction of harm which the defendant had a reasonable opportunity to avoid at the time of the acts or omissions which were its proximate cause." O.W. Holmes, Jr., The Common Law 145 (1881). The failure to take care when there is a reasonable opportunity to do so--i.e., fault--is the cornerstone of much of our tort law.

or mistakenly but reasonably, understands that it was intended to refer"); [5] W. Prosser & W. Keeton, Torts section 111, at 783 (5th ed.1984) ("the understanding that the plaintiff is meant must be a reasonable one"); id. section 113, at 808-810 (discussing whether plaintiff must prove that defendant was negligent in publishing words which reasonably could be interpreted to refer to the plaintiff).

It is arguable that our later opinions have already moved away from the Hanson subjective test and have adopted this

---

[5] Restatement (Second) of Torts section 564 comment b (1977) states: "<u>Person mistakenly but reasonably believed to be intended</u>. If the communication is reasonably understood by the person to whom it is made as intended to refer to the plaintiff, it is not decisive that the defamer did not intend to refer to him.... It is not enough however, that the defamatory matter is actually understood as intended to refer to the plaintiff; the interpretation must be reasonable in the light of all the circumstances. It is not necessary that the plaintiff be designated by name; it is enough that there is such a description of or reference to him that those who hear or read reasonably understand the plaintiff to be the person intended. Extrinsic facts may make it clear that a statement refers to a particular individual although the language used appears to defame nobody.... It is not necessary that everyone recognize the other as the person intended; it is enough that any recipient of the communication reasonably so understands it. However, the fact that only one person believes that the plaintiff was referred to is an important factor in determining the reasonableness of his belief. If the applicability of the defamatory matter to the plaintiff depends upon extrinsic circumstances, it must appear that some person who saw or read it was familiar with the circumstances and reasonably believed that it referred to the plaintiff...." (Emphasis in original.)

Comment f states: "(T)he defamer is subject to liability if he knew that the communication would be understood by the recipient to refer to the plaintiff or was negligent in failing to recognize that this might happen. If the recipient reasonably understood the communication to be made concerning the plaintiff, it may be inferred that the defamer was negligent in failing to realize that the communication would be so understood.... <u>It is ... necessary for the plaintiff to prove that a reasonable understanding on the part of the recipient that the communication referred to the plaintiff was one that the defamer was negligent in failing to anticipate</u>. This is particularly important when the recipient knew of extrinsic facts that make the communication defamatory of the plaintiff but these facts were not known to the defamer." (Emphasis supplied.) Id.

rule of negligent defamation. See, e.g., Merrill v. Post Publishing Co., 197 Mass. 185, 192, 83 N.E. 419 (1908); Ingalls v. Hastings & Sons Publishing Co., 304 Mass. 31, 33-34, 22 N.E.2d 657 (1939); Brauer v. Globe Newspaper Co., 351 Mass. 53, 55-56, 217 N.E.2d 736 (1966). In any event, we take this opportunity to make clear that a plaintiff may establish that the defendant's words were of and concerning the plaintiff by proving at least that the defendant was negligent in publishing words which reasonably could be interpreted to refer to the plaintiff. This position brings the proof of this aspect of a defamation claim into line with the proof of other aspects of a defamation claim: "As to defamatory impact, the issue is whether in the circumstances of this case a reasonably prudent person, writing an article for publication, would realize that attribution of the racial reference (to the plaintiff) would discredit the plaintiff in the minds of a 'considerable and respectable segment in the community.'" Schrottman v. Barnicle, 386 Mass. 627, 641, 437 N.E.2d 205 (1982), quoting Stone v. Essex County Newspapers, Inc., supra 367 Mass. at 853, 330 N.E.2d 161. Also, in determining whether an allegedly defamatory statement is fact or opinion, "the test is whether the challenged language can reasonably be read as stating a fact." Myers v. Boston Magazine Co., 380 Mass. 336, 340, 403 N.E.2d 376 (1980). Moreover, an objective test--i.e., inquiry into a reasonable recipient's understanding of the words rather than the speaker's intent--has been used over the years to prove that words are defamatory. Rue v. Mitchell, 2 U.S. (2 *1011 Dall.) 58, 59, 1 L.Ed. 288 (1790) ("The sense in which words are received by the world, is the sense which Courts of Justice ought to ascribe to them, on the trial of actions for slander"). Washington Post Co. v. Chaloner, 250 U.S. 290, 293, 39 S.Ct. 448, 63 L.Ed. 987 (1919), quoting Commercial Publishing Co. v. Smith, 149 F. 704, 706-707 (6th Cir.1907) ("A publication claimed to be defamatory must be read and construed in the sense in which the readers to whom it is addressed would ordinarily understand it").

In holding that a plaintiff must prove that a defendant negligently wrote and published words which reasonably could be interpreted to refer to the plaintiff, we in no way depart from the rule that the plaintiff may plead and prove extrinsic facts tending to show that the words could be so interpreted. "(I)f the person is not referred to by name or in such manner as to be readily identifiable from the descriptive matter in the publication, extrinsic facts must be alleged and proved showing that a third person other than the person libeled understood it to refer to him." Brauer v. Globe Newspaper Co., supra 351 Mass. at 56, 217 N.E.2d 736.

(4, 5) While we favor the use of summary judgment procedures in defamation cases, see Cefalu v. Globe Newspaper Co., 8 Mass.App. 71, 74, 391 N.E.2d 935 (1979), appeal dismissed and cert. denied, 444 U.S. 1060, 100 S.Ct. 944, 62 L.Ed.2d 738 (1980), we hold in this case that the trial judge erred in granting summary judgment for the Globe. The affidavits presented several genuine issues of material fact relating to the question whether the Globe articles were of and concerning NETT-Conn. These issues are (1) whether the Globe intended to refer to NETT-Conn and was so understood, and (2) if it did not so intend, whether it was negligent in publishing articles which reasonably could be understood to refer to NETT-Conn.

The Globe filed an affidavit of the principal reporter in charge of investigating and writing the articles in issue. In his affidavit, the reporter states that he researched only NETTT-Mass, and that he did not intend to refer to NETTT-Conn. This affidavit is not conclusive on the question of the Globe's intent. To rebut this claim NETTT-Conn filed two affidavits of Arlan Greenberg, president of both NETTT-Conn and NETTT-Mass, the second of which stated that Greenberg had explained to the Globe reporter that "(t)he New England Tractor-Trailer Training School is one school with a branch in Quincy, Massachusetts and a branch in Somers, Connecticut." NETTT-Conn argues that the Globe intended to refer to NETTT-Conn as well as to NETTT-Mass. Despite the reporter's assertions, we conclude that it is an unresolved question of fact whether the Globe actually intended to refer to NETTT-Mass and NETTT-Conn, or simply to NETTT-Mass.

Moreover, even if a fact finder should conclude that the Globe did not intend to refer to NETTT-Conn, there is a material issue of fact as to whether the Globe was negligent in publishing articles which reasonably could be interpreted to refer to NETTT-Conn. This issue breaks into two distinct components. The first is whether the Globe articles reasonably could be interpreted to refer to NETTT-Conn. The second is, if the articles reasonably could be so understood, whether the Globe was negligent in publishing them. Of course, "(i)f the recipient reasonably understood the communication to be made concerning the plaintiff, it may be inferred that the defamer was negligent in failing to realize that the communication would be so understood. (However,) (i)t is ... necessary for the plaintiff to prove that a reasonable understanding on the part of the recipient that the communication referred to the plaintiff was one that the defamer was negligent in failing to anticipate." Restatement (Second) of Torts section 564 comment f. See supra note 5.

The Globe articles published on March 29, April 12, and June 6, 1974, referred to "New England Tractor-Trailer School." *1012 The March 29, 1974, article begins, "On a windswept abandoned air strip in Quincy, (Massachusetts,) dozens of young men sit in their cars for hours each day awaiting their turns to drive run-down tractor trailers." The Globe argues that this initial reference to Quincy, Massachusetts, makes it clear that this article (and the April 12 and June 6 articles which refer back to this article) refers only to NETT-Mass. We do not agree. We believe that it is a question of fact whether the article reasonably could be understood as referring to NETTT-Conn as well as to NETTT-Mass. Nowhere does the article specifically state that it describes NETTT-Mass. Also, no explicit reference to NETTT-Conn is made. Numerous statements in the article could be construed as describing a regional school. The school is referred to as "New England." The article alleges that New England violated the laws "of at least two states," Massachusetts and New Hampshire. It stated that "New England calls itself the largest such school in the region." Id. Moreover, it quoted statements of Arlan Greenberg, whom it described as "N.E. Tractor president"; Greenberg's affidavits state that he is the president of both NETTT-Conn and NETTT-Mass.

If a jury were to find that the Globe articles reasonably could be interpreted to refer to NETTT-Conn, it would then be presented with another issue of material fact: Whether the Globe was negligent in writing and publishing articles which could be so interpreted. Pertinent to this issue are the questions whether NETTT-Mass and NETTT-Conn hold themselves out to be one school with two locations; if so, whether the Globe knew, or reasonably should have known, that they did so. NETTT-Conn has submitted evidence from which a jury could infer that NETTT-Conn and NETTT-Mass held themselves out to the public as one school, and that the Globe knew, or reasonably should have known, this fact. Appended to the first Greenberg affidavit are numerous pieces of literature describing and advertising the school. In many instances the brochures refer simply to "New England Tractor Trailer Training, Inc.," and provide two sets of addresses and telephone numbers, one in Connecticut and one in

Massachusetts. A company letterhead and an announcement both refer to "New England Tractor Trailer Training of Connecticut, Inc.," but give addresses and telephone numbers in Connecticut and Massachusetts. Moreover, the Globe reporter's affidavit states that he applied for admission to NETTT-Mass; a jury could infer that he received brochures from NETTT-Mass which indicated the existence of NETTT-Conn. The reporter's affidavit does not disavow knowledge of the existence of NETTT-Conn. Greenberg, in his second affidavit, states that he told the Globe reporter that the school had two separate corporate identities but that "(e)ach corporation held itself out as, and has been known as part of, the same school." The plaintiffs also submitted an affidavit showing that these articles, and the Globe, were published in Connecticut.

In conclusion, we hold that a defamation plaintiff must prove that the defendant's words are of and concerning the plaintiff. To do so, the plaintiff must prove either that the defendant intended its words to refer to the plaintiff and that they were so understood, or that the defendant's words reasonably could be interpreted to refer to the plaintiff and that the defendant was negligent in publishing them in such a way that they could be so understood. NETTT-Conn has raised genuine issues of material fact which preclude the entry of summary judgment for the Globe.

Judgment reversed.

Supp. Ch. 3

BISHOP
v.
E. A. STROUT REALTY AGENCY, Inc.

United States Court of Appeals Fourth Circuit.
182 F.2d 503.

Argued April 19, 1950.
Decided May 29, 1950.

Benjamin Fitzhugh Bishop and another brought action for deceit against E. A. Strout Realty Agency, Inc. A judgment for defendant on a verdict was entered by the United States District Court for the District of Maryland, at Baltimore, William C. Coleman, J., and the plaintiffs appealed. The Court of Appeals, Parker, Chief Judge, held that purchasers of tract of land with water frontage for purpose of using it as an angler's camp was not precluded from recovering damages for deceit from real estate company which handled the transaction based on agent's alleged false representations that water adjacent to the land was deep enough that boats could be brought in.

Judge reversed and case remanded.

*504 Before PARKER, Chief Judge, and SOPER and DOBIE, Circuit Judges.

PARKER, Chief Judge.

This is an appeal by plaintiffs from a judgment for defendant on a directed verdict in an action to recover damages for deceit. Plaintiffs are husband and wife who purchased a tract of land with water frontage for the purpose of using it as an angler's camp. The defendant is the real estate agency that is alleged to have sold the property acting through its local representative or "associate", one Oscar C. Davis, who was not joined in the action. The complaint alleges that plaintiffs were induced to purchase the land through the false and fraudulent representations of Davis as to the depth of the adjacent water and that they suffered damage as a result. The case was heard before a jury and the trial judge directed verdict for defendant on the ground that the falsity of the representations could have been discovered by plaintiffs by an examination of the property purchased. Defendant contends that the direction of the verdict should be sustained on the ground given by the trial judge and also on the additional grounds that no fraudulent intent was shown, that there was no proof of damage and that it was not shown that Davis was acting for defendant in the sale of the property.

As the case must be tried again it is not desirable to discuss the evidence in detail. It is sufficient to say that when taken in the light most favorable to plaintiffs, as it must be on motion for directed verdict, it was amply sufficient to take the case to the jury. There was evidence tending to show that the property was listed with defendant for sale, that Davis handled business for defendant in the locality where the land was situate and that defendant afterwards recognized the sale as having been made through its agency. There was evidence that plaintiffs notified Davis of the purpose for which they desired the property and of the necessity of having deep water adjacent to it so that boats could be brought in, and that they were assured by him that this property would suit them to a "T" and that the water adjacent was not less than six feet deep at low tide and nine feet or more deep at high tide. They testified that they were shown the property at high tide and relied upon these statements of Davis without making soundings because they trusted him and had no reason to believe that he was not telling the truth. Plaintiffs paid $3,000 down, giving a $4,000 mortgage for the remainder of the purchase price, and entered into possession and made certain expenditures for improvements. Shortly thereafter they discovered that the water adjacent to the property was very shallow. Because of this, it was not at all suited for the purpose for which it had been purchased and plaintiffs had to abandon it. When they attempted to see Davis, they were unable to get him to meet with them to discuss the matter. The mortgage given by plaintiffs was foreclosed and the property was bought in at the foreclosure sale for the amount of the mortgage debt. The evidence thus presents all the elements necessary to a recovery on the ground of actionable fraud, which are set forth by the Court of Appeals of Maryland in Gittings *505 v. VonDorn, 136 Md. 10, 15, 109 A. 553, 554, as follows:

"To entitle the plaintiff to recover it must be shown: 1. That the representation made is false; 2. that its falsity was either known to the speaker, or the misrepresentation was made with such a reckless indifference to truth as to be equivalent to actual knowledge; 3. that it was made for the purpose of defrauding the person claiming to be injured thereby; 4. that such person not only relied upon the misrepresentation, but had a right to rely upon it in the full belief of its truth, and that he would not have done the thing from which the injury resulted had not such misrepresentation been made; and 5. that he actually suffered damage directly resulting from such fraudulent misrepresentation. McAleer v. Horsey, 35 Md. 439; Buschman v. Codd, 52 Md. 202; Robertson v. Parks, 76 Md. 118, 24 A.411; Cahill v. Applegarth, 98 Md. 493, 56 A. 794; Boulden v. Stilwell, 100 Md. 543 (551) 60 A. 609, 1 L.R.A., N.S., 258."

We do not think that plaintiffs are precluded of recovery because they accepted and relied upon the representations of Davis as to the depth of the water without making soundings or taking other steps to ascertain their truth or falsity. The depth of the water was not a matter that was apparent to ordinary observation; Davis professed to know whereof he was speaking; and there was nothing to put plaintiffs on notice that he was not speaking the truth. There is nothing in law or in reason which requires one to deal as though dealing with a liar or a scoundrel, or that denies the protection of the law to the trustful who have been victimized by fraud. The principle underlying the caveat emptor rule was more highly regarded in former times than it is today; but it was never any credit to the law to allow one who had defrauded another to defend on the ground that his own word should not have been believed. The modern and more sensible rule is that applied by the Court of Appeals of Maryland in Standard Motor Co. v. Peltzer, 147 Md. 509, 510, 128, A. 451, where it was held not to be negligence or folly for a buyer to rely on what had been told him. This is in accord with the modern trend in all jurisdictions which is summed up in A.L.I. Restatement of Torts, sec. 540 as follows:

"The recipient in a business transaction of a fraudulent misrepresentation of fact is justified in relying upon its truth, although he might have ascertained the falsity of the representation had he made an investigation."

The rule is thus stated with citation of the pertinent authorities in 55 Am.Jur.p. 539:

"The tendency of the courts, however, is not to deny relief to a defrauded purchaser on the ground that he was negligent in relying on the vendor's representations, and the mere fact that he could have ascertained by inquiry and investigation the falsity of express representations of existing facts, the truth of which was known to the vendor and unknown to the purchaser, will not necessarily bar him from relief. In this connection it has been said that the unmistakable drift is toward the doctrine that the vendor cannot shield himself from liability by asking the law to condemn the credulity of the purchaser."

Defendant places particular reliance upon the old case of Buschman v. Codd, 52 Md. 202, where the rule is stated: "Where the real quality of the thing is an object of sense, obvious to a person of ordinary intelligence, and the parties have equal knowledge or means of acquiring information by the exercise of ordinary inquiry and diligence, and nothing is said for the purpose of preventing such inquiries as every prudent person ought to make, under such circumstances there is no warranty of the seller's knowledge of the truth of his representations, or of the fact being as it is stated to be." We do not think that this indicates that the law of Maryland differs from the law prevailing in other jurisdictions. See A.L.I. Restatement of Torts sec. 541.[1] The case here, however, is not one of a representation *506 obviously false but of a representation of fact which plaintiffs had no reason to doubt, made by one who professed to know whereof he was speaking and who made it for the purpose of influencing their judgment and bringing about a sale of the property. The rule applicable in such a situation is the general rule as set forth in the Restatement, which was

---

[1] Maryland Cases dealing with the right to recover on the ground of deceit are McAleer v. Horsey, 35 Md. 439; Buschman v. Codd, 52 Md. 202; Weaver v. Shriver, 79 Md. 530, 30 A. 189; Boulden v. Stilwell, 100 Md. 543, 60 A. 609, 610, 1 L.R.A.N.S., 258; Gittings v. VonDorn, 136 Md. 10, 109 A. 553; Standard Motor Co. v. Peltzer, 147 Md. 509, 128 A. 451; Purdum v. Edwards, 155 Md. 178, 141 A. 550; Babb v. Bolyard, Md. 72 A.2d 13. While these hold that mere statements of opinion or intent or statements which are obviously false do not furnish the basis for an action of deceit, there is nothing in any of them to indicate that the law of Maryland is not in accord with the general law on the subject to the effect that one who has made to another false representations as to material and subsisting facts, which are reasonably relied upon by the party to whom they are made and are acted upon by him to his damage, is liable for the damage resulting from the fraud. While statements the falsity of which should have been as obvious to the person to whom made as to the maker have been held not to furnish grounds of action, there is no holding that a defrauded person is not justified in relying upon a false statement of material fact which he has no reason to doubt.

applied by the Court of Appeals of Maryland in Standard Motor Company v. Peltzer, supra, where the false representation was that a 1917 model truck offered for sale was a 1920 model and had been used for only a very short while. In answer to an argument based on Buschman v. Codd, supra, that the plaintiff was not justified in relying upon the representation, the court said:

"The evidence showed that the buyer here had some experience as an owner and user of a truck, and that the truck was displayed for his inspection without restriction. On some of his visits to the salesrooms he remained an hour and more. He testified, however, that his illiteracy rendered him unable to read marks or names on the truck and its engine, and that, having the statements of the selling agents to depend upon, he did not undertake to determine any of the facts for himself. He was not an expert in motor vehicles; he was a farmer. The selling agents, on the other hand, were presumably experts with exact information as to the truck they were selling. And the court could not say that it was negligence and folly for this buyer to accept and rely on whatever had been told him." (147 Md. 509, 128 A. 453.)

Little need be said as to the other grounds urged to sustain the direction of the verdict. It is said that there was no evidence of fraudulent intent; but the misrepresentations were made for the purpose of inducing a sale and, if Davis did not make them with knowledge of their falsity, it is a fair inference that he made them with "reckless indifference to truth." The fact that he avoided an interview with the plaintiffs after they had discovered the wrong that had been done them was a circumstance tending to show guilty knowledge on his part. It is said there is no proof of damage resulting from the fraud; but plaintiffs are out more than $3,000 as a result of their experience and the fact that the property brought no more than the mortgage when offered at public sale is some evidence that it was not worth what plaintiffs paid for it when they were led to believe that it had deep water adjacent and was just the sort of property that they were looking for to establish an angler's camp. It is significant that in the motion for directed verdict no question was raised as to the sufficiency of the proof on the issue of damages; and the trial judge gave no such reason for directing the verdict. As to proof of agency, the evidence that the property was listed with defendant and that after the sale defendant recognized it as having been made through its agency, is sufficient to take the case to the jury. Defendant could not do business through Davis and escape responsibility for his conduct by relying upon limitations in a contract of which plaintiffs had no notice. The rules of law applicable to such a situation are too elementary to justify discussion.

The judgment appealed from will be reversed and the case will be remanded for a new trial.

Reversed and remanded.

Supp. Ch. 3

CHAMBERLAIN
v.
MATHIS

Supreme Court of Arizona. Nov. 24, 1986.
729 P.2d 905

Employees of Department of Health Services brought defamation action against Director of Department. The Superior Court, Maricopa County, Warren L. McCarthy, J., dismissed employees' complaint on grounds that Director enjoyed absolute privilege, and employees appealed. The Supreme Court, Feldman, J., held that: (1) Director was entitled to qualified immunity from liability; (2) Director would forfeit his immunity if and only if he acted outside outer perimeter of his required or discretionary functions, or acted with malice in that he knew his statements regarding employees were false or acted in reckless disregard of truth; and (3) reasonableness of Director's conduct should be measured by objective standard.

Reversed and remanded.

*907 FELDMAN, Justice.

This defamation action was brought by William Chamberlain, Wilda Dearie, Sue Ann Gundy, Arthur Reeves, and Michael J. Savino (plaintiffs) against Donald Mathis (Mathis), Director of the Arizona Department of Health Services (ADHS). The trial court dismissed plaintiffs' complaint on the grounds that Mathis enjoyed an absolute privilege. The court of appeals reversed, holding that there was no absolute privilege and that whether Mathis was entitled to "high level executive" immunity was a question of fact for the jury. Chamberlain v. Mathis, No. 1 CA-CIV 7750 (Ariz.Ct.App. Aug. 27, 1985) (memorandum decision). We accepted review to clarify the law regarding immunity for executive government officials. Rule 23(c)(4), Ariz.R.Civ.App.P., 17A A.R.S. We have jurisdiction pursuant to Ariz. Const. art. 6, section 5(3) and A.R.S. section 12-120.24.

FACTS

Plaintiffs, ADHS employees, comprised the internal audit staff of the Arizona Health Care Cost Containment System (AHCCCS). The AHCCCS was administered by McAuto Systems Group, Inc. (MSGI) pursuant to an administrator contract between the State of Arizona and MSGI. Plaintiffs audited the administrator contract and submitted a draft of that audit to Mathis on May 4, 1983. Plaintiffs allege that the audit was performed in accordance with generally accepted auditing standards and that the audit report's recommendations were made in good faith.

Mathis refused public access to the audit report. However, in the presence of several individuals, including a newspaper reporter, Mathis made several allegedly defamatory comments regarding the audit and ADHS employees:

> The (audit) was prepared by Department of Health personnel who are incompetent and unqualified as auditors.
>
> I've got a bunch of employees in this department, who, I think, have a rich fantasy life.
>
> Charges of covering up failings in the AHCCCS were made by uninformed dissidents in my own department.
>
> I am convinced that McAuto Systems Group, Inc. would sue me if I released the (audit) before the Attorney General reviewed it.

Mathis's comments were published in The Arizona Republic on Sunday, August 14, 1983. Plaintiffs contend that Mathis, acting in his capacity as ADHS director, made the above statements maliciously, knowing that they were false.

Mathis was appointed ADHS director by the governor. A.R.S. section 36-102(C). He served at the governor's pleasure, id., and was responsible for the "direction, operation and control of" ADHS. A.R.S. section 36-102(B). Mathis was to oversee "(p)rogram coordination, evaluation and development" and was charged with administering the department's accounting functions. A.R.S. sections 36-104(1)(a), (d)(ii). He also was authorized to "(p)rovide information and advice on request by (public) agencies and by private citizens, business enterprises and community organizations on matters within the scope of (ADHS's) duties...." A.R.S. *908 section 36-104(9). His position in state government is roughly comparable to that of a federal cabinet officer.

In considering the propriety of Mathis's motion to dismiss, see Rule 12(b)(6), Ariz.R.Civ.P., 16 A.R.S., we assume plaintiffs' allegations are true. Summerfield v. Superior

Court, 144 Ariz. 467, 470, 698 P.2d 712, 715 (1985). Viewing the facts in this light, we examine the procedural propriety of Mathis's motion to dismiss and then the scope of immunity for executive officials.

DISCUSSION

A. Procedural Issues

Plaintiffs argue that Mathis's motion to dismiss should have been denied because absolute immunity is an affirmative defense that should have been raised in Mathis's answer, rather than in a motion to dismiss for failure to state a claim. In general, Rule 8(d), Ariz.R.Civ.P., 16 A.R.S., requires defendants to plead affirmative defenses in their answer. However, we have previously held that the defense of immunity "may be properly raised in a motion to dismiss, if the facts establishing the occasion for the privilege[1] appear in the pleadings." Green Acres Trust v. London, 141 Ariz. 609, 613, 688 P.2d 617, 621 (1984) (footnote added); see also Sierra Madre Dev., Inc. v. Via Entrada Townhouses Ass'n, 20 Ariz.App. 550, 552, 514 P.2d 503, 505 (1973); 2A J. MOORE, MOORE'S FEDERAL PRACTICE 8.28, at 8-209 (1986) ("The affirmative defense raised by a motion to dismiss may be handled entirely under Rule 12(b)(6) ... where the defense appears on the face of the complaint itself."). We adhere to this exception to Rule 8(d) because it "is more in keeping with the general purpose" of our rules of civil procedure "to avoid decisions based on pleading technicalities rather than the merits of a case." 2A J. MOORE, supra 8.28, at 8-207 to 208.

(1) Defendant properly raised the immunity defense in his motion to dismiss because its factual framework was established in plaintiffs' complaint. Plaintiffs had alleged that Mathis was acting in his capacity as ADHS director. Because immunity protects official conduct, the allegation that Mathis was acting in his capacity as director of ADHS is sufficient to support an immunity defense.

(2-4) Once an immunity defense has been raised properly,

---

[1] The terms "immunity" and "privilege" are used interchangeably. Although courts have traditionally used "privilege" in defamation actions against government officials, we use "immunity" because we think it better describes the substantive effect of the asserted defense.

the court determines whether defendants are entitled to immunity. Green Acres, 141 Ariz. at 613, 688 P.2d at 621; Restatement (Second) of Torts section 619 (1977). If the existence of immunity turns on disputed factual issues, the jury determines the facts and the court then determines whether those facts are sufficient to establish immunity. If the court finds that Mathis is entitled only to qualified immunity, then the jury generally determines whether he abused his immunity by acting for an improper purpose or in an improper manner. Restatement (Second) of Torts section 619, comment b (1977).

(5) Having determined that Mathis properly raised the defense of immunity in this case and that defining the scope of immunity is a legal question for the court, we turn to the question whether he is entitled to absolute or qualified immunity. The primary distinction between qualified and absolute immunity is that the former protects only those acts done in good faith, while the latter shields all acts, no matter how malicious. Barr v. Matteo, 360 U.S. 564, 79 S.Ct. 1335, 3 L.Ed.2d 1434 (1959).

B. Absolute or Qualified Immunity

1. Competing Interests

(6) The rationale for granting executive government officials immunity for conduct within the scope of their employment is that government must be allowed to govern. If executive officials are denied immunity, they may elevate personal interest *909 above official duty. Public servants would be obligated to spend their time in court justifying their past actions, instead of performing their official duties. Ultimately, government, including good government, may be hampered and qualified individuals may be hesitant to serve in positions that require great responsibility. See generally Grimm v. Arizona Bd. of Pardons and Paroles, 115 Ariz. 260, 264-65, 564 P.2d 1227, 1231-32 (1977) (discussing various rationales for judicial and official immunity); Schuck, Suing Our Servants: The Court, Congress, and the Liability of Public Officials for Damages, 1980 SUP.CT.REV. 281.

The arguments favoring official immunity are countered by the legitimate complaints of those injured by government officials. Grimm, 115 Ariz. at 265, 564 P.2d at 1231. One's reputation is a significant, intensely personal possession that the law strives to protect. The entire common law of defamation attests to the importance we attach to an individual's right to seek compensation for damage to his reputation. Dombey v. Phoenix Newspapers, Inc., 150 Ariz. 476, 479-80, 724 P.2d 562, 565-66 (1986). Not even the critical need for open and robust public debate on issues of public concern is sufficient to completely shield malicious defamations. New York Times v. Sullivan, 376 U.S. 254, 280, 84 S.Ct. 710, 726, 11 L.Ed.2d 686 (1964).

The interests furthered by absolute official immunity are also countered by basic principles of equal justice. "Our system of jurisprudence rests on the assumption that all individuals, whatever their position in government, are subject to (the) law." Butz v. Economou, 438 U.S. 478, 506, 98 S.Ct. 2894, 2910, 57 L.Ed.2d 895 (1978) (federal executive officials entitled only to qualified immunity when "constitutional tort" is alleged). As we stated in Grimm, "(t)he more power bureaucrats exercise over our lives, the more ... some sort of ultimate responsibility (should) lie for their most outrageous conduct." 115 Ariz. at 266, 564 P.2d at 1233. Grimm recognized that imposing liability for wrongful acts serves two important goals: compensating victims and deterring wrongdoers. Id.

This case requires us to reconcile the competing interests furthered by immunity and responsibility. In Arizona, as elsewhere, courts generally have reconciled these interests by granting public officials either absolute or qualified immunity. E.g., Green Acres, 141 Ariz. at 613, 688 P.2d at 621 (absolute immunity from defamation action for statements made in connection with judicial proceedings); Portonova v. Wilkinson, 128 Ariz. 501, 503, 627 P.2d 232, 234 (1981) (qualified immunity for police officer accused of defamation); Grimm, 115 Ariz. at 265, 564 P.2d at 1232 (qualified immunity for board of pardons and paroles); see also A.R.S. section 41-621(G) (relieving state employees of personal liability for acts within the employee's discretion "done in good faith without wanton disregard of his statutory duties"). Because the decisions just cited establish that government executive employees are presumptively entitled to some immunity, our analysis is limited to a comparison of qualified and absolute immunity. Before proceeding to that comparison, however, it is important to note that not all official conduct is protected by immunity.

2. When is Immunity Available?

(7) Both qualified and absolute immunity protect only acts

reasonably within the employee's discretionary authority. Thus, immunity generally will be recognized when officials are setting policy or performing an act that inherently requires judgment or discretion. For example, Mathis's statements regarding plaintiffs' audit were within his discretion because the director of ADHS is charged with overseeing the department's accounting functions and is authorized to provide information on matters within the scope of ADHS's duties. Ante at 553, 729 P.2d at 907. Because Mathis had discretion in making a public *910 statement regarding the audit, he is entitled to some level of immunity.[2]

(8) In contrast, it is possible to characterize those situations in which no immunity exists as those involving the performance of ministerial acts, such as driving a car or moving furniture. For example, even though the director of ADHS may drive from point A to point B to carry out his official duties, he has no immunity to drive negligently. Driving is not a discretionary governmental function that must be shielded by immunity for government to function effectively. Cf. Ryan v. State, 134 Ariz. 308, 656 P.2d 597 (1982). See generally W. PROSSER & W. KEETON, THE LAW OF TORTS section 132, at 1059-69 (5th ed. 1984).

The distinction between ministerial and discretionary acts is often made, but has not proved entirely satisfactory. See W. PROSSER & W. KEETON, supra section 132, at 1062. The important point is that certain types of activity, such as driving cars, posting warning signs, or moving office furniture are the types of activity for which immunity serves no worthwhile purpose; other types of activity, such as evaluating reports or employees' performances or deciding upon parole release warrant at least qualified immunity in order to advance important public objectives: effective government administered by skilled government officials. See, e.g., Grimm, 115 Ariz. at 263, 564 P.2d at 1230; W. PROSSER & W. KEETON, supra section 132, at 1062-69.

Because Mathis was acting within his discretionary

---

[2] Of course, even executive officials do not have discretion to make statements in every conceivable situation. E.g., Cheatum v. Wehle, 5 N.Y.2d 585, 159 N.E.2d 166, 186 N.Y.S.2d 606 (1959) (dinner speech attacking other officials not within state conservation commissioner's discretion).

authority, he is entitled to some level of immunity. The question is whether Mathis is protected by absolute or qualified immunity.

3. Previous Case Law

Absolute immunity from defamation actions for so-called executive officials became the norm with the United States Supreme Court's decision in Barr v. Matteo, supra. See, e.g., Restatement (Second) of Torts section 591 (1977) (following Barr and granting superior executive state officials an "absolute privilege to publish defamatory matter concerning another in communications made in the performance of his official duties"). Barr involved a press release issued by the director of a federal agency. The release announced the director's intention to suspend two employees involved in conduct for which the agency had been criticized. The Court recognized that the director was not required to issue the press release and that a jury may have found that the director acted with malice. Nevertheless, the Court held that because the press release was within the "outer perimeter" of the director's discretion, the director was entitled to absolute immunity. 360 U.S. at 575, 79 S.Ct. at 1341.

Barr reasoned that government officials

should be free to exercise their duties unembarrassed by the fear of damage suits in respect of acts done in the course of those duties--suits which would consume time and energies which would otherwise be devoted to governmental service and the threat of which might appreciably inhibit the fearless, vigorous, and effective administration of policies of government.

360 U.S. at 571, 79 S.Ct. at 1339. It is not enough, the Court reasoned, that honest, good faith mistakes will be protected by qualified immunity or that, presumably, only well-grounded complaints will result in actual liability. The Court held that society's interest in relieving government officials from any judicial inquiry into their motives outweighs the victim's interest in compensation.

"(I)f it were possible in practice to confine such complaints to the guilty, it would be monstrous to deny recovery. The justification for doing so is that it is impossible to know whether the claim is well founded until the case has been *911 tried, and that to submit all officials, the innocent as well as the guilty, to the burden of a trial and to the inevitable danger of its outcome would dampen the ardor of all but the most resolute, or the most irresponsible, in the unflinching discharge of their duties."

360 U.S. at 571, 79 S.Ct. at 1339 (quoting Gregoire v. Biddle, 177 F.2d 579, 581 (2d Cir.1949) (opinion of Judge Learned Hand)).

Our court of appeals followed Barr in Long v. Mertz, 2 Ariz.App. 215, 407 P.2d 404 (App.1965). Long granted absolute immunity to a state highway department official who had commented on the qualifications of a private contractor. With one minor exception,[3] the court of appeals consistently has adhered to the position advocated in Long. E.g., Bugarin v. Wilson Sch. Dist. No. 7, 17 Ariz.App. 541, 499 P.2d 119 (1972) (allegedly defamatory statement by school district superintendent regarding Mexican-American teachers); Grande v. State, 115 Ariz. 394, 565 P.2d 900 (App.1977) (state tax commission officials' statements in notice of dismissal); Petroni v. Board of Regents, 115 Ariz. 562, 566 P.2d 1038 (App.1977) (statements by professors and regents in tenure proceedings); Wyatt v. Ruck Const., Inc., 117 Ariz. 186, 571 P.2d 683 (App.1977) (statements of city contract administrator).

This court has not expressly adopted Barr or its rationale. We relied indirectly on Barr in White Mountain Apache Indian Tribe v. Shelley, 107 Ariz. 4, 480 P.2d 654 (1971), to hold that Indian tribe executive officers and the tribe's general counsel are absolutely immune from defamation charges for "actions ... within the scope of (their) duties as ... public official(s)." 107 Ariz. at 7, 480 P.2d at 657. However, the holding in White Mountain was premised in part on the tribe's status as a dependent sovereign not subject to state court jurisdiction. 107 Ariz. at 5, 480 P.2d at 655. The court referred to Barr to support its holding that the tribe's general counsel was entitled to the same immunity from state court jurisdiction as the tribe. Nevertheless, White Mountain comes close to adopting Barr as the rule to be

---

[3] Division Two refused to follow Long in Martinez v. Cardwell, 25 Ariz.App. 253, 542 P.2d 1133 (1975). However, it soon overruled Cardwell and adopted Long in Petroni v. Board of Regents, 115 Ariz. 562, 566 P.2d 1038 (App.1977).

applied to government executive officials.

More recently, we refused to extend absolute immunity to police officers, Portonova, supra, or the board of pardons and paroles, Grimm, supra. In both cases we found the protection offered by qualified immunity sufficient to protect government officials acting within the scope of their official duties. Our rejection of absolute immunity in Grimm is significant because, like defendant in the instant case, members of the board of pardons and paroles are executive officials appointed by the governor. A.R.S. section 31-401(A) (Supp.1985). Also, the board enjoys wide discretion in the exercise of its duties. A.R.S. section 31-412 (Supp.1985); Stinson v. Arizona Bd. of Pardons and Paroles, 151 Ariz. 60, 725 P.2d 1094 (1986). Grimm held "that absolute immunity for public officials in their discretionary functions acting in other than true judicial proceedings is not required and, indeed, is improper." 115 Ariz. at 265, 564 P.2d at 1232.

Although Grimm abolished absolute immunity for some public officials exercising discretionary authority by overruling earlier cases affording such immunity, it did not explicitly foreclose absolute immunity for "high level" government officials. 115 Ariz. at 266, 564 P.2d at 1233. Statements in our subsequent decisions can be read fairly as giving conflicting signals on this issue. Compare Ryan v. State, 134 Ariz. at 310, 656 P.2d at 599 ("(W)e must hasten to point out that certain areas of immunity must remain. The more obvious of such immunities are legislative immunity, judicial immunity, and high-level executive immunity.") with Carlson v. Pima County, 141 Ariz. 487, 492, 687 P.2d 1242, 1247 (1984) ("There is no absolute privilege in Arizona for public officers and employees of the state and its political subdivisions.").

*912 4. Resolution

(9) Although there may be some government offices that require absolute immunity, e.g., Nixon v. Fitzgerald, 457 U.S. 731, 102 S.Ct. 2690, 73 L.Ed.2d 349 (1982), we believe the general rule of qualified immunity announced in Grimm should govern the case before us. Qualified immunity protects government officials from liability for acts within the scope of their public duties unless the official knew or should have known that he was acting in violation of established law or acted in reckless disregard of whether his activities would deprive another person of their rights.

Butz v. Economou, 438 U.S. at 497-98, 98 S.Ct. at 2906; Wood v. Strickland, 420 U.S. 308, 322, 95 S.Ct. 992, 1001, 43 L.Ed.2d 214 (1975); Green Acres, 141 Ariz. at 616, 688 P.2d at 624; Restatement (Second) of Torts section 600 (1977). We believe this to be the better rule for several reasons.

We explained in Grimm that because immunity "deprives individuals of a remedy for wrongdoing(, it) should be bestowed only when and at the level necessary." Grimm, 115 Ariz. at 265, 564 P.2d at 1232. Thus, although we have recognized an absolute immunity for persons participating in judicial proceedings, we have narrowly construed the requirement that the act raising the privilege have a close, direct relationship to such proceedings. Green Acres, 141 Ariz. at 614, 688 P.2d at 622. Similarly, in Ryan v. State, 134 Ariz. at 311, 656 P.2d at 600, we endorsed the use of governmental "immunity as a defense only when its application is necessary to avoid a severe hampering of a governmental function or thwarting of established public policy."

The case for absolute official immunity is premised on the assumption that the possibility of inquiry into official motives or conduct will deter proper and necessary official action. Barr, 360 U.S. at 571, 79 S.Ct. at 1339; Halperin v. Kissinger, 606 F.2d 1192, 1214 (D.C.Cir.1979) (Gesell, J., concurring). This argument was made with respect to government immunity, Ryan v. State, 134 Ariz. at 309, 656 P.2d at 598, immunity for police officers, Portonova, 128 Ariz. at 503, 627 P.2d at 234, and immunity for the board of pardons and paroles, Grimm, 115 Ariz. at 270, 564 P.2d at 1237 (Hays, J., dissenting). However, after we limited government immunity and granted police officers and members of the parole board qualified, rather than absolute, immunity, neither government, law enforcement, nor the parole system came to a standstill. We are therefore reluctant to base a rule that eliminates both deterrence of public officials and compensation of victims on such speculative grounds. Barr, 360 U.S. at 589-90, 79 S.Ct. at 1349 (Brennan, J., dissenting) ("This, I fear, is a gossamer web self-spun without a scintilla of support to which one can point.").[4] We believe that in the vast majority of cases,

---

[4] See also 2 F. HARPER & F. JAMES, THE LAW OF TORTS section 29.10, at 1645 (1956) (emphasis in original), quoted in Barr, 360 U.S. at 588, 79 S.Ct. at 1348-49 (Brennan, J., dissenting):

Where the charge is one of honest mistake we exempt the

qualified immunity will adequately protect state executive officials. W. PROSSER & W. KEETON, supra section 114, at 822 ("It does not appear" that government has been hindered "in those states where only the qualified privilege is recognized....").

We recognize, however, that qualified immunity may offer executive public officials insufficient protection if plaintiffs, by merely alleging malice, can force public officials to engage in intensive discovery and cumbersome, time-consuming trials. See Harlow v. Fitzgerald, 457 U.S. 800, 817, 102 S.Ct. 2727, 2737, 73 L.Ed.2d 396 (1982) ("the subjective element of a good *913 faith defense frequently has proved incompatible with our admonition in Butz that insubstantial claims should not proceed to trial"). As Professor Schuck has noted:

> (T)he qualified "good-faith" immunity standard, far from assuring an official that vigorous decision making will be rewarded, is pregnant with risk to him: a rather small risk that he will ultimately be held liable, a somewhat higher risk that the immunity will ultimately be denied, and a substantial risk that a full-dress trial will be necessary to establish its applicability and scope.... It is within the shadow cast by those risks that the official will decide what his duty--to himself as well as to the public--requires of him.

Schuck, supra, 1980 SUP.CT.REV. at 330.

(10, 11) We believe the negative aspects of suits against public officials will be minimized if plaintiffs, instead of merely alleging subjective malice, are required to establish

---

officer because we deem that an <u>actual holding of liability</u> would have worse consequences than <u>the possibility of an actual mistake</u> (which under the circumstances we are willing to condone). But it is stretching the argument pretty far to say that the mere inquiry into malice would have worse consequences than the possibility of actual malice (which we would not, for a minute, condone). Since the danger that official power will be abused is greatest where motives are improper, the balance here may well swing the other way.

proof of objective malice.[5] Thus, in a defamation case, qualified immunity will protect a public official if the facts establish that a reasonable person, with the information available to the official, "could have formed a reasonable belief that the defamatory statement in question was true and that the publication was an appropriate means for serving the interests which justified the privilege." Handler & Klein, The Defense of Privilege in Defamation Suits Against Government Executive Officials, 74 HARV.L.REV. 44, 68 (1960); see also Harlow v. Fitzgerald, 457 U.S. at 816-17, 102 S.Ct. at 2737-39.[6]

Although a subjective inquiry may suffice in most common law actions, we believe it is inappropriate for public officials. The loss of time and expense incurred by claims brought against public officials will be minimized by avoiding lengthy discovery procedures that delve into the mind of the defendant in an attempt to ascertain his subjective motives. The use of an objective test for public officials is not a favor bestowed upon such officials. Instead, it flows from the need to keep public officials available to perform their duties and from recognition that lawsuits are filed against the innocent as well as the guilty. Halperin v. Kissinger, 606 F.2d at 1214-15 (Gesell, J., concurring).

In our view, the adoption of an objective test for determining malice, use of rigid pretrial scrutiny to eliminate frivolous claims, cf. Anderson v. Liberty Lobby, Inc., --- U.S. ----, 106 S.Ct. 2505, 91 L.Ed.2d 202 (1986), and willingness of trial judges to impose sanctions under Rule 11 for claims that are frivolous or intended to harass will provide sufficient protection against the perils

---

[5] If plaintiffs are public officials and the allegedly defamatory statements raise matters of public concern, plaintiffs must establish actual malice with clear and convincing evidence. Anderson v. Liberty Lobby, Inc., --- U.S. ----, 106 S.Ct. 2505, 91 L.Ed.2d 202 (1986); Dombey, supra.

[6] Of course, this objective standard does not shield a public official who knew his statements were false, even though a reasonable person in the official's situation may have had reasonable grounds for believing the statements were true.

described in Barr v. Matteo.[7] At the same time, the adoption of a general rule of qualified immunity for executive government officials will deter those who would intentionally misuse power and will compensate those who are wronged by abuse of power. Harlow v. Fitzgerald, 457 U.S. at 819, 102 S.Ct. at 2739.

Our conclusion is bolstered by recent federal caselaw. Since its pronouncement of absolute immunity in Barr, the United States Supreme Court has granted federal and state officials only qualified immunity for violation of statutory and constitutional rights. Thus, state governors, presidential aides, and executive cabinet officials now enjoy only qualified immunity for statutory *914 and constitutional violations. E.g., Scheuer v. Rhodes, 416 U.S. 232, 94 S.Ct. 1683, 40 L.Ed.2d 90 (1974) (state governor); Harlow v. Fitzgerald, supra (presidential aides); Butz, supra (presidential cabinet officials). In addition, the Court has adopted an objective standard to determine whether qualified immunity is available. Harlow v. Fitzgerald, 457 U.S. at 816-17, 102 S.Ct. at 2737-39.

In its more recent decisions recognizing only qualified immunity, the Supreme Court has distinguished Barr solely on the grounds that it involved a common law action, instead of a statutory or constitutional claim. E.g., Butz, 438 U.S. at 494-95, 98 S.Ct. at 2904-05. We think the distinction between statutory or constitutional violations and common law wrongs is insignificant at best. The rationale for absolute immunity is that officials will be deterred by the fear of liability from performing their duties. But it "cannot be seriously argued that an official will be less deterred by the threat of liability for unconstitutional conduct than for activities which might constitute a common-law tort." Butz, 438 U.S. at 522-23, 98 S.Ct. at 2919 (Rehnquist, J., dissenting). Also, common law actions often can be rephrased in statutory or constitutional terms; it makes little

---

[7] On a case by case basis some officials may be able to establish a need for absolute immunity. See Nixon v. Fitzgerald, supra. However, government officials seeking absolute exemption from personal liability bear "the burden of showing that public policy requires an exemption of that scope." Butz, 438 U.S. at 506, 98 S.Ct. at 2911. Also, public officials are obviously immune from liability for completely nondiscretionary acts that they are required to perform in a certain manner.

difference to the victim whether he was injured by a common law, constitutional, or statutory violation. Id.; Schuck, supra, 1980 SUP.CT.REV. at 324. If qualified immunity offers sufficient protection against liability for constitutional wrongs, then it is also sufficient in cases alleging common law torts.

CONCLUSION

(12) We hold that Mathis is entitled to qualified immunity from liability for his allegedly defamatory statements concerning plaintiffs. He forfeits his immunity if, and only if, he (1) acted outside the outer perimeter of his required or discretionary functions, or (2) acted with malice in that he knew his statements regarding plaintiffs were false or acted in reckless disregard of the truth. The reasonableness of Mathis's conduct should be measured by an objective standard. Ante at 558-559, 729 P.2d at 912-913.

The trial court's order of dismissal is reversed. The court of appeals' decision is vacated. This case is remanded for further proceedings consistent with this opinion.

HOLOHAN, C.J., GORDON, V.C.J., and HAYS and CAMERON, JJ., concur.

Supp. Ch. 3

McKEE
v.
AMERICAN HOME PRODUCTS CORPORATION

Supreme Court of Washington, En Banc. Nov. 30, 1989.
782 P.2d 1045, 113 Wash.2d 701

Consumer sued pharmacists, prescribing physician, and drug manufacturer seeking damages for physical and psychological injuries allegedly sustained as a result of her addiction to plegine. The Superior Court, King County, Herbert M. Stephens, J., entered summary judgment in favor of pharmacists, and consumer appealed. The Supreme Court, Callow, C.J., held that pharmacists did not have a duty to warn consumer of potential hazards of prescription drug.

Affirmed.

*1046 Dore, J., dissented and filed opinion in which Utter and Brachtenbach, JJ., and Pearson, J., pro tem., concurred.

CALLOW, Chief Justice.

The plaintiff, Elaine McKee, appeals a summary judgment dismissing her cause of action against defendant pharmacists Gerald Sidran and Leonard Mezistrano. The trial court ruled that the pharmacists, who had filled McKee's drug prescriptions for 10 years, had no duty to warn her of the adverse side effects of long-term administration of that drug. We affirm.

From 1974 through 1984 McKee received prescriptions for Plegine, an appetite suppressant, from her family physician to control an ostensible weight problem. Plegine is an amphetamine and is potentially addictive. It is a class III drug, requiring either an oral or written prescription from a physician each time it is filled. WAC 360-36-010 and WAC 360-36-020. The manufacturer's information contained in the Physician's Desk Reference (1984) (PDR) states, among other things, that Plegine "is indicated in the management of exogenous obesity as a short term adjunct (a few weeks)...." It further warns:

> Amphetamines and related stimulant drugs have been extensively abused, and the possibility of abuse of PLEGINE should be kept in mind when evaluating the desirability of including a drug as part of a weight

reduction program....

> Tolerance to the anorectic effect of PLEGINE ... develops within a few weeks. When this occurs, its use should be discontinued....

The desk reference for physicians also lists various side effects from overuse, such as: extreme fatigue and mental depression after abrupt cessation, intense psychological dependence and severe social dysfunction, and at an extreme, psychosis.[1]

*1047 McKee filled nearly all her Plegine prescriptions at a pharmacy in Seward Park in Seattle. From 1974 through 1981, the prescriptions were filled by Sidran, who owned the pharmacy. In April 1981, Sidran sold the pharmacy to Mezistrano, who continued to fill McKee's prescriptions until they were discontinued by a second physician in 1984. It is undisputed that the pharmacists filled the prescriptions accurately and pursuant to either a written prescription or oral refill authorization from McKee's physician.

McKee's prescriptions were for 100 tablets each. The manufacturer packaged Plegine in 100-tablet bottles; attached to the outside of each was the manufacturer's package insert. Before giving McKee a bottle of Plegine, the pharmacists would remove the package insert and place their own label on the bottle to comply with state and federal labeling laws.[2] It is undisputed that at no time did either pharmacist warn McKee of the possible side effects of extended use of Plegine or give her the manufacturer's insert.

In 1985, McKee brought this action against the prescribing physician, the drug manufacturer, and the defendant

---

[1] The Physician's Desk Reference is supplied by drug manufacturers for the guidance of physicians, not pharmacists.

[2] RCW 18.64.246 requires that all prescription drugs bear a label containing, inter alia, the name and address of the pharmacy, the name of the prescribing doctor and his directions, the name and strength per unit dose of the drug, the name of the patient, the date of the prescription, and the expiration date. See also WAC 360-16-255. 21 U.S.C. section 353(b)(2) contains similar federal requirements.

pharmacists, seeking damages for physical and psychological injuries allegedly sustained as a result of her addiction to Plegine. Only the claims against the pharmacists are at issue in this appeal.

McKee alleged the pharmacists were negligent in selling her Plegine for such an extended length of time without warning her of its adverse effects and were negligent in failing to give her the manufacturer's package insert. She also alleged strict liability and breach of express and implied warranties. The pharmacists moved for summary judgment and dismissal of all claims against them, contending they had no duty to warn their customers of the potential hazards of a prescription drug. The trial court granted the pharmacists' motion and dismissed McKee's claims. We granted direct review.

(1) Initially we note that McKee did not assign error to the trial court's dismissal of her strict liability and breach of warranty claims, as required by RAP 10.3. Aside from citing the Product Liability Act and arguing that the defendant pharmacists are "product manufacturers" thereunder, McKee provides no argument or legal authority in support of her strict liability and breach of warranty claims. We will not consider issues on appeal that are not raised by an assignment of error or are not supported by argument and citation of authority. Transamerica Ins. Group v. United Pac. Ins. Co., 92 Wash.2d 21, 28-29, 593 P.2d 156 (1979). Therefore, we will address McKee's negligence claim only.

I

A summary judgment motion may be granted under CR 56(c) only if the pleadings, affidavits, depositions, and admissions on file demonstrate there is no genuine issue concerning any material fact, and the moving party is entitled to judgment as a matter of law. Wilson v. Steinbach, 98 Wash.2d 434, 437, 656 P.2d 1030 (1982); Barrie v. Hosts of Am., Inc., 94 Wash.2d 640, 646, 618 P.2d 96 (1980). All facts submitted and all reasonable inferences from the facts must be considered by the court in the light most favorable to the nonmoving party. Wilson, 96 Wash.2d at 437, 656 P.2d 1030; Yakima Fruit & Cold Storage Co. v. Central Heating & Plumbing Co., 81 Wash.2d 528, 530, 503 P.2d 108 (1972); Barber v. Bankers Life & Cas. Co., 81 Wash.2d 140, 142, 500 P.2d 88 (1972). Motions for summary judgment should only be granted, if reasonable persons could only reach but one conclusion from all the evidence. Wilson, 96

Wash.2d at 437, 656 P.2d 1030; Morris v. McNicol, 83 Wash.2d 491, 494-95, 519 P.2d 7 (1974).

*1048 (2) For purposes of CR 56(e) the affidavit must: (1) be made on personal knowledge, (2) set forth admissible evidentiary facts, and (3) affirmatively show that the affiant is competent to testify to the matters stated therein. Bernal v. American Honda Motor Co., 87 Wash.2d 406, 412, 553 P.2d 107 (1976); Meadows v. Grant's Auto Brokers, Inc., 71 Wash.2d 874, 878, 431 P.2d 216 (1967). Competency to testify can reasonably be found by the trial court. Bernal, 87 Wash.2d at 413, 553 P.2d 107. Furthermore, "(t)he qualifications of an expert are to be judged by the trial court, and its determination will not be set aside in the absence of a showing of abuse of discretion." Bernal, at 413, 553 P.2d 107, quoting Nordstrom v. White Metal Rolling & Stamping Corp., 75 Wash.2d 629, 642, 453 P.2d 619 (1969).

(3) The gravamen of this case is whether the plaintiff met her burden under RCW 7.70.040,[3] of proving the defendants failure to exercise the degree of care, skill, and learning expected of a reasonably prudent pharmacist licensed in the State of Washington at the time.

The only evidence offered by McKee concerning the standard of care of a pharmacist practicing in Washington was an affidavit of an Arizona physician. The physician was not licensed to practice medicine in Washington, nor was he a pharmacist. We recently reiterated the rule that to establish the standard of care required of professional practitioners, that standard must be established by the testimony of experts who practice in the same field. The

---

[3] RCW 7.70.040 reads:

"The following shall be necessary elements of proof that injury resulted from the failure of the health care provider to follow the accepted standard of care.

"(1) The health care provider failed to exercise that degree of care, skill, and learning expected of a <u>reasonably prudent health care provider at that time in the profession or class to which he belongs, in the state of Washington</u>, acting in the same or similar circumstances;

"(2) Such failure was a proximate cause of the injury complained of." (Italics ours.)

duty of physicians must be set forth by a physician, the duty of structural engineers by a structural engineer and that of any expert must be proven by one practicing in the same field--by one's peer. Young v. Key Pharmaceuticals, Inc., 112 Wash.2d 216, 770 P.2d 182 (1989). So here, only a pharmacist who knew the practice and standard of care in this state could establish the standard of care for the defendants. Contrary to the requirements of RCW 7.70.040 the affidavit does not assert the standard of care of a pharmacist in this state. Therefore, for purposes of CR 56(e) the affidavit does not show that the affiant was qualified to prove the standard of care of a pharmacist in the State of Washington.

The trial court determined that no genuine issues of material fact remained. Therefore, the moving parties were entitled to judgment as a matter of law. We have thoroughly reviewed all the pleadings, affidavits, depositions and admissions on file and affirm the granting of the summary judgment by the trial court.

II

While we need go no further, it is appropriate that we discuss the merits of the primary issue raised because of the importance of the issue and the public interest therein. McKee contends the pharmacists had a duty to warn her of the harmful side effects of long-term use of Plegine, and that she should recover from the defendants under RCW 7.70.030(1). Recovery is provided under RCW 7.70.030(1) where: "(t)hat injury resulted from the failure of a health care provider to follow the accepted standard of care(.)"

Chapter 7.70 of the RCW outlines actions for injuries resulting from health care. A pharmacist is defined as a health care provider under RCW 7.70.020. RCW 7.70.030 requires that the plaintiff prove each fact essential to an award by a preponderance of the evidence.

(4) The elements required to prove that an injury resulted from a failure to follow the accepted standard of care are stated in RCW 7.70.040. Although a pharmacist's duty to warn of potential hazards associated with a prescription drug is an issue of *1049 first impression in Washington, we choose to join the majority of those states with statutes similar to RCW 7.70.040 which have addressed this issue holding that

a pharmacist has no duty to warn. In Florida[4], in a case almost factually identical, the court answered two questions which are applicable here: First, does a licensed pharmacist have a duty not only to properly fill a prescription but to warn the customer of dangerous propensities of the prescription drug? Second, does a licensed pharmacist who has actual or constructive knowledge of a customer's dependency and addiction have a duty to warn the treating physician of this fact? The court answered in the negative to both questions.

> (A) supplier of drugs has no duty to fail or refuse to supply a customer with drugs for which the customer has a valid and lawful prescription from a licensed physician, nor any duty to warn said customer of the fact that one using the prescribed drug for any period of time could or would become addicted to the use thereof and would become physically and psychologically dependent thereon ....

Pysz v. Henry's Drug Store, 457 So.2d 561, 561-62 (Fla.Dist.Ct.App.1984). The physician has the duty to know the drug that he is prescribing and to properly monitor the patient. Here the druggist properly filled a lawful prescription.

Similarly, the Michigan Court of Appeals held that a pharmacist owes a duty to properly fill the lawful prescriptions of its customers. Adkins v. Mong, 168 Mich.App. 726, 729, 425 N.W.2d 151 (1988). "(A) pharmacist is held to a very high standard of care in performing this duty and may be held liable in tort for any breach." Adkins,

---

[4] Fla.Stat. section 768.45 (1985) is renumbered as 766.102 (1988) and provides for standards of recovery in medical negligence actions. Like our RCW 7.70.040, Florida provides that in an action against a health care provider:

"... the claimant shall have the burden of proving by the greater weight of evidence that the alleged actions of the health care provider represented a breach of the prevailing professional standard of care for that health care provider. The prevailing professional standard of care for a given health care provider shall be that level of care, skill, and treatment which, in light of all relevant surrounding circumstances, is recognized as acceptable and appropriate by reasonably prudent similar health care providers."

at 729, 425 N.W.2d 151. However, "'a pharmacist has no duty to warn the patient of possible side effects of a prescribed medication where the prescription is proper on its face and neither the physician nor the manufacturer has required that any warning be given to the patient by the pharmacist.'" Adkins, at 728, 425 N.W.2d 151 quoting, Stebbins v. Concord Wrigley Drugs, Inc., 164 Mich.App. 204, 218, 416 N.W.2d 381 (1987). Indeed, "there exists no legal duty on the part of a pharmacist to monitor and intervene with a customer's reliance on drugs prescribed by a licensed treating physician." Adkins, 168 Mich.App. at 732, 425 N.W.2d 151. It is the physician who owes the duty to the patient to monitor prescription drug usage and a pharmacist will not be found liable for lawfully filling a prescription issued by a licensed physician. Adkins, at 730, 425 N.W.2d 151.

(5) This court has addressed a closely related issue--the manufacturer's duty to warn. Adopting the "learned intermediary" doctrine, we held in Terhune v. A.H. Robins Co., 90 Wash.2d 9, 577 P.2d 975 (1978) that a prescription drug manufacturer's duty to warn of dangers associated with its product runs only to the physician; it is the physician's duty to warn the ultimate consumer.

The reasons for this rule are apparent.

> Where a product is available only on prescription or through the services of a physician, the physician acts as a "learned intermediary" between the manufacturer or seller and the patient. It is his duty to inform himself of the qualities and characteristics of those products which he prescribes for or administers to or uses on his patients, and to exercise an independent judgment, taking into account his knowledge of the patient as well as the product. The patient is expected to and, it can be presumed, does place primary reliance upon that judgment. *1050 The physician decides what facts should be told to the patient. Thus, if the product is properly labeled and carries the necessary instructions and warnings to fully apprise the physician of the proper procedures for use and the dangers involved, the manufacturer may reasonably assume that the physician will exercise the informed judgment thereby gained in conjunction with his own independent learning, in the best interest of the patient.

(Footnote omitted.) Terhune, at 14, 577 P.2d 975.

The Illinois court's have also adopted the learned intermediary doctrine. In Leesley v. West, 165 Ill.App.3d 135, 116 Ill.Dec. 136, 518 N.E.2d 758 (1988), the court expanded the learned intermediary doctrine to apply to pharmacies. In Kirk v. Michael Reese Hosp. & Med. Ctr., 117 Ill.2d 507, 111 Ill.Dec. 944, 952, 513 N.E.2d 387, 395 (1987), cert. denied, 485 U.S. 905, 108 S.Ct. 1077, 99 L.Ed.2d 236 (1988), the court held a doctor, as a learned intermediary, decides which available drug fits the patient's needs, choosing which facts from the various warnings should be conveyed to the patient. The extent of disclosure is a matter of medical judgment. Kirk, at 523, 111 Ill.Dec. 944, 513 N.E.2d 387. The opinion continues:

> "It is the physician who is in the best position to decide when to use and how and when to inform his patient regarding risks and benefits pertaining to drug therapy." (W. Prosser & W. Keeton, The Law of Torts sec. 96, at 688 (5th ed. 1984).) As such, the manufacturer is only obligated to adequately warn the physicians, who decide which drug to use and which warnings to provide. The drug companies are not required to warn hospital personnel because they do not select the proper drugs for the patient and prescribe them.

Kirk, 117 Ill.2d at 523, 111 Ill.Dec. 944, 513 N.E.2d 387. Indeed "(t)he foreseeability of injury to an individual consumer in the absence of any particular warning also varies greatly depending on the medical history and condition of the individual--facts which we cannot reasonably expect the pharmacist to know." Leesley, 165 Ill.App.3d at 142, 116 Ill.Dec. 136, 518 N.E.2d 758.

In North Carolina, the court held that physicians offered their professional services and skill for which they are paid by their patients. This is the basis of the relationship between the physician and his patient. Only the doctor knows the myriad of factors that went into deciding upon the proper medication, proper amount and proper frequency of ingestion. The pharmacist must fill the prescription as directed. Where there is no allegation that the product was other than what it was supposed to be, there is no negligence. Batiste v. American Home Prods. Corp., 32 N.C.App. 1, 231 S.E.2d 269,

274 (1977).[5]

The relationship between the physician-patient-manufacturer applies equally to the relationship between the physician-patient and pharmacist. In both circumstances the patient must look to the physician, for it is only the physician who can relate the propensities of the drug to the physical idiosyncrasies of the patient. "It is the physician who is in the best position to decide when to use and how and when to inform *1051 his patient regarding risks and benefits pertaining to drug therapy." W. Keeton, R. Keeton & D. Owen, Prosser and Keeton on Torts section 96, at 688 (5th ed. 1984).

In Young v. Key Pharmaceuticals, Inc., 112 Wash.2d 216, 770 P.2d 182 (1989), we stated, "proper dosages of medication is not within the scope of matters on which nonphysicians are competent...." Young, at 230, 770 P.2d 182. We went on to hold that "pharmacists are not doctors and are not licensed to prescribe medication because they lack the physician's rigorous training in diagnosis and treatment." Young, at 230, 770 P.2d 182.

Neither manufacturer nor pharmacist has the medical education or knowledge of the medical history of the patient

---

[5] The Batiste opinion states in part:

"She alleged that she obtained a prescription from her physician and that defendant druggist filled that prescription. There is no allegation that defendant druggist added anything thereto or selected anything for plaintiff to take. Nor is this a situation where plaintiff made her choice from items selected and displayed by the druggist for sale to the general public. Here the drug purchased by plaintiff was not available to the general public in the sense that it was available for purchase by any customer who came in the drug store, selected it from the shelf, and paid the price therefor. It was available only to those who had previously seen their physician and obtained from the physician a prescription directing the druggist to supply the drug. Obviously the plaintiff patient did not rely on the druggist's skill or judgment in assuming that the drug would be fit for its intended purpose. This reliance had been properly placed with her physician. We are not willing to extend the applicability of implied warranties of fitness and merchantability to this situation and agree with the trial court in dismissing these two claims for relief." (Citations omitted.) Batiste, 32 N.C.App. at 12, 231 S.E.2d 269.

which would justify a judicial imposition of a duty to intrude into the physician-patient relationship. In deciding whether to use a prescription drug, the patient relies primarily on the expertise and judgment of the physician. Proper weighing of the risks and benefits of a proposed drug treatment and determining what facts to tell the patient about the drug requires an individualized medical judgment based on knowledge of the patient and his or her medical condition. The physician is not required to disclose all risks associated with a drug, only those that are material. Smith v. Shannon, 100 Wash.2d 26, 31, 666 P.2d 351 (1983). It is apparent that a pharmacist would not be qualified to make such a judgment as to materiality. Moreover, circumstances may exist justifying nondisclosure of even material risks. See Holt v. Nelson, 11 Wash.App. 230, 240-41, 523 P.2d 211, 69 A.L.R.3d 1235 (1974) (enumerating exceptions to the informed consent doctrine). Requiring the pharmacist to warn of potential risks associated with a drug would interject the pharmacist into the physician-patient relationship and interfere with ongoing treatment. We believe that duty, and any liability arising therefrom, is best left with the physician.

A majority of other jurisdictions that have addressed the issue have likewise refused to impose a duty to warn on the pharmacist. E.g., Jones v. Irvin, 602 F.Supp. 399 (S.D.Ill.1985); Ramirez v. Richardson-Merrell, Inc., 628 F.Supp. 85, 88 (E.D.Pa.1986); Eldridge v. Eli Lilly & Co., 138 Ill.App.3d 124, 92 Ill.Dec. 740, 485 N.E.2d 551 (1985); Makripodis v. Merrell-Dow Pharmaceuticals, Inc., 361 Pa.Super. 589, 597-98, 523 A.2d 374 (1987) (strict liability theory). As said in Ramirez, at 88:

> To impose a duty to warn on the pharmacist, however, would be to place the pharmacist between the physician who, having prescribed the drug presumably knows the patient's present condition as well as his or her complete medical history, and the patient. Such interference in the patient-physician relationship can only do more harm than good. As the court in Batiste v. American Home Products Corp., 32 N.C.App. 1, 231 S.E.2d 269, 274 (1977) emphasized, when holding that a pharmacy could not be held liable in negligence for its failure to warn the plaintiff of the potential side effects associated with an oral contraceptive drug, defendant is not a physician and is not qualified or licensed to advise plaintiff with respect to the best medication for her use. See also Ingram v. Hook's Drugs, Inc.,

Ind.App., 476 N.E.2d 881 (1985).

(6, 7) McKee cites RCW 18.64.011(11) as supporting a duty to warn. RCW 18.64.011(11) defines the "practice of pharmacy." RCW 18.64.011(11) reads:

> "Practice of Pharmacy" includes the practice of and responsibility for: Interpreting prescription orders; the compounding, dispensing, labeling, administering, and distributing of drugs and devices; the monitoring of drug therapy and use; the initiating or modifying of drug therapy in accordance with written guidelines or protocols previously established and approved for his or her practice by a practitioner authorized to prescribe drugs; the participating in drug utilization reviews and drug product selection; the proper and safe storing and distributing of drugs and devices and maintenance of proper records thereof; the providing of information on legend drugs which may include, but is not limited to, the advising of therapeutic values, *1052 hazards, and the uses of drugs and devices.

RCW 18.64.011(11) is applicable to pharmacists. However contrary to McKee's contentions it does not require that warnings concerning the prescription be given to the patient. Initially we note this statute is definitional and does not purport to set forth duties. Further, WAC 360-12-150 states that the term "monitoring drug therapy" as used in the statute shall include duties such as measuring patient vital signs and ordering and evaluating laboratory test results. The provision is not meant to apply to the neighborhood pharmacy but only to pharmacists practicing in an institutional setting.[6] Nor does the latter quoted

---

[6] WAC 360-12-150 reads:

> Monitoring of drug therapy by pharmacists. The term "monitoring (of) drug therapy" used in RCW 18.64.011(11) shall mean a review of the drug therapy regimen of patients by a pharmacist for the purpose of evaluating and rendering advice to the prescribing practitioner regarding adjustment of the regimen. Monitoring of drug therapy shall include, but not be limited to:
>
> (1) Collecting and reviewing patient drug use histories;
>
> (2) Measuring and reviewing routine patient vital signs including, but not limited to, pulse, temperature, blood pressure

definition create a mandatory duty on all pharmacists to warn customers of all dangers associated with a drug.[7] That duty may be appropriate where the pharmacist has prescriptive authority, a question not presented here. See RCW 18.64.011(11) and WAC 360-12-140.

III

McKee contends that although a pharmacist may not have a duty to warn of hazardous side effects in every case, here the pharmacists knew or should have known from the manufacturer's literature and from the fact that McKee did

---

and respiration; and

    (3) Ordering and evaluating the results of laboratory tests relating to drug therapy including, but not limited to, blood chemistries and cell counts, drug levels in blood, urine, tissue or other body fluids, and culture and sensitivity tests when performed in accordance with policies and procedures or protocols applicable to the practice setting, which have been developed by the pharmacist and prescribing practitioners and which include appropriate mechanisms for reporting to the prescriber monitoring activities and results.

We are unaware of any practice wherein pharmacists must collect and review patient drug use histories. Such activity could intrude into the privacy of the customer and bring forth a number of issues not before us in this action. Further, we are unaware of any practice by pharmacists which includes taking the pulse, temperature, and blood pressure, and checking the respiration of a customer who enters a drug store bearing, in hand, a prescription from his doctor.

[7] WAC 360-16-250 specifically requires the pharmacist to orally explain the directions for use and give any additional information necessary to assure proper use of the drug. We interpret this to include nonjudgmental information, not affecting a decision to take or continue using a drug, such as: whether to take the drug on an empty or full stomach, substances to avoid while using the drug, or not to drive or use heavy machinery while taking the drug. We do not decide whether failure to give this information is actionable. See Brushwood & Simonsmeier, Drug Information for Patients: Duties of the Manufacturer, Pharmacist, Physician, and Hospital, 7 J.Legal Med. 279, 282, 308-20 (1986).

not appear obese,[8] that her physician was misprescribing Plegine, giving rise to a duty to warn her or to question the physician. In support of her argument, McKee relies on Hand v. Krakowski, 89 A.D.2d 650, 453 N.Y.S.2d 121 (1982) and Riff v. Morgan Pharmacy, 353 Pa.Super. 21, 508 A.2d 1247 (1986).

In Hand, a pharmacy dispensed drugs which were contraindicated with alcohol to an alcoholic, resulting in the patient's death. It was undisputed that the pharmacist had personal knowledge that the patient was an alcoholic. The court held that since the pharmacy knew the customer was alcoholic and knew or should have known the drugs were contraindicated for that particular customer, an issue of fact existed as to whether the pharmacy had a duty to warn the decedent and to question the prescribing physician.

Riff involved a prescription on which the doctor had failed to state the maximum *1053 safe dosage. The pharmacy took no steps to correct the error and the patient suffered an overdose. Expert testimony established that the pharmacy was negligent in failing to be aware of obvious inadequacies on the face of the prescription and to warn the patient or notify the prescribing physician.

(8) Both of these cases involved obvious or known errors in the prescription. In Hand, the court emphasized that the drug was contraindicated, "refer(ring) to a circumstance under which the drug must never be given. It is absolute and admits of no exceptions(.)" 89 A.D.2d at 651, 453 N.Y.S.2d 120, citing Baker v. St. Agnes Hosp., 70 A.D.2d 400, 402, 421 N.Y.S.2d 81 (1979). We agree pharmacists should have a duty to be alert for patent errors in a prescription, for example: obvious lethal dosages, inadequacies in the instructions, known contraindications,[9] or incompatible prescriptions,[10] and

---

[8] McKee is 54 tall and states that her maximum weight while using Plegine was 138 pounds.

[9] Pharmacies in Washington are required to maintain a patient medication record for each patient, which may include information on "allergies, idiosyncrasies, or chronic condition which may relate to drug utilization." WAC 360-19-030(1)(i), -040(1)(g). We recognize, however, that a pharmacist typically does not have the patient's complete medical history and there may be occasions where the pharmacist is unaware a drug is contraindicated.

to take corrective measures.

The alleged negligence in this case, however, involved an exercise of the physician's judgment in determining whether Plegine was an appropriate drug for McKee's condition and the length of time she could safely use it. It is undisputed that McKee's physician monitored her condition throughout the time she used Plegine, requiring periodic checkups during which he would check her weight and blood pressure. On at least one occasion he required her to stop using Plegine for several months. Imposing a duty such as McKee urges would, in essence, require the pharmacist to question the physician's judgment regarding the appropriateness of each customer's prescription. Sound policy reasons exist for not imposing such a duty.

As noted, without benefit of a patient's medical history, the pharmacist is not qualified to determine the propriety of a particular drug regimen. That determination certainly cannot be made from a patient's physical appearance alone. As an Illinois court observed:

> The propriety of a prescription depends not only on the propensities of the drug but also on the patient's condition. A prescription which is excessive for one patient may be entirely reasonable for the treatment of another. To fulfill the duty which the plaintiff urges us to impose would require the pharmacist to learn the customer's condition.... To accomplish this, the pharmacist would have to interject himself into the doctor-patient relationship and practice medicine without a license.

Eldridge v. Eli Lilly & Co., 138 Ill.App.3d at 127, 92 Ill.Dec. 740, 485 N.E.2d 551.

A physician may often have valid reasons for deviating from

---

[10]. WAC 360-19-050 requires a pharmacist to review a patient's medication record upon receipt of a prescription for possible drug interactions, reactions or duplications, and to contact the prescriber if needed. WAC 360-19-080(2) states: "If in the judgment of the dispenser, the prescription presented for dispensing is determined to cause a potentially harmful drug interaction or other problem due to a drug previously prescribed by another practitioner, the dispenser may communicate this information to the prescribers."

the drug manufacturer's recommendations based on a patient's unique condition. The duty which McKee urges would result in the pharmacist second guessing numerous prescriptions to avoid liability. This would not only place an undue burden on pharmacists, but would likely create antagonistic relations between pharmacists and physicians. As stated in Jones v. Irvin, 602 F.Supp. at 402:

> It is the duty of the prescribing physician to know the characteristics of the drug he is prescribing, to know how much of the drug he can give his patient, to elicit from the patient what other drugs the patient is taking, to properly prescribe various combinations of drugs, to warn the patient of any dangers associated with taking the drug, to monitor the *1054 patient's dependence on the drug, and to tell the patient when and how to take the drug. Further, it is the duty of the patient to notify the physician of the other drugs the patient is taking. Finally, it is the duty of the drug manufacturer to notify the physician of any adverse effects or other precautions that must be taken in administering the drug. Placing these duties to warn on the pharmacist would only serve to compel the pharmacist to second guess every prescription a doctor orders in an attempt to escape liability.

(Citation omitted.) Moreover, unnecessary warnings to the patient could cause unfounded fear and mistrust of the physician's judgment, jeopardizing the physician-patient relationship and hindering treatment.

Pharmacists are defined as health care providers under RCW 7.70.020. The elements necessary to prove that a health care provider did not follow the accepted standard of care are found in RCW 7.70.040 previously quoted.

It is inappropriate to interpret this statute to allow any testimony regarding the practice of pharmacy as the proper standard of care. RCW Ch. 18.64 discusses pharmacists and their expected duties. The "practice of pharmacy" as defined by RCW 18.64.011(11) reads:

> "Practice of pharmacy" includes the practice of and responsibility for: Interpreting prescription orders; the compounding, dispensing, labeling, administering, and distributing of drugs and devices; ... <u>the providing of information on legend drugs which may include, but is not limited to</u>, the advising of therapeutic values, hazards,

and the uses of drugs and devices.

(Italics ours.)

Nowhere in RCW Ch. 18.64 are pharmacists required to disclose all information when filling a prescription. RCW 18.64.011(11) provides that information may include therapeutic values, hazards and the use of the drug. Further, WAC 360-16-250 provides "the pharmacist ... must orally explain to the patient or the patient's agent the directions for use and any additional information, in writing if necessary, to assure the proper utilization of the medication or device prescribed."

Plegine is a legend drug, it may be dispensed on prescription only. As a legend drug, the pharmacists may have given McKee information about the therapeutic values or hazards of plegine, however, they were not required to do so. McKee had a prescription for every refill she received, therefore, she was constantly monitored by her physician.

Nothing in RCW Ch. 18.64 nor in WAC 360-16 requires pharmacists to disclose all contraindications or warnings. If the Legislature intended pharmacists to be liable for failure to warn, the Legislature could have so provided.

IV

(9) McKee also contends the pharmacists were negligent in failing to provide her with the manufacturer's package insert. Prescription drugs are exempt from the package labeling requirements for drugs sold over the counter. 21 U.S.C. section 353(b)(2). Instead, the Food and Drug Administration (FDA) requires manufacturers to accompany each package of prescription drugs with a package insert describing the drug and detailing its uses, contraindications, potential harmful effects, and directions to the physician for use. 21 C.F.R. sections 201.100(d), 201.56, 201.57. Consistent with the learned intermediary doctrine, the insert is directed to the physician or other health care provider; its contents are reprinted in the PDR. Brushwood, The Informed Intermediary Doctrine and the Pharmacist's Duty to Warn, 4 J. Legal Med. 349, 356 (1983). There is no regulatory requirement that pharmacists provide consumers with this insert. We decline to impose such a duty for several reasons.

First, such a requirement would place an unknown burden on

pharmacists. As noted, manufacturers are not required to provide consumers with their warnings. Although here the amount of McKee's prescription coincided with the size of the manufacturer's *1055 package, drugs are often packaged in large units, containing only one package insert, and must be divided to fill numerous prescriptions. Thus, pharmacists would have the economic and logistic burden of copying the inserts as well as developing a storage, filing and retrieval system to ensure the current insert is dispensed with the proper drug. From a liability standpoint, the pharmacist may also need a system for proving the patient received the insert.

More importantly, such a duty may not be without risk. Package inserts, written for the physician, are detailed and technical, and may confuse and frighten the patient. In 1980, the FDA adopted regulations requiring patient package inserts (PPI) directed to the consumer. These were information leaflets, in lay language, to be produced by manufacturers and distributed by pharmacists at the time a prescription was filled. 40 Fed.Reg. 60,754 (1980). This program was rescinded, however, in 1982. 47 Fed.Reg. 39,147 (1982). Patient inserts are still required for oral contraceptives and several other drugs, but not Plegine. See Brushwood & Simonsmeier, Drug Information For Patients: Duties of the Manufacturer, Pharmacist, Physician, and Hospital, 7 J.Legal Med. 270, 280 n. 6 (1986) (listing PPI requirements).

Some have argued that direct warnings to the consumer, once the patient has made the decision to use a drug and the physician is no longer available to counsel, may be counterproductive and are contrary to the rationale behind the learned intermediary doctrine. Brushwood & Simonsmeier, 7 J.Legal Med. at 283-84; Brushwood, 4 J.Legal Med. at 357; Makripodis, 361 Pa.Super. at 597, 523 A.2d 374. As one commentator stated:

> The most innocuous of drugs, and those generally considered safe, effective, and best for a given problem may, nevertheless, produce serious side effects in some patients. A description of risks in a package insert drafted for the self-protection of the drug company and the FDA could disturb even the most sophisticated patient. Placing this type of information in the hands of patients after the course of treatment had been agreed on with the physician would add an uncontrollable and often unknown factor to the treatment process. The

patient might make a new judgment not to take the medication as directed.

Curran, Package Inserts for Patients: Informed Consent in the 1980s, 305 New Eng.J.Med. 1564, 1565-66 (1981).

Moreover, a requirement that consumers receive the manufacturer's insert effectively abrogates the learned intermediary doctrine and could impact not only pharmacists' liability, but that of manufacturers and physicians as well.

While some form of written warnings to consumers may well be beneficial, in light of the potential ramifications of such a decision and the pervasive regulation in this area, if such warnings are to be required, the duty should be imposed by the Legislature. The Legislature can better assess the relative costs and benefits involved, and determine what form any warnings should take. The legislative process can better reconcile the interests of all persons concerned with the imposition of such a duty: pharmaceutical manufacturers, medical societies, retail pharmacists, health care insurers, consumer groups and patient representative groups. We find before us a single injured plaintiff and two drug store owners. Holding that the drug store owners could be negligent for failing to warn her about the drug her doctor prescribed would muddy the waters as to where responsibility lies up and down the chain of health care. We decline to do so.

CONCLUSION

(10) In summary, our holding is narrow. The pharmacist still has a duty to accurately fill a prescription, see Annot. Liability of Manufacturer or Seller for Injury Caused by Drug or Medicine Sold, 79 A.L.R.2d 301 (1961), and to be alert for clear errors or mistakes in the prescription. The pharmacist does not, however, have a duty to question a judgment made by the physician as to the propriety of a prescription *1056 or to warn customers of the hazardous side effects associated with a drug, either orally or by way of the manufacturer's package insert.

Summary judgment is appropriate when "there is no genuine issue as to any material fact and ... the moving party is entitled to a judgment as a matter of law." CR 56(c). Hontz v. State, 105 Wash.2d 302, 311, 714 P.2d 1176 (1986). The defendants owed no duty to the plaintiff and are entitled to judgment as a matter of law. The trial court's order is affirmed.

DOLLIVER, DURHAM, ANDERSEN and SMITH, JJ., concur.

DORE, Justice (dissenting).

The claims of plaintiff, Elaine McKee, relevant to this appeal, arise from the defendant pharmacists' continual refilling of a prescription of Plegine for a period of 10 years. During 1974 plaintiff, Elaine McKee, believed that she had a weight problem. At that time, Elaine was 20 years of age and otherwise in good health. She went to see her longtime family physician, defendant Dr. Michael Shanahan. Dr. Shanahan prescribed the drug, Plegine and the defendant pharmacy dispensed it to McKee for a period of 10 years. The plaintiff stated in her deposition that during portions of the time these amphetamines were dispensed to her she was well within her target weight range, but felt the drug was saving her life because she felt she was a defective person.

Prior to dispensing Plegine to the plaintiff, the defendant pharmacists elected to remove the manufacturer's warnings from the medication. Defendant Mezistrano testified that he removed the manufacturer's package insert warning instructions in dispensing bottles of 100 Plegine tablets (the quantities dispensed to Elaine). In fact, Mezistrano testified that he had decided that the package warnings were too complicated for the customers to understand them. There was testimony that the druggist could have placed his label on the other side of the capsule container without disturbing the manufacturer's warning.

The nature of the drug, Plegine, is vital to the plaintiff's contentions concerning the duty of the pharmacists. Plegine is an amphetamine. The drug was utilized for weight control, but was potentially addictive and possessed a number of very dangerous side effects.

The majority admits that for 10 years the pharmacists Sidran and Mezistrano removed a label from the Plegine prescription sold to McKee, which contained the following warning:

> Indications: PLEGINE (phendimetrazine tartrate) is indicated in the management of exogenous obesity as a short term adjunct (a few weeks) in a regimen of weight reduction based on caloric restriction. The limited usefulness of agents of this class should be measured

against possible risk factors inherent in their use. (See Actions).

Warnings: DRUG DEPENDANCE: Plegine is related chemically and pharmacologically to the amphetamines. Amphetamines and related stimulant drugs have been extensively abused, and the possibility of abuse of Plegine should be kept in mind when evaluating the desirability of including a drug as part of a weight reduction program ... Tolerance to the anorectic effect of Plegine (phendimetrazine tartrate) develops within a few weeks. When this occurs, its use should be discontinued; the maximum recommended dose should not be exceeded.

Precautions: ...The least amount feasible should be prescribed or dispensed at one time in order to minimize the possibility of an overdose.

Clerk's Papers, at 115, 749, 756. Majority, at 1046. Incredibly, the pharmacists never mentioned the "few weeks" warning and possible side effects to McKee, or the recommendation that the drug should be discontinued after several weeks. Maybe one might understand a delay of such a warning over several months, but not a delay of 10 years.

I would have no difficulty holding that Sidran and Mezistrano were negligent as a matter of law in not warning McKee of Plegine's side effects. But that issue is *1057 not presented here. The sole issue is whether McKee presented enough evidence in response to the defendants' motion for summary judgment to take the issue of negligence to a jury. Since McKee did present evidence from which a jury could infer that the pharmacists had failed to exercise the due care required of a reasonably prudent health care provider, the defendant's summary judgment motion should have been denied.

I would reverse the trial court's decision and remand for trial.

PHARMACISTS OWE A DUTY OF DUE CARE

There is no question that a pharmacist has a duty of due care. It is established and defined by statute. A pharmacist is defined as a "health care provider" in RCW 7.70.020. RCW 7.70.040 provides in part:

> The following shall be necessary elements of proof that injury resulted from the failure of the health care provider to follow the accepted standard of care:
>
> (1) The health care provider failed to exercise that degree of care, skill, and learning expected of a reasonably prudent health care provider at that time in the profession or class to which he belongs, in the state of Washington, acting in the same or similar circumstances(.)

The "reasonably prudent practitioner" standard of this statute is distinct from and higher than the "average practitioner" standard of the common law. The question is what the public would expect a reasonably prudent practitioner to do, not what his peers would expect. Harris v. Groth, 99 Wash.2d 438, 444-445, 663 P.2d 113 (1983).

Since the question is what the public judgment of reasonable prudence is, the issue of due care under RCW 7.70.040 is an issue of fact on which expert testimony will ordinarily be received. This court wrote in Harris:

> In general, expert testimony is required when an essential element in the case is best established by an opinion which is beyond the expertise of a layperson. Medical facts in particular must be proven by expert testimony unless they are "observable by (a layperson's) senses and describable without medical training". Thus, expert testimony will generally be necessary to <u>establish the standard of care</u> and most aspects of causation.

(Footnote and citations omitted. Italics mine.) Harris, at 449, 663 P.2d 113. The court in a footnote stated:

> This will remain true even under the reasonable prudence standard of care, since the <u>factual question of whether a particular medical practice is reasonably prudent</u> is generally neither observable by or describable by a layperson. In some exceptional circumstances, laypersons may be capable of balancing the costs and benefits of a particular procedure and deciding whether it was reasonably prudent.

(Italics mine.) Harris, at 449 n. 6, 663 P.2d 113. The issue of a pharmacist's duty of due care is therefore a question of fact for a jury, not an issue of law for the court.

The majority cites several cases for the proposition that the existence of a duty is a question of law. All of these cases consider the existence of a common law duty of due care. None of the cases involved conduct governed by an applicable statute, like RCW 7.70.040, which itself imposes a duty of care. The cases cited by the majority are distinguishable. RCW 7.70.040 supersedes the common law, and whether or not a duty should be imposed is no longer an open question. The only remaining issue is the specific content or application of the duty in the particular case, and that is a question for the jury. Put another way, if the existence of a duty is a question of law, in this case the statute provides a clear answer to that question: yes. The majority's wrestling with the question of whether a duty of due care exists is, at best, unnecessary and, at worst, a usurpation of the Legislature's power.

The majority argues that RCW 18.64.011(11) determines the standard of care for pharmacists, rather than a jury with the assistance of experts under RCW 7.70.040. *1058 Majority, at 1054. The passage the majority relies on states that:

> "Practice of pharmacy" includes the practice of and responsibility for: Interpreting prescription orders; the compounding, dispensing, labeling, administering, and distributing of drugs and devices; ... the providing of information on legend drugs which may include, but is not limited to, the advising of therapeutic values, hazards, and the uses of drugs and devices.

Stressing the word "may" in this passage, the majority concludes that the pharmacist's duty of due care does not include providing warnings on dangerous drugs because such warnings are optional. This argument has no merit because the passage has been taken out of context. It has nothing whatever to do with the standard of care which governs pharmacists.

RCW 18.64.011(11) is a definition of what constitutes the "practice of pharmacy" for the purposes of RCW Ch. 18.64 generally. For example, RCW 18.64.020 makes it unlawful for a person "to practice pharmacy" without a license. The passage quoted by the majority, when placed in the proper context, means that one who advises on the therapeutic values and hazards of drugs may be committing an act which is illegal without a license. In drafting RCW 18.64.011(11) the Legislature was considering an entirely different question from due care, and the majority reads something into the statute which is not there. Furthermore, the proposition that RCW 18.64.011(11) defines the standard of due care is directly contrary to the holding of Harris that the due care of health care providers under RCW 7.70.040 is a question of fact to be decided by the jury with the assistance of expert testimony. Harris, at 449, 663 P.2d 113.

Since the majority concludes that the pharmacists owed McKee no duty to warn of the adverse effects of Plegine, it affirms the grant of summary judgment. It is impossible to tell from the majority opinion, however, which of two distinct questions it is attempting to answer. It is clear that neither one is presented here. First, to ask whether a pharmacist owes a duty to warn as a matter of law might mean: Is there a legal duty, distinct from the duty of due care, which the pharmacists owed McKee? Second, to ask whether a pharmacist owes a duty to warn as a matter of law might mean: Was the pharmacists' failure to warn McKee so extreme a failure that it breached their duty of due care as a matter of law? The pharmacists' motion for summary judgment raises neither of these questions. The only issue is whether there is evidence from which a jury could infer that the pharmacists violated their duty of due care.

These distinctions can be illustrated by our prior cases on the duties of health care professionals. In Gates v. Jensen, 92 Wash.2d 246, 595 P.2d 919 (1979) we recognized a duty to warn distinct from the general health care professional's duty of due care. The plaintiff had offered a jury instruction which read in part:

> "You are instructed that an ophthalmologist has a duty to advise his patient of all relevant, material information concerning the condition of the patient's eyes that the patient will need to make an informed decision respecting the alternative methods of examination for eye disease, of the reasonably foreseeable risks of each alternative, and of no such examination at all. Failure to so advise the patient is negligence."

Gates, at 249 n. 2, 595 P.2d 919. This duty to warn was not part of the duty of due care, but a separate duty grounded in the physician's status as a fiduciary entrusted with the care of the patient's body. Gates, at 250, 595 P.2d 919. The majority at times seems to be discussing a duty to warn distinct from the duty of due care, similar to that recognized in Gates. McKee, however, has never argued such a theory. Instead, she contends only that there was evidence of a violation of the duty of due care under RCW 7.70.040 sufficient to preclude summary judgment. Aside from its patently flawed contention that RCW 18.64.011(11) defines the standard of care, the majority ignores that question.

*1059 The majority at other times seems to be discussing whether the pharmacist violated the standard of due care as a matter of law. That was the ground of our decision in Helling v. Carey, 83 Wash.2d 514, 519, 519 P.2d 981, 67 A.L.R.3d 175 (1974) in which we recognized that, as a matter of law, failure to test for glaucoma in patients under 40 violated the health care professional's duty to exercise reasonable prudence.

> Under the facts of this case reasonable prudence required the timely giving of the pressure test to this plaintiff. The precaution of giving this test to detect the incidence of glaucoma to patients under 40 years of age is so imperative that irrespective of its disregard by the standards of the ophthalmology profession, it is the duty of the courts to say what is required to protect patients under 40 from the damaging results of glaucoma.
>
> We therefore hold, as a matter of law, that the reasonable standard that should have been followed under the undisputed facts of this case was the timely giving of this simple, harmless pressure test to this plaintiff and that, in failing to do so, the defendants were negligent ....

In Helling, the judgment appealed from had been entered on a jury verdict for defendants, and so the question whether the defendant had been negligent as a matter of law was before the court. That question might also be raised by a plaintiff's motion for summary judgment. However, the issue of negligence as a matter of law is not raised by a defendant's motion for summary judgment, such as the one we have here. Where the defendant moves for summary judgment, the plaintiff need only establish that there is an issue of fact for the jury, not that the defendant violated the standard of due care as a matter of law. McKee established that there was a question of fact for the jury as to whether the pharmacist had breached the ordinary negligence standard of due care.

WASHINGTON STATUTORY LAW, REGULATION, AND POLICY CONSIDERATIONS REQUIRE IMPOSITION OF A PHARMACIST'S DUTY TO ADVISE CUSTOMERS

Two commentators in 1986 pharmacological literature identified Washington as a state that imposes a statutory duty on pharmacists to advise customers regarding prescriptive drugs. Brushwood & Simonsmeier, Drug Information for Patients, 7 J. of Legal Med. 279, 302 (1986); Duckworth, The Potential Liability of Pharmacists Arising from Announcements of New Standards and Codes of Practice, 43 Food Drug Cosm.L.J. 1, 3 (1988). This should not be surprising given the definition of "Practice of pharmacy" as found in RCW 18.64.011(11), which provides:

> "Practice of pharmacy" includes the practice of and _responsibility for_: Interpreting prescription orders; the compounding, dispensing, labeling, administering, and distributing of drugs and devices; the _monitoring_ of drug therapy and use; ... _the providing of information_ on legend drugs which may include, but is not limited to, the _advising_ of therapeutic values, hazards, and the uses of drugs and devices.

(Italics mine.) The use of the phrase "and responsibility for" indicates this definition is more than merely descriptive, but also speaks to affirmative duties required of a pharmacist.

RCW 18.64.005(11)[1] empowers the Washington State Board of Pharmacy to

> Promulgate rules for the dispensing, distribution, wholesaling, and manufacturing of drugs and devices and the practice of pharmacy for the _protection and promotion of the public health, safety, and welfare_. Violation of any such rules shall constitute grounds for refusal, suspension, or revocation of licenses or any other authority to practice issued by the board(.)

(Italics mine.)

The regulations adopted by the board are consistent with

---

[1] In 1989 18.64.005(11) was amended. There were no textual changes, but that statute now appears as 18.64.005(7).

recognition of RCW 18.64.*1060 011(11) as imposing a duty to advise on the pharmacist.

SUMMARY JUDGMENT SHOULD HAVE BEEN DENIED

The issue is, analyzing all the evidence in the light most favorable to the nonmoving party, is there a genuine issue of material fact for the jury to resolve? Hartley v. State, 103 Wash.2d 768, 774, 698 P.2d 77 (1985). McKee offered sufficient evidence in response to the defendants' motion to create an issue of fact, precluding summary judgment.

Depositions in the case were filed and published in connection with the summary judgment motion. According to the deposition of Leon Mezistrano, one of the respondent pharmacists, Plegine is distributed in bottles of 100 tablets, with a warning attached to the bottle. The warning was based on the Physicians' Desk Reference (hereafter PDR) entry for Plegine. Clerk's Papers, at 749, 756. The PDR and the attached label both stated the warnings quoted above. Clerk's Papers, at 115.

Mezistrano testified that he filled McKee's prescriptions for Plegine on numerous occasions between 1981 and 1984. Clerk's Papers, at 765-73. Mezistrano believed it is important for a pharmacist to determine whether a drug he dispenses is potentially addictive, but that at the time he dispensed Plegine to McKee, he did not believe that Plegine had such a potential. Clerk's Papers, at 691-93. Mezistrano also testified that, to fill a prescription for 100 tablets of Plegine, such as that submitted by McKee, he dispensed the drug in the manufacturer's bottles of 100. While he did not rebottle the medicine, he removed the warnings attached to the bottles by the manufacturer because he thought consumers might misunderstand the information and be frightened by it. Clerk's Papers, at 755, 756, 757-58, 777-78.

Gerald Sidran, the other respondent pharmacist, testified that he filled McKee's prescriptions for Plegine on numerous occasions between 1977 and 1981, when he sold the pharmacy to Mezistrano. Clerk's Papers, at 563-68. He testified that he was aware that McKee had been receiving Plegine for an extended period of time. Clerk's Papers, at 591. He maintained that it is common practice for a pharmacy to fill repeated prescriptions for drugs which the literature recommends should not be taken over a long period of time. Clerk's Papers, at 588-89. This, of course, would be no justification, since the standard of due care under RCW

7.70.040 is reasonable prudence, not customary practice. Harris v. Groth, 99 Wash.2d 438, 444-45, 663 P.2d 113 (1983).

During the period from 1974 to 1984, McKee never weighed more than 138 pounds. She is 5 feet 4 inches tall. Her weight during the 1982-1983 period dropped at one point to 105 pounds. Clerk's Papers, at 292-93, 331-32.

McKee submitted an affidavit of an expert, Dr. Andrew Weil, who was sharply critical of the defendants' conduct, which was included with her response to defendants' motion for summary judgment. Clerk's Papers, at 117-18. Attached to that affidavit was the Curriculum Vitae of Dr. Weil, which shows that Dr. Weil is currently licensed to practice medicine in seven states: Arizona, California, Maryland, Massachusetts, New York, Oregon and Virginia. Dr. Weil states in his affidavit that during his tenure as professor at the University of Arizona, where he has taught for 10 years, he has lectured on the subject of drug abuse at the pharmacy school of the University of Arizona and has lectured to organizations of professional pharmacists regarding the duties and responsibilities of pharmacists to their customers. Additionally, Dr. Weil's affidavit demonstrates that he has written several books on the subject of drug abuse which have received national attention and distribution.

Dr. Weil unequivocally states that he is familiar with the duties and standards of care relative to the duties of pharmacists to their customers during the period involved in this case:

> 3. ... I have lectured to organizations of professional pharmacists. The courses which I have taught deal with *1061 the duties and responsibilities of pharmacists to their customers and _I am familiar with such duties and the standards of care relative to the duties of pharmacists to their customers during the period involved in this case_.

(Italics mine.) Clerk's Papers, at 116. Affidavit of Dr. Weil.

Defendants claim the affidavit of Dr. Weil fails to qualify him as an expert capable of rendering an opinion in the present case. For example, they place significance on the fact Dr. Weil was not licensed to practice medicine in the state of Washington nor was he a pharmacist, but the majority cites no authority which would show that an expert has to be licensed in his particular field in Washington in order to qualify as an expert. To the contrary, an expert, if otherwise qualified, need not be licensed to practice his profession in the state of Washington in order to qualify as an expert witness. Walker v. Bangs, 92 Wash.2d 854, 601 P.2d 1279 (1979), involved the qualification of an attorney who was not licensed to practice law in Washington, but who stated in his affidavit that he was a "specialist" in trial work. This court approved the consideration of his testimony on the standard of care applicable to attorneys in Washington. In reversing the lower court's dismissal of the cause for failure to prove negligence, this court held:

> Generally, one who holds himself out as specializing and as possessing greater than ordinary knowledge and skill in a particular field, will be held to the standard of performance of those who hold themselves out as specialists in that area....
>
> ... Brotsky's personal participation in trials in a federal district court of the Ninth Circuit in litigation concerning similar maritime personal injury cases would seem to meet the necessary experiential requirements for qualification as an expert witness in this case, and the exclusion of his testimony was error.

Walker, at 860, 601 P.2d 1279.

Under Harris, the standard of due care is not what the pharmacists' peers would do, but what the public has a right to expect. Harris, 99 Wash.2d at 444-45, 663 P.2d 113. Harris encourages the use of expert testimony for the purpose of aiding the jury in "balancing the costs and benefits of a particular procedure and deciding whether it was reasonably prudent." Harris, at 449 n. 6, 663 P.2d 113. As to this question, the testimony of a physician from this or any other state is entirely relevant and obviously admissible for the purpose of aiding the jury.

Dr. Weil in his affidavit testified:

> 5. In my opinion the drug plegine which possesses the attributes of an amphetamine should never be prescribed by any physician, or be dispensed by any pharmacist, for a period of more than approximately one month. This drug should never, under any circumstances, be given to any person who is not overweight. In my

opinion any pharmacist filling a prescription should be aware of the fact that the drug should not be given for a period of more than one month and should be especially aware that this drug should not be dispensed over a long period of time to anyone and especially to a person who is not overweight.

6. In my opinion it was below the standard of care expected of a reasonable and prudent pharmacist acting under the same or similar circumstances (hereinafter "substandard") for Defendants Mezistrano and Sidran (hereinafter the "pharmacists") to dispense the drug plegine to Elaine McKee for the prolonged periods of time it was dispensed to her, under the circumstances of this case. The prescription and prolonged dispensation of this drug over a period of approximately ten years was grossly substandard and inexcusable. Furthermore, in my opinion, the dispensation of this drug caused very serious long term physical and emotional problems to Elaine McKee and was a cause of two suicide attempts by Ms. McKee. The pharmacists in this case had moral and legal duties to advise the patient of the risks of long term therapy with plegine and to make her aware of the side effects and toxicity of the drug when used over long period(s) of time. Their failure to so advise Ms. *1062 McKee was also substandard and the drug as dispensed, without appropriate warnings and instructions was, in my opinion, dangerous and defective.

6. (7.) In my opinion the pharmacists had a duty to reasonably inform themselves of the dangers of drugs which they dispensed.

This duty included a responsibility to become reasonably acquainted with the risks of addiction and long term toxicity of these drugs. Pharmacists also have a duty to inform patients about these risks and to question Physicians about their continued prescriptions of drugs when there is reasonable question about the appropriateness of their prescription andor the safety of the use of such drugs. In my opinion, the pharmacists in this case failed to reasonably inform themselves of the dangers of the drug plegine and its prolonged use and the risks of addiction and long term toxicity. In my opinion, it was substandard for the pharmacists in this case to fail to advise Elaine McKee of these risks andor to provide her with the manufacturer's printed warnings relating to plegine.

Clerk's Papers, at 117-18. Affidavit of Dr. Weil.

The drug Plegine is not recommended for persons who are not overweight. In any event, it is not recommended for a period of more than "a few weeks". Those recommendations were clearly stated by the manufacturer on labels which the pharmacists, at least, were aware of. In addition, those recommendations were made in the PDR, the standard reference work for the profession. McKee was obviously not overweight and the pharmacists dispensed Plegine to her for at least 10 years. A jury could have concluded that a reasonably prudent pharmacist would take some action in these circumstances; that he would not dispense drugs which are clearly contraindicated, would warn the consumer that the drug is contraindicated or would specifically discuss the contraindication with the prescribing physician.

The jury could also conclude that the pharmacists violated their statutory duty of due care when they removed the manufacturer's warnings from bottles intended for consumers. Given that the warnings were actually glued onto the consumer-size bottles, the jury could conclude that the warnings were intended for consumers and that a reasonably prudent health care provider, dispensing an obviously powerful drug, would have passed that warning on to the consumer. The majority's argument that some manufacturers' warnings do not accompany individual, consumer-size units, and that requiring pharmacists to pass on such warnings would be a hardship, is completely irrelevant. In this case the warnings did accompany individual bottles; consequently, it could never establish the precedent the majority fears.

The majority's reasoning on the issue of warnings illustrates perfectly why the standard of care is a question of fact and not of law. The majority argues that warnings on drugs "could disturb even the most sophisticated patient." Majority, at 13 (quoting Curran, Package Inserts for Patients: Informed Consent in the 1980's, 305 New Eng.J.Med. 1564, 1565-66 (1981)). In effect the majority accepts Mezistrano's argument that consumers ought to be protected from alarming facts concerning the drugs their physicians have prescribed. I find this sort of paternalism offensive. Is the majority seriously suggesting that a patient has no right to be informed of the dangers of the medication he takes? It may be that the question is a proper one for the Legislature, but the Legislature has determined in RCW 7.70.040 that it is also a question of fact for juries. The warning should be passed on to the consumer if a reasonably prudent health care provider would do so. McKee produced sufficient evidence here to be entitled to a jury's judgment on that issue.

I believe the jury could determine factually that the pharmacist had a duty to warn that this particular drug should be discontinued after several weeks. But for argument sake, assume there was no duty to warn, did the defendants have the right to destroy the warning of the manufacturer? This is a factual issue and the jury might find that the destruction of the manufacturer's *1063 warning to the consumer McKee was negligence.

Had the druggist not intervened, the plaintiff would have received the "few weeks" warning and she possibly would have been spared her ordeal. The drug was dispensed directly from the druggist to the consumer--in a small 100-pill container and he could have placed his own label on the capsule container on the opposite side from the manufacturer's label without disturbing it. By what authority did the druggist prevent the consumer from knowing that the drug should only be taken for a few weeks at a time? The cases cited by the majority are factually incorrect as the physician here did not act as a "learned intermediary" between the manufacturer and the client.

The majority concludes its opinion with the startling concession: "We agree pharmacists should have a duty to be alert for patent errors in a prescription, for example: obvious lethal dosages, inadequacies in the instructions, known contraindications, or incompatible prescriptions, and to take corrective measures." (Footnotes omitted.) Majority, at 16.

Isn't knowing that Plegine, an amphetamine, should be prescribed only for several weeks rather than 10 years within the definition of the majority's "obvious lethal dosages, inadequacies in the instructions" or "known contraindications"? Aren't there factual issues on these matters which prevent a summary judgment from being granted?

CONCLUSION

McKee produced evidence from which a jury could conclude that the pharmacists failed to act in a reasonably prudent manner and that they breached their duty of due care under RCW 7.70.040. For 10 years the pharmacists Sidran and

Mezistrano removed labels from the Plegine prescription sold to McKee which would have warned her that the medication she was receiving was not necessary and was endangering her health. Not only did they remove the manufacturer's warning, the pharmacists never heeded the warning themselves and never took steps to warn McKee verbally of the drug's possible side effects or the recommendation that the drug should be discontinued after several weeks. Their failure was repeated, not over a few weeks or a few months, but for 10 years. Since McKee's evidence was clearly sufficient to go to the jury on the issue of statutory due care, the trial court erred in granting the pharmacists' motion for summary judgment.

I would reverse and remand for trial.

UTTER and BRACHTENBACH, JJ., and PEARSON, J. Pro Tem., concur.

Supp. Ch. 3

WARDS COVE PACKING COMPANY, INC.
v.
ATONIO
109 S.Ct. 2115

Argued Jan. 18, 1989.
Decided June 5, 1989.

CIVIL RIGHTS: statistical evidence failed to establish disparate impact in Title VII case.

Former salmon cannery workers brought class action suit alleging employment discrimination on basis of race. The United States District Court for the Western District of Washington, Walter T. McGovern, Chief Judge, dismissed action for lack of jurisdiction. The Court of Appeals, 703 F.2d 329, affirmed in part and reversed and remanded in part. On remand, the District Court, Justin L. Quackenbush, J., entered judgment for employers. On appeal, the Court of Appeals for the Ninth Circuit, 768 F.2d 1120, affirmed. On rehearing en banc, the Court of Appeals, 810 F.2d 1477, determined that disparate impact analysis could be applied, and returned case to original panel. The Court of Appeals, 827 F.2d 439, then reversed and remanded. On certiorari, the Supreme Court, Justice White held that statistical evidence showing high percentage of nonwhite workers in employer's cannery jobs and low percentage of such workers in noncannery positions did not establish prima facie case of disparate impact in violation of Title VII.

Reversed and remanded.

Justice Stevens filed dissenting opinion in which Justices Brennan, Marshall and Blackmun joined.

Justice Blackmun filed dissenting opinion in which Justices Brennan and Marshall joined.

Syllabus[1]

---

[1] The syllabus constitutes no part of the opinion of the Court but has been prepared by the Reporter of Decisions for the convenience of the reader. See United States v. Detroit Lumber Co., 200 U.S. 321, 337, 26 S.Ct. 282, 287, 50 L.Ed. 499.

*2116 Jobs at petitioners' Alaskan salmon canneries are of two general types: unskilled "cannery jobs" on the cannery lines, which are filled predominantly by nonwhites; and "noncannery jobs," most of which are classified as skilled positions and filled predominantly with white workers, and virtually all of which pay more than *2117 cannery positions. Respondents, a class of nonwhite cannery workers at petitioners' facilities, filed suit in the District Court under Title VII of the Civil Rights Act of 1964, alleging, inter alia, that various of petitioners' hiring/promotion practices were responsible for the work force's racial stratification and had denied them employment as noncannery workers on the basis of race. The District Court rejected respondents' claims, finding, among other things, that nonwhite workers were overrepresented in cannery jobs because many of those jobs were filled under a hiring hall agreement with a predominantly nonwhite union. The Court of Appeals ultimately reversed in pertinent part, holding, inter alia, that respondents had made out a prima facie case of disparate impact in hiring for both skilled and unskilled noncannery jobs, relying solely on respondents' statistics showing a high percentage of nonwhite workers in cannery jobs and a low percentage of such workers in noncannery positions. The court also concluded that once a plaintiff class has shown disparate impact caused by specific, identifiable employment practices or criteria, the burden shifts to the employer to prove the challenged practice's business necessity.

Held:

1. The Court of Appeals erred in ruling that a comparison of the percentage of cannery workers who are nonwhite and the percentage of noncannery workers who are nonwhite makes out a prima facie disparate-impact case. Rather, the proper comparison is generally between the racial composition of the at-issue jobs and the racial composition of the qualified population in the relevant labor market. Hazelwood School Dist. v. United States, 433 U.S. 299, 308, 97 S.Ct. 2736, 2741, 53 L.Ed.2d 768. With respect to the skilled noncannery jobs at issue, the cannery work force in no way reflected the pool of qualified job applicants or the qualified labor force population. Petitioners' selection methods or employment practices cannot be said to have had a disparate impact on nonwhites if the absence of minorities holding such skilled jobs reflects a dearth of qualified nonwhite applicants for reasons that are not petitioners' fault. With respect to the unskilled noncannery jobs, as long as there are no barriers or practices deterring qualified nonwhites from applying, the

employer's selection mechanism probably does not have a disparate impact on minorities if the percentage of selected nonwhite applicants is not significantly less than the percentage of qualified nonwhite applicants. Where this is the case, the percentage of nonwhite workers found in other positions in the employer's labor force is irrelevant to a prima facie statistical disparate-impact case. Moreover, isolating the cannery workers as the potential labor force for unskilled noncannery jobs is both too broad--because the majority of cannery workers did not seek noncannery jobs-- and too narrow--because there are many qualified persons in the relevant labor market who are not cannery workers. Under the Court of Appeals' method of comparison, any employer having a racially imbalanced segment of its work force could be haled into court and made to undertake the expensive and time-consuming task of defending the business necessity of its selection methods. For many employers, the only practicable option would be the adoption of racial quotas, which has been rejected by this Court and by Congress in drafting Title VII. The Court of Appeals' theory is also flawed because, if minorities are over-represented in cannery jobs by virtue of petitioners' having contracted with a predominantly nonwhite union to fill those positions, as the District Court found, petitioners could eliminate respondents' prima facie case simply by ceasing to use the union, without making any change whatsoever in their hiring practices for the noncannery positions at issue. Pp. 2120-2123

2. On remand for a determination whether the record will support a prima facie disparate-impact case on some basis other than the racial disparity between cannery and noncannery workers, a mere *2118 showing that nonwhites are underrepresented in the at-issue jobs in a manner that is acceptable under the standards set forth herein will not alone suffice. Rather, the courts below must also require, as part of respondents' prima facie case, a demonstration that the statistical disparity complained of is the result of one or more of the employment practices respondents are attacking here, specifically showing that each challenged practice has a significantly disparate impact on employment opportunities for whites and nonwhites. This specific causation requirement is not unduly burdensome, since liberal discovery rules give plaintiffs broad access to employers' records, and since employers falling within the scope of the Uniform Guidelines on Employee Selection Procedures must maintain records disclosing the impact of tests and selection procedures on employment opportunities of persons by

identifiable race, sex, or ethnic group. Pp. 2123-2125.

3. If, on remand, respondents establish a prima facie disparate-impact case with respect to any of petitioners' practices, the burden of producing evidence of a legitimate business justification for those practices will shift to petitioners, but the ultimate burden of persuasion will remain with respondents at all times. This rule conforms with the usual method for allocating persuasion and production burdens in the federal courts and with the rule in disparate-treatment cases that the plaintiff bears the burden of disproving an employer's assertion that the adverse employment practice was based solely on a legitimate neutral consideration. See Texas Dept. of Community Affairs v. Burdine, 450 U.S. 248, 256-258, 101 S.Ct. 1089, 1095-1096, 67 L.Ed.2d 207. To the extent that some of this Court's decisions speak of an employer's "burden of proof" with respect to the business justification defense, they should be understood to mean an employer's burden of production, not persuasion. Even if respondents cannot persuade the trier of fact on the business necessity question, they may still prevail by coming forward with alternatives that reduce the disparate impact of petitioners' current practices, provided such alternatives are equally effective in achieving petitioners' legitimate employment goals in light of the alternatives' costs and other burdens. Pp. 2125-2126.

827 F.2d 439, (CA9 1987) reversed and remanded.

WHITE, J., delivered the opinion of the Court, in which REHNQUIST, C.J., and O'CONNOR, SCALIA, and KENNEDY, JJ., joined. STEVENS, J., filed a dissenting opinion, in which BRENNAN, MARSHALL, and BLACKMUN, JJ., joined. BLACKMUN, J., filed a dissenting opinion, in which BRENNAN and MARSHALL, JJ., joined.

Justice WHITE delivered the opinion of the Court.

(1) Title VII of the Civil Rights Act of 1964, 42 U.S.C. section 2000e-2(a) makes it an unfair employment practice for an employer to discriminate against any individual with respect to hiring or the terms and condition of employment because of such individual's race, color, religion, sex, or national origin; or to limit, segregate or classify his employees in ways that would adversely affect any employee because of the employee's race, color, religion, sex, or

national origin.[1] Griggs v. Duke Power Co., *2119 401 U.S. 424, 431, 91 S.Ct. 849, 853, 28 L.Ed.2d 158 (1971), construed Title VII to proscribe "not only overt discrimination but also practices that are fair in form but discriminatory in practice." Under this basis for liability, which is known as the "disparate impact" theory and which is involved in this case, a facially neutral employment practice may be deemed violative of Title VII without evidence of the employer's subjective intent to discriminate that is required in a "disparate treatment" case.

I

The claims before us are disparate-impact claims, involving the employment practices of petitioners, two companies that operate salmon canneries in remote and widely separated areas of Alaska. The canneries operate only during the salmon runs in the summer months. They are inoperative and vacant for the rest of the year. In May or June of each year, a few weeks before the salmon runs begin, workers arrive and prepare the equipment and facilities for the canning operation. Most of these workers possess a variety of skills. When salmon runs are about to begin, the workers who will operate the cannery lines arrive, remain as long as there are fish to can, and then depart. The canneries are then closed down, winterized, and left vacant until the next spring. During the off season, the companies employ only a small number of individuals at their headquarters in Seattle and Astoria, Oregon, plus some employees at the winter shipyard in Seattle.

---

[1] Title VII of the Civil Rights Act of 1964, 42 U.S.C. section 2000e-2(a), provides:

"(a) It shall be an unlawful employment practice for an employer-

"(1) to fail or refuse to hire or to discharge any individual, or otherwise to discriminate against any individual with respect to his compensation, terms, conditions, or privileges of employment, because of such individual's race, color, religion, sex, or national origin; or

"(2) to limit, segregate, or classify his employees or applicants for employment in any way which would deprive or tend to deprive any individual of employment opportunities or otherwise adversely affect his status as an employee, because of such individual's race, color, religion, sex, or national origin."

The length and size of salmon runs vary from year to year and hence the number of employees needed at each cannery also varies. Estimates are made as early in the winter as possible; the necessary employees are hired, and when the time comes, they are transported to the canneries. Salmon must be processed soon after they are caught, and the work during the canning season is therefore intense.[2] For this reason, and because the canneries are located in remote regions, all workers are housed at the canneries and have their meals in company-owned mess halls.

Jobs at the canneries are of two general types: "cannery jobs" on the cannery line, which are unskilled positions; and "noncannery jobs," which fall into a variety of classifications. Most noncannery jobs are classified as skilled positions.[3] Cannery jobs are filled predominantly by nonwhites, Filipinos and Alaska Natives. The Filipinos are hired through and dispatched by Local 37 of the International Longshoremen Workers Union pursuant to a hiring hall agreement with the Local. The Alaska Natives primarily reside in villages near the remote cannery locations. Noncannery jobs are filled with predominantly white workers, who are hired during the winter months from the companies' offices in Washington and Oregon. Virtually all of *2120 the

---

[2] "Independent fishermen catch the salmon and turn them over to company-owned boats called 'tenders,' which transport the fish from the fishing grounds to the canneries. Once at the cannery, the fish are eviscerated, the eggs pulled, and they are cleaned. Then, operating at a rate of approximately four cans per second, the salmon are filled into cans. Next, the canned salmon are cooked under precise time-temperature requirement established by the FDA, and the cans are inspected to ensure that proper seals are maintained on the top, bottom and sides." 768 F.2d 1120, 1123, vacated, 787 F.2d 462 (CA9 1985).

[3] The noncannery jobs were described as follows by the Court of Appeals: "Machinists and engineers are hired to maintain the smooth and continuous operation of the canning equipment. Quality control personnel conduct the FDA-required inspections and recordkeeping. Tenders are staffed with a crew necessary to operate the vessel. A variety of support personnel are employed to operate the entire cannery community, including, for example, cooks, carpenters, store-keepers, bookkeepers, beach gangs for dock yard labor and construction, etc." 768 F.2d, at 1123.

noncannery jobs pay more than cannery positions. The predominantly white noncannery workers and the predominantly nonwhite cannery employees live in separate dormitories and eat in separate mess halls.

In 1974, respondents, a class of nonwhite cannery workers who were (or had been) employed at the canneries, brought this Title VII action against petitioners. Respondents alleged that a variety of petitioners' hiringpromotion practices--e.g., nepotism, a rehire preference, a lack of objective hiring criteria, separate hiring channels, a practice of not promoting from within--were responsible for the racial stratification of the work force, and had denied them and other nonwhites employment as noncannery workers on the basis of race. Respondents also complained of petitioners' racially segregated housing and dining facilities. All of respondents' claims were advanced under both the disparate-treatment and disparate-impact theories of Title VII liability.

The District Court held a bench trial, after which it entered 172 findings of fact. App. to Pet. for Cert. I-1-I-94. It then rejected all of respondents' disparate-treatment claims. It also rejected the disparate-impact challenges involving the subjective employment criteria used by petitioners to fill these noncannery positions, on the ground that those criteria were not subject to attack under a disparate-impact theory. Id., at I-102. Petitioner's "objective" employment practices (e.g., an English language requirement, alleged nepotism in hiring, failure to post noncannery openings, the rehire preference, etc.) were found to be subject to challenge under the disparate-impact theory, but these claims were rejected for failure of proof. Judgment was entered for petitioners.

On appeal, a panel of the Ninth Circuit affirmed, 768 F.2d 1120 (CA9 1985), but that decision was vacated when the Court of Appeals agreed to hear the case en banc, 787 F.2d 462 (CA9 1985). The en banc hearing was ordered to settle an intra-circuit conflict over the question whether subjective hiring practices could be analyzed under a disparate-impact model; the Court of Appeals held--as this Court subsequently ruled in Watson v. Fort Worth Bank & Trust, 487 U.S. ----, 108 S.Ct. 2777, 101 L.Ed.2d 827 (1988)-that disparate-impact analysis could be applied to subjective hiring practices. 810 F.2d 1477, 1482 (CA9 1987). The Ninth Circuit also concluded that in such a case, "(o)nce the plaintiff class has shown disparate-impact caused by specific, identifiable employment practices or criteria, the burden shifts to the employer," id., at 1485, to "prov(e the) business necessity" of the challenged practice. Id., at 1486. Because the en banc holding on subjective employment practices reversed the District Court's contrary ruling, the en banc Court of Appeals remanded the case to a panel for further proceedings.

On remand, the panel applied the en banc ruling to the facts of this case. 827 F.2d 439 (CA9 1987). It held that respondents had made out a prima facie case of disparate-impact in hiring for both skilled and unskilled noncannery positions. The panel remanded the case for further proceedings, instructing the District Court that it was the employer's burden to prove that any disparate impact caused by its hiring and employment practices was justified by business necessity. Neither the en banc court nor the panel disturbed the District Court's rejection of the disparate-treatment claims.[4]

---

[4] The fact that neither the District Court, nor the Ninth Circuit en banc, nor the subsequent Court of Appeals panel ruled for respondents on their disparate treatment claims--i.e., their allegations of intentional racial discrimination--warrants particular attention in light of the dissents' comment that the canneries "bear an unsettling resemblance to aspects of a plantation economy." Post, at 2127-2128 n. 4 (STEVENS, J., dissenting); post, at 2136 (BLACKMUN, J., dissenting).

Whatever the "resemblance," the unanimous view of the lower courts in this litigation has been that respondents did not prove that the canneries practice intentional racial discrimination. Consequently, Justice BLACKMUN's hyperbolic allegation that our decision in this case indicates that this Court no longer "believes that race discrimination against nonwhites is a problem in our society," post, at 2136, is inapt. Of course, it is unfortunately true that race discrimination exists in our country. That does not mean, however, that it exists at the canneries-or more precisely, that it has been proven to exist at the canneries.

Indeed, Justice STEVENS concedes that respondents did not press before us the legal theories under which the aspects of cannery life that he finds to most resemble a "plantation economy" might be unlawful. Post, at 2128 n. 4. Thus, the question here is not whether we "approve" of petitioners' employment practices or the society that exists at the canneries, but rather, whether respondents have properly established that these practices violate Title VII.

*2121 Petitioners sought review of the Court of Appeals' decision in this Court, challenging it on several grounds. Because some of the issues raised by the decision below were matters on which this Court was evenly divided in Watson v. Fort Worth Bank & Trust Co., supra, we granted certiorari, 487 U.S. ----, 108 S.Ct. 2777, 101 L.Ed.2d 827 (1988), for the purpose of addressing these disputed questions of the proper application of Title VII's disparate-impact theory of liability.

II

(2) In holding that respondents had made out a prima facie case of disparate impact, the court of appeals relied solely on respondents' statistics showing a high percentage of nonwhite workers in the cannery jobs and a low percentage of such workers in the noncannery positions.[5] Although statistical proof can alone make out a prima facie case, see Teamsters v. United States, 431 U.S. 324, 339, 97 S.Ct. 1843, 1856, 52 L.Ed.2d 396 (1977); Hazelwood School Dist. v. United States, 433 U.S. 299, 307-308, 97 S.Ct. 2736, 2741-2742, 53 L.Ed.2d 768 (1977), the Court of Appeals' ruling here misapprehends our precedents and the purposes of Title VII, and we therefore reverse.

(3) "There can be no doubt," as there was when a similar mistaken analysis had been undertaken by the courts below in Hazelwood, supra, at 308, 97 S.Ct., at 2741, "that the ... comparison ... fundamentally misconceived the role of statistics in employment discrimination cases." The "proper comparison (is) between the racial composition of (the at-issue jobs) and the racial composition of the qualified ... population in the relevant labor market." Ibid. It is

---

[5] The parties dispute the extent to which there is a discrepancy between the percentage of nonwhites employed as cannery workers, and those employed in noncannery positions. Compare, e.g., Brief for Petitioners 4-9 with Brief for Respondents 4-6. The District Court made no precise numerical findings in this regard, but simply noted that there were "significant disparities between the at-issue jobs (i.e., noncannery jobs) and the total workforce at the canneries" which were explained by the fact that "nearly all employed in the 'cannery worker' department are non-white." See App. to Pet. for Cert. I-111, I-42.

For reasons explained below, the degree of disparity between these groups is not relevant to our decision here.

such a comparison--between the racial composition of the qualified persons in the labor market and the persons holding at-issue jobs--that generally forms the proper basis for the initial inquiry in a disparate impact case. Alternatively, in cases where such labor market statistics will be difficult if not impossible to ascertain, we have recognized that certain other statistics--such as measures indicating the racial composition of "otherwise-qualified applicants" for at-issue jobs--are equally probative for this purpose. See, e.g., New York City Transit Authority v. Beazer, 440 U.S. 568, 585, 99 S.Ct. 1355, 1366, 59 L.Ed.2d 587 (1979).[6]

It is clear to us that the Court of Appeals' acceptance of the comparison between the racial composition of the cannery *2122 work force and that of the noncannery work force, as probative of a prima facie case of disparate impact in the selection of the latter group of workers, was flawed for several reasons. Most obviously, with respect to the skilled noncannery jobs at issue here, the cannery work force in no way reflected "the pool of qualified job applicants" or the "qualified population in the labor force." Measuring alleged discrimination in the selection of accountants, managers, boat captains, electricians, doctors, and engineers--and the long list of other "skilled" noncannery positions found to exist by the District Court, see App. to Pet. for Cert. I-56-I-58--by comparing the number of nonwhites occupying these jobs to the number of nonwhites filling cannery worker positions is nonsensical. If the absence of minorities holding such skilled positions is due to a dearth of qualified nonwhite applicants (for reasons that are not petitioners' fault),[7] petitioners' selection methods or

---

[6] In fact, where "figures for the general population might accurately reflect the pool of qualified job applicants," cf. Teamsters v. United States, 431 U.S. 324, 340, n. 20, 97 S.Ct. 1843, 1856 n. 20, 52 L.Ed.2d 396 (1977), we have even permitted plaintiffs to rest their prima facie cases on such statistics as well. See, e.g., Dothard v. Rawlinson, 433 U.S. 321, 329-330, 97 S.Ct. 2720, 2726, 53 L.Ed.2d 786 (1977).

[7] Obviously, the analysis would be different if it were found that the dearth of qualified nonwhite applicants was due to practices on petitioner's part which--expressly or implicitly--deterred minority group members from applying for noncannery positions. See, e.g., Teamsters v. United States, supra, 431 U.S., at 365, 97 S.Ct., at 1869.

employment practices cannot be said to have had a "disparate impact" on nonwhites.

One example illustrates why this must be so. Respondents' own statistics concerning the noncannery work force at one of the canneries at issue here indicate that approximately 17% of the new hires for medical jobs, and 15% of the new hires for officer worker positions, were nonwhite. See App. to Brief for Respondents B-1. If it were the case that less than 15-17% of the applicants for these jobs were nonwhite and that nonwhites made up a lower percentage of the relevant qualified labor market, it is hard to see how respondents, without more, cf. Connecticut v. Teal, 457 U.S. 440, 102 S.Ct. 2525, 73 L.Ed.2d 130 (1982), would have made out a prima facie case of disparate impact. Yet, under the Court of Appeals' theory, simply because nonwhites comprise 52% of the cannery workers at the cannery in question, see App. to Brief for Respondents B-1, respondents would be successful in establishing a prima facie case of racial discrimination under Title VII.

Such a result cannot be squared with our cases or with the goals behind the statute. The Court of Appeals' theory, at the very least, would mean that any employer who had a segment of his work force that was--for some reason--racially imbalanced, could be haled into court and forced to engage in the expensive and time-consuming task of defending the "business necessity" of the methods used to select the other members of his work force. The only practicable option for many employers will be to adopt racial quotas, insuring that no portion of his work force deviates in racial composition from the other portions thereof; this is a result that Congress expressly rejected in drafting Title VII. See 42 U.S.C. section 2000e-2(j); see also Watson v. Fort Worth Bank & Trust Co., 487 U.S. at ---- - ----, and n. 2, 108 S.Ct., at ---- - ----, and n. 2 (opinion of O'CONNOR, J.). The Court of Appeals' theory would "leave the employer little choice ... but to engage in a subjective quota system of employment selection. This, of course, is far from the intent of Title VII." Albemarle Paper Co. v. Moody, 422 U.S. 405, 449, 95 S.Ct. 2362, 2387, 45 L.Ed.2d 280 (1975) (BLACKMUN, J., concurring in judgment).

(4, 5) The Court of Appeals also erred with respect to the unskilled noncannery positions. Racial imbalance in one segment of an employer's work force does not, without more, establish a prima facie case of disparate impact with respect to the selection of workers for the employer's other positions, even where workers for the different positions may have somewhat fungible skills (as is arguably the case for cannery and unskilled noncannery workers). As long as there are no barriers or practices deterring qualified nonwhites from applying *2123 for noncannery positions, see supra, n. 6, if the percentage of selected applicants who are nonwhite is not significantly less than the percentage of qualified applicants who are nonwhite, the employer's selection mechanism probably does not operate with a disparate impact on minorities.[8] Where this is the case, the percentage of nonwhite workers found in other positions in the employer's labor force is irrelevant to the question of a prima facie statistical case of disparate impact. As noted above, a contrary ruling on this point would almost inexorably lead to the use of numerical quotas in the workplace, a result that Congress and this Court have rejected repeatedly in the past.

Moreover, isolating the cannery workers as the potential "labor force" for unskilled noncannery positions is at once both too broad and too narrow in its focus. Too broad because the vast majority of these cannery workers did not seek jobs in unskilled noncannery positions; there is no showing that many of them would have done so even if none of the arguably "deterring" practices existed. Thus, the pool of cannery workers cannot be used as a surrogate for the class of qualified job applicants because it contains many persons who have not (and would not) be noncannery job applicants. Conversely, if respondents propose to use the cannery workers for comparison purposes because they represent the "qualified labor population" generally, the group is too narrow because there are obviously many qualified persons in the labor market for noncannery jobs who

---

[8] We qualify this conclusion--observing that it is only "probable" that there has been no disparate impact on minorities in such circumstances--because bottom-line racial balance is not a defense under Title VII. See Connecticut v. Teal, 457 U.S. 440, 102 S.Ct. 2525, 73 L.Ed.2d 130 (1982). Thus, even if petitioners could show that the percentage of selected applicants who are nonwhite is not significantly less than the percentage of qualified applicants who are nonwhite, respondents would still have a case under Title VII, if they could prove that some particular hiring practice has a disparate impact on minorities, notwithstanding the bottom-line racial balance in petitioners' workforce. See Teal, supra, at 450, 102 S.Ct., at 2532; see also n. 8, infra.

are not cannery workers.

The peculiar facts of this case further illustrate why a comparison between the percentage of nonwhite cannery workers and nonwhite noncannery workers is an improper basis for making out a claim of disparate impact. Here, the District Court found that nonwhites were "overrepresent(ed)" among cannery workers because petitioners had contracted with a predominantly nonwhite union (Local 37) to fill these positions. See App. to Pet. for Cert. I-42. As a result, if petitioners (for some permissible reason) ceased using Local 37 as its hiring channel for cannery positions, it appears (according to the District Court's findings) that the racial stratification between the cannery and noncannery workers might diminish to statistical insignificance. Under the Court of Appeals' approach, therefore, it is possible that with no change whatsoever in their hiring practices for noncannery workers--the jobs at-issue in this lawsuit-- petitioners could make respondents' prima facie case of disparate impact "disappear." But if there would be no prima facie case of disparate impact in the selection of noncannery workers absent petitioners' use of Local 37 to hire cannery workers, surely the petitioners' reliance on the union to fill the cannery jobs not at-issue here (and its resulting "overrepresentation" of nonwhites in those positions) does not--standing alone--make out a prima facie case of disparate impact. Yet it is precisely such an ironic result that the Court of Appeals reached below.

Consequently, we reverse the Court of Appeals' ruling that a comparison between the percentage of cannery workers who are nonwhite and the percentage of noncannery workers who are nonwhite makes out a prima facie case of disparate impact. Of course, this leaves unresolved whether the record made in the District Court will support a conclusion that a prima facie case of disparate impact has been established on *2124 some basis other than the racial disparity between cannery and noncannery workers. This is an issue that the Court of Appeals or the District Court should address in the first instance.

III

Since the statistical disparity relied on by the Court of Appeals did not suffice to make out a prima facie case, any inquiry by us into whether the specific challenged employment practices of petitioners caused that disparity is pretermitted, as is any inquiry into whether the disparate impact that any employment practice may have had was justified by business considerations.[9] Because we remand for further proceedings, however, on whether a prima facie case of disparate impact has been made in defensible fashion in this case, we address two other challenges petitioners have made to the decision of the Court of Appeals.

A

First is the question of causation in a disparate-impact case. The law in this respect was correctly stated by Justice O'CONNOR's opinion last Term in Watson v. Fort Worth Bank & Trust, 487 U.S., at ----, 108 S.Ct., at 2788:

"(W)e note that the plaintiff's burden in establishing a prima facie case goes beyond the need to show that there are statistical disparities in the employer's work force. The plaintiff must begin by identifying the specific employment practice that is challenged.... Especially in cases where an employer combines subjective criteria with the use of more rigid standardized rules or tests, the plaintiff is in our view responsible for isolating and identifying the specific employment practices that are allegedly responsible for any observed statistical disparities."

Cf. also Id., at ----, 108 S.Ct., at ---- (BLACKMUN, J., concurring in part and concurring in judgment).

Indeed, even the Court of Appeals--whose decision petitioners assault on this score--noted that "it is ... essential that the practices identified by the cannery workers be linked causally with the demonstrated adverse impact." 827 F.2d, at 445. Notwithstanding the Court of Appeals' apparent adherence to the proper inquiry,

---

[9] As we understand the opinions below, the specific employment practices were challenged only insofar as they were claimed to have been responsible for the overall disparity between the number of minority cannery and noncannery workers. The Court of Appeals did not purport to hold that any specified employment practice produced its own disparate impact that was actionable under Title VII. This is not to say that a specific practice, such as nepotism, if it were proved to exist, could not itself be subject to challenge if it had a disparate impact on minorities. Nor is it to say that segregated dormitories and eating facilities in the workplace may not be challenged under 42 U.S.C. section 2000e-2(a)(2) without showing a disparate impact on hiring or promotion.

petitioners contend that that court erred by permitting respondents to make out their case by offering "only (one) set of cumulative comparative statistics as evidence of the disparate impact of each and all of (petitioners' hiring) practices." Brief for Petitioners 31.

(6) Our disparate-impact cases have always focused on the impact of particular hiring practices on employment opportunities for minorities. Just as an employer cannot escape liability under Title VII by demonstrating that, "at the bottom line," his work force is racially balanced (where particular hiring practices may operate to deprive minorities of employment opportunities), see Connecticut v. Teal, 457 U.S., at 450, 102 S.Ct., at 2532, a Title VII plaintiff does not make out a case of disparate impact simply by showing that, "at the bottom line," there is racial imbalance in the work force. As a general matter, a plaintiff must demonstrate that it is the application of a specific or particular employment practice that has created the disparate impact under attack. Such a showing is an integral part of the plaintiff's *2125 prima facie case in a disparate-impact suit under Title VII.

(7) Here, respondents have alleged that several "objective" employment practices (e.g., nepotism, separate hiring channels, rehire preferences), as well as the use of "subjective decision making" to select noncannery workers, have had a disparate impact on nonwhites. Respondents base this claim on statistics that allegedly show a disproportionately low percentage of nonwhites in the at-issue positions. However, even if on remand respondents can show that nonwhites are underrepresented in the at-issue jobs in a manner that is acceptable under the standards set forth in Part II, supra, this alone will not suffice to make out a prima facie case of disparate impact. Respondents will also have to demonstrate that the disparity they complain of is the result of one or more of the employment practices that they are attacking here, specifically showing that each challenged practice has a significantly disparate impact on employment opportunities for whites and nonwhites. To hold otherwise would result in employers being potentially liable for "the myriad of innocent causes that may lead to statistical imbalances in the composition of their work forces." Watson v. Fort Worth Bank & Trust, supra, 487 U.S., at ----, 108 S.Ct., at 2787.

Some will complain that this specific causation requirement is unduly burdensome on Title VII plaintiffs. But liberal civil discovery rules give plaintiffs broad access to employers' records in an effort to document their claims. Also, employers falling within the scope of the Uniform Guidelines on Employee Selection Procedures, 29 CFR section 1607.1 et seq. (1988), are required to "maintain records or other information which will disclose the impact which its tests and other selection procedures have upon employment opportunities of persons by identifiable race, sex, or ethnic group(s.)" See section 1607.4(A). This includes records concerning "the individual components of the selection process" where there is a significant disparity in the selection rates of whites and nonwhites. See section 1607.4(C). Plaintiffs as a general matter will have the benefit of these tools to meet their burden of showing a causal link between challenged employment practices and racial imbalances in the work force; respondents presumably took full advantage of these opportunities to build their case before the trial in the District Court was held.[10]

Consequently, on remand, the courts below are instructed to require, as part of respondents' prima facie case, a demonstration that specific elements of the petitioners' hiring process have a significantly disparate impact on nonwhites.

B

(8) If, on remand, respondents meet the proof burdens outlined above, and establish a prima facie case of disparate impact with respect to any of petitioners' employment practices, the case will shift to any business justification petitioners offer for their use of these practices. This phase of the disparate-impact case contains two components: first, a consideration of the justifications an employer offers for his use of these practices; and second, the availability of alternate practices to achieve the same business ends, with less racial impact. See, e.g., Albemarle Paper Co. v. Moody, 422 U.S., at 425, 95 S.Ct., at 2375. We consider these two components in turn.

---

[10]. Of course, petitioners' obligation to collect or retain any of these data may be limited by the Guidelines themselves. See 29 CFR section 1602.14(b) (1988) (exempting "seasonal" jobs from certain record-keeping requirements).

(1)

(9) Though we have phrased the query differently in different cases, it is generally well-established that at the justification stage of such a disparate impact case, the dispositive issue is whether a challenged practice serves, in a significant way, the legitimate employment goals of the employer. *2126 See, e.g., Watson v. Fort Worth Bank & Trust Co., 487 U.S., at ----, 108 S.Ct., at ----; New York Transit Authority v. Beazer, 440 U.S., at 587, n. 31, 99 S.Ct., at 1366, n. 31; Griggs v. Duke Power Co., 401 U.S., at 432, 91 S.Ct., at 854. The touchstone of this inquiry is a reasoned review of the employer's justification for his use of the challenged practice. A mere insubstantial justification in this regard will not suffice, because such a low standard of review would permit discrimination to be practiced through the use of spurious, seemingly neutral employment practices. At the same time, though, there is no requirement that the challenged practice be "essential" or "indispensable" to the employer's business for it to pass muster: this degree of scrutiny would be almost impossible for most employers to meet, and would result in a host of evils we have identified above. See supra, at 2122.

(10) In this phase, the employer carries the burden of producing evidence of a business justification for his employment practice. The burden of persuasion, however, remains with the disparate-impact plaintiff. To the extent that the Ninth Circuit held otherwise in its en banc decision in this case, see 810 F.2d, at 1485-1486, or in the panel's decision on remand, see 827 F.2d, at 445, 447--suggesting that the persuasion burden should shift to the petitioners once the respondents established a prima facie case of disparate impact--its decisions were erroneous. "(T)he ultimate burden of proving that discrimination against a protected group has been caused by a specific employment practice remains with the plaintiff at all times." Watson, supra, 487 U.S., at ----, 108 S.Ct., at 2790 (O'CONNOR, J.) (emphasis added). This rule conforms with the usual method for allocating persuasion and production burdens in the federal courts, see Fed. Rule Evid. 301, and more specifically, it conforms to the rule in disparate-treatment cases that the plaintiff bears the burden of disproving an employer's assertion that the adverse employment action or practice was based solely on a legitimate neutral consideration. See Texas Dept. of Community Affairs v. Burdine, 450 U.S. 248, 256-258, 101 S.Ct. 1089, 1095-1096, 67 L.Ed.2d 207 (1981). We acknowledge that some of our

earlier decisions can be read as suggesting otherwise. See Watson, supra, 487 U.S., at ----, 108 S.Ct., at ---- (BLACKMUN, J., concurring). But to the extent that those cases speak of an employers' "burden of proof" with respect to a legitimate business justification defense, see, e.g., Dothard v. Rawlinson, 433 U.S. 321, 329, 97 S.Ct. 2720, 2726, 53 L.Ed.2d 786 (1977), they should have been understood to mean an employer's production--but not persuasion--burden. Cf., e.g., NLRB v. Transportation Management Corp., 462 U.S. 393, 404, n. 7, 103 S.Ct. 2469, 2475, n. 7, 76 L.Ed.2d 667 (1983). The persuasion burden here must remain with the plaintiff, for it is he who must prove that it was "because of such individual's race, color," etc., that he was denied a desired employment opportunity. See 42 U.S.C. section 2000e-2(a).

(2)

(11) Finally, if on remand the case reaches this point, and respondents cannot persuade the trier of fact on the question of petitioners' business necessity defense, respondents may still be able to prevail. To do so, respondents will have to persuade the factfinder that "other tests or selection devices, without a similarly undesirable racial effect, would also serve the employer's legitimate (hiring) interest(s);" by so demonstrating, respondents would prove that "(petitioners were) using (their) tests merely as a 'pretext' for discrimination." Albemarle Paper Co., supra, 422 U.S., at 425, 95 S.Ct., at 2375; see also Watson, 487 U.S., at ----, 108 S.Ct., at 2779 (O'CONNOR, J.); Id., at ----, 108 S.Ct., at 2781 (BLACKMUN, J.). If respondents, having established a prima facie case, come forward with alternatives to petitioners' hiring practices that reduce the racially-disparate impact of practices currently being used, and petitioners refuse to adopt these alternatives, *2127 such a refusal would belie a claim by petitioners that their incumbent practices are being employed for nondiscriminatory reasons.

(12) Of course, any alternative practices which respondents offer up in this respect must be equally effective as petitioners' chosen hiring procedures in achieving petitioners' legitimate employment goals. Moreover, "(f)actors such as the cost or other burdens of proposed alternative selection devices are relevant in determining whether they would be equally as effective as the challenged practice in serving the employer's legitimate business goals." Watson, supra, at ----, 108 S.Ct., at 2790

(O'CONNOR, J.). "Courts are generally less competent than employers to restructure business practices," Furnco Construction Corp. v. Waters, 438 U.S. 567, 578, 98 S.Ct. 2943, 2950, 57 L.Ed.2d 957 (1978); consequently, the judiciary should proceed with care before mandating that an employer must adopt a plaintiff's alternate selection or hiring practice in response to a Title VII suit.

IV

For the reasons given above, the judgment of the Court of Appeals is reversed, and the case is remanded for further proceedings consistent with this opinion.

It is so ordered.

Justice STEVENS, with whom Justice BRENNAN, Justice MARSHALL, and Justice BLACKMUN join, dissenting.

Fully 18 years ago, this Court unanimously held that Title VII of the Civil Rights Act of 1964[1] prohibits employment practices that have discriminatory effects as well as those that are intended to discriminate. Griggs v. Duke Power Co., 401 U.S. 424, 91 S.Ct. 849, 28 L.Ed.2d 158 (1971). Federal courts and agencies consistently have enforced that interpretation, thus promoting our national goal of eliminating barriers that define economic opportunity not by aptitude and ability but by race, color, national origin, and other traits that are easily identified but utterly irrelevant to one's qualification for a particular job.[2]

---

[1] 78 Stat. 253, as amended, 42 U.S.C. section 2000e et seq.

[2] Title VII also bars discrimination because of religion or sex. 42 U.S.C. section 2000e-2(a). Discrimination based on other characteristics has been challenged under other statutes. See, e.g., School Board of Nassau County v. Arline, 480 U.S. 273, 107 S.Ct. 1123, 94 L.Ed.2d 307 (1987) (determining scope of protection for handicapped schoolteacher under section 504 of the Rehabilitation Act of 1973, 87 Stat. 394, 29 U.S.C. section 794); Newport News Shipbuilding & Dry Dock Co. v. EEOC, 462 U.S. 669, 103 S.Ct. 2622, 77 L.Ed.2d 89 (1983) (Pregnancy Discrimination Act of 1978, Pub.L. 95-555, section 1, 92 Stat. 2076, 42 U.S.C. section 2000e(k)); Lorillard v. Pons, 434 U.S. 575, 98 S.Ct. 866, 55 L.Ed.2d 40 (1978) (Age Discrimination in Employment Act of 1967, 81 Stat. 602, as amended, 29 U.S.C. section 621 et seq.); Corning Glass Works v. Brennan, 417 U.S. 188, 94 S.Ct. 2223, 41 L.Ed.2d 1 (1974)

Regrettably, the Court retreats from these efforts in its review of an interlocutory judgment respecting the "peculiar facts" of this lawsuit.³ Turning a blind eye to the meaning and purpose of Title VII, the majority's opinion perfunctorily rejects a longstanding rule of law and underestimates the probative value of evidence of a racially stratified work force.⁴ I cannot *2128 join this latest

---

(Equal Pay Act of 1963, 77 Stat. 56, section 3, enacted as section 6(d) of the Fair Labor Standards Act of 1938, 29 U.S.C. section 206(d)).

³ See ante, at 2123. The majority purports to reverse the Court of Appeals but in fact directs the District Court to make additional findings, some of which had already been ordered by the Court of Appeals. Compare 827 F.2d 439, 445 (CA9 1987), with ante, at 2124-2125. Furthermore, nearly half the majority's opinion is devoted to two questions not fairly raised at this point: "the question of causation in a disparate impact case," ante, at 2124, and the nature of the employer's defense, id., at 2125. Because I perceive no urgency to decide "these disputed questions," ante, at 2121, at an interlocutory stage of such a factually complicated case, I believe the Court should have denied certiorari and allowed the District Court to make the additional findings directed by the Court of Appeals.

⁴ Respondents comprise a class of present and former employees of petitioners, two Alaskan salmon canning companies. The class members, described by the parties as "nonwhite," include persons of Samoan, Chinese, Filipino, Japanese, and Alaska Native descent, all but one of whom are United States citizens. 34 EPD 34,437, pp. 33,822, 33,836-33,838 (WD Wash.1983). Fifteen years ago they commenced this suit, alleging that petitioners engage in hiring, job assignment, housing, and messing practices that segregate nonwhites from whites, in violation of Title VII. Evidence included this response in 1971 by a foreman to a college student's inquiry about cannery employment:

"'We are not in a position to take many young fellows to our Bristol Bay canneries as they do not have the background for our type of employees. Our cannery labor is either Eskimo or Filipino and we do not have the facilities to mix others with these groups.'" Id., at 33,836.

Some characteristics of the Alaska salmon industry described in this litigation-in particular, the segregation of housing and dining facilities and the stratification of jobs along racial and ethnic lines-bear an unsettling resemblance to aspects of a plantation economy. See generally Plantation, Town, and County, Essays on the Local History

sojourn into judicial activism.

I

I would have thought it superfluous to recount at this late date the development of our Title VII jurisprudence, but the majority's facile treatment of settled law necessitates such a primer. This Court initially considered the meaning of Title VII in Griggs v. Duke Power Co., 401 U.S. 424, 91 S.Ct. 849, 28 L.Ed.2d 158 (1971), in which a class of utility company employees challenged the conditioning of entry into higher paying jobs upon a high school education or passage of two written tests. Despite evidence that "these two requirements operated to render ineligible a markedly disproportionate number of Negroes,"[5] the Court of Appeals had held that because there was no showing of an intent to discriminate on account of race, there was no Title VII violation. Id., at 429, 91 S.Ct. at 852. Chief Justice Burger's landmark opinion established that an employer may violate the statute even when acting in complete good faith without any invidious intent.[6] Focusing on section

---

of American Slave Society 163-334 (E. Miller & E. Genovese eds. 1974). Indeed the maintenance of inferior, segregated facilities for housing and feeding nonwhite employees, see 34 EPD 34,437, pp. 33,836, 33,843-33,844, strikes me as a form of discrimination that, although it does not necessarily fit neatly into a disparate impact or disparate treatment mold, nonetheless violates Title VII. See generally Brief for National Association for the Advancement of Colored People as Amicus Curiae. Respondents, however, do not press this theory before us.

[5] This Court noted that census statistics showed that in the employer's State, North Carolina, "while 34% of white males had completed high school, only 12% of Negro males had done so.... Similarly, with respect to standardized tests, the EEOC in one case found that use of a battery of tests, including the Wonderlic and Bennett tests used by the Company in the instant case, resulted in 58% of whites passing the tests, as compared with only 6% of the blacks." Griggs, 401 U.S., at 430, n. 6, 91 S.Ct., at 853, n. 6.

[6] "The Court of Appeals held that the Company had adopted the diploma and test requirements without any 'intention to discriminate against Negro employees.' We do not suggest that either the District Court or the Court of Appeals erred in examining the employer's intent; but good intent or absence of discriminatory intent does not redeem

703(a)(2),⁷ he explained:

"The objective of Congress in the enactment of Title VII is plain from the language of the statute. It was to achieve equality of employment opportunities and remove barriers that have operated in the past to favor an identifiable group of white employees over other employees. Under the Act, practices, procedures, or tests neutral on their face, and even neutral in terms of intent, cannot be *2129 maintained if they operate to 'freeze' the status quo of prior discriminatory employment practices." Griggs, 401 U.S., at 429-430, 91 S.Ct., at 852-853.

The opinion in Griggs made it clear that a neutral practice that operates to exclude minorities is nevertheless lawful if it serves a valid business purpose. "The touchstone is business necessity," the Court stressed. Id., at 431, 91 S.Ct., at 853. Because "Congress directed the thrust of the Act to the consequences of employment practices, not simply the motivation(,).... Congress has placed on the employer the burden of showing that any given requirement must have a manifest relationship to the employment in question."⁸

---

employment procedures or testing mechanisms that operate as 'built-in headwinds' for minority groups and are unrelated to measuring job capability." Id., at 432, 91 S.Ct., at 854 (emphasis added) (citation omitted).

⁷ See id., at 426, n. 1, 91 S.Ct., at 851, n. 1. This subsection provides that "(i)t shall be an unlawful employment practice for an employer-

"(a) to limit, segregate, or classify his employees or applicants for employment in any way which would deprive or tend to deprive any individual of employment opportunities or otherwise adversely affect his status as an employee, because of such individual's race, color, religion, sex, or national origin." 42 U.S.C. section 2000e-2(a)(2).

⁸ The opinion concluded:

"Nothing in the Act precludes the use of testing or measuring procedures; obviously they are useful. What Congress has forbidden is giving these devices and mechanisms controlling force unless they are demonstrably a reasonable measure of job performance. Congress has not commanded that the less qualified be preferred over the better qualified

Id., at 432, 91 S.Ct., at 854 (emphasis in original). Congress has declined to act--as the Court now sees fit--to limit the reach of this "disparate impact" theory, see Teamsters v. United States, 431 U.S. 324, 335, n. 15, 97 S.Ct. 1843, 1854, n. 15, 52 L.Ed.2d 396 (1977); indeed it has extended its application.[9] This approval lends added force to the Griggs holding.

The Griggs framework, with its focus on ostensibly neutral qualification standards, proved inapposite for analyzing an individual employee's claim, brought under section 703(a)(1),[10] that an employer intentionally discriminated on

---

simply because of minority origins. Far from disparaging job qualifications as such, Congress has made such qualifications the controlling factor, so that race, religion, nationality, and sex become irrelevant. What Congress has commanded is that any tests used must measure the person for the job and not the person in the abstract." 401 U.S., at 436, 91 S.Ct., at 856 (emphasis added).

[9] Voting Rights Act Amendments of 1982, Pub.L. 97-205, 96 Stat. 131, 134, as amended, codified at 42 U.S.C. sections 1973, 1973b (1982 ed. and Supp. V). Legislative reports leading to 1972 amendments to Title VII also evince support for disparate impact analysis. H.R.Rep. No. 92-238, pp. 8, 20-22 (1971); S.Rep. No. 92-415, p. 5, and n. 1 (1971); accord Connecticut v. Teal, 457 U.S. 440, 447, n. 8, 102 S.Ct. 2525, 2531, n. 8, 73 L.Ed.2d 130 (1982). Moreover, the theory is employed to enforce fair housing and age discrimination statutes. See Note, Business Necessity in Title VIII: Importing an Employment Discrimination Doctrine into the Fair Housing Act, 54 Ford.L.Rev. 563 (1986); Note, Disparate Impact Analysis and the Age Discrimination in Employment Act, 68 Minn.L.Rev. 1038 (1984).

[10]. This subsection makes it unlawful for an employer:

"to fail or refuse to hire or to discharge any individual, or otherwise to discriminate against any individual with respect to his compensation, terms, conditions, or privileges of employment, because of such individual's race, color, religion, sex, or national origin...." 42 U.S.C. section 2000e-2(a)(1).

account of race.[11] The means for determining intent absent direct evidence was outlined in McDonnell Douglas Corp. v. Green, 411 U.S. 792, 93 S.Ct. 1817, 36 L.Ed.2d 668 (1973), and Texas *2130 Dept. of Community Affairs v. Burdine, 450 U.S. 248, 101 S.Ct. 1089, 67 L.Ed.2d 207 (1981), two opinions written by Justice Powell for unanimous Courts. In such a "disparate treatment" case, see Teamsters, 431 U.S., at 335, n. 15, 97 S.Ct., at 1854, n. 15, the plaintiff's initial burden, which is "not onerous,"450 U.S., at 253, 101 S.Ct., at 1093, is to establish "a prima facie case of racial discrimination," 411 U.S., at 802, 93 S.Ct., at 1824, that is, to create a presumption of unlawful discrimination by "eliminat(ing) the most common nondiscriminatory reasons for the plaintiff's rejection."[12] 450 U.S., at 254, 101 S.Ct.,

---

[11]. In McDonnell Douglas Corp. v. Green, 411 U.S. 792, 93 S.Ct. 1817, 36 L.Ed.2d 668 (1973), Justice Powell explained:

"Griggs differs from the instant case in important respects. It dealt with standardized testing devices which, however neutral on their face, operated to exclude many blacks who were capable of performing effectively in the desired positions. Griggs was rightly concerned that childhood deficiencies in the education and background of minority citizens, resulting from forces beyond their control, not be allowed to work a cumulative and invidious burden on such citizens for the remainder of their lives. Respondent, however, appears in different clothing. He had engaged in a seriously disruptive act against the very one from whom he now seeks employment. And petitioner does not seek his exclusion on the basis of a testing device which overstates what is necessary for competent performance, or through some sweeping disqualification of all those with any past record of unlawful behavior, however remote, insubstantial, or unrelated to applicant's personal qualifications as an employee. Petitioner assertedly rejected respondent for unlawful conduct against it and, in the absence of proof of pretext or discriminatory application of such a reason, this cannot be thought the kind of 'artificial, arbitrary, and unnecessary barriers to employment' which the Court found to be the intention of Congress to remove." Id., 411 U.S., at 806, 93 S.Ct., at 1826 (citations omitted).

[12]. "This may be done by showing (i) that he belongs to a racial minority; (ii) that he applied and was qualified for a job for which the employer was seeking applicants; (iii) that, despite his qualifications, he was rejected; and (iv) that, after his rejection, the position remained open and the employer continued to seek applicants from persons of complainant's qualifications." Id., at 802, 93 S.Ct., at 1824.

at 1094. "The burden then must shift to the employer to articulate some legitimate, nondiscriminatory reason for the employee's rejection." 411 U.S., at 802, 93 S.Ct., at 1824; see 450 U.S., at 254, 101 S.Ct., at 1094. Finally, because "Title VII does not ... permit (the employer) to use (the employee's) conduct as a pretext for the sort of discrimination prohibited by section 703(a)(1)," the employee "must be given a full and fair opportunity to demonstrate by competent evidence that the presumptively valid reasons for his rejection were in fact a coverup for a racially discriminatory decision." 411 U.S., at 804-805, 93 S.Ct., at 1825; see 450 U.S., at 256, 101 S.Ct., at 1095. While the burdens of producing evidence thus shift, the "ultimate burden of persuading the trier of fact that the defendant intentionally discriminated against the plaintiff remains at all times with the plaintiff."[13] 450 U.S., at 253, 101 S.Ct., at 1093.

Decisions of this Court and other federal courts repeatedly have recognized that while the employer's burden in a disparate treatment case is simply one of coming forward with evidence of legitimate business purpose, its burden in a disparate impact case is proof of an affirmative defense of business necessity.[14] Although the majority's opinion blurs

---

[13]. Although disparate impact and disparate treatment are the most prevalent modes of proving discrimination violative of Title VII, they are by no means exclusive. See generally B. Schlei & P. Grossman, Employment Discrimination Law 13-289 (2d ed. 1983) (four chapters discussing "disparate treatment," "present effects of past discrimination," "adverse impact," and "reasonable accommodation" as "categories" of discrimination). Cf. n. 4, supra. Moreover, either or both of the primary theories may be applied to a particular set of facts. See Teamsters v. United States, 431 U.S. 324, 336, n. 15, 97 S.Ct. 1843, 1854, n. 15, 52 L.Ed.2d 396 (1977).

[14]. See McDonnell Douglas, 411 U.S., at 802, n. 14, 93 S.Ct., at 1824, n. 14. See also, e.g., Teal, 457 U.S., at 446, 102 S.Ct., at 2530 ("employer must demonstrate that 'any given requirement (has) a manifest relationship to the employment in question'"); New York City Transit Authority v. Beazer, 440 U.S. 568, 587, 99 S.Ct. 1355, 1366, 59 L.Ed.2d 587 (1979) (employer "rebutted" prima facie case by "demonstration that its narcotics rule 'is job related'"); Dothard v. Rawlinson, 433 U.S. 321, 329, 97 S.Ct. 2720, 2726, 53 L.Ed.2d 786 (1977) (employer has to "prov(e) that the challenged requirements are job related"); Albemarle Paper Co. v. Moody, 422 U.S. 405, 425, 95 S.Ct. 2362, 2375, 45 L.Ed.2d

that distinction, thoughtful reflection on common-law pleading *2131 principles clarifies the fundamental differences between the two types of "burdens of proof."[15] In the ordinary civil trial, the plaintiff bears the burden of persuading the trier of fact that the defendant has harmed her. See, e.g., 2 Restatement (Second) of Torts sections 328 A, 433 B (1965) (hereinafter Restatement). The defendant may undercut plaintiff's efforts both by confronting plaintiff's evidence during her case in chief and by submitting countervailing evidence during its own case.[16] But if the plaintiff proves the existence of the harmful act, the defendant can escape liability only by persuading the

---

280 (1975) (employer has "burden of proving that its tests are 'job related'"); Griggs, 401 U.S., at 432, 91 S.Ct., at 854 (employer has "burden of showing that any given requirement must have a manifest relationship to the employment"). Court of Appeals opinions properly treating the employer's burden include Bunch v. Bullard, 795 F.2d 384, 393-394 (CA5 1986); Lewis v. Bloomsburg Mills, Inc., 773 F.2d 561, 572 (CA4 1985); Nash v. Consolidated City of Jacksonville, Duval Cty., Fla., 763 F.2d 1393, 1397 (CA11 1985); Segar v. Smith, 238 U.S.App.D.C. 103, 121, 738 F.2d 1249, 1267 (1984), cert. denied sub nom. Meese v. Segar, 471 U.S. 1115, 105 S.Ct. 2357, 86 L.Ed.2d 258 (1985); Moore v. Hughes Helicopters, Inc., a Div. of Summa Corp., 708 F.2d 475, 481 (CA9 1983); Hawkins v. Anheuser-Busch, Inc., 697 F.2d 810, 815 (CA8 1983); Johnson v. Uncle Ben's, Inc., 657 F.2d 750 (CA5 1981), cert. denied, 459 U.S. 967, 103 S.Ct. 293, 74 L.Ed.2d 277 (1982); contra Croker v. Boeing Co., 662 F.2d 975, 991 (CA3 1981) (en banc). Cf. Equal Employment Opportunity Comm'n Uniform Guidelines on Employee Selection Procedures, 29 CFR section 1607.1 et seq. (1988).

[15]. See, e.g., 9 J. Wigmore, Evidence sections 2485-2498 (J. Chadbourn rev.1981); D. Louisell & C. Mueller, Federal Evidence sections 65-70 (1977) (hereinafter Louisell); 21 C. Wright & K. Graham, Federal Practice and Procedure section 5122 (1977) (hereinafter Wright); J. Thayer, A Preliminary Treatise on Evidence 353-389 (1898) (hereinafter Thayer); C. Langdell, Equity Pleading 108-115 (2d ed. 1883).

[16]. Cf. Thayer 357 (quoting Caldwell v. New Jersey S. B. Co., 47 N.Y. 282, 290 (1872)) ("'The burden of maintaining the affirmative of the issue, and, properly speaking, the burden of proof, remained upon the plaintiff throughout the trial; but the burden or necessity was cast upon the defendant, to relieve itself from the presumption of negligence raised by the plaintiff's evidence'").

factfinder that the act was justified or excusable. See, e.g., Restatement sections 454-461, 463-467. The plaintiff in turn may try to refute this affirmative defense. Although the burdens of producing evidence regarding the existence of harm or excuse thus shift between the plaintiff and the defendant, the burden of proving either proposition remains throughout on the party asserting it.

In a disparate treatment case there is no "discrimination" within the meaning of Title VII unless the employer intentionally treated the employee unfairly because of race. Therefore, the employee retains the burden of proving the existence of intent at all times. If there is direct evidence of intent, the employee may have little difficulty persuading the factfinder that discrimination has occurred. But in the likelier event that intent has to be established by inference, the employee may resort to the McDonnell Burdine inquiry. In either instance, the employer may undermine the employee's evidence but has no independent burden of persuasion.

In contrast, intent plays no role in the disparate impact inquiry. The question, rather, is whether an employment practice has a significant, adverse effect on an identifiable class of workers--regardless of the cause or motive for the practice. The employer may attempt to contradict the factual basis for this effect; that is, to prevent the employee from establishing a prima facie case. But when an employer is faced with sufficient proof of disparate impact, its only recourse is to justify the practice by explaining why it is necessary to the operation of business. Such a justification is a classic example of an affirmative defense.[17]

---

[17]. Accord Fed.Rule Civ.Proc. 8(c) ("In pleading to a preceding pleading, a party shall set forth affirmatively ... any ... matter constituting an avoidance or affirmative defense"). Cf. Thayer 368-369:

"An admission may, of course, end the controversy; but such an admission may be, and yet not end it; and if that be so, it is because the party making the admission sets up something that avoids the apparent effect of it.... When this happens, the party defending becomes, in so far, the actor or plaintiff. In general, he who seeks to move a court in his favor, whether as an original plaintiff whose facts are merely denied, or as a defendant, who, in admitting his adversary's contention and setting up an affirmative defence, takes the role of actor (reus excipiendo fit actor), must satisfy the court of the truth and adequacy of the grounds of his claim, both in point of fact and law."

*2132 Failing to explore the interplay between these distinct orders of proof, the Court announces that our frequent statements that the employer shoulders the burden of proof respecting business necessity "should have been understood to mean an employer's production--but not persuasion--burden."[18] Ante, at 2126. Our opinions always have emphasized that in a disparate impact case the employer's burden is weighty. "The touchstone," the Court said in Griggs, "is business necessity." 401 U.S., at 431, 91 S.Ct., at 853. Later, we held that prison administrators had failed to "rebu(t) the prima facie case of discrimination by showing that the height and weight requirements are ... essential to effective job performance," Dothard v. Rawlinson, 433 U.S. 321, 331, 97 S.Ct. 2720, 2727, 53 L.Ed.2d 786 (1977). Cf. n. 14, supra. I am thus astonished to read that the "touchstone of this inquiry is a reasoned review of the employer's justification for his use of the challenged practice.... (T)here is no requirement that the challenged

---

Similarly, in suits alleging price discrimination in violation of section 2 of the Clayton Act, as amended by the Robinson Patman Act, 15 U.S.C. section 13, it is well settled that the defendant has the burden of affirmatively establishing as a defense either a cost justification, under the proviso to subsection (a), United States v. Borden Co., 370 U.S. 460, 467, 82 S.Ct. 1309, 1313, 8 L.Ed.2d 627 (1962), or a good-faith effort to meet a competitor's equally low price, pursuant to subsection (b), Standard Oil Co. v. FTC, 340 U.S. 231, 250, 71 S.Ct. 240, 250, 95 L.Ed. 239 (1951).

[18]. The majority's only basis for this proposition is the plurality opinion in Watson v. Fort Worth Bank & Trust, 487 U.S. ----, ----, 108 S.Ct. 2777, ----, 101 L.Ed.2d 827 (1988), which in turn cites no authority. As Justice BLACKMUN explained in Watson, 487 U.S., at ---- - ----, 108 S.Ct., at ---- - ---- (concurring in part and concurring in judgment), and as I have shown here, the assertion profoundly misapprehends the difference between disparate impact and disparate treatment claims.

The Court also makes passing reference to Federal Rule of Evidence 301. Ante, at 2126. That Rule pertains only to shifting of evidentiary burdens upon establishment of a presumption and has no bearing on the substantive burdens of proof. See Louisell sections 65-70; Wright section 5122.

practice be ... 'essential,'" ante, at 2126. This casual--almost summary--rejection of the statutory construction that developed in the wake of Griggs is most disturbing. I have always believed that the Griggs opinion correctly reflected the intent of the Congress that enacted Title VII. Even if I were not so persuaded, I could not join a rejection of a consistent interpretation of a federal statute. Congress frequently revisits this statutory scheme and can readily correct our mistakes if we misread its meaning. Johnson v. Transportation Agency, Santa Clara, Cty., Cal., 480 U.S. 616, 644, 107 S.Ct. 1442, 1458-1459, 94 L.Ed.2d 615 (1987) (STEVENS, J., concurring); Runyon v. McCrary, 427 U.S. 160, 190-192, 96 S.Ct. 2586, 2604-2605, 49 L.Ed.2d 415 (1976) (STEVENS, J., concurring). See McNally v. United States, 483 U.S. 350, 376, 107 S.Ct. 2875, 2890, 97 L.Ed.2d 292 (1987) (STEVENS, J., dissenting); Commissioner v. Fink, 483 U.S. 89, 102-105, 107 S.Ct. 2729, 2736-2738, 97 L.Ed.2d 74 (1987) (STEVENS, J., dissenting); see also Rodriguez de Quijas v. ShearsonAmerican Express, Inc., 490 U.S. ----, ---- - ----, 109 S.Ct. 1917, ---- - ----, --- L.Ed.2d ---- (1989) (STEVENS, J., dissenting).

Also troubling is the Court's apparent redefinition of the employees' burden of proof in a disparate impact case. No prima facie case will be made, it declares, unless the employees "'isolat(e) and identif(y) the specific employment practices that are allegedly responsible for any observed statistical disparities.'" Ante, at 2124 (quoting Watson v. Fort Worth Bank & Trust, 487 U.S. ----, ----, 108 S.Ct. 2777, 2788, 101 L.Ed.2d 827 (1988) (plurality opinion)). This additional proof requirement is unwarranted.[19] It is elementary that a plaintiff cannot recover upon proof of injury alone; rather, the plaintiff must connect the injury to an act of the defendant in order to establish prima facie that the defendant is liable. E.g., Restatement section 430. Although the causal link must have substance, the act need

---

[19]. The Solicitor General's brief amicus curiae on behalf of the employers agrees:

"(A) decision rule for selection may be complex: it may, for example, involve consideration of multiple factors. And certainly if the factors combine to produce a single ultimate selection decision and it is not possible to challenge each one, that decision may be challenged (and defended) as a whole." Brief for United States as Amicus Curiae 22 (footnote omitted).

not constitute the sole or primary cause of the harm. sections 431-433; cf. Price *2133 Waterhouse v. Hopkins, 490 U.S. ----, 109 S.Ct. 1775, 104 L.Ed.2d 268 (1989). Thus in a disparate impact case, proof of numerous questionable employment practices ought to fortify an employee's assertion that the practices caused racial disparities.[20] Ordinary principles of fairness require that Title VII actions be tried like "any lawsuit." Cf. USPS Board of Governors v. Aikens, 460 U.S. 711, 714, n. 3, 103 S.Ct. 1478, 1481, n. 3, 75 L.Ed.2d 403 (1983). The changes the majority makes today, tipping the scales in favor of employers, are not faithful to those principles.

II

Petitioners seek reversal of the Court of Appeals and dismissal of this suit on the ground that respondents' statistical evidence failed to prove a prima facie case of discrimination. Brief for Petitioners 48. The District Court concluded "there were 'significant disparities'" between the racial composition of the cannery workers and the noncannery workers, but it "made no precise numerical findings" on this and other critical points. See ante, at 2121, n. 5. Given this dearth of findings and the Court's newly articulated preference for individualized proof of causation, it would be manifestly unfair to consider respondents' evidence in the aggregate and deem it insufficient. Thus the Court properly rejects petitioners' request for a final judgment and remands for further determination of the strength of respondents' prima facie case. See ante, at 2123. Even at this juncture, however, I believe that respondents' evidence deserves greater credit than the majority allows.

Statistical evidence of discrimination should compare the racial composition of employees in disputed jobs to that "'of the qualified ... population in the relevant labor market.'" Ante, at 2121 (quoting Hazelwood School District v. United

---

[20]. The Court discounts the difficulty its causality requirement presents for employees, reasoning that they may employ "liberal civil discovery rules" to obtain the employer's statistical personnel records. Ante, at 2125. Even assuming that this generally is true, it has no bearing in this litigation, since it is undisputed that petitioners did not preserve such records. Brief for Respondents 42-43; Reply Brief for Petitioners 18-19.

States, 433 U.S. 299, 308, 97 S.Ct. 2736, 2741, 53 L.Ed.2d 768 (1977)). That statement leaves open the definition of the qualified population and the relevant labor market. Our previous opinions, e.g., New York City Transit Authority v. Beazer, 440 U.S. 568, 584-586, 99 S.Ct. 1355, 1365-1366, 59 L.Ed.2d 587 (1979); Dothard v. Rawlinson, 433 U.S. 321, 329-330, 97 S.Ct. 2720, 2726-2727, 53 L.Ed.2d 786 (1977); Albemarle Paper Co. v. Moody, 422 U.S. 405, 425, 95 S.Ct. 2362, 2375, 45 L.Ed.2d 280 (1975); Griggs, 401 U.S., at 426, 430, n. 6, 91 S.Ct., at 851, 853, n. 6, demonstrate that in reviewing statistical evidence, a court should not strive for numerical exactitude at the expense of the needs of the particular case.

The District Court's findings of fact depict a unique industry. Canneries often are located in remote, sparsely populated areas of Alaska. 34 EPD 34,437, p. 33,825 (WD Wash.1983). Most jobs are seasonal, with the season's length and the canneries' personnel needs varying not just year-to-year but day-to-day. Ibid. To fill their employment requirements, petitioners must recruit and transport many cannery workers and noncannery workers from States in the Pacific Northwest. Id., at 33,828. Most cannery workers come from a union local based outside Alaska or from Native villages near the canneries. Ibid. Employees in the noncannery positions--the positions that are "at issue"--learn of openings by word of mouth; the jobs seldom are posted or advertised, and there is no promotion to noncannery jobs from within the cannery workers' ranks. Id., at 33,827-33,828.

In general, the District Court found the at-issue jobs to require "skills," ranging from English literacy, typing, and "ability to use seam micrometers, gauges, and mechanic's hand tools" to "good health" and a *2134 driver's license.[21] Id., at 33,833-33,834. All cannery workers' jobs, like a handful of at-issue positions, are unskilled, and the court found that the intensity of the work during canning season precludes on-the-job training for skilled noncannery

---

[21]. The District Court found that of more than 100 at-issue job titles, all were skilled except these 15: kitchen help, waiterwaitress, janitor, oildock crew, night watchman, tallyman, laundry, gasman, roustabout, store help, stockroom help, assistant caretaker (winter watchman and watchman's assistant), machinist helpertrainee, deckhand, and apprentice carpentercarpenter's helper. 34 EPD 34,437, p. 33,835.

positions. Id., at 33,825. It made no findings regarding the extent to which the cannery workers already are qualified for at-issue jobs: individual plaintiffs testified persuasively that they were fully qualified for such jobs,[22] but the court neither credited nor discredited this testimony. Although there are no findings concerning wage differentials, the parties seem to agree that wages for cannery workers are lower than those for noncannery workers, skilled or unskilled. The District Court found that "nearly all" cannery workers are nonwhite, while the percentage of nonwhites employed in the entire Alaska salmon canning industry "has stabilized at about 47% to 50%." Id., at 33,829. The precise stratification of the work force is not described in the findings, but the parties seem to agree that the noncannery jobs are predominantly held by whites.

Petitioners contend that the relevant labor market in this case is the general population of the "'external' labor market for the jobs at issue." Brief for Petitioners 17. While they would rely on the District Court's findings in this regard, those findings are ambiguous. At one point the District Court specifies "Alaska, the Pacific Northwest, and California" as "the geographical region from which (petitioners) draw their employees," but its next finding refers to "this relevant geographical area for cannery worker, laborer, and other nonskilled jobs," 34 EPD 34,437, p. 33,828. There is no express finding of the relevant labor market for noncannery jobs.

Even assuming that the District Court properly defined the relevant geographical area, its apparent assumption that the population in that area constituted the "available labor supply," ibid., is not adequately founded. An undisputed requirement for employment either as a cannery or noncannery worker is availability for seasonal employment in the far reaches of Alaska. Many noncannery workers, furthermore, must be available for preseason work. Id., at 33,829, 33,833-33,834. Yet the record does not identify the portion of the general population in Alaska, California, and the

---

[22]. Some cannery workers later became architects, an Air Force officer, and a graduate student in public administration. Some had college training at the time they were employed in the canneries. See id., at 33,837-33,838; App. 38, 52-53; Tr. 76, 951-952, 1036, 1050, 2214.

Pacific Northwest that would accept this type of employment.[23] This deficiency respecting a crucial job qualification diminishes the usefulness of petitioners' statistical evidence. In contrast, respondents' evidence, comparing racial compositions within the work force, identifies a pool of workers willing to work during the relevant times and familiar with the workings of the industry. Surely this is more probative *2135 than the untailored general population statistics on which petitioners focus. Cf. Hazelwood, 433 U.S., at 308, n. 13, 97 S.Ct., at 2742, n. 13; Teamsters, 431 U.S., at 339-340, n. 20, 97 S.Ct., at 1856, n. 20.

Evidence that virtually all the employees in the major categories of at-issue jobs were white,[24] whereas about

---

[23]. The District Court's justification for use of general population statistics occurs in these findings of fact:

"119. Most of the jobs at the canneries entail migrant, seasonal labor. While as a general proposition, most people prefer full-year, fixed location employment near their homes, seasonal employment in the unique salmon industry is not comparable to most other types of migrant work, such as fruit and vegetable harvesting which, for example, may or may not involve a guaranteed wage.

"120. Thus, while census data is (sic) dominated by people who prefer full-year, fixed-location employment, such data is (sic) nevertheless appropriate in defining labor supplies for migrant, seasonal work." 34 EPD 34,437, p. 33,829.

The court's rather confusing distinction between work in the cannery industry and other "migrant, seasonal work" does not support its conclusion that the general population composes the relevant labor market.

[24]. For example, from 1971 to 1980, there were 443 persons hired in the job departments labeled "machinists," "company fishing boat," and "tender" at petitioner Castle & Cooke, Inc.'s Bumble Bee cannery; only three of them were nonwhites. Joint Excerpt of Record 35 (Exh. 588). In the same categories at the Red Salmon cannery of petitioner Wards Cove Packing Co., Inc., 488 whites and 42 nonwhites were hired. Id., at 36 (Exh. 589).

two-thirds of the cannery workers were nonwhite,[25] may not by itself suffice to establish a prima facie case of discrimination.[26] But such evidence of racial stratification puts the specific employment practices challenged by respondents into perspective. Petitioners recruit employees for at-issue jobs from outside the work force rather than from lower-paying, overwhelmingly nonwhite, cannery worker positions. 34 EPD 34,437, pp. 33,828-33,829. Information about availability of at-issue positions is conducted by word of mouth;[27] therefore, the maintenance of housing and mess halls that separate the largely white noncannery work force

---

[25]. The Court points out that nonwhites are "overrepresented" among the cannery workers. Ante, at 2123-2124. Such an imbalance will be true in any racially stratified work force; its significance becomes apparent only upon examination of the pattern of segregation within the work force. In the cannery industry nonwhites are concentrated in positions offering low wages and little opportunity for promotion. Absent any showing that the "underrepresentation" of whites in this stratum is the result of a barrier to access, the "overrepresentation" of nonwhites does not offend Title VII.

[26]. The majority suggests that at-issue work demands the skills possessed by "accountants, managers, boat captains, electricians, doctors, and engineers." See ante, at 2122. It is at least theoretically possible that a disproportionate number of white applicants possessed the specialized skills required by some at-issue jobs. In fact, of course, many at-issue jobs involved skills not at all comparable to these selective examples. See 34 EPD 34,437, pp. 33,833-33,834. Even the District Court recognized that in a year-round employment setting, "some of the positions which this court finds to be skilled, e.g., truckdriving on the beach, (would) fit into the category of jobs which require skills that are readily acquirable by persons in the general public." Id., at 33,841.

[27]. As the Court of Appeals explained in its remand opinion:

"Specifically, the companies sought cannery workers in Native villages and through dispatches from ILWU Local 37, thus securing a work force for the lowest paying jobs which was predominantly Alaska Native and Filipino. For other departments the companies relied on informal word-of-mouth recruitment by predominantly white superintendents and foremen, who recruited primarily white employees. That such practices can cause a discriminatory impact is obvious." 827 F.2d, at 446.

from the cannery workers, id., at 33,836, 33,843-33,844, coupled with the tendency toward nepotistic hiring,[28] are obvious barriers to employment opportunities for nonwhites. Putting to one side the issue of business justifications, it would be quite wrong to conclude that these practices have no discriminatory consequence.[29] Thus I agree with the Court of Appeals, 827 F.2d 439, 444-445 (CA9 1987), that when the District Court makes the additional *2136 findings prescribed today, it should treat the evidence of racial stratification in the work force as a significant element of respondents' prima facie case.

III

The majority's opinion begins with recognition of the settled rule that that "a facially neutral employment practice may be deemed violative of Title VII without evidence of the employer's subjective intent to discriminate that is required in a 'disparate treatment' case." Ante, at 2119. It then departs from the body of law engendered by this disparate impact theory, reformulating the order of proof and the weight of the parties' burdens. Why the Court undertakes these unwise changes in elementary and eminently fair rules is a mystery to me.

I respectfully dissent.

---

[28]. The District Court found but downplayed the fact that relatives of employees are given preferential consideration. See 34 EPD 34,437, p. 33,840. But "of 349 nepotistic hires in four upper-level departments during 1970-75, 332 were of whites, 17 of nonwhites," the Court of Appeals noted. "If nepotism exists, it is by definition a practice of giving preference to relatives, and where those doing the hiring are predominantly white, the practice necessarily has an adverse impact on nonwhites." 827 F.2d, at 445.

[29]. The Court suggests that the discrepancy in economic opportunities for white and nonwhite workers does not amount to disparate impact within the meaning of Title VII unless respondents show that it is "petitioners' fault." Ante, at 2122; see also ante, at 2122-2123. This statement distorts the disparate impact theory, in which the critical inquiry is whether an employer's practices operate to discriminate. E.g., Griggs, 401 U.S., at 431, 91 S.Ct., at 853. Whether the employer intended such discrimination is irrelevant.

Justice BLACKMUN, with whom Justice BRENNAN and Justice MARSHALL join, dissenting.

I fully concur in Justice STEVENS' analysis of this case. Today a bare majority of the Court takes three major strides backwards in the battle against race discrimination. It reaches out to make last Term's plurality opinion in Watson v. Fort Worth Bank & Trust, 487 U.S. ----, 108 S.Ct. 2777, 101 L.Ed.2d 827 (1988), the law, thereby upsetting the longstanding distribution of burdens of proof in Title VII disparate-impact cases. It bars the use of internal workforce comparisons in the making of a prima facie case of discrimination, even where the structure of the industry in question renders any other statistical comparison meaningless. And it requires practice-by-practice statistical proof of causation, even where, as here, such proof would be impossible.

The harshness of these results is well demonstrated by the facts of this case. The salmon industry as described by this record takes us back to a kind of overt and institutionalized discrimination we have not dealt with in years: a total residential and work environment organized on principles of racial stratification and segregation, which, as Justice STEVENS points out, resembles a plantation economy. Post, at 2128, n. 4. This industry long has been characterized by a taste for discrimination of the old-fashioned sort: a preference for hiring nonwhites to fill its lowest-level positions, on the condition that they stay there. The majority's legal rulings essentially immunize these practices from attack under a Title VII disparate-impact analysis.

Sadly, this comes as no surprise. One wonders whether the majority still believes that race discrimination--or, more accurately, race discrimination against nonwhites--is a problem in our society, or even remembers that it ever was. Cf. City of Richmond v. J.A. Croson Co., --- U.S. ----, 109 S.Ct. 706, 102 L.Ed.2d 854 (1989).

CHAPTER 4

VALUES IN REASONED DECISIONMAKING

DAVIS
v.
WYETH LABORATORIES, INC.

United States Court of Appeals Ninth Circuit.
399 F.2d 121.
Jan. 22, 1968, As Modified on Denial of Rehearing Sept. 10, 1968.

Action by consumer against manufacturer of polio vaccine seeking damages resulting from plaintiff's contraction of polio after taking the vaccine. The United States District Court for the District of Idaho, Fred M. Taylor, Chief Judge, gave judgment for manufacturer, and appeal was taken. The Court of Appeals, Merrill, Circuit Judge, held that instruction should have been given, either in warranty or in tort, stating that manufacturer of polio vaccine was strictly liable if its drug caused plaintiff to contract polio, since manufacturer had a duty to warn consumer, or to make adequate provision for his being warned, as to risks involved in taking the drug, which failure rendered the drug unfit in the sense that it was thereby rendered unreasonably dangerous.

Reversed and remanded for new trial.

Hamlin, Circuit Judge, dissented.

*122 Before HAMLIN, MERRILL and DUNIWAY, Circuit Judges.

MERRILL, Circuit Judge:

This case presents the question whether appellee Wyeth Laboratories, Inc., a manufacturer of Sabin polio vaccine, should be held to strict tort liability to one who took the drug and contracted polio as a result.

Appellant Glynn Richard Davis took appellee's Type III polio vaccine at a mass immunization clinic conducted in West Yellowstone, Montana, in March, 1963. At that time he was thirty-nine years old, in good health, and engaged in the lumber business. Within thirty days he evidenced paralysis and other symptoms of polio, and has remained paralyzed from the waist down ever since. He brought suit in the District Court for the District of Idaho asserting jurisdiction founded on diversity of citizenship and here appeals from judgment for appellee following jury trial.

I. THE BACKGROUND

A. The Vaccine

The vaccine involved is Sabin oral polio vaccine, as developed by Dr. Albert Sabin after many years of research. There are three separate types of Sabin vaccine: Type I, Type II and Type III. Each is designed to immunize the person taking the vaccine from contracting paralytic poliomyelitis from a corresponding type of polio virus. Differing from the earlier Salk vaccine, administered by injection, the Sabin vaccine utilizes live virus.

The use of a live virus polio vaccine which could be taken orally had been under study throughout the world for a number of years. In the United States it has been determined that the Sabin vaccine strains should be licensed. Licensing was handled by The Division of Biologic Standards of the National Institutes of Health, a part of the United States Department of Health, Education and Welfare. Ultimately the United States licensed three manufacturers of the vaccine, including appellee Wyeth Laboratories. Appellee was licensed to sell Type III vaccine on May 17, 1962.

Licensing in the United States was preceded by worldwide clinical testing on between 700,000 and 1,000,000 people.

The vaccine is licensed for sale only as a prescription drug. It is usually manufactured in what the producers call "lots." Each lot of the vaccine is manufactured *123 under extremely complex and technical standards devised by The Division of Biologic Standards. The virus used in the vaccine, without regard to who manufactures it, comes from a common source. Appellee obtained from Dr. Sabin a so-called "seed" virus and this original seed, still maintained, is the parent of each separate lot of vaccine manufactured by appellee. Each individual lot is, in turn, run through a number of tests in the manufacturing laboratory.

Following manufacture and satisfactory testing within the laboratory, the lot involved in this case was sent to The Division of Biologic Standards where it was again subjected to rigorous testing. The Government, being satisfied with the result of the test, granted authorization for the release of this lot on January 31, 1963.

B. The Mass Immunization Clinics

In the fall of 1960 an advisory committee was established by the Surgeon General of the United States to review all phases of polio prevention. In February, 1962, the Communicable Disease Center of the Public Health Service, Department of Health, Education and Welfare, issued recommendations and reports of this committee. It was stated:

> "With the licensing of type III monovalent vaccine, which is anticipated in the near future, the complete oral polio virus vaccine will become available. Recommendations as to planning and policies which will assure its maximally effective use are now essential for the guidance of the medical profession and official health authorities."

The goal of this compaign to disseminate the oral vaccine was stated as "the complete elimination of paralytic poliomyelitis from the United States." Community mass immunization centers were recommended and guidelines were given for setting them up. The following month the Surgeon General, on behalf of the Public Health Service, issued recommendations for the use of the vaccine in the 1962 season, giving further guidance for the conduct of community programs.

That month, March, 1962, representatives of the Public Health Service held a meeting with Idaho public health officials and medical association officers at which a joint release was issued recommending the holding of community clinics. The holding of such clinics in Eastern Idaho was later officially authorized by the Idaho Falls Medical Society and its Public Health Committee, who then selected appellee's product as the vaccine to be administered. At a subsequent meeting it was decided to include West

Yellowstone, Montana, in the Eastern Idaho program since there were no doctors there and the residents relied on medical facilities in Ashton, Idaho. In the absence of a doctor the administration of the vaccine for the West Yellowstone clinic was delegated to a pharmacist.

The clinics in Eastern Idaho were originally scheduled for the fall of 1962. On September 14, 1962, a statement was issued by the Association of State and Territorial Health Officers through the subcommittee on epidemic intelligence of its committee on infections diseases. It stated:

> "The Sub-committee * * * has reviewed data showing a temporal association between the incidence of paralytic poliomyelitis and the administration of Type 3 oral poliomyelitis vaccine. The Sub-committee believes that the data indicate a causal relationship and show that a small but definite risk attends the use of presently available Type 3 oral polio vaccines. The data further suggest that the risk is almost exclusively limited to adult populations. While the Subcommittee acknowledges the presence of a small risk, it recognizes the tremendous value of oral poliomyelitis vaccines and the detrimental effect the unqualified withdrawal at this time would have on their future use. In view of the very small magnitude of the risk and the enormous potential *124 value of oral vaccines, the Sub-committee therefore recommends that the Surgeon General issue a statement which will: 1. Apprise the public of the nature of the risk. 2. Recommend that the non-epidemic use of Type 3 oral vaccine be restricted to preschool and school age children. 3. Recommend that the vaccine continue to be available for epidemic use. 4. Reaffirm the desirability of restricting mass application to the late Fall, Winter and Spring."

The following day a statement was issued by the Surgeon General respecting his own special advisory committee's review of occurrences of polio cases associated with the administration of the vaccine. It stated:

> "The level of this risk can only be approximated but clearly is within range of less than I case per million doses. Since the cases have been concentrated among adults the risk to this group is greater; whereas, the risk to children is exceedingly slight or practically nonexistent.

The Committee therefore recommends that the use of Type III vaccine in mass campaigns be limited to preschool and school age children. Plans for mass programs using Type I and II vaccines in all age groups should continue. Furthermore, Type III vaccine is still indicated for use among adults in high risk groups, which include tourists to hyperendemic areas and persons residing in epidemic areas.

A special report is being prepared and will be sent to the members of the medical and public health profession within the next few days and will be made public."

The special report followed on September 21, 1962. It stated:

"Present data indicate that for 1962, the paralytic poliomyelitis rate for those under 20 will be approximately 7.6 per million; for those over 20, about 0.9 per million. These rates will represent a record low for the 52 year period since the reporting began."

It reiterated the recommendation earlier made in the Surgeon General's statement:

"With the incidence of poliomyelitis at a low level in this country, the Committee therefore recommended that the Type III vaccine be restricted to preschool and school age children and to those adults in high risk groups, such as those travelling to hyperendemic areas or in areas where a Type III epidemic is present or impending.

Since the vast majority of poliomyelitis cases occur among young children and since children are the principal disseminators of the virus, continued intensive immunization programs among this group are clearly indicated. If this group can be adequately immunized, the spread of the poliomyelitis viruses will be sharply restricted, if not essentially eradicated."

In December, 1962, a further report was issued. It stated:

"It is therefore recommended: (1) that community plans for immunization be encouraged, using all three types; and (2) that immunization be emphasized for children in whom the danger of naturally occurring poliomyelitis is greatest and who serve as the natural source of poliomyelitis infection in the community. Because the need for immunization diminishes with advancing age and because potential risks of vaccine are believed by some to exist in adults, especially above the age of 30, vaccination should be used for adults only with the full recognition of its very small risk. Vaccination is especially recommended for those adults who are at higher risk of naturally occurring disease; for example, parents of young children,[1] pregnant women, persons in epidemic *125 situations and those planning foreign travel.

Of greatest importance is the continuing vaccination of oncoming generations."

With these recommendations before them the East Idaho officials postponed their clinics scheduled for the fall of 1962, but determined to proceed in the spring of 1963. Adults were included in their immunization program.

C. Appellee's Participation

When Eastern Idaho chose appellee's vaccine for its clinics, Mr. John Franklin, one of appellee's salesmen, was assigned to handle the sales and assist in setting up the clinics. He was sent by appellee to Nevada to receive special training in setting up and conducting such clinics. Thereafter he managed the campaign for the Idaho Falls Medical Society. He furnished books to those in charge of clinics, setting forth schedules and procedures to be followed and details of the physical manner in which the clinics were to be set up and also showing sample promotional letters and advertising matter. He arranged for delivery of the vaccine from headquarters at Idaho Falls to the various clinics, including that in West Yellowstone, by the Idaho Falls Jeep Patrol. He arranged for the printing of forms and immunization cards and posters urging "KO Polio" and took charge of sending them to West Yellowstone. He organized meetings and conferred with those in charge of the separate clinics as to the procedures to be followed. For expenses incurred by him in connection with these activities he was reimbursed by the medical society.

---

[1] Appellant fell in this class.

Each person who received the vaccine was charged 25 [cents] (although it was given free of charge if the recipient so requested). Appellant paid this amount for his dosage. Funds collected from the clinics were used to pay the medical society's bill from Wyeth for the vaccine, with the remainder retained by the society.

D. Warnings

The Surgeon General's March statement was the subject of a news story in a Pocatello, Idaho, newspaper and was read by Franklin. It was his first information respecting the subject and he promptly informed the medical society of the release. The society confirmed the information by a telephone call to the office of the Surgeon General.

The drug when sold to the medical society had a printed insert with each bottle containing 100 doses. This insert contained directions for use and pertinent excerpts from the Surgeon General's report.

A fact sheet put out by appellee and contained in the book it supplied to clinics was published prior to the Surgeon General's report and represented the vaccine as completely safe for all ages. A collection of news clippings from Idaho newspapers introduced in evidence by appellant shows not only a complete lack of warning but assurances that the vaccine was safe for all.

No effort was made by Franklin or the medical society to inform the West Yellowstone pharmacist of the existence of risk. The latter did not read the package insert, nor did appellant. The advertising posters made no disclosure of risk and none was made directly to those who took the drug in West Yellowstone. Appellant testified that he had no knowledge of the risk, relied on the posters and was convinced by the campaign's advertising that it was his civic duty to participate.

II. THE ISSUES AS PRESENTED

Appellant stated claims founded on (1) negligent manufacture, (2) failure to warn of known dangers, (3) strict liability in tort and (4) breach of an implied warranty of fitness. The District Court dismissed all save that of breach of warranty.

We agree with the District Court that there was nothing in

the record to create a jury issue as to negligence *126 in manufacture. On the contrary, the record shows scrupulous attention in the matter of preparation and testing. The resulting product was precisely what was intended.[2] For this reason we also reject appellant's claim that it was error for the District Court to refuse to give an instruction that under Montana law appellee was held to an implied warranty that there was no "impurity" in the vaccine.

We find no error in the District Court's choice to present the case to the jury on warranty rather than on strict liability in tort. The law as emerging is tending toward the latter treatment[3] but under either approach the elements remain the same. The difference is largely one of terminology.[4]

We do find reversible error, however, in the manner in which the breach of warranty claim was given to the jury in the light of the court's dismissal of the claim for breach of a duty to warn.

Appellant contends that the District Court erred in instructing, on warranty, that the test is whether the drug was "reasonably fit and reasonably safe for use by the public

---

[2] In this respect our case differs from Gottsdanker v. Cutter Laboratories, 182 Cal.App.2d 602, 6 Cal.Rptr. 320, 79 A.L.R.2d 290 (1960), involving the Salk vaccine. There harm resulted because through inadequate testing procedures live virus remained in a product from which they supposedly had been eliminated.

[3] Greenman v. Yuba Power Products, Inc., 59 Cal.2d 57, 27 Cal.Rptr. 697, 377 P.2d 897, 13 A.L.R.3d 1049 (1963).

[4] See Prosser, The Fall of the Citadel (Strict Liability to the Consumer), 50 Minn.L.Rev. 791, 804-05 (1966). Greeno v. Clark Equipment Co., 237 F.Supp. 427, 429 (N.D.Ind.1965), noted that strict liability as imposed by Restatement (Second) of Torts 402A (1965) is "hardly more than what exists under implied warranty when stripped of the contract doctrines of privity, disclaimer, requirements of notice of defect, and limitation through inconsistencies with express warranties."

as a whole."[5] He contends that the warranty was that the drug was fit and safe as to him.

As a general proposition we would question the correctness of appellant's contention. It would, if generally applied, be equivalent to an imposition of absolute enterprise liability whereby all those who suffer unanticipated harm from the use of drugs are compensated out of profits from the sale of such products as a cost of doing business to the manufacturer. Although there are those who regard such a result as just,[6] it has so far been found inappropriate for the courts to impose such a farreaching change in the law of products liability.

Under the circumstances of this case, however, we conclude that strict liability does attach to sale of the drug to appellant and that the jury should have been so instructed, either by such an instruction as that requested by appellant or otherwise. Our conclusion in this respect is based upon our determination that a duty to warn existed, as to which none of appellant's requested instructions was given.

*127 While appellant alleged negligent breach of a duty to warn as an independent claim, we regard failure to warn, where the circumstances of sale imposed that duty, as

---

[5] "In considering the question of breach of an implied warranty, you are instructed that the implied warranty involved in this case is that the vaccine was reasonably fit for the particular purpose for which it was manufactured. In other words, under such circumstances the law imposes upon defendants a warranty that the Sabin vaccine, which it manufactured and supplied, was reasonably fit and reasonably safe for consumption by members of the public as a whole. This warranty does not mean, however, that this vaccine could be used with absolute safety, but means only that the vaccine must have been reasonably fit and reasonably safe for use by the public as a whole."

[6] Cochran v. Brooke, 409 P.2d 904, 907 (Ore.1966); James, The Untoward Effects of Cigarettes and Drugs: Some Reflections on Enterprise Liability, 54 Calif. L.Rev. 1550, 1558 (1966); Traynor, The Ways and Meanings of Defective Products and Strict Liability, 32 Tenn.L.Rev. 353 (1965). See also Keeton, Products Liability--Some Observations About Allocation of Risks, 64 Mich.L.Rev. 1329, 1347-48 (1966).

exposing the vendor to strict liability in tort[7] (or to liability for breach of warranty if that approach is used).

It was stipulated below that Montana law governed this case. We can find no Montana decision in point on the issue of a drug manufacturer's duty to warn of dangers inherent in its product. Privity of contract between buyer and seller as a prerequisite to recovery in an implied warranty action has long been abolished in that state in cases involving food, and strict liability has been imposed on those who sold it.[8] It would seem that the same approach would be adopted by the Montana Supreme Court in cases involving drugs meant for internal use. Faced with the absence of controlling state precedent, we choose to assume that Montana would follow the majority of other states in finding that liability can attach to the sale of drugs, in either tort or warranty, despite lack of privity, and would adopt the views set forth below on the manufacturer's duty to warn of dangers in "nondefective" but potentially harmful products.[9]

III. THE LAW OF STRICT LIABILITY AS APPLICABLE HERE

The clearest statement of the law as it exists today is in our view that set forth in the Restatement (Second) of Torts

---

[7] See Crane v. Sears, Roebuck & Co., 218 Cal.App.2d 855, 32 Cal.Rptr. 754 (1963); Canifax v. Hercules Powder Co., 237 Cal.App.2d 44, 46 Cal.Rptr. 552 (1965); Traynor, supra note 6; 2 Frumer & Friedman, Products Liability 16A(4) (e) (1967).

[8] Kelley v. John R. Daily Co., 56 Mont. 63, 181 P. 326 (1919); Bolitho v. Safeway Stores, 109 Mont. 213, 95 P.2d 443 (1938).

[9] In vicariously creating state law in such cases, we must look to the same sources that would be used by the state court-- Restatement of Law, treatises, law review commentary and both state and federal decisions. Wright, Federal Courts 206 (1963); Corbin, The Laws of the Several States, 50 Yale L.J. 762, 775-76 (1941). We have been proven wrong before when we predicted that a state court would refuse to follow a more enlightened rule of personal injury recovery. Compare Summers v. Wallace Hospital 276 F.2d 831 (9th Cir. 1960), with Owens v. White, 342 F.2d 817 (9th Cir. 1965).

(1965). Relevant to our case are 402A and comments j and k. They are set forth in the margin.[10]

---

[10] 402A. Special liability of Seller of Product for Physical Harm to User or Consumer

(1) One who sells any product in a defective condition unreasonably dangerous to the user or consumer or to his property is subject to liability for physical harm thereby caused to the ultimate user or consumer, or to his property, if

    (a) the seller is engaged in the business of selling such a product, and

    (b) it is expected to and does reach the user or consumer without substantial change in the condition in which it is sold.

(2) The rule stated in Subsection (1) applies although

    (a) the seller has exercised all possible care in the preparation and sale of his product, and

    (b) the user or consumer has not bought the product from or entered into any contractual relation with the seller.
....
    j. Directions or warning. In order to prevent the product from being unreasonably dangerous, the seller may be required to give directions or warning, on the container, as to its use. The seller may reasonably assume that those with common allergies, as for example to eggs or strawberries, will be aware of them, and he is not required to warn against them. Where, however, the product contains an ingredient to which a substantial number of the population are allergic, and the ingredient is one whose danger is not generally known, or if known is one which the consumer would reasonably not expect to find in the product, the seller is required to give warning against it, if he has knowledge, or by the application of reasonable, developed human skill and foresight should have knowledge, of the presence of the ingredient and the danger. Likewise in the case of poisonous drugs, or those unduly dangerous for other reasons, warning as to use may be required.

    But a seller is not required to warn with respect to products, or ingredients in them, which are only dangerous, or potentially so, when consumed in excessive quantity, or over a long period of time, when the danger, or potentiality of danger, is generally known and recognized. Again the dangers of alcoholic beverages are an example, as are also those of foods containing such substances as saturated

*128 The general proposition as there stated (subject to certain exceptions) is that strict liability shall attach to one who sells a product "in a defective condition, unreasonably dangerous" to the consumer.

At the outset we reject appellee's contention that the rule applies only where unreasonable danger results because of an ascertainable "defect" or "impurity" in the product, and that since this product was precisely what it was intended to be

---

fats, which may over a period of time have a deleterious effect upon the human heart.

Where warning is given, the seller may reasonably assume that it will be read and heeded; and a product bearing such a warning, which is safe for use if it is followed, is not in defective condition, nor is it unreasonably dangerous.

k. Unavoidably unsafe products. There are some products which, in the present state of human knowledge, are quite incapable of being made safe for their intended and ordinary use. These are especially common in the field of drugs. An outstanding example is the vaccine for the Pasteur treatment of rabies, which not uncommonly leads to very serious and damaging consequences when it is injected. Since the disease itself invariabily leads to a dreadful death, both the marketing and the use of the vaccine are fully justified, notwithstanding the unavoidably high degree of risk which they involve. Such a product, properly prepared, and accompanied by proper directions and warning, is not defective, nor is it unreasonably dangerous. The same is true of many other drugs, vaccines, and the like, many of which for this very reason cannot legally be sold except to physicians, or under the prescription of a physician. It is also true in particular of many new or experimental drugs as to which, because of lack of time and opportunity for sufficient medical experience, there can be no assurance of safety, or perhaps even of purity of ingredients, but such experience as there is justifies the marketing and use of the drug notwithstanding a medically recognizable risk. The seller of such products, again with the qualification that they are properly prepared and marketed, and proper warning is given, where the situation calls for it, is not to be held to strict liability for unfortunate consequences attending their use merely because he has undertaken to supply the public with an apparently useful and desirable product, attended with a known but apparently reasonable risk.

there was no such defect. The true test in a case of this kind is whether the product was unreasonably dangerous.[11]

Comment j recognizes that to prevent a product from being unreasonably dangerous, direction or warnings as to its use must be given in appropriate cases.

Comment k deals with the unavoidably unsafe product. Here the fact that a product is dangerous does not result in strict liability if, on balance, public interest demands that it be made available notwithstanding its dangerous characteristics. This situation, as the comment notes, is especially common in the field of drugs, and, in particular, new and experimental drugs. We agree with appellee that the Sabin vaccine qualifies for such treatment. As the comment stresses, however, strict liability is avoided in these situations only where sale is accompanied by proper directions and proper *129 warnings.[12] Thus we are returned to the problem of the duty to warn.

The duty seems clear where the drug's danger is directed to a foreseeable and ascertainable class of persons, such as those prone to certain allergies.[13] Such a warning constitutes a caution that certain persons should not take

---

[11] See Wade, Strict Tort Liability of Manufacturers, 19 S.W.L.J. 5, 14-15 (1965):

"The more difficult problem arises with a product which was made in the way it was intended to be made and in the condition planned and which yet proves to be dangerous. Is such an article defective? * * * In cases of this general type the phrase 'defective condition' has no independent meaning, and the attempt to use it is apt to prove misleading. The only real problem is whether the product is 'unreasonably dangerous,' because 'defective condition,' if it is to be applied at all, depends on that." See also Rapson, Products Liability Under Parallel Doctrines: Contrasts Between the Uniform Commercial Code and Strict Liability in Tort, 19 Rutgers L.Rev. 692, 702 (1965).

[12] See Prosser, supra note 3, at 808. In one sense, the lack of adequate warning is what renders the product "defective." See 2 Frumer & Friedman, Products Liability 16A(4)(e) (1967), and sources cited.

[13] E.g., Wright v. Carter Products, Inc., 244 F.2d 53 (2d Cir. 1957).

the drug; that as to certain persons it is not "fit."

There are many cases, however, particularly in the area of new drugs, where the risk, although known to exist, cannot be so narrowly limited and where knowledge does not yet explain the reason for the risk or specify those to whom it applies. It thus applies in some degree to all, or at least a significant portion, of those who take the drug. This is our case; there seems to be no certain method of isolating those adults who may be affected adversely by taking Type III Sabin vaccine.[14]

In such cases, then, the drug is fit and its danger is reasonable only if the balance is struck in favor of its use. Where the risk is otherwise known to the consumer, no problem is presented, since choice is available. Where not known, however, the drug can properly be marketed only in such fashion as to permit the striking of the balance; that is, by full disclosure of the existence and extent of the risk involved.

As comment k recognizes, human experimentation is essential with new drugs if essential knowledge ever is to be gained. No person, however, should be obliged to submit himself to such experimentation. If he is to submit it must be by his voluntary and informed choice or a choice made on his behalf by his physician.

In such cases, then, the drug is fit and its danger is reasonable only if the balance is struck in favor of its use. It can properly be marketed only in such fashion as to permit the striking of that balance; that is, by full disclosure of the existence and extent of the risk involved.

When Type III Sabin vaccine was first licensed by the Government in early 1962 and first manufactured and sold by Wyeth, there was no known or foreseeable risk involved in taking it. Thus Wyeth could not initially be expected to warn

---

[14] Such apparently was also the case in Toole v. Richardson-Merrell, Inc., 251 A.C.A. 785, 60 Cal.Rptr. 398 (Dist.Ct.App.1967), where it was held that the traditional "defect" in the product was unnecessary for recovery by a person who developed cataracts from using MER/29, a treatment for arteriosclerosis; and that "strict liability is justified on the ground that the product was marketed without proper warning of its known dangerous result." Id. at 807, 60 Cal.Rptr. at 414.

of unknown dangers. But its responsibility did not end there. When, after further experience, the danger became apparent a duty to warn attached.[15] We do not need to fix the precise point at which it attached. Certainly by March, 1963, when appellant took the vaccine, six months after the Surgeon General's first report on the subject, it was the responsibility of Wyeth to see that such warning was given.

There will, of course, be cases where the personal risk, although existent and known, is so trifling in comparison with the advantage to be gained as to be de minimis. Appellee so characterizes this case. It would approach the problem from a purely statistical point of view: less than one out a million is just not unreasonable. This approach we reject. When, in a particular case, the risk qualitatively (e.g., of death or major disability) as well as quantitatively, on balance with the end sought to be achieved, is such as to call for a true choice judgment, *130 medical or personal, the warning must be given.[16]

Appellee contends that even under such a test no true choice situation is presented here. It asserts that "common sense and knowledge of the mainstreams of human conduct would unavoidably bring one to the conclusion" that appellant would have chosen to take the risk. It says, "Simply stated that proposition is this: A man has less than one in a million chance of contracting the dreaded disease of polio if he takes the vaccine. If he does not take the vaccine his chances of contracting polio are abundantly increased."

---

[15] See Note, The Manufacturer's Duty to Warn of Dangers Involved in Use of a Product, 1967 Wash.U.L.Q. 206, 211.

[16] The purely statistical approach has been abandoned in many recent cases in the allergy field, and a duty to warn a small hypersensitive group has been found where the potential side effect of a cosmetic or drug was serious. In Wright v. Carter Products, Inc., supra note 13, the court stated that, despite the fact that only a miniscule number of users of the deodorant in question were endangered, "duties to warn are not, in all cases, measured by quantitative standards," and that a manufacturer may in some circumstances have a duty to warn "those few persons who it knows cannot apply its product without serious injury." Id. at 56, 58. Accord, Sterling Drug Inc. v. Cornish, 370 F.2d 82 (8th Cir. 1967); Gober v. Revlon, Inc., 317 F.2d 47 (4th Cir. 1963); Braun v. Roux Distrib. Co., 312 S.W.2d 758 (Mo.1958).

We do not so read the record. The Surgeon General's report of September, 1962, as we have quoted it, predicted that for the 1962 season only .9 persons over 20 years of age out of a million would contract polio from natural sources. While appellant was the father of two young children, he resided in an area that not only was not epidemic but whose immediate past history of incidence was extremely low. We have no way of knowing the extent to which either factor would affect the critical statistics. Thus appellant's risk of contracting the disease without immunization was about as great (or small) as his risk of contracting it from the vaccine. Under these circumstances we cannot agree with appellee that the choice to take the vaccine was clear.

We may note further that where the end sought is prevention of disease (and the likelihood of contracting the disease from natural sources is a relevant factor) the situation is a different one from that in which the disease has already struck and the end sought is relief or cure. Risks are far more readily taken in the latter case.

We conclude that the facts of this case imposed on the manufacturer a duty to warn the consumer (or make adequate provision for his being warned) as to the risks involved, and that failure to meet this duty rendered the drug unfit in the sense that it was thereby rendered unreasonably dangerous. Strict liability, then, attached to its sale in absence of warning.

Appellee contends that its duty to warn was met by Franklin's disclosures to the medical society. It points out that its only direct sale of vaccine was to the medical society and that it was the society's judgment and not appellee's to proceed with the clinics.

Ordinarily in the case of prescription drugs warning to the prescribing physician is sufficient.[17] In such cases the choice involved is essentially a medical one involving an assessment of medical risks in the light of the physician's knowledge of his patient's needs and susceptibilities. Further it is difficult under such circumstances for the manufacturer, by label or direct communication, to reach the

---

[17] Sterling Drug Inc. v. Cornish, supra note 16; Magee v. Wyeth Laboratories, 214 Cal.App.2d 340, 29 Cal.Rptr. 322 (1963).

consumer with a warning. A warning to the medical profession is in such cases the only effective means by which a warning could help the patient.[18]

*131 Here, however, although the drug was denominated a prescription drug it was not dispensed as such. It was dispensed to all comers at mass clinics without an individualized balancing by a physician of the risks involved. In such cases (as in the case of over-the-counter sales of nonprescription drugs[19]) warning by the manufacturer to its immediate purchaser will not suffice. The decision (that on balance and in the public interest the personal risk to the individual was worth taking) may well have been that of the medical society and not that of appellee. But just as the responsibility for choice is not one that the manufacturer can assume for all comers, neither is it one that he can allow his immediate purchaser to assume. In such cases, then, it is the responsibility of the manufacturer to see that warnings reach the consumer, either by giving warning itself or by obligating the purchaser to give warning. Here appellee knew that warnings were not reaching the consumer. Appellee had taken an active part in setting up the mass immunization clinic program for the society and well knew that the program did not make any such provision, either in advertising prior to the clinics or at the clinics themselves. On the contrary, it attempted to assure all members of the community that they should take the vaccine.

We conclude that appellee did not meet its duty to warn.

---

[18] Love v. Wolf, 226 Cal.App.2d 378, 394, 38 Cal.Rptr. 183, 192 (1964). In Wolf the profit from the sale of a drug was held admissible to show motive for alleged overpromotion of that drug to the medical profession that might be held to cancel out the effectiveness of an insert warning. Appellant claims that the trial court erred in refusing to allow him to gain, through interrogatories, evidence of Wyeth's profits on the sale of Sabin vaccine. Since we find that, in any event, the package insert did not fulfill Wyeth's obligation to warn in this case, we need not rule on this contention.

[19] Stottlemire v. Cawood, 213 F.Supp. 897, 899 (1963). The consumer may, of course, choose to sue the retailer rather than the manufacturer in such cases. See Crotty v. Shartenberg's-New Haven, Inc., 147 Conn. 460, 162 A.2d 513 (1960).

This duty does not impose an unreasonable burden on the manufacturer. When drugs are sold over the counter to all comers warnings normally can be given by proper labeling. Such method of giving warning was not available here, since the vaccine came in bottles never seen by the consumer. But other means of communication such as advertisements, posters, releases to be read and signed by recipients of the vaccine, or oral warnings were clearly available and could easily have been undertaken or prescribed by appellee.

For these reasons we hold that it was error to fail to instruct the jury, either in warranty or in tort, that appellee was strictly liable if its drug caused appellant to contract polio and if appellant's taking of the drug was without knowledge of risk.[20]

Reversed and remanded for new trial.

HAMLIN, Circuit Judge (dissenting).

I respectfully dissent.

Appellee brought to the attention of the Medical Society the report of the Surgeon General. After this, the Medical Society, which was in charge of the mass immunization program, decided to proceed and the program was thereafter under the direction of that organization. On each of the bottles containing 100 doses of that vaccine which appellee sold to the Medical Society, appellee included a printed insert containing pertinent portions of the Surgeon General's report. Under the circumstances of this case I cannot agree with the court's holding that there was as a matter of law an *132 absolute breach by appellee of its duty to warn.

---

[20] The Surgeon General's Advisory Committee on Poliomyelitis Control in 1964 reviewed 87 cases in which paralytic illness had occurred within 30 days of the taking of Sabin vaccine, of which 57 were found "compatible" with having been caused by the vaccine. These 57 cases were further subdivided into "probable" and "possible" categories. Appellant's case was placed in the "compatible-probable" group. There seems to be no method of knowing with medical certainty whether any such attack of poliomyelitis has been caused by external virus or by the vaccine. The issue of causation was properly left to the jury in the trial below, but no special verdict on this issue was returned. On remand this question remains for jury determination.

The court's instruction to the jury that there was an implied warranty on the part of appellee that the vaccine was reasonably fit for the particular purpose for which it was manufactured was proper, and the jury verdict in favor of appellee apparently found that there was no breach of that warranty.

I would affirm.

HAMLIN, Circuit Judge, would grant the petition for rehearing.

A Note on Reconsidering Cases in Chapters 1-3

After reading Chapter 4 of the Text, reconsider cases in Chapters 1-3 from the perspective of value implications of the court's lawmaking choices. In particular, read again the opinions in <u>Shackil</u>, in Chapter 2, and <u>Hustler Magazine</u>, in Chapter 3.

Supp. Ch. 4

Liability Insurance Materials

Liability Insurance Policy Provisions

First Illustration -- Personal Automobile Insurance

[The Company]

Agrees with the insured, named in the declarations made a part hereof, in consideration of the payment of the premium and in reliance upon the statements in the declarations and subject to all of the terms of this policy:

Part I -- Liability

Coverage A -- Bodily Injury Liability:
Coverage B -- Property Damage Liability: To pay on behalf of the insured all sums which the insured shall become legally obligated to pay as damages because of

    A. Bodily injury, sickness or disease, including death resulting therefrom, hereinafter called "bodily injury," sustained by any person,

    B. injury to or destruction of property, including loss of use thereof, hereinafter called "property damage";

arising out of the ownership, maintenance or use of the owned automobile or any non-owned automobile, and the company shall defend ***

* * *

EXCLUSIONS: This policy does not apply under Part I:

    * * *

    (b) to bodily injury or property damage caused intentionally by or at the direction of the insured.

    * * *

LIABILITY INSURANCE — Supp. Ch. 4

Second Illustration -- Homeowners' Insurance

AGREEMENT

We will provide the insurance described in this policy in return for the premium and compliance with all applicable provisions of this policy.

DEFINITIONS

In this policy "you" and "your" refer to the "named insured" shown in the Declaration and the spouse if a resident of the same household. "We," "us" and "our" refer to the Company providing this insurance. In addition, certain words and phrases are defined as follows:

1. "bodily injury" means bodily harm, sickness or disease, including required care, loss of services and death that results.

   * * *

2. "insured" means you and residents of your household who are:

    a. your relatives; or

    b. other persons under the age of 21 and in the care of any person named above.

   * * *

5. "occurrence" means an accident, including exposure to conditions, which results during the policy period, in

    a. bodily injury; or

    b. property damage.

   * * *

Supp. Ch. 4   **LIABILITY INSURANCE**

Third Illustration -- Lawyers Professional Liability Insurance
(CLAIMS MADE)

1. COVERAGE -- LAWYERS PROFESSIONAL LIABILITY

    The company will pay on behalf of the insured all sums which the insured shall be legally obligated to pay as damages for claims to which this insurance applies because of any act or omission of the insured, or of any other person for whose act or omission the insured is legally responsible, for which claim is first made against the insured and reported to the company during the policy period, arising out of the performance of professional services for others in the insured's profession as a lawyer.

    * * *

EXCLUSIONS

This insurance does not apply to any claim:
   (a) arising out of any dishonest, fraudulent, criminal or malicious act or omission of any insured or employee of any insured;

   * * *

   (i) arising out of any acts or omissions occurring prior to the effective date of this policy if the insured at the effective date knew or could have reasonably foreseen that such acts or omissions might be expected to be the basis of a claim or suit.

   * * *

LIABILITY INSURANCE   **Supp. Ch. 4**

Fourth Illustration -- Physicians Professional
Liability Insurance
(CLAIMS MADE)

1. COVERAGE AGREEMENTS

    The company will pay on behalf of the insured:
    COVERAGE M -- INDIVIDUAL PROFESSIONAL LIABILITY
       All sums which the insured shall be legally obligated to pay as damages because of injury to which this insurance applies caused by a medical incident, occurring subsequent to the retroactive date, for which claim is first made against the insured and reported to the company during the policy period, arising out of the practice of the insured's profession as a physician, surgeon or dentist.

    * * *

CHAPTER 5

A JUDGE'S WRITING AND SPEAKING

Exercise 5.1

Your law clerk has prepared for you the following draft Memorandum and Final Judgment in Faithful Liability Insurance Company v. Edward Edwards and The Pub, Inc., Civil Action No. 90-234, pending before you.

Rewrite or revise it as you think appropriate.

EXERCISES Supp. Ch. 5

UNITED STATES DISTRICT COURT
DISTRICT OF xxxxxxxxxxx

FAITHFUL LIABILITY)
INSURANCE COMPANY,)
   Plaintiff)
)
v.) CIVIL ACTION
) NO. 90-234
EDWARD EDWARDS, and)
THE PUB, INC.,)
   Defendants)

Memorandum
_____, 199_

This is a declaratory judgment action filed by Faithful Liability Insurance Company against the parties to a lawsuit filed by one of the defendants, Edward Edwards, against the other defendant. Edwards sued The Pub in another court on the ground that he sustained injuries as a result of the negligence of The Pub in selling and serving alcoholic beverages to an individual who thereafter struck Edwards with an automobile. Faithful seeks a declaration from this court that it is not obligated to defend or indemnify The Pub against the claims brought by Edwards against it in that suit.

At the time of the accident, The Pub was the named insured of a policy issued by Faithful. Faithful argues, however, that it is not required to defend and indemnify The Pub because liability resulting from the serving and selling of alcoholic beverages is specifically exempted from coverage in its insurance contract with The Pub. Faithful now moves for summary judgment on that basis. The Pub has filed no responsive pleadings in this case. Defendant Edwards has filed an opposition to the motion for summary judgment on two grounds. First, Edwards argues that plaintiff is not entitled to summary judgment because it has failed to submit affidavits in support of its allegations. Second, Edwards argues that the public should be able to rely on the fact that licensed liquor facilities should have insurance, and therefore certain minimum compulsory insurance should be required and insurance carriers such as the plaintiff should be held responsible for such minimum compulsory coverage.

The contract states:

This insurance does not apply: ...
(b) to <u>bodily injury</u> or <u>property damage</u> for which the <u>insured may be held liable</u>
    (1) as a person or organization engaged in the business of manufacturing, distributing, selling or serving alcoholic beverages, or
    (2) if not so engaged, as an owner or lessor of premises used for such purposes if such liability is imposed
        (i) by or because of the violation of, any statute, ordinance or regulation

pertaining to the sale, gift, distribution or use of an alcoholic beverage, or

(ii) by reason of the selling, serving or giving of any alcoholic beverage to a minor or to a person under the influence of alcohol or which causes or contributes to the intoxication of any person;

but part (ii) of this exclusion does not apply with respect to liability of the <u>insured</u> as an owner or lessor described in (2) above.

Edwards has made two claims against The Pub in the action pending in another court. Count I claims that defendant violated a statute of this state by negligently causing or allowing alcoholic beverages to be sold to an intoxicated patron. Count II alleges that the defendant was negligent in serving an intoxicated patron and then allowing the patron to operate a motor vehicle upon leaving the establishment.

This standard exemption language, although it has not been specifically addressed by courts of this state, has been upheld in a number of other states as a valid insurance exemption. <u>See, e.g.</u>, <u>Wilson</u> v. <u>United States Fidelity and Guaranty Ins. Co.</u>, 830 F.2d 588 (5th Cir. 1987); <u>United States Fidelity and Guaranty</u> v. <u>Griggs</u>, 341 Pa. Super. 286, 491 A.2d 267 (1985); <u>Stewart</u> v. <u>Bohnert's Estate</u>, 101 Cal. App.3d 978, 162 Cal. Rptr. 126 (1980); <u>Mt. Hope Inn</u> v. <u>Travelers Indemnity Co.</u>, 157 N.J. Super. 431, 384 A.2d 1159 (1978); <u>New Hampshire Ins. Co.</u> v. <u>Hillwinds Inn, Inc.</u>, 117

N.H. 350, 373 A.2d 354 (1977); <u>Marston</u> v. <u>Merchants Mutual Insurance Co.</u>, 319 A.2d 111 (Me. 1974).

The fact that public policy arguments may favor requiring those who serve liquor to have insurance for claims of the kind brought by Edwards does not give this court authority to modify the contract between these parties so as to require this particular insurance company to provide The Pub with insurance coverage it did not purchase.

Summary judgment is appropriate because there is no genuine dispute of fact that Faithful is entitled to a declaration that it is not obligated to defend or indemnify The Pub against the claims asserted by defendant Edwards.

ORDER

For the foregoing reasons, it is ORDERED:

Plaintiff's motion for summary judgment is allowed. Judgment will be entered accordingly.

/s/
United States District Judge

EXERCISES Supp. Ch. 5

UNITED STATES DISTRICT COURT
DISTRICT OF xxxxxxxxxxxx

FAITHFUL LIABILITY
INSURANCE COMPANY,
   Plaintiff

v.

EDWARD EDWARDS, and
THE PUB, INC.,
   Defendants

CIVIL ACTION
NO. 90-234

Judgment
_____, 199_

For the reasons stated in the Memorandum of this date, it is ORDERED:

(1) The Court hereby declares:

Faithful Liability Insurance Company has no duty to defend or indemnify The Pub, Inc., against the claims of Edward Edwards for (1) violation of a statute of this state by causing or allowing to be sold alcoholic beverages to an intoxicated patron, and (2) negligence in serving an intoxicated patron and allowing said patron to operate a motor vehicle upon leaving the establishment.

(2) Final judgment for plaintiff, with costs.

_____/s/_____
United States District Judge

Exercise 5.2

Ask a classmate to select for you a recently published judicial opinion that your classmate considers to be an especially good one. Select any segment of the opinion you wish to rewrite. Assume that you are a law clerk for the author of the opinion, who has asked you to try to make the opinion clearer and shorter without loss of content.

Exercise 5.3

Read Kavados v. Lorenzen, the first case in Chapter 6 of this Course Supplement, infra.

Assume that you are a law clerk to the trial judge who is trying another case almost identical on the facts to Kavados. The judge directs you to draft appropriate instructions to the jury on the meaning of the statutory phrases "act in concert" and "aid or encourage a tortious act."

CHAPTER 6

JUDGING STATUTES

KAVADAS
v.
LORENZEN

Supreme Court of North Dakota. Nov. 20, 1989.
448 N.W.2d 219

Police officer brought action against arrestee and establishment which allegedly served arrestee alcohol prior to arrest, seeking to recover for damages allegedly sustained when arrestee resisted arrest and assaulted officer. The District Court, Grand Forks County, Northeast Central Judicial District, Joel D. Medd, J., entered judgment against defendants, apportioning 75% fault to arrestee and 25% fault to establishment, and awarded costs and disbursements against defendants jointly and severally. On cross appeals by officer and establishment, the Supreme Court, Gierke, J., held that: (1) statute prohibiting imposition of joint and several liability on tort-feasors who do not act in concert does not violate equal protection; (2) requested instruction and special verdict form focusing on "in concert" language of statute were properly refused; and (3) trial court did not abuse discretion in awarding costs and disbursements from defendants jointly and severally.

Affirmed.

*220 GIERKE, Justice.

Jeffrey Kavadas appealed from a district court order denying his post-trial motion in his personal injury action against Jeffrey Lorenzen and Poor Richard's, Inc., and Poor Richard's cross-appealed from the court's decision to award Kavadas certain costs and disbursements against Lorenzen *221 and Poor Richard's jointly and severally. We affirm.

KAVADAS V. LORENZEN

Kavadas sued Lorenzen and Poor Richard's for injuries he sustained when, in the course of his employment as a Grand Forks police officer, he arrested Lorenzen for driving while under the influence of alcohol on the morning of July 16, 1987. Kavadas alleged that Lorenzen resisted the lawful arrest and assaulted him, seriously injuring his right wrist. Kavadas further alleged that, on the evening of July 15, 1987, Poor Richard's, through its employees, knowingly served Lorenzen alcoholic beverages while he was obviously intoxicated and that Poor Richard's conduct proximately caused Kavadas' injuries.

A jury found that Kavadas sustained $254,000.52 in damages and apportioned 75% fault to Lorenzen and 25% fault to Poor Richard's. Because Lorenzen had no insurance and is judgment proof, Kavadas' recovery was effectively limited under the several liability provisions of Section 32-03.2-02, N.D.C.C.,[1] to $63,500 in damages attributable to Poor Richard's.

Kavadas then moved to have the several liability provisions of Section 32-03.2-02, N.D.C.C., declared unconstitutional so that Lorenzen and Poor Richard's would be jointly and severally liable for the entire judgment. Alternatively, Kavadas moved for a new trial, contending that the trial court erred in failing to give a requested instruction entitled "acting in concert/aiding or encouraging."

The trial court denied Kavadas' motion and entered a judgment awarding Kavadas $190,500.39 from Lorenzen and $63,500.13 from Poor Richard's. The court further determined that it was "difficult, if not impossible, to delineate most of the costs and disbursements attributable to each defendant" and accordingly, except for $78.10 in clearly

---

[1] Section 32-03.2-02, N.D.C.C., provides, in part:

"32-03.2-02. Modified comparative fault.... When two or more parties are found to have contributed to the injury, the liability of each party is several only, and is not joint, and each party is liable only for the amount of damages attributable to the percentage of fault of that party, except that any persons who act in concert in committing a tortious act or aid or encourage the act, or ratifies or adopts the act for their benefit, are jointly liable for all damages attributable to their combined percentage of fault."

identifiable costs, awarded Kavadas $6,095.58 costs and disbursements against both defendants jointly and severally. Kavadas appealed, and Poor Richard's cross-appealed.

We initially consider Kavadas' claim that Section 32-03.2-02, N.D.C.C., violates the equal protection provisions of Article I, section 21, N.D. Const.[2] Under that statute plaintiffs injured by two or more tortfeasors who do not act in concert in committing a tortious act or aid or encourage the act can not recover under joint and several liability, while plaintiffs injured by two or more tortfeasors who act in concert in committing a tortious act or aid or encourage the act can recover under joint and several liability.

(1-3) Our standard of review for analyzing equal protection claims depends on the right allegedly infringed upon by the challenged legislative classification. We apply strict scrutiny to legislative classifications that are inherently suspect or infringe upon fundamental rights, and we strike down the challenged classification unless it promotes a compelling government interest and the distinction drawn is necessary to further its purpose. State ex rel. Olson v. Maxwell, 259 N.W.2d 621 (N.D.1977). If a legislative classification infringes upon important substantive rights, we apply an intermediate standard of review, and we uphold the classification if it bears a close correspondence to the legislative goals. Mund v. Rambough, 432 N.W.2d 50 (N.D.1988); Bellemare v. Gateway Builders, Inc., 420 N.W.2d 733 (N.D.1988); Hanson v. Williams County, 389 N.W.2d 319 (N.D.1986). We apply a rational basis test to legislative classifications *222 that are not inherently suspect, or do not infringe upon fundamental or important substantive rights, and we uphold the classification unless it is patently arbitrary and bears no rational relationship to a legitimate governmental purpose. Lee v. Job Service of North Dakota, 440 N.W.2d 518 (N.D.1989); Gange v. Clerk of Burleigh Co. District Court, 429 N.W.2d 429 (N.D.1988);

---

[2] Article I, section 21, N.D. Const., provides:

"No special privileges or immunities shall ever be granted which may not be altered, revoked or repealed by the legislative assembly; nor shall any citizen or class of citizens be granted privileges or immunities which upon the same terms shall not be granted to all citizens."

Kadrmas v. Dickinson Public Schools, 402 N.W.2d 897 (N.D.1987), aff'd, --- U.S. ----, 108 S.Ct. 2481, 101 L.Ed.2d 399 (1988).

Relying on Hanson v. Williams County, supra, Kavadas argues that the intermediate level of scrutiny[3] is applicable to this classification because it infringes upon a plaintiff's important substantive rights. Kavadas contends that this classification affects a plaintiff's right to recover for injuries under joint and several liability which, he asserts, is an important substantive right. Poor Richard's responds that the rational basis test applies to this case because recovery under joint and several liability does not rise to the level of an important substantive right.

In Hanson v. Williams County, supra, we applied the intermediate level of scrutiny to an equal protection challenge to Section 28-01.1-02, N.D.C.C., a products liability statute of repose. That statute precluded an action by persons who were injured by a product that was initially purchased more than ten years or manufactured more than eleven years before an injury, while permitting actions by persons who were injured within those time periods. Because that classification completely eliminated the right to sue for some injuries before they occurred, we concluded that it involved an important substantive right.

Hanson follows our equal protection cases in which we have generally applied the intermediate level of scrutiny to classifications which have completely prevented a class of injured persons from maintaining an action to recover for their injuries. Bellemare v. Gateway Builders, Inc., supra (intermediate level of scrutiny applicable to statute that prevented a class of plaintiffs from suing for damages for

---

[3] In Kadrmas v. Dickinson Public Schools, --- U.S. ----, 108 S.Ct. 2481, 101 L.Ed.2d 399 (1988), the United States Supreme Court recognized that, under the Federal Constitution, the "intermediate" or "heightened" level of scrutiny generally has not been extended beyond discriminatory classifications based on sex, illegitimacy, or "unique circumstances" like denying the children of illegal aliens free public education available to other residents. Under our dual constitutional system, our equal protection analysis under Article I, section 21, N.D. Const., is not necessarily governed by the Federal Court's analysis of the parallel Federal constitutional provision. Johnson v. Hassett, 217 N.W.2d 771 (N.D.1974).

any deficiency in the design, planning, supervision or observation of construction, or construction of an improvement to real property); Patch v. Sebelius, 320 N.W.2d 511 (N.D.1982) (intermediate level of scrutiny applicable to statute that prevented a class of plaintiffs from suing the state or a state agency); Benson v. North Dakota Workmen's Compensation Bureau, 283 N.W.2d 96 (N.D.1979) (intermediate level of scrutiny applicable to statute that excluded a class of employees from workmen's compensation); Herman v. Magnuson, 277 N.W.2d 445 (N.D.1979) (intermediate level of scrutiny applicable to statute that prevented a class of plaintiffs from suing a municipality for defective streets or bridges); Johnson v. Hassett, 217 N.W.2d 771 (N.D.1974) (intermediate level of scrutiny applicable to automobile guest statute that prohibited a class of plaintiffs from suing for ordinary negligence of host).

In contrast, we have generally applied the rational basis test to statutory classifications which involve economic or social matters and do not deprive a class of plaintiffs from access to the courts. Mauch v. Manufacturers Sales & Service, Inc., 345 N.W.2d 338 (N.D.1984) (rational basis test applicable to comparative negligence provisions of Section 9-10-07, N.D.C.C.); Law v. Maercklein, 292 N.W.2d 86 (N.D.1980) (rational basis test applicable to statute allowing only residents to participate in the Unsatisfied Judgment Fund); Tharaldson v. Unsatisfied Judgment Fund, 225 N.W.2d 39 (N.D.1974) (rational basis test applicable to statute limiting recovery from Unsatisfied Judgment Fund to $5,000 in cases in *223 which the tortfeasor can not be ascertained, while permitting a $10,000 recovery from the Fund in other cases).

(4) We believe the interest involved in this case is similar to the interests involved in cases in which we have applied the rational basis test. Although the doctrine of joint and several liability provides plaintiffs a measure of protection from insolvent tortfeasors when there are additional tortfeasors who are financially able to bear the total damages, we are not aware of any authority, and none has been cited, which suggests that that doctrine is a constitutionally mandated rule of law, immune from legislative modification or revision. The elimination of joint and several liability affects the amount of damages that an injured party may recover; however, that party is not denied access to the courts. Under this statute, an injured party is not prevented from suing the tortfeasors, obtaining a judgment, and collecting damages in proportion

to the relative share of fault of each tortfeasor. The joint and several liability doctrine thus involves allocation of the amount of damages recoverable by a class of injured persons, an issue with economic implications, and is not "a limitation upon the authority of an injured party to bring an action against the tortfeasor." Herman v. Magnuson, supra, 277 N.W.2d at 451. We conclude that the rational basis test is applicable to this equal protection challenge. See Evangelatos v. Superior Court, 246 Cal.Rptr. 629, 44 Cal.3d 1188, 753 P.2d 585 (1988) (rational basis test applicable to equal protection challenge to an initiated measure which limited a tortfeasor to several liability for noneconomic damages and allowed joint and several liability for economic damages); Beeler v. Van Cannon, 376 N.W.2d 628 (Iowa 1985) (rational basis test applicable to equal protection challenge to statute barring application of joint and several liability doctrine to defendants who were found to bear less than fifty percent of the total fault assigned to all the parties).

Accordingly, we analyze this classification under the rational basis test, which requires us to sustain it unless it is patently arbitrary and bears no rational relationship to a legitimate governmental purpose. Tharaldson v. Unsatisfied Judgment Fund, supra.

(5) Section 32-03.2-02, N.D.C.C., is part of "tort liability" modification enacted in 1987. 1987 N.D.Sess.Laws Ch. 404. A statement of legislative intent indicates that the legislative goals of this act were to "limit, clarify, and improve the method of determining and fixing responsibility for and paying of damages" and to reduce the cost and increase the availability of liability insurance. No party has asserted that these goals are not legitimate.

We believe that a statutory scheme which makes a tortfeasor's liability for damages dependent upon the degree of fault of that tortfeasor and not upon the degree of solvency of other tortfeasors is not patently arbitrary and bears a rational relationship to the legitimate legislative goal of improving "the method of determining and fixing responsibility for and paying of damages." Moreover, in our view, this legislative classification, which eliminates joint and several liability unless two or more tortfeasors act in concert in committing a tortious act or aid or encourage the act, is also rationally related to "fixing responsibility for and paying of damages." The difference in degree and type of conduct necessary to trigger the benefits of joint and several liability is rationally related to the imposition of the broader responsibility of joint and several liability for that conduct.

Kavadas nevertheless argues that the public interest is not furthered by eliminating joint and several liability for multiple tortfeasors because, under several liability, a plaintiff is denied full recovery when one or more of the tortfeasors is insolvent. However, Kavadas' argument ignores that it is a legislative function to assess public interests and, under our applicable standard of review, we do not interfere with a legislative assessment unless it is patently arbitrary and bears no rational relationship to a legitimate legislative goal. The standard necessary to invalidate this legislative classification has not been met in this case. *224 We conclude that the legislative classification in Section 32-03.2-02, N.D.C.C., is rationally related to a legitimate legislative goal of "fixing responsibility for and paying of damages" and therefore does not violate equal protection.

(6) Kavadas next argues that the trial court erred in refusing to give an instruction entitled "acting in concert/aiding or encouraging":

"A person is acting in concert with another if he knows that the other's conduct constitutes a breach of a duty and gives substantial assistance or encouragement to the other to conduct himself in that manner.

"In determining whether a person is acting in concert with another, you should consider the nature of the act encouraged, the amount of assistance given, the person's presence or absence at the time of the unlawful act, his relation to the other and his state of mind.

"If the person's assistance or encouragement is a substantial factor in the other's harming a third person, the fact that the person giving the assistance or encouragement neither foresaw nor should have foreseen the manner in which the harm occurred does not matter."

The trial court also denied part of Kavadas' requested special verdict form which asked if Poor Richard's acted "in concert with JEFFREY LORENZEN in bringing about the harm."

As previously noted, Section 32-03.2-02, N.D.C.C., allows joint liability for all damages attributable to the combined percentage of fault for tortfeasors who "act in concert in committing a tortious act or aid or encourage the act." That statutory language addresses two different types of conduct by tortfeasors, those who act in concert in committing a tortious act and those who aid or encourage a tortious act.

On appeal, Kavadas "does not contend that Poor Richards action rose to the level of acting in concert as provided in" Section 32-03.2-02, N.D.C.C. Instead, Kavadas asserts that his requested instruction should have been given because there was evidence that Poor Richard's "aided or encouraged" Lorenzen's conduct by serving him alcoholic beverages when he was obviously intoxicated. However, Kavadas' requested instruction and special verdict form only focused on the "in concert" language of Section 32-03.2-02, N.D.C.C. Kavadas did not request an instruction on "aiding or encouraging" and his requested special verdict form only asked if Poor Richard's acted "in concert" with Lorenzen. Under these circumstances, we do not believe that the trial court erred in refusing to give Kavadas' requested instruction. Moreover, we do not believe the trial court abused its discretion in denying Kavadas' motion for a new trial on the basis of the failure to give that instruction. Neither do we believe that the court erred in failing to find, as a matter of law, that Poor Richard's and Lorenzen acted in concert in committing a tortious act or that Poor Richard's aided or encouraged Lorenzen's conduct.

(7) On its cross-appeal, Poor Richard's contends that the trial court erred in awarding Kavadas $6,095.58 in costs and disbursements from the defendants jointly and severally. Poor Richard's argues that because the defendants were severally liable for Kavadas' damages, the taxing of costs and disbursements should have been based upon the percentage of fault attributable to each defendant. Poor Richard's also argues that some of the costs and disbursements taxed by the trial court were unreasonable and unnecessary.

It is well established that the allowance of reasonable and necessary costs and disbursements is within the discretion of the trial court and will not be overturned on appeal absent an abuse of discretion. E.g., Richter v. Jones, 378 N.W.2d 209 (N.D.1985); Keller v. Vermeer Manufacturing Co., 360 N.W.2d 502 (N.D.1984); Moser v. Wilhelm, 300 N.W.2d 840 (N.D.1980). We have defined an abuse of discretion as action that is unreasonable, arbitrary, or unconscionable. E.g., Moser v. Wilhelm, supra.

Although a trial court may award costs and disbursements based upon the percentage *225 of fault attributable to the parties (see Craft Tool & Die Co., Inc. v. Payne, 385 N.W.2d 24 (Minn.Ct.App.1986)), no unreasonable, arbitrary, or unconscionable conduct has been shown in the trial court's decision to award Kavadas costs and disbursements from the defendants jointly and severally. Moreover, after reviewing the contested costs and disbursements, we conclude that the trial court did not abuse its discretion in determining that those costs and disbursements were reasonable and necessary.

In accordance with this opinion, the order and judgment are affirmed.

ERICKSTAD, C.J., VANDE WALLE and MESCHKE, JJ., and VERNON R. PEDERSON, Surrogate Justice, concur.

VERNON R. PEDERSON, Surrogate Justice, sitting in place of LEVINE, J., disqualified.

GULDEN
v.
CROWN ZELLERBACH CORPORATION

United States Court of Appeals, Ninth Circuit.
890 F.2d 195

Argued and Submitted Nov. 1, 1988.
Decided Nov. 24, 1989.

WORKERS' COMPENSATION: ordering clean up of PCBs without protective clothing could fall within intentional injury exception.

Employees who had been ordered to finish cleanup of PCB spill on their hands and knees without protective clothing sued employer alleging battery, and one of them asserted fraud claims. Summary judgment for employer was granted by the United States District Court for the District of Oregon, Helen J. Frye and James A. Redden, JJ., and employees appealed. The Court of Appeals, James R. Browning, Circuit Judge, held that: (1) there was issue of fact, precluding summary judgment, as to whether employer's conduct showed deliberate intention to injure within exception to exclusive remedy provision of Oregon workers' compensation law, and (2) fraud claim was not preempted by the Labor Management Relations Act.

Reversed and remanded.

*196 Appeal from the United States District Court for the District of Oregon.

Before BROWNING, TANG and FARRIS, Circuit Judges.

JAMES R. BROWNING, Circuit Judge:

A transformer failure released a toxic level of polychlorinated biphenyls (PCBs) onto the floor of Crown Zellerbach's mill in West Linn, Oregon. After three attempts by hazardous waste specialists failed to reduce the PCB level to nontoxic levels, Crown Zellerbach ordered employees Robert Gulden and Gregory Steele to finish the cleanup by scrubbing the floor while on their hands and knees without protective clothing. Both workers acquired body levels of PCBs beyond that considered safe. They filed separate diversity-based suits in federal district court. The district court granted summary judgment to Crown Zellerbach on Gulden's and Steele's causes of action, holding their battery claims to be preempted by the Oregon workers' compensation scheme. The court rejected Steele's fraud claim as preempted by section 301 of the Labor Management Relations Act.[1] We consolidated Gulden's and Steele's appeals and reverse.

I.

The district court granted summary judgment for Crown Zellerbach on Gulden's and Steele's causes of action for battery on the ground there was no evidence Crown Zellerbach intended to injure Gulden and Steele and therefore workers' compensation was their exclusive remedy. Viewing the evidence in the light most favorable to Gulden and Steele, we conclude a reasonable jury could find Crown Zellerbach "had a deliberate intention to injure (Gulden and Steele) or someone else and that (they were) in fact injured as a result of that deliberate intention." Duk Hwan Chung v. Fred Meyer, Inc., 276 Or. 809, 556 P.2d 683, 685 (1976); see Or.Rev.Stat. section 656.156(2).

(1) A jury could conclude that coming into contact with PCBs at a strength 500 times Environmental Protection Agency standards--sufficient to produce a body level of PCBs six-to-ten times higher than normal and to trigger serious health concerns--constituted an injury. See Bakker v. Baza'r, Inc., 275 Or. 245, 551 P.2d 1269, 1271 & 1273-74 (1976) (harmful contact constitutes battery).

(2, 3) Under Oregon law, a jury could conclude that the intention to injure--in this case, to expose Gulden and Steele to toxic levels of PCB--was deliberate where the employer had an opportunity to weigh the consequences and to make a conscious *197 choice among possible courses of action. See Lusk v. Monaco Motor Homes, Inc., 97 Or.App. 182, 775 P.2d 891, 894 (1989);[2] see also Weis v. Allen, 147

---

[1] The district court also granted summary judgment against Gulden's fraud claim, a judgment from which Gulden does not appeal.

[2] There is no merit in Crown Zellerbach's contention that we should not consider Lusk to be supplemental authority because it was cited to us after briefing and "does not announce a departure from Oregon law." Fed.R.App.P. 28(j) allows a party to "promptly advise" this court "(w)hen pertinent and significant authorities come to the attention of a party

Or. 670, 35 P.2d 478, 482 (1934); Palmer v. BiMart Co., 92 Or.App. 470, 758 P.2d 888, 891-92 (1988). Here, a jury could conclude that Crown Zellerbach made a conscious choice to injure Gulden and Steele based on the following factors: (1) Crown Zellerbach ordered Gulden's and Steele's contact with toxic levels of PCBs without any protective clothing; (2) Crown Zellerbach ordered that contact to continue not for just a short period but for a period of five days; (3) during this five-day period, Crown Zellerbach knew that Gulden's and Steele's clothing was soaked with PCBs; (4) Crown Zellerbach had been warned that the concentration of PCBs greatly exceeded levels authorized by the Environmental Protection Agency standards; and (5) Crown Zellerbach assigned the task of cleanup to two temporary workers unfamiliar with such work rather than contracting with specialists as it had in the past.

It is true that Crown Zellerbach offered evidence that would support an inference that it did not intentionally injure Gulden and Steele by exposing them to toxic levels of PCBs, but that does not justify summary judgment in its favor. As the Oregon Court of Appeals recently explained:

> Here, a jury could infer, from all the circumstances, that defendant failed to provide (safety equipment) _because_ it wished to injure plaintiff.... A specific intent to produce injury is not the only permissible inference to be drawn from defendant's apparent obstinacy, but it is one that a jury should be permitted to consider. It is for the finder of fact, not the court on summary judgment, to determine what inferences to draw. Summary judgment is particularly inappropriate where the inferences which the parties seek to have drawn deal with questions of motive, intent and subjective feelings and reactions.

Lusk, 775 P.2d at 895 (quotations, citations and footnote omitted) (emphasis in original).

(4) Crown Zellerbach relies on several cases to establish that Oregon courts strictly construe the deliberate intention exception. See Duk Hwan Chung, 556 P.2d at 683; Caline v. Maede, 239 Or. 239, 396 P.2d 694 (1964); Heikkila v. Ewen

---

after the party's brief has been filed, or after oral argument but before decision." Lusk is such an authority.

Transfer Co., 135 Or. 631, 297 P. 373 (1931); Jenkins v. Carman Mfg. Co., 155 P. 703 (Or.1916). We agree the exception is strictly construed, but none of these cases prevents a plaintiff from maintaining a cause of action against an employer where the evidence is sufficient to support an inference the employer deliberately instructed an employee to injure himself. In all the cases cited by Crown Zellerbach, workers' compensation was held to be the exclusive remedy because the only inference that could be drawn from the evidence was that the employer's actions constituted "'mere carelessness, recklessness, or negligence.'" Duk Hwan Chung, 556 P.2d at 685 (quoting Heikkila, 297 P. at 374). In Jenkins, for example, the plaintiff was injured by improperly maintained machinery, 155 P. at 704; in Heikkila, by a truck with defective brakes, 297 P. at 373. The cases relied upon by Crown Zellerbach were distinguished on this ground by the Oregon Supreme Court in Weis, 35 P.2d at 482, and the Oregon Court of Appeals in Lusk, 775 P.2d at 894-95.

In contrast, Gulden and Steele have alleged facts which, if true, would support an inference that although Crown Zellerbach was aware that contact with the PCBs would injure Gulden and Steele, Crown Zellerbach nonetheless ordered the two workers to perform their task in a manner requiring them to initiate and maintain contact with the PCBs. An inference from these facts of deliberate intention to injure *198 Gulden and Steele--that is, to expose them to toxic levels of PCBs--would fall easily within the strictest construction of section 656.156(2).[3]

II.

The district court granted summary judgment for Crown Zellerbach on Steele's state law fraud claim on the ground this claim was preempted by section 301 of the Labor Management Relations Act.

---

[3] The district court believed its finding of no evidence of intent compelled the court to strike that portion of Steele's fraud claim alleging that Crown Zellerbach's failure to warn of the risks of PCB exposure constituted intentional infliction of injury. Since we reverse the district court's original finding that the evidence was insufficient to defeat summary judgment on the issue of intent, we also reverse the district court's grant of Crown Zellerbach's motion to strike based on the original finding.

(5) Recent Supreme Court opinions establish two bases upon which a state-law claim may be preempted by section 301. First, section 301 may preempt a state claim "on the basis of the subject matter of the law in question," Lingle v. Norge Div. of Magic Chef, Inc., 486 U.S. 399, 108 S.Ct. 1877, 1883, 100 L.Ed.2d 410 (1988), as where the "'claims (are) founded directly on rights created by collective-bargaining agreements,'" id. 108 S.Ct. at 1884 n. 10 (quoting Caterpillar Inc. v. Williams, 482 U.S. 386, 394, 107 S.Ct. 2425, 2430, 96 L.Ed.2d 318 (1987)). Second, where the right is created by state law and not by the collective-bargaining agreement, a claim based upon that right is preempted "if (the application of state law) requires the interpretation of a collective-bargaining agreement." Id. 108 S.Ct. at 1885; see Caterpillar Inc., 482 U.S. at 394, 107 S.Ct. at 2430 ("Section 301 governs claims ... 'substantially dependent on analysis of a collective-bargaining agreement.'") (quoting Electrial Workers v. Hechler, 481 U.S. 851, 859 n. 3, 107 S.Ct. 2161, 2166 n. 3, 95 L.Ed.2d 791 (1987)).

Accordingly, if, as Steele asserts, his claim is neither based upon Crown Zellerbach's collective-bargaining agreement nor dependent upon an interpretation of that agreement, it is not preempted.[4]

(6) Steele contends that ordering him to clean the PCB spill without warning him of the hazards inherent in that task worked a fraud upon him because Oregon law creates a right to be warned of the health and safety risks posed by the cleanup independent of any rights conferred under the collective-bargaining agreement. The district court held Oregon law did not confer such a right because Or.Rev.Stat. section 654.196, which codified the "right to know," was enacted in 1985, after the incident at issue. Long before the "right to know" was codified, however, Oregon courts had held employers liable for breach of an employee's right to be "warned of latent dangers incident to his service." Voshall v. Northern Pac. Terminal Co., 116 Or. 237, 240 P.

---

[4] We reject Steele's assertion that Farmer v. United Brotherhood of Carpenters, 430 U.S. 290, 97 S.Ct. 1056, 51 L.Ed.2d 338 (1977), precludes section 301 preemption of his fraud claim. Farmer does not apply to section 301 cases. See Vincent v. Trend W. Technical Corp., 828 F.2d 563, 565 (9th Cir.1987).

891, 893 (1925); see also, e.g., Ferrari v. Beaver Hill Coal Co., 102 P. 1016, 1021-22 (Or.1909). Since Steele's claim rests upon state law and not upon the collective-bargaining agreement, it is not preempted because of its subject matter.

The district court held Steele's claim was preempted because "(e)xamination of plaintiff's claim will require reference to the collective bargaining agreement on several points." The test is somewhat more restrictive. "'(N)ot every dispute ... tangentially involving a provision of a collective-bargaining agreement is preempted by section 301.'" Lingle, 108 S.Ct. at 1885 n. 12 (quoting Allis-Chalmers Corp. v. Lueck, 471 U.S. 202, 211, 105 S.Ct. 1904, 1911, 85 L.Ed.2d 206 (1985)). Rather, Steele's claim is preempted only if it "turn(s) on any collective-bargaining interpretation." Id. 108 S.Ct. at 1881 n. 5.

*199 Neither of the references to the collective-bargaining agreement identified by the district court requires preemption.

The district court held Steele's claim required the court "to look to the agreement to determine what assignments of work defendant was permitted to make." This was error; Steele's claim does not "turn on" the job assignment provisions in the collective-bargaining agreement. All Steele need prove to succeed on his fraud claim is that Oregon law conveyed an independent right to be warned; that Crown Zellerbach's failure to warn Steele of these risks constituted a fraudulent omission upon which Steele relied to his detriment by agreeing to perform the work for less than its true value;[5] and that Steele sustained damage measured by the normal cost to employers of convincing forewarned employees to assume such a risk. See Complaint 11-20. None of these elements depends upon an interpretation of the job assignment provisions in Crown Zellerbach's collective-bargaining agreement.

The district court also held that calculation of the damages Steele seeks may require interpretating the wage scale established by the collective-bargaining agreement. Again, it would not follow that Steele's claim is preempted.

---

[5] Whether or not this actually constitutes fraud under Oregon law is irrelevant for purposes of this appeal. Only the preemption issue is before us.

As the Supreme Court noted in Lingle:

> A collective-bargaining agreement may, of course, contain information such as rate of pay and other economic benefits that might be helpful in determining the damages to which a worker prevailing in a state law suit is entitled. Although federal law would govern the interpretation of the agreement to determine the proper damages, the underlying state law claim, not otherwise pre-empted, would stand. Thus, as a general proposition, a state law claim may depend for its resolution upon both the interpretation of a collective-bargaining agreement and a separate state law analysis that does not turn on the agreement. In such a case, federal law would govern the interpretation of the agreement, but the separate state law analysis would not be thereby preempted.

108 S.Ct. at 1885 n. 12 (citation omitted).

REVERSED and REMANDED.

CHAPTER 7

JUDGING IN PRETRIAL PROCEEDINGS

HEILEMAN BREWING CO., INC.
v.
JOSEPH OAT CORPORATION

United States Court of Appeals, Seventh Circuit.
871 F.2d 648

Argued May 20, 1987.
Rehearing En Banc Sept. 27, 1988.
Decided March 27, 1989.

PRETRIAL PROCEDURE: federal district court could order party represented by counsel to personally appear at pretrial conference.

In disputes over waste water treatment system for waste water treatment plant, the United States District Court for the Western District of Wisconsin, Barbara B. Crabb, Chief Judge, 107 F.R.D. 275, sanctioned corporate defendant for failing to send corporate representative to settlement conference as ordered and appeal was taken. The Court of Appeals, Manion, Circuit Judge, 848 F.2d 1415, reversed. On rehearing en banc, the Court of Appeals, Kanne, Circuit Judge, held that: (1) district court was entitled to order represented litigant to appear before it in person at pretrial conference for purpose of discussing posture and settlement of case, and (2) district court was entitled to impose sanctions upon corporation for failing to comply with such order.

Affirmed.

Posner, Circuit Judge, filed dissenting opinion.

Coffey, Circuit Judge, filed dissenting opinion in which Easterbrook, Ripple, and Manion, Circuit Judges, joined.

Easterbrook, Circuit Judge, filed dissenting opinion in which Posner, Coffey and Manion, Circuit Judges, joined.

Ripple, Circuit Judge, filed dissenting opinion in which Coffey, Circuit Judge, joined.

Manion, Circuit Judge, filed dissenting opinion in which Coffey, Easterbrook and Ripple, Circuit Judges, joined.

*650 Before BAUER, Chief Judge, CUMMINGS, WOOD, Jr., CUDAHY, POSNER, COFFEY, FLAUM, EASTERBROOK, RIPPLE, MANION and KANNE, Circuit Judges.

KANNE, Circuit Judge.

May a federal district court order litigants--even those represented by counsel--to appear before it in person at a pretrial conference for the purpose of discussing the posture and settlement of the litigants' case? After reviewing the Federal Rules of Civil Procedure and federal district courts' inherent authority to manage and control the litigation before them, we answer this question in the affirmative and conclude that a district court may sanction a litigant for failing to comply with such an order.

I. BACKGROUND

A federal magistrate ordered Joseph Oat Corporation to send a "corporate representative with authority to settle" to a pretrial conference to discuss disputed factual and legal issues and the possibility of settlement. Although counsel for Oat Corporation appeared, accompanied by another attorney who was authorized to speak on behalf of the principals of the corporation, no principal or corporate representative personally attended the conference. The court determined that the failure of Oat Corporation to send a principal of the corporation to the pretrial conference violated its order. Consequently, the district court imposed a sanction of $5,860.01 upon Oat Corporation pursuant to Federal Rule of Civil Procedure 16(f). This amount represented the costs and attorneys' fees of the opposing parties attending the conference.

II. THE APPEAL

Oat Corporation appeals, claiming that the district court did not have the authority to order litigants represented by counsel to appear at the pretrial settlement conference. Specifically, Oat Corporation contends that, by negative implication, the language of Rule 16(a)(5) prohibits a district court from directing represented litigants to attend pretrial conferences.[1] That is, because Rule 16 expressly refers to "attorneys for the parties and any unrepresented parties" in introductory paragraph (a), a district court may not go beyond that language to devise procedures which direct the pretrial appearance of parties represented by counsel. Consequently, Oat Corporation concludes that the court lacked the authority to order the pretrial attendance of its corporate representatives and, even if the court possessed such authority, the court abused its discretion to exercise that power in this case. Finally, Oat Corporation argues that the court abused its discretion to enter sanctions.

A. Authority to Order Attendance

First, we must address Oat Corporation's contention that a federal district court lacks the authority to order litigants who are represented by counsel to appear at a pretrial conference. Our analysis requires us to review the Federal Rules of Civil Procedure and district courts' inherent authority to manage the progress of litigation.

Rule 16 addresses the use of pretrial conferences to formulate and narrow issues for trial as well as to discuss means for dispensing with the need for costly and unnecessary litigation. As we stated in Link v. Wabash R.R., 291 F.2d 542, 547 (7th Cir.1961), aff'd, 370 U.S. 626, 82 S.Ct. 1386, 8 L.Ed.2d 734 (1962):

---

[1] Rule 16(a)(5) provides:

(a) Pretrial Conferences; Objectives. In any action, the court may in its discretion direct the attorneys for the parties and any unrepresented parties to appear before it for a conference or conferences before trial for such purposes as
.....
(5) facilitating the settlement of the case.

Fed.R.Civ.P. 16(a)(5).

Pre-trial procedure has become an integrated part of the judicial process on the *651 trial level. Courts must be free to use it and to control and enforce its operation. Otherwise, the orderly administration of justice will be removed from control of the trial court and placed in the hands of counsel. We do not believe such a course is within the contemplation of the law.

The pretrial settlement of litigation has been advocated and used as a means to alleviate overcrowded dockets, and courts have practiced numerous and varied types of pretrial settlement techniques for many years. See, e.g., Manual for Complex Litigation 2d, sections 21.1-21.4 (1985); Federal Judicial Center, Settlement Strategies for Federal District Judges (1988); Federal Judicial Center, The Judge's Role in the Settlement of Civil Suits (1977) (presented at a seminar for newly-appointed judges); Federal Judicial Center, The Role of the Judge in the Settlement Process (1977). Since 1983, Rule 16 has expressly provided that settlement of a case is one of several subjects which should be pursued and discussed vigorously during pretrial conferences.[2]

(1) The language of Rule 16 does not give any direction to the district court upon the issue of a court's authority to order litigants who are represented by counsel to appear for pretrial proceedings. Instead, Rule 16 merely refers to the participation of trial advocates--attorneys of record and pro se litigants. However, the Federal Rules of Civil Procedure do not completely describe and limit the power of the federal courts. HMG Property Investors, Inc. v. Parque Indus. Rio Canas, Inc., 847 F.2d 908, 915 (1st Cir.1988) (citations omitted).

The concept that district courts exercise procedural

---

[2] Rule 16(c)(7) states:

(c) Subjects to be Discussed at Pretrial Conferences. The participants at any conference under this rule may consider and take action with respect to
....
(7) the possibility of settlement or the use of extrajudicial procedures to resolve the dispute;....

Fed.R.Civ.P. 16(c)(7).

authority outside the explicit language of the rules of civil procedure is not frequently documented, but valid nevertheless. Brockton Sav. Bank v. Pete, Marwick, Mitchell & Co., 771 F.2d 5, 11 (1st Cir.1985), cert. denied, 475 U.S. 1018, 106 S.Ct. 1204, 89 L.Ed.2d 317 (1986). The Supreme Court has acknowledged that the provisions of the Federal Rules of Civil Procedure are not intended to be the exclusive authority for actions to be taken by district courts. Link v. Wabash R.R., 370 U.S. 626, 82 S.Ct. 1386, 8 L.Ed.2d 734 (1962).

In Link, the Supreme Court noted that a district court's ability to take action in a procedural context may be grounded in "'inherent power,' governed not by rule or statute but by the control necessarily vested in courts to manage their own affairs so as to achieve the orderly and expeditious disposition of cases." 370 U.S. at 630-31, 82 S.Ct. at 1389 (footnotes omitted).[3] This authority likewise forms the basis for continued development of procedural techniques designed to make the operation of the court more efficient, to preserve the integrity of the judicial process, and to control courts' dockets.[4] Because the rules *652 form

---

[3] The Supreme Court has long held that "the inherent powers of federal courts are those which 'are necessary to the exercise of all others.'" Roadway Express, Inc. v. Piper, 447 U.S. 752, 764, 100 S.Ct. 2455, 2463, 65 L.Ed.2d 488 (1980) (quoting United States v. Hudson & Goodwin, 7 Cranch 32, 34, 11 U.S. 32, 3 L.Ed. 259 (1812)).

[4] See Newman-Green, Inc. v. Alfonzo-Larrain R., 854 F.2d 916, 921-22 (7th Cir.1988) (en banc) (court discussing examples of specific procedures, such as the power to punish for contempt, power to sanction persons who file frivolous pleadings, power to determine whether there is jurisdiction), cert. granted, --- U.S. ----, 109 S.Ct. 781, 102 L.Ed.2d 773; Strandell v. Jackson County, 838 F.2d 884, 886 (7th Cir.1988); Thompson v. Housing Auth. of Los Angeles, 782 F.2d 829, 831 (9th Cir.), cert. denied, 479 U.S. 829, 107 S.Ct. 112, 93 L.Ed.2d 60 (1986); Halaco Eng'g Co. v. Costle, 843 F.2d 376, 380 (9th Cir.1988) (court stating that the Supreme Court has recognized that a district court has inherent authority to impose sanctions for discovery abuses which may not be a technical violation of discovery rules).

The practice of some district judges requiring represented parties to appear in person (or by corporate representative) has been part and parcel of such settlement conferences for many years. See In re LaMarre, 494 F.2d 753, 756 (6th Cir.1974) (court stating that it is well within

and shape certain aspects of a court's inherent powers, yet allow the continued exercise of that power where discretion should be available, the mere absence of language in the federal rules specifically authorizing or describing a particular judicial procedure should not, and does not, give rise to a negative implication of prohibition. See Link, 370 U.S. at 629-30, 82 S.Ct. at 1388;[5] see also Fed.R.Civ.P. 83 ("In all cases not provided for by rule, the district judges and magistrates may regulate their practice in any manner not inconsistent with these rules or those of the district in which they act.").

(2) Obviously, the district court, in devising means to control cases before it, may not exercise its inherent authority in a manner inconsistent with rule or statute. As we stated in Strandell v. Jackson County, 838 F.2d 884, 886 (7th Cir.1988), such power should "be exercised in a manner that is in harmony with the Federal Rules of Civil Procedure." This means that "where the rules directly mandate a specific procedure <u>to the exclusion of others</u>, inherent authority is proscribed." Landau & Cleary, Ltd. v. Hribar Trucking, Inc., 867 F.2d 996, 1002 (7th Cir.1989) (emphasis added).

In this case, we are required to determine whether a court's power to order the pretrial appearance of litigants who are represented by counsel is inconsistent with, or in derogation of, Rule 16. We must remember that Rule 1 states, with unmistakable clarity, that the Federal Rules of Civil Procedure "shall be construed to secure the just, speedy, and

---

the scope of a district court's authority to compel the appearance of a party's insurer at a pretrial conference and to enforce the order).

[5] In Link, plaintiff's counsel, who was aware of a pretrial conference, deliberately failed to attend the conference. The district court dismissed the suit even though the Federal Rules of Civil Procedure did not expressly provide for it. Our court recognized the district court's inherent authority to do so and found that it was not an abuse of discretion to dismiss the lawsuit. "Courts may exercise their inherent powers and invoke dismissal as a sanction in situations involving disregard by parties of orders, rules, or settings." Link, 291 F.2d at 546 (citations omitted). The Supreme Court affirmed this rationale. Link, 370 U.S. at 627, 82 S.Ct. at 1387, 8 L.Ed.2d 734 (1962).

inexpensive determination of every action." This language explicitly indicates that the federal rules are to be liberally construed. Cf. Hickman v. Taylor, 329 U.S. 495, 507, 67 S.Ct. 385, 392, 91 L.Ed. 451 (1947). There is no place in the federal civil procedural system for the proposition that rules having the force of statute, though in derogation of the common law, are to be strictly construed. C. Wright & A. Miller, Federal Practice and Procedure: Civil 2d section 1029 (1987).

"(The) spirit, intent, and purpose (of Rule 16) is broadly remedial, allowing courts to actively manage the preparation of cases for trial." In re Baker, 744 F.2d 1438, 1440 (10th Cir.1984) (en banc), cert. denied, 471 U.S. 1014, 105 S.Ct. 2016, 85 L.Ed.2d 299 (1985). Rule 16 is not designed as a device to restrict or limit the authority of the district judge in the conduct of pretrial conferences. As the Tenth Circuit Court of Appeals sitting en banc stated in Baker, "the spirit and purpose of the amendments to Rule 16 always have been within the inherent power of the courts to manage their affairs as an independent constitutional branch of government." Id. at 1441 (citations omitted).

(3) We agree with this interpretation of Rule 16. The wording of the rule and the accompanying commentary make plain that the entire thrust of the amendment to Rule 16 was to urge judges to make wider use of their powers and to manage actively their dockets from an early stage. We therefore conclude that our interpretation of Rule 16 to allow district courts to order represented parties to appear at pretrial settlement conferences merely represents another application of a district judge's inherent authority to preserve the efficiency, and more importantly the integrity, of the judicial process.

To summarize, we simply hold that the action taken by the district court in this case constituted the proper use of inherent authority to aid in accomplishing the purpose *653 and intent of Rule 16. We reaffirm the notion that the inherent power of a district judge-derived from the very nature and existence of his judicial office--is the broad field over which the Federal Rules of Civil Procedure are applied.[6] Inherent authority remains the means by which

---

[6] The Federal Rules of Civil Procedure are not the only set of rules grounded in the district courts' inherent authority. Circumstances not explicitly authorized in the Federal Rules of Evidence such as in limine

district judges deal with circumstances not proscribed or specifically addressed by rule or statute, but which must be addressed to promote the just, speedy, and inexpensive determination of every action.

B. Exercise of Authority to Order Attendance

Having determined that the district court possessed the power and authority to order the represented litigants to appear at the pretrial settlement conference,[7] we now must examine whether the court abused its discretion to issue such an order.

(4, 5) At the outset, it is important to note that a district court cannot coerce settlement. Kothe v. Smith, 771 F.2d 667, 669 (2d Cir.1985).[8] In this case, considerable concern has been generated because the court ordered "corporate representatives with authority to settle" to attend the conference. In our view, "authority to settle," when used in the context of this case, means that the "corporate representative" attending the pretrial conference was required to hold a position within the corporate entity allowing him to speak definitively and to commit the corporation to a particular position in the litigation. We do not view "authority to settle" as a requirement that corporate representatives must come to court willing to settle on someone else's terms, but only that they come to court in order to consider the possibility of settlement.

---

rulings are derived from the district court's inherent authority to manage the course of trials. See Luce v. United States, 469 U.S. 38, 41 n. 4, 105 S.Ct. 460, 463 n. 4, 83 L.Ed.2d 443 (1984) (citations omitted).

[7] The district court had authorized the magistrate to resolve all pretrial matters pursuant to 28 U.S.C. section 636(b)(1)(A).

[8] Likewise, a court cannot compel parties to stipulate to facts. J.F. Edwards Constr. Co. v. Anderson Safeway Guard Rail Corp., 542 F.2d 1318 (7th Cir.1976) (per curiam). Nor can a court compel litigants to participate in a nonbinding summary jury trial. Strandell, 838 F.2d at 887. In the same vein, a court cannot force a party to engage in discovery. Identiseal Corp. v. Positive Identification Sys., Inc., 560 F.2d 298 (7th Cir.1977).

As Chief Judge Crabb set forth in her decision which we now review:

> There is no indication ... that the magistrate's order contemplated requiring Joseph Oat ... to agree to any particular form of settlement or even to agree to settlement at all. The only requirement imposed by the magistrate was that the representative (of Oat Corporation) be present with full authority to settle, should terms for settlement be proposed that were acceptable to (Oat Corporation).

G. Heileman Brewing Co., Inc. v. Joseph Oat Corporation, 107 F.R.D. 275, 276-77 (1985).

If this case represented a situation where Oat Corporation had sent a corporate representative and was sanctioned because that person refused to make an offer to pay money—that is, refused to submit to settlement coercion—we would be faced with a decidely different issue—a situation we would not countenance.

The Advisory Committee Notes to Rule 16 state that "(a)lthough it is not the purpose of Rule 16(b)(7) to impose settlement negotiations on unwilling litigants, it is believed that providing a neutral forum for discussing (settlement) might foster it." Fed.R.Civ.P. 16 advisory committee's note, subdivision (c) (1983). These Notes clearly draw a distinction between being required to attend a settlement conference and being required to participate in settlement negotiations. Thus, under the scheme of pretrial settlement conferences, the corporate representative remains free, on behalf of the corporate entity, to propose terms of *654 settlement independently—but he may be required to state those terms in a pretrial conference before a judge or magistrate.

(6) As an alternative position, Oat Corporation argues that the court abused its discretion to order corporate representatives of the litigants to attend the pretrial settlement conference. Oat Corporation determined that because its business was a "going concern":

> It would be unreasonable for the magistrate to require the president of that corporation to leave his business (in Camden, New Jersey) to travel to Madison, Wisconsin, to participate in a settlement conference. The expense and burden on the part of Joseph Oat to

comply with this order was clearly unreasonable.

Consequently, Oat Corporation believes that the district court abused its authority.

We recognize, as did the district court, that circumstances could arise in which requiring a corporate representative (or any litigant) to appear at a pretrial settlement conference would be so onerous, so clearly unproductive, or so expensive in relation to the size, value, and complexity of the case that it might be an abuse of discretion. Moreover, "(b)ecause inherent powers are shielded from direct democratic controls, they must be exercised with restraint and discretion." Roadway Express, Inc. v. Piper, 447 U.S. 752, 764, 100 S.Ct. 2455, 2463, 65 L.Ed.2d 488 (1980) (citation omitted). However, the facts and circumstances of this case clearly support the court's actions to require the corporate representatives of the litigants to attend the pretrial conference personally.

This litigation involved a claim for $4 million--a claim which turned upon the resolution of complex factual and legal issues.[9] The litigants expected the trial to last from one to three months and all parties stood to incur substantial

---

[9] G. Heileman Brewing Company hired RME Associates, Inc., a consulting firm, to build a waste water treatment plant at Heileman's brewery in LaCrosse, Wisconsin. Subsequently, RME entered into a contract with Joseph Oat Corporation whereby Oat Corporation agreed to design, engineer, construct and test the system. Oat Corporation was the exclusive licensee in the United States for the system's developer, N.V. Centrale Suicker Maatschappij (CSM), a Dutch corporation.

A contract dispute arose between Oat Corporation, Heileman, and RME involving the malfunctioning of the waste water treatment system. In December, 1982, Oat Corporation initiated federal diversity litigation against Heileman and RME in New Jersey. RME counterclaimed. The case was transferred to the court below. RME then joined CSM as a third-party defendant. On the same day, Heileman filed an action in Wisconsin state court against Oat Corporation and RME. RME cross-claimed against Oat Corporation and counter-claimed against Heileman.

In the early phase of trial preparation, Heileman and Oat Corporation agreed to withdraw all claims between them. In addition, Oat Corporation dismissed its complaint against RME. After these events, the lawsuit consisted of RME's claims against Oat Corporation and CSM.

legal fees and trial expenses. This trial also would have preempted a large segment of judicial time--not an insignificant factor. Thus, because the stakes were high, we do not believe that the burden of requiring a corporate representative to attend a pretrial settlement conference was out of proportion to the benefits to be gained, not only by the litigants but also by the court.

Additionally, the corporation did send an attorney, Mr. Fitzpatrick, from Philadelphia, Pennsylvania to Madison, Wisconsin to "speak for" the principals of the corporation. It is difficult to see how the expenses involved in sending Mr. Fitzpatrick from Philadelphia to Madison would have greatly exceeded the expenses involved in sending a corporate representative from Camden to Madison. Consequently, we do not think the expenses and distance to be traveled are unreasonable in this case.

Furthermore, no objection to the magistrate's order was made prior to the date the pretrial conference resumed. Oat Corporation contacted the magistrate's office concerning the order's requirements and was advised of the requirements now at issue. However, Oat Corporation never objected to its terms, either when it was issued or when Oat Corporation sought clarification. Consequently, Oat Corporation was left with only one course of action: it had to comply fully with the letter and *655 intent of the order and argue about its reasonableness later.[10]

We thus conclude that the court did not abuse its authority and discretion to order a representative of the Oat

---

[10]. In Malone v. United States Postal Serv., 833 F.2d 128 (9th Cir.1987), cert. denied, --- U.S. ----, 109 S.Ct. 59, 102 L.Ed.2d 37 (1988), the Ninth Circuit addressed the same general issue we confront here. Malone appealed the imposition of the sanction of dismissal. Malone argued that the pretrial order was invalid and thus her noncompliance was justified. Id. at 133. Specifically, Malone claimed that the order of dismissal was erroneous since the court lacked the authority to require Malone to supply a list of questions and answers for all potential witnesses. The Ninth Circuit Court of Appeals disagreed with Malone's argument and held that counsel who believes a court order to be erroneous is not relieved of the duty to obey it. Malone's refusal to abide with the pretrial order was not justified. Id.; see also Maness v. Meyers, 419 U.S. 449, 458, 95 S.Ct. 584, 591, 42 L.Ed.2d 574 (1975).

Corporation to appear for the pretrial settlement conference on December 19.

C. Sanctions

Finally, we must determine whether the court abused its discretion by sanctioning Oat Corporation for failing to comply with the order to appear at the pretrial settlement conference. Oat Corporation argues that the instructions directing the appearance of corporate representatives were unclear and ambiguous. Consequently, it concludes that the sanctions were improper.

(7) Absent an abuse of discretion, we may not disturb a district court's imposition of sanctions for failure of a party to comply with a pretrial order. The issue on review is not whether we would have imposed these costs upon Oat Corporation, but whether the district court abused its discretion in doing so. National Hockey League v. Metropolitan Hockey Club, Inc., 427 U.S. 639, 642, 96 S.Ct. 2778, 2780, 49 L.Ed.2d 747 (1976) (citations omitted).

(8) Oat Corporation contends that the presence of Mr. Fitzpatrick, as an attorney authorized to speak on behalf of the principals of Oat Corporation, satisfied the requirement that its "corporate representative" attend the December 19 settlement conference. Oat Corporation argues that nothing in either the November 19, 1984 order or the December 14, 1984 order would lead a reasonable person to conclude that a representative or principal from the Joseph Oat Corporation was required to attend the conference personally--in effect arguing that sanctions cannot be imposed because the order failed to require a particular person to attend the conference.

We believe that Oat Corporation was well aware of what the court expected. While the November order may have been somewhat ambiguous, any ambiguity was eliminated by the magistrate's remarks from the bench on December 14, the written order of December 18,[11] and the direction obtained by

---

[11]. On December 18, 1984, the oral order was reduced to writing.

It stated:

The progress of the conference was impaired by the fact that neither plaintiff Joseph Oat Corporation, or its carrier National Union, was

counsel from the magistrate's clerk.

On December 14, in the presence of Oat Corporation's attorney of record and all those in the courtroom, the magistrate announced that the pretrial conference had *656 been impaired because Oat Corporation[12] had not complied with Paragraph 5(c) of the November order requiring it to send to the conference a corporate representative.[13] The magistrate

---

represented, in addition to counsel, by a representative having full authority to settle the case....

It appearing that a substantial possibility exists that a number of the claims and issues in these cases may be susceptible of settlement, and that other related matters might be considered (including the avoidance of unnecessary proof, cumulative evidence, and redundant litigation; the possibility of adopting amendments to the pleadings, the restructuring of the parties; and the adoption of special procedures for managing this complex and protracted litigation) so as to secure the just and speedy determination of this litigation as the least expense to the parties,

IT IS HEREBY ORDERED:
....
2. In addition to counsel, each party and the insurance carriers of plaintiff Oat and defendant RME, shall be represented at the conference in person by a representative having full authority to settle the case or to make decisions and grant <u>authority to counsel with respect to all matters that may be reasonably anticipated to come before the conference</u>;....

(Order of Dec. 18, 1984) (emphasis supplied).

[12]. Except for the Oat Corporation, all the parties complied, sending their counsel and corporate representatives to the pretrial conference (a principal of CSM was standing by a telephone in the Netherlands). The Oat Corporation was represented by his attorney of record, John Possi. In addition, the Oat Corporation's liability insurance carrier, National Union Fire Insurance Company, was represented by an adjuster.

[13]. In pertinent part, the order stated:

5. A settlement conference, which shall include the Heileman Brewing Company, shall be held herein on December 14, 1984 at 2:00 p.m.

In addition to counsel, each party shall be represented at the

clearly stated that the order's purpose was to insure the presence of the parties personally at the conference. From that moment on, Oat Corporation had notice that it was ordered to send a corporate representative to the resumed conference. Moreover, prior to the December 19 conference, Oat Corporation's counsel contacted the magistrate's office to determine if the magistrate really intended for corporate representatives to be in Madison, Wisconsin, for the settlement conference. Counsel was assured that such was the case.

When the conference resumed on December 19, Mr. Possi was present acting in his capacity as Oat Corporation's attorney of record. Mr. Fitzpatrick, who was not an attorney of record in the case, asserted that he was directed to attend the conference and speak on behalf of Oat Corporation's principals.[14] Mr. Fitzpatrick also stated that he interpreted

---

conference by a representative having full authority to settle the case

(Order of Nov. 19, 1984).

[14]. On December 19, the following dialogue took place between the magistrate and Mr. Fitzpatrick:

THE COURT: I made it clear on December 14th, that for purposes of this conference that each party in addition to be represented by counsel would have present the party itself for purposes of authorizing or discussing settlement in this case, speaking specifically about the order which is dated December 18th but was entered I think clearly enough on the 14th. That in addition to counsel, each party shall be represented at the conference in person by a representative having full authority to settle the case or make decisions relevant to all matters reasonably anticipated to come before the conference....

As a matter of fact, Mr. Possi called yesterday to find out from my secretary if that is what I really meant he was informed that it is what I really meant; and I would like to have your explanation as to why no one from Joseph Oat is here from (sic) that authority.

MR. FITZPATRICK: I am here as a representative of Joseph Oat which I understood your order to be. I have discussed this thing thoroughly with the principals of Joseph Oat. They directed me to come to the conference. They directed me that I could speak for them, with authority to speak for them. Their direction was I should make no offer to settle the case. That is their position. That is the position they choose to

the November order not as requiring the presence of a principal of Oat Corporation at the conference scheduled for December 14, but as requiring the presence of the insurance carriers with authority to discuss settlement.

The distinction is clearly drawn between an attorney representing a corporation and a corporate representative. As we define in this opinion--consistent with the meaning given by the magistrate--a corporate representative is a person holding "a position with the corporate entity." Although Mr. Fitzpatrick was representing the corporate principals and Mr. Possi the corporation, no corporate representative attended as required by the magistrate's order. We therefore conclude that the court properly sanctioned Oat Corporation pursuant to Rule 16(f) for failing to send a corporate representative to the settlement conference.

III. CONCLUSION

We hold that Rule 16 does not limit, but rather is enhanced by, the inherent authority of federal courts to order litigants represented by counsel to attend pretrial conferences for the purpose of discussing settlement. Oat Corporation violated the district court's order requiring it to have a corporate representative attend the pretrial settlement *657 conference on December 19, 1984. Under these circumstances, the district court did not abuse its discretion by imposing sanctions for Oat Corporation's failure to comply with the pretrial order. The judgment of the district court is hereby AFFIRMED.

POSNER, Circuit Judge, dissenting.

Rule 16(a) of the Federal Rules of Civil Procedure authorizes a district court to "direct the attorneys for the parties and any <u>unrepresented</u> parties to appear before it for a (pretrial) conference." The word I have italicized could be thought to carry the negative implication that no <u>represented</u> party may be directed to appear--that was the panel's conclusion--but I hesitate to so conclude in a case

---

take and they designated me as the representative to communicate that to the Court.

(Transcript of Dec. 19, 1984).

that can be decided on a narrower ground.

The main purpose of the pretrial conference is to get ready for trial. For that purpose, only the attorneys need be present, unless a party is acting as his own attorney. The only possible reason for wanting a represented party to be present is to enable the judge or magistrate to explore settlement with the principals rather than with just their agents. Some district judges and magistrates distrust the willingness or ability of attorneys to convey to their clients adequate information bearing on the desirability and terms of settling a case in lieu of pressing forward to trial. The distrust is warranted in some cases, I am sure; but warranted or not, it is what lies behind the concern that the panel opinion had stripped the district courts of a valuable settlement tool--and this at a time of heavy, and growing, federal judicial caseloads. The concern may well be exaggerated, however. The panel opinion may have had little practical significance; it is the rare attorney who will invite a district judge's displeasure by defying a request to produce the client for a pretrial conference.

The question of the district court's power to summon a represented party to a settlement conference is a difficult one. On the one hand, nothing in Rule 16 or in any other rule or statute confers such a power, and there are obvious dangers in too broad an interpretation of the federal courts' inherent power to regulate their procedure. One danger is that it encourages judicial high-handedness ("power corrupts"); several years ago one of the district judges in this circuit ordered Acting Secretary of Labor Brock to appear before him for settlement discussions on the very day Brock was scheduled to appear before the Senate for his confirmation hearing. The broader concern illustrated by the Brock episode is that in their zeal to settle cases judges may ignore the value of other people's time. One reason people hire lawyers is to economize on their own investment of time in resolving disputes. It is pertinent to note in this connection that Oat is a defendant in this case; it didn't want its executives' time occupied with this litigation.

On the other hand, die Not bricht Eisen ("necessity breaks iron"). Attorneys often are imperfect agents of their clients, and the workload of our district courts is so heavy that we should hesitate to deprive them of a potentially useful tool for effecting settlement, even if there is some difficulty in finding a legal basis for the tool. Although few attorneys will defy a district court's request to produce the client, those few cases may be the very ones where the client's presence would be most conducive to settlement. If I am right that Rule 16(a) empowers a district court to summon unrepresented parties to a pretrial conference only because their presence may be necessary to get ready for trial, we need not infer that the draftsmen meant to forbid the summoning of represented parties for purposes of exploring settlement. The draftsmen may have been unaware that district courts were asserting a power to command the presence of a represented party to explore settlement. We should hesitate to infer inadvertent prohibitions.

The narrowly "legal" considerations bearing on the question whether district courts have the power asserted by the magistrate in this case are sufficiently equivocal to authorize--indeed compel--us to consider the practical consequences for settlement before deciding what the answer should be. Unfortunately we have *658 insufficient information about those consequences to be able to give a confident answer, but fortunately we need not answer the question in this case--so clear is it that the magistrate abused his discretion, which is to say, acted unreasonably, in demanding that Oat Corporation send an executive having "full settlement authority" to the pretrial conference. This demand, which is different from a demand that a party who has not closed the door to settlement send an executive to discuss possible terms, would be defensible only if litigants had a duty to bargain in good faith over settlement before resorting to trial, and neither Rule 16 nor any other rule, statute, or doctrine imposes such a duty on federal litigants. See Strandell v. Jackson County, 838 F.2d 884, 887 (7th Cir.1987); Kothe v. Smith, 771 F.2d 667, 669 (2d Cir.1985); Del Rio v. Northern Blower Co., 574 F.2d 23, 26 (1st Cir.1978); Perez v. Maine, 760 F.2d 11, 12 (1st Cir.1985); National Ass'n of Government Employees, Inc. v. National Federation of Federal Employees, 844 F.2d 216, 223 (5th Cir.1988); Advisory Committee Notes to 1983 Amendments to Fed.R.Civ.P. 16. There is no federal judicial power to coerce settlement. Oat had made clear that it was not prepared to settle the case on any terms that required it to pay money. That was its prerogative, which once exercised made the magistrate's continued insistence on Oat's sending an executive to Madison arbitrary, unreasonable, willful, and indeed petulant. This is apart from the fact that since no one officer of Oat may have had authority to settle the case, compliance with the demand might have required Oat to ship its entire board of directors to Madison. Ultimately Oat did make a money settlement, but there is no indication that it would have settled sooner if only it had complied with the magistrate's demand for the dispatch of an executive possessing "full settlement authority."

Sufficient unto the day is the evil thereof: We should reverse the district court without reaching the question whether there are any circumstances in which a district court may compel a party represented by counsel to attend a pretrial conference.

COFFEY, Circuit Judge, with whom EASTERBROOK, RIPPLE and MANION, Circuit Judges, join, dissenting.

Because Rule 16 of the Federal Rules of Civil Procedure, amended by the Supreme Court and Congress as recently as 1983, specifically designates who may be ordered to appear at a pretrial conference, I disagree with the majority's determination "that the action taken by the district court in this case constituted the proper use of inherent authority to aid in accomplishing the purpose and intent of Rule 16." Majority Opinion at 652. Rule 16 of the Federal Rules of Civil Procedure states in relevant part:

"(a) Pretrial Conferences; Objectives. In any action, the court may in its discretion direct the attorneys for the parties and any unrepresented parties to appear before it for a conference or conferences before trial for such purposes as (1) expediting the disposition of the action; (2) establishing early and continuing control so that the case will not be protracted because of lack of management; (3) discouraging wasteful pretrial activity; (4) improving the quality of the trial through more thorough preparation; and (5) facilitating the settlement of the case."

Unlike the majority, I am convinced that Rule 16 does not authorize a trial judge to require a represented party litigant to attend a pretrial conference together with his or her attorney because the rule mandates in clear and unambiguous terms that only an unrepresented party litigant and attorneys may be ordered to appear.

Although I recognize that all courts, including those of federal jurisdiction, possess certain inherent authority, such as the contempt power and the power to determine whether the court has jurisdiction, this authority is limited. We recently warned that:

"'Inherent authority'" is not a substitute for good reason.... 'Inherent authority' *659 like its cousin in criminal law the 'supervisory power', is just another name for the power of courts to make common law when statutes and rules do not address a particular topic. Cf. United States v. Widgery, 778 F.2d 325, 328-29 (7th Cir.1985)."

Soo Line R. Co. v. Escanaba & Lake Superior R. Co., 840 F.2d 546, 551 (7th Cir.1988). The Supreme Court has placed clear limits on judicial reliance on "inherent authority" or, as it is labeled in the criminal law context, "supervisory power":

"Even a sensible and efficient use of the supervisory power ... is invalid if it conflicts with constitutional or statutory provisions. A contrary result 'would confer on the judiciary discretionary power to disregard the considered limitations of the law it is charged with enforcing.'"

Thomas v. Arn, 474 U.S. 140, 148, 106 S.Ct. 466, 471, 88 L.Ed.2d 435 (1985) (quoting United States v. Payner, 447 U.S. 727, 737, 100 S.Ct. 2439, 2447, 65 L.Ed.2d 468 (1980)). Thus, as the majority recognizes, "the district court, in devising means to control cases before it, may not exercise its inherent authority in a manner inconsistent with rule or statute." Majority Opinion at 652.

The Supreme Court very recently underscored the fact that district courts are not to attempt to utilize an alleged inherent authority in a manner that contravenes the balance between varying interests that has previously been struck in a federal procedural rule, such as Federal Rule of Civil Procedure 16. In Bank of Nova Scotia v. United States, --- U.S. ----, 108 S.Ct. 2369, 2374, 101 L.Ed.2d 228 (1988), the Court held that a judge may not invoke inherent authority (labeled "supervisory" power by the Court) to dismiss an indictment based upon "harmless error" in a grand jury proceeding:

"We now hold that a federal court may not invoke supervisory power to circumvent the harmless error inquiry prescribed by Federal Rule of Criminal Procedure 52(a). The balance struck by the Rule between societal costs and the rights of the accused may not casually be overlooked 'because a court has elected to analyze the question under the supervisory power.' United States v. Payner, 447 U.S. (727, 736, 100 S.Ct. 2439, 2447, 65 L.Ed.2d 468 (1980))."

As the Supreme Court observed in an earlier decision rejecting the broad use of the supervisory power (inherent authority) to justify an individual court's determination that public policy required criminal defendants to be extended certain protections beyond those allowed in the Constitution, such

> "reasoning ... amounts to a substitution of individual judgment for the controlling decisions of this Court. Were we to accept this use of the supervisory power, we would confer on the judiciary discretionary power to disregard the considered limitations of the law it is charged with enforcing. We hold that the supervisory power does not extend so far."

United States v. Payner, 447 U.S. 727, 737, 100 S.Ct. 2439, 2447, 65 L.Ed.2d 468 (1980) (footnote omitted). Like the procedural rule involved in Bank of Nova Scotia, the Federal Rules of Civil Procedure, including Rule 16, "are the product of a careful process of study and reflection designed to take 'due cognizance both of the need for expedition of cases and the protection of individual rights.'" Strandell v. Jackson County, 838 F.2d 884, 886 (7th Cir.1987) (quoting S.Rep. No. 1744, 85th Cong., 2d Sess., reprinted in 1958 U.S.Code Cong. & Admin.News 3023, 3026). Furthermore, "in those areas of trial practice where the Supreme Court and the Congress, acting together, have addressed the appropriate balance between the needs for judicial efficiency and the rights of the individual litigant, innovation by the individual judicial officer must conform to that balance." Id. at 886-87.

Prior to 1983, Rule 16 only provided district court judges with the discretion to require the attendance of attorneys for parties at such proceedings. As pointed out earlier in this opinion, the Supreme Court and Congress took a good hard look at Rule 16 in hopes of improving judicial efficiency *660 and only increased the power of district court judges to the extent of authorizing them to compel the attendance of "unrepresented parties" at pretrial conferences.

However, it is very clear that the amendment explicitly stopped short of providing trial judges with the broad and sweeping authority to compel the presence of "represented parties" at pretrial conferences that the majority now seeks to achieve by judicial fiat. "(T)he Supreme Court and Congress, acting together, ... addressed the appropriate balance between the needs for judicial efficiency and the rights of the individual litigant,"[1] when they chose to amend Rule 16 in a limited manner. The majority upsets this careful balance and acts contrary to the Supreme Court's mandate in the Bank of Nova Scotia case when it relies upon an alleged "inherent authority" to permit district court judges to exercise a power which the drafters of Rule 16 explicitly denied them. See United States R. Retirement Board v. Fritz, 449 U.S. 166, 179, 101 S.Ct. 453, 461, 66 L.Ed.2d 368 (1980) ("The language of the statute is clear, and we have historically assumed that Congress intended what it enacted.")[2] The obvious intent of the Supreme Court and Congress that only attorneys and unrepresented parties be required to participate in pretrial conferences is clearly supported by the specific references to "attorneys" and "unrepresented parties" throughout Rule 16. Rule 16(a), as noted previously, allows for the court to "direct the attorneys for the parties and any unrepresented parties to appear before it." Rule 16(b), concerning scheduling, requires a judge to "consult( ) with the attorneys for the parties and any unrepresented parties." Rule 16(c), regarding subjects to be discussed at a pretrial conference, states that "(a)t least one of the attorneys for each party participating in any conference before trial shall have authority to enter into stipulations and to make admissions regarding all matters that the participants may reasonably anticipate may be discussed." Similarly, Rule 16(d), concerning final pretrial conferences, provides that "(t)he conference shall be attended by at least one of the attorneys who will conduct the trial for each of the parties and by any unrepresented parties."

---

[1] Strandell, 838 F.2d at 886-87.

[2] Justice Scalia pointed toward a similarly circumscribed construction of "supervisory power" when he recently noted: "Even less do I see a basis for any court's 'supervisory powers to discipline the prosecutors of its jurisdiction,' except insofar as concerns their performance before the court and their qualifications to be members of the court's bar." Bank of Nova Scotia, 108 S.Ct. at 2379 (Scalia, J., concurring) (quoting United States v. Hasting, 461 U.S. 499, 505, 103 S.Ct. 1974, 1978, 76 L.Ed.2d 96 (1983)). Likewise, there is no basis for a court's possession of broad inherent powers to force party litigants to participate in settlement discussions where the party litigants have not expressed a desire to participate.

The majority's creation of this new inherent authority to compel attendance of litigants (represented parties) also contravenes the terms of at least one other rule regulating compulsory attendance at judicial proceedings. Federal Rule of Civil Procedure 45 does not authorize subpoenas to be issued for pretrial conferences and permits the invocation of the subpoena power only for hearings and trials. On the federal level neither the Supreme Court nor Congress has given the courts the authority to direct litigants' attendance much less the power to subpoena them to pretrial conferences whose sole purpose is to discuss the upcoming trial, to frame and define the issues, and through custom to explore with the consent of the litigants' attorneys, in very limited situations, the discussion of settlement possibilities. Furthermore, the extension of the "inherent authority" doctrine to substitute for the subpoena power at pretrial conferences raises a due process question in that the court's rule authority to issue a subpoena is subject to a motion to quash, which is not available to challenge the alleged inherent authority. Assuming that the court would issue a contempt citation for failure to appear, I know of no avenue for an unwilling litigant to challenge the alleged "inherent authority" other than an attempt *661 to offer a defense to an unjustified contempt citation.

The newly created "inherent authority" to require represented litigants to appear at a pretrial conference is based upon a legal foundation of quicksand. Exercise of this power has posed and will continue to pose a substantial invitation for judicial abuse. The purpose of a pretrial conference is to set the parameters of litigation, clarify the issues and organize its presentation with the aid of the respective attorneys, and now, unrepresented party litigants in the hope of improving judicial efficiency at trial.

As Charles Richey, District Judge for the United States District Court for the District of Columbia, has noted, "Rule 16 provides an important mechanism for narrowing the issues in a case, saving time and expense for the litigants and easing the burden on the courts by facilitating the handling of congested dockets." C. Richey, Modern Management Technique for Trial Courts to Improve the Quality of Justice: Requiring Direct Testimony to be Submitted in Written Form Prior to Trial, 72 Geo.L.J. 73, 78 (1983). As the majority admits, "'it is not the purpose of Rule 16(b)(7) to impose settlement negotiations on unwilling litigants.'" Majority Opinion at 653 (quoting Fed.R.Civ.P. 16 Advisory Committee's Note (c) (1983)). We emphasized this fact when we noted that there is "nothing in the amended rule (16) or in the Advisory Committee Notes (that) suggests that the amendments were intended to make the rule coercive." Strandell, 838 F.2d at 888. In our judicial system all party litigants are entitled to their day in court to present their claims or defenses before an impartial judge or jury. Our trial judges must never fall prey to becoming part of a process that even subliminally suggests a pressure to forego the essential right of trial.

An example of the possible abuse that can result from creation of an inherent authority to require the attendance of represented party litigants at a pretrial conference is found in a case in which a trial judge in this circuit sought to compel the attendance of a represented party, the Secretary of Labor, to discuss a settlement after the Department of Labor's attorney refused to agree to a settlement proposal suggested by the district court.[3] The trial court judge in that case stated:

"I think I want to set a hearing as soon as I get back in which I want the Secretary of Labor to be here, not even Mr. Lilly. I'm tired of horsing around with people who sit in the Solicitor's Office, spending the taxpayer's money, having these kinds of, to me, difficult to understand, to put it gently, positions, and say, 'We want to take the position that any breach, however infinitesimal, however irrelevant, however immaterial, however inadvertent, however innocent, is going to be of significance in a determination as to whether or not compensation can be paid under an indemnification agreement to ERISA trustees.' I want the Secretary to tell me that that's the Department of Labor's position. I want the Secretary to tell me that he wants a hole in this decree so that the other court would have to decide whether or not what the Trustees and Senator Saxbe (Independent Special Counsel) and the Fund did--the staff recommendation and all--should be determined by a new and different judge who has never had anything to do with the case, has no background in it, has no knowledge of the facts, etcetera."

No. 85-1640, unpublished order at 2-3 (7th Cir. April 23,

---

[3] No. 85-1640, unpublished order at 2 (7th Cir. April 23, 1985). This order is not cited as precedent, but merely for its description of the involved factual situation.

1985). The district court added that:

"I will tell you now that I am through with the Department of Labor's waltzing around, taking ridiculous positions, and saying that this is the Government. The Government is the Secretary of Labor, so far as I'm concerned. And I want to see him at 10:00 o'clock on the 23rd of April in this courtroom to tell me why the Secretary of Labor is taking these idiotic positions."

*662 Creation of an "inherent authority" to require the presence of a party litigant at a pretrial conference presents a host of problems. Certainly, the court has the power to command the attendance of attorneys at the conference under the provisions of Rule 16 and as "officers of the court." However, I am convinced that if the attorney does not wish to have the litigant personally appear before the court at the pretrial conference, he is not bound to do so, lest, among other problems, the litigant make an admission of some type which would be damaging to the case and which had not previously been elicited in discovery proceedings. I believe we are all aware of the fact that the appearance of fairness, impartiality and justice is all imperative, and based upon logic I fail to understand how a litigant sitting at a command appearance before a judge who injects himself into an adversarial role for either of the parties' positions during settlement negotiations can feel that he or she (the litigant) will have a fair trial before the judge if he or she fails to agree with the judge's reasoning or direction regarding a recommended settlement. We may express in grandiose terms all sorts of theory and postulation about being careful not to influence, intimidate andor coerce a settlement, but under the pressure that our trial judges experience today from their ever-burgeoning caseloads, we would be foolhardy not to anticipate an undesirable and unnecessary psychological impact upon the litigant in circumstances of this nature. The difficulties associated with active judicial participation in settlement negotiations is expressly exacerbated when the trial is scheduled before the court rather than a jury of one's peers. The appearance of partiality and impropriety must be avoided at all lengths if our nation is to continue to show respect for its judicial judgments. Since litigants are neither trained in the law nor have the basic understanding of the nuances of legal proceedings that we as lawyers have gained through years of education, professional training and experience, they could well be confused and dismayed with judicial participation in settlement negotiations.

My conclusion that judges lack the inherent authority to require the presence of a represented party litigant at a pretrial conference does not deprive trial judges of the ability to effectively handle their caseloads. Judges remain free to require the attendance of attorneys and unrepresented parties at pretrial conferences. However, if further measures are taken to coercively require the presence and active participation of a represented party at a pretrial conference, it is my considered belief that judges will be no longer worthy of the aura of impartiality for "the guiding consideration is that the administration of justice should reasonably appear to be disinterested as well as be so in fact." Public Utilities Commission v. Pollack, 343 U.S. 451, 466-67, 72 S.Ct. 813, 822-23, 96 L.Ed. 1068 (1952) (Frankfurter, J., in chambers).[4]

Rule 16 is an example of "the Supreme Court and the Congress, acting together (to address) the appropriate balance between the needs for judicial efficiency and the rights of the individual litigant." Strandell, 838 F.2d at 886-87. If we are to maintain the appearance of fairness and impartiality that is so important to preservation of confidence and respect for our cherished judicial system, "innovation by the individual judicial officer must conform to that balance." Id. at 887. The majority, in their attempt to permit judicial officers the right to exercise their personal judgment to require the attendance at pretrial conferences of entities other than those specifically enumerated in Rule 16, upsets the delicate balance the Supreme Court and *663 Congress struck between the needs for judicial efficiency and the rights of the individual litigant. But on the other hand, if we wish to grant federal trial judges the power, let it be accomplished through the

---

[4] It should be noted that those who advocate expansive use of "supervisory power" or inherent authority in the criminal context rely upon the integrity of the judicial process as a justification for allowing courts to exercise this authority. See United States v. Payner, 447 U.S. 727, 745-46, 100 S.Ct. 2439, 2451-52, 65 L.Ed.2d 468 (1980) (Marshall, J., dissenting). In our case, creation of the appearance of impropriety with a judge actively injecting himself into the settlement procedure in the presence of the party litigants compromises, rather than furthers, the "protect(ion of) the integrity of the court," the "major purpose behind the exercise of the supervisory powers." 447 U.S. at 748, 100 S.Ct. at 2453.

accepted channels of the Supreme Court and Congress of the United States.[5] Because district court judges lack authority to require the attendance of represented litigants at a pretrial conference as of this date, I dissent.[6]

EASTERBROOK, Circuit Judge, with whom POSNER, COFFEY and MANION, Circuit Judges, join, dissenting.

Our case has three logically separate issues. First, whether a district court may demand the attendance of someone other than the party's counsel of record. Second, whether the court may insist that this additional person be an employee rather than an agent selected for the occasion. Third, whether the court may insist that the representative have "full settlement authority"--meaning the authority to agree to pay cash in settlement (maybe authority without cap, although that was not clear). Even if one resolves the first issue as the majority does, it does not follow that district courts have the second or third powers, or that their exercise here was prudent.

The proposition that a magistrate may require a firm to send an employee rather than a representative is puzzling. Corporate "employees" are simply agents of the firm. Corporations choose their agents and decide what powers to give them. Which agents have which powers is a matter of internal corporate affairs. Joseph Oat Corp. sent to the conference not only its counsel of record but also John Fitzpatrick, who had authority to speak for Oat. Now Mr. Fitzpatrick is an attorney, which raised the magistrate's hackles, but why should this count against him? Because Fitzpatrick is a part-time rather than a full-time agent of

---

[5] "If such radical surgery is to be performed, we can expect that the national rule-making process outlined in the Rules Enabling Act will undertake it in quite an explicit fashion." Strandell, 838 F.2d at 888 (footnote omitted).

[6] Although I am convinced that the district court lacked the authority to require represented parties to attend the pretrial conference, if it did have such power I would conclude, for the reasons enumerated by Judge Posner, that the magistrate acted improperly in exercising this power to require that Oat Corporation send to the settlement conference an executive possessing "full settlement authority."

the corporation? Why can't the corporation make its own decision about how much of the agent's time to hire? Is Oat being held in contempt because it is too small to have a cadre of legal employees--because its general counsel practices with a law firm rather than being "in house"?

At all events, the use of outside attorneys as negotiators is common. Many a firm sends its labor lawyer to the bargaining table when a collective bargaining agreement is about to expire, there to dicker with the union (or with labor's lawyer). Each side has a statutory right to choose its representatives. 29 U.S.C. section 158(b)(1)(B). Many a firm sends its corporate counsel to the bargaining table when a merger is under discussion. See Ronald J. Gilson, Value Creation by Business Lawyers: Legal Skills and Asset Pricing, 94 Yale L.J. 239 (1984). Oat did the same thing to explore settlement of litigation. A lawyer is no less suited to this task than to negotiating the terms of collective bargaining or merger agreements. Firms prefer to send skilled negotiators to negotiating sessions (lawyers are especially useful when the value of a claim depends on the resolution of legal questions) while reserving the time of executives for business. Oat understandably wanted its management team to conduct its construction business.

As for the third subject, whether the representative must have "settlement authority": the magistrate's only reason for ordering a corporate representative to come was to facilitate settlement then and there. As I understand Magistrate Groh's opinion, and Judge Crabb's, the directive was to send a person with "full settlement authority". Fitzpatrick was deemed inadequate *664 only because he was under instructions not to pay money. E.g.: "While Mr. Fitzpatrick claimed authority to speak for Oat, he stated that he had no authority to make a (monetary) offer. Thus, no representative of Oat or National having authority to settle the case was present at the conference as the order directed" (magistrate's opinion, emphasis added). On learning that Fitzpatrick did not command Oat's treasury, the magistrate ejected him from the conference and never listened to what he had to say on Oat's behalf, never learned whether Fitzpatrick might be receptive to others' proposals. (We know that Oat ultimately did settle the case for money, after it took part in and "prevailed" at a summary jury trial--participation and payment each demonstrating Oat's willingness to consider settlement.) The magistrate's approach implies that if the Chairman and CEO of Oat had arrived with instructions from the Board to settle the case without paying cash, and to negotiate and bring back for the Board's consideration any financial proposals, Oat still would have been in contempt.

Both magistrate and judge demanded the presence not of a "corporate representative" in the sense of a full-time employee but of a representative with "full authority to settle". Most corporations reserve power to agree (as opposed to power to discuss) to senior managers or to their boards of directors--the difference depending on the amounts involved. Heileman wanted $4 million, a sum within the province of the board rather than a single executive even for firms much larger than Oat. Fitzpatrick came with power to discuss and recommend; he could settle the case on terms other than cash; he lacked only power to sign a check. The magistrate's order therefore must have required either (a) changing the allocation of responsibility within the corporation, or (b) sending a quorum of Oat's Board.

Magistrate Groh exercised a power unknown even in labor law, where there is a duty to bargain in good faith. 29 U.S.C. section 158(d). Labor and management commonly negotiate through persons with the authority to discuss but not agree. The negotiators report back to management and the union, each of which reserves power to reject or approve the position of its agent. We know from Fed.R.Civ.P. 16--and especially from the Advisory Committee's comment to Rule 16(c) that the Rule's "reference to 'authority' is not intended to insist upon the ability to settle the litigation"--that the parties cannot be compelled to negotiate "in good faith". A defendant convinced it did no wrong may insist on total vindication. See Hess v. New Jersey Transit Rail Operations, Inc., 846 F.2d 114 (2d Cir.1988), and Kothe v. Smith, 771 F.2d 667 (2d Cir.1985), holding that a judge may not compel a party to make a settlement offer, let alone to accept one. Rule 68, which requires a party who turns down a settlement proposal to bear costs only if that party does worse at trial, implies the same thing. Yet if parties are not obliged to negotiate in good faith, on what ground can they be obliged to come with authority to settle on the spot--an authority agents need not carry even when the law requires negotiation? The order we affirm today compels persons who have committed no wrong, who pass every requirement of Rules 11 and 68, who want only the opportunity to receive a decision on the merits, to come to court with open checkbooks on pain of being held in contempt.

Settling litigation is valuable, and courts should promote

it. Is settlement of litigation more valuable than settlement of labor disputes, so that courts may do what the NLRB may not? The statutory framework--bona fide negotiations required in labor law but not in litigation--suggests the opposite. Does the desirability of settlement imply that rules of state law allocating authority within a corporation must yield? We have held in other cases that settlements must be negotiated within the framework of existing rules; the desire to get a case over and done with does not justify modifying generally applicable norms. E.g., Dunn v. Carey, 808 F.2d 555, 560 (7th Cir.1986) (consent decrees, and hence settlement, may be more attractive if parties may agree not to follow state law, but the value of settlement does not authorize *665 that); Kasper v. Board of Election Commissioners, 814 F.2d 332, 340-42 (7th Cir.1987) (same); In re Memorial Hospital of Iowa County, Inc., 862 F.2d 1299 (7th Cir.1988) (parties' desire to settle does not justify vacating a judicial opinion that may be valuable to other persons). See also, e.g., Tiedel v. Northwestern Michigan College, 865 F.2d 88 (6th Cir.1988) (a district court lacks the power to promote settlement by requiring a party who rejects a mediator's proposal to pay the prevailing side's attorneys' fees).

The majority does not discuss these problems. Its approach implies, however, that trial courts may insist that representatives have greater authority than labor negotiators bring to the table. And to create this greater authority, Oat Corp. might have to rearrange its internal structure--perhaps delegating to an agent a power state law reserves to the board of directors. Problems concerning the reallocation of authority are ubiquitous. For example, only the Assistant Attorney General for the Civil Division has authority to approve settlements of civil cases, and his authority reaches only to $750,000; above that the Deputy Attorney General must approve. 28 C.F.R. sections 0.160(a)(2), 0.161. An attorney for the government, like Fitzpatrick, lacks the authority to commit his client but may negotiate and recommend. Does it follow that, in every federal civil case, a magistrate may require the presence of the Assistant or Deputy Attorney General or insist that they redelegate their authority? If such a demand would be improper for the Department of Justice, is it more proper when made of Joseph Oat Corporation?

These issues will not go away. The magistrate's order was to send a representative with the authority to bind Oat to pay money. What is the point of insisting on such authority if not to require the making of offers and the acceptance of "reasonable" counteroffers--that is, to require good faith negotiations and agreements on the spot? Fitzpatrick had the authority to report back to Oat on any suggestions; he had the authority to participate in negotiations. The only thing he lacked--the only reason Oat was held in contempt of court--was the ability to sign Oat Corp.'s check in the magistrate's presence. What the magistrate found unacceptable was that Fitzpatrick might say something like "I'll relay that suggestion to the Board of Directors", which might say no. Oat's CEO could have done no more. We close our eyes to reality in pretending that Oat was required only to be present while others "voluntarily" discussed settlement.

RIPPLE, Circuit Judge, with whom COFFEY, Circuit Judge, joins, dissenting.

I join the dissenting opinions of Judge Coffey and Judge Manion. I write separately only to emphasize that the most enduring--and dangerous--impact of the majority's opinion will not be its effect on the conduct of the pretrial conference, but on the relationship between the Judiciary and the Congress in establishing practice and procedure for the federal courts. Recognizing that the line between substance and procedure is at best an indistinct and vague one, the two branches of government have established a long tradition of shared responsibility for this aspect of governance. That tradition is embodied principally--although not exclusively--in the Rules Enabling Act. 28 U.S.C. section 2072. That Act was designed to foster a uniform system of procedure throughout the federal system, supplemented but not altered, by local rules to take care of local problems. Experimentation at the local level in areas where policy choices have not been made at the national level is permitted. Moreover, there is no question that the judicial officer retains a substantial degree of inherent authority to deal with individual situations--as long as that authority is exercised in conformity with the policies embodied in the national rules. However, the Rules Enabling Act hardly contemplates the broad, amorphous, definition of the "inherent power of a district judge," at 652, articulated by the majority.

It is significant that, just months ago, in the Judicial Improvements and Access to Justice Act, Pub.L. No. 100-702, 102 Stat. 4642 (1988), Congress made clear its concern *666 with district courts' frustrating the careful process of evaluation and consensus set up by the Rules Enabling Act through the proliferation of local rules. sections 401-407, 102 Stat. 4648-52. Today's decision is indeed hard to reconcile with the underlying Congressional concern for uniformity of practice in the federal courts. Indeed, the majority encourages the individual district court to march to its own drummer. Before long, we shall no doubt see the rhetoric of its opinion used to justify far more questionable "innovations" than the strong-arm settlement methodology of the magistrate at issue in this opinion.

MANION, Circuit Judge, joined by COFFEY, EASTERBROOK and RIPPLE, Circuit Judges, dissenting.

Federal Rule of Civil Procedure 16 states that district courts may order "the attorneys for the parties and any unrepresented parties" to appear at pretrial settlement conferences. Despite this seemingly clear language, the majority holds that district courts have "inherent power" to compel parties represented by counsel to appear in court to discuss settlement. Because Rule 16 leaves no room for any such use of inherent power, I respectfully dissent.

Inherent power is not a license for federal courts to do whatever seems necessary to move a case along. Inherent power is simply "another name for the power of courts to make common law when statutes and rules do not address a particular area." Soo Line R. Co. v. Escanaba & Lake Superior R. Co., 840 F.2d 546, 551 (7th Cir.1988). Since inherent power's purpose is to fill gaps left by statute or rule, it necessarily follows that where a statute or rule specifically addresses a particular area, it is inappropriate to invoke inherent power to exceed the bounds the statute or rule sets. Cf. Bank of Nova Scotia v. United States, --- U.S. ----, 108 S.Ct. 2369, 2373-74, 101 L.Ed.2d 228 (1988) (a federal court may not invoke its supervisory--i.e. inherent--power over criminal proceedings to circumvent Fed.R.Crim.P. 52(a)'s harmless error inquiry).

We recently applied this principle in Strandell v. Jackson County, 838 F.2d 884 (7th Cir.1988). In Strandell, we recognized that district courts must exercise their inherent power "in harmony with the Federal Rules of Civil Procedure." After carefully examining Rule 16 and its accompanying advisory committee note, we held in Strandell that a district court may not order an unwilling litigant to participate in a summary jury trial because Rule 16, which addresses the district courts' power to insist on pretrial settlement proceedings, did not authorize district courts to conduct mandatory summary jury trials. See id. at 186-88. Implicit in this holding is that no inherent power exists to conduct mandatory summary jury trials; Rule 16 shut the door on such proceedings.

The issue here--whether a district court may order a represented party to appear at a settlement conference--is slightly different from the issue in Strandell. But the proper analysis is the same. Since Rule 16 specifically addresses the use of settlement conferences in the federal courts, we must determine whether Rule 16 limits a district court's power over who the court may order to appear at those conferences.

As with any rule or statute, the proper starting point in interpreting Rule 16 is the rule's language. We should not be content to rely on general statements about "liberal construction," and Rule 16's "broadly remedial" "spirit." See majority opinion at 652-53. It is true that Rule 1 commands us to construe the federal rules "to secure the just, speedy, and inexpensive determination of every action;" but that command is not an excuse for us to ignore the words the drafters used to pursue that goal.

As originally enacted, Rule 16 provided that district courts could "direct the attorneys for the parties" to appear for pretrial conferences. In 1983, Rule 16 was amended to provide, among other things, that the possibility of settlement is an appropriate subject to consider at pretrial conferences. Fed.R.Civ.P. 16(c)(7); see also Fed.R.Civ.P. 16(a)(5) ("facilitating" settlement). But Rule 16(c) states only that "the _participants_ *667 at any conference under this rule" may consider settlement (emphasis added); Rule 16(c) does not say who those "participants" may be. Rule 16(a), on the other hand, provides that a district court may "<u>direct the attorneys for the parties and any unrepresented parties</u>" to appear for a pretrial conference. Rule 16(a) thus defines who the "participants" at a pretrial conference are: attorneys and unrepresented parties.

As Judge Coffey notes, dissenting opinion at 660, other parts of Rule 16 echo Rule 16(a)'s reference to attorneys and unrepresented parties. Rule 16(b) requires courts to enter scheduling orders after consulting with "the attorneys for the parties and any unrepresented parties...." Rule 16(d) requires that "one of the attorneys who will conduct the trial for each of the parties and ... any unrepresented parties" must attend the final pretrial conference.

The language of Rule 16's sanctions provision, Rule 16(f), reinforces Rule 16's distinction between represented and unrepresented parties. The only language in Rule 16(f) specifically addressing appearance does <u>not</u> authorize sanctions if "a party fails to appear;" instead, sanctions are appropriate if "no appearance is made <u>on behalf of a party</u>...." (Emphasis added.) This choice of language is significant. In the normal course, an attorney appears "on behalf of" a represented client at a pretrial conference. An unrepresented party has nobody to appear on his behalf except himself.

Congress has provided that litigants may "conduct their own cases personally <u>or by counsel</u>...." 28 U.S.C. section 1654 (emphasis added). Rule 16's distinction between represented and unrepresented parties is consistent with a litigant's statutory right to representation by an attorney. It is also consistent with the attorney's traditional role in litigation. Litigants hire attorneys to take advantage of the attorneys' training and skill and, as Judge Posner notes, "to economize on their own investment of time in resolving disputes." Dissenting opinion at 657, Part of an attorney's expertise includes evaluating cases, advising litigants whether or not to settle, and conducting negotiations. I realize that attorneys may sometimes convey inadequate information to their clients regarding settlement. But an attorney has a strong self interest in realistically conveying to the client relevant information necessary for the client to make an informed settlement decision, and in accurately conveying the client's settlement position to the court and opposing litigants. The attorney also has an ethical duty to convey that information. The threat of malpractice suits and disciplinary proceedings should be sufficient to make any attorney think twice before trying to mislead his client or the court. Attorneys play an important role in our adversary system, and we should not denigrate that role by presuming that attorneys will be incompetent to perform one of the most important functions for which their clients hire them. Nor should we presume that Rule 16's drafters meant to encroach on a litigant's right to conduct his case through counsel. Rule 16's clear language shows that the rule's drafters presumed otherwise.

The majority asserts that Rule 16 "does not give any direction to the district court upon the issue of a court's authority to order litigants who are represented by counsel to appear for pretrial proceedings." Majority opinion at 651. But given Rule 16's clear language and consistent distinction between represented and unrepresented parties (a consistent distinction the majority ignores), that assertion is specious. The majority seems to be saying that district courts can order represented parties to appear at settlement conferences because Rule 16 does not explicitly say that district courts cannot order represented parties to appear.[1]

But that ignores the *668 drafters' decision in 1983 to specifically add "unrepresented parties" to the people a district court can order to appear under Rule 16. It also ignores the drafters' language in Rule 16(f) specifically addressing a failure to appear "on behalf of a party" at a pretrial conference. If the drafters had intended to allow district courts to order represented parties to appear, or to sanction parties for failing to appear (as opposed to failing to send someone to appear), the drafters could have easily said so.

---

[1] The majority, citing Link v. Wabash R. Co., 370 U.S. 626, 82 S.Ct. 1386, 81 L.Ed.2d 734 (1962), asserts that "the mere absence of language in the federal rules specifically authorizing or describing a particular judicial procedure should not, and does not, give rise to a negative implication of prohibition." Majority opinion at 652. That sweeping statement reads far too much into Link's narrow holding. Link held that a district court retained the inherent power to dismiss a case sua sponte for failure to prosecute in the face of Fed.R.Civ.P. 41(b), which merely authorized defendants to move for such dismissals. The Court in Link reasoned that given the longstanding--indeed, ancient--authority of trial courts to dismiss cases for want of prosecution, "it would require a much clearer expression of purpose than Rule 41(b) provides for us to assume that it was intended to abrogate" that power. 370 U.S. at 630-32, 82 S.Ct. at 1388-90.

Link did not hold that negative implication is always an inappropriate tool to use in interpreting the federal rules. Link only held that in the context of the particular rule and the particular power involved in that case, any negative implication was not enough, by itself, to convince the Court that the rule's drafters meant to limit that power. While negative implication may not, by itself, completely answer what limits a particular rule places on a district court's power, it does provide a starting point for that analysis. As demonstrated in the text, this case involves much more than the "mere absence" of a particular procedure in Rule 16. Link does not relieve us of the responsibility of analyzing the language the drafters used--and did not use--in Rule 16.

The majority offers no reason why the drafters used the language they did in Rule 16 if they did not intend to limit the district courts' authority to order represented parties to appear. No reason appears on Rule 16's face or in the advisory committee note. Apparently, the majority would chalk up the drafters' choice of language to inadvertence or sloppy draftsmanship. But a rule's words are meant to convey a meaning to those who read the rule. This court should give the drafters credit for being able to communicate what they actually intended. Furthermore, the process for amending the federal rules belies any inadvertence or sloppy draftsmanship. As Professors Wright and Miller have noted,

> (w)hen the Civil Rules are amended, the process is extremely careful. The Advisory Committee on Civil Rules includes lawyers, judges, and scholars with a national reputation for their expertness on matters of procedure, and it is assisted by a scholar of rank who acts as its Reporter. When it has agreed on a preliminary draft of amendments, thousands of copies of that draft are sent out to the profession. Many comments on the draft, and suggestions for improvement in it, then come back to the committee from bar association committees, individual lawyers and scholars, and in law review commentary. The draft is reevaluated and refined in the light of these comments. When the Advisory Committee has completed its work, the amendments still must be approved by the Standing Committee on Rules of Practice and Procedure, by the Judicial Conference of the United States, and by the Supreme Court, and Congress retains the power, though it never has exercised it, to disapprove the amendments. The process is calculated to ensure that any changes reflect the best thinking of the entire profession.

12 C. Wright & A. Miller, Federal Practice and Procedure section 3152, at 220 (1973). It is incredible to believe that after this careful process, amended Rule 16 would expressly authorize district courts to order only attorneys and unrepresented parties to appear if the drafters also intended to allow district courts to order represented parties to appear. This is especially so given Rule 16's consistent distinction between represented and unrepresented parties, and that distinction's congruence with the statutory right to representation by an attorney and the attorney's traditional role in litigation.

The advisory committee note accompanying the 1983 amendment of Rule 16 reinforces the conclusion that Rule 16 leaves no room for any inherent power to order represented parties to attend pretrial settlement *669 conferences. While the majority makes much of the drafters' general intent to allow district courts "to make wider use of their powers and to manage actively their dockets," the majority offers little in the way of specifics. The advisory committee note does not discuss settlement conferences in much detail. The note does state, however, that "(A)lthough it is not the purpose of Rule 16(b)(7) to impose settlement negotiations on unwilling litigants it is believed that providing a neutral forum for discussing the subject might foster it."

The majority brushes aside this admonition by drawing a distinction between being required to attend a settlement conference and being required to negotiate. This distinction is puzzling. I suppose that if a represented party is required to come to court to state his position--even if that position is simply, "I refuse to settle. See you at trial."--that would not be requiring the represented party to "negotiate." But if that is all the majority is requiring, then the majority has recognized nothing more than a district court's inherent power to waste litigants' time doing what their attorneys could have done (and were hired to do). Rule 16's drafters could hardly have meant to approve (or allow) such a pointless exercise.

The majority obviously does not envision that a settlement conference should be the pointless exercise sketched out above. The majority cites with approval the district court's statement that "'(t)he only requirement imposed by the magistrate was that (Oat's) representative be present with full authority to settle, should terms for settlement be proposed that were acceptable to (Oat).'" Majority opinion at 653. The majority also states that a district court may require represented parties "to come to court to consider the possibility of settlement." But requiring that a party consider the possibility of settlement and that the party have authority to settle if another party proposes acceptable terms presupposes that besides stating his own position, the party must sit and listen to other parties' (and, possibly, the court's) proposals. How else could a representative with "authority to settle" act on terms he might find acceptable, except by listening to possible terms? It appears that the court is saying that a district court may order a represented party to appear in court both to talk and listen about settlement--in other words, to actually discuss settlement. I cannot see any meaningful distinction between this kind of activity and "negotiation;" after all, negotiation in large measure simply involves discussion. If a distinction does exist, it is so blurry as to be almost invisible, and certainly difficult, if not impossible, to enforce. The distinction is especially elusive in this case because, as Judge Easterbrook notes, dissenting opinion at 664, the magistrate's order that Oat send a representative with "authority to settle" could only mean that Oat's representative had to have the ability to settle by paying money--even if, as the majority claims, "authority to settle" did not mean that the representative had to be willing to use that ability. What is the point of insisting on such authority if not to require negotiation?

The majority errs by interpreting the advisory committee's admonition against forced negotiations too narrowly. Rule 16 is dead set against any coercive settlement practices. The advisory committee note speaks only of facilitating--that is, providing a forum for the parties to voluntarily pursue--settlement. Cf. Strandell, 838 F.2d at 837. Even if it is possible to draw a distinction between "discussing" and "negotiating" that is reasonably possible to enforce, the kind of coerced participation by represented parties in settlement conferences that the majority seems to approve is close enough to forced negotiation to fall within the advisory committee's general admonition against forced settlement. Moreover, Rule 16 "was not intended to require that an unwilling litigant be sidetracked from the normal course of litigation." Id. Rule 16's language and structure--its consistent distinction between represented and unrepresented parties--leave no doubt that in the normal course of litigation, including settlement discussions, the rule's drafters envisioned that courts would work with attorneys, not the attorneys' clients. Given *670 Rule 16's clear language, the advisory committee's comments leave no room for construing that rule to allow a district court to order represented parties, under threat of contempt (see Fed.R.Civ.P. 16(f) and 37(b)(2)(D)), to appear in court to discuss settlement.

One may ask why the majority strains to get around Rule 16's clear language and the advisory committee's admonition against coercive settlement practices. Implicit in the majority's opinion--and explicit in the dissent to the panel opinion--is the notion that to effectively manage their case loads, district courts need the power to order represented parties to appear at settlement conferences. See majority opinion at 650-51; G. Heileman Brewing Co. v. Joseph Oat Corp., 848 F.2d 1415, 1427 (7th Cir.1988) (dissenting opinion); see also Judge Posner's dissenting opinion at 657. Even if this is so (and I do not think it is), it does not justify expansively interpreting the district courts' inherent power to exceed the bounds Rule 16 sets. Moreover, as Judge Coffey and Judge Posner demonstrate, if any benefits do result from allowing district courts to order represented parties to attend settlement conferences, those benefits do not come without substantial costs. One of those costs is that expansively construing inherent power encourages judicial high-handedness. This case (in which Judge Posner has accurately labeled the magistrate's actions as "arbitrary, unreasonable, willful, and indeed petulant," dissenting opinion at 658) and the case uninvolving the Secretary of Labor, Will, cited by Judge Coffey, dissenting opinion at 661-62, aptly demonstrate that danger. Another cost is the expense and imposition on litigants that litigants try to avoid by hiring attorneys. A third cost is the denigration of the attorney's role in litigation. Perhaps the greatest cost, as Judge Coffey explains in detail, dissenting opinion at 662, is the damage to the appearance of fairness and the federal court's image as a neutral forum, factors that are essential to the court's proper functioning. Say what we will about the difference between coercing settlement and coercing attendance, it is difficult to believe that a litigant who has been forced to appear against his will, and possibly to listen to the opposing party or a judicial officer berate his litigation position, is going to walk away from that experience feeling he will get a fair shake from the court at trial if he resists the pressure to capitulate.

Obdurate litigants who unreasonably refuse to settle may cause headaches for the courts and opposing litigants. But litigants have no duty to settle, or even negotiate, and Rule 16 makes clear that federal courts have no business trying to force litigants to negotiate. If a litigant's position is legally or factually unsound, procedures such as judgment on the pleadings, Rule 12(b) dismissal, and summary judgment exist to dispose of the case at an early stage. District courts also have substantial power--of which they should take full advantage--to deter and punish frivolous litigation and undue delay. See 848 F.2d at 1421-22 (mentioning, among other things, the district courts' scheduling power under Rule 16 and the courts' sanctioning powers under Rule 16, Rule 11, and 28 U.S.C. section 1927). And district courts still have other methods--without forcing unwilling litigants to appear in court under threat of contempt--to facilitate settlements, including the time-honored method of pushing cases to early trials. See id; see also Strandell, 838 F.2d at 887. Where these methods do not produce settlements, it is unlikely that coercion will. And where coercion does succeed in producing a settlement, it is unlikely that success will advance the cause of justice or the federal court's image as a neutral forum.

In what seems to be an attempt to justify its result by implying that coercing represented parties to appear at settlement conferences has received widespread judicial approval, the majority asserts that "requiring represented parties to appear in person ... has been part and parcel of ... settlement conferences for years." Majority opinion at 651 n. 4. The only case the majority cites for this statement is In re LaMarre, 494 F.2d 753 (6th Cir.1974). In LaMarre, counsel for plaintiffs and defendants indicated to the district court on the morning of trial that they had reached a *671 settlement. The defendant's insurer's claims manager, however, would not accept the settlement. The district court ordered the claims manager to appear in court to discuss the matter and, when the claims manager failed to appear, held him in criminal contempt. Id. at 754-55. The court of appeals upheld the court's general authority to order the claims manager to appear. Id. at 756.

LaMarre is distinguishable. Because of the conflict between the defendant, his counsel (hired by the insurance company), and the insurance company, it is arguable that the insurance company was not a represented party (assuming that it was a party at all); even though the insurer hires and pays the attorney, the attorney's allegiance is to the defendant, not the insurer. If that's so, even the amended Rule 16 would not prohibit ordering the insurer's representative to appear in court because amended Rule 16 expressly authorizes district courts to order unrepresented parties to appear.

More importantly, LaMarre, despite its broad language, see id. at 756, does not stand for any widespread judicial approval for ordering represented parties to appear at settlement conferences. LaMarre is the only appellate case (besides this case) that has even dealt with the issue. More importantly, the Sixth Circuit decided LaMarre long before the 1983 amendments to Rule 16. Since the Sixth Circuit could not consider Rule 16 as amended, LaMarre simply does not address whether Rule 16, as it now stands, limits the district court's power to order represented parties to appear at settlement conferences.

The answer to the question that LaMarre could not address is clear. Rule 16, as amended, authorizes district courts to order only attorneys and unrepresented parties to appear at pretrial conferences. The rule consistently distinguishes between attorneys and unrepresented parties on one hand, and represented parties on the other. That distinction is consistent with litigants' statutory right to representation by counsel and with the attorney's traditional role in litigation, including settlement. No reason exists why Rule 16's drafters wrote the rule as they did if they did not mean what they said. Finally, the advisory committee note to the 1983 amendment of Rule 16 states that Rule 16 was not meant "to impose settlement negotiations on unwilling litigants," and, more generally, that Rule 16 is dead set against any coercion in settlement. Taken together, all this can lead to only one conclusion: Rule 16 leaves no room for any inherent power in the district courts to order represented parties to appear at settlement conferences.

"Federal judges spend lots of time telling other officials to stay within constitutional and statutory bounds, however those bounds may chafe in particular circumstances." Newman-Green, Inc. v. Alfonzo-Larrain R., 854 F.2d 916, 926 (7th Cir.1988). However much federal courts may desire the power to address unwilling parties directly in endeavoring to induce settlements, Rule 16 commands that the courts work through the parties' attorneys if that is what the parties desire. Rather than straining to circumvent Rule 16's clear command, we should demand that those of us in the federal judiciary practice what we preach so much to others, and work within the entirely reasonable limits that Rule 16 sets. Because the magistrate did not have the power to order Oat to send a corporate representative to the settlement conference, I would reverse the district court's judgment.[2]

---

[2] The majority also holds that Oat has waived any objection to the magistrate's order because Oat did not object before the settlement conference. See majority opinion at 654-55. For the reasons stated in the panel opinion, 848 F.2d at 1418, I would hold that Oat has not waived its right to object to the magistrate's order. I also agree with Judge Posner that even if the magistrate had the power to order Oat to send a corporate representative, other than its attorney, to the settlement conference, the magistrate abused his discretion in exercising that power. Even if a district court may order a corporate representative to appear, the court may not insist that the representative have "authority to settle." See Fed.R.Civ.P. 16, advisory committee note

Exercise 7.1

Prepare a draft, in 1,000 words or less, of a reasoned explanation of your position on either or both of the following questions:

(1) Is it appropriate for trial judges to confer with the parties in a pending case, together with their attorneys, for the purpose of bringing about either a settlement or an agreement to use some method of dispute resolution other than a traditional adversary trial?

(2) If so, what self-imposed limitations would you observe in such conferences if you were a trial judge?

("The reference to 'authority' in Rule 16(c) is not intended to insist upon the ability to settle the litigation"); see also Judge Easterbrook's dissenting opinion at 664.

CHAPTER 8

CONDUCTING JURY AND NONJURY TRIALS

BULL
v.
McCUSKEY

Supreme Court of Nevada. Aug. 21, 1980.
615 P.2d 957

Physician sued attorney to recover damages for abuse of process, contending that the attorney instituted a medical malpractice suit against him for the ulterior purpose of coercing a nuisance settlement, knowing that there was no basis for the claim of malpractice. The Second Judicial District Court, Washoe County, William N. Forman, J., rendered judgment for the physician and attorney appealed. The Supreme Court, Thompson, J., held that: (1) evidence of abuse of process was sufficient for the jury; (2) the fact that the trial court allowed the underlying suit to go to the jury did not bar by collateral estoppel the abuse of process suit; (3) the award of $35,000 in compensatory damages and $50,000 in punitive damages was supported by the evidence; and (4) though the denigrating comments of the attorney concerning the physician during the trial of the malpractice case were privileged and should not have been admitted in evidence in the abuse of process case, their admission was not prejudicially erroneous.

Affirmed.

*959 OPINION

THOMPSON, Justice:

Dr. Charles McCuskey commenced this action against attorney Samuel Bull to recover damages for abuse of process. It was his contention that attorney Bull, acting for Catherine Doucette, instituted a malpractice suit against him for the ulterior purpose of coercing a nuisance settlement knowing that there was no basis for the claim of malpractice. A jury returned its verdict for Dr. McCuskey, awarding him $35,000 as compensatory and $50,000 as punitive damages. Bull has appealed from the judgment entered upon jury verdict and from denial of his post-trial motion for judgment n. o. v., or in the alternative, a new trial. The main claim of error is that the evidence does not show an abuse of process. Other errors also are assigned and will be considered.

On May 20, 1974, Catherine Doucette, an 86-year-old woman, was admitted to St. Mary's Hospital following an automobile accident. She had sustained multiple injuries, including fractures of the left wrist, the patellas, and the right femur. Because of her age, she also suffered from an arteriosclerotic heart disease, and was senile. Dr. Charles McCuskey was called to take care of the orthopedic problems, while other doctors managed her other disabilities. The following August, she was transferred from St. Mary's Hospital to the Physicians' Hospital for Extended Care. She was depressed, uncooperative and uncommunicative. While there, she developed bed sores on her hips and heels. Because of this, her nephew, Milan Jeffers, who had been appointed her guardian, dismissed Dr. McCuskey and replaced him with Dr. Jack Sargent. Soon after the substitution, Jeffers inquired of Dr. Sargent whether there had been malpractice by Dr. McCuskey and was told that there was none. Apparently, her bed sores resulted either from her refusal to follow directions, or her inability to do so, and were not traceable to any conduct of the doctor.

In October 1974, Milan Jeffers contacted attorney Bull. An action charging Dr. McCuskey with malpractice, and the Physicians' Hospital with negligence then was filed. The complaint was filed on the basis of Jeffers' statement that the condition of his aunt, Catherine Doucette, had greatly deteriorated, and upon photographs showing bed sores, which photographs were taken by Bull's assistant.

Before filing suit, attorney Bull did not examine nor did he obtain medical records from St. Mary's Hospital or Physicians' Hospital. He did not confer with a doctor. Neither did he submit his client's claim to the Joint Screening Panel, established pursuant to an agreement between the Washoe County Medical Society and the Washoe County Bar Association.[1]

After filing suit, attorney Bull did not secure the

---

[1] Since April 30, 1975, state statute provides for the joint medical-legal screening panel. See 1975 Nev.Stats. ch. 302.

deposition of Dr. McCuskey, nor of any doctor. He did not retain an expert for trial, nor attempt to do so.

Shortly before trial, the claim against Physicians' Hospital was settled for $750. Dr. McCuskey refused to authorize his carrier to settle for any amount, although settlement of the claim against him also could have been made for $750.

During trial, attorney Bull called Dr. McCuskey incompetent, a fumble-fingered fellow, a liar, a scoundrel, a damned idiot. He also said, "(i)t will be a cold day in hell when I let that dum-dum take care of my mother." Of the doctor he also stated, "(h)e will lie under oath, steel an elderly woman's redress, cheat if he can get away with it, and all that is left for him is to make a pact with the devil and murder those who would oppose him."

The jury to whom the medical malpractice action was presented, quickly returned its verdict for Dr. McCuskey. Dr. McCuskey then commenced this action against attorney Bull for abuse of process.

*960 (1) 1. The main assignment of error is that the evidence may not be viewed as establishing the elements of the tort of abuse of process. Recently, this court had occasion to consider that tort. Nevada Credit Rating Bur. v. Williams, 88 Nev. 601, 503 P.2d 9 (1972). We there noted that the two essential elements of abuse of process are an ulterior purpose, and a willful act in the use of the process not proper in the regular conduct of the proceeding. The malice and want of probable cause necessary to a claim of malicious prosecution are not essential to recovery for abuse of process. Moreover, we mentioned that abuse of process hinges on the misuse of regularly issued process in contrast to malicious prosecution which rests upon the wrongful issuance of process.

In Nevada Credit Rating Bur. we sustained an award of compensatory and punitive damages for abuse of process. In that case, property valued at more than $30,000 was attached to secure an alleged debt of less than $5,000. We deemed that to be a willful misuse of the ancillary remedy of attachment for the ulterior purpose of coercing payment of the sum claimed to be due.

In the case at hand, it is asserted that the process (complaint and summons) charging Dr. McCuskey with malpractice was misused for the ulterior purpose of coercing a nuisance settlement. In considering all evidence presented, it was permissible for the jury to conclude that attorney Bull had utilized an alleged claim of malpractice for the ulterior purpose of coercing a nuisance settlement. His offer to settle the case for the minimal sum of $750 when considered in the light of his failure adequately to investigate before deciding to file suit and the total absence of essential expert evidence, supports such a conclusion by the jury, and we may not set it aside.

(2) 2. Next, it is asserted that certain rulings of the trial court in the medical malpractice action preclude recovery by Dr. McCuskey in this case by reason of the doctrine of collateral estoppel. This contention is without substance.

In the malpractice case the district court denied Dr. McCuskey's pre-trial motion for summary judgment, and also his motion for a directed verdict tendered during trial. It is asserted that those rulings conclusively establish that the Doctor's instant action for abuse of process is without merit.

(3) The relitigation of an issue that has been finally resolved in a prior case may be barred by the doctrine of collateral estoppel. Clark v. Clark, 80 Nev. 52, 389 P.2d 69 (1964). The mentioned rulings in the earlier malpractice action were interlocutory rather than final. The only final determination in that action was a judgment entered upon a jury verdict that Dr. McCuskey was not liable for malpractice. The doctrine of collateral estoppel is not concerned with interlocutory rulings.

(4) 3. It is asserted that the evidence simply does not support either the award of $35,000 in compensatory damages or $50,000 in punitive damages.

(5) a. The compensatory damages recoverable in an action for abuse of process are the same as in an action for malicious prosecution, Prosser, Law of Torts at 858 (4th ed. 1971), and include compensation for fears, anxiety, mental and emotional distress. Spellens v. Spellens, 49 Cal.2d 210, 317 P.2d 613 (Cal.1957). In Miller v. Schnitzer, 78 Nev. 301, 371 P.2d 824 (1962), a malicious prosecution case, we wrote:

> (T)he plaintiff may recover general money damages to compensate for injury to reputation . . .,

humiliation, embarrassment, mental suffering and inconvenience, provided they are shown to have resulted as the proximate consequence of the defendant's act. These elements of damage are wholly subjective. The monetary extent of damage cannot be calculated by reference to an objective standard. The extent of such damage, by its very nature, falls peculiarly within the province of the trier of fact, in this case, a jury. (Citations) The only limitation upon the judgment of the jury in this regard is that the damages thus awarded must not have been given under the influence *961 of passion or prejudice. NRCP 59(a)(6).

In the Miller case we affirmed a compensatory damage award of $30,000, noting that the record, when read in the light most favorable to plaintiff, contained substantial evidence tending to prove damage to reputation, extreme embarrassment, humiliation, mental suffering and inconvenience as the proximate consequence of the defendant's conduct. That observation applies with equal force to the record now before us. The compensatory damage award of $35,000 is fully supported by the evidence.

b. In an action for the breach of an obligation not arising from contract, punitive damages may be recovered where the defendant has been guilty of oppression, fraud or malice, express or implied. NRS 42.010. It is suggested that malice is not shown, and, in any event, that the award of $50,000 is too high.

(6) Malice may be established by showing that the defendant's conduct was willful, intentional and done in reckless disregard of its possible consequences. Nevada Credit Rating Bur. v. Williams, 88 Nev. 601, 503 P.2d 9 (1972). It was permissible for the jury to conclude that suit was filed against Dr. McCuskey and an offer to settle made with the intention to force a nuisance payment, and that this occurred intentionally and in reckless disregard of possible consequences. Accordingly, an award of punitive damages was within the province of the jury to allow.

Heretofore, we have recognized the subjective nature of punitive damages, Caple v. Raynel Campers, Inc., 90 Nev. 341, 526 P.2d 334 (1974), and the absence of workable standards by which to evaluate the propriety of such an award. Accordingly, we have allowed that determination to rest with the discretion of the trier of the fact, Midwest Supply, Inc. v. Waters, 89 Nev. 210, 510 P.2d 876 (1973), unless the evidence introduced at trial shows that the amount awarded by the jury would financially destroy or annihilate the defendant, Miller v. Schnitzer, supra, in which event we would attempt an appropriate adjustment of the award.

In the case at hand, trial evidence as to attorney Bull's net worth was not produced. Therefore, we are unable to conclude that the award was excessive.

(7) 4. The denigrating comments of attorney Bull concerning Dr. McCuskey during the trial of the malpractice case (incompetent, a liar, a scoundrel, a damned idiot, etc.) were received in evidence in this case to show malice. A prior motion in limine to preclude such evidence was tendered and denied. This ruling is asserted to be reversible error.

(8) As a general proposition an attorney at law is absolutely privileged to publish defamatory matter concerning another in communications preliminary to a proposed judicial proceeding, or in the institution of or during the course and as a part of, a judicial proceeding in which he participates as counsel, if it has some relation to the proceeding. Restatement (Second) of Torts § 586 (1976); Richards v. Conklin, 94 Nev. 84, 575 P.2d 588 (1978). The privilege rests upon a public policy of securing to attorneys as officers of the court the utmost freedom in their efforts to obtain justice for their clients.

The malpractice complaint placed in issue Dr. McCuskey's competence as a physician. When Dr. McCuskey testified in that case, he placed in issue his credibility. Attorney Bull's comments may be understood to pertain to either Dr. McCuskey's competence or his credibility, and therefore, are privileged. The motion in limine should have been granted.

It does not follow, however, that the error in admitting such evidence requires this court to set aside the judgment entered upon jury verdict. An error in the reception of evidence which does not affect the substantial rights of the parties must be disregarded as harmless. NRCP 61.

We already have mentioned the evidence that would allow the jury to find malice and award punitive damages. With this in mind, it is evident that the reception of *962 attorney Bull's denigrating comments was not essential to the punitive damage issue and, therefore, may be deemed harmless.

Although the denigrating comments of attorney Bull

regarding Dr. McCuskey were privileged, and alone would not supply a basis for liability in damages, it does not follow that an attorney may so conduct himself without fear of discipline. Indeed the oath taken by an attorney licensed to practice in Nevada states in part "that I will abstain from all offensive personalities and advance no fact prejudicial to the honor or reputation of a party or witness, unless required by the justice of the cause with which I am charged . . . ." Moreover, SCR 188(4) commands that a lawyer should never be unfair or abusive or inconsiderate to adverse witnesses or opposing litigants. His obligation to present his client's cause vigorously does not contemplate violation of the attorney's oath or of the standards of conduct.

5. We shall not comment upon the remaining assignment of error that of the impeachment of a witness by reference to his prior felony conviction, when that conviction had been satisfied by an honorable discharge from probation and the witness released from all penalties and disabilities resulting therefrom since the impeaching evidence already was before the jury through an earlier witness without objection.

Affirmed.

MOWBRAY, C. J., BATJER and MANOUKIAN, JJ., and ZENOFF,[2] Senior Justice, concur.

---

[2] The Chief Justice designated the Hon. David Zenoff, Senior Justice, to sit in the place of the Hon. E. M. Gunderson, Justice. Nev.Const. art. 6, s 19; SCR 10.

ROSSELL
v.
VOLKSWAGEN OF AMERICA

Supreme Court of Arizona, En Banc. Oct. 28, 1985.
Reconsideration Denied Dec. 17, 1985.
709 P.2d 517, 147 Ariz. 160

Guardian ad litem filed suit on behalf of automobile passenger for negligence against automobile manufacturer and distributor. The Superior Court, Maricopa County, Roger G. Strand, J., entered judgment in favor of passenger, and manufacturer appealed. The Court of Appeals, 709 P.2d 533, reversed, and review was granted. The Supreme Court, Feldman, J., held that: (1) the jury was free to reach conclusion that manufacturer had negligently placed battery system inside passenger compartment on basis of its own experience and knowledge of what was "reasonable," even in absence of expert opinion, and (2) replacement of original battery with battery too large to fit in designed restraint system was not intervening, superseding cause sufficient to excuse manufacturer's negligent placement of battery system within passenger compartment.

Opinion of Court of Appeals vacated; judgment affirmed.

*519 FELDMAN, Justice.

This is a product liability action brought by Phyllis A. Rossell, as guardian ad litem on behalf of her daughter, Julie Ann Kennon (plaintiff), against the manufacturer and the North American distributor of Volkswagen automobiles. The defendants will be referred to collectively as "Volkswagen." The case involves the design of the battery system in the model of the Volkswagen automobile popularly known as the "Beetle" or "Bug." The jury found for the plaintiff and awarded damages in the sum of $1,500,000. The court of appeals held that the plaintiff had failed to establish a prima facie case of either negligence or proximate cause and that the trial judge had erred in denying Volkswagen's motion for judgment n.o.v. (Rossell v. Volkswagen of America, 147 Ariz.App. 176, 709 P.2d 533 (1984.) Believing that the court of appeals had incorrectly stated the applicable law with respect to both *520 issues, we granted review. Rule 23, Ariz.R.Civ.App.P., 17A A.R.S. We have jurisdiction under Arizona Constitution art. 6, section 5(3) and A.R.S. section 12-120.24.

FACTS

We view the facts in the light most favorable to the party who prevailed at trial. McFarlin v. Hall, 127 Ariz. 220, 224, 619 P.2d 729, 733 (1980). This action arises from a 1970, one-vehicle accident. At the time of the accident Julie, then eleven months old, was sleeping in the front passenger seat of a 1958 Volkswagen driven by her mother. At approximately 11:00 p.m., on State Route 93, Ms. Rossell fell asleep and the vehicle drifted to the right, off the paved roadway. The sound of the car hitting a sign awakened Rossell, and she attempted to correct the path of the car, but oversteered. The car flipped over, skidded off the road and landed on its roof at the bottom of a cement culvert. The force of the accident dislodged and fractured the battery which was located inside the passenger compartment. In the seven hours it took Rossell to regain full consciousness and then extract herself and her daughter from the car, the broken battery slowly dripped sulfuric acid on Julie. The acid severly burned her face, chest, arm, neck, part of her back and shoulder, and both hands. Since the accident Julie has undergone extensive corrective surgery but remains seriously disfigured and in need of additional surgery.

Plaintiff filed the complaint in May, 1978. She alleged four theories of recovery: negligent design of the battery system and strict liability for the defective design of the battery system, the heating system and for the propensity of the vehicle to roll over. Prior to trial, the court entered partial summary judgment for Volkswagen on the theory of strict liability for battery system design. This ruling was based on the replacement of the original battery with a larger battery which did not fit the designed restraints and which the court felt constituted "a substantial change in the condition in which the vehicle was sold." See Restatement (Second) of Torts 402A(b) (1965) (hereafter Restatement, section). The summary judgment order preserved the claim based on negligent design for placement of the battery. After the close of the plaintiff's case, the court granted a directed verdict on the issues involving heating system design and roll-over propensity. Plaintiff has not taken a cross-appeal from these rulings. Thus, the case was submitted to the jury only on the question of Volkswagen's negligence in locating the battery inside the passenger compartment.

Plaintiff argued at trial that battery placement within the passenger compartment created an unreasonable risk of harm and that alternative designs were available and practicable. In their trial motions and later motion for judgment n.o.v., Volkswagen argued that plaintiff had failed to make a prima facie case. First, it claimed that in a negligent design case the defendant must comply with the standard of a reasonably prudent designer of automobiles and that

> knowledge of automobile design principles and engineering practices often is beyond the knowledge of laymen, (so that) plaintiff in a case such as this must produce expert testimony establishing the minimum standard of care and deviation therefrom in designing the automobile....

(Defendant's Supplemental Brief at 11.) Concluding its argument, Volkswagen pointed out that plaintiff produced no testimony

> expert or otherwise, (to) describe what was expected of (or done by) a reasonable automobile designer or manufacturer in 1958 ... or that defendants failed to meet (that) standard of care.

(Id. at 14.)

DID PLAINTIFF MAKE A PRIMA FACIE CASE OF NEGLIGENCE?

Legal Principles Applicable to a Negligent Design Case

The trial judge characterized Volkswagen's position as a contention that plaintiff could not prevail in the

> *521 absence of testimony ... from a qualified expert as opposed to simply permitting the jury to infer it, ... that the standard of care required of a prudent manufacturer would require that the battery be placed elsewhere (or that) it was negligent ... not to have placed it outside of the passenger compartment.

(Transcript of January 29, 1980.)

The trial judge disagreed with Volkswagen and denied the motion for judgment n.o.v. However, a majority of the court of appeals held that such evidence was required for a prima facie case. That court held

> (i)n order to establish the duty element of its negligence theory, (plaintiff) would have to provide expert witness testimony regarding the expert's opinion concerning the battery system design of ordinary careful manufacturers of automobiles in 1957. This was not done.

(Slip op. at 9.)

> The state ... of the art can be established by expert testimony.... Here the questions were not asked, and this aspect of duty was not established by the evidence.

(Id. at 12.)

We do not agree with the views expressed by the court of appeals. First, the concept of "duty," mentioned twice by the court's majority, is irrelevant to the issues presented by this case. Duty, of course, is a necessary element in a negligence case. To satisfy that element, the court must find that the relation between plaintiff and defendant was such that it imposed upon the latter a legal obligation to use some degree of care for the protection of the former. Coburn v. City of Tucson, 143 Ariz. 50, 52, 691 P.2d 1078, 1080 (1984), quoting W. Prosser & W. Keeton, THE LAW OF TORTS section 53 at 356 (5th ed. 1984). Ever since MacPherson v. Buick Motor Co., 217 N.Y. 382, 111 N.E. 1050 (1916) it has been accepted that even in the absence of privity of contract an automobile manufacturer is under a duty of care to those who use the automobile. MacPherson is still the rule in Arizona. Crouse v. Wilbur-Ellis Co., 77 Ariz. 359, 366, 272 P.2d 352, 357 (1954).

(1) Intimations about limitations of duty based on unforeseeability also appear in the majority opinion. (Slip op. at 12.) Palsgraf v. Long Island Railway Co., 248 N.Y. 339, 162 N.E. 99 (1928), teaches that the duty of care does not extend to potential victims outside the zone of foreseeable risk. Palsgraf is the law in Arizona. See McFarlin v. Hall, supra; West v. Cruz, 75 Ariz. 13, 251 P.2d 311 (1952). However, a passenger in a motor vehicle is not an "unforeseeable plaintiff" as to the manufacturer of that vehicle. Palsgraf has no application to the present case. In short, we see no duty issue here and note that Volkswagen has raised none. Its primary argument is directed to problems connected with the standard of care applied when

duty does exist.[1]

We turn, then, to the central issue presented. What type of proof must plaintiff produce in order to make a prima facie case of negligent design against a product manufacturer? What is the standard of care? In the ordinary negligence case, tried under the familiar rubric of "reasonable care," plaintiff's proof must provide facts from which the jury may conclude that defendant's behavior fell below the "reasonable man" standard. Prosser, supra section 31 at 169. This question is ordinarily decided without providing the jury with any direct evidence about the details of what may or may not comply with the standard of care.[2] The risk/benefit analysis *522 involved in deciding what is reasonable care under the circumstances is generally left to the jury, id. at 173,

> ... and the function of the jury in fixing the standard of reasonable conduct is so closely related to law that it amounts to a mere filling in of the details of the legal standard.

Prosser, supra section 37, at 238.

Thus, in the usual negligence case the jury is left to reach its own conclusion on whether defendant's conduct

---

[1] Volkswagen has argued the lack of foreseeability of the accident as it relates to the issues of negligence and proximate cause. See infra at 525-528.

[2] Cf. Moorer v. Clayton Mfg. Corp., 128 Ariz. 565, 627 P.2d 716 (App.1981). Moorer is a strict liability, defective design case in which, as here, the court disagreed with defendant's contention that appellee (plaintiff) had not sustained its burden of proof by failing to present evidence of the product's non-conformance with the applicable standard. The court explained:

> Appellee's expert witness testified that the "nip-point" made it hazardous. The jury saw pictures of the machine and heard testimony describing how the emissions control test was performed and how the accident happened. Whether the design there satisfied the strict liability standard was a question of fact for the jury.

Id. at 568, 627 P.2d at 719.

complied with the legal standard of reasonable care. There need be no opinion testimony on the subject; the jury is encouraged, under proper instruction, to consider the circumstances, use its own experience and apply community standards in deciding what is or is not negligence. Id. at 237; section 32, at 173-74.

Volkswagen claims that negligent design cases are an exception. They contend that product manufacturers are held to an expert's standard of care, as are professionals such as lawyers, doctors and accountants. In professional malpractice cases the reasonable man standard has been replaced with the standard of "what is customary and usual in the profession." Prosser, supra section 32, at 189. This, of course, requires plaintiff to establish by expert testimony the usual conduct of other practitioners of defendant's profession and to prove, further, that defendant deviated from that standard.

>It has been pointed out often enough that this gives the medical profession, and also the (other professions), the privilege, <u>which is usually emphatically denied to other groups</u>, of setting their own legal standards of conduct, merely by adopting their own practices.

Id. (emphasis supplied) (citations omitted).

Should we adopt for manufacturers in negligent design cases a rule "emphatically denied to other groups" but similar to those applied to defendants in professional malpractice cases? Such a rule, of course, would require--not just permit--plaintiff to present explicit evidence of the usual conduct of other persons in the field of design by offering expert evidence of what constitutes "good design practice." Plaintiff would also be required to establish that the design adopted by the defendant deviated from such "good practice." We believe that such a rule is inappropriate.

(2) The malpractice requirement that plaintiff show the details of conduct practiced by others in defendant's profession is not some special favor which the law gives to professionals who may be sued by their clients. It is, instead, a method of holding such defendants to an even higher standard of care than that of an ordinary, prudent person. Prosser, supra section 32 at 185. Such a technique has not been applied in commercial settings, probably because the danger of allowing a commercial group to set its own standard of what is reasonable is not offset by professional

obligations which tend to prevent the group from setting standards at a low level in order to accommodate other interests. Thus, it is the general law that industries are not permitted to establish their own standard of conduct because they may be influenced by motives of saving "time, effort or money." Prosser, supra section 33 at 194. Long ago, Judge Learned Hand expressed the rule in a case in which the defendant claimed that it had not been negligent in failing to put Mr. Marconi's invention on its tugboats:

> Is it then a final answer that the business had not yet generally adopted receiving sets? ... Indeed in most cases reasonable prudence is in fact common prudence; but strictly it is never its measure; a whole calling may have unduly lagged in the adoption of new and available devices. It never may set its own *523 tests, however persuasive be its usages. Courts must in the end say what is required; there are precautions so imperative that even their universal disregard will not excuse their omission.

The T. J. Hooper, 60 F.2d 737, 740 (2d Cir.1932). This, of course, is not to say that evidence of custom and usage is inadmissible.

> What usually is done may be evidence of what ought to be done, but what ought to be done is fixed by a standard of reasonable prudence, whether it usually is complied with or not.

Texas & Pacific Railway Co. v. Behymer, 189 U.S. 468, 470, 23 S.Ct. 622, 623, 47 L.Ed. 905 (1903) (Holmes, J.). Holmes' view has been previously considered and approved by this court. Atchison, Topeka & Santa Fe Railway Co. v. Parr, 96 Ariz. 13, 17, 391 P.2d 575, 578 (1964).

Volkswagen argues that case law already recognizes that in negligent design cases a manufacturer is not liable absent a showing that he failed to conform to the standard of care in design followed by other manufacturers. We do not agree. Darner Motor Sales, Inc. v. Universal Underwriters Insurance Co., 140 Ariz. 383, 682 P.2d 388 (1984); Boyce v. Brown, 51 Ariz. 416, 77 P.2d 455 (1938); and Riedisser v. Nelson, 111 Ariz. 542, 534 P.2d 1052 (1975), are, for instance, cases involving professionals (insurance broker and physicians) sued by their clients or patients. National Housing Industries, Inc. v. E.L. Jones Development Co., 118 Ariz. 374, 576 P.2d 1374 (App.1978) involves the liability of a professional engineer to the assignee of its client, a developer. None of these cases consider the liability of a manufacturer for defects in mass-produced products. They do involve, instead, the liability of professionals who generally work in close relationship with their clients or patients. Cardullo v. General Motors Corp., 378 F.Supp. 890 (E.D.Pa.1974), affirmed, 511 F.2d 1392 (3rd Cir.1975) is inapposite but illustrates the difference. In Cardullo the court held that plaintiff's case failed for lack of expert evidence that the use of a single master brake cylinder was hazardous. Proof that the alternative of a dual master cylinder system was available was not, in itself, sufficient to make a prima facie case because plaintiff was also required to prove that the use of the single system was unreasonably dangerous. That is quite different from holding that plaintiff was obligated to prove, additionally, that industry practice required the use of a dual master cylinder. The latter ruling would, of course, tend to permit commercial defendants to prevail as a matter of law if their conduct complied with a general, negligent practice prevailing in their industry. This is exactly the rule criticized in Prosser, rejected by both Justice Holmes and Judge Hand, and rejected by this court in Parr, supra.

In view of public policy and existing law, we decline to transform defective design cases into malpractice cases. We believe the law is best left as it is in this field. Special groups will be allowed to create their own standards of reasonably prudent conduct only when the nature of the group and its special relationship with its clients assure society that those standards will be set with primary regard to protection of the public rather than to such considerations as increased profitability. We do not believe that automobile manufacturers fit into this category. This is no reflection upon automobile manufacturers, but merely a recognition that the necessities of the marketplace permit manufacturers neither the working relationship nor the concern about the welfare of their customers that the professions generally permit and require from their practitioners.

(3-5) Therefore, in Arizona the rule in negligence cases shall continue to be that evidence of industry custom and practice is generally admissible as evidence relevant to whether defendant's conduct was reasonable under the circumstances. In determining what is reasonable care for manufacturers, the plaintiff need only prove the defendant's conduct presented a foreseeable, unreasonable risk of harm.

As in all other negligence cases, the jury is permitted *524 to decide what is reasonable from the common experience of mankind. We do not disturb the rule that in determining what is "reasonable care," expert evidence may be required in those cases in which factual issues are outside the common understanding of jurors. Atchison, Topeka & Santa Fe Railway Co. v. Parr, 96 Ariz. at 18, 391 P.2d at 578-79. However, unlike most malpractice cases, there need not be explicit expert testimony establishing the standard of care and the manner in which defendant deviated from that standard. M. Udall & J. Livermore, LAW OF EVIDENCE section 25 at 43-44 (2d ed. 1982). With these principles in mind, we now turn to a consideration of the evidence in order to determine whether plaintiff did prove a prima facie case.

Application to the Evidence

Plaintiff presented two experts, Jon McKibben, an automotive engineer, and Charles Turnbow, a safety engineer. Their testimony established that the great majority of cars on the road at the time the Beetle in question was designed had batteries located outside the passenger compartment, usually in the engine compartment and occasionally in the luggage compartment. There was evidence from which the jury could find that from both an engineering and practical standpoint the 1958 Volkswagen could have been designed with the battery outside the passenger compartment, as was the Karmann Ghia, an upscale model which used the same chassis as the Beetle. There was further testimony that placement of the battery inside the passenger compartment was unreasonably dangerous because "batteries do fracture in crashes, not infrequently." According to McKibben,

> the degree to which the battery inside the compartment is a hazard depends to some extent on how likely it is that that battery is going to become dislodged or fractured or somehow spill acid. And certainly in a roll-over type crash, a battery in that location is more likely to be a hazard to the occupants. So the fact that this model Volkswagen tends to turn over with relatively high frequency makes the battery placement inside the car a more serious hazard than it might be in other types of vehicles.

(Trial transcript of October 9, 1979, at 42; see also transcript of October 10, 1979 at 48-49 (Turnbow).)

Volkswagen argues that the danger of interior battery

location was unforeseeable to a designer/manufacturer in the relevant time frame 1957-58. Of course, the contemporaneous foreseeability of unreasonable danger is the litmus test for negligent conduct.[3] Restatement section 289 comment b. If Volkswagen could not have foreseen that locating the battery within the passenger compartment posed an unreasonable risk of harm, then its design would not be negligent. Volkswagen argues that the only danger was Ms. Rossell's unforeseeable use of a battery too big to fit the restraints provided in Volkswagen's design.[4] However, the jury could have found that this did not affect the design hazard involved. While the battery in question was too large to fit in the designed restraints, *525 there was a danger of battery fracture during an accident even when batteries were properly restrained. Finally, there was testimony that various factors, including natural corrosion and deterioration, would often impair restraint systems, so that even a properly sized battery might be dislodged in a roll-over type accident.

(6) We conclude that the plaintiff did present expert evidence that the battery design location presented a foreseeable, unreasonable risk of harm, that alternative designs were available and that they were feasible from a technological and practical standpoint. We reject

---

[3] This distinguishes a negligent design case from a strict liability design case. In the latter, the quality of the product is the issue and is determined in light of knowledge which is obtained after manufacture. See, e.g., Phillips v. Kimwood Machine Co., 269 Or. 485, 491, 525 P.2d 1033, 1036 (1974).

[4] There was some conflict in the testimony with respect to the foreseeability of the use of over-sized replacement batteries. Plaintiff's experts claimed that the original equipment battery was unavailable in America and could not be used for replacement, so that a replacement battery would be larger than the designed system. Volkswagen counters with the argument that vehicles manufactured for the export market, particularly in America, were designed for and equipped with a larger battery. This difficult factual issue is not as important as it might seem, at least to our review, because there was testimony from plaintiff's experts that replacement on most Volkswagens was with a battery even larger than either of those. This larger battery would fit neither the domestic nor the export battery restraint systems of the Beetle. It was, in fact, this larger battery that the Rossell vehicle was using at the time of the accident.

Volkswagen's contention that in addition to the evidence outlined above, plaintiff was compelled to produce expert opinion evidence that the standard of "good design practice" required Volkswagen to design the car so that the battery system was located outside the passenger compartment. Unlike a malpractice case, the jury was free to reach or reject this conclusion on the basis of its own experience and knowledge of what is "reasonable," with the assistance of expert opinion describing only the dangers, hazards and factors of design involved.[5]

PROXIMATE CAUSE

Volkswagen argues that "foreseeability must be established as an element of proximate cause" (Defendant's Supplemental Brief at 21), and that the real proximate cause of plaintiff's injury in the present case was the intervening, superseding negligence of the unknown person that installed a battery too large to be contained by the restraint system of Rossell's car. (Id. at 8.) The court of appeals agreed. (Slip op. at 12-16.) Since the trial judge did instruct the jury on the proximate cause issue, all questions of fact on that issue have been resolved in plaintiff's favor.[6]

(7) An intervening cause is one which intervenes between

---

[5] We need not concern ourselves with whether any of these issues could have been submitted to the jury without expert evidence. The evidence was presented; there is no need to go beyond that.

[6] In part, the instruction read as follows:

Not all intervening causes are superseding causes. A superseding cause is an intervening cause which by its nature becomes the proximate cause of the injury and relieves the defendant of any liability for said injury.

For an intervening cause to be a superseding cause it must be a cause which could not have been reasonably foreseen or anticipated by the defendant.

Defendant has not claimed that the trial court erred in this instruction. As will be seen, infra, at 526, the instruction was probably more favorable to defendant's position than is justified by the current state of the law.

defendant's negligent act and the final result and is a necessary component in bringing about that result. Prosser, supra section 44 at 301, et seq. Given the complexity of life, there is little that can be attributed to any single act, and the law does not relieve a defendant from liability simply because of the intervening act of a third person. It is only when the intervening act is considered superseding cause that the original actor is relieved of liability for his negligence. Id. The test for a superseding cause is simpler to articulate than it is to apply and has been a frequent source of litigation and confusion.

In the final analysis, the question of superseding cause

> has been determined by asking whether the intervention of the later cause is a significant part of the risk involved in defendant's conduct, or so reasonably connected with it that the responsibility (of defendant) should not be terminated. It is therefore said that the defendant is to be held liable if, but only if, the intervening cause is "foreseeable."
>
> But here, ... this overworked and undefined word covers a multitude of sins. It is at least clear that in many cases recovery has been allowed where the intervening cause was not one which any reasonable actor could be expected to anticipate or have in mind, but it is regarded as 'normal' to the situation which the actor has created. In other words, although the theory of the cases is one of *526 foreseeability, a considerable element of hindsight may have entered into its practical application.

Id. at 302-03; see also Restatement, section 435 comment d.

Thus, the text writers and commentators generally acknowledge that an intervening force becomes a superseding cause only when its operation was both unforeseeable and when with the benefit of "hindsight" it may be described as abnormal or extraordinary. These principles have been acknowledged in Arizona whenever the issues have been raised. See, e.g., Ontiveros v. Borak, 136 Ariz. 500, 506, 667 P.2d 200, 206 (1983) (superseding cause is one which is unforeseeable and, viewed through hindsight, extraordinary); Parness v. City of Tempe, 123 Ariz. 460, 464, 600 P.2d 764, 768 (App.1979) (where the intervening negligent or intentional act was within the scope of the original risk created by defendant's negligence, it is not a superseding cause); Central Alarm of Tucson v. Ganem, 116 Ariz. 74, 567 P.2d 1203 (App.1977) (burglar alarm company which left a key to deactivate the alarm system where it was accessible to unauthorized persons is not relieved of liability by intervening criminal acts of a third party).

These cases encompass the rule that the scope of the risk created by the negligence of the original actor may include the foreseeable negligent or criminal conduct of others. Hemet Dodge Corp. v. Gryder, 23 Ariz.App. 523, 534 P.2d 454 (1975) (Installer of incorrect radiator cap is liable notwithstanding the intervening act of the driver who negligently removed the cap from an overheated engine in the presence of others, including the plaintiff.); Brand v. J.H. Rose Trucking Co., 102 Ariz. 201, 427 P.2d 519 (1967); Prosser, supra section 44 at 304. The Restatement indicates that the intervening negligence of a third person is not a superseding cause if the original actor's conduct was a substantial factor in bringing about the result and if "a reasonable man knowing the situation existing when the act of the third person was done would not regard it as highly extraordinary that the third person had so acted" Restatement section 447(b) (emphasis supplied); Serrano v. Kenneth A. Ethridge Contracting Co., 2 Ariz.App. 473, 409 P.2d 757 (1966); see also Restatement sections 435 and 442(b).

(8) Thus, defendant is not relieved of liability simply because he could not have foreseen the manner in which the accident occurred, including the negligent intervention of third parties. Schnyder v. Empire Metals, Inc., 136 Ariz. 428, 430, 666 P.2d 528, 530 (App.1983). The question is whether the plaintiff was in the foreseeable range of defendant's negligent conduct (designing the vehicle with a battery located inside the driver's compartment) and whether the injury resulted from the recognizable risk that made that conduct negligent. Id.

With these principles in mind we turn again to the evidence to determine whether the trial court was required to rule as a matter of law that defendant's negligence was superseded by the intervening acts of the battery installer and the driver. The record indicates that the vehicle was made with a battery which foreseeably would need replacement every two to four years. According to one of plaintiff's experts, the car was designed with

> ... a battery size and battery cover size which was

almost impossible to fit in terms of an available (replacement) battery here in the United States or into which it was almost impossible to fit an available battery size.

(Trial transcript of October 4, 1979 at 113 (McKibben).)

Defendant's version of the facts was that properly sized replacement batteries were available and it was unforeseeable that properly sized replacement batteries would not be used. Nevertheless, there was evidence that the risk in locating the battery inside the passenger compartment was raised by the foreseeable non-use of the restraint system. McKibben testified:

> I believe I mentioned before the fact that hold-down systems tend to deteriorate with the passage of time. They tend to *527 corrode. They tend to become unusable so that when batteries are replaced, it is often not possible to reuse the previous restraint system or hold-down system. And obviously from my own personal experience, whoever installs the battery under those circumstances does not go out and seek additional or alternate hold-down parts ... to hold the battery back down.
>
> Secondly, in this particular case, assuming that this vehicle came with a 66-amp-hour battery of dimensions described in the Volkswagen's drawings that I have reviewed, I don't think that the cover and that ... the standard hold-down system would be usable and on a readily obtainable battery. It just flat won't fit on a battery that someone would be able to go down and buy at a typical battery outlet.

(Trial transcript of October 9, 1979 at 44.)

(9) In the final analysis, then, the intervening act of some third person consisted of installing a battery of any size without using the designed restraint system. In the present case the failure to use the restraint system may have been the result of using an oversized battery, of deterioration of the system through corrosion, of the installer's negligence, or of another cause. There was evidence that properly restrained batteries may break loose from the tie down system in a roll-over accident, so that design must also account for the danger of a properly restrained battery coming loose because of the nature of the

accident. There was even further evidence that batteries that did not come loose could be fractured in accidents. The jury could find, in other words, that the hazard created by Volkswagen's location of the battery in the passenger compartment was that the battery, when fractured for any one of a variety of reasons, would expose occupants to the danger of burns from sulfuric acid. We do not believe that it can be said as a matter of law that the fracture of a battery resulting in burns to someone within the passenger compartment was not attributable to the recognizable risk. Schnyder v. Empire Metals, supra. The injury was within the scope of the risk created by defendant's original design; whether the exact manner in which the accident occurred was foreseeable to defendant is not the determining factor. Id.; Restatement section 449.[7]

We hold that plaintiff did make a prima facie case of negligence and proximate cause. The trial court did not err in failing to direct a verdict or grant judgment n.o.v. Because we must vacate the court of appeals opinion, we now turn to the remaining issues which defendant raised on appeal and which the court of appeals did not address.

DID THE TRIAL COURT ERR BY ALLOWING PLAINTIFF TO REFER TO THE BEETLE'S PROPENSITIES TO ROLL-OVER AND TO INTRODUCE CARBON MONOXIDE INTO THE PASSENGER COMPARTMENT?

At the end of plaintiff's case Volkswagen moved for directed verdicts on plaintiff's theories pertaining to strict liability for the Beetle's propensities to roll over, strict liability for the propensity to introduce carbon monoxide into the passenger compartment, and negligent design of the battery system. The trial court granted the motion only with respect to the two strict liability claims. Volkswagen argues that plaintiff's persistent references, after the directed verdicts, to the Beetles' roll-over and carbon monoxide problems denied it a fair trial. It contends

---

[7] Cf: Peck v. Ford Motor Co., 603 F.2d 1240 (7th Cir.1979) (applying Indiana law), the case on which Volkswagen relies most heavily. Peck may well be a case in which defendant's tort had "spent its force." Id. at 1244. Indiana law on superseding cause is so substantially different from Arizona's that Peck has no application to the case at hand. Compare for example, Conder v. Hull Lift Truck, Inc., 435 N.E.2d 10, 14-15 (Ind.1982) with Ontiveros v. Borak, 136 Ariz. 500, 506, 667 P.2d 200, 206 (1983).

that the many examples of plaintiff's "continu(ing) to try issues removed by the directed verdict" (Defendant's Opening Brief to the Court of Appeals at 43) include such questions as the *528 following, posed by plaintiff's counsel to one of defendant's expert witnesses:

> If a vehicle had a propensity to roll-over with a fairly high frequency, do you think that ought to be taken into account in designing the placement of the battery in that vehicle and the retention system?

(10) The grant of a directed verdict does not cleanse the record of facts adduced to support the legal theories taken from the jury. Evidence which fails to establish the theory at which it was aimed may, nevertheless, be considered on any other issue to which it is relevant. The trial court responded to defendant's objections by ruling that carbon monoxide was removed from the case with respect to the issue of defective heater design, but not with respect to its possible soporific effect on the car's occupants. The court also ruled that the evidence of roll-over propensity was still admissible because it related to the question of whether the interior location of the battery system was negligent. Both rulings were correct. Plaintiff could argue all evidence relevant to her theory of negligent battery design, whether she originally brought the case under that theory alone or under several theories, some of which were later dismissed. Directed verdicts on some theories do not change what is relevant to remaining theories. See, e.g., Brady v. Melody Homes Manufacturer, 121 Ariz. 253, 589 P.2d 896 (App.1979).

Finally, the court explicitly told the jury during plaintiff's closing argument that two of the three issues had been removed from the case, that battery location was the only issue remaining and that evidence regarding roll-over danger and carbon monoxide were to be considered only if relevant on the issue of battery location and the conduct of plaintiff and her mother. The jury instructions given later repeated this. We find no error.

JURY INSTRUCTIONS

(11) Volkswagen claims to be entitled to a new trial because Instructions Nos. 14 and 22 pertained to theories of law not supported by the facts, and invited speculation as to abstract circumstances. Instruction No. 14 given by the trial court was as follows:

> You are instructed that the negligence, if any, of Phyllis Rossell may not be imputed to Julie Ann Kennon.

Volkswagen argues that it was never its theory that Ms. Rossell's action could or should be "imputed' to Julie, but only that Ms. Rossell's actions were the sole proximate cause of Julie's injuries. It argues that instruction on imputation, combined with the instruction on superseding cause, could only have rendered the jurors "hopelessly confused." We disagree.

Jury instructions should inform the jury of the law that they are to apply to the facts. Noland v. Wootan, 102 Ariz. 192, 194, 427 P.2d 143, 145 (1967). They should also limit consideration to those issues which the jury is to determine. Embrey v. Galentin, 76 N.M. 719, 418 P.2d 62, 64 (1966). Here the instruction on imputation was clearly intended to limit the jury's attention to the issues properly before it.[8] Defendant's reliance on Noland v. Wootan, supra, is misplaced. In that case we found the jury instruction to be reversible error because it had two mutually exclusive meanings; because the jury could have applied the wrong meaning, we held that the instruction was misleading and prejudicial. We cannot come to the same conclusion in this case. Instructions prohibiting speculation about imputed negligence and defining proximate cause are not mutually exclusive. The jury could have and should have applied both instructions.

(12) Instruction No. 22 given by the trial court was as follows:

> If you decide for the plaintiff on the question of liability, you must then fix the amount of money which will reasonably and fairly compensate for any of the *529 following elements of damages proved by the evidence to have resulted from the defendant's negligence:

* * *

---

[8] Because plaintiff was eleven months old at the time of the accident, contributory negligence was of course precluded as a defense. The reasonable foreseeability of the mother's conduct was relevant to the issue of proximate cause.

4. *Any decrease in earning power or capacity in the future.*

Whether any of these elements of damages has been proved by the evidence is for you to determine.

(emphasis supplied). Volkswagen argues that the instruction is reversible error for two reasons. First, because it claims: "(i)f a plaintiff can work *at all, an award for total loss of earning capacity is improper.*" (Emphasis in original.) However, the instruction in question does not require that the jury make an award for "total loss of earning capacity," only for "any decrease" which is proved.

(13) Second, Volkswagen claims that the trial court erred in giving Instruction No. 22 because there was no evidence to support an award for decreased earning capacity. We disagree because there was evidence of decreased earning capacity. That evidence consisted of the jurors' view of the plaintiff, the pictures of the plaintiff and the medical testimony about the permanent, disfiguring injuries sustained by the plaintiff. There is a difference between loss of earnings--not an issue in this case--as an item of special damages and decrease of earning capacity as an item of general damages. Mandelbaum v. Knutson, 11 Ariz.App. 148, 149, 462 P.2d 841, 844 (1969). To sustain an award for the former, the plaintiff must produce evidence of specific losses which are ordinarily reduced to present value. Id. To sustain an award for the latter, the plaintiff must establish only the fact of diminished capacity and its permanence. Atchison, Topeka & Santa Fe Ry. Co. v. Parr, supra. The photographs of plaintiff's scars create a jury question with regard to whether her disfiguring injuries would affect plaintiff's earning capacity. It is certain that plaintiff's ability to perform some jobs has not been affected and her ability to perform others has been diminished or destroyed. No doubt some interviewers will be able to overlook the scars and some will not, no matter how hard they try. Perhaps plaintiff will overcome the impediment, perhaps not. Such questions are properly left to the jury.

There was no error in giving either instruction.

DID THE TRIAL COURT ABUSE ITS DISCRETION BY PERMITTING ILLUSTRATIVE EVIDENCE INTO THE JURY ROOM?

(14, 15) Volkswagen first complains that components of

various Beetle battery systems, admitted for illustrative purposes only, should not have been allowed into the jury room during the jury's deliberations. The problem to be avoided is allowing the jury to conduct its own experiments.

> In attempting to distinguish between proper and improper use of tangible exhibits, the most commonly drawn distinction is between experiments which constitute merely a closer scrutiny of the exhibit and experiments which go "beyond the lines of evidence' introduced in court and thus constitute the introduction of new evidence in the jury room.

McCormick on Evidence section 217 at 541 (E. Cleary, ed., 2d ed. 1972). The decision as to what testimonial exhibits are to be permitted into the jury room is within the trial court's discretion. Falcher v. St. Luke's Hospital Medical Center, 19 Ariz.App. 247, 252, 506 P.2d 287, 292 (1973); McCormick, supra. There is no indication that the jury did use or could have used the exhibits for any particular experimental purpose beyond those presented in the evidence. The components, therefore, were of the type useful for "closer scrutiny." There was no abuse of discretion in sending them to the jury room.

(16) Defendant also complains the trial court erred by admitting four large charts concerning the effects on humans of certain levels of carbon monoxide. The charts were prepared by Mr. Turnbow. Three of the charts contained summaries of data from clinical studies made by others; the fourth summarized Turnbow's opinions. *530 Volkswagen argues that because they were not the original treatises the first three charts do not fit into the "learned treatise" hearsay exception of Rule 803(18), Ariz.R.Evid. 17A A.R.S., and were therefore inadmissible. Furthermore, even if the exception was applicable, Volkswagen argues that Rule 803(18) permits admissible statements from treatises only to be read into the record, not received physically into evidence.

The learned treatise exception to the hearsay rule stems from three independent guarantees of trustworthiness of such works. Treatises admissible under Rule 803(18) are written impartially in favor of truth as the authors see it; they are subject to careful professional scrutiny for inaccuracies by the author's colleagues; and the author has an interest in its accuracy because his or her reputation is at stake. 6 J. Wigmore, EVIDENCE section 1692 (Chadbourn rev. 1976). The purpose served by limiting the jury's exposure to an oral reading at the time the expert is being examined is to avoid the jurors' possible misunderstanding and misuse of the technical treatise when it is later examined in the jury room with no one present to explain or be cross-examined. 4 J. Weinstein & M. Berger, WEINSTEIN'S EVIDENCE section 803(18)(01).

The dangers at which the rule's restrictions are aimed, were not present in this case. The charts did not purport to be excerpts from the treatises, but only the opinions of the witness as to what the articles established. When the trial judge admitted the charts, he specifically admonished the jury that they should not regard the charts as substantive evidence of the material contained in them, but only as illustrative of the witness' opinions as to the effects of carbon monoxide. The limitation of the rule to oral recitation of the text of a learned treatise was not violated and it was within the trial court's discretion to allow the charts into the jury room.

Finally, defendants argue that they are entitled to a new trial because the verdict is not justified by the evidence and is contrary to the law. This contention is disposed of by our previous discussion.

The opinion of the court of appeals is vacated. The judgment is affirmed.

HOLOHAN, C.J., GORDON, V.C.J., and HAYS and CAMERON, JJ., concur.

Exercise 8.1

Attached is a draft Charge to the Jury, prepared for proposed use in a case based on a claim against prison officers for use of excessive force. Pick any segment of two to five pages and rewrite it to make it more understandable to the jury without loss of content material to jury deliberations.

The verdict form associated with this draft charge is reproduced at pages 275-78, supra.

Supp. Ch. 8   CHARGE TO JURY

UNITED STATES DISTRICT COURT
DISTRICT OF MASSACHUSETTS

ANTHONY DION,
   Plaintiff

v.   CIVIL ACTION
                                            NO. 90-3030-K
MICHAEL KATZ, et al.,
   Defendants

Charge to the Jury

MEMBERS OF THE JURY:

It is now time for me to give you instructions on the law. To help you understand and remember the instructions, I will divide them into two main parts: <u>first</u>, general instructions, intended to guide you throughout your deliberation, <u>second</u>, instructions about the particular issues before you in this case.

Part I

General Instructions

The general instructions that I give you apply not only to the present case but also to other cases. I do not mean any of my instructions to be understood by you as a comment by me on the evidence in this case. It is your function to determine the facts, and although the law allows a trial judge in this court to comment on evidence, I deliberately do not do so and instead leave the factfinding entirely in your hands.

It is your duty as jurors to follow the law as stated in the instructions of the court, and to apply the rules of law so given to the facts as you find them from the evidence in the case. Counsel have quite properly referred to some of the governing rules of law in their arguments. If, however, any difference appears to you between the law as stated by counsel and that stated by the court in these instructions, of course you are to be governed by these instructions.

You are not to single out one instruction alone as stating the law, but must consider the instructions as a whole. You are not to be concerned with the wisdom of any rule of law stated by the court. Regardless of any opinion you may have as to what the law ought to be, it would be a violation of your sworn duty to base a verdict upon any other view of the law than that given in the instructions of the court; just as it would be a violation of your sworn duty, as judges of the facts, to base a verdict upon anything but the evidence in the case.

Justice through trial by jury must always depend upon the willingness of each individual juror to seek the truth as to the facts from the same evidence presented to all the jurors; and to arrive at a verdict by applying the same rules of law, as given in the instructions of the court. In your factfinding, of course, you are not to be swayed by bias, prejudice, sympathy, or antagonism. It is your function to find the facts fairly and impartially, on the basis of the evidence.

The evidence in the case consists of the sworn testimony of the witnesses, all exhibits received in evidence, and all facts which may have been admitted or stipulated.

Statements and arguments of counsel are not evidence in the case, unless made as an admission or stipulation of fact. When the attorneys for opposing parties stipulate or agree as to the existence of a fact, however, there is no need for evidence for any party on that point. You must accept the stipulation as evidence, and take that fact as proved.

Anything you may have seen or heard outside the courtroom is not evidence, and you must disregard it entirely. You are to consider only the evidence in the case. But of course in your consideration of the evidence, you are permitted to draw, from facts which you find have been proved, such reasonable inferences as you feel are justified in the light of experience and common sense.

Where oral testimony or an exhibit was limited in a particular way, you are bound by that limitation. You are not to consider any question or evidence that has been excluded or stricken. Nor are you to regard any argument of counsel as though it were evidence.

If any reference by the court or by counsel to matters of evidence is inconsistent with your own recollection, it is your recollection which should control during your deliberations.

At times during the trial you heard lawyers make objections to questions asked of witnesses, or to answers of witnesses. It is a proper function of lawyers to make objections. In objecting, a lawyer is requesting that I make a decision on a particular rule of law. Do not draw from objections, or from my rulings on the objections, any inferences about facts. The objections and my rulings related only to legal questions that I had to determine. They should not influence your thinking about the facts. Remember, however, that when I sustained an objection to a question, the witness was not allowed to answer it after my ruling. And if you heard an answer to the question before my ruling, you are to disregard it. Do not discuss or attempt to guess what answer might have been given, had I permitted it, to a question that was not answered. Also, when I told you not to consider a particular statement, whether made by a witness or by an attorney, you were told in effect to put that statement out of your mind. Do not discuss or refer to that statement in your deliberations.

Facts in dispute may be proved or disproved by direct evidence, or by circumstantial evidence, or by both. Direct evidence is the testimony of one who asserts actual knowledge of a fact, such as an eyewitness. Circumstantial evidence is proof of events or circumstances on the basis of which the jury, from common experience, may infer the existence or nonexistence of a fact. Direct and circumstantial evidence have equal standing in law. That is, with respect to what weight shall be given to evidence before you, the law makes no distinction between direct and circumstantial evidence. Also, no greater degree of certainty is required of circumstantial evidence than of direct evidence. You are to consider all the evidence in the case and give each item of evidence the weight you believe it deserves.

Now I turn to considerations bearing on evaluating witnesses' testimony.

As I have told you, it is your job to decide all material questions of fact. An important part of that job will be making judgments about the testimony of the witnesses who testified in this case. You should decide whether you believe what each person had to say, and how important that testimony was. In making that decision I suggest that you ask yourself a few questions: Did the person impress you as honest? Did he or she have any particular reason not to tell the truth? Did he or she have a personal interest in the outcome of the case? Did the witness seem to have a good memory? Did the witness have the opportunity and ability to observe accurately the things he or she testified about? Did he or she appear to understand the questions clearly and answer them directly? Did the witness's testimony differ from the testimony of other witnesses? These are a few of the considerations that will help you determine the accuracy of what each witness said.

This case is brought by a prisoner against certain defendants who are state officials and state employees. I instruct you that the testimony of state officials and state employees is entitled to no special sanctity. The testimony of a state official or employee should be considered by you just as any other evidence in the case, and in evaluating his credibility you should use the same guidelines which you apply to the testimony of any witness. In no event should you give either greater or lesser credence or weight to the testimony of any witness merely because he is a state official or employee.

Also, you are instructed that you should not give either greater or lesser credence or weight to the testimony of a witness merely because he is a prisoner.

Members of the jury, I now remind you of a limiting instruction I gave during the trial with respect to evidence of prior convictions of a witness.

Evidence of prior convictions is received for a limited purpose. You may take it into account for the purpose of giving whatever weight you think it has, if any, in determining the credibility of the witness. This is the sole purpose for which this evidence is received.

Inconsistencies or conflicts within the testimony of a witness, or between the testimony of different witnesses, may or may not cause the jury to discredit part or all of that testimony. Two or more persons witnessing an incident or a transaction may see or hear it differently; and innocent misrecollection, like failure of recollection, is not an uncommon experience. In weighing the effect of an inconsistency, always consider whether it concerns a matter of importance or an unimportant detail, and whether it results from innocent error or intentional falsehood.

After making your own judgment, you will give the testimony of each witness such weight, if any, as you think it deserves.

Now I will instruct you about what effect you may give to evidence of what in law is called "prior inconsistency." In this context, "prior" simply means "before this trial." One kind of "evidence of prior inconsistency" is evidence that at some other time a witness has said or done something which is inconsistent with the witness's testimony at the trial. Another kind of evidence of prior inconsistency is evidence that the witness failed to say or do something at an earlier time and that this failure is inconsistent with the testimony of the witness at trial.

You may consider evidence of prior inconsistency for the purpose of judging the credibility of the witnesss. Unless an exception I will tell you about applies, this is the only purpose for which you may consider such evidence; you must not consider it as evidence or proof of the truth of any matter stated or implied in previous statement or conduct.

Here is one exception: If the witness is a party in the case (that is, a plaintiff or a defendant) or is a person who was authorized to speak for a party (that is, was, when speaking or acting, then doing so within the scope of authority to speak for a party on the matter stated), and, by an earlier statement, act or omission admitted some fact, then you may consider the earlier statement, act or omission both for the purpose of judging the credibility of the person as a witness and as evidence of the truth of the fact so admitted.

During the trial of this case, certain testimony has been read to you from depositions, which are sworn, recorded answers to questions asked of the witness in advance of trial by one or more of the attorneys for the parties. Deposition testimony is entitled to the same consideration, and is to be judged as to credibility, and weighed, and otherwise considered by you, insofar as possible, in the same way as testimony from the witness stand, and under the same rules as to any limiting or other special instructions you have been given.

On each issue submitted to you, one party or another has the burden of proof to establish that party's contention by a preponderance of the evidence.

To "establish by a preponderance of the evidence" means to prove that something is more likely so than not so. In other words, a preponderance of the evidence in the case means such evidence as, when considered and compared with that opposed to it, has more convincing force, and produces in your minds the belief that what is sought to be proved is more likely true than not true.

"Preponderance of the evidence" does not refer to the number of witnesses or exhibits. Rather it refers to the quality of the evidence and the weight you decide to give it. In determining whether any fact in issue has been proved by a preponderance of the evidence in the case, the jury may, unless otherwise instructed, consider the testimony of all witnesses, regardless of who may have called them, and all exhibits received in evidence, regardless of who may have produced them. The burden of proof has not been carried on an essential element of the claim or defense if, after you have considered all the evidence bearing on this matter you find that the evidence is evenly balanced, or you find that you must speculate, guess, or imagine that this essential element of the claim or defense is true.

Although, on each issue one party or the other has the burden to prove that party's contention on that issue by a preponderance of the evidence in the case, this rule does not, of course, require proof to an absolute certainty, since proof to an absolute certainty is seldom possible in any case.

In a civil action such as this, it is proper to find that a party has carried the burden of proof on an issue of fact if, after considering all the evidence in the case, and on the basis of the evidence, you find that what is sought to be proved on that issue is more likely true than not true.

Part II

Now I turn to instructions about the claims and defenses in this case, and the questions stated on the verdict form.

This case arises under a federal statute found in Title 42 of the United States Code at § 1983. That statute provides that any person may seek redress in this court, by way of damages, against a state official or employee who, acting in his official capacity, deprives the person of any rights, privileges, or immunities, secured or protected by the Constitution or laws of the United States.

The plaintiff in this case has made claims under § 1983, alleging that his constitutional rights were violated. The disputed facts which you must determine regarding all of the claims which the plaintiff is making are summarized on a special verdict form, which I will explain to you in more detail in the instructions I am now giving you.

To establish a claim under § 1983, a plaintiff must establish, by a preponderance of the evidence, each of the following three elements:

First, that the conduct complained of was committed by a person acting under color of state law;

Second, that the conduct deprived him of rights guaranteed to him by the United States Constitution; and

Third, that the defendants' acts were the cause of the injuries or deprivation of rights suffered by the plaintiff.

"Acting under color of law" simply means acting in one's capacity as a state official or employee. It is undisputed in this case that the defendant correction officers and prison officials were acting under color of law at the time of this incident. You must accept that fact as proved, therefore the first element of the plaintiff's claim is proved.

The plaintiff claims that one or more of the defendants violated his constitutional rights in two distinct and separate ways. First, the plaintiff claims one or more of the defendants, while in the plaintiff's cell, violated his constitutional rights by using excessive force to restrain the plaintiff and to remove his television set and caused him injury. Second, the plaintiff claims that one or more of the defendants shackled him to his metal bed frame in four-point restraints and kept him there for a period of approximately twenty-four (24) hours, and that this deprived plaintiff of a constitutional right and caused him injury.

The defendants admit that on September 24, 1984, while the defendants were acting under color of state law and regulation, force was used against the plaintiff and that he was held in four-point restraint for approximately twenty-four hours. They deny that any act or conduct of theirs deprived the plaintiff of any rights or privileges or immunities secured to him by the Constitution or laws of the United States; and they further deny that the plaintiff was injured as a result of any of their actions. The defendants deny that any act or conduct of theirs was maliciously or wantonly or oppressively done. The defendants assert that all of their acts and conduct were done pursuant to their lawful authority and lawful duty as correctional officers and officials and that they acted to enforce regulations governing the conduct and orderly operation of the prison. The defendants allege that they acted reasonably and in good faith and that they are therefore entitled to immunity.

To help you keep the two incidents separate, the verdict form addresses each incident separately. I will now go through that form with you.

[Read Question 1(a).]

In considering Question 1(a), you will consider the force used during the entire period that the extraction team was in the plaintiff's cell. In making the determination whether the force used was grossly disproportionate, you may weigh as factors in your consideration, along with any other relevant evidence, the evidence before you bearing upon:

1. Whether there was a need for the application of force;

2. The relationship between the need and the amount of force that was used;

3. The extent of injury inflicted, if any; and

4. Whether the force was applied in response to an existing need to act in order to maintain order and discipline.

It is not necessary that severe or permanent injuries result for the amount of force to be so grossly disproportionate as to violate the plaintiff's constitutional rights. Under the test I have given you this is only one factor to be considered. If the force used is grossly disproportionate to the force reasonably required, the plaintiff's constitutional rights can be violated even though the resulting injuries are slight. Thus, if you find by a preponderance of the evidence that one or more members of the extraction team used grossly disproportionate force while they were inside the plaintiff's cell, you must answer Question 1 YES.

Plaintiff's claims that his constitutional rights have been violated are based on a provision in the Eighth Amendment of the Constitution of the United States. That provision prohibits the use of cruel and unusual punishment. Cruel and unusual punishment is a kind or degree of punishment that is offensive to society's standards of humanity, dignity, and decency.

The Supreme Court of the United States has determined that a prison officer can be held liable to a prisoner for violation of this constitutional right by the use of force against the prisoner if, but only if, the prison officer has violated a right that is "clearly established" by law in a particularized sense. That is, the contours of the right -- the ways the law describes and defines it -- must be sufficiently clear that a <u>reasonable official</u> would understand that <u>what he is doing</u> violates that right.

I must give you instructions now about the way the right claimed by the plaintiff is described and defined in the law, as particularly applied to claims that grossly disproportionate force was used against the plaintiff.

I instruct you that, in this case, in order to determine whether force used by a defendant at a particular time was grossly disproportionate, you should first consider what information an ordinarily prudent person in the position of that defendant would have had at that time about whether there was then a set of circumstances that created a need for use of some force to maintain order and discipline in the prison and, if so, what kind and degree of force it would have been reasonable to use in response to that need.

In considering these questions, you will bear in mind that when there is a need for some force, the degree of force that is reasonable will be greater as the need for action to preserve order and discipline grows greater or more urgent, and the degree of force that is reasonable will be less as the need for action to preserve order and discipline becomes less substantial or less urgent.

Bear in mind, however, that the question you are to answer in this verdict form is not whether a defendant used force that was merely somewhat excessive -- that is, somewhat more than would have been reasonable. Rather, the question is whether a defendant used grossly disproportionate force.

After considering these two matters that I have been explaining and all the evidence bearing upon them, you may find that a defendant used grossly disproportionate force if and only if you make one or the other or both of the following findings: First, that in the circumstances a reasonably prudent officer would have known that order and discipline could be maintained without the use of force and that the defendant nevertheless used significant and substantial force which, because of the absence of need, cannot reasonably be found to have been used in response to a need to use force to maintain order and discipline and is therefore grossly disproportionate. Second, that even though some force was reasonably needed the force used by the defendant was grossly disproportionate to the force that an ordinarily prudent officer would have considered it proper to use at that time in response to the need to preserve order and discipline in that set of circumstances. If you make either of these findings against a defendant by a preponderance of the evidence, you will answer Question 1(a) YES as to that defendant. If you do not make either of these findings against a defendant by a preponderance of the evidence, you will answer Question 1(a) NO as to that defendant.

[Read Question 1(b).]

The words maliciously and sadistically are used in their ordinary sense. Thus, for example, a person acts maliciously when acting with hatred, spite, or ill-will. And, for example, a person acts sadistically when taking satisfaction or pleasure in causing pain or harm to another person.

I will now explain to you why I am asking you this Question 1(b), as well as Question 2(b).

When a prison security measure is undertaken to resolve a disturbance that poses significant risks to the safety of inmates and prison staff, the question whether the measure taken inflicted unnecessary and wanton pain and suffering and thereby violated a clearly established right ultimately turns on "whether force was applied in a good faith effort to maintain or restore discipline or maliciously and sadistically for the very purpose of causing harm." Such factors as the need for the application of force, the relationship between the need and the amount of force that was used, and the extent of injury inflicted are relevant to that ultimate determination. From such consideration inferences may be drawn as to whether the use of force could plausibly have been thought necessary, or instead show such wantonness with respect to the unjustified infliction of harm as is tantamount to a knowing willingness that it occur.

When the potential for violent confrontation in a prison ripens into actual unrest and conflict, the prison administrators are entitled to great deference in decisionmaking regarding the appropriate course of action to deal with the situation. In this situation, the plaintiff, in order to show a violation of constitutional rights, must prove that the force used against him was malicious or sadistic.

If there is merely a question over the reasonableness of the particular force used, or if there is simply a question of arguably superior alternatives, the plaintiff cannot prevail in a claim of violation of constitutional rights. The plaintiff must prove by a preponderance of the evidence wantonness and that the force was used maliciously or sadistically.

[Read Question 2(a).]

The explanation of "grossly disproportionate force" that I gave you a few minutes ago, in relation to Question 1(a), applies here also.

[Read Question 2(b).]

The explanation of "maliciously and sadistically" that I gave you in relation to Question 1(b) applies here also.

[Read Question 3(a).]

As I have stated in explaining Questions 1(b) and 2(b), we need your answer to this question and to Question 4(a) because, if you answer YES, it makes a difference with respect to what the plaintiff has to prove to show a violation of his constitutional rights. That is, if you answer this question YES, the plaintiff then must prove that a defendant acted maliciously and sadistically in order to prove a claim against that defendant.

The burden of proof as to Question 3(a) and 4(a) is upon the defendants. As to all other questions on this verdict form, the burden of proof is upon plaintiff.

[Read Question 3(b).]

Now I turn to explanation of what we mean by

"compensatory damages" as those words are used in Questions 3 and 4, and throughout my instructions to you.

Compensatory damages are damages which compensate an injured party for any injuries sustained. You may find that the plaintiff is entitled to compensation for physical injury such as pain and suffering.

You may also find that the plaintiff is entitled to compensation for emotional and mental harm suffered during and after the incident, including apprehension of harmful or offensive physical touching, fear, humiliation, intimidation, frustration, indignation and mental anguish.

If you should find that the plaintiff in this case has proved by a preponderance of the evidence that the defendants have deprived him of his constitutional rights, you must award him such damages, and only such damages, as will reasonably compensate him for any injury, harm, or damage that you find he has sustained as a result.

I will now define "cause" for you as it is used in these questions and throughout my instructions. The definition applies as well to associated words such as "caused" or "causing," and also to "result" and such associated words as "resulted" or "resulting."

Injury of any kind, including violation of constitutional rights, is caused by an act if the injury would not have occurred but for the act and the injury was a natural and probable consequence of the act. Similarly, injury of any kind is caused by a failure to act in a situation where a person has a duty act. Thus, applying this definition together with the other instructions I have given you, you will find that injury is caused by an act, or a failure to act, if you find from a preponderance of the evidence that the injury would not have occurred but for the act or failure to act and that the injury was a natural and probable consequence of the act or failure to act.

Naturally there may be more than one cause of an injury, especially where the act or failure to act of more than one person is combined in a single incident. Where two or more persons act together and cause a wrong to another, they incur a joint liability for the acts of each other. The law does not require the injured party to establish how much of the injury was done by one person and how much of the injury was done by another. Rather, when two or more persons act together the law permits the injured party to treat all concerned in the injury jointly and all are liable.

In addition, where one or more persons act alone or together and cause a wrong to another, and at the same time other persons who are in a position to act to prevent the wrong from occurring fail to do so, all are liable. All those who actively participate in a wrongful act, by cooperation or request, or who lend aid or encouragement to the wrong-doer, or ratify and adopt his acts for their benefit, or who fail to act to prevent the wrongful conduct, are equally liable with him. Express agreement is not necessary, and all that is required is that there should be a common design or understanding, even if it is an unspoken one.

Thus, if you find that one or more of the defendants personally acted to deprive the plaintiff of a constitutional right, you may find that one or more of the remaining defendants liable if they aided or encouraged the wrongdoer, or if they knew the wrongful act was occurring and were in a position to stop it but did not intervene.

[Read Questions 4(a) and 4(b).]

The instructions I gave you in explaining Question 3(a) and 3(b) apply here also.

[Read Question 5.]

Thus far I have been speaking of compensatory damages. If violations of constitutional rights have been found, a jury may in certain circumstances award punitive damages in addition to compensatory damages.

The function of punitive damages is to punish the defendant for reckless conduct and to deter similar conduct by others. Unlike compensatory damages, punitive damages are not awarded as of right but only when a defendant's conduct merits such award. You may award punitive damages against a defendant if you find that a defendant acted with a reckless or callous disregard of, or indifference to the plaintiff's constitutional rights.

Punitive damages may be awarded even if the violation of plaintiff's rights resulted in only nominal compensatory damages. That is, even if the plaintiff can show no severe injury as a result of a defendant's actions, if these actions were done with reckless disregard of plaintiff's constitutional rights, you may assess punitive damages in addition to any award of actual damages. The amount of punitive damages assessed against any defendant may be such sum as you believe will serve to punish that defendant and to deter him and others from like conduct. If you determine that one or more of the defendants acted with a reckless or callous disregard of, or indifference to the plaintiff's constitutional rights, you must answer Question 5 YES and indicate which of the defendants is liable. Then if you decide to award punitive damages, you must indicate in Question 5 the amount of damages for each defendant you find liable.

If it becomes necessary during your deliberations to

communicate with the court, you may send a note by the marshal, signed by your foreperson, or by one or more members of the jury. No member of the jury should ever attempt to communicate with the court by any means other than a signed writing; and the court will never communicate with any member of the jury on any subject touching the merits of the case, otherwise than in writing, or orally here in open court.

Bear in mind also that you are never to reveal to any person -- not even to the court -- how the jury stands, numerically or otherwise, on any issue before you, until after you have reached a unanimous verdict.

You may communicate with the marshal regarding such matters as arrangements for coffee or lunch.

You may select your foreperson.

The foreperson will preside over your deliberations, and will act for you here in court, in your presence, when you return with your verdict.

[A form of verdict has been prepared for your convenience, and I have read it to you.]

You will take this form to the jury room and, when you have reached unanimous agreement as to your verdict, you will have your foreperson fill in, date and sign the form to state the verdict upon which you unanimously agree, and then return with your verdict to the court room.

Members of the jury, before I send you out for a brief recess, I will tell you about my usual practice as to the schedule for jury deliberations. You will understand that my giving you this information is not to be interpreted as any comment by me on the length of your deliberations. That is a matter in your hands.

When a jury is deliberating into the late afternoon, it is my usual practice, absent special circumstances, to allow a jury either to recess before dinner and begin deliberations again the following morning, or else, if the jurors prefer, to have dinner and then continue deliberations in the evening, but not later than 9:30 or 10:00 p.m. You may ask the marshal to report to me your preference. If you wish to continue deliberations after dinner the marshal will need advance notice of at least two hours as to when you will wish to recess for dinner. A dinner recess usually requires 1-1/2 to 2 hours.

It is not yet time for you to start deliberating. I will ask you to go to the jury room and remain at ease for a few minutes. I still have some more brief instructions to give you before it will be time for you to deliberate.

[Objections to the charge, if any.]

[Alternates, if any, to be separated.]

Members of the jury, it is now time for the case to

be submitted to you. The first thing you should do is select one of the members of the jury to act as your foreperson. Then, you may commence your deliberations. All of you who are the jury must be together at all times when you are deliberating. Whenever you need a recess for any purpose, your foreperson may declare a recess. Do not discuss the case during a recess in your deliberations. All your discussion of the case should occur only when you are all together and your foreperson has indicated that deliberations may proceed. This should be your procedure so that everyone in the jury will have equal opportunity to participate and to hear all that other members of the jury say.

You may go to the jury room and may commence your deliberations as soon as you have selected your foreperson.

INDEX

This is an index of only the following parts of this book:

(a) the Text (pages 1-256);

(b) the names of authors of all **recent** (1980 or later) judicial opinions cited in the text, and **authors** of selected earlier opinions cited in the text;

(c) the names of authors of all judicial opinions reproduced in the Course Supplement.

The judicial opinions in the Course Supplement are listed in the Table of Cases at the front of the book. They are not indexed by subject matter. They are arranged, however, in chapters of the Course Supplement that focus respectively on the same subject matter as the corresponding chapter of the Text.

Following is the key to the meaning of entries in this Index:

1. Numbers alone indicate pages. E.g., under "ABNORMALLY DANGEROUS ACTIVITIES," in the entry, "Aircraft, crop dusting, 2F, 64," the number "64" refers to page 64 of the book.

2. Combined number-letter entries indicate sections or subsections of the book. E.g., under "ABNORMALLY DANGEROUS ACTIVITIES," in the entry, "Aircraft, crop dusting, 2F, 64," the entry "2F" refers to chapter 2, section F. The chapter and section numbers appear at the top outside corners of pages of the text.

3. In this index, chapter designations are in the form "ch." followed by the chapter number.

4. Hypothetical cases are designated by the case number followed by parentheses in which appear the page where the statement of the case commences -- e.g., Case 1.1 (5).

5. Forms are designated by the form number followed by parentheses in which appear the number of the first page of that form -- e.g., Form 7.A (185).

INDEX

ABNORMALLY DANGEROUS ACTIVITIES,
See also STRICT LIABILITY
Aircraft, cropdusting, 2F, 64
Duty formulation, ambiguity
    of, 3F2
Explosives, 119
Field burning, 76 n.13
Philosophical issues, relevance,
    76 n.13
Policies served, bearing on
    lawmaking choice, 3B2
Premise facts, 58
Transportation of explosives, 58,
    64, 4B
Values of, relevance, 76 n.13

ABRAMS, HON. RUTH I.,
<u>Cody v. Connecticut General Life
    Ins. Co.</u>, 134 n.5

ABSOLUTE IMMUNITY, 3D

ABSOLUTE LIABILITY,
See ABNORMALLY DANGEROUS
    ACTIVITIES

ABSOLUTE PRIVILEGE, 3D

ACCIDENT INSURANCE, 134-35
Collateral source rule, 134
Coordination of benefits, 134-35

ACCOUNTABILITY,
Legal Tests for determining,
    ch. 3
State-of-mind elements, 3B

ACCOUNTANTS,
Defamation of, Case 3.1 (95)

ACT,
    In general, 5C, 5D, 6E
Duty to, 3F2, 4D
"Intentional act," 5C, 5D,
    Case 6.1 (146),
    Case 6.2 (148), 6E

ACT--Cont'd
Omission distinguished,
    Not doing, 3F2, 4D
    Not speaking, 6C
"Voluntary act," 155-57
Willful, 82, 155-61,
    Case 6.1 (146),
    Case 6.2 (148),
    Case 6.5 (165)

ACTIVISM,
Constrained by candid
    explanation, 4B
Inevitable lawmaking
    distinguished, 1C, 2E2, 2E3,
    4C

ACTORS IN PROFESSIONAL ROLES,
See PROFESSIONALISM; ROLES

ADHESION CONTRACTS, 133

ADJUDICATIVE FACTS,
    In general, 2C, 2F, 68 n.3
Cause, 2F
Substantial similarity,
    Copyright, 2F, 58 n.4

ADMINISTRATION OF JUSTICE,
See JUDGING; JUDICIAL
    MANAGEMENT; JUSTICE; LAW

ADVERSARY SYSTEM,
See also ADVOCATES;
    PROFESSIONALISM; ROLES
Clarifying issues, 4E2
Contentiousness, see that title
Quality of advocacy, 8A
    Changing, 244
Speed, 210
Time Limits as incentives, 8A
Tradition as influence, 8A

ADVOCATES,
See also ADVERSARY SYSTEM
Aids to judge's decision, 163-64
Civility, 242

INDEX

ADVOCATES--Cont'd
Contentiousness, see that title
Discipline of, onerous responsibility, 183
Jury instructions, 3B3, 3F3
Sensitivity to judge's obligations, 137-38
Showing how to decide favorably, 137-38
Tailoring objective tests, 3C2

AGE OF COMPETENCY, 3A2, 3A3

AGENCY,
Insurance cases, 133
Master-servant tests, 3C3
Municipal liability, 3B4, 4E1
Scope-of-employment tests, 70, 94-95, 3C3

AGGRAVATION,
Pre-existing condition, 3F3

AIRCRAFT,
Crop dusting by, 2F, 64

ALCOHOL,
Medical need resulting from intoxication, 85

ALDERMAN, HON. JAMES E.,
Insurance Co. of North America v. Pasakarnis, 162 n.9

ALDISERT, HON. RUGGERO,
The Judicial Process (1976), 151 n.1

ALLOCATING,
Burdens, 134-36
Damages, Case 6.1 (146), Case 6.2 (148), Case 6.5 (165)
Risks of insolvency, Case 6.1 (146), Case 6.2 (148), Case 6.5 (165)

ALTERNATIVE DISPUTE RESOLUTION,
See DISPUTE RESOLUTION

ALTERNATIVE LIABILITY,
Infant vaccine victim, Case 2.1 (31)
Managing ignorance, 2D3

AMERICAN LEGAL HISTORY,
See LEGAL HISTORY

AMBIGUITY,
See MEANING

ANALOGY, 1A, 4B, 4E2

AND,
Compared with "or" as connective, 160

APPELLATE JUDGING,
See also JUDGING
Supreme courts, 2B1
Intermediate courts, 2B1

ARIZONA,
Department of Health Services, Case 3.1 (95), 3D3

ARNOLD, HON. RICHARD S.,
Janklow v. Newsweek, Inc., 74

ARREST,
Claim against officer, verdict, Form 8.C (247)
Injury to officer during, 158-60

ARTIFICIAL INTELLIGENCE,
Informative reasoning compared, 140

ASBESTOS HAZARDS, Case 2.2 (40), 2F, 2H

ASSOCIATION,
State of mind, 3B4

INDEX

ATTORNEY FEES,
Discovery disputes, 7D,
    Form 7.A (185)

AUERBACH, PROF. CARL,
The Anatomy of an Unusual Economic Substantive Due Process Case: Workers' Compensation Insurers Rating Association v. State, 174 n.7, 176 nn.12, 13

AUTHORITY,
Answering previously unanswered questions, 2E2
Power distinguished, 1A, 2E2
Respect for,
    Changing attitudes, 7C
    Formal and substantive, 5C, 5D, 6G
    Statutes, 150, 158, 6G

AUTONOMY,
Local, 2B5

BALANCING,
See TESTS FOR DECIDING CASES

BARTLETT,
Familiar Quotations, 66 n.1

BASEBALL,
Injury expected or intended, 158-59 n.7

BATTERED CHILD, Case 1.2 (8)

BEAUTY,
Eye of the beholder, 74

BECKER, HON. EDWARD,
In re Asbestos Litigation (concurring), 58 n.5, 413

BEES, Case 4.2 (115)

BENEFITS,
Coordination of, 134
Costs compared, 4D

BLACKMUN, HON. HARRY,
Daniels v. Williams (concurring), 274
DeShaney v. Winnebago County Department of Social Services (dissenting), 300
Wards Cove Packing Co. v. Atonio (dissenting), 661

BODILY INJURY,
Expected or intended, insurance law, 158-59

BORDERLAND BETWEEN LAW AND FACT, 2H
See also FACTS; LAW

BOSTON GLOBE, 115 n.5

BOWMAN, HON. PASCO M. III,
Janklow v. Newsweek, Inc. (dissenting), 74 n.11

BOWNES, HON. HUGH H.,
O'Neill v. Dell Publishing Co., 58 n.4, 60 n.1
United States v. Bank of New England, 538

BRANDEIS, HON. LOUIS,
State of Washington v. Dawson & Co. (dissenting), 46 n.15
Olmstead v. United States, 50 n.1

BRAUCHER, PROF. JEAN,
Toward a Broader Perspective on the Role of Economics in Legal Policy Analysis: A Retrospective and Agenda from Albert O. Hirschman, 13 Law & Social Inquiry 741 (1988), 127-28 n.4

INDEX

BRENNAN, HON. WILLIAM J. JR.,
New York Times Co. v. Sullivan, 83
Sandstrom v. Montana, 80 n.1, 470
Zobel v. Williams, (concurring), 24 n.7, 26 nn.8-11, 27 n.12, 323
DeShaney v. Winnebago County Department of Social Services (dissenting), 293

BREYER, HON. STEPHEN G.,
Oxford Shipping Co. v. New Hampshire Trading Corp., 16 n.6, 88 n.12, 527

BRIGHT-LINE TESTS,
In general, 3A2, 3A3,
Joint liability, 168
Statutory sunset, 6H
Within totality-of-the-circumstances, 3A3

BROODING OMNIPRESENCE, 52

BROWNING, HON. JAMES R.
Gulden v. Crown Zellerbach Corp., 702

BURDENS,
Allocation of, 134-36
Clash of high-value interests, 3D3
Costs, 4E2
Immunity and privilege, 3D3
Techniques for decisionmaking, 2D3, 55, 3E, 3F

BURGER, HON. WARREN E.,
Zobel v. Williams, 24 n.7, 26 nn.8-11, 27 n.12, 314

BUT-FOR RULE, 3F3
See also CAUSE

CABINET-LEVEL IMMUNITY, 3D3

CALABRESI, DEAN GUIDO,
A Common Law for the Age of Statutes (1982), 173 nn.4, 5
The Costs of Accidents (1970), 127 n.3

CALABRESI, DEAN GUIDO and HIRSCHOFF, JON,
Toward a Test for Strict Liability in Torts, 81 Yale L. J. 1055 (1972), 127 n.3

CALCULUS, SOCIAL,
In lawmaking, 4D

CALLOW, HON. KEITH M.
McKee v. American Home Products Corp., 594

CALOGERO, HON. PASCAL F. JR.,
Breland v. Schilling, 158-59 n.7

CAMPBELL, HON. LEVIN H.
International Paper Co. v. Inhabitants of the Town of Jay, Maine, 12 n.3

CANDOR,
In general, 1C, 1D
Difficulty,
In general, 1C1
Decisions of panel, 10
Decisions on cause, 3F
Decisions on duty, 3F
Judicial commitment to, 1C1, 138
Temptation to use burden as explanation, 3E

CAPS,
Noneconomic damages, 59

CARDOZO, HON. BENJAMIN,
The Growth of the Law. 133 (1924), 46 n.15

CARRIERS,
Slight negligence, 91

INDEX

CASELOADS,
    See WORKLOAD OF COURTS

CASES,
Development, ch. 7, ch. 8
Disposition, ch. 7, ch. 8
First impression, 2E2, 2E3
    See also CHOICE
Hypothetical cases,
    Case 1.1 The Injured Inmate, 5
    Case 1.2 The Battered Child, 8
    Case 1.3 The Favored Older
        Resident, 24
    Case 2.1 An Infant Vaccine
        Victim, 31
    Case 2.2 Knowledge of Asbestos
        Hazards, 40
    Case 3.1 A Cost Containment
        Controversy, 95
    Case 3.2 The Ruptured Spleen,
        106
    Case 4.1 The Adult Vaccine
        Victim, 114
    Case 4.2 Gypsy Moths and
        Honeybees, 115
    Case 6.1 Rich, Cabbie, and
        Luce, 146
    Case 6.2 After Luce's
        Settlement, 148
    Case 6.3 Wrongful Death and
        Punitive Damages, 148-49
        n.2
    Case 6.4 Electronic
        Eavesdropping, 148-49 n.2
    Case 6.5 Toxic Waste Disposal,
        165
Pretrial development, ch. 7

CAUSE,
Adjudicative fact, 2F
Baseball injury, expected or
    intended, 158-59 n.7
But-for rule, 3F3
Community values, 104
Conclusion, 3F
Discretion in determining, 2H, 3F
Discrimination cases, 3E, 3F
Fact, 3F

CAUSE--Cont'd
Holmes' comment on, 166-68
Jury instructions, 3F3
Objective tests, 79
Patterns of decisions as
    precedent, 59
Substantial factor, 3F3
Tests of uncertain meaning, 2H
"The" cause, 3F2

CHAMBERS GUIDELINES, 145

CHANGE,
Premises of lawmaking,
    See PREMISES, Transitory

CHARGE TO THE JURY,
    See JURY, Instructions

CHARITIES,
Immunity, 3D

CHICKEN,
Meaning, 142 n.1

CHIEF EXECUTIVE,
Required attendance at Rule 16
    conference, 7A2

CHILD,
Battered, Case 1.2 (8)
Consent,
    Age of competency, 3A2, 3A3
    Tests for determining, 3A2, 3A3
Vaccine victim, Case 2.1 (31)

CHOICE,
Arbitrary, 1A, 4A
Authority, 2E2
Committing resources in managing
    cases, 7F
Constraints upon, 4C, 158, 173,
    174
Deciding disputes of fact, 2B,
    2E, 2G, 2H
Deciding disputes of law, 2C, 2F,
    2G, 2H

INDEX

CHOICE--Cont'd
Disciplined by necessity of explaining, 137
Discretion, see that title
Employment discrimination tests, 77-78
Fiat, 79, 4D n.5
Hard, 138
Holmes' comment on, 166-68
Incomplete information, 7F3
Issues of first impression, 32-34, 2E, 62
Judging as, 1A1, 1D, 2E2, 4A, 4B, 4C, 4D, 138
Making and explaining, in decisions, ch. 3, ch. 4, ch. 5, ch. 6
Necessity in judging, 50 n.1, 4A, 4B, 4C
Opinion that won't write, 137
Power of, 2E2
Premises, Case 1.3 (24), 4B
Professional commitment regarding, 137,
   See also COMMITMENT; PROFESSIONALISM
Reasoned, 1A, 1D, 4A-B-C-D, 138, 7A1
Value-laden, 4A, 4B
Who pays, 4E

CIRCUMSTANCES,
Totality of, 3C3

CIRCUMSTANTIAL EVIDENCE,
Direct evidence compared, 81-82
Permissible inferences, 80-82

CITY,
   See MUNICIPALITY

CIVILITY, 242

CIVIL RIGHTS CLAIMS,
   In general, Case 1.1 (5), 1B2, 1D1, Case 1.2 (8), Case 3.2 (106), Form 8.C (247)
Insurance for, 4E1

CIVIL RIGHTS CLAIMS--Cont'd
Jury verdict, Form 8.C (247)
Privacy, 150

CLARITY,
   See MEANING

CLASSIFICATION,
Disputes of fact, 2F
Facts, 2F
Invidious, Case 1.3 (24)
Suspect, Case 1.3 (24), Case 2.2 (40)

CLIFFORD, HON. ROBERT L.,
Shackil v. Lederle Laboratories, 31 n.1, 342

CLUB,
State of mind, 3B4

COFFEY, HON. JOHN L.,
Heileman Brewing Co. v. Joseph Oat Corp. (dissenting), 726

COFFIN, HON. FRANK, 39 n.5
EEOC v. Trabucco, 59 n.9
Planned Parenthood League of Massachusetts v. Bellotti, 73 n.9
Dance v. Ripley, 101 n.13
Book Review, 91 Yale L. J. 827 (1982), 173 n.5

COLLATERAL SOURCE RULE, 134

COMMITMENT,
To justice, 1A, 2E2
To law, 1A, 2E
To professionalism, 1A, 1C, 4A, 137
To representing community interests, 1A, 2E2, 76, 4A, 137

COMMON LAW,
Lawmakers, 2B1

INDEX

COMMUNICATIONS,
See also MEANING
Interpreting, 5D
Judge's, ch. 1, ch. 5

COMMUNITY STANDARDS,
Sources of law, 1A, 2E2, 76, 4A, 137

COMPARATIVE FAULT,
Case 6.1 (146), Case 6.2 (148)

COMPENSATION SYSTEMS, 133

COMPLETE PRIVILEGE, 3D

COMPLEXITY,
Facts, 2C
Law, 2B
Opinion, 144

CONCEALMENT,
See also DISCOVERY
Rules designed to prevent, 8A

CONCLUSIONS OF LAW,
See also REVIEW; DUTY; CAUSE
Cause as, 3F1
Duty as, 3F1
Stated orally, 139

CONDITIONAL PRIVILEGE, 3D

CONDITIONAL SUMMARY TRIAL,
Resources used, 7F
Stipulation and order,
Form 7.C (193)

CONFLICTS OF INTEREST,
Accommodating in lawmaking, ch. 4
Between defendant and others, 134
Between plaintiff and other
potential plaintiffs, 134
Judge's personal interest, 2E2

CONGRESS,
See also STATUTES
Intent, 5D, 6D, 6G

CONGRESS--Cont'd
Lawmaker, 2B1
Policy of, as to limitation of
liability of ships, 52 n.2
Preemption,
see PREEMPTION, FEDERAL

CONSENT,
Tests for determining, 3A2, 3A3

CONSPIRACY,
Distinguished from entity, 89
Joint liability, Case 6.1 (146),
Case 6.2 (148)

CONSTITUTIONAL TORTS,
See also DUE PROCESS; EQUAL
PROTECTION
Burdens, 3E
Court-fashioned, 85
Insurance for, 4E1
Recklessness, Case 1.1 (5),
Case 1.2 (8), 1B2, 1D1, 82,
Case 3.2 (106),
Form 8.C (247)

CONSTITUTIONS,
See also DUE PROCESS; EQUAL
PROTECTION
State, 2B
Federal, 2B

CONSTRAINTS ON JUDGING,
See JUDGING; PROFESSIONALISM

CONSUMER FRAUD,
Deceptive act or practice, 150
Statutes, 84

CONTENTIOUSNESS,
Discovery sanctions, 7D,
Form 7.A (185)
Incentives to control, 7D
Discovery, Form 7.A (185)
Tailored jury trial,
Form 8.A (217)
Tailored nonjury trial,
Form 8.B (232)

INDEX

CONTENTIOUSNESS--Cont'd
Rules of proof, 8C

CONTRACT,
Adhesion, 133
Competency, 3A2
Damages, payment of, 4E
Death of, 133
Gaps, filling, 5C, 5D
Insurance, see that title
Lawmakers, 2B1
Manifested meaning, 5C, 5D
Payment of damages, 4E
Unconscionability, 133

CONTRACTOR,
Spraying, Case 4.2 (115)

COORDINATION OF BENEFITS, 134-35

COPYRIGHT,
Substantial similarity,
  Adjudicative fact, 2F
  Mixed fact and law, 58 n.4

CORPORATION,
State-of-mind, 84, 3B4
Representative,
  Attendance at conditional
    summary trial,
    Form 7.C (193)
  Attendance at Rule 16
    conference, 7A2, 200
  Attendance at summary jury
    trial, Form 7.B (189)

COST,
Containment, Case 3.1 (95)
Burdens, 4E2

COST BENEFIT ASSESSMENT, 4D

COURTS,
  See also JUDGES; JUDGING;
  JUDICIAL MANAGEMENT
Lawmakers, 2B

COUNSELING,
Settlement, see that title

COX, PROF. ARCHIBALD, 144 n.2

CREATING LAW,
  See LAWMAKING

CREATIVE LABELING, 3A
  See also MEANING

CREDIBILITY,
Asking one witness to assess
  another's, 242-43

CRIMES,
Conspiracy, 89
Intent,
  As element, 57, 79, 3A2
  Not required, 79
Officers, committed by, 50 n.1
Tests of accountability, 79
Without intent, 57

CRISIS,
Insurability, 4E
Premise fact, 2D2, 2D3, 4B
Proving, 2D3
Transitory, 6H

CRITERIA FOR DECISION,
  See TESTS

CROP DUSTING, 2F, 64

CROSS-EXAMINATION,
Rules of proof regarding, 242-43

DAMAGES,
Aggravation of pre-existing
  condition, 3F3
Allocating, Case 6.1 (146),
  Case 6.2 (148)
Burden of paying, 4E
Caps on noneconomic, 59
Economic, as element of,
  Case 2.1 (31), Case 4.1 (114)
Natural persons seldom pay, 4E

INDEX

DAMAGES--Cont'd
Pain and suffering,
    Case 3.2 (106),
    Case 4.1 (114)
  Caps on, 59
  Precluding, 126
Payment of, 4E
Punitive,
  Claims, Case 6.3 (148-49 n.2)
  Liability insurance, 3B2, 4E

DATA,
Use as premise facts, 59

DAVIES, SEN. JACK,
A Response to Statutory
    Obsolescence: The Nonprimacy
    of Statutes Act,
    4 Vt. L. Rev. 247 (1979),
    174 n.6

DAVIS, PROF. KENNETH,
An Approach to Problems of
    Evidence (1942), 39 n.4,
    42 n.11

DEATH,
Statutes, 29,
    Case 6.3 (148-49 n.2)

DECENTRALIZATION OF LAWMAKING, 2B

DECEPTIVE ACT OR PRACTICE, 150

DECISIONMAKING,
Based on incomplete information,
    7F3
Introduction to, ch. 1, ch. 2
Incomplete, 4E2
Judicial, see JUDGING
Municipal, Case 4.2 (115)
Private, 77
Reasoned, 5C-D-E
Structured, discrimination cases,
    3E

DECISION POINTS,
Multiple, disadvantages of, 6G

DEDUCTIVE REASONING,
See REASONING

DEFAMATION,
Accountants, Case 3.1 (95)
Clash of high-value interests, 3E
Obviously false statement, 92
Of and concerning, 77 n.14, 92-93
Publisher's intent, 77 n.14
State-of-mind tests, 3B2

DEFECTIVE PRODUCTS,
    Case 2.1 (31), Case 4.1 (114)

DEFENSE, PRIVILEGE OF,
Person, 3D
Private necessity, 3D
Property, 3D
Public necessity, 3D
Self, 3D

DEFENSE REPRESENTATION,
See ADVOCATES

DEFERENTIAL REVIEW,
    See also REVIEW, STANDARDS OF
Evidence rulings, 241
Mixed law-fact questions, 2G, 2H

DELIBERATE INDIFFERENCE,
Constitutional tort,
    Case 1.1 (5), 1B2, 1D1, 62,
    4E1
Medical need, 62, 85, 4E1
Municipality, 3B4, 4E1
State of mind, 82, 4E1

DENNIS, HON. JAMES L.,
Bazley v. Tortorich, 155
Pique v. Saia, 158

DE NOVO REVIEW,
Mixed law-fact questions, 2G, 2H

813

INDEX

DESUETUDE, 172-73

DEVELOPMENT OF CASES IN COURT,
Pretrial, ch. 7
Trial, ch. 8

DICTIONARY MEANINGS,
  See also MEANING
Hand's caution about, 141 n.5

DIFFICULTY OF DECISION,
Affecting choice of legal test,
  2D3

DIRECT EVIDENCE,
Circumstantial evidence compared,
  81-82

DISCIPLINE,
Onerous responsibility, 183

DISCOVERY,
Abuse, 7C
Disputes, resolving, 7C
Memorandum and Order Regarding,
  Form 7.A (185)

DISCRETION,
Burdens in discrimination case,
  3E
Criminal sentencing, 181
Evidence rulings, 8C
Fine tuning, see that title
Incident to uncertain meaning, 2H
Judicial management, 7D
Lawmaking tests, ch. 3
Leading questions 242
Objective tests, 3A3
Pretrial proceedings, 7D
Procedure, 7A
Promoting settlement, 7E
Rule contrasted,
  Lawmaking tests, ch. 3
  Procedure, 7B
Subjective tests, 3A3
Tailoring, see that title

DISCRIMINATION,
Burdens, 3E
Employment, 77-78, 3E
McDonnell-Douglas criteria, 3E

DISMISSAL,
Grounds of immunity, 3D3

DISPOSAL OF TOXIC WASTE,
Case 6.5 (165)

DISPUTE RESOLUTION,
Choices committing resources, 7F
Conditional summary trial,
  Form 7.C (193)
Discovery, 7C
Summary jury trial, 7A2
Without trial, 7E, 8A

DIVISIBLE LIABILITY,
Case 6.1 (146)

DOLLIVER, HON. JAMES M.,
Langan v. Valicopters, Inc., 446

DORE, HON. FRED H.,
McKee v. American Home Products
  (dissenting), 612

DPT VACCINE, Case 2.1 (31)

DRIVERS,
Accident cases, 38, 58, 85, 91,
  3C2, 119, Case 6.1 (146),
  Case 6.2 (148)
Host drivers, test of
  accountability, 3C2
Taxicab, Case 6.1 (146),
  Case 6.2 (148)

DRUGS, Case 2.1 (31),
  Case 4.1 (114)

DUE PROCESS,
Deliberate indifference,
  Constitutional tort,
    Case 1.1 (5), 1B2, 1D1, 62,
    4E1

INDEX

DUE PROCESS--Cont'd
Medical need, 62, 85, 4E1
Municipality, 3B4, 4E1
State of mind, 82, 4E1
Excessive force, Case 3.2 (106),
 Form 8.C (247)
Joint liability, ch. 6,
 Case 6.1 (146),
 Case 6.2 (148),
 Case 6.5 (165), 8E,
 Form 8.C (247),
 Form 8.D (254)
Officer's negligence,
 Case 1.1 (5), 1B2, 1D1,
 Case 1.2 (8), Case 3.2 (106),
 82, Form 8.C (247)
Presumed intent, 80-82
Punitive damages, 3B2
Rate regulation, workers
 compensation insurance,
 174-76
Recklessness, Case 1.1 (5),
 Case 1.2 (8), 1B2, 1D1, 82,
 Case 3.2 (106),
 Form 8.C (247)

DUTY,
Ambiguity as to standard of
 conduct, 3F2
Conclusion, 3F
Fact, 3F
Policy reasons, varied, 3F2
To act, 3F2, 4D
When acting, 3F2, 4D

DWORKIN, PROF. RONALD,
Law's Empire (1986), 127 n.3,
 172 n.2

EASTERBROOK, HON. FRANK H.,
*Heileman Brewing Co. v. Joseph
 Oat Corp.* (dissenting), 734

EAVESDROPPING,
Electronic, Case 6.4 (148-49 n.2)

**ECONOMIC IMPLICATIONS OF
LAWMAKING**, 4A, 4D, 4E

ECONOMIC LOSS,
 See DAMAGES

ELECTRONIC EAVESDROPPING,
Case 6.4 (148-49 n.2)

ELEEMOSYNARY ENTITIES,
Immunity, 3D

EMERGENCY,
Excusing conduct, 71
Legal test regarding, 3A2

EMOTIONAL DISTRESS,
 See also DAMAGES
Malicious parody, 75-76

EMPLOYMENT,
Discrimination in, 77-78
Master-servant tests, 3C3
Scope of, 3C3
Workers compensation, 155, 158,
 174-76

EMPLOYMENT DISCRIMINATION,
Racial, 77-78

ENGLISH, PLAIN,
Charge to jury, 8D
Opinion, 144

ENTITLEMENT, ch. 4

ENTITY,
Conspiracy distinguished, 89
Defined, 3B4
State of mind, 84, 3B4

ENVIRONMENTAL INTERESTS,
Preemption, see that title
Spraying, 2F, 64, Case 4.2 (115)
Toxic waste, Case 6.5 (165)

INDEX

EQUAL PROTECTION,
Asbestos hazards, Case 2.2 (40)
Invidious classification,
    Case 1.3 (24)
Residence, Case 1.3 (24)
Suspect classification,
    Case 1.3 (24), Case 2.2 (40)

EVALUATIVE TESTS,
   In general, 3A
Caution about using, 3A2, 3C3,
   5C, 6G
Consent, 3A2, 3A3
Copyright, substantial
    similarity, 2F
Court or jury, 2H
Knowability of asbestos hazards,
    Case 2.2 (40)
Mixed questions of law-fact, 2G
On-balance tests, 3A2, 5C
Substantial similarity,
    copyright, 2F

EVENHANDED TREATMENT, 4C, 6C

EVIDENCE,
   In general, 8C
Discretion, 240-41
Rulings, 8C

EXCESSIVE FORCE, Case 3.2 (106)
Verdict, Form 8.C (247)

EXCUSE,
Emergency, 71

EXECUTIVES,
Immunity, 3D

EXHIBITS,
Marking, 228

EXPECTED OR INTENDED INJURY,
Insurance law, 158-59

EXPERTS,
Basis for opinion, disclosure,
    243-44

EXPERTS--Cont'd
Knowability of asbestos hazards,
   62
Rules of proof, 243-44
Scientific knowledge,
    Case 2.2 (40), 2F
Tendering, 243

EXPLAINING LAWMAKING CHOICES,
   ch. 3, ch. 4, ch. 5, ch. 6

EXPLOSIVES,
Transportation, 58, 64

EYE,
Of the beholder, 74

FACTS,
   As related to judging
    generally, ch. 2
Adjudicative, 2C
Becoming, 2D2
Being, 2D1
Borderland between law and fact,
   2H
Characteristics, 2D
Classifying, ways of, 2C, 2F
Elements of legal tests, 3A2
Evaluative, 2F
Historical,
   Defined, 2F
   State of mind as, 2D4, 57
   Truth about, 2D4
Human relations, realities
    concerning, 2D4
Independent of proclamation, 2D4
Interpretive, 2F
Law distinguished, ch. 2
Laws of human relations, 2D4
Laws of the physical universe,
   2D4
Legislative facts, 2C
Mixed questions of law-fact, 2G
Opinion distinguished, 3A3
Predictions as, 2F
Premise facts, 2C
Proclamation as, 2D4
Truth or falsity, 2D4, 2F

INDEX

FACTS--Cont'd
Unknown, 2D3
Who decides, 2C

FACTORS,
Caution about tests that use, 3A2, 3C3, 5C, 6G
Elements of tests of accountability, 3A2, 3C3

FAGG, HON. GEORGE G.,
<u>Janklow v. Newsweek, Inc.</u> (dissenting), 74 n.11

FARMERS,
Crop dusting, 2F, 64
Field burning, 76 n.13

FAVORED OLDER RESIDENT,
Case 1.3 (24)

FEDERAL PREEMPTION,
See PREEMPTION, FEDERAL

FELDMAN, HON. STANLEY G.,
<u>Chamberlain v. Mathis</u>, 95 n.1, 98 nn.3-4, 99 nn.5-7, 580
<u>Rossel v. Volkswagen</u>, 757

FIAT,
Applying tests of accountability, 79, 4D n.5
Value-laden choice as, 4D n.5

FICTIONS, LEGAL,
Avoiding, 144, 6G
Entity intent, 80-82, 3B4, 143, 6C, 6D
Presumed intent, 80-82, 143, 6C

FIELD BURNING, 76 n.13

FIFTH AMENDMENT,
See also DUE PROCESS
Corporations, 87 n.11

FINANCIAL IRRESPONSIBILITY,
Effect on settlement, Case 6.5 (165)
Risks of, Case 6.1 (146), Case 6.2 (148), Case 6.5 (165)

FINANCIAL RESPONSIBILITY LAWS, 136

FINDINGS OF FACT,
See also REVIEW
Stated orally, 139

FINE TUNING TO DO JUSTICE,
Complexity, 36
Discretion as means of, 2H
Evaluative tests, 2H, 3A
Refining rules as means of, 36
Risks of, 2H

FIRE,
As incentive, 2D4

FIRST AMENDMENT,
Clash of high-value interests, 3E
Defamation, see that title
Subjective and objective tests, 3A3

FIRST IMPRESSION, ISSUES OF,
See also GAPS
Deciding, 32-34, 2E, 62
Deductive and informative reasoning, 4C
Disclosed by writing opinion, 137
Gaps,
  Filling, 5D, 6A, 6B, 6C, 163, 166-69
  In existing law, 2E4
Refusing to decide as deciding, 32
Written opinion, 139, 143

FOOL,
Unable to recover against knave, 92

817

INDEX

FORFEITURE,
Assets of conspirator, 89

FORMS,
Form 7.A Memorandum and Order Regarding Discovery, 185
Form 7.B Stipulation and Order for Summary Jury Trial, 189
Form 7.C Stipulation and Order for Conditional Summary Trial, 193
Form 7.D A Grid for Evaluating Techniques of Judicial Involvement in Dispute Resolution, 206
Form 8.A Stipulation and Order for Tailored Jury Trial, 217
Form 8.B Stipulation and Order for Tailored Non-Jury Trial, 232
Form 8.C Verdict in Phase I of Trial, 247
Form 8.D Judgment, 254

FOURTEENTH AMENDMENT,
See DUE PROCESS; EQUAL PROTECTION

FOWL, 142 n.1

FRAUD,
Increased claims, 3B2
Used car sale, 85

FREEDOM OF ACTION, 3D

FREEDOM OF EXPRESSION,
See also FIRST AMENDMENT
Privilege, 3D

FRIENDLY, HON. HENRY,
<u>Frigaliment Importing Co. Ltd v. B.N.S. International Sales Corp.</u>, 142 n.1
<u>United States v. Hooker Chemicals & Plastics Corp.</u>, 72 n.1

FULLER, PROF. LON,
<u>The Law in Quest of Itself</u> (1940), 53

GAPS,
See also FIRST IMPRESSION, ISSUES OF
Filling, 5D, 6A-C, 163, 166-69
In existing law, 2E
Law in development, 2B, 2E2, 4B

GIERKE, HON. H.F. III,
<u>Kavadas v. Lorenzen</u>, 734

GIGO PRINCIPLE,
Case management decisions, 202

GILMORE, PROF. GRANT,
<u>Death of Contract</u> (1974), 133 n.3
<u>Putting Senator Davies in Context</u>, 4 Vt. L. Rev. 233 (1979), 173-74 & n.4

GOOD FAITH,
Argument for extension or modification of precedent, 2E3

GOVERNMENTAL IMMUNITY,
In genneral, 3D
National Childhood Vaccine Injury Act, Case 2.1 (31)
Tort Claims Acts, 3D3
Waiver, 3D3

GOVERNMENTAL SUBSIDY, 4E

GOVERNOR,
Participant in legislative intent, 153, 170
Proclamation of, 2D4

GRAVITY, LAW OF, 2D4

GROSS NEGLIGENCE,
Duty formulation, ambiguity of, 3F2
Host drivers, 3C2

INDEX

GROWTH OF LAW, 2E2

GUEST STATUTES,
Host drivers, 3C2

GURU,
Discovery supervisor, 215

GYPSY MOTHS, Case 4.2 (115)

HAMLIN, HON. OLIVER D. JR.,
Davis v. Wyeth Laboratories, Inc.
    (dissenting), 679

HAND, HON. LEARNED,
Cabell v. Markham, 141 n.5
Hardy v. United States, 82 n.3
Sinram v. Pennsylvania R. R., 79
    n.19, 103 n.2, 128 n.5

HART, PROF. HENRY, and SACKS,
DEAN ALBERT,
The Legal Process (tent. ed.
    1958), 19 n.2

HAZARDS,
Abnormally dangerous activity,
    76 n.13
Asbestos, Case 2.2 (40), 2F,
    60 n.1, 62
Field burning, 76 n.13

HEALTH, STATE DEPARTMENT,
Official of, defamation claim,
    Case 3.1 (95)

HELICOPTER,
  See SPRAYING

HIGHWAY ACCIDENTS,
  In general, 38, 58, 85, 91,
    3C2, 119, Case 6.1 (146),
    Case 6.2 (148)
Host drivers, 3C2
Taxicab, Case 6.1 (146),
    Case 6.2 (148)

HIRSCHMAN, PROF. ALBERT O.,
    Cited, 127-28 n.4

HIRSCHOFF, JON and CALABRESI,
DEAN GUIDO,
Toward a Test for Strict
    Liability in Torts,
    81 Yale L. J. 1055 (1972),
    127 n.3

HISTORICAL FACTS,
Defined, 2F

HISTORY,
Legal, see LEGAL HISTORY
Legislative, 57
    Analogy to obiter dicta, 6C, 6D

HOLMES, HON. OLIVER WENDELL, JR.,
    46 n.15, 142 n.1
Chastleton Corp v. Sinclair,
    175 nn.8-10, 176
Olmstead v. United States,
    50 n.1
Southern Pacific Co. v. Jensen
    (dissenting), 52
Brooding omnipresence, 52
The Common Law, Lecture IV,
    Fraud, Malice and Intent --
    The Theory of Torts" (1881
    ed.), 166-68
The Path of the Law, 178 n.1

HOMEOWNERS LIABILITY INSURANCE,
Injury expected or intended,
    158-59

HONEYBEES, Case 4.2 (115)

HONORING REASONABLE EXPECTATIONS,
    133

HORSE AND BUGGY ORDINANCE, 6H

HOST DRIVERS,
Test for accountability, 3C2

INDEX

HUMAN BEHAVIOR,
Incentives affecting, 2D4
Realities concerning, 2D4

HUNTER, HON. JAMES III
<u>In re Asbestos Litigation</u>
(dissenting), 58 n.5, 426

HYPOTHETICAL CASES,
See CASES, Hypothetical

IGNORANCE,
Burden of proof, 2D3
Managing, 2D3

ILLOGICAL,
Jargon, professional,
Case 1.3 (24), Case 2.2 (40),
2D2, 171

IMMUNITIES,
In general, 3D
Abuse, 3D3
Employer, workers compensation acts, 155
Motive and purpose, 3D3
Terminology, 3D2

IMMUNIZATION, Case 2.1 (31),
Case 4.1 (114)

IMPUTED NEGLIGENCE,
Claim against agent, 88 n.12

INCENTIVES,
Human behavior influenced by, 2D4
Judicial management, use in, 7C, 8A
Jury trial, 8A
Nonjury trial, 8A
Professional conduct affected by, 7C, 7D
Sanctions designed to affect, 7D, Form 7.A (185)
Time limits, 8A

INCOMPLETE DECISIONMAKING, 4E

INCOMPLETE INFORMATION,
Decisions based on, 7F3

INDEPENDENT CONTRACTOR, 94

INDEPENDENT INTERVENING CAUSE, 109

INDIVIDUAL AUTONOMY,
Case 4.1 (114)

INDIVIDUAL ENTITLEMENT IN LAWMAKING, 4D

INFANT,
Battered, Case 1.2 (8)
Consent,
Age of competency, 3A2, 3A3
Tests for determining, 3A2, 3A3
Statutory rape, objective test, 3A3
Vaccine victim, Case 2.1 (31)

INFERENCES,
Irrebuttable presumptions distinguished, 80-82

INFORMATIVE REASONING,
See REASONING

INJURED INMATE, Case 1.1 (5)

INJURY,
Expected or intended, insurance law, 158-59

INMATE, INJURED, Case 1.1 (5)

INSOLVENCY OF TORTFEASOR,
Allocating risks of,
Case 6.1 (146),
Case 6.2 (148),
Case 6.5 (165)
Effect on settlement,
Case 6.5 (165)

INDEX

INSTRUCTIONS TO JURY,
See JURY, Instructions

INSURABLE INTEREST, 29

INSURANCE,
Agency doctrines, 133
Collateral source rule, 134
Coordination of benefits, 134
Expected or intended injury, 158-59
Honoring reasonable expectations, 133
Insurable interest, 29
Liability insurance, 3B2
Malpractice insurance, 2D2, 59
Managing ignorance, 2D3
Rates, workers compensation, 174-76
Reasonable expectations, 133
Unconscionability, 133
Workers compensation, rates, 174-76

INTENT,
Clarity about test, 5D
Consequences, focus on, 81-82, 156-60
Holmes' comment on, 166-68
"Intentional act," see that title
Knowledge of substantial certainty, 81-82
Legal accountability, without, 79
Manifested, 5D
Manifested meaning contrasted, 6D
Motive compared, 156-57, 160-61
Negligence distinguished, 81-82
Presumed, 80-82, 143, 6C
State of mind, 81-82, 5D
Statutes, 6D
Substantial certainty, knowledge of, 81-82, 156-60
Tests, 3A2, 3A3
"Voluntary act," 155-57

"INTENTIONAL ACT", 5D, ch. 6
Compared with "willful act," 155-61

INTENTIONAL INFLICTION OF EMOTIONAL DISTRESS, 75-76

INTEREST,
Award in judgment, 8E

INTERESTS,
Weighed in lawmaking, ch. 4

INTERROGATORIES TO JURY,
See also JURY, Instructions
Civil rights case, Form 8.C (247)
Complex cases, 5F
State-of-mind tests, 3B1

INTERSTICES,
See FIRST IMPRESSION, ISSUES OF; GAPS

INTERVENTION AS OF RIGHT, 71-72

INTRODUCTION TO JUDICIAL DECISIOMMAKING, ch. 1, ch. 2

INVIDIOUS CLASSIFICATION,
See also DISCRIMINATION
Residence, Case 1.3 (24)
Suspect, Case 1.3 (24), Case 2.2 (40)

IRRATIONAL,
Jargon, professional, Case 1.3 (24), Case 2.2 (40), 2D2, 171

JARGON, PROFESSIONAL,
Illogical, Case 1.3 (24), 2D2, 171
Irrational, Case 1.3 (24), 2D2, 171
Jury charge, 144
Opinions, use in, 5C
Rationality, Case 1.3 (24), 2D2, 171
Use for objections to evidence, 8C

INDEX

JOHNSON, SAM D.
Salinas v. Roadway Express, Inc., 19 n.1, 302

JOINT LIABILITY, ch.6,
Case 6.1 (146), Case 6.2 (148),
Case 6.5 (165), 8E,
Form 8.C (247), Form 8.D (254)

JUDGES,
Discretion,
  Tailoring, see that title
  Under rules of procedure, 7A, 7B
Eye, as subjective beholder, 3A3
Immunity, 3D
Lawmakers, see LAWMAKERS; LAWMAKING
Shepherds, 215
Speaking, ch. 5
Subjective and objective decisionmaking, 3A3
Trial Judges,
  Lawmakers, 1C, 51, 4C
  Perspective of, 1B1
  Speaking, ch. 5
  Writing, ch. 5

JUDGMENT,
  See also JUDGING
Form of, 8E, Form 8.D (254)
Joint liability, 8E,
  Form 8.D (254)
Summary, grounded on immunity, 3D3

JUDGING,
Activism,
  Constrained by candid explanation, 4B
  Inevitable lawmaking distinguished, 1C, 151, 4C
Choice, see that title
Commitments,
  To justice, 1A, 2E2
  To law, 1A, 2E
  To professionalism, 1A, 1C, 4A, 137

JUDGING--Cont'd
  To representing community interests, 1A, 2E2, 76, 4A, 137
Community standards, 1A, 2E2, 76, 4A, 137
Compelled to unjust result, 2E2
Conflicting personal interest, 2E2
Introduction to, ch. 1, ch. 2
Justice,
  Commitment to, 1A
  Unjust law, 2E2
Lawfully, 2E2
Managerial, 7D-F, 8A, 240
Method of reasoned choice, 1A, 1D, 4A-B-C-D, 138, 7A1
Moral issues, 2E2, ch. 4
Perspectives on, ch. 1
Post-trial proceedings, 8E
Professional commitments,
  To justice, 1A, 2E2
  To law, 1A, 2E
  To professionalism, 1A, 1C, 4A, 137
  To representing community interests, 1A, 2E2, 76, 4A, 137
Proof, 8C
Reasoned decision,
  Obligation of, 1A, 1D, 4A-B-C-D, 138, 7A1
Representative of community interests, 1A, 2E2, 76, 4A, 137
Rules of procedure, 7A
Subjective and objective, 3A3

JUDICIAL ACTIVISM,
Constrained by candid explanation, 4B
Inevitable lawmaking distinguished, 1C, 2E2, 2E3, 4C

JUDICIAL DECISIONMAKING,
  See also JUDGING
Introduction to, ch. 1, ch. 2

INDEX

JUDICIAL INTERVENTION,
See also JUDICIAL MANAGEMENT
To promote settlement, 7E,
    Form 7.B (189),
    Form 7.C (193)

JUDICIAL MANAGEMENT,
Choices committing resources, 7F
Disposition without trial, 7E
Grid for evaluating techniques,
    Form 7.D (136)
Incentives, using, see INCENTIVES
Qualitative evaluation, 7F4
Qualitative perspective, 7F4
Pretrial, 7D
Settlement, see that title
Trial, ch. 8

JUDICIAL NOTICE, 68 n.3, 175

JURISDICTION,
Limit on judicial immunity, 3D3

JURY,
Adjudicative facts, see that
    title
Burdens in discrimination cases,
    3E
Cause, 58, 3F3
Charges, 5F, 8D
  See also Instructions, in this
    title, below
Genuinely disputed facts, 2C
Instructions,
    In general, 5F, 8D
  Aggravation of preexisting
    condition, 3F3
  Burdens in discrimination
    cases, 3F
  Cause, 58, 3F3
  Examples, 94-95, 114-15, 3F3,
    229
  Note-taking, 229
  Plain English, 3F3, 5F
  Scope of employment, 94-95
  State-of-mind tests, 3B1, 3B3
  Substantial factor, 3F3
  Tailored to case, 3B3, 5F, 8D

JURY--Cont'd
  Unreasonably dangerous drugs,
    114-15
Interrogatories,
  Civil rights case,
    Form 8.C (247)
  Complex cases, 5F
  State-of-mind tests, 3B1
Material facts, 2C
Mixed questions of law and fact,
    2G
Premise (legislative) facts,
  See PREMISE FACTS
Proximate cause, 58, 3F3
State-of-mind tests, explanation
    of, 3B1
Trials, ch. 8
Verdict,
  Forms, Form 8.C (247), 247-252
  Judicial control over, 2C, 8D

**JUSTICE, RELATION OF LAW AND
FACTS TO,**
In general, ch. 2, ch. 4
Accommodating conflicting
    interests, 4A, 4B
Aim of procedural rules, 7A1
Conflicting interests
    accommodated, 4A, 4B
Evenhanded treatment of cases,
    4C, 6C
Facts, 2D
Judge's commitment to, 1A, 2E2
Law, 1A, 2E
Reasoned choice, 4B
  See also CHOICE; REASONING
Unjust law, 2E2

KANNE, HON. MICHAEL S.,
Heileman Brewing Co. v. Joseph
    Oat Corp., 709

KEETON, DEAN W. PAGE,
Prosser & Keeton, Torts (5th ed.
    1984), 82 n.2, 156 nn.4, 5,
    157 n.6, 164 nn.10-13

INDEX

KEETON, ROBERT E.,
Creative Continuity in the Law of Torts (1962), 58 n.7, 69 n.4
Entitlement and Obligation, 46 U. Cin. L. Rev. 1 (1977), 113 n.2, 125 n.1
Legal Cause in the Law of Torts (1963), 58 n.7, 59 n.8, 103 n.2, 104 nn.3, 4
Legislative Facts and Similar Things: Deciding Disputed Premise Facts (1988), 38 n.1, 40 n.6, 42 n.12, 58 n.5, 62 n.2, 244 n.3
Statutes, Gaps, and Values in Tort Law (1978), 33 n.3, 149 n.2, 150 n.1
The Function of Local Rules and Tension With Uniformity, 50 U. Pitt. L. Rev. 853 (1989), 177 n.2, 180 n.6, 181 nn.2, 3, 184 n.1
Time Limits as Incentives in an Adversary System, 137 U. Pa. L. Rev. 2053 (1989), 209 n.2
Venturing to Do Justice (1969), 11 n.1, 58 n.7, 151 n.1
Judicial opinions,
    Carapellucci v. Town of Winchester, 62 n.1
    United States v. Vest, 148-49 n.2
    Wallace v. United States, 17 n.8

KEETON, ROBERT E. and WIDISS, PROF. ALAN I.,
Insurance Law (1988), 84 n.7, 130 n.2

KNAVE,
Escapes liability to fool, 92

KNOWABLE HAZARDS,
  Case 2.2 (40), 2F, 2H

KNOWLEDGE,
Hazards, Case 2.2 (40), 2F, 2H

KNOWLEDGE--Cont'd
Intent, see that title
Negligence, 77

LABELING, 3A
  See also MEANING

LABOR LAW,
Federal preemption, 67 n.2

LAMBROS, HON. THOMAS D.,
The Summary Jury Trial and Other Alternative Methods of Dispute Resolution, 103 F.R.D. 461 (1984), 191-92

LANGBEIN, PROF. JOHN,
The German Advantage in Civil Procedure, 52 U. Chi. L. Rev. 823 (1985), 210 & n.3

LAW,
  See also LAWS
  Relating to judging generally, ch. 2
Becoming, 2E2
Being, 2E1
Characteristics, 2E
Community's standards reflected, 1A, 2E2, 76, 4A, 137
Criminal, see CRIMES
Facts, distinguished, ch. 2
Federal,
  Preemption, see PREEMPTION, FEDERAL
Gaps in, see FIRST IMPRESSION, ISSUES OF; GAPS
Gravity, 2D4
Growth, 2B, 2E2
Human behavior, 2D4
In action, 1B2
In being, 2E1
Incompleteness, 2E, 5D, 6A-C, 163, 166-69
In development, 1B3, 2B, 2E2, 4B
Judging, relation to, ch. 2
Justice, relation to, ch. 2
Living quality, 2B, 2E2

INDEX

LAW--Cont'd
Makers, see LAWMAKERS; LAWMAKING
Morals, relation to, 2E2
Natural, 2E1, 2E2, 55
Physical universe, 2D4
Positive, 2E1, 2E2, 55
Preemption, see PREEMPTION, FEDERAL
Private, 2B1
Proclaimed, 2E4
Public and private, 2B1
Purposes of, objectively manifested, 55
Reform, annual legislative agenda, 134-36
State,
  Common law, 2B1
  Proclamation, 2D4
  Statutes, see that title
Unanswered questions, see that title
Unknown, 2E2, 2E3
  See also FIRST IMPRESSION, ISSUES OF; GAPS
Who decides, 2B

LAWMAKERS,
  In general, 2B
  See also LAWMAKING
Administrative agencies, 35
Municipal authorities, 35
Panels, different reasons for choice, 10
Respect for, 5C
Trial judges, 1C, 51

LAWMAKING,
  In general, 2B
Administrative agencies and officials, 35
Case-by-case advantages, 2E2
Choice, see that title
Employment discrimination, 77-78
Explaining, ch. 3, ch. 4, ch. 5, ch. 6
Executive agencies and officials, 35
Judges, see JUDGES; JUDGING

LAWMAKING--Cont'd
Municipal agencies and officials, 35
Necessity, 1C, 2E2, 2E3, 4C
Rules, changing, B2
State, see STATE LAW
Tests, see TESTS FOR DECIDING CASES
Who pays, 4E

LAWS,
  See also LAW
Gravity, 2D4
Human behavior, 2D4
Physical universe, 2D4

LEADING QUESTIONS,
Discretion, 242
Rules of proof, 242

LEGAL AUTHORITIES,
Respect for, 5C, 5D

LEGAL FICTIONS,
Avoiding, 144, 6G
Entity intent, 80-82, 3B4, 143, 6C, 6D
Presumed intent, 80-82, 143, 6C

LEGAL HISTORY,
  See also LEGAL FICTIONS
Caseloads, 2B1
Changes in adversary system, 8A, 244
Common law lawmakers, 2B1
Developing American trends, ch. 2
Holmes' influence, see HOLMES
Increasing role of statutes, see STATUTES
Negligence in 20th century, 3B2
Professionalism, 1930s-1990s, 7C
Realists, 55 n.6
Respondeat superior refashioned, 136

INDEX

LEGAL MALPRACTICE,
See also MALPRACTICE INSURANCE
Settlement appraisal,
　Case 6.5 (165)

LEGAL PROTECTION,
Cause, 3F
Duty, 3F
Immunity and privilege, 3D
Scope, 3D, 3F

LEGAL TESTS,
See TESTS

LEGISLATION,
See Statutes

LEGISLATIVE FACTS,
　In general, 2C, 2D2, 2F, 2H,
　　4B, 6H
Authoritative, 4B
Changed, 2D2, 4B, 6H, 7C
Crisis as, 2D2, 2D3, 4B, 4E
Chosen, 4A, 4B
Data as, 59
Derived by logic, 4B
Disclosure, 1A, 4A
Need as, 2D2, 2D3, 4B, 4E
Proving, 2D3
Rate regulation, 174-76
Transitory, 2D2, 4B, 6H, 7C
Transporting explosives, 58

LEGISLATIVE HISTORY,
Analogy to obiter dicta, 6C, 6D
Premises,
　Nation at war, 57
　Transitory, 2D2, 4B, 6H

LEGISLATIVE INTENT, 5D, 6D, 6G
Governor's participation, 153

LEGISLATORS,
Immunity, 3D
Intent, as fiction, 5D, 6D, 6G

LEMMON, HON. HARRY T.,
<u>Citizen v. Daigle</u>, 155, 156 n.3

LEVAL, HON. PIERRE N., 216

LIABILITY INSURANCE,
Availability and cost, 4E
Claims-made coverage, 130
Expected or intended injury,
　158-59
Intended consequences, 3B2,
　158-59
Malpractice,
　Crisis alleged, 2D2
　Data used, 59
Punitive damages, 3B2
Settlement, Case 6.5 (165)
Source of paying damages, 4E
State-of-mind tests, 3B2
Taxicab, Case 6.1 (146),
　Case 6.2 (148)

LIACOS, HON. PAUL J.,
<u>New England Tractor-Trailer
　Training of Connecticut, Inc.
　v. Globe Newspaper Co.</u>,
　77 n.14, 93 n.4, 592

LIGHTS
Traffic, Case 6.1 (146),
　Case 6.2 (148)

LIMITS, SPEED,
Accidents, 3A2, Case 6.1 (146),
　Case 6.2 (148)
Multi-choice tests, 3A2

LINDE, HON. HANS,
<u>Koos v. Roth</u>, 76 n.13

LOCAL AUTONOMY,
National uniformity contrasted,
　2B5

LOGIC,
Affecting choice of premises,
　Case 1.3 (24)
Limits of, 50 n.1

826

INDEX

LOGICAL,
Professional jargon,
    Case 1.3 (24), Case 2.2 (40),
    2D2, 171

LONG-TAIL RISKS, 130

LOVELACE, RICHARD, 66 n.1

LYING,
Reluctance to note, 3E

MAKING LAWMAKING CHOICES,
    In general, 1A, 1D, chs. 3-6
    See also CHOICE

MALICIOUS PARODY, 75

MALICIOUS PROSECUTION,
Pendent state claim, 8D,
    Form 8.C (247)

MALPRACTICE,
Insurance,
    Crisis alleged, 2D2
    Data used, 59
Legal, Case 6.5 (165)

MANAGEMENT,
    See also JUDICIAL MANAGEMENT
Ignorance, 2D3
Risk, 2D3

MANAGERIAL JUDGING, 7D-F, 8A, 240

MANIFESTED MEANING,
    In general, 5C, 5D, ch. 6
Entity state of mind
    distinguished, 90
Guidelines for determining, 6B,
    6C, 6G
Intent distinguished, 6D

MANION, HON. DANIEL A.,
<u>Heileman Brewing Co. v. Joseph
    Oat Corp.</u> (dissenting), 739

MANUFACTURERS,
State-of-the-art defense,
    Case 2.2 (40)
Knowable hazards, Case 2.2 (40),
    2F
Vaccines,
    DPT, Case 2.1 (31)
    Polio, Case 4.1 (114)

MARCH,
Reasoned explanation, 144

MARKET,
Redistribution of burdens, 133

MARKET SHARE LIABILITY,
Infant vaccine victim,
    Case 2.1 (31)
Managing ignorance, 2D3

MARSHALL, HON. JOHN,
<u>Dartmouth College v. Woodward</u>,
    87 n.11

MARSHALL, HON. THURGOOD,
<u>Zobel v. Williams</u> (concurring),
    24 n.7, 26 nn.8-11, 27 n.12

MAYOR,
Decisionmaker, Case 4.2 (115)
Lawmaker, 35

<u>**McDONNELL-DOUGLAS**</u> **CRITERIA,** 3E

McREYNOLDS, HON. JAMES C.,
<u>Southern Pacific Co. v. Jensen</u>,
    52 n.2

MEANING,
    In general, 3A, 3C3, 3D2
    See also UNANSWERED QUESTIONS
Act, 5C, 5D, 6E
Ambiguous phrases, 5C
Chicken, 142 n.1
Clarity about, 5C
Commonsense reading, 5C
    Presumptions contrary to, 5C
Communications, interpreting, 5D

INDEX

MEANING--Cont'd
Conclusions, see CONCLUSIONS OF LAW
Dictionary, caution about, 5C
Duty, 3F
Hand's caution, 141 n.5
Immunity and privilege, 3D2
"Intentional act," see that title
Literal, but unlikely, 141 n.5
Logical, Case 1.3 (24),
    Case 2.2 (40), 2D2, 171
Manifested, 5C, 5D, ch. 6
  Entity state of mind
    distinguished, 90
  Guidelines for determining, 6B, 6C, 6G
  Intent distinguished, 6D
Multi-choice tests, 3A2
Presumptions, 5C
Rational, Case 1.3 (24),
    Case 2.2 (40), 2D2, 171
Rational basis, Case 1.3 (24),
    Case 2.2 (40), 2D2
Tests for scope of
    accountability, 3A2
Uncertainty about,
    In general, 3A
  Adverse effect on
    predictability, 2H
  Burdens of obligation, 4E
  Cause, 3E, 3F
  Deliberate indifference, 82
  Duty, 3F
  Effect on discretion, 2H
  Evaluative tests, 2H
  Generalized instructions to
    jury, 3B3
  "Intentional act," see that
    title
  Judicial opinions, 2H
  Obvious, 92
  Procedural rules, 7A2, 8A
    Settlement initiatives, 7A2
  Reckless, 82
  Reckless disregard, 82
  State-of-mind elements, 3B1
  Totality-of-the-circumstances
    tests, 3C3

MEANING--Cont'd
  Wanton, 82
  "Voluntary act," 155-57

MEDIA,
Clash of high-value interests, 3E
Defamation, 85, 93
Malicious parody, 75

MEDICAL NEED,
Deliberate indifference, 62, 85

MERRILL, HON. CHARLES M.,
Davis v. Wyeth Laboratories, Inc., 662

METHOD,
  In general, 1A
  Reasoned choice, see REASONING

MINIMUM RATIONALITY
  See RATIONALITY

MISTAKES,
Logic and choice, 5C

MIXED MOTIVES,
Affecting immunity or privilege, 3D3
Structured decisionmaking, 3E

MIXED QUESTIONS OF LAW AND FACT,
  In general, 2G
Cause, 3F
Duty, 3F

MORALS,
  See also VALUES IN LAWMAKING
Law and, 2E2, ch. 4

MOTION TO DISMISS,
Asserting privilege or immunity, 3D3
Writing decision on, 139

MOTIVE,
Affecting immunity or privilege, 3D3

INDEX

MOTIVE--Cont'd
Compared with intent, 156-57, 160-61
Structured decisionmaking, 3E

MULTIPLE DECISION POINTS, 6G

MUNICIPALITY,
Civil rights claims against, 4E1
   See also OFFICERS
Insurance, 4E1
Liability for spraying,
   Case 4.2 (115)
Respondeat superior, limitation
   of, 3B4, 4E1
State of mind, 3B4, 4E1

MUNICIPAL OFFICIALS,
Claims against, 4E1
   See also OFFICERS
Lawmakers, 35
Mayor as decisionmaker,
   Case 4.2 (115)

MURDER,
State-of-mind test, 80-82

MUSCULAR MOVEMENT,
   See ACT

NATIONAL CHILDHOOD VACCINE INJURY ACT, Case 2.1 (31)

NATIONAL UNIFORMITY,
Local autonomy contrasted, 2B5

NATURAL AND PROBABLE CONSEQUENCES,
   See also CAUSE
Jury instruction, 3F3
Presumed intent, 80-82

NATURAL LAW, 2E1, 2E2, 55

NATURAL PERSONS,
As payers of damages, 4E

NECESSITY,
For lawmaking, 1C, 2E2, 2E3, 4C
Private, privilege based on, 3D
Public, privilege based on, 3D

NEED,
Premise fact, 2D2, 2D3, 4B, 4E
Proving, 2D3
Transitory, 2D2, 4B, 6H, 7C

NEGLIGENCE,
Adjudicative fact, 2F
Crimes and torts, 79
Defamation, 93
Driving too fast, 58
Failing to know, 81-82
Fraud, 84-85
Highway accidents, 58, 119,
   Case 6.1 (146),
   Case 6.2 (148)
Incompetence, 3C1
Intent distinguished, 81-82
Joint liability, ch. 6,
   Case 6.1 (146),
   Case 6.2 (148),
   Case 6.5 (165), 8E,
   Form 8.D (254)
Levels of care, 3C2
Objective test, 77, 3C
Per se, 29, 71
Role in lawmaking choices, 20th
   century, 3B2
Seat belt, failure to fasten,
   Case 6.1 (146),
   Case 6.2 (148)
Slight, 91
Slippery road, 38
Speed limit, 58
Subjective or objective, 77
Truck driving, 58
Vaccines, Case 2.1 (31),
   Case 4.1 (114)

NEGOTIATING,
   See also SETTLEMENT
Judicial intervention, 7E,
   Form 7.B (189),
   Form 7.C (193)

INDEX

NET LOSS,
Coordination of benefits, 134

NEW JERSEY SUPREME COURT,
Asbestos hazards, Case 2.2 (40)
Infant vaccine victim,
　Case 2.1 (31)
Skackil v. Lederle Laboratories,
　342

NONDEFERENTIAL REVIEW,
Mixed law-fact questions, 2G, 2H

NONJURY TRIALS, ch. 8
Order regulating, Form 8.B (232)

NOT DOING, 3F2, 4D

NOT SPEAKING, 6C

OBJECTIVE,
Malice, 3D3
Subjective contrasted, 3A3
Tests of Accountability, 3A3, 3C

OBJECTIONS TO EVIDENCE,
Deferential review, 240-41
Harmless error, 241
Rulings, 68, 8C

OBJECTIVELY MANIFESTED MEANING,
　See MEANING, Manifested

OBLIGATION, ch. 4

OBSCENITY,
Subjective and objective tests,
　3A3

OBVIOUS,
Danger, failure to heed, 92
Falsity, alleged reliance, 92

O'CONNOR, HON. SANDRA DAY,
Browning-Ferris Industries of
　Vermont v. Kelco Disposal,
　Inc., 87 n.11

O'CONNOR, HON. SANDRA DAY--Cont'd
Philadelphia Newspapers, Inc. v.
　Hepps, 46 n.16, 100 n.9,
　101 nn.10, 11
Zobel v. Williams (concurring),
　26 n.8, 328

OFFICERS,
Accountant, Case 3.1 (95)
Civil rights claims against,
　Case 1.1 (5), 1B2, 1D1,
　Case 1.2 (8), Case 3.2 (106),
　Form 8.C (247)
Crimes committed by, 50 n.1
Defamation of, 93, Case 3.1 (95)
Injury to, 159
Jury verdict, Form 8.C (247)

O'HERN, HON. DANIEL J.,
Shackil v. Lederle Laboratories
　(dissenting), 371

OMISSION,
Not doing, 3F2, 4D
Not speaking, 6C

OMNIPRESENCE, BROODING, 52

ON-BALANCE TESTS, 3A2, 5C
　See also EVALUATIVE TESTS
Review of application, 74

OPINIONS,
Argumentative form, 143
Judicious, 143
Publishing, 139
Won't write, 137
Writing, ch. 5

OR,
Compared with "and" as
　connective, 160

ORAL PROMISES, 29

ORDINANCE,
Horse and buggy, 6H

INDEX

OUTRAGEOUSNESS AS LEGAL TEST, 75

OVERRULING,
Changed premise facts, 2D2, 4B, 6H, 7C
Increased incidence, 11

PAIN AND SUFFERING,
See DAMAGES

PANELS OF JUDGES,
Different reasons for choice, 10

PARKER, HON. JOHN J.,
Bishop v. E.A. Strout Realty Agency, 574

PARODY, MALICIOUS, 75

PARTY,
Attendance,
   Rule 16 conference, 7A2
   Conditional summary trial, Form 7.C (193)
   Summary jury trial, Form 7.B (189)
Representation of, see ADVOCATES

PATENT CASES,
Test for preliminary injunction, 73-74

PATTERN OF RACKETEERING, 150

PATTERNS OF DECISIONS AS PRECEDENT,
Proximate cause, 59

PEERLESS, TWO SHIPS, 154

PENSIONS,
Federal preemption, 67 n.2

PERSPECTIVES ON JUDGING,
In general, ch. 1
Law in action, 1B2
Law in development, 1B3, 2B, 2E2, 4B

PERSPECTIVES ON JUDGING--Cont'd
Professionalism, see that title
Trial judges, 1B1, 1C, 51

PESTICIDE,
See SPRAYING

PHILOSOPHICAL ISSUES,
See also VALUES IN LAWMAKING
Relevance to legal tests for strict liability, 76 n.13

PLAINTIFFS,
Representation, see ADVOCATES

PLANNING,
Uncertainty, effect on, 2D3

POLICE OFFICER,
Injury to, 159
Liability of, see OFFICERS

POLICY REASONING,
In general, 1D2, 50 n.1, 4A, 4B, 4D, 4E
See also VALUES IN LAWMAKING
Causation issues, 3F2
Economics and law, 4E
Holmes views, 50 n.1
Judging statutes, 6C
Philosophical issues, 76 n.13

POLIO, Case 4.1 (114)

POSITIVE LAW, 2E1, 2E2, 55

POSNER, HON. RICHARD,
Economic Analysis of Law (3d ed. 1986), 127 n.3
Heileman Brewing Co. v. Joseph Oat Corp. (dissenting), 723

POST-JUDGMENT INTEREST, 8E

POST-TRIAL PROCEEDINGS,
Attorney fees, 252
Form of judgment, Form 8.D (254)

INDEX

POUND, DEAN ROSCOE, 69 n.4

POWELL, HON. LEWIS F. JR.,
Harlow v. Fitzgerald, 99 n.8
Kassel v. Consolidated
    Freightways Corp., 176 n.13
Texas Department of Community
    Affairs v. Burdine, 101 n.14
Zobel v. Williams (joining),
    24 n.7, 26 nn.8-11, 27 n.12

POWER,
Authority distinguished, 1A, 2E2

PRECEDENT,
Causation issues, 3F2
Evaluative tests, see that title
Overruling, 11, 2D2, 4B, 6H, 7C
Policy within, 50 n.1
Respect for, 5C

PREEMPTION, FEDERAL,
    In general, 2B1
Defamation, 92-93
First amendment, 92-93
Labor law, 67 n.2
Limitation of liability of ships,
    52 n.2
National Childhood Vaccine Injury
    Act, Case 2.1 (31)
Pensions, 67 n.2
Products liability, Case 2.1 (31)
State law privileges, defamation,
    92-93

PREJUDGMENT INTEREST, 8E

PRELIMINARY INJUNCTION, TESTS
    FOR, 73-74

PREMISE FACTS,
    In general, 2C, 2D2, 2F, 2H,
    4B, 6H
Authoriative, 4B
Changed, 2D2, 4B, 6H, 7C
Chosen, 4A, 4B
Crisis as, 2D2, 2D3, 4B, 4E
Data as, 59

PREMISE FACTS--Cont'd
Derived by logic, 4B
Disclosure, 1A, 4A
Need as, 2D2, 2D3, 4B, 4E
Proving, 2D3
Rate regulation, 174-76
Transitory, 2D2, 4B, 6H, 7C
Transporting explosives, 58

PREMISES,
Legal and factual, 4A
Outmoded, 2D2, 4B, 6H, 7C
Probing for value implications,
    4A, 4B
Transitory, 2D2, 4B, 6H, 7C
Value implications, 4A, 4B
    See also VALUES IN LAWMAKING

PREPONDERANCE OF THE EVIDENCE,
    reck3F3

PRESUMED INTENT, 80-82, 143, 6C

PRESUMPTIONS,
Irrebuttable, 80-82
Techniques for decisionmaking,
    2D3, 3E, 3F

PRETRIAL PROCEEDINGS,
    In general, ch. 7
Conferences, Rule 16, 7A2, 8A
Privilege to avoid, 3D3
Tailoring, 7B

PRIMA FACIE CASE,
Discrimination cases, 3E

PRIMARY MOTIVE,
Affecting immunity or privilege,
    3D3
Structured decisionmaking, 3E

PRINCIPLES,
    See also CHOICE; REASONING;
    VALUES IN LAWMAKING
Judging statutes, 6C
Policy, 50 n.1, 4A, 4B, 4D, 4E

INDEX

PRIVACY,
Corporations, 87 n.11
Natural persons, 150

PRIVATE LAW,
Lawmakers, 2B1

PRIVILEGED OCCASION, 3D3

PRIVILEGES, 3D

PROBABLE CAUSE,
Civil rights claim,
  Verdict, Form 7.C (193)

PROCEDURAL RULES,
Discretion under, 7B
Judging under, 7A
Objectives of, 7A1
Questions not answered by, 7A2

PROCLAMATION,
As law, 2E4
As truth, 2D4

PRODUCTS LIABILITY,
Knowable hazards, Case 2.2 (40), 2F
Preemption, Case 2.1 (31)
State-of-the-art defense,
  Case 2.2 (40)
Vaccines,
  DPT, Case 2.1 (31)
  Polio, Case 4.1 (114)

PROFESSIONALISM,
  In general, 1A
Acting in role, see ROLES
Civility, 242
Changes, 1930s-1990s, 7C
Commitment to, by judges, see
    JUDGING, Commitments
Discipline, onerous
    responsibility, 183
Experts, see that title
Incentive structures, 7C
Insurance, 130
Officers of the court, 7C

PROFESSIONALISM--Cont'd
Roles, see ROLES
Sanctions, 7D, Form 7.A (185), 215

PROMISES, ORAL, 29

PROOF,
Compared with rules of evidence, 241-42
Experts, 243-44
Judging, 213, 8C
Rules of, 213, 8C
Standards of, 2D3

PROSECUTOR,
Discretion as to outmoded laws, 1/3

PROSSER, DEAN WILLIAM,
Prosser & Keeton, Torts (5th ed. 1984), 82 n.2, 156 nn.4, 5, 157 n.6, 164 nn.10-13

PROVINE, PROF. D. MARIE,
Settlement Strategies for Federal District Judges (1986), 198 n.1

PROXIMATE CAUSE,
See CAUSE

PUBLIC FIGURE,
Defamation, 93
Malicious parody, 75

PUBLIC LAW,
Lawmakers, 2B1

PUBLIC OFFICIALS,
See OFFICERS

PUBLISHERS,
See MEDIA

PUNITIVE DAMAGES,
Claims, Case 6.3 (148-49 n.2)
Liability insurance, 3B2, 4E

INDEX

PURPOSES OF LAW,
See LAW

QUALIFIED IMMUNITY, 3D

QUALIFIED PRIVILEGE, 3D

QUALITY,
See JUDGING; JUDICIAL MANAGEMENT; LAW; TESTS FOR DECIDING CASES; TRIAL

QUESTIONS UNANSWERED,
See FIRST IMPRESSION, ISSUES OF; GAPS

RACKETEERING, 150

RAPE, STATUTORY,
Objective test, 3A3

RATIONAL,
As professional jargon,
Case 1.3 (24), Case 2.2 (40), 2D2, 171
Limits of, 50 n.1

RATIONAL BASIS,
In general, Case 1.3 (24), Case 2.2 (40), 2D2
Outmoded statutes, 6H
Time of application, 6H

RATIONALITY, MINIMUM,
Case 1.3 (24), Case 2.2 (40)

REALISTS, 55 n.6

REASONABLE EXPECTATIONS,
Honoring, 133

REASONING,
See also RATIONAL; RATIONAL BASIS
Deductive, 1A, 1D, 4C, 5C, 6G
Informative, 1A, 1D, 4C, 5C, 6G,
Labels, 3A, 5C

REASONING--Cont'd
Method, reasoned choice, 1A, 1D, 4A, 4B, 4D, 138
Policy, 1D2, 50 n.1, 4A, 4B, 4D, 4E
Substantive, 5C

RECORD,
Adjudicative facts, see that title
Premise (legislative) fact disputes, see that title

RECKLESS,
Constitutional tort,
Case 1.1 (5), Case 1.2 (8), 1B2, 1D1, 82, Case 3.2 (106), Form 8.C (247)
Joint liability, ch. 6,
Case 6.1 (146),
Case 6.2 (148),
Case 6.5 (165), 8E,
Form 8.C (247),
Form 8.D (254)
Meaning, 82
Duty formulation, ambiguity of, 3F2
Driver, 85, 91
See also DRIVERS

RECKLESS DISREGARD,
Constitutional tort,
Case 1.1 (5), 1B2, 1D1, 62, 82, 85, 4E1
Defamation, 3B2, 85, 92-93
Meaning, 82
Other tests, 3B2

REFORM, LAW,
See also LAW; LAWMAKING
Annual legislative agenda, 134-36

INDEX

REHNQUIST, HON. WILLIAM H.,
Daniels v. Williams, 5 n.1, 2,
6 n.3, 7 n.4, 265
DeShaney v. Winnebago County
Department of Social
Services, 8 n.5, 279
Hustler Magazine v. Falwell,
37 n.9, 76 n.12, 83 n.6, 458
Zobel v. Williams (dissenting),
26 n.8, 337
Sandstrom v. Montana
(concurring), 80 n.1   487

RENFREW, HON. CHARLES, 231

RENT-A-JUDGE, 211

RENT CONTROL, 175-76

REPORTERS,
See MEDIA

RESIDENT, FAVORED, Case 1.3 (24)

RESOURCES,
Choices committing limited
resources,
Managing cases, 7F
Judicial, 7F
Party, 198, 207
Private, 7F, 207
Public, 7F
Value reasoning, in general,
ch. 4

RESPECT FOR AUTHORITY,
Changing attitudes, 7C
Formal and substantive, 5C, 5D,
6G
Statutes, 150, 158, 6G

RESPONDEAT SUPERIOR,
Municipal liability, limited,
3B4, 4E1
Refashioned in 20th century, 136

RESTATEMENT (SECOND) OF TORTS,
158-59 n.7

RESTRAINT OF TRADE, 150

REVIEW, STANDARDS OF,
Clearly erroneous, 2F
Deferential, 2G, 2H, 241
De novo, 2G, 2H
Evidence rulings, 241
Findings and conclusions, 2G
Law-fact borderland, 2H
Mixed questions of law-fact, 2G,
2H
Nondeferential, 2G, 2H
On-balance tests, 74
Preliminary injunction, 74
Preserving objections,
State-of-mind issues, 3B1
Presumed intent, 80-82

RICO, 150

RILEY, HON. DOROTHY COMSTOCK,
Lowe v. Estate Motors Ltd.,
162 n.9

RIPPLE, HON. KENNETH F.,
Heileman Brewing Co. v. Joseph
Oat Corp. (dissenting), 738

RISK,
Avoidance, 4E
Hazard compared, Case 2.2 (40)
Long-tail, 130
Management, 2D3, 4E
Retention, 4E
Transference, 4E

ROLES,
See ADVOCATES; COUNSELING;
JUDGES; JUDGING; LAWMAKING;
NEGOTIATING; SETTLEMENT

ROSS, HON. DONALD R.,
Janklow v. Newsweek, Inc.
(dissenting), 74 n.11

RUBIN, HON. ALVIN,
Diggs v. Hood, 169-71

INDEX

RULE 16 CONFERENCES, 7A2, 8A

RULES,
Discretion, contrasted,
   Lawmaking tests, ch. 3
   Rules of procedure, 7B, 240
Evidence, 8C
Incentive structures created by, 7C
Law, in general, ch. 3
Premises transitory, see
     PREMISES, Transitory
Procedural,
   Judging under, 7A
   Objectives of, 7A1
   Questions not answered by, 7A2
Proof, 8C
Rulings compared, 3A2
Standards compared, 3A2, 181 n.1

RULINGS,
Patterns as precedents, 59
Rules compared, 3A2

SACKS, DEAN ALBERT,
The Legal Process (tent. ed. 1958), 19 n.2

SANCTIONS,
Changing professional incentives, 7D, Form 7.A (185), 215
Onerous responsibility, 183

SANCTUARY, WILDLIFE,
Case 4.2 (115)

SCIENTIFIC KNOWLEDGE,
In general, Case 2.2 (40), 2F
Experts, see that title

SCOPE OF EMPLOYMENT,
See AGENCY

SCOPE OF LEGAL ACCOUNTABILITY,
Duty and cause, 3F
Immunities and privileges, 3D3

SCRUTINY,
In general, Case 1.3 (24), Case 2.2 (40)
Factfinding, 2G
Findings and conclusions, 2G
Outmoded statutes, 6H

SEAT BELTS, Case 6.1 (146), Case 6.2 (148)

SEAVEY, PROF. WARREN, 77 n.15

SECURITIES FRAUD,
Claims increased, 84

SEGREGATION,
Educational,
   Brown v. Board of Education, 39 n.3

SELF-DEFENSE, 3D, 160

SELF-INSURERS, 4E

SELYA, HON. BRUCE M.,
Montplaisir v. Leighton, 67 n.2,
In re San Juan Dupont Plaza Hotel Fire Litigation, 215 & n.9

SERVANT,
See AGENCY

SETTLEMENT,
   See also JUDICIAL MANAGEMENT
Attributing causation, 203-04
Conditional summary trial,
   Form 7.C (193)
Effect on court dockets, 51
Effect on joint liability,
   Case 6.2 (148),
   Case 6.5 (165)
Grid for evaluating intervention,
   Form 7.D (206)
Judicial intervention, 7E,
   Form 7.B (189),
   Form 7.C (193)
Most cases, 51, 204-05

INDEX

SETTLEMENT--Cont'd
Resolving most disputes, 51, 204-05
Strategies, 198 n.1
Summary jury trial, Form 7.B (189)

SEVERAL LIABILITY,
Case 6.1 (146), Case 6.2 (148), Case 6.5 (165)

SHAPIRO, PROF. DAVID L.,
<u>Federal Rules, Local Rules, and State Rules: Uniformity, Divergence, and Emerging Procedural Patterns</u>, 137 U. Pa. L. Rev. 1999 (1989), 209 n.2, 211-13 & nn.5-8

SHEPHERDS,
Judges as, 215
Professors as, 215

SHOULDER HARNESS, Case 6.1 (146), Case 6.2 (148)

SIMPLICITY,
Opinion writing, 144

SLIGHT NEGLIGENCE, 91

SLIPPERY ROADS, 38

SMITH, EDWARD S.,
<u>Hybritech, Inc. v. Abbott Laboratories</u>, 73 n.10

SOCIAL CALCULUS IN LAWMAKING, 4D

SOCIAL NORMS,
See also COMMUNITY; POLICY REASONING; STANDARDS; VALUES IN LAWMAKING
Elements in lawmaking, 76 n.13

SOLE PURPOSE,
Affecting immunity, 3D3
Structured decisionmaking, 3E

SOLIDARY LIABILITY,
Case 6.1 (146), Case 6.2 (148), Case 6.5 (165)

SOVEREIGN IMMUNITY
In general, 3D
Tort Claims Act, 3D
Waiver, 3D

SPEED,
Accidents caused by, 3A2, Case 6.1 (146), Case 6.2 (148)
Limits, multi-choice tests, 3A2

SPEEDY TRIAL,
Incomplete guarantee, 4E2

SPLEEN, RUPTURED, Case 3.2 (106)

SPRAYING,
Farm, 2F, 64
Gypsy moths, Case 4.2 (115)

STANDARDS, COMMUNITY,
Sources of law, 1A, 2E2, 76, 4A

STANDARDS OF LAW,
Rules compared, 3A2, 181 n.1

STANDARDS OF REVIEW,
See REVIEW, STANDARDS OF

STATE FLOWER,
Proclamation, 2D4

STATE LAW,
Common law, 2B1
Proclamation, 2D4
Statutes, ch. 6

STATE-OF-MIND ELEMENTS OF LEGAL ACCOUNTABILITY,
In general, 3A2, 3B
Changing significance, 3B2
Entity state-of-mind, 3B4
Historical fact, 2D4
Insurability, 4E1

INDEX

STATE-OF-MIND ELEMENTS OF LEGAL ACCOUNTABILITY--Cont'd
Municipality, 3B4, 4E1
Murder, 80-82
Tailoring tests, 3B3

STATE-OF-THE-ART DEFENSE,
Case 2.2 (40), 58 n.5

STATUTES,
    In general, ch. 6
    Applying, ch. 6
    Cases involving, Case 1.3 (24),
        Case 2.1 (31),
        Case 6.1 (146),
        Case 6.2 (148),
        Case 6.3 (148-49 n.2),
        Case 6.4 (148-49 n.2),
        Case 6.5 (165)
Consumer fraud, 84
Financial responsibility laws, 136
Frauds, statutes of, 29
Gaps in, 2E, 5D, 6A-C, 163, 166-69
Guidelines for deciding meaning, 6B, 6C, 6G
Increase in, 84, 146, 176
Insurable interest, 29
Interpreting, ch. 6
Joint liability, Case 6.1 (146),
    Case 6.2 (148),
    Case 6.5 (165)
Legislative history,
    Analogy to obiter dicta, 6C, 6D
    Premises,
        Nation at war, 57
        Transitory, 2D2, 4B, 6H, 7C
        Unemployment, 57
Outmoded, 2D2, 4B, 6H, 7C
Securities fraud, 84
Significance in judging, 84, 146, 176
Sunset provisions, 6H
Survival, 29, Case 6.3 (148-49 n.2)
Tort law affected by, 146

STATUTES--Cont'd
Transitory premises, 2D2, 4B, 6H, 7C
Wrongful death, 29,
    Case 6.3 (148-49 n.2)

STATUTORY RAPE,
Objective test, 3A3

STEVENS, HON. JOHN PAUL,
<u>NAACP v. Claiborne Hardware Co.</u>, 37 n.9
<u>Daniels v. Williams</u> (concurring), 265
<u>Wards Cove Packing Co. v. Atonio</u> (dissenting), 644

STRICT LIABILITY,
    In general, Case 2.1 (31),
        Case 4.1 (114)
    See also ABNORMALLY DANGEROUS ACTIVITIES
Asbestos hazards, Case 2.2 (40), 2F, 2H
Philosophical issues, relevance, 76 n.13
Policies served, bearing on lawmaking choice, 3B2
Duty formulation, ambiguity of, 3F2

STRUCTURED DECISIONMAKING,
Burdens in discrimination cases, 3E

STYLE AND SUBSTANCE, 5E

SUBJECTIVE TESTS OF ACCOUNTABILITY,
Objective tests contrasted, 3A3

SUBSIDY, GOVERNMENTAL, 133

SUBSTANCE AND STYLE, 5E

SUBSTANTIAL FACTOR, 3F3
    See also CAUSE

INDEX

SUBSTANTIALLY CERTAIN, 81-82, 156-60
   See also INTENT

SUMMARY JUDGMENT,
Grounded on immunity, 3D3

SUMMARY JURY TRIAL,
Lambros proposal, 191-92
Order for, Form 7.B (189)
Resources used, 7F
Rule 16, relation to, 7A2

SUNSET PROVISIONS, 6H

SUPPRESSION OF EVIDENCE, Case 6.4 (148-49 n.2)

SUPREME COURTS,
Lawmakers, 2B1

SURPRISE,
   See also DISCOVERY
Rules designed to prevent, 8A

SURVIVAL ACTS, 29, Case 6.3 (148-49 n.2)

SUSPECT CLASSIFICATIONS,
   Case 1.3 (24), Case 2.2 (40)

TAILORING,
Discovery sanction, 7D, Form 7.A (185)
Jury charge, 144
Objective tests, 3C2
Policy, relation to, 104
Pretrial conferences, 7B
State-of-mind tests, 3B3
Tests for deciding cases, ch. 3
Tests for scope of accountability, 3F3, Case 3.2 (106)
Trials, 8A, 8B

TAX INCENTIVES, 133

TAXICAB, Case 6.1 (146), Case 6.2 (148)

TERMINOLOGY,
   See MEANING

TESTS FOR DECIDING CASES,
   In general, ch. 3
Difficulty of use, as factor, 2D3
Evaluative, 3A2
Kinds, and how described, 3A2
Objective, 3A3, 3D3
Multi-choice, 3A2
On-balance, 3A2
One-choice, 3A2
Rules and rulings, 3A2
State-of-mind elements, 3B, 3D3
Subjective, 3A3, 3D3

THOMPSON, HON. GORDON,
<u>Bull v. McCuskey</u>, 750

TIME LIMITS,
Incentives, in trials, 8A
Orders for, Form 8.A (217), Form 8.B (232)

TORTS,
   See ABNORMALLY DANGEROUS ACTIVITIES; CAUSE; CIVIL RIGHTS CLAIMS; CONSTITUTIONAL TORTS; DAMAGES; DEFAMATION; FRAUD; HIGHWAY ACCIDENTS; MANUFACTURERS; MARKET SHARE LIABILITY; NEGLIGENCE; STRICT LIABILITY; WRONGFUL DEATH

TOTALITY OF THE CIRCUMSTANCES, 3A2, 3C3

TOXIC WASTE, Case 6.5 (165)

TRAFFIC,
Accidents, 38, 58, 85, 91, 3C2, 119, Case 6.1 (146), Case 6.2 (148)

INDEX

TRAFFIC--Cont'd
Lights, Case 6.1 (146), Case 6.2 (148)
Taxicab, Case 6.1 (146), Case 6.2 (148)

TRANSACTION COSTS,
Applying legal tests, 2D3, 3A
Coordination of benefits, 134-35

TRANSITORY PREMISES,
See PREMISES, Transitory

TRANSPORTATION OF EXPLOSIVES, 58, 64, 4B

TRIAL JUDGES,
Lawmakers, 1C, 51
Perspective of, 1B1
Speaking, ch. 5
Writing, ch. 5

TRIAL,
In general, ch. 8
Contrast between jury and nonjury, 239-40
Jury, order regulating, Form 8.A (217)
Nonjury, order regulating, Form 8.B (232)
Privilege to avoid, 3D3
Proof, 8C
Tailored, 8B

TRUST,
Wildlife sanctury, Case 4.2 (115)

TRUTH,
See also FACTS
As related to judging, 2D

UNANSWERED QUESTIONS,
In general, 3A
See also MEANING
Ambiguity, 5C
Analogy in resolving, 1A, 4B
Burdens of obligation, 4E

UNANSWERED QUESTIONS--Cont'd
Cause, 3E, 3F
Community's values, relevance to, 4B
Deliberate indifference, 82
Duty, 3F
Effect on discretion, 2H
Evaluative tests, 2H
Existing law, 4A
Generalized instructions to jury, 3B3
Good reasons for, 2E2
Incomplete decisionmaking, 4E
"Intentional act," see that title
Judicial opinions, 2H
Obvious, meaning of, 92
Procedural rules, 7A2, 8A
Reckless, meaning of, 82
Reckless disregard, meaning of, 82
Settlement initiatives, 7A2
State-of-mind tests, 3B1
Statutes, 6B
Value-laden choice in answering, 4B
Wanton, meaning of, 82

UNCERTAINTY,
See also MEANING; UNANSWERED QUESTIONS
Burdens, 2D3
Managing, 2D3

UNCONDITIONAL PRIVILEGE, 3D

UNFAIR COMPETITION, 150

UNKNOWN FACTS,
Burdens as techniques of decisionmaking, 3E

UTILITARIAN, 4D

VACCINE,
Adult Victim, Case 4.1 (114)
Infant Victim, Case 2.1 (31)

INDEX

VALUES IN LAWMAKING,
In General, ch. 4
See also POLICY REASONING
Abnormally dangerous activities, 76 n.13
Cause, 3F2
Choice of legal test, 79
Community standards, 1A, 2E2, 76, 4A
Criminal law tests of accountability, 79
Duty, 3F2
Individual entitlement premises, 4D
Probing premises, 4B
Social calculus premises, 4D

VERDICT FORM, 5F, 8D,
Form 8.C (247)

VIRUS,
In computer software, 140
In vaccine, Case 2.1 (31), Case 4.1 (114)

"VOLUNTARY ACT", 155-57
Holmes usage, 166-67

WAGERING, INSURABLE INTEREST, 29

WANTON,
Constitutional tort,
Case 1.1 (5), 1B2, 1D1, 82
Meaning, 82

WAR EMERGENCY,
Rent control based on, 175-76

WARNINGS,
Duty regarding, Case 2.1 (31), Case 4.1 (114)

WASTE, TOXIC, Case 6.5 (165)

WEATHER,
Effect on spraying, Case 4.2 (115)

WEIGHING,
See TESTS FOR DECIDING CASES

WEINSTEIN, HON. JACK B., 215

WEIS, HON. JOSEPH F., JR.,
In re Asbestos Litigation, 41 nn.6-8, 42 n.10, 55 n.6, 58 n.5, 394

WHITE, HON. BYRON R.,
Wards Cove Packing Co. v. Atonio, 77, 78 n.17, 102 n.15, 629
Hustler Magazine v. Falwell (concurring), 469

WHO DECIDES FACTS, 2C

WHO DECIDES LAW, 2B

WHO PAYS, 4E

WIDISS, PROF. ALAN I.,
Keeton & Widiss, Insurance Law (1988), 84 n.7, 130 n.2

WILDLIFE SANCTUARY,
Case 4.2 (115)

WILLFUL ACT, Case 6.1 (146), Case 6.2 (148), Case 6.5 (165)
Compared with "intentional act," 155-61

WILLFULLY,
See also WILLFUL ACT
Constitutional tort,
Case 1.1 (5), 1B2, 1D1, 82
Meaning, 82

WORDS,
See MEANING

WORKERS COMPENSATION,
"Intentional act" of employer, 155, 158
Rate regulation, 174-76

WORKLOAD OF COURTS,
   In general, 2B1, ch. 7, ch. 8
Federal, 2B1
Increasing, 2B1
State, 2B1

WORKS, PUBLIC,
Gypsy moth spraying,
    Case 4.2 (115)

WRITING BY JUDGES,
   In general, ch. 5
How much, 139
Jury charges, see JURY,
   Instructions
Reasoned explanation, 1A, 4A, 5C
   See also REASONING
Style, 5E
Substance, 5E

WRONGDOERS,
Liability insurance, 3B2
Punitive damages, 3B2, 4E,
    Case 6.3 (148-49 n.2)

WRONGFUL DEATH, 29,
  Case 6.3 (148-49 n.2)

WYZANSKI, HON. CHARLES
<u>Whereas -- A Judge's Premises</u>
    (1965), 12 n.2

YOUTH,
Battered child, Case 1.2 (8)
Consent,
   Age of competency, 3A2, 3A3
   Tests for determining, 3A2, 3A3
Statutory rape, objective test,
   3A3
Vaccine victim, Case 2.1 (31)

ZONE,
Wildlife, Case 4.2 (115)

Notes

Notes

Notes

Notes

Notes

Notes

Notes

Notes

Notes

Notes

Notes

Notes